D1134012

In Trouble *and* In Wonder

A Spiritual Commentary on The Gospel of Thomas

Lynn C. Bauman

PRAXIS PUBLISHING
2014

In Trouble and in Wonder:
A Spiritual Commentary on the Gospel of Thomas
Lynn C. Bauman © 2014
(Second printing 2015)

All rights reserved.
No part of this book may be reproduced in any form
without written permission,
except in the case of brief quotations
embodied in critical articles or reviews.

Inquiries should be addressed to:
PRAXIS PUBLISHING
268 PR 249
Telephone, Texas 75488
www.praxisofprayer.com

Printed in the United States of America

ISBN-13 978-0-9801371-4-9
ISBN-10 0-9801371-4-4

Cover and Interior Design by
Lynn C. Bauman

The painting that is featured on the cover
is from the hand of the artist, Sharon Grimes
of Longview, Texas.
Painted in 2014,
it was done in Acrylic
and is titled
"After the Storm"

Preface
and
Dedication

This is indeed a large volume. It contains a treasury of traditional wisdom based on a stream coming from the tradition of Jesus.

It is meant to be comprehensive, but in the end it is not. You yourself must complete the work by adding to its growth, for Wisdom lives. She is not dead, but alive and growing, not only from her own ancient sources and during her maturation in humankind through the centuries, today she breathes life into our world, and will continue to do so until she moves humanity forward to its ultimate destiny. As in any sapiential text, therefore, Wisdom is not confined to these pages, she is also active in you—not just in your head, but in the depths of your soul—the human heart.

So I dedicate this volume, first, to my loving wife Jackie, with whom I have shared a long and generous life, and who has lived the wisdom that she knew from her own inner depths.

I also dedicate this volume to you, O Lover of Wisdom. May you track her scent through these many pages.

L. Bauman
September 2014

Acknowledgments

I wish to acknowledge and express my deepest gratitude to the many colleagues and friends who have shared in living and working with the wisdom of Yeshua, its Master, as it is expressed in the Gospel of Thomas.

First, there is the community of many friends and monks in the Oriental Orthodox Order in the West all across North America who have worked with this text in its various volumes and given me invaluable feedback helping me bring it to completion. Then, there are my own close colleagues Ron and Karen Poidevin, Ann Johnson, Blake Burleson, and my brother, Ward Bauman, as well as Cynthia Bourgeault, who have walked alongside me and shared their own extraordinary insights as I worked through this material. I have listen very closely to one individual in particular, Les Killian, whose insights have always proven of immense value seeking to grasp the wisdom of Thomas' Gospel.

This volume, however could not have come to completion without the dedicated help of such individuals as Lesley Morgan, Diane Walker, Linda Elston, Paul Griffiths, and Ed Clifford. Ed never left my virtual side until it was finished, and Diane Walker has carefully edited a much cleaner and more accurate text for the second printing. Each of these in their own way have graciously and unselfishly given of their time and energies to see that the language, punctuation, and flow of the work achieved higher levels of coherence and accuracy than I could have provided. I am entirely grateful.

L. Bauman
September 2014, 2015

Contents

Introduction

The Discovery of the Gospel of Thomas

When they came to light in the mid-Twentieth Century, the collection of manuscripts known as the Nag Hammadi Library fell like pieces of a puzzle into the yawning gaps of early Christian history. The Gospel of Thomas, perhaps the most prized of all the documents in that Library, was a rare find. Known to have existed in the first centuries of Christianity, it had vanished as a complete text—surviving only in a few shards whose origins were unknown. Now in its full form (although a Coptic translation from what is believed to be its Greek original), it provided a more direct access to two important elements in the early Jesus tradition: a clear wisdom stream without the narration which characterizes the canonical Gospels, and an early literary form of collected sayings proposed by many biblical scholars as the source of the Gospels. Most scholars had concluded that the Gospels of Mark and Luke were based upon a collection of sayings they called "Q" for ***quella***. Here was evidence. Though the Gospel of Thomas was not the exact document many scholars have speculated to have existed, the text nonetheless appeared in the exact form they had imagined to be the primitive source for the synoptic Gospels.

Almost half of the Gospel of Thomas, however, is made up of sayings which were never recorded in the canonical texts. Many of them are so different that they seem to be completely unrelated to Jesus'* original teaching (and unfamiliar to us and to the Christian tradition as we have known it). If, however, they do represent an early, but independent transmission of sayings coming from Jesus, then they add considerable new material, broadening our understanding of Yeshua's sapiential teachings. This commentary devotes itself to this possibility, seeking to understand this hidden or unknown layer of the early tradition and what it might tell us about Yeshua's original wisdom. As many who have studied this text in depth now feel, this fresh infusion of sayings certainly throws new light upon our traditional conclusions about the Gospel, putting some of our most cherished beliefs in doubt. In the end, as we shall see, the insights gained from an in-depth study of the Gospel of Thomas also requires that we re-examine many of our normal assumptions about Yeshua himself.

The Wisdom Tradition

It is clearer to us now that to understand this remarkable Gospel, we must first place it within the wider context of traditional Jewish wisdom, and not second-century Gnosticism. The wisdom tradition of the Hebrew people was in fact an ancient stream that flowed through the centuries from a long line of Hebrew sages and seers extending back, many believe, to its headwaters in the Prophetic upwelling during the Axial Age (around 500 BCE). From that period forward the sages of Jewish wisdom began to articulate an alternative vision that was linked to the prophetic seeing which questioned and transcended the norms of conventional religion. New insights were born and flourished, and wisdom's stream swelled through the ages as new texts and voices were added. The negative impact of the conquests of Alexander the Great in Palestine forced an even greater outpouring of sapiential insight, compelling fresh

* *The western name of **Jesus** is, of course, based on the Greek language. He was known, however in his own day and in his own language as **Yeshua**, which is the preferred name used in this commentary.*

expressions of mystical and spiritual vision. These became the roots of the Jewish mystical tradition (of which Yeshua was also a part), predating and influencing him. They were absorbed and extended through his own unique understanding, and can be clearly seen in the Gospel of Thomas.

It is obvious from this and the canonical Gospel texts that Yeshua was indeed a powerful wisdom teacher. He expressed his insights in a compelling and often original way through the abundant use of aphorisms and parables, which was a characteristic feature of Jewish ***mashal*** (the genre of wisdom instruction) and its teachers, ***moshelim*** (wisdom sages). While the teachings of Yeshua in the canonical Gospels contain much of this wisdom tradition, they are linked with a narrative that frames them in theological categories that appear not to have been original with Yeshua himself, but with later interpreters like the Apostle Paul. It is also clear that Yeshua's teaching was not standard wisdom instruction even in his own day. Many of his contemporaries were troubled by the fact that he was not simply repeating the wisdom that they were used to, but was introducing them to new ideas and insights which they had never heard before (Mark 6:1-4, Matthew 13:54-58).

Whether or not all of the sayings found in the Gospel of Thomas are "from the lips of Jesus" will remain an unanswered question no matter how astute our scholarship may be. What is important to remember, however, is that the Gospel of Thomas does represent an early wisdom stream that flourished in the context of first-century Judaism and early Christianity. This wisdom stream, which appeared in Oriental Christianity, is an alternative one from the teachings we have heard in the Occidental Christianity. Thomas' Gospel opens a new window onto that unique world which has for centuries remained hidden to us. No matter who spoke the aphorisms in Thomas, or what we now call them, they express "the wisdom of the twin." Not only does the name Thomas mean twin, but the entire emphasis of the Gospel which now bears his name is upon understanding how "two" (twoness or "twinness") evolved from the One, and how return to Oneness (out of twoness) is the ultimate goal in the spiritual evolution of humanity. This commentary takes us into that world of non-dual Oneness, which may become an important interpretive lens for us. It allows us to gain fresh insights into the early Christian tradition that we may have not thought possible. It is hoped that such interpretive possibilities will assist the modern reader to take a fresh look at the sapiential nature of Yeshua's original teachings.

How this Commentary Came to Be

When I first encountered the Gospel of Thomas some forty years ago, I was stunned by its power and originality. If indeed these were the words of Jesus, then here was something entirely new, altogether different from what I, as a well-taught Christian, was used to. I also realized then that this Gospel text challenged all my previous assumptions about Yeshua and the meaning of his teachings in a profound way. Although I was greatly puzzled by many of the logia, and knew that I did not have a clear understanding of their meaning, I also felt compelled by that lack to plunge more deeply into the text. I could not let it go, and it seemed it would not let go of me. That sense has remained with me to this day. It has compelled me to deeper and deeper study. I was forced eventually to learn and translate the Coptic words afresh. And then, more importantly, I was led into some of the deepest contemplative reflection that I had ever known. Through the use of this commentary it is my desire want to invite you also into this same process, and to explain some of the discoveries I have made so that you may also enter more fully into the profundity of this most ancient and mysterious text.

When scholars first encountered the Gospel of Thomas in the context of the Nag Hammadi Library, they concluded that it was a late collection of Gnostic sayings that had little or no real relationship to Jesus himself. This was due in part to the number of the manuscripts found there that were indeed Gnostic (from the second-century Gnostic period). But guilt by association does not make this Gospel a Gnostic text. Neither do sayings that throw our previous understandings and presuppositions into some doubt that mean they are necessarily Gnostic. If we do not understand something (or if it is strange or unfamiliar to our ears), it is easy to protect ourselves from such strangeness by calling it "Gnostic." Because of that preliminary judgment, the text came to be known as the "Gnostic Gospel of Thomas," and the name has stuck to this day. This is an unfortunate and anachronistic label which, I and many other are convinced, is not only false, but which keeps the average person at arms length from this important text. In fact, it has made many Christians suspicious and mistrustful of even reading the text, let alone studying it, because the label says it is heretical and must be avoided. This is not only regrettable, but it also treats a significant discovery with disrespect. I like to point out that if, in any other tradition, possible sayings of the founder of a faith (let's imagine Buddhism, for example), had been discovered from such an early period of its history, there would be rejoicing. But in the Christian tradition, Thomas was met with distrust and skepticism by many Christian authorities and a largely ignored by the faithful.

Two Initial Problems

As I began my in-depth exploration of the Gospel of Thomas, there were two looming problems. First was the translation itself. The translations available at the time were all academic, designed to help academicians deal with the complexities of the original language. They were wooden, inflexible, and often impenetrable. I understood why they existed, but found them, in the end, to be limiting and unhelpful. I longed to read the original Coptic manuscript and eventually I did.

The second problem was even more intractable. The early conclusion about Thomas being a second century Gnostic text was compounded by the fact that many scholars concluded that not only were these sayings put into the mouth of Jesus by later Gnostics, the text itself appeared to be random—a compilation of sayings put into a collection without rhyme or reason and in no ordered way. The logia were therefore virtually indecipherable and meaningless for us in our world today. One could never reasonably expect to unravel their meaning or get to their semantic core. The Gospel of Thomas would therefore remain an odd and anomalous document meant for academics and scholars, but consigned to the museums of ancient history. As I continued to read the Gospel on an almost daily basis, however, I intuitively felt that not only were these conclusions off the mark (the first readers had reached these conclusion perhaps too quickly), but that the text was alive with meaning. The question was, however, how might I access it?

Slowly, over years of daily study and reflection, I became aware of patterns within the text. It felt as if I was making some headway in "cracking the code," as it were, and I was not alone. There were others like the early Stevan Davis, and then April DeConick, and more recently Samuel Zinner, who also had a very different sense of things. Opinions about its origins and meanings began to change. My conclusions along with these other scholars and readers, was that this was not a random collection of late sayings tainted by Gnosticism, but an early independent stream of authentic Jesus-wisdom compiled by followers of the Apostle Thomas in the Aramaic speaking regions of upper Syria.

Translation and the Interpretive Process

But first I needed to apply my own linguistic skills and re-translate the text for myself using the original Coptic and other methods of translation. Principles of translation depend, of course, on their purpose. For my purposes, I used the same method that linguists and translators employ at the United Nations when someone is translating from one language to another. The goal is for the listeners to understand exactly what is being said in the speaker's language, but in such a way that the dynamics of both languages are preserved. This is not impossible. It requires work and familiarity with the way languages are used and an understanding of both linguistic and hermeneutical principles. I had developed such skills in my first work in the Middle East and subsequent post-graduate studies.

The result was a fresh new translation of dynamic equivalency for the Gospel of Thomas alongside a more academic version with notes as to the choices made and their alternatives. This volume with questions for interpretative study made it into print as: **The Gospel of Thomas: Wisdom of the Twin** (White Cloud Press, Second Edition 2012), which is also the basis for this commentary.

After this work was completed, for the next several years I sat daily with the text and its translations, and began an exploration based on my previous hermeneutical studies to see if I could make new discoveries about its meaning. Slowly a new picture began to emerge. Essentially I started from the beginning and stayed with each logion until its possible meanings began to unfold (as well as the perplexing questions which they raised for me). I would then move on to the next and the next, beginning all over again with each logion. Using that process, I made a series of startling discoveries.

Here is what I found. Not only did Thomas appear to be carefully and sequentially arranged (but without a narrative structure per se), it was intended to raise and then later answer questions in the reader's mind in an almost dialogical way. It was as if I was having a conversation not only with the text, but with the "living Master" behind the text. Essentially I saw it not only to be dialogical, but also to be a synchronic text—each logion once read was to remain "in play" so that the next logia could be properly understood. The whole Gospel was more like an orchestra playing a symphony of meaning than it was a story being told diachronically as in the narrative style of the canonical Gospels. The Gospel of Thomas was a wisdom text expressed in a sapiential way meant for those who wished to be in a dialogue with its living Master. I also found that if I kept in mind the questions which each saying raised, later logia would often directly address those very questions while also raising new ones.

MANY CLEAR THEMES

As I worked and collected more and more material, cross-referencing and comparing the logia, many clear themes began to emerge. The original wisdom of Yeshua that I was encountering in the Gospel of Thomas, though quite unlike what I had grown used to in my western theological education, was powerful and compelling. For example, at its core, the teaching coming from the lips of Yeshua in this Gospel appears to focus on the singularity (or oneness) of a unified being— ***monachos***—who has stood up out of the ***kosmos*** (the human order) in order to rise along the vertical axis into the Kingdom of Heaven. Such an image is vividly expressed in Logion 28 where Yeshua himself speaks of his own personal experience:

I stood to my feet in the midst of the cosmos,
appearing outwardly in flesh.
I discovered that all were drunk and none were thirsty,
for their hearts are blind
and they cannot see from within.
They have come into the cosmos empty,
and they are leaving it empty.
At the moment you are inebriated,
but free from the effects of wine,
you too may turn and stand.

Coupled with this image is another which further elucidates Thomas' distinctive teaching of non-duality expressed in its Jewish form from the Semitic stream of traditional wisdom. Yeshua says,

Blessed are those chosen and unified.
The Realm of the Kingdom is theirs.
For out of her you have come,
and back to her you are returning.
(Logion 49)

This Gospel focuses our attention, therefore, on the conditions necessary for the possibility of becoming a chosen and unified being. It urges its readers to struggle with the obstacles that prevent this from happening. It also urges his students and followers forward on a journey of return back into the Realm from which they have come by awakening, turning and standing up out of the ***kosmos*** of human affairs. On such a journey many complications are encountered along the way. There is much to be learned, and so a Teacher who knows the Way is crucial. There are challenges to be overcome, and new places inside and outside one's own being to which one must go. Finally, there is the coordination and integration between the outer experience of a seeker who is journeying along the path, and his or her own inner experience before wisdom can be grasped. This is not an easy passage. One experiences "trouble" of many sorts, but Yeshua explains that in such experiences one's life is also a "wonder" for it is lived in a state of blessedness in the only way possible—because one has found its Source not on the outside, but abiding deep within the interiority of one's own being.

It is true, of course, that none of us are ready, for we are all asleep. The affairs of the ***kosmos*** have swallowed us up in a stream of never-ending activity. We are swamped by the events of time and space, and by our own projections and neediness. Each of us, in our own way, seeks for solace in the external world around us. But these will never suffice. There is a key, however, and it leads to a door that exists at the core of one's being—in the heart. One must go there, move through that door, and give birth in the outer world to that which lies in the womb of one's own inner reality.

The sayings in the Gospel of Thomas are Wisdom's voice from the Master of Wisdom who wields the "sword of gnosis," which is the instrument that will bring a direct knowing of these mysteries which then can never be taken away. In such a state wisdom does not exist as mere precepts in the head. If we will practice them, they become qualities alive within the heart.

THE STRUCTURE AND CONTENT OF THIS COMMENTARY

As I became more confident in my hermeneutical approach to the text, and as I compiled material for a possible commentary, its many themes and meanings began to emerge. I realized then that to comment on these insights required that whatever form it took, a commentary must be multi-layered and many-dimensioned and not limited to a single, linear historical-critical expression. The text itself would not allow for such a limitation. For the purposes of this commentary, therefore, I created a structure that allowed for a "hyper-layering" of its content, giving each reader various entry points and a way of not only reading, but reflecting upon and practicing its principles as a form of personal integration. The knowledge available through this Gospel is meant not simply to be understood intellectually, but to be experienced as transformational because it is grasped inwardly and fully lived. This is a distinction that is often forgotten in conventional religious and theological circles where we are satisfied to know facts surrounding the latest textual discoveries, and about their contribution to historical and form-critical scholarship in New Testament studies. Or we are often content to have the dogmas that our particular tradition espouses confirmed, but resist experimenting with the truth in such a way that we know it through lived experience, which is precisely the intent of the Gospel of Thomas.

This commentary is in many ways unique. It situates itself between a historical and form-critical work of scholarship and a complete hermeneutic of mystical discourse. It attempts to take seriously both the semiotics of the text (its internal semantic content and semiotic structures), as well as its intended purpose to have direct spiritual impact upon the reader as a guide to wisdom. "Reader response" theory is now an accepted approach in modern hermeneutics. How the reader hears, understands, and responds to a text is as important as its original intent and meaning—the two, in some sense, can never be entirely separated. The following commentary, therefore, attempts to place you, the reader, at the center of the work of interpreting Thomas (and by extension, the teachings of Yeshua). But in order for you to enter and understand the text (and Yeshua's teaching), and for it to become truly integrated as your own, you must first engage it in a reflective process of spiritual practice that includes you and, hopefully, a community around you.

Personal Integration and Integral Knowing

If the Gospel of Thomas is a wisdom text, and it clearly is, one important definition for wisdom is knowledge that has been grasped and integrated personally because it has been lived inwardly. From a sapiential point of view, the only way to fully grasp the meaning of its content is through integral knowing.

Your personal work with this commentary, therefore, is like owning a cookbook whose cuisine and recipes intrigue you. To own the book is wonderful. To take it off the shelf and read through the mouthwatering descriptions and their accompanying illustrations is another important step, but they pale in comparison to collecting ingredients, taking down the pots and pans, stirring and mixing the contents together in their intended proportions, cooking as needed, and (now comes the best part and the real test) savoring the results. To linger over the meal that has been created, to enjoy the feast, to share it with others—that is what a cookbook is ultimately all about. The Gospel of Thomas is gourmet fare. It is meant to be cooked, loved, shared, savored and eaten until you are able to enjoy the entire cuisine. This is not an intellectual exercise—never—it is a sapiential feast, and this commentary attempts to invite you to such a banquet!

Many intellectual and academic issues are, however, raised by this commentary. Many questions and textual issues remain to be resolved. In your own way perhaps, you can help answer questions through your own personal explorations and practice. You yourself may find solutions to unsettled issues by living the results. Your own "take" on certain problems, and your answers to the questions the Gospel raises, can be a process of individual discovery much like amateur astronomers who, scanning the heavens on their own, often make important discoveries which they then pass along to the professionals in the field. You yourself will see interpretive possibilities and make new discoveries that are not even mentioned in this commentary. Breakthroughs go both ways.

A Strategy for Working with this Commentary

Everyone, of course, must develop their own pace and their own plan for working with this Gospel and its commentary. It is important, therefore, to be acquainted with some of its key features in order to work with its complexity.

First, **you** are the most important element in the work. Without your attention and readiness to plunge in, the work will not get done, and no real understanding will arrive. Second, it takes time for understanding to unfold even when you are attentive. So do not rush the process. Some people try to complete a logion in a fixed amount of time. It is better to let the teaching (and your own process of understanding) be the guide as to how long you remain with a particular portion of the text. You can, of course, take one section at a time (for example, the Focal Point, which seeks to establish the logion's sapiential focus) and starting with the first, read quickly through the entire volume in order to get the overall picture. But then you would want to return to each of the logia and move more deeply and carefully into its many layers.

In the end it is important that you sit with the Commentary itself over an extended period of time (perhaps reading it over a series of days). Let this section raise questions for you. Underline what you do and do not understand. Both are crucial. Make notes for yourself about these. Turn then to the Questions for Reflection, and the Exercises and Meditations and write out your responses, practicing its truths in daily life, and journaling your discoveries. Allow these to lead you even deeper into an understanding of the Gospel's teaching. It is easy to rush through this section. The more deeply focused you become in *praxis*, the more you will ultimately understand. Why? Because this is the place where you learn to apply and embody the wisdom of Yeshua according to Thomas. It is here you turn from the text itself and examine your own experience. You are invited to engage the wisdom found there by applying it to your own personal circumstances in "real time."

The final section is the Readings for Insight.* It can be used in two ways, first, to add depth and meaning to the wisdom of each logion. Second, these short readings act as another form of commentary from wisdom expressed across the ages and often in other traditions. As you read them, you will see the truth of each logion in new light. Again, it would be good to journal your insights. You might also wish to use these readings as a form of *Lectio Divina* (sacred reading during periods of personal meditation). Read each of them slowly, deliberately, and reflectively at the level of the heart more than once. Do so on several consecutive days. Allow their truths to sink deeply into you.

Finally, it must always be remembered that gaining wisdom is an art form or a skill that you learn through deep personal practice. It must be experienced and lived from the inside out. As was said earlier, it involves the whole of your being and your entire life in the context of your normal circumstances. It is exploratory, inviting you into unexplored territory as an adventurer. Such exploration will ultimately be visionary, taking you from your limited perspectives and propelling you forward into a greater seeing past the surface structures and into the deep-structure of Reality. This commentary is meant to be a pilgrim's guide into new territory—an ancient sapiential landscape—so that you are no longer a stranger in a strange, strange land. It is to this quest of interior seeing and interpretation that the opening words of the Gospel of Thomas invite you. You are called upon to engage these words not merely as a curious bystander, but as an eager reader and interpreter, uncovering its many hidden dimensions through personal encounter. As this Gospel suggests, you were made for such a vision and Thomas' Gospel was meant to ignite it. Through such vision you live, without it you perish, for as Thomas says:

I assure you, whoever grasps the meaning of these words
will not know the taste of death.
(Logion 1)

— L. Bauman
September 2014

* *Through the years I have amassed a large library of short sayings, aphorisms, poetry, quotes and other references from the world's sacred traditions. I have used these to populate this section of the text. Where I have them, I have given authors, sources, and references. Where I do not, I have let them stand without appellation or reference.*

Commentary

LOGION 1:

I who write this am Thomas,
the Double, the Twin.
Yeshua, the Living Master spoke,
and his secret sayings I have
written down.

I assure you, whoever grasps their
meaning will not know the taste of
death.

Sapiential Themes

- *The tradition of the transmission of the wisdom sayings of Yeshua the Master included many streams, more than the common four Gospels.*
- *In this stream the Master lives and continues to teach.*
- *Active participation by the reader is also required if one is to grasp the meaning of what he teaches.*
- *The result of knowing their meanings will nourish one with life rather than death.*

Parallel Texts

Jeremiah 23:18, Luke 1:1-2, 8:10, 9:27
John 8:51, 21:25

FOCAL POINT

In this opening Logion we are introduced to Yeshua, the Living Master of Wisdom, and to Thomas, the transmitter of these sayings. Thomas calls himself a "twin" which is no doubt literal, but which may also be the first important clue to the meaning of this Gospel. Clearly the sayings he records are shaped by Thomas' own interests and ability to see, as are those preserved in the canonical Gospels. His seeing and hearing are astute, and he invites us into the mystery of their meanings, bidding us to become active seekers and learners of the Wisdom from one who is still alive and teaching any who will come near to receive. The promise of knowing truth beyond the "taste of death" is a profound one which both describes something of the difficulty of our human condition and offers us a way forward into a life which lies beyond it.

Links

This Gospel of the collected sayings of Yeshua appears not to be random, but created deliberately as a kind of symphony of wisdom, each saying a musical note in harmony with all of the other sayings. The logia, therefore, are synchronic. Each relates in harmonic ways to others until the whole sapiential orchestra is playing in concert. The sayings, therefore, are linked to one another, often sequentially, but at other times referentially to previous or future sayings in the text. Attempts will be made in this section to highlight these semantic and metaphoric relationships.

Notes

*The name **Thomas** means twin in Aramaic. **Didymous** is the same word, twin, in Greek. So right at the beginning this text, called Thomas, emphasizes twinness or twoness as an important meaning that will be amplified and expressed in multiple ways throughout the Gospel.*

COMMENTARY

Jesus (or ***Yeshua*** in his own language) appeared on the horizon of the first century as a wisdom teacher of extraordinary power. He was a sage, speaking from the tradition of Hebrew wisdom, but teaching from a spiritual vision that went well beyond the normal boundaries of local expectations. What was said about him in the canonical Gospels (that he taught nothing without using a parable) is highlighted in the sayings of Thomas. And so, coming perhaps from an early and independent source, Thomas' collection of the sayings (***mashal***, Hebrew or ***logia***, Greek) becomes a powerful vehicle for the transmission of the original wisdom of Yeshua.

Thomas, the gatherer and guardian of these sayings, called them "hidden" or "secret." In the canonical Gospels the same idea is expressed by the term "the mysteries" (***musterion***) to describe their hidden or inner nature. The word ***musterion*** (used also in the Greek Septuagint) translated an old Persian word ***raz*** used in the Hebrew texts. These terms express two important ideas. First, there is an ancient tradition of wisdom teaching originating from the Hebrew exile in Babylon and Persia. This tradition appears to be honored both by Jesus and the Essenes as well as other first-century Jewish communities where wisdom was an important category. Clearly Jesus used this same type of material within the circle of his first students where it was spoken privately, in contrast to that which was publicly expressed (Matt. 13:11, Mark 4:11, 13, Luke 8:9-10). Later this same theme was expressed within early Christianity. For example, St. Paul speaks of teachings which were "hidden in mystery" (I Cor. 2: 6-7, and Ephesians 3). These teachings are directed inwardly to the deep levels of the heart for those who are beyond spiritual infancy and growing into maturity. Second, this term emphasizes the many difficult and challenging aspects of Jesus' teaching which were "hidden" because they were expressed as symbolic truth through metaphor. As Jesus notes in the canonical Gospels, these teachings simply went "over the heads" of many of his listeners (and often even of his own students) who were as yet unprepared to understand their meaning or hear their truth.

These words are said to be from the living Jesus, as opposed to the words of someone who is dead and gone. We might understand, then, that the Thomas tradition passed on these sayings in order that the Teacher might continue to interact with his students through time. The early community felt themselves to be in constant communion with the one who was still speaking and challenging them from beyond death. To see the tradition in this way places stress upon the present moment as the place of learning. In whatever ages they are read, these sayings bring a sense of immediacy to the listener. The wisdom of these sayings is present and repeatable, to be experienced through personal interaction with the "living Jesus" at the level of the heart.

The focus of this text is upon discovery. You the reader must seize the meaning for yourself because your life depends on it. Don't let it slip away from you as truth normally does. How often do you grasp it only to find a little later it is suddenly gone? You can't seem to hold onto it. (Note that the words **discover** or **seize** used throughout this Gospel are extremely important and invite you to actively participate). This process of discovery invests you with great authority and power to interpret for yourself. You do not need an intermediary. The strategy of this text is to strengthen you so that you become an active participant—a collaborator in grasping the wisdom of Jesus. Your hearing and understanding, and (more importantly) your response, are essential to how it turns out.

Ultimately the goal of this Gospel is to inspire you in your discovery of the meaning of these sayings: that you will no longer taste (experience) death. Their meaning leads to a significant state—an alternative way of experiencing your life—to live in this world in an un-death-like state. As a result of making these meaningful discoveries you will be eating (or drinking) life. The inner wisdom of these sayings is all that is necessary for you to know the fullness of life, to arise from among the "dead" and remain alive in that domain of spiritual consciousness and being where the Living One dwells. Yeshua's wisdom, however, must be actively present in your consciousness in order for you to be transformed into a being filled with life.

*Sayings and parables (or **logia**) play a very critical role in the wisdom tradition. They are an important part of Hebrew wisdom, and Jesus is Master of that tradition. Some of the Gospel writers say that Jesus taught nothing without using a parable (Matt. 13:34). The purpose of the parables was both to reveal and conceal meaning according to the spiritual aptitude of the individual. Ultimately Jesus used them as tools for awakening, so that those who deeply heard and understood might enter a realm he called "God's kingdom."*

QUESTIONS FOR REFLECTION

1. Imagine that you not only stumble across an ancient document from early Christianity, but that twenty centuries later the contents of that document challenge every perception you have about who Yeshua is. What adjustments in your thinking might you need to make in order to receive this ancient wisdom?

2. Yeshua is presented in this first saying as a living teacher and not simply a figure of ancient history. Suppose this teacher is actually active in the present moment and wants to use this text to teach you wisdom now. How might you need to respond?

3. As in Psalm 1, the theme of a path leading to life and one leading to death is part of ancient wisdom teaching (read this Psalm carefully). What would be the difference between these two paths or experiences now? Carefully look at your life currently. Which of these two paths predominates?

Many good translations of the Psalms exist. You might want to examine this Psalm using a poetic version like ***Ancient Songs Sung Anew*** *(Lynn Bauman from Praxis), or* ***Psalms for Praying*** *(Ann Merrill).*

EXERCISES AND MEDITATIONS

1. In reading the Gospel of Thomas you are embarking on an adventure of discovery. You could simply read it as an interesting piece of ancient literature. Or, you could read it to bring you into contact with the living Jesus, who is addressing you directly through these sayings. These are very different ways of reading the text. The outcome depends, of course, on which reading strategy you choose. A good way to begin is to read the entire text all the way through at one sitting.
2. The next exercise is "Meeting the Teacher." You need to be assured that you are in personal, living contact with Jesus as the Teacher of wisdom, or this work will become merely an intellectual exercise. To "meet the Teacher" you must open and activate a place inside yourself through an act of choice, courage and will. With intention, invite the Teacher inside yourself to teach and to speak to you directly. Ask the Teacher for a sign that the relationship has been established. Be attentive to it.
3. Now begin your dialogue within with a saying (a ***logion***). In your reading of the whole set of sayings one may have leapt out at you for special attention. Write that particular ***logion*** on a card. Read it several times a day. Remain alert to how the saying affects you and what you begin to learn from it. Write down what you discover. The truth of these sayings and the inner relationship you establish with the Teacher should become self-authenticating—no one need convince you from the outside. The conviction, when it comes, will come from within.
4. The final exercise is "Tasting Death/Tasting Life." These two phrases are clearly metaphoric. We develop "tastes" for things. What could it mean that you develop a taste for death or life? How would that flavor change your experience? Imagine that you "eat" one of these states or conditions daily. At what level or in what ways do these two "foods" come to you?

Be aware that the Teacher may have his own way of making himself known to you that is very different from what you are expecting. Stay open for surprises.

READINGS FOR INSIGHT

I

Wisdom is a living stream,
not an icon preserved in a museum.
Only when we find the spring of wisdom in our own life can it flow
to future generations.

Thich Nhat Hanh

II

The format of Thomas, ***logoi sophon***, has a long and distinguished history in the Wisdom tradition of Judaism. It was a format used to convey Jesus' teachings which, by the late first century, was in decline. Narrative gospels, dialogues of the risen Christ, legends about the infant Jesus and the apostles, parenthetic letters, theological treatises, were in the ascendancy. The ***logoi sophon*** format is not simply early; it seems to have been *the* earliest form of the preservation of Jesus' sayings. Certainly, collections of sayings were in existence before any narrative gospels were written. This is not to say that collections of miracle stories were not in circulation at a very early time, but our concern here is with sayings traditions only.

Stevan L. Davies
The Gospel of Thomas and Christian Wisdom
16

III

The light inside my heart flows from Your wonderful mysteries.
My eyes have been privileged to gaze on eternal realities.
I have beheld wisdom hidden from human beings and knowledge
and sagacity sequestered from the sons of men.
I have drunk from a fountain of righteousness and from a well of strength.
I have swallowed deep drafts from a spring of glory,
concealed from the assembly of flesh....
The track of my steps is over solid, unmovable rock.
The truth of the Eternal is the rock of my steps.

Manual of Discipline
Col. 11:4-7
Dead Sea Scrolls

IV

Sutras (the oldest form of recorded spiritual teaching) are powerful pointers to the truth in the form of aphorisms or short sayings, with little conceptual elaboration. The Vedas and Upanishads are the early sacred teachings recorded in the form of sutras, as are the words of the Buddha. The sayings and parables of Jesus, too, when taken out of their narrative context, could be regarded as sutras, as well as the profound teachings contained in the ***Tao Te Ching***, the ancient Chinese book of wisdom. The advantage of the sutra form lies in its brevity. It does not engage the thinking mind more than is necessary. What it doesn't say—but only points to—is more important than what it says.

Eckhart Tolle
Stillness Speaks
x-xi

V

So long as you haven't experienced this:
to die and to grow,
you are only a troubled guest
on the dark earth.

Goethe

LOGION 2:

Sapiential Themes

- *The six states of wisdom in three sets of pairs are expressed as a process of learning.*
- *The first set is well known. The next two seem to be original to Yeshua and a further elaboration of the wisdom tradition.*
- *This progression may be recognized as a spiraling movement leading to higher and deeper expansions.*

Yeshua says...

If you are searching, you must not stop until you find.

When you find, however, you will become troubled.
Your confusion will give way to wonder.
In wonder you will reign over all things.
Your sovereignty will be your rest.

Parallel Texts

Daniel 7:27
Proverbs 2:4-6, 8:17, 35,25:2
Sirach 6:18, 7:29-31, 39:1-3
Wisdom of Solomon 4:7
Matthew 7:7
Luke 1:29, 11:9
Revelations 1:6, 3:21, 5:10, 20:4

Links

The first Logion sends the reader out looking for the meaning of the sayings of Yeshua with the promise that if it is found, then the taste of death will disappear from the palette. So, then, the obvious questions are, how does one search, and where does one find such meaning? We are ready, perhaps then, to listen to wisdom's answer.

FOCAL POINT

This second Logion places great trust in any seeker who will not give up the search to find the meaning of Yeshua's wisdom. One who searches will find, but that is never the end of the story. The early roots of the wisdom tradition as it was expressed in Hebrew Scripture was content to stop with the finding—or believed that this was the end point. Yeshua sees differently. By personal experience perhaps, Yeshua knows that finding will inevitably lead to confusion, but if one stays with the process and does not seek to avoid this troubling intermediate state, it will eventually give way to wonder as something greater unfolds. When one learns, gaining mastery over this greater truth, it can be said that one has reached the state of rest or equilibrium.

Notes

Something of Yeshua's own experience seems to be expressed in this Logion. Could it not be that Yeshua went through this progression in his own journey and recognized it as the deeper wisdom that he now knew?

The ancient wisdom tradition speaks of movement, growth and transformation experienced as ***helikos tropon*** *(in the manner of a spiral). Spiraling movement through states and stages of being and consciousness is the "natural course" transformation takes. Wisdom understands this as a continuously repeating pattern that we experience over and over again.*

Searching and finding (the two components of discovery) are constants for human beings. God is an infinite horizon of never-ending possibility and wonder toward which we forever move. We will, therefore, never cease our searching, and there will always be the adventure of new discovery. But if we are ever to change and grow, then the discovery must fundamentally disturb (break up) the solid structure already established in us to allow for new growth. It is this part of the cycle which we resist. Allowing the "break-up" to occur leads to wonder and astonishment in the face of new realities that are now unfolding. It also permits a new sovereignty in the Realm of the All where an equilibrium establishes itself and prepares us for the next "adventure" of search and discovery and its completion in the spiral of transmutation.

COMMENTARY

The theme of seeking and finding, so fundamental to traditional Wisdom, is universal. In this second Logion, however, we are invited not only into the initial stages of discovery (seeking and finding), but beyond it toward that which will unfold in us as we continue (and do not cease) our spiritual search. Interestingly, the search for wisdom will not simply bring new knowledge, it will bring transformation. The process, if it is pursued long enough, will have a transformative effect, changing the very nature and being of the searcher.

This second Logion presents us with a mysterious six-stepped process as the catalytic means of finding life and the wisdom that sustains it. Beginning in the ancient Hebrew literature of wisdom (the Psalms and Proverbs in particular), seeking and finding is the great theme at the heart of the tradition. In this Logion, Yeshua adds significant and powerful insight to the tradition, perhaps never expressed before. He describes the experience of discovery with an awareness of its inner complexity. He discloses the effects of the process on us and the ultimate goal to which wisdom will bring us.

This complex and sophisticated progression takes us step by step through six states and stages of knowing into the realm of wisdom. As a progression, it describes the art of learning through a series of doublets: seeking/finding, troubled/astonished, reigning/rest. Each of these reflects two modes: an active mode of engagement and a passive mode of receptivity. These six states express a progressive maturation from the initial seeking and finding to ultimate rest. In a natural sequence, finding, of course, follows seeking. Formerly, this first binary would express the beginning and end of the process, but here more is disclosed. Finding is a prelude to a deeper stage in the search. Finding unsettles, disturbs, and bewilders the seeker because, typically, what is found is larger or different from the expectations of what one had to begin with. This wider domain leads inevitably to a state of disorientation and instability. Breaking up the norms to which one has grown accustomed leads the searcher beyond that first finding to a new unknowing. One passes through an initial state of confusion until what has been found fits into some larger perspective. From this unsettling state, a truer seeing can occur, a larger perspective that astonishes. Wonder does not debilitate, but empowers the seeker to mastery (or sovereignty) in this new realm described as "the All" (or everything), where nothing is ultimately excluded. In this sovereign reign one reaches the rest, harmony, and equilibrium of royal wisdom.

In the wisdom tradition of the Hebrew people, the word "rest" (***anapausis***) is one of great significance. It suggests the perfection or completion in the Sabbath rest of God following the creation of the world. Resting, therefore, is a state in which wisdom reigns in full without seeming effort. In the wisdom tradition of the Far East, it has also been described as "effortless action" (***wu-wei*** in Chinese—a condition central to the understanding of Taoism). In the letter to the Hebrews, the word "rest" is used to signify a sublime state where strife and conflict subside into attunement. Rest also equals immortality, which is described by T.S. Eliot as the "still point of the turning world." It is a vibrant state where everything is inwardly alive and in balance with everything else (the All) in an equipoise of harmony and right-relatedness which is the true condition of Ultimate Reality.

QUESTIONS FOR REFLECTION

1. Think about your own journey of personal search and discovery. When and where did it begin? Where has it been the strongest? When is it at its weakest?

At some point in this work of discovery, because it ultimately concerns yourself, you might want to outline the major stages and events of your own pilgrimage.

2. What have you found so far that you consider to be answers in your search?

3. When have you found yourself totally confused? What confused you? Explore reasons why you may have been confused.

4. Have you ever experienced wonder or astonishment after a time of confusion? Describe that experience.

5. If sovereignty is a form of mastery (where you and the truth of what you know are one thing because truth has been fully incorporated into your own being), what have you mastered?

EXERCISES AND MEDITATIONS

1. This second saying provides the reader (or searcher) with a primary key to learning wisdom from Yeshua the Sage. Wisdom is inherently transformative. Its purpose is not to provide either entertainment or information, but to transmute the energies of human beings toward a new completion. This Logion gives us insight into the mode and goal of that transformation.
2. First, begin by engaging this Logion from the premise upon which it is based—search and discovery. This is an exercise called, "Finding the Questions." Ask yourself, do I have a real question (or set of questions) for which I am searching answers? What is (are) my question(s)—those deeply provocative issues which remain open for me and which are fundamental to whether I change and grow or remain where I am? These questions are not simply "trivial pursuit"—"My, wouldn't it be nice to know if…" They are what remains hidden to me and what I now want and need to learn.

The inquiry method has a long and venerable history. For example, in the Platonic dialogues, Socrates is described as teaching and mentoring his students through penetrating questions. The same method is also used extensively in this Gospel text.

3. When was the last time you were disturbed to the very core of your being (rocked or knocked off your foundations)? When was the last time you stood in wonder and awe before the sight of some greater truth? If neither of these have happened within recent memory, then this may indicate that your journey into wisdom has slowed or ceased. What can renew it again? Begin a new search for understanding
4. This raises another question. Is there a time to search and a time not to search? And another question, when is our comfort level a gracious gift, and when does it become a danger? Can we actually tell the difference between these two conditions? Remember, modern society has made the procurement of "creature comforts" the highest value in a consumer culture. Is that perhaps a reason for the loss of wisdom in the modern world or in you? What comfort might you need to give up?

READINGS FOR INSIGHT

I

Phil Cousineau
The Art of Pilgrimage
9

It is down the path to the deeply real
where time stops and we are seized by the mysteries.
This is the journey we cannot not take.

II

van der Post

Meaning transfigures all.

III

Pema Chödrön
Comfortable with Uncertainty
174

The world we find ourselves in, the person we think we are—these are our working bases. This charnel ground called life is the manifestation of wisdom. This wisdom is the basis of freedom and also the basis of confusion. In every moment, we make a choice: Which way do we go? How do we relate with the raw material of our existence?

IV

Houston Smith
Introduction to
Phil Cousineau's
The Art of Pilgrimage
xii-xiv

...be prepared to discover that from the spiritual point of view a journey is always something of a two-edged sword because of the dispersion which can result from contact with so much that is new. We cannot simply shut ourselves off from this newness or we might just as well stay at home—if we are going to travel we naturally wish to learn something. But if the newness threatens to overwhelm us, it can occasion periodic hardenings of the ego, as if in reaction to the fear of losing ourselves through dispersal we find it necessary to shore up our identities. The smallness of these identities is certain to bring suffering, however, beginning with the feeling of impatience and annoyance. The art is to learn to master today's unavoidable situation with as much equanimity as we can muster, in preparation for facing its sequel tomorrow.

IV

Phil Cousineau
The Art of Pilgrimage
xix-xx

...the unsettling, but inescapable fact (is) that we are all strangers in this world and that part of the elusive wonder of travel is that during those moments far away from all that is familiar, we are forced to face that truth, which is to say, the sacred truth of our *soul's journey* here on earth. This is one reason the stranger has always been held in awe and why the stranger on the move is perpetually a soul in wonder.

V

Paul Fussell

The traveler is a student of what he sought.

LOGION 3:

Sapiential Themes

- *In religious matters and spiritual search one often looks to external authority for truth—this may be misleading.*
- *The Sources of divine Reality are closer at hand.*
- *The first step in spiritual search leads to the truth about oneself.*
- *Without true self-knowledge one remains a poverty-stricken being.*

Yeshua says. . .

If your spiritual guides say to you,
"Look, the divine Realm is in the sky,"
well then the birds will get there ahead of you.
If they say, "It is in the sea,"
then the fish will precede you.

No, divine Reality exists inside and all around you.
Only when you have come to know your true Self will you be fully known
—realizing at last that you are a child of the Living One.
If however you never come to know who you truly are,
you are a poverty-stricken being,
and it is your "self"
which lies impoverished.

Parallel Texts

Genesis 6:2
Deut. 30:10-14
Hosea 1:10
Mal. 2:10
Wisdom of Sol. 6:17-20
Luke 17:21
Gal. 4:8-9
I Cor. 8:1-3, 13:12
*Plato's **Philebus** 48c, 63c*

Links

This Logion follows directly from the previous saying in which we are introduced to the six states of wisdom. In our searching we pass through inner changes, but questions remain, and many new ones emerge. In the flow of wisdom teaching Logion 3 takes the next step toward answering many of these questions and teaching about the true nature of the search. .

FOCAL POINT

When one begins a search, a number of questions arise almost automatically. What am I really looking for? Who can help me, and will I recognize it when I find it? The third Logion gives Yeshua's insight and answer to these crucial questions. Typically we look for guidance from outside ourselves, and think, also, that the answer lies somewhere on the outside as well. Neither of these are entirely true, according to this saying. There is a place that we often fail to explore—on the inside of ourselves. What we seek outside, we do well to explore within. When we explore within we come to that central question—the most personal question we can ever ask: who am I? Failure to know the answer to that question leaves us poverty-stricken beings.

Notes

*It is of interest that the word translated **sky** could also be translated **heaven.** The two are the same in Coptic. If we take the metaphors of sea and sky as representative of that which lies either above or below earth, then these may signify transcendent realms otherwise inaccessible to human contact, about which we presumably need guidance.*

COMMENTARY

At the beginning this saying sets up a stark contrast between outside authority (the leaders who represent exteriorized and objectified religious knowledge) and interior truth. Leaders of this realm seldom bring you to the Kingdom because exoteric faith typically makes wisdom a religious or dogmatic object. It tends to locate truth specifically in time and space—within history and one particular tradition alone. But you, the reader of this text, do not necessarily need outside authority for what you are pursuing. External authority of this nature can often lead one astray. In this search, acting as an inner guide, Yeshua empowers you to find God's realm both within and without. True spiritual leadership will never take that authority away from you, but will enable you to seek both inwardly and outwardly within a "unified field."

It is important to know that Thomas' Gospel spans the thought-world of both the Hebrews and Greeks. These are linked together, it seems, in the mind and heart of Yeshua. Therefore, in Hebrew the word ***Kingdom*** *is an idiom for the divine Reality or Realm which encompasses all things in a single whole (inside and outside). In Hellenic culture the equivalent idea is expressed by the Greek phrase, the All (****ta panta****). In the All the inside and outside become one whole, or everything.*

So what does one discover in the divine realm where nothing is excluded and where the inside and the outside exist as one unified field--inclusive of everything? The first, and perhaps most critical learning to come is to know your true Self. Clearly Yeshua has recognized here the truth of the ancient imperative—"Know Thyself." It is at this juncture, however, that real confusion may occur. Often we "think" we know who we are, but do we? Is who we think we are the truth about ourselves, or is it some kind of deception?

From our own personal perspective, limited by the only history we know from our birth date forward, who we appear to be is the "only" truth we believe there is to know. But from a spiritual perspective that same "truth" is a kind of falsehood because it is only a part of who we are and not the whole—in fact, certainly not even the most important part. Spiritual teaching says that if we only know this partial self recognized out of our temporal experience, we have not yet met our True Self.

In the Wisdom of Sol. 6:17-20, a pre-Christian text from Hellenic Judaism which Yeshua knew, the search for wisdom leads to a Kingdom: "The beginning of wisdom is the most sincere desire for instruction, and concern for instruction is the love of her, and the love of her is the keeping of her laws, and giving heed to her laws is the assurance of immortality, and immortality brings one near to God' so the desire for wisdom leads to a kingdom." This is obviously not an idea new either to Yeshua or his religious world.

Whether we yet know it or not, this "other Self" already exists outside the temporal world. Its reality is "in God"—that is, it is a transcendent Self (or being) expressing the full image of who we are meant to be. This other Self (as opposed to the one we know in space-time) is more "me" than I am to myself at this moment in time. It is the "truer me" as opposed to the "limited me" because it expresses the fullness of the divine image. The limited self I know becomes "false" when I take it to be the only self there is of me. This is, of course, a great mystery, and the purpose of the Gospel of Thomas is to help us "seize the meaning" of this most important of all discoveries. If we live on earth our whole lives and never discover this true Self, we are in fact, cheating ourselves of our Self.

Another very important insight follows immediately from the Semitic world of Yeshua's teaching. It complements true Self-knowledge. When you come to know the truth about your Self, you will then be fully known (or, as it says elsewhere, "know as you are known," Gal. 4:8-9, I Cor. 8:1-3, 13:12). To clarify what this means, we might use the analogy of one's own child (if one is a parent). When you raise a child you truly know that child in a way that the child perhaps never will—from inception to the present moment. But the child must grow up into full self-knowledge. He or she must come to know who he or she is as a being separate from the parents. An individual must gain personal self-awareness and accept him or her self as they are. Once the child reaches this level of self-knowledge, then the parents are also recognized for who they are, and for what they know even about their child.

All of these steps lead to a deeper form of intimacy—an experience of deep knowing—between parent and child that nothing else can quite duplicate.

Words of gender in relationship to God are problematic because they often insinuate social mores conditioned by history and culture. On the other hand, the metaphors of the divine Father and the divine Mother can be extremely helpful in understanding something of the personal nature of our relationship with God. Yeshua uses the familiar name for God as Father perhaps also because of his own difficult upbringing, where he was commonly considered to be the offspring of an illicit liaison—a bastard.

Self-knowledge, as we have explained it, leads to an ultimate revelation—it reveals the truth about our divine parentage. The truth of our origins does not lie here in space-time at all, but elsewhere, in transcendence. The truth is, you and I (and all human beings) carry divine DNA. You are not simply "adopted" by a distant heavenly Father (though this image is also used, and useful, for different purposes in Scripture), but you are a child (the offspring) of the living Father. Note here the emphasis on the present reality of a Father who is alive. As elsewhere in the teachings of Yeshua, the word Father denotes not male patriarchy, but intimacy with a parent. Yeshua uses the word for loving intimacy, ***Abba,*** which signifies the deepest inner relationship with the divine Parent as both Source and Origin. It is a word used when there is profound care and love between a parent and a child. In various forms it is still in current use in the Middle East today.

Without an interior knowledge of the True Self (and of our divine origins) we are left poverty-stricken beings. Poverty is the absence of wealth. Knowledge of this kind is true riches. This constitutes a whole new redefinition of poverty and wealth in terms of spirit and wisdom and not in terms of material goods. The truth is further clarified here; wealth is not something you **have**, it is something you **are**. You are either "walking in poverty" or "living in wealth."

QUESTIONS FOR REFLECTION

You might want to think about how good external authority becomes toxic or unhelpful in the end. What makes that happen?

1. External authority is often extremely helpful and important in life. Think, for example, about your own need for parenting, or the guidance of professors, mentors, and friends. Think also about when religious leadership and authority has been important for you.

2. Why, in this case, would Yeshua believe that external authority or leadership would be more apt to lead us astray then to help us?

3. How would you describe the characteristics of a "false self?" What would that self be like or act like?

4. Now imagine the characteristics of a "True Self " (as opposed to the false self). What are the True Self's characteristics?

5. To be impoverished at the very center of one's being is something that Yeshua sees as particularly destructive. We have all felt impoverished, inadequate, and deficient (not enough). Is this true? When is it true?

Like so many of the metaphors used in Yeshua's teaching, there is both a positive and a negative aspect to each one. For example, impoverished people are also called "blessed" by Yeshua.

EXERCISES AND MEDITATIONS

*In Greek, the word **philosopher** is actually the "lover of wisdom."*

1. Logion 3 raises many important questions for "lovers of wisdom." The first is, in what realm or kingdom are you seeking for wisdom, and who are you listening to? Do you trust yourself at all, or is all your trust external? Perhaps if you are distrustful of anyone but "your leaders," you are not yet ready for this kind of search. Readiness is achieved when you learn to move beyond trust in your leaders to trust in yourself.
2. We are complex and compound beings—that is, we are more than meets the eye, and even our own eyes may deceive us. According to sacred tradition, there are parts of ourselves that we do not know yet. Only God knows. So to come to know as we are known, and to be truly **known** we must begin a journey of discovery that will take us into the unknown (hidden) parts of ourselves that exist in God. Those parts may be hidden from us, because we, in fact, hide from ourselves or from God. Or there may be parts of ourselves that we simply have not yet encountered, but which are there, awaiting our discovery. Self-knowledge is therefore a long and interesting journey of discovery. How would you know if you've begun it?
3. You may want to begin the step of self-discovery with an exercise called "The Onion." Many teachers of wisdom speak about the human self as multi-layered like an onion. Once you pull back one layer, you discover another one nested beneath it. So imagine the first layer as the one that your acquaintances know or see—the public persona. Just below that is another layer that your close friends and family know, which often is hidden from full public view. Below that is another layer, the one you know more fully, and often hide, even from relatives and close friends. Suppose there are other layers that you hide from yourself, but only glimpse occasionally. They may be frightening to you. Now imagine that there are layers of your being beyond these that only God knows. These are layers yet to be discovered. Imagine that these layers constitute actual "parts" of yourself so that the human "self" as we know it actually has "invisible members" because they are hidden from us—they have not yet been discovered or revealed. Imagine that these hidden members do not lie in space-time, but in a realm transcendent to it and just as real as this one. Suppose that beyond those levels exist others, where, again, aspects of your True Self also exist. So reflect on this: if I am only operating out of the known areas and these others also exist, what am I missing? How might those missing pieces, if discovered, change the course of my life?

You may want to make an inventory of the various parts of yourself that you know about—for example, the roles you play, the masks you wear. If you are willing, show that list to a trusted friend, and ask whether or not they agree with it, and from their perspective, what they might add or take away.

4. There are many wisdom stories, legends, or mythic tales told of "pauper children" who are actually royal sons or daughters (heirs to the kingdom) hidden in the world. Perhaps they know it. Perhaps they do not, but once they discover it, everything changes. They may still be externally poor, but once they know their true origins, everything changes. Imagine yourself in that position and use the following exercise called, "Heaven's Child."
5. Suppose that you are actually "heaven's child" on earth, a divine representative sent here (some say, exiled here for a purpose). How would you act if you didn't know it? How might you act if you did? If you came to know it, what would enrich you? What would impoverish you? What might frustrate you? What would give you courage and energy? These are complex questions and they raise many issues. Spend time looking at this problem from all sides.

READINGS FOR INSIGHT

I

We are impoverished in our longing and devoid of imagination when it comes to our reaching out to others. We need to be introduced to our longings, because they guard our mystery. Ask yourself, what mystery is being guarded by your longing? Are you taking the time to find out? The time for this never appears; it is discovered.

Alan Jones

II

A bumptious man dismissed a wandering sage by shouting at him,
"Be off, nobody knows you here."
"But I know myself," said the sage.
"How sad it would be if the reverse were true."

A story of Sufi Origins

III

Wisdom is not a product of thought. The deep *knowing* that is wisdom arises through ... full attention. Attention is primordial intelligence, consciousness itself. It dissolves the barriers created by conceptual thought, and with this comes the recognition that nothing exists in and by itself. It joins the perceiver and the perceived in a unifying field of awareness. It is the healer of separation.

Pema Chödrön
Comfortable with Uncertainty
174

IV

The Truth is yourself,
But not your mere bodily self,
Your real self is higher than "you" and "me".
This visible "you" which you fancy to be yourself
Is limited in place, the real "you" is not limited.
Why, O pearl, linger trembling in your shell?
Esteem not yourself mere sugar-cane, but real sugar.
This outward "you" is foreign to your real "you";
Cling to your real self, quit this dual self.

Jalal-uddin Rumi
Spiritual Couplets
317

V.

The mind is incessantly looking not only for food for thought; it is looking for food for its identity, its sense of self. This is how the ego comes into existence and continuously re-creates itself.... When you think or speak about yourself, when you say, "I," what you usually refer to is "me and my story." This is the "I" of your likes and dislikes, fears and desire, the "I" that is never satisfied for long. It is a mind-made sense of who you are, conditioned by the past and seeking to find its fulfillment in the future. Can you see that this "I" is fleeting, a temporary formation, like a wave pattern on the surface of the water? Who is it that sees this? Who is it that is *aware* of the fleetingness of your physical and psychological form? I Am. This is the deeper "I" that has nothing to do with past and future.

Eckhart Tolle
Stillness Speaks
27-28

VI

T.S. Eliot

Where is the wisdom we have lost in knowledge?
Where is the knowledge we have lost in information?

VII

Marietta T. Stepaniants
Sufi Wisdom
41

Man's ignorance is due to the fact that he has forgotten his high predestination and has looked for the treasure of Truth everywhere except within himself. The path to the knowledge of God should take Man through rejection of his external self to affirmation of his real self.

VIII

Pema Chödrön
Comfortable with Uncertainty
209

When our attitude toward fear becomes more welcoming and inquisitive, a fundamental shift occurs. Instead of spending our lives tensing up, we learn that we can connect with the freshness of the moment and relax. The practice is compassionate inquiry into our moods, our emotions, our thoughts. Compassionate inquiry into our reactions and strategies is fundamental to the process of awakening. We are encouraged to be curious about the neurosis that's bound to kick in when our coping mechanisms start falling apart. This is how we get to the place where we stop believing in our personal myths, the place where we are not always divided against ourselves, always resisting our own energy. This is how we learn to abide in basic goodness.

IX

Anthony de Mello
One Minute Wisdom
60

"Help us find God."
"No one can help you there."
"Why not?"
"For the same reason that no one can help the fish find the ocean."

X

A.H. Almaas
Diamond Heart: Book One
22

Our whole society is set up to teach us that we should get our value from the outside to fill our holes—get value, love, strength, whatever—from the outside. We talk about how wonderful it is to do things for other people, or to fall in love, or have a meaningful profession—things like that. Society is arranged in general for people to fill each other's holes. Civilization as we know it, is a product of the false personality. It is the product of the false personality and it is the home of the false personality. It is what sustains and nourishes the false personality.

XI

Jalaluddin Rumi
The Book of Love
12-13

Why ask about behavior when you are soul-essence,
and a way of seeing into presence! ....
You are soul, and you are love,
not a sprite or an angel or a human being!
You're a *Godman-woman-Godman-God-Godwoman!*
No more questions now
as to what it is we're *doing* here.

LOGION 4:

Sapiential Themes

- *To find one's true Self at a later stage in life, one must return to the original source of one's being—to a form of infancy.*
- *The metaphor of a "seven-day-old" infant is understandable within the Hebrew context of creation.*
- *An understanding of transcendent topography becomes essential in the wisdom tradition.*
- *Inquiry is the methodology used to interrogate the infant about origination.*
- *The mysterious goal of this query is unification.*

Yeshua says. . .

A person of advanced age
must go immediately and ask
an infant born just seven days
about life's source.

Such asking leads to life
when what is first becomes last.
United they become a single whole.

Parallel Texts

Genesis 2:2-3, 17:12
Matthew 11:25-26, 18:2-4
Mark 10:13-16
Luke 10:21

FOCAL POINT

Logion 4 is the first true parable of this Gospel (the first paradoxical saying, a characteristic of many Semitic and Eastern wisdom texts). Its focus is on the experience of inversion where the symbolic figures of the infant and the elder are juxtaposed and then inverted in a non-logical way that forces new understanding beyond the rational mind. Symbolically, the elder speaks of chronological age and the knowledge that is accrued through temporal existence. The infant seven days old in the Hebrew tradition is an uncircumcised child (circumcision occurs on the 8th day). This is a child newly emerging from the Sabbath week of creation symbolizing the eternal day of Rest (Gen. 2:2-3). This parable sets up a logical reversal of expectations: normally, a child ought to be led by adults, not lead them. Children ought to ask questions of adults, not to answer them. Children need guidance to find their way to the place of life, not to instruct on that place (Valantasis). So a critical point of reversal is being made in order to open human understanding.

Links

Though this Logion may appear to have no relationship to the last, the connecting linkage of meaning concerns coming to know one's true Self. Where does one go to get that kind of information? Many answers can be given, but the most unexpected answer is found in this saying. The subject of seeking and asking is explored more fully in this Logion.

Notes

An important commentary and interpretation of the Gospel of Thomas has been prepared by Richard Valantasis. The basis of this commentary is the historical-critical method used by most modern commentators.

***The Gospel of Thomas**, London and New York: Routledge, 1977.*

COMMENTARY

Logion 3 has already instructed us in many things that lead us away from spiritual impoverishment to the true wealth of self-knowledge, becoming known, and to the knowledge that we are children of the Living One. This saying invites us into the meaning and realization of that spiritual wealth which is true self-knowledge. We discover that to be known we must meet and integrate with our Original form and in this way become true children of the Living One. In this way we come to be fully alive.

The image of the child is an important subject within the sacred traditions of the East (especially the Middle East and the teachings of Jesus). Something about the "child" leads a human being towards fullness of life—what is it? The child symbolizes what the East calls "the beginner's mind"—the readiness to see anew—to see as a child sees. The older we get, the more barriers we put up to the beginner's mind. It is hard to go back, to be vulnerable, to say to yourself, "I don't know anything." What blocks spiritual transformation and growth is the assumption that we already know, or that we don't need to know. In the parable, however, wisdom is signified by the metaphor of an elder who is wise enough not to delay or hesitate in asking the child from the standpoint of the beginner's mind.

The child also symbolizes the original "place" out of which the creation emerges—its Source and Origin. It signifies the original luminous state of the creation as it emerged into time. The Greek word ***topos*** is used in this Coptic version of the Gospel of Thomas and is critical, for it suggests a particular place of origination with its own special "topography." This "place," then, is one of great power; it is also one of harmony, rest and equilibrium as the centerpoint of all existence and the fountainhead of all that comes into being. To be there puts one into a state of unitive experience. The child represents that which has just arrived from its Origin and Source into the paradise of God, where heaven and earth are united. It is, therefore, proximate to unitive being for separative experience has not had "time" to make its effect in this paradisiacal state. This "garden of paradise" is the original home of humanity, and the home for which we long.

The beginning and ending points are the same—both are located in a topography of transcendence. It is this Source of life which is closer to the child and more distant to the elder. So the elder can ask and receive "news" from his or her own "child-mind" concerning this place of human origination. To know it (in order to find, ask, and receive from the beginning), however, there must be a recapitulation of steps, or change of direction, which brings the person of advanced age to the beginning point which is also the ending point. In some sense, the elder must reverse course (***metanoia***) and begin a journey of return to the place of revelation (or Original vision) to receive its full wisdom and self-knowledge.

It must be understood, however, that this Logion is not suggesting the return to a simple naiveté. Something has been gained – a new form of wisdom. Having passed through temporality, the elder now gains the state of the child as a new and yet ancient state. The ancient state is now entirely swallowed up in something fresh as it emerges out of temporality into eternity with the painful experience of having passed through space-time.

The basis of such a possibility of knowing (of receiving unitive knowledge) is grounded in two basic principles: many (but not all) of the first will be last, and the two (first and last, elder and child) will become one and the same—a single or unified whole. Duality is overcome by non-duality (a unification of the polarities, overcoming of opposites) which appears to be the great theme of this text. Interestingly, the "first" to arrive (as the elder), also becomes the "last" to arrive (as the child)...in which event they are united as one.

Throughout the Gospel of Thomas, returning to the original state of oneness (non-duality) will become a central focus. This paradoxical state, which unites opposites, cannot be adequately described. It can only be hinted at through metaphors and images which are liberally sprinkled throughout this Gospel by way of illustration. The state of oneness overcomes the dualities that manifest in this world, not by forcing them together or making one the other, but by transcending both through entry into the Realm of oneness—the Kingdom of God. There, the beginning and the end, the first and the last, temporal being and eternal being, exist together in perfect unity.

QUESTIONS FOR REFLECTION

1. Using the image below, begin your personal reflections upon the meaning of this Logion as it relates to you. Where are you in the experience of the "elder"— having already made part of your passage through time? Label this diagram with your own titles, times and places. What does the circle represent? What does the horizontal line signify?

2. If you understood the "child-mind" to be a way of talking about the "intuitive mind" how might this affect your understanding of Yeshua's teaching?

3. Have you ever used your unitive mind for inquiry? What happened? What has been your experience of this?

4. If you (as a person advanced in time) can ask the child-mind anything you need to know in this search, what might you want to ask?

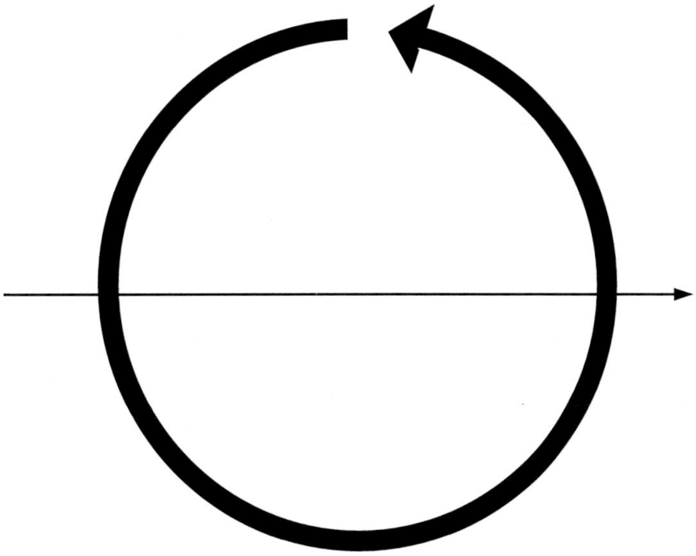

For an important perspective on the Zen-Buddhist view of the child-mind and its relationship to Christianity see:
J.K. Kadowaki, SJ
Zen and the Bible: A Priest's Experience
London, Boston: Routledge & Kegan Paul 1980

No diagram ever perfectly describes the complexity of these ideas. It is only an approximation. You may, therefore, want to change the diagram in some way to help you better understand this Logion..

EXERCISES AND MEDITATIONS

As this commentary unfolds there will be more exploration of this transcendent topography and its implications for the sapiential tradition.

1. Imagine that the first stage of the human journey is out of a "place" where one has the pure experience of the divine. The second stage of the journey is to enter into space-time and lose this awareness. The third stage begins a reflective process upon the question, who am I, really? Answers to that question begin to be understood, and then through assimilation into thought, feeling and memory, the implications of one's origins are integrated into one's being. The fourth stage formulates that understanding into words and actions so that it becomes communicable and is realized as a part of one's own experience. These steps constitute the journey of return, and in experience, move back through these layers to one's origins. Where are you in this process? How can you move from where you are now?
2. Another line of reflection has to do with play. The child is a symbol of playfulness—the seven days of creative play and the rest that God enacted. After much experience in time, the elder perhaps can begin to return to a state of play—effortless action, creative skill, and the capacity for turning work into play. He or she returns to the state of a child where consciousness is concentrated without effort—attention and awareness are completed and undivided in that original state which is serious play (not infantile play). However, the work of the elder has been indispensable. She or he is now ready to ask and be received into a new creative dimension. Wisdom is not merely the accumulation of experience in chronological age within space-time, but the state of being made ready for integration or oneness—the ultimate goal of this text—in which something entirely new and original can emerge. What is your experience of the playful elder?

READINGS FOR INSIGHT

I

Matthew 18:1-4

At that time the disciples came to Jesus saying,
"Who is the greatest in the kingdom of heaven?"
And calling to him a child, he put him in the midst of them, and said,
"Truly, I say to you, unless you turn and become like children, you will never enter the kingdom of heaven. Whoever humbles himself like this child, he is the greatest in the kingdom of heaven."

II

J.K. Kadowaki, SJ
Zen and the Bible
155

In both Zen and Christianity, the person who has reached the pinnacle of truth is simple and docile, like a little child. In that simplicity, however, there lies hidden infinite riches.

III

Qur'an 7:189

God it is who has created all of you from One Soul,
and made there from its spouse.

IV

Being at One with the Holy One of Being is not about becoming the same as God, but about forgetting the boundaries of self. You now realize who you have been all along. You forget, at least for a moment, the mind game of where you end and Creation begins. You understand that you are an expression of Creation: it is in you and you are everywhere in it .... The primary obstacle to becoming one is self-awareness, self-consciousness, talking to oneself. And for this reason, high awareness involves stopping, ignoring, forgetting the conversation we routinely carry on inside our heads between different parts of our personalities. Such amnesia is another word for self-unification.

When the one who asks and the one who hears are the same, we are who we are. We realize, to our embarrassment, that we have been ourselves all along and only linguistic convention tricked us into thinking that we were someone else .... The outer person is an illusion, a figment of language. Only an un-self-awareness remains.

Rabbi Lawrence Kushner
The Book of Words
15-17

V

We shall not cease from exploration
And the end of all our exploring
Will be to arrive where we started
And know that place for the first time.

T.S. Eliot
Four Quartets

VI

Through Returning Home all things are reunited with God .... Returning Home is, in essence, an effort to return to one's original status, to the source of life and higher being in their fullness, without limitation and diminution, in their highest spiritual character, as illumined by the simple, radiant divine light .... It is only through the great truth of returning to oneself that the person and the people of the world and all the words, the whole of existence, will return to their Creator, to be illumined by the light of life. This is the mystical meaning of the light of the Messiah, the manifestation of the soul of the universe, by whose illumination the world will return to the source of its being, and the light of God will be manifest on it.

Abraham Isaac Kook
Abraham Isaac Kook: The Lights of Penitence
10

VII

...In accordance with the Prophet's saying: "God created Adam according to His Image." The Divine Image is not at all the same as the image we have of ourselves. The creation of Adam is not a past event, that occurred millennia ago in the physical world—the fact that we are born in human form does not mean that we are born as Man. This second birth, the real birth of Adam, is a spiritual event that has to occur internally. In truth, our humanity does not begin until this is known. However, we must also realize that this is not simply a one-off event: it is a constant renewal of our being, for we are constantly inseminated by the Divine Spirit. At each moment we have the possibility to be truly human. At each moment we have the capacity to be a "mother" to what is presented to us, as we receive the influx of revelation: we were created to give birth to spiritual realizations and these depend upon the quality of receptivity and manifestation—or we may remain, albeit only for a time, attached to the illusions of independent selfhood.

Stephen Hirtenstein
The Unlimited Mercifer
49

VII

How long will you move backward?
Don't go, come near!
Do not stray in unbelief,
come dancing to religion.
Look, the elixir is hidden in the poison
Come, return to the root of the root of your Self.
Molded of clay you think you are an earthly being,
but you have been kneaded from the substance of certainty,
You are a guardian at the Treasury of Holy Light,
Come, return to the root of the root of your Self.
Once you get a hold of selflessness
you'll be dragged from your own ego,
and freed from its many traps,
So come, return to the root of the root of your Self.
You were born vice-regent
a child of the children of God,
but you have fixed your sights too low.
How can you be happy with these scraps?
Come, return to the root of the root of your Self.
Though you are a talisman
protecting the world's treasure,
yet within yourself you are the mine.
Open your hidden eyes and see,
Come, return to the root of the root of your Self.
You were born from the ray of God's majesty,
and have the blessing of the morning star,
so how long will you suffer
at the hands of things that do not exist?
Come, return to the root of the root of your Self.
You came here from the presence of the Friend,
a little drunk, but gentle, that look so full of fire,
How long will you try to deceive us,
we can see the truth in your eyes?
So come, return to the root of the root of your Self..
The King is here, our master and host,
and has placed the cup of eternity before you,
Glory, glory be to God, what a rare wine!
Come drink now
and return to the root of the root of your Self.

Jalal ud-din Rumi,
Diwan-e Shams-e Tabrizi

IX

The first human being was the first clairvoyant. To him, all appeared as spirit. What are children, but the first humans? The fresh eye of a child is more prolific than the insight of the most determined seer. What is a human being? A perfect spiritual metaphor. All true communication, then, takes place in images—and are not caresses therefore true communications?

Georg von Hardenberg
"Fragments"
An Endless Trace
220-221

LOGION 5:

Yeshua says. . .

Come to know the One in the presence before you,
and everything hidden from you will be revealed.

For there is nothing concealed that will not be revealed,
and nothing buried that will not be raised.

Sapiential Themes

- *Conscious presence and being present to consciousness is at the heart of searching and finding.*
- *There is an I AM Presence which fills the whole creation.*
- *The promise of the wisdom tradition is to reveal what has been hidden away and raise everything that bas been buried.*
- *The fulfillment of that promise lies close at hand; right in front of one's own face.*

Parallel Texts

Logia 52, 59, 77, 91, 109, 111
Exodus 3:14
Matthew 10:26
Mark 14:62

FOCAL POINT

This fifth saying of Yeshua posits the existence and presence of realities and persons invisible to the naked eye, but which can be "seen" nonetheless if one develops a certain form of attention. This Logion focuses on the **praxis** (practice) of spiritual attention to what is immediate and present (right in front of one's face), because what is actually present is often simply hidden in plain view. Coming to attention and remaining present to whatever or whoever exists in our field of awareness in the present moment is the key that unlocks the door to what is invisible and hidden behind the veil of visible reality. Knowing this presence is the doorway to knowing one's true self and place of origination. There is no doubt about the eventual full disclosure of these hidden things, or that hidden reality will become known and clear, and all that was buried raised. Immediate perception holds the key.

Links

Where would one go to ask the child about life's source? Where would that place be? How might one meet the child of one's origins? The answers to those important questions are given in this Logion, and again, they are surprising, but they come with a promise. This saying also has links to each of the earlier sayings in different ways. It links to Logion 1 when the living Yeshua becomes personally present. It links to the process of searching and finding and all that follows. It links as well to the discovery of the true Self that has remained hidden until it becomes revealed.

Notes

This Logion helps to illustrate why Thomas is not Gnostic in any formal way. Gnostic philosophy often posited "secret knowledge" possessed only by an elite few. Thomas declares a process available not to the few, but to all. Such knowledge is based, however, upon attentive recognition. In the end, nothing shall remain hidden... it will all "appear." This appearance of what lies hidden behind the surfaces of the world is the meaning of the term ***epiphany****.*

COMMENTARY

According to the Abrahamic traditions, the universe is filled with Presence. It is not empty as many modern men and women believe. The word Presence suggests that we inhabit a universe filled with ***anima*** or consciousness, not an inanimate and dead structure made entirely of matter. But there is more. The intuition of the Semitic peoples was that this consciousness is personal and invites us into a direct, personal encounter as Presence. In this Logion Yeshua instructs us to know the One who inhabits consciousness as another "I AM." Yeshua's own spiritual practice led him into that Presence which he knew as **Abba**. We ourselves are to become as fully aware as he was by being present to something (or someone) besides ourselves in the now-moment we currently inhabit.

Logion 5 has two versions, and multiple ways of translating the first line. The two versions are a Greek version in fragments which appears to be earlier, and the entire Coptic version used as the primary text. It is the Greek version which is used in this text and considered to be the fullest and most complete. Translation of the first phrase is critical to an understanding of the text. If it is translated in the form given above, then it suggests the student must come to know a living Presence by personal knowledge. Another possible, but perhaps more mundane, translation is as follows: "(Learn to) recognize what is present before your face,…" This translation is less direct and personal, and suggests, perhaps, only a simple attention to the present moment.

The availability of the divine Presence to the knowing heart is central to all spiritual teaching. If the One in the Presence is invisible to the naked eye, but nevertheless present before one's face, how do we come to know the I AM in an intense, personal way? What form of knowing is required? The words **face** and **presence** are metaphors having to do with the direct knowledge or experience of someone or something. If you are standing before the face of someone, you are in their presence, having direct personal knowledge. Yeshua's wisdom is based, not upon doctrinal correctness, but personal knowledge in a relationship of encounter between persons. This was the entire foundation of his own relationship with the **Abba**, and this Logion lays the groundwork for our participation in that same wisdom. This wisdom appears to be two-fold.

First, as we have previously seen, true self-knowledge is the master key to wisdom and to knowing who we are and the meaning of our existence. Logion 3 used the phrase, "When you come to know your self, you will be known…" In this Logion the important phrase is literally, "…know the One in the in the presence before your face." Together these suggests a double meaning. To be in the presence before your own face is to have direct personal knowledge not only of another Presence, but of yourself as well. Knowledge of your true Self and of the I Am Presence go hand-in-hand because both inhabit the same consciousness.

Second, if we juxtapose this Logion with the one just before it, we begin to get answers to the questions, how does one find the child? How does one reach the beginning-ending point? Here we see that the ancient past and the coming future are contained in this very moment and in what is available or "visible" to the gaze (or awareness) of one who is attentive to this present moment with its double centers of consciousness. Recognition of what is presently available (the Presence of One who is already here) is the key to the revelation of what has been heretofore unknown and unseen by us. Here revelation precedes resurrection—when what is buried (and perhaps dead as well) is ultimately raised into life. The theme of revelation and resurrection amplifies the meaning of the appearance (**epiphany**) of the One present in the midst of consciousness itself. Such an appearance brings with it revelation and resurrection. As a human being, you are presently a "hidden and buried reality." You will ultimately be revealed for who you are and the final revelation will come through being raised up. Your resurrection is dependent upon (and the result of) a new and final form of revelation (***apocalypsis***), which will be the unveiling of the entire creation. In that unveiling, all appearances will be stripped away and the original design and purpose of all things will be made known. This is the promise of resurrection.

QUESTIONS FOR REFLECTION

1. Have you ever noticed that you were not truly alone—but that in your awareness or consciousness something or someone else was present?

2. How attentive are you to your own experience and to what is right around you? How much of your attention is occupied with simply having experience, or being sure you are "enjoying" your experience, but not on what or who might be there, present in that experience?

The subject of consciousness is very complex. We seldom pay attention to consciousness itself, but only to the content of consciousness—our thoughts. Yet, we can become fully present to (or aware of) consciousness itself.

3. It is easy to look at our own experience through a limited "frame" or "lens"—for example, the expectations of an "other," of society, what we want for ourselves through anticipations of our own personal happiness, success, etc. Notice how much time you spend judging your experience by external standards, without truly looking at and recognizing your own consciousness and gaining understanding as you go.

4. Often we are simply preoccupied with the thoughts going through our heads. Most of the time our attention is focused on the surface of the outer world which is simply a backdrop for our thoughts. Observe yourself. How often is this true?

5. What "hidden things" have come to light for you? What are they?

EXERCISES AND MEDITATIONS

1. The state of inner attention (or watchfulness) is of utmost importance in this saying. To understand this as a form of spiritual practice, we must know that we inhabit time, but only in the present moment. We are never anywhere but in the present moment, but we are rarely ever "here." Typically we are somewhere else—"in our thoughts," or in some time other than where we currently are. We often live in our memories of the past, or we have taken off into the future and live there. Learn to recognize these two states in yourself.
2. Watchfulness entails recollection (or recollected awareness)—collecting those parts of us that are scattered across time and memory, so that our attention is re-collected where we are now in the present moment. This is a state of heightened awareness where we are fully awake to ourselves as well as to everything else around us.

3. Seeing what is really here (before or in front of us) is the next step in awareness, or in coming to know the unseen or the invisible structures behind the reality we experience. Attention in the present moment unlocks a door and allows us to step through into deeper structures behind external reality. The purpose of Thomas is to help us discover these invisible forms of wisdom.
4. So the next reflection we need to make is, to what are we to become "present?" What is to fill the screen of our attention in the present moment? The first answer has to do with an immediate awareness of our own being (our own presence) in a new form of self-observation. If we are to unlock the door to the invisible, then self-knowledge by recognition and by presence is required. To stay attentive to your own presence and your immediate experience of the world, and to recognize what is true about that experience, becomes a basic, daily practice. The truth is we are often blind or oblivious to our own experience. We are constantly "having experiences" but the truth of them, and the truth about ourselves in them, often goes unrecognized. No true self-knowledge comes from them. True self-knowledge is the foundation upon which any deeper knowledge or wisdom rests. Often we wish to rush into the invisible world behind appearances without this firm foundation of self-knowledge in the present moment.

Knowledge-by-presence is a very important spiritual and philosophical theme. It has an ancient lineage, but has not been well known in the West until the work of Michael Polanyi in the important text, ***Personal Knowledge: Towards a Post-Critical Philosophy*** *(London: Routledge & Kegan Paul, 1958).*

5. As the commentary suggests, the Presence of the Other, and the One who inhabits that Presence, is the second critical awareness. Humans know almost by instinct that divine Presence fills the universe—a Presence which inhabits and haunts the universe—but often they have no direct knowledge of that Presence, no sense of personal encounter. This saying invites us to get acquainted with that Presence in a personal way—perhaps by way of friendship, as one would with a person one had just met. What are the steps that you would need to take to make a new friendship? How would this apply as you get acquainted with the One who inhabits the universe?

In the Islamic tradition, the statement, "He who knows himself, knows his Lord," also suggests its reversal – the one who comes to know the Lord (as Presence) comes then to know the true Self. The two are inextricably tied together. One cannot happen without the other.

6. Waiting patiently for what is hidden to appear is a final aspect of the practice that is here directed by Yeshua. Spend time each day observing the world that is right in front of you and all around you. Watch that world (and yourself in it) as an observant scientist or anthropologist might do, trying to discover things that are missing from your knowledge. Each time you move back inside your head (spending more time with your own thoughts, expectations, and preconceived notions than you do with actual experience of yourself in the world around you), move back out of the flow of your thoughts and simply attend to what is right there in front of you in a state of watchfulness. Attention coupled with patience is implied as the basis of the practice of this saying.

READINGS FOR INSIGHT

I

And lo, the Lord passed by. There was a great and mighty wind; splitting mountains and shattering rocks by the power of the Lord; but the Lord was not in the wind. After the wind, an earthquake; but the Lord was not in the earthquake. After the earthquake, fire; but the Lord was not in the fire. And after the fire, the soft barely audible sound of almost breathing.

I Kings 19:11-12

II

O you who live in God's transcendent being,
know that you are sheltered by a mighty power.
You can truly say,
"You are the sanctuary in which I hide, my God.
You are the citadel of my trust."
For you release me from the snares the trappers set,
you save me from the poisonous bait put out for me.
Your wings are ever over me,
I hide among their feathers nested close to you.
In truth your presence is my shield,
protecting from the terrors of the night
And from the arrows flying through the day.
Near you, I do not fear the scourge which stalks my shadowlands,
nor the evils that set their ambush in my way.
You may walk among a pride of lions or through a viper's den,
but these will only be your stepping stones.
When you have set your love on God,
God has already place you under loving care.
And as you come to know the real name of God,
God is ever knowing yours, protecting you.
When you call out for me, God says,
I AM has already answered you.
I AM is with you in deep trouble.
I AM is saving you.
I AM will bring you to your destination.
Your length of life I will extend, says God,
And you will know my saving power restoring you.

Psalm 91: 1-6, 13-16
Ancient Songs Sung Anew

III

There are times when I am with you,
when there is no beginning or ending in time;
when the day is dateless and the rhythm of time has ceased to record the hours,
and the calendar, the days;
when no birds sing, but rest; and no winds blow, but breathe;
and the air is drenched with the white silence of love,
and my fingers trace the lineaments of your face.

Brother Thomas More Page

IV

Bodhichitta is a Sanskrit word that means "noble or awakened heart." Just as butter is inherent in milk and oil is inherent in a sesame seed, the soft spot of ***bodhichitta*** is inherent in you and me. No matter how committed we are to unkindness, selfishness, or greed, the genuine heart of ***bodhichitta*** cannot be lost. It is here in all that lives, never marred and completely whole.

It is said that in difficult times, it is only ***bodhichitta*** that heals. When inspiration has become hidden, when we feel ready to give up, this is the time when healing can be found in the tenderness of pain itself. ***Bodhichitta*** is also equated, in part, with compassion—our ability to feel the pain that we share with others. Without realizing it we continually shield ourselves from this pain because it scares us. Based on a deep fear of being hurt, we erect protective walls made out of strategies, opinions, prejudices, and emotions. Yet just as a jewel that has been buried in the earth for a million years is not discolored or harmed in the same way this noble heart is not affected by all of the ways we try to protect ourselves from it. The jewel can be brought out into the light at any time, and it will glow as brilliantly as if nothing has ever happened.

Pema Chödrön
Comfortable with Uncertainty
3-4

V

We live in a haunted house,
for a mysterious Presence fills the universe
and haunts us all.

L. Bauman

VII

One day some friends came to my house looking for me. I hid in the closet. They happened to hear the noise I made climbing inside. Although they didn't see me, they knew I was there (figuring it had to be me). We were all present in the same little house together. And so with joyful excitement and heightened anticipation mingled with fearful trepidation, they began to seek out my exact whereabouts. To them, the most real thing, certainly the most influential at the moment, was my unseen presence. Well, that is what religious experience is like. Finally, they opened the closet door, saw me standing there, and even though they knew what they were going to find, when they saw me with their own eyes, came into direct contact with my actual presence which was until that moment merely a suggested presence, haunting, telltale noise in the room, they stood still and screamed. That is what mystical experience is like.

Robert McNamara
The Human Adventure
146

VII

O God you have come searching for me.
You know me inside and out.
You know where I rise up and where I fall.
Before I think them, my thoughts are already clear to you.
The track of my journey you discern ahead of me.
All the pathways my life shall take are known to you.
Indeed before I speak them the meaning of every word is understood by you.
I am encircled by your presence, embraced by your hands.
These things I can hardly grasp, O my God,
they transport me to heights beyond myself.
Is it possible, then, to be absent from your presence?
Is there anywhere I could escape your Spirit?

Psalm 139
Ancient Songs Sung Anew

LOGION 6:

His students asked him,

Do you want us to fast?
How shall we pray?
Should we give offerings?
From what foods must we abstain?

Yeshua answered,

"Stop lying.
Do not do what you hate,
because everything here lies open
before heaven.
Nothing hidden will remain secret,
for the veil will be stripped away from
all that lies concealed behind it."

Sapiential Themes

- *The conscious awareness between his students in their early understanding, and the wisdom way of seeing in Yeshua are contrasted.*
- *The contrast between external religious duty and inner states of being is explored.*
- *The key to inner integrity has to do with truth and love.*
- *There are no "secrets" in the divine realm. Everything lies open to the unveiling movement of revelation.*

Parallel Texts

Psalms. 97:10, 119:163
Proverbs. 10:18, 13:5
Matthew 5:43-44, 6:24, 10:26, 16:17
Luke 6:27, 10:21, 12:2
Romans 1:25, 7:15
Ephesians 4:25
Colossians 3:9
I Timothy 2:7
I John 1:6

FOCAL POINT

The level of religious and spiritual awareness in Yeshua's students becomes clearer in this Logion. Their questions focus upon external form and religious duty. The emphasis of the Jewish tradition in Yeshua's day was upon doing what is right in the external world. The students' four questions center on their religious responsibilities as they perceive them. Yeshua's answer is an indirect one that changes the focus from outside performance to their inner state. Lying and doing what one hates are behaviors, but each of these manifests the interior state in relationship to external action. The rationale for change in the inner state and its subsequent consequences in the outer world is that in heaven's gaze nothing is hidden or secret—everything is open, and this same openness will bring about the divine action of revealing the hidden.

Links

The issue of religious practice comes to center stage in this Logion. From the beginning of the Gospel Yeshua's teaching has emphasized the practice of wisdom in many ways, none of which appear normal to his students. As followers of common Jewish practice they expect something more conventional. So their questions highlight the concept of common spiritual and religious practice performed by the normal Jew. Yeshua's answer pushes past their conventional concerns to the heart of the matter.

Notes

Religious life comes in two forms, one exterior and one interior. The concern of Yeshua was that the practitioners of religion know both forms, and not simply the first. The conventional religion of Yeshua's day was focused upon "correct form." In an attempt to point to the Reality at the heart of religion, Yeshua would often disregard or contravene accepted religious form and speak directly to the issues of the heart.

COMMENTARY

Heaven represents a vertical dimension. Its truth is a "plumb line" that descends into our world, often bisecting (and thus contradicting) the realities we take for granted. The standards set out in the Sermon on the Mount, and in much of the Gospel of Thomas, contradict conventional common sense – but these are the standards of a reality called "heaven" and "truth" seen from a vertical perspective. We are asked to live in that perspective. It is not possible to do this ideologically, but only through practice.

The setting of this Logion is a conversation. Yeshua and his students are in dialogue over issues of personal and religious concern. Many voices appear to be speaking. Their questions and his answer must be heard within the social context of the religious community of Yeshua's day. Everything in the Gospel up to this point suggests that personal experience through spiritual awareness and practice are the primary means of gaining wisdom. Jewish tradition is a religion of practice—the fulfillment of the precepts of the Torah in daily life. Yeshua's students therefore want to know what is required of them, since their previous experience of religion is based in the practice of Jewish duty. They can only think in terms of exterior religious practices, however. They list, therefore, the common practices: fasting, prayer, alms giving, and diet. What does Yeshua require of them in regards to these? For them it is a logical and important question. Perhaps, also, on the minds of all who gather to hear Yeshua's words.

Yeshua's answer (like all of his answers) moves far beyond the immediate (or surface) level to deeper issues essential to wisdom. His concern is not upon external practice per se, but upon interior realities and an inner integrity of spirit as the source of all spiritual and religious expression. The two imperatives: "do not lie" and "do not do what you hate" relate to the denial or distortion of truth, and the denial or distortion of the true Self. Nothing could be more central to spiritual life than these. External religious duties pale in comparison to these.

So what is lying? What does it mean to do what you hate? These are complex issues, but in essence they relate to one's own integrity and self-awareness. If we think of truth as that which conforms to reality, then much of our understanding and living is a distortion of reality. Often the distortion is self-deception, either a deliberate or an unknowing misrepresentation of the truth. If we speak or live a lie, we distort reality deliberately. If it is unconscious then we are experiencing confusion. Its opposite would be to tell or live the truth as fully and completely as possible—a difficult thing to do in a world full of systemic distortion.

Any form of spiritual practice is done not before the eyes of humanity, but before the gaze of heaven (or in Greek, before truth—(which means literally "the unforgetting").

Equally, we often act in direct opposition to what we deeply love or to love itself. Sometimes we act in conformity to social pressures around us or in direct violation of our own personal sense of integrity. In either case, the results are disastrous—spoiling the world around us and contravening our own inner sense of rightness and balance. Yeshua asks us to put an end to the patterns within us that destroy love.

Spiritual practice (and religious duty) is done in accordance with the three principles of disclosure: 1) Everything here lies open before heaven; 2) Hidden things will be revealed; 3) Anything that is covered or veiled will be unveiled. These principles underscore that clear seeing (enlightenment as opposed to blindness) is the crucial state of heaven, and that enlightenment through unveiling, uncovering, and disclosure raises everything into the divine light. Each of these actions is the energetic force of divine Reality. This is what is wanted and needed by Cosmic Mind and Intelligence—everything is pushing towards this goal. External piety, then, misses the point entirely. The issue of practice within the tradition of wisdom is the praxis of openness from an interior point of view. Everything else is "false piety" and done for the wrong reasons or with the wrong ultimate ends in view.

QUESTIONS FOR REFLECTION

1. If you could, what would be your "top ten" questions for Yeshua? In terms of religious practice, what are your main concerns?

2. How would you define lying and doing what you hate? How have you participated in these practices? In what way have these two patterns of life or activities been destructive for you?

3. If you knew that all the activities of earth lie open and transparent to every dimension above space-time, how might that affect you? Why would transparency be a characteristic along the vertical axis?

Implicit in this saying is a cosmology that is radically different from the modern view that the only reality is the material universe. In the ancient viewpoint the cosmos was a realm of multiple dimensions. This older viewpoint, however, is coming to be seen as true by the most modern physicists.

4. The question for every follower of Yeshua is, where do we put our spiritual priorities—on external religious demands or inner realities? Reflect on the relationship between these aspects of religious practice in your own life. Where does the weight lie?

EXERCISES AND MEDITATIONS

1. Esoteric spiritual practice uses altogether different criteria from external obligation set out here under the two injunctions: "do not lie," and "do not do what you hate." These may be interpreted literally (for example the simple telling of lies in terms of what is spoken), or they may point toward deeper distortions that are lived through our thoughts. If truth is an "unforgetting" (the derivation of the word in Greek), then a lie has something to do with forgetfulness, and hence distortion because of what cannot be (or is not) remembered.
2. An Exercise: "Do What You Love." To do what one hates is to contravene some inner compass of heart or conscience. How often do we violate that inner truth telling and so "sin" against our own best and highest knowledge? This is a difficult question to answer because the contravention may have something to do with our blind spot. It may also be that the actual effects of self-hatred come after an event and not before it. An increase in the sensitivity of practice would, therefore, involve a form of fore-knowledge about what one hates, and not 20/20 hindsight. Better in this practice would be to "do what one loves"—that is, live according to an inner law of right-relatedness about which one can be passionately committed.

READINGS FOR INSIGHT

I

Muhammad

When God wishes a servant well,
God causes that one to see the faults of the soul.

II

A.H. Almaas
Elements of the Real in Man
99, 155

When you have compassion for yourself you begin to trust yourself,
and you begin to see that it is the truth that saves you.
When truth is present,
it is as if you are tasting something within your heart.

III

A.H. Almaas
Elements of the Real in Man
98

...the process of learning to see the truth will bring up a lot of pain, fear and humiliation. So when you are faced with the choice of seeing the truth about yourself or someone else, or avoiding the pain, which is the compassionate action? If you choose to hide the truth in any situation, no matter how devastatingly painful it might be to face it, you are sentencing yourself to living the World of Lies.

IV

Meister Eckhart
Love Poems from God
113

What a cruel act to be untruthful.
Earthquakes happen in the heart that hears sounds that are amiss.
Havoc is created in the mind that can no longer trust someone once loved,
and schisms devour alliances that helped support life.
Words can enrich and be as wonderful spices
mixed into the days we imbibe with all our senses.
There are fields in the soul—lush organic meadows,
though sounds and words that fall there can be, at times, a poison.
A plague is spread by one who cannot tell the truth.

V

Anthony de Mello
Taking Flight
186

There was a loud knocking in the seeker's heart.

"Who's there?" asked the frightened seeker.
"It is I, Truth," came the answer.
"Don't be ridiculous," said the seeker. "Truth speaks in silence."

That effectively stopped the knocking—to the seeker's great relief. What he did not know was that the knocking was produced by the fearful beating of his heart.

VI

St. Augustine

Love God
and do what you like.

LOGION 7:

Yeshua says,

A lion eaten by a man is blessed as it changes to human form,

but a human devoured by a lion is cursed as lion becomes human.

Sapiential Themes

- *The first parable presented as a paradox.*
- *The first* **makarios** *or blessing.*
- *The two images, lion and human, possess both positive and negative qualities.*
- *Eating (or ingestion) describes the metaphoric action of this parable.*
- *Eating results in change—alterations in consciousness and being.*

Parallel Texts

Psalm 1
Psalm 7:2, 17:2, 22:13, 49:12, 21
Ezekiel 1:10
Daniel 7:4
I Peter 5:8

FOCAL POINT

In a visual play of opposites, this parable introduces two processes: downward and upward transmutation as the cause of blessedness and woe. Through the metaphor of a lion and a human, two interior states come into existence in the act of eating. When human and lion-like forms ingest qualities from the other they are transformed. Clearly these are not external realities (humans becoming literal lions, and lions becoming literal humans), but transformations of consciousness leading to interior states of being. In both cases the parable focuses upon the "lion becoming human"—leonine qualities emerging as human realities. The issue is the direction of metamorphic change, downward or upward. In each case human and leonine characteristics must be interpreted differently. In the end, two very different kinds of humans beings—one which has eaten the lion, and other which the lion has consumed—illustrating the states of blessedness and curse.

Links

In the previous saying Yeshua's imperative is to stop lying and doing what one hates. What could this mean, and how would it affect the human condition if these commands were carried out in practice? Through image and symbol, Logion 7 illustrates what happens when lies are told and hatred is lived. The result is a state of woe or curse. Released from this state, however, one enters the realm of blessedness.

Notes

This saying expresses a classic parable in the form of a paradox. The metaphors in the parable concern relationships illustrated by a lion and a human consuming each other. As paradox, it is a direct assault on the logical or rational mind. The asymmetry between the two propositions concerning lions and humans makes it appear illogical and irrational. One would think that it should read: Blessed is the lion which a man eats so that the lion becomes human, but cursed is the human which a lion eats so that the human becomes a lion.

COMMENTARY

To understand how the metaphors work in this saying, begin by imagining both positive and negative qualities for the images: lion and human. The point is not that animals and humans eat each other (lions do eat humans (though humans seldom eat lions), but that certain qualities or characteristics that these creatures represent overtake one's being. Lions can be both brave and strong, but they can also be ferocious and brutal. Humans can be kind, caring, strong and "royal," but they too, can descend into a state of cruelty and viciousness. It all depends on which qualities are in control. Metaphorically, eating signifies an interior (and even intimate) relationship between each creature—for each is taking qualities or forms of the other into itself and internalizing them.

The word ***makarios*** *used here is the same one used in the Sermon on the Mount for the beatitudes.*

A blessed human being (perhaps even a "true" human being) is one who has "eaten the lion." If eating signifies integration and assimilation, then an un-integrated or a disintegrated individual lives under a "curse" (perhaps even under the "original curse" of alienation and disintegration).

Imagine yourself encountering a lion alone in the wild. It would be a heart-stopping experience. Each of you possesses certain energies and power, but they are not the same, or even equal. The might and power of a lion is legendary, and a human unarmed and unaided is no match. The lion appears to be unassailable, but is it? What the lion possesses in power, the human possesses in intelligence. Given the opportunity, a human could out-think and perhaps trap the lion. Strategically, a higher order intelligence has power over a lower order intelligence despite the lion's massive strength.

The purpose of this saying is to match the brute force of lower orders (symbolized by the lion) with the higher and subtler force of heaven (the human). It is possible, but it all depends on the action of eating. The lion represents the bestial level of eating merely for the sake of survival—the shadow side of the human condition. The image of the human signifies something "higher" than the fulfillment of life centered only on basic instincts. The bipedal, anthropomorphic symbolism of a human being standing up in the cosmos and eating suggests a spirituality greater than the instinctual. In each case of eating, the integration and transmutation of certain energies from one level into the other is in focus. The bestial level can be integrated upward into a new fullness where two great forces (the instinctual and the relational) form a new identity—creating a state of blessedness experienced as an inner flowering of joy, bliss, poise, and radiance. Or if, as the image suggests, the lion devours the human, reducing the higher order to the level of the instinctual, there is curse (opposite the state of ***makarios,*** blessedness). Higher qualities are downgraded and made to serve the lower. What is blessing becomes affliction.

It is clear from Yeshua's teachings that entering the state of blessedness has to do with a **hierarchy of being** called "the Kingdom." The difference between a human and a lion is not simply that they are dissimilar objects or creatures, but that each lives in entirely different realms or domains where different principles and values apply. On the natural level, there are important distinctions between the human and animal worlds and the image of a lion and a human symbolize these differences. The higher one moves up the chain of being the greater are the choices available and the wider their implication for the cosmos. Lions eat their prey in the natural course of ecological balance. Humans eat, are nourished and extend the act of eating into a higher world of hospitality and relationship. The human image symbolizes transformational ascent from a lower to a higher order. In Thomas, Yeshua is inviting us to eat higher up the chain of being—consuming life-giving qualities from the realm of the Kingdom and thereby experiencing metamorphosis.

The key to understanding the wisdom of this saying, therefore, rests on the meaning of eating (ingesting lion-like or human-like qualities into one's being as a kind of food). Humans eat for both survival and pleasure. Lions eat presumably at a more instinctual level to keep their kind alive. Humans, however, have elevated eating to a social act surrounded with elaborate ritual in which the benefit is a state of blessedness shared by a family or a community. The act of eating not only results in personal pleasure, but establishes new or renewed relationships which ultimately transforms the world of the eaters. This parable symbolizes this form of transformation occurring on many different levels. Yeshua invites us to move into the Kingdom's state of blessedness through the transformation of the lower into the higher. It all depends on what qualities are ingested and take control of one's being.

QUESTIONS FOR REFLECTION

1. Imagine being taken over by a lion who has turned itself into a human inside of you. What might you expect from this transformation?

There was a movie made with a similar theme, "The Invasion of the Body Snatchers."

2. Suppose that the "forces of the lion" stand not only for animal energies (or attachments to the passions, as the early Desert Fathers and Mothers will say), but also for the erratic and unpredictable nature of your ego. How have you experienced these wild, ferocious forces, and your ego being out of control?

The early Christian tradition put great emphasis upon what they called the "passions"—those attachments that "ate up" the soul and prevented it from transformation. For a study of this see: Metropolitan Hierotheos ***Orthodox Psychotherapy*** *(Levadia, Greece: Birth of the Theotokos Monastery, 1994)*

3. How do you picture the "uncontrollable" forces of your own nature? Do you give them animal symbolism? What would that symbolism be?

4. In practice, how do you integrate the wild, animal-like leonine forces within your own nature into something higher?

5. Have you ever experienced the "curse" of being assimilated into the lower nature? Why was that a curse? Why is the other a blessing? Define "blessedness."

Many metaphors for the ego and egoic consciousness will be used in Thomas and across Christian tradition. Wisdom teaching among the Semitic peoples tended to use graphic metaphors to illustrate the energetic nature of the ego at work within human beings.

6. If the lion symbolizes egoic forces how does the image of a human symbolize higher realities? What name would you give to this new image?

EXERCISES AND MEDITATIONS

1. Though the metaphors in this saying present us with animal symbolism, the focus is upon two states of humanity—a blessed state in which the leonine nature has been taken up into the human realm and subdued, and a cursed state in which humanness has been subsumed by leonine qualities which devour the soul. A human can live in either state; it all depends upon "eating"—the relational exchange between one level of the hierarchy and another. What does it mean to feast on the being of another creature? What does it mean to dine or take a meal with someone else? What are we doing when we are eating?

Living in the state of "curse" may be directly related to the injunctions in Logion 6. The Lion may define the actions of lying and hating.

2. Eating is, of course, central to the symbolism of historic Christianity in the Eucharist. Based upon the words of Jesus in St. John "...for unless you eat of the flesh of the Son of Man and drink his blood you have no life within you." The meaning of Jesus' words here has to do with communion (or co-union) with the Son of Humanity, and assimilating the greater being of Yeshua into one's own self. In communion with the body of Christ, a human takes another step forward in an ascending hierarchy from human to the divine nature.

John 6:51-54

READINGS FOR INSIGHT

I

Yehuda Berg
The Power of Kabbalah
219

When the accumulated, intolerant actions of man can become so great, they create a mass of negativity that literally bocks the Light....This is how chaos is born.

II

Gillian Feeley-Harnick
The Lord's Table

Food exchanges are able to act as symbols of human interaction. Eating is a behavior which symbolizes feelings and relationships, mediates social status and power, expresses the boundaries of group identity.

III

Richard Rohr
Jesus' Plan for a New World
11

The world as it would be if God were directly in charge would be a world of right relationships. It would not be a world without pain or mystery but simply a world where we would be in good contact with all things, where we would be connected and in communion. Conversely, the world of the Evil One is always to separate, divine and throw (tear) apart (*dia-bolical*).

IV

Anthony de Mello
One Minute Wisdom
207

Much advance publicity was made for the address the Master would deliver on "The Destruction of the World" and a large crowd gathered at the monastery grounds to hear him. The address was over in less than a minute. All he said was: "These things will destroy the human race:

politics without principle
progress without compassion
wealth without work
learning without silence
religion without fearlessness
worship without awareness."

V

Jalal uddin Rumi
The Soul of Rumi
167

A lover loves death,
which is God's way of helping us evolve
from mineral to vegetable to animal,
the one incorporating the others.
Then animal becomes Adam,
and the next will take us beyond what we can imagine,
into the mystery of *we are all returning*.
So do not fear death.

LOGION 8:

Yeshua says,

A true human being can be compared to a wise fisherman who casts his net into the sea and draws it up from below full of small fish.

Hidden among them is one large, exceptional fish which he seizes immediately, throwing back all the rest without a second thought. Whoever has ears let them understand this.

Sapiential Themes

- *Fishing is a familiar image in the teaching and experience of Yeshua. Here it becomes a metaphor for wisdom.*
- *Water, another metaphor, is used here to refer to symbolic depth and the surface of the world.*
- *Discernment, a crucial faculty in the wisdom tradition, is expressed in this Logion as immediate recognition and choice.*
- *Numeration, quantity and size stand for quality, meaning, and value.*

Parallel Texts

Matthew 13:47-48, 17:27
Luke 5:4-9
John 21:3-9

FOCAL POINT

You may have seen the sign, "Gone fishin'!" This could be the heading placed not only above the picture this parable creates, but over the whole of human existence. We human beings are on a deep-sea fishing expedition across the surface of life, pulling up our catch from mysterious depths. While our vessel moves across the horizons of space and time, we human beings search for that which lies deeper, below the surface. True human beings are by nature searchers after meaning, fishers of the mystery, adventurers sailing across the vast expanse of existence. This parable tells the tale of wisdom's work in all of these activities.

Links

How would you describe a true human being—the one who consumes the lion? The two logia which follow Logion 7 (as well as many other Logia throughout the Gospel) define this new form of humanity by who they are and how they act. This is the second mention of the sea in Thomas. The first reference (either neutral or perhaps negative) was mentioned in the third saying. In this Logion, however, it has positive value, for great, good fish come to the surface from its depths.

Notes

Notice that the vertical relationships of ascent and descent in the previous saying are continued in this Logion. Here, however, the horizontal is added, for the ship floats across the surface of the sea. All the while the wise fisherman acts along the vertical axis casting his net down into the depths and raising fish up into the boat. These bi-axial spatial relationships are symbolically significant in sapiential teaching.

*The term used here, the "Human One" (**anthropos**) is perhaps the same individual who becomes a blessed human in Logion 7. In traditional literature this term is very significant and can also refer to the primordial human, as well as the collectivity of humanity gathered in the original Adam.*

COMMENTARY

In this saying Yeshua is teaching humanity not only about the wise person, but also about the nature of a true human being—the "Human One." (***anthropos***). He clarifies what it means to be truly human (as opposed to a human being of lesser wisdom). It is one who knows how to fish the depths; who is at work fishing in the sea of existence—in the realm of space and time as we know it and yet going beneath the surface to the unknown resources of the deep. There is much that lies hidden below the surface of the world waiting to be caught. This mysterious fact is the impetus that fills any serious fisherman with the urge to fish.

Clearly Yeshua is not teaching his students (many of whom are already veteran fishermen from Galilee) some new technique. He is applying what they already know to the higher pursuits of wisdom in human existence. In that realm they can also become **wise** fishermen, for in its height and in its depth there exist the mysteries. This unknown sea contains many things great and small. In it, however, are large, good fish, something quite different (perhaps unique) from the small, ordinary fish that are normally caught. All avid fishermen are after the "the big one"—the fish that easily gets away. This distinction between great and good, and small and perhaps ordinary (and the ability to tell the difference between them), is central to wisdom.

In this scene, fishing is by net, which means it is an indiscriminate drawing up out of the sea of existence whatever is captured and held in its mesh. Indiscriminate "netting" is followed by a discriminate choosing from the sea of existence and lifting it into higher reality, space and time. When the objects caught in the net reach the surface of space-time, it is time to choose and decide between them. This is the key. The wise fisherman can immediately tell the difference between a good fish (the one you keep) and the ones that you must let back into the sea.

The parable unfolds in a series of actions: casting a net, drawing it up, discovering the good fish, lifting it out, throwing back all the rest. Each of these completes the picture describing the abilities of a wise fisherman. The human being who acts with wisdom brings to the surface what is crucial and important from out of the depths. At the critical moment he or she can discern the large, good fish without difficulty or hesitation. He or she acts to throw everything else immediately back into the sea (keeping what is better, and of more value), all part of the expression of choice.

So what is this form of fishing all about, and what is the sea out of which good fish are caught? For millennia, the image of the ocean has signified the mysteries of the conscious and unconscious mind and the depths of the Divine Intelligence out of which all such consciousness comes. We fish in that depth with our creative imagination, gathering images from this sea of intelligence—raising objects of meaning to the surface. Only when the myriad of objects come to light on the surface can we make the decision to keep what is mature and ready and let the still-too-small fall away. The one large and good fish is the unified form that wisdom discerns which has now surfaced out of the watery darkness.

Anyone listening to (or, perhaps, seeing) this picture with the proper ears (eyes) can understand and learn.

QUESTIONS FOR REFLECTION

1. What is the difference between an experienced and a first-time fisherman? If the picture was changed and the man was either bait fishing or fly-fishing, would it change the meaning in any way? How?

Metaphorically, the sea is very symbolic. You might think about your own dreams of water and the ocean and make a determination about its significance and meaning for you.

2. Wise action in the midst of life as a sacred domain is likened to the process of fishing. In life we are seeking for something (fishing, either by vocation or as a game). We are seeking something out of the sea of existence. The actions of this parable raise very specific questions. First, what is "fishing" and how do you cast a net in the sea of existence? Second, how do you draw usable material up out of that sea? Third, how do you discover what is great and good? Fourth, how can you choose without difficulty, and willingly throw back everything else?

3. Have you ever "come up" with a really good idea? Where did it come from? How did you get it? How did you know it was a really good idea?

4. What is this region of the unknown in which you fish?

EXERCISES AND MEDITATIONS

1. At first glance, this parable seems so simple—but is it? What if you dreamed it, what would it mean for you? Do you really fish the sea, or are you simply passing over existence? Can you draw material out for yourself, or does it remain hidden—and someone else has to provide you with fish? Can you make discoveries of great, good material without difficulty, discriminating it from all the rest? Do you have the ability to choose well, and relinquish the rest? Each of these questions concerns discernment, which is the essence of wisdom—making wise choices.
2. Discernment is expressed metaphorically by size (a quantitative property). However, the parable adds the key word of quality (good) to indicate a critical issue in discernment. The external eye can see size without difficulty. Can the inner eye discern greatness and goodness without difficulty? Quantity shifts to quality in this parable. Journal your reflection on your own criteria for discerning quality: knowing what to hold on to and what can be let go.
3. The metaphor of choosing the one good thing distinct from the many things of lesser quality puts us into the realm of practical spiritual experience. This motif of the "one good thing" (a pearl, a treasure, a fish, a coin) is expressed repeatedly in the teaching of Yeshua. Existence is a sea filled with multiple entities, experiences and realities. It is easy to be lost at sea, unable to fish, unable to choose. Wisdom is the ability to fish and choose well. The question in your practice is: "In the sea of existence am I a wise fisherman? Do I choose well?"

Finding meaning is one of the major tasks of human life. We do it constantly in "reading" the body language of another human, trying to understand complex interactions and the hidden motivations in the world of human interaction. When you fish for meaning, how good are you?

Inner discernment is a faculty that is traditionally linked to the powers of the cognitive organ called the heart. Learning to use this faculty is central to the practice of wisdom.

READINGS FOR INSIGHT

I

The soul never thinks without a mental image.

Aristotle

II

Live deep enough
and there is only one direction.

Author Unknown

III

Hasan of Basra was given to extreme ascetic practices. Through these, he won certain occult powers which he took great pride in flaunting.

One day he saw Rabia on the bank of the river. He threw his prayer rug onto the water and shouted to her, "Rabia, come! Let's pray together!"

Rabia replied, "Is it really necessary for you to sell yourself like this? If it is, it is because you are weak."

Then, Rabia ascended into the air on her prayer rug and called down. "Hasan, come up here! Everyone will see us!" Hasan, who was not as advanced as she, stayed silent.

Rabia said to him, "What you did a fish can do. What I did a fly can do. The real work is beyond either of our tricks. The one thing necessary is to do the real work."

Andrew Harvey
Perfume in the Desert
121

IV

Purity of heart is to will one thing, but to will one thing could not mean to will the world's pleasure and what belongs to it, even if a person only named one thing as his choice, since this one thing was one only by a deception. Nor could willing one thing mean willing it in the vain sense of mere bigness which only to a man in a state of giddiness appears to be one. *For in truth to will one thing a man must will the Good.* On the other hand, as for each act of willing the Good which does not will it in truth, it must be declared to be double-mindedness. ... If then, a man in truth wills the Good, then *he must be willing to do all for it or he must be willing to suffer all for it.*

Sören Kierkegaard
Purity of Heart

V

"I am ready to go anywhere in search of Truth," proclaimed the ardent disciple.

The Master was amused. "When are you going to set out?" he asked.

"The moment you tell me where to go."

"I suggest you travel in the direction your nose is pointed."

"Yes. But where do I stop?"

"Anywhere you wish."

"And will the Truth be there?"

"Yes. Right in front of your nose, staring your unseeing eyes in the face."

Anthony de Mello
One Minute Nonsense
143

VI

A heart that has been completely emptied of mental images gives birth to divine, mysterious intellections that sport within it like fish and dolphins in a calm sea. The sea is fanned by a soft wind, the heart's depth by the Holy Spirit.

St/ Hesychios
***Philokalia**. Vol. I, 190*

LOGION 9:

Sapiential Themes

- *The agricultural metaphor of planting and harvesting illustrates wisdom's work in the cosmos.*
- *The profligate and hopeful sower is generous with the seed.*
- *Different soil types and conditions receive the seed reflecting the human ground.*
- *The goal of all planting is the harvest which, as this saying suggests, means sending it heavenward.*

Yeshua says,

A farmer went out to plant; seed in hand he scattered it everywhere.
Some fell on the surface of the road. Birds came and ate it.

Other seed fell on rocky ground and could not take root in the earth, or send grain heavenward, so never germinated. Still other seed fell among weeds and brambles which choked it out and insects devoured it.

Some, however, fell onto fertile soil, which produced fruit of high quality yielding as much as sixty
and one-hundred-and-twenty percent.

Parallel Texts

Psalm 126
Matthew 13:18-32
Mark 4:3-9
Luke 10:2
John 4:35
Ephesians 3: 10-12
James 3:15-18
I Peter 1:23

Links

Continuing the theme of the true human, this saying develops a third metaphor by way of illustration. Those familiar with the canonical Gospels will recognize this parable told by Yeshua to illustrate the interaction taking place within a human being who engages with divine Reality. Wisdom understands the true nature of the human condition, and what is required to become productive in the field of divine life.

FOCAL POINT

This and the last two logia utilize the most fundamental survival skills of humanity as spiritual symbols: hunting, fishing, and farming are metaphors for divine activity and the spiritual energies which sustain human life in the tradition of wisdom. Following the metaphors of hunting and net fishing, Yeshua takes up the great agricultural symbol of farming to illustrate the divine work in the cosmos—and more particularly in the field of the human heart. In the rural lands of the Middle East, each of these metaphors represents the source of human existence. In the wisdom tradition, they also speak of truths crucial to survival.

Notes

Twice in the original Coptic, the text says that the grain is meant to be sent heavenward. This emphasis means that the great goal of productivity is destined for something transcendent to either the grain or the earth itself.

COMMENTARY

If we think of farming as a cosmic rather than a provincial enterprise, then this saying takes us to the heart of wisdom's vision for the universe. Like the passionate gardener or the serious farmer, the creation is designed for harvest, perhaps provisioning the future with the labors of present-day existence.

Fishing and farming are clearly two favorite metaphors in the teaching tradition of Yeshua. Sea and soil are the two constituent elements of physical reality along the horizontal axis. Symbolically, however, each stands for something far more crucial—interior elements of human reality: the sea of human consciousness, and the soil of human being. Consciousness and being are at the heart of the divine concern.

This parable, told in expanded form in the canonical Gospels, is expressed here very directly and simply with little commentary. Its powerful image, so common to the majority of human beings who subsist through farming the earth, points toward mysteries beyond earth which concern the divine agenda for all existence and every human being. For millennia humans have farmed the earth, sustaining physical existence, but a far larger "agricultural enterprise" is going on just beneath (or above) the surface of ordinary reality. Divine seeds fall as God "farms" the universe of intelligent beings, and as this saying suggests, these beings are cast onto the ground of the human condition (the horizontal realm of space-time) with the hope that some will germinate and bear fruit. In the end some seeds indeed do, sending their produce heavenward.

At the center of this saying is the unknown sower who, in an act of great generosity, takes seed and scatters it in every direction along the horizontal plane of temporal and spatial reality. This seed, belonging to the farmer, is sown with no hesitation and falls wherever it will onto a diversity of soils and conditions. The first is the highly traveled surface of the road, illustrating perhaps the surface structure of human social reality, where the seed lies unable to gain ground and is carried off by observant birds. The second is similar, but even harder to penetrate: rocky ground which gives no room to root and so fails the test of germination. Nothing is able to penetrate below its surface or grow above ground, in order to move heavenward. The third soil condition is already occupied with other life forms which will allow no competition and so the seed is swallowed up and destroyed by outside forces. Finally, however, there is a portion of fertile ground which is able to produce a high-quality product that sends multiples of itself heavenward.

Because the sower is an unknown figure, it is possible to read this parable in a different way. Responsibility for sowing the seed might also belong to humanity. The sower may also represent a human, or at least a particular kind of human—one perhaps like the Anointed One. On the other hand, consistent with the way other passages of the Christian Scriptures are interpreted, the sower more clearly can be identified as the divine gardener who is sowing seed, and humanity as the recipient of this divine care.

Only in the last soil type is there increase. All else is decrease and diminution. If we are to understand this parable from the perspective of wisdom, clearly the seed contains the germ of divine life and only certain kinds of soil conditions can receive and benefit from it. The universal law of cause and effect (or "karmic law" as it is called in eastern traditions), therefore, is being represented in this saying by the relationship of the sown seed to the various soil types. An "if...then" correspondence expresses this law. There is, however, indeterminacy about where these seeds might fall and how much grain is ultimately produced out of the good soil.

Metaphorically, then, the soil types stand for regions of human receptivity to the divine seed. Typically these soil types are interpreted as four different kinds of human beings whose inner condition is represented by one of these types. However, one might also conclude that all four types exist within every human being. The four zones of receptivity (and the four outcomes) express the four ways that a human being relates to the divine action.

QUESTIONS FOR REFLECTION

1. Imagine yourself to be a field in which the four soil types exist. What are the hard-packed, well-trafficked conditions that receive nothing new—no exterior life-form other than what already moves there? What carries "life" away from you?

2. Imagine the other soil types inside your being: the rocky, infertile soil where there is no depth, but lots of obstructions. Think about the "jungle within," the weed patch of overgrowth, full of devouring insects that choke out and eat away whatever is productive. Imagine these metaphors are pointing you toward clarity about your inner condition. What are they teaching you?

3. What is fruitful, productive, and creative in your life that you send up and out into the cosmos? Where is the energy in your life? Where is itcoming from?

EXERCISES AND MEDITATIONS

1. If you imagine God to be the divine gardener, then this saying makes you "ground" for the living grain that is sown in the human condition. There are many practical questions raised by this understanding. It is imperative, therefore, for you to reflect on the soil types that are represented here:

   A road: ground which is hard-packed through traffic and overuse.
   Rocks: ground which is not yet soil and has no nutritive elements to sustain life.
   Thorns: useable soil that is overgrown with insect infested weeds which choke out and destroy life.
   Good ground: soil that is arable and produces good fruit.

   What is the primary (or largest) soil condition inside your being? Do you know the answer to this question? Typically where does the germ of divine life fall in you, and what has been the result? What has been harvested from your being?
2. Creating and expanding arable land within your being is possible as a form of spiritual practice. In the natural world soil types seem passive, so it is counter-intuitive to think that we could actively rework the ground of our own being. To the degree that we each have some control over this process, we can create fertile soil within; that is, we can prepare ground through an inner state of openness to the transcendent and the divine. There is a synchronicity between the appearance of the divine seed and the inner configuration of the soul which becomes the precise state that is able to receive and germinate the seed, producing fruit. Imagine your work is to expand the acreage of available land to the seeds of Spirit through receptivity and emptiness of heart. What does this mean for you? How is this accomplished?

The ground of one's being in traditional wisdom is said to be the heart. This is the foundation, the soil from which grows the "rose of enlightenment."

A seed has no energy of its own, but it can come alive in the right environment. Every form of life has a capacity for response but none so much as the human being. In an infertile environment this capacity for response may be dormant. The cultivation we need to provide is through conscious awareness. This makes the difference between nominally being alive and being alive abundantly. With awareness we can develop all our faculties. The body, mind, spirit, and ecology form an interconnected whole. When a harmonious relationship exists among all of these, we have abundant life

Kabir Helminski,
from Living Presence
11

*Note that the heads of grain are represented by vertical growth sent heavenward. This is the driving force and destiny of divine life. This is the inner destiny (**entelechy**) which moves us toward the transcendent—the Sun of divine Light. This striving, longing, and fruitfulness produces "grain," nutritive elements that ultimately can become "bread" and "wine."*

READINGS FOR INSIGHT

I

Author Unknown
"The Song of a Grain of Wheat"

I'm not afraid of the furrow, someday I'll germinate,
Tomorrow I shall be bread.
Death awaits in the furrow, warm wedded embrace,
Death, you do not know my secret,
Tomorrow I shall be bread.
Death, I shall bury myself in your womb,
And the world will forget me;
Your embrace will be painful,
But tomorrow, I shall be bread.

II

David Appelbaum
"Parabola"
Volume 26, No.1

Traditions of knowledge speak of humankind as a seed. But of what? From what planting? We admit to wondering little about the matter of growth. We barely discern the seed-like nature of ourselves: that the outer life is a husk protecting or concealing a fragile inner life, embryo of a new being. Since both pod and living germ have their part to play if the whole self ever is to be born, we search for ways to harmonize these often quarrelsome aspects. Will we succeed? If not, the difficult task of bearing new life onto the planet—life with vision and will—is bound to fail, with seed falling "on fallow ground." Traditions also speak of the calamitous consequences of ignoring this enormous human responsibility.

III

Bahauddin
The Drowned Book
29

Give yourself in the way seeds get planted. Disappear in the ground, no trace, as a tree begins to grow with branches that reach their blind trust into the air. Great multiples grow from trusting.

IV

Mary Oliver
New and Selected Poems
"Rice" 38

It grew in the black mud.
It grew under the tiger's orange paws.
Its stems thinner than candles, and as straight
Its leaves like the feathers of egrets, but green.
The grains cresting, wanting to burst.
Oh, blood of the tiger.
I don't want you just to sit down at the table.
I don't want you just to eat, and be content.
I want you to walk out into the fields
    where the water is shining, and the rice has risen.
I want you to stand there, far from the white tablecloth.
I want you to fill your hands with the mud, like a blessing.

V

Jalauddin Rumi
Coleman Bark's
Rumi: the Book of Love
30

The moment this love comes to rest in me,
many beings in one being.
In one wheat grain a thousand sheaf stacks.
Inside the needle's eye, a turning night of stars.

LOGION 10:

Yeshua says,

See, I have sown fire into the cosmos, and I shall guard it carefully until it blazes.

Sapiential Themes

- *Fire is an ancient sacred symbol for a category of divine reality that both attracts and frightens us.*
- *Yeshua is the Master of this fire and the Lord of the Cosmos. His careful tending is at the heart of our world.*
- *This saying points towards metaphysical structures behind the ordinary surface of reality in space-time.*

Parallel Texts

Logion 82
Psalm 21:9, 97
Zechariah 13:8-9
Malachi 4:2
Matthew 3:11-12, 13:43, 17:2
Mark 9:2
Luke 12:49
John 1: 3-9, 8:12
I Corinthians 3:11-15
Ephesians 5:8-14
Hebrews 12:18-21, 28-29
James 1:17
I Peter 1:3-8
I John 1:5-7

FOCAL POINT

The word "Fire!" uttered in earnest can spread instant alarm. Just the mention of fire is so immediately compelling that we are forced to pay attention in a new way. This Logion is meant to bring us to attention and to raise questions and concerns that heighten our sense of awareness and alertness to the divine activity in the world. In the end, though this saying may frighten us, the image of fire is also a powerful and positive one, giving us insight into the nature of wisdom's true work in the world through the alchemical fire.

Links

After reading the previous saying, the question may rightly be asked, what is the seed being scattered so profusely across the terrain of human habitation? What fruit is it meant to produce? Answers to these questions come through understanding that the answer, according to this Logion, is fire!

Notes

This saying suggests that we take special note and look to see what is actually happening to our human world—the cosmos. Wisdom acts and then demands that we pay close attention to what is going on all around and within us from the viewpoint of the divine perspective.

COMMENTARY

Fire, a universal sacred symbol, fills this short saying with extraordinary metaphoric significance. Its powerful imagery is meant to fuel the human imagination. The image of fire in this context is a startling and perhaps problematic one. Yet clearly its purpose is to get and hold our attention. Thomas introduces this saying here deliberately and provocatively, and the image of fire will continue to be used in multiple ways throughout the rest of the Gospel. The cosmic gardener that is seeding the cosmos in Logion 9 is juxtaposed here with fire, which defines the nature of that seed. The word seed is prosaic until we attach to it this second image—fire as seed. The world of humanity receives first the gardener's deliberate attention and action only to be followed by the second: the gardener's watchfulness over the world until the fire blazes. Watchfulness, however, is not passive, it is focused and attentive. Yeshua as watcher is actively guarding and tending the fire he has set until the whole cosmos is ablaze. Nothing less will do. So how are we to perceive this new mystery across history? Throughout its unfolding there is a kind of divine guardianship of history, a careful tending of the holy fire that has been sent deliberately into the world. The intention is to ignite it into some new blaze of energy.

*The actual Greek word, **kosmos,** is used here since in the writings of early Christian literature, it typically signifies not the physical cosmos as such, but the human constructions that make up the world as we know it. These constructs are understood to be dominated by negative forces which destroy and choke out the divine life. It is into this "world-structure" (the **kosmos**) that Yeshua throws the divine fire.*

In the biblical tradition, there are many references to fire based upon its presence and utility in the ancient world. To the ancients, fire and light were physically and inextricably linked so that, often, the very words used for either were the same. The effects of fire are, of course, powerful and convincing. Fire burns and purifies, but it also gives light and illumines. Fire is, thus, a multiple image with contrasting functions that must be balanced. These two effects (purification and enlightenment) work hand in hand. It is easy to think of fire in either way alone, or negatively as a form of destruction so that the meaning of this saying suggests nothing but a punitive act on the part of Yeshua. We must, however, balance this aspect with its opposite: the positive sense of fire as the power of illumination and the burning light of the divine glory. The fire of God both consumes and glorifies. It burns and it enlightens. The tree Moses beheld in the desert (the "burning bush") blazed with the light of God and yet it was never consumed. The holy mountain, Sinai, was set ablaze with the glory of God, and yet remained as witness to the divine Presence touching earth. The opposite images of the purifying fires of holocaust on the altar and the blazing glory of God were somehow united in ancient Hebrew thought. The image used here, therefore, has ancient and multiple references. Fire in the sacred tradition is nothing less than the light of the divine glory which ignites every created form, destroying all that is burnable, while filling it full of the light of glory.

*An interesting example of this is found in Mark 14:54 where the word translated as fire is actually the Greek word for light (**phos**).*

In the western traditions of wisdom, fire is an alchemical symbol which stands for the secret inner energy that unites the polarities. This alchemy of transformation applies to the whole transmutation of human being and consciousness beginning in the heart.

Ultimately, the whole cosmos is to be set ablaze, but in the end, by a fire that both purifies and glorifies it. This is accomplished through the great ***Shekinah*** Presence which, throughout the Abrahamic traditions, is said to leave nothing unaffected. And so here the guardian of the fire jealously watches over all until everything is ignited. This, then, becomes the ultimate goal of the Messiah. The one who himself is Anointed anoints all who follow him with Spirit and with Light. As his mission unfolds he will manifest that same transformative light in an epiphany on the Mount of Transfiguration while will hold and clothe him in utter transcendence. This same process of transfiguration witnessed on Mount Tabor is in later tradition seen to catch hold and blaze up, until it fills every being with light. There is nothing that is not to be transformed, dissolved, and melted away inside of glory.

*The Hebrew word **shekinah** stands for the fiery (or shining) Presence of God. It is this glory which is understood to set whatever it touches ablaze.*

QUESTIONS FOR REFLECTION

1. This Logion suggests that we look at our own experience in the cosmos as an encounter with fire. When we notice this and accept it, then we are seeing something of the divine design and desire for the outer cosmos as well as our own inner cosmos. The ultimate purpose is to set us (our cosmos) ablaze with light, but first, inevitably, comes the burning. How have you noticed this divine fact in your own experience?

2. Where is the burning in your experience? Where are you being set afire? You might notice it both through pain and by illumination. If fire is therefore the seed of the divine life, then where is that seed falling in your experience? Where does the pain occur? Where is the light coming?

3. Is your tendency to dampen out the fire, to not allow it to blaze up? If this is the case, we are going against the inner purpose for the cosmos. Acceptance and rejection are played out on many different levels. How might you better assist the fire, and therefore willingly participate in the divine purpose? Is it possible for you to be a "fire-keeper" yourself?

Fire is used in almost every sacred tradition to signify the divine energies which transcend us, and yet for which we long. The Sun, which is our natural source of light, energy, and fire, is seen to be the symbolic image of the divine power to create and hold all life in existence. Without light-energy life could not exist. Light is ultimately transformative and life giving even though it has also the capacity to destroy.

EXERCISES AND MEDITATIONS

1. Though we speak of the "inner fires" of imagination and desire as natural (or a native element) we are particularly careful with fire. It could harm us, and yet we need fire for warmth and energy, or we become incapacitated by cold immobility. To receive into ourselves the divine fire will be profoundly "dangerous" to our system of the self as we know it, and yet if the image holds, an extraordinary positive possibility will also exist: that fire will radically change and transfigure us. It is important to understand that our spiritual life and practice is predicated upon human beings experiencing a living relation to the divine Light as fire in both its purifying and transformative aspects. When we open ourselves to divine Light, we accept into our being the fire of burning and, ultimately, glorification. So we must "play with fire" and **be** burned by it. A question for your deep reflection and meditation is, how do you play with the divine fire in your life? Where or in what ways are you engaged with this energetic form in your ordinary world? After reflecting on this and examining it, journal your conclusions.
2. What is your vision of glory? Each of us has the capacity, if we will exercise it, of perceiving something of the eschatology (the ultimate unveiling and destiny) of our own being. Perhaps we can also glimpse the end and destiny of the cosmos as well. Your vision can be (and perhaps already has been) "ignited" by the divine fire. What have you seen? What could you see?

The one response that is called for by this saying is to "look"— to pay attention and behold something that may have been unnoticed before. It therefore has personal application, and is not simply informative. We are commanded to notice, and we cannot notice something that is outside our sphere of comprehension or experience. Our awareness must be within the circle of our personal human experience.

READINGS FOR INSIGHT

I

A traditional wisdom saying

What is to give light
must endure the burning.

II

Andrew Harvey
Teachings of the Christian Mystics
xxi-xxiii

What is needed is the flaming-out, on a global scale, of an unstoppable force of Divine-human love wise enough to stay in permanent humble contact with the Divine and brave enough to call for, risk, and implement change at every level and in every arena before time runs out and we destroy ourselves. Such a love has to spring from an awakened mystical consciousness, and must be rooted in habits of fervent meditation, adoration of the Divine, and prayer; for only then will it be illuminated enough to act at all times with healing courage, and strong enough to withstand the ordeals and torments that are inevitable. Teilhard de Chardin wrote, "Some day, after we have mastered the winds, the waves, the tides and gravity, ... we shall harness the energies of love. Then, for the second time in the history of the world, man will have discovered fire."

III

Rumi
Mathnawi I, 1721

I am burning.
If anyone lacks tinder,
let him set his rubbish ablaze with my fire.

IV

Majnun in Nizami's
Leyla and Majnun
Perfume in the Desert
109

I have not only lost you; I no longer know myself. Who am I? I keep turning and turning around myself, asking, "What is your name? Are you in love? With whom? Are you loved? By whom?

A flame keeps leaping in my heart, a vast immeasurable flame which has charred my entire being to ashes. Do I still know where I live? Can I still taste what I eat? I am lost in my own desert… I am pulled towards death; death lives within me.

V

Kharaqani
Perfume in the Desert
131

When you heart is consumed with longing and burned to ashes, the breeze of Love arises and sweeps up the ashes, and fills heaven and earth with the utterly burnt one.

VI

Bhai Sahib
Perfume in the Desert
110

When does gold ore become gold? When it is put through a process of fire. So the human being during the training becomes as pure as gold through suffering. It is the burning away of the dross. Suffering has great redeeming quality. As a drop of water falling in the desert sand is sucked up immediately, so we must become nothing and nowhere...and disappear.

LOGION 11:

Yeshua says,

The sky and all that lies in the dimensions above it will cease to exist.

The dead know nothing of life, and the living will never die.

When you consume that which is already dead, you are turning it back into life.

So, then, when you too re-emerge into the Light, what will you do?

For on the day when you were created one, you also became two, but when you come to realize your twoness again, what will you do?

Sapiential Themes

- *This is a Logion made up of five different sayings which seem unrelated but are connected in interesting ways.*
- *If you thought of each saying as being aligned along a central, vertical axis rather than just a collection of sayings strung together in a linear way, they create an interesting structure.*
- *Each saying relates to changes being made in relationships with the cosmos and the results of those relationships.*
- *The reader is asked a question twice. The answer is crucial.*

Parallel Texts

Logion 7, 60
I Kings 8:27
Isaiah 34:4, 65:17
Matthew 24:35
II Corinthians 12:2-4
Ephesians 5:6-14
Revelations 21:1, 3, 23

FOCAL POINT

As in most wisdom traditions, the Gospel of Thomas uses aphorisms and proverbs in ways that puts stress upon the rational mind. Here five sayings are juxtaposed to create a new understanding out of the resonances and tensions generated by the interactions between them. Though they may seem entirely unrelated, each speaks to the changes that will occur when the divine fire begins to interact with the cosmos and humanity. As a collectivity, these unusual sayings are not easy to interpret. This Logion may have been deliberately constructed to create rational mayhem.

Links

The direct link between this Logion and the one before it is connected to the fourth saying in the list. When fire is cast into the cosmos, certain things begin to happen. There is light, and through the fire and the light, changes begin to occur. Each change triggers another in a chain of events described by this complex Logion.

Notes

The five Logia of this saying form a single Logion of great complexity. One could begin to interpret their meaning from the top of the list and move down to the final saying. However, it also makes sense to begin at the final saying in the list, since it is there at the very bottom where fire has been cast that the conflagration begins and burns its way to the top.

COMMENTARY

If we explore the many meanings in this layered collection through an inversion, starting with the final saying in the series—at the place where the fire falls—we must start to think about the mystery of our twoness. This is opposed to the common sense view that we are one individual being. The subject of the twin which is introduced in the very first saying in this Gospel is reintroduced here, but now it involves the individual reader and not just Thomas. Move in a logical progression from this discovery to the next saying above it, and proceed back up to the first saying in the list. Seek to understand the entire collection in both directions.

Richard Valantasis
The Gospel of Thomas
Routledge
1997.

Logion 11 layers the many mysteries of life in the cosmos, one over against the other. This is a grouping of five sayings placed together to form one Logion. Though they seem unrelated, it must be assumed that they have been purposefully juxtaposed either by Thomas or Yeshua, creating a multi-layered text with many meanings and pointing toward alternative realities.

The contemporary commentator, Richard Valantasis, asserts that this arrangement of staccato-like statements is meant to "challenge rational reflection." Initially it produces the effect of confusion and bewilderment (described earlier in the second Logion). Ultimately, however, after their meanings and relationships have become clearer, these enigmatic aphorisms cause us to marvel. We must read them in the context of fire from the previous Logion 10. When fire interacts with the world there is not only conflagration, but transformation and change. Fire changes known realities. Its energy provokes new possibilities and contrary ways of perceiving the world.

The first statement in this series of sayings is cosmological and ultimately eschatological. Its context is a multidimensional understanding of the cosmos, with lower realms embedded within higher realms. Elsewhere in early Christian Scripture, St. Paul spoke of a "third heaven," indicative of a complex cosmological view. Imagine this same complexity exists for Yeshua, so when he spoke this saying he pointed towards the sky and indicated "this (starry) heaven" and then next to the heaven above it. If those two "heavens" were to pass away, what would remain is the third heaven. There would no longer be three, but one that includes everything that heretofore had been separate from the rest.

Suppose the passing away of these intermediate heavens is precisely the effect of the fire which Yeshua casts into the cosmos. It smolders, then blazes until nothing is left but the one, ultimate and divine Reality—the Source of all other realities. This is the final goal of fire: to undo all barriers and unite the world in the blaze of divine light. It isn't that realms are being annihilated; rather, through the force of fire distinct and separate identities are passing away into a new unity.

The phrase "passing away" suggests, of course, death—the subject of the next statement. Imagine in your mind's eye that Yeshua then points his finger to the crowd around him and speaks the following words: "The dead are not alive, and the living will never die." If such a visual context is possible, then the subject matter of this saying is not an obvious truism, but a profound seeing into the inner state of those right around him as he speaks these words. Most of those who count themselves "alive" are, from his point of view, dead. However, his second phrase asserts another outcome as the final eschatological goal—the state of deathlessness, where men and women are no longer eating death or form the company of the "walking dead."

If the purpose of fire is to make something come to life again (into the deathless state), then the third saying describes the method of transformation as a kind of divine alchemy. Dead matter is turned into living being in the very way we ingest our food and continue to live. The principle of such a transmutation described here applies to a higher order as well. This is the process already suggested in Logion 7. Here it is in direct relationship to the power and purpose of fire and light.

As the dead come to life, they emerge back into the light. The fire which has been cast into the cosmos burns, eating and consuming its objects, turning things into itself—to light and fire. So, then, for you who are touched by fire, who also receive light (which, as we shall see, is the condition for seeing who you truly are), the question is what will you do? How will you live and interact with light? If light is our true homeland, the environment for all spiritual beings, the question again is, what will you do in that domain? What will you see? This question implies that some form of active cooperation is required here—your willingness to work with and assist the light. But how does one assist light? What are one's responsibilities to the light? The answer appears in the final saying, but points to the ones above it as well—to take what is darkness and turn it back into the light by eating what is dead and turning it back into life means that one moves toward some ultimate state.

The final saying in the series expresses a mystery concerning human existence and history embedded within the cosmos. At a specific moment in the creation of humanity, we made our appearance in creation as a "twin." This strange phraseology might best be understood as the primordial emergence of humankind into temporality—the moment when singularity became duality and when humanity fell into the realm of "the many" in time.

Presently we find ourselves carried along by the flow of time in the midst of a realm characterized by duality. When the divine fire touches us and we begin to come back into light, we will discover the truth of this "twoness" again. This final step suggests a link between this saying and the one above it: when you come to be in the light" (the light of awareness and recognition), you will know that you are, in fact, two—a twin or a double. At the moment of recognition, when the light blazes for you, what will you do?

There are many cosmological and practical implications suggested by this final saying. The first is that your point of origination may not be in space-time at all, but elsewhere, in the realm from which you descended as a double or twin into time. You think you are a single being here—you alone as you know yourself—but suppose this "you" here is an analog of some higher, greater Self which is your origin and template.

The second implication is that Yeshua's ultimate goal (the reason for casting fire into the cosmos) is to bring you back to singularity or oneness again through the conquest (or overcoming) of your duality. First, however, you have to know the truth of your twinness. The ultimate object of all our seeking and finding is to enter the state of oneness as the primordial beginning point and the final outcome of our journey through time. Only then can the experience of oneness (as a result of our journey through the "round of time") become a grounded and secure knowledge. It becomes true wisdom, the ultimate reality, and the eschatological destiny of all temporal beings.

It is quite clear that this collection of sayings is meant to involve you, the reader, in a direct way. It asks two direct questions in the final two statements, "What will you do?" By turning to face you, Yeshua's questions become personal, breaking into your safety zone. His voice "jumps off the page," past the narration of Thomas, and speaks directly to you in your own world. These two questions initially create a form of confusion (and perhaps a conflagration—a fire released into your cosmos). How should one answer such a direct question from the Master of Wisdom? What, in fact, should one do? It may be that Yeshua is not wanting an immediate answer, but seeking to provoke profound reflection on possibilities which lie in your future.

QUESTIONS FOR REFLECTION

1. When you first read this group of sayings, what was your reaction? Did some part of it bother you in particular? What was it? Did anything in particular seem to strike you as important?

It might be important for you to begin to construct a cosmology based in part upon your study of Thomas. Keep that map handy and add to it as you learn more.

2. In the first saying, how do you understand and describe the dimensions above the sky? What exists beyond the great cosmic universe that we can see with our eyes and detect with our telescopic instruments? What is going on in this saying? Is it destruction or something else more interesting? Have you ever seen into (or felt) any dimensions beyond space and time?

3. Do you know any "dead people walking?" Have you ever experienced being alive but feeling dead? What was that like? What is the opposite sense, and how have you experienced it?

4. Suppose that beyond physical eating and ingestion you can spiritually take in what is dead and transmute it back into life. What is this saying talking about in the spiritual realm?

5. What is it like to be in the dark about something, and then suddenly to have "all the lights turned on?" What happens as a result? How might greater light change the way you live? Where is that greater light coming from for you?

6. Have you ever had the sense that you are not simply one being, but that there are two of you, or at least parts of you that are hidden, but there nonetheless? If you started to get to know the hidden parts, or the "other Self" that is also said to be you, what might that mean? Where would you look?

EXERCISES AND MEDITATIONS

1. You, the reader, are being directly addressed in this Logion. From that standpoint, there is no "safe haven" from which you can escape the probing questions of Yeshua. Through these five sayings you are being led into new territory and a different understanding of yourself. Yeshua's words have the potential to create a conflagration, hurling you into a world opposite your normal

expectations and perspectives. In a time of meditation, allow yourself to move through these sayings beginning with the first (or in reverse order, from the last to the first). Let each saying reverberate with a meaning all its own and then link it to the next like beads on a necklace. What happens when you do? What do you discover from this meditation?

2. This collectivity of sayings suggests a reorientation of consciousness (a true ***metanoia)*** along the vertical axis where these realities hold true. If we begin to interact with truths different from our common-sense reality, we may see the illusory nature of our world. Things around us perhaps seem permanent and stable, but they are rapidly passing away. What we take to be alive is, in fact, already dead or dying—while those truly alive never die. The creation of this eternal life-form is through ingestion. This is the truth about transmutation into eternal life. So we are challenged to live in light, and come to understand the principle of unitive ingestion as the highest mode of existence. What impact will these realities have upon you? What can you do to create unity from your own duality? First, though, you must come to terms with your twin nature. You may ask to receive knowledge of this other Self. We are told in this Gospel that such seeking is rewarded.
3. "What will you do?" is not just a question that is asked about the future. It is asked of you now. In light of everything Yeshua has said, what will you do **now**? There is something to do in the present moment relative to the eschatological fire which smolders (perhaps secretly) inside you. Will you live oriented to the temporal (horizontal) realities of space-time, or will you begin to reorient to the vertical realities and come to see all that exists around you for what it really is? What happens when you do that? Journal your thoughts, experiences, and the outcomes of any changes that you are making.
4. We live "in time," in the temporal mode of exile (descent into temporality). Here we are being moved by light and fire to the point of ultimate ascent as a final revelation after fire and light have done their work. This is a sacred journey. The fire that has been cast into us is meant to blaze up into light in order that we might come to know (and taste by experience) these hidden realities. Yeshua's words are meant to fan this fire into flame, and initiate the "journey of return." Remember, though, his fire is dangerous, for it pushes us out of our safe zones and into another reality. When have you not felt "safe" around the divine Reality? Is that bad for you?
5. These sayings have Eucharistic significance. Ingestion is a central symbol in Christian tradition. Through its liturgy and ritual we are invited to eat divine food as we ourselves are taken up (ingested) into the divine Reality. This is known as reciprocal feeding, for in both cases there is a "lifting up" into a higher mode of being. These two actions (eating and being eaten) symbolize our ultimate re-making—the goal of the divine life. These symbols echo across the centuries and are found in many other sacred traditions. You might want to renew your connection to this principle by participating in a Mass or some other Eucharistic celebration, or you may want to create a celebration of your own—enacting this sacred ritual using bread and wine symbolically.

Metanoia *is a Greek word that is used extensively in early Christian literature. Its fundamental meaning is a change or reorientation of conscious awareness, in which case it would shift from orientation along the horizontal axis of space-time to a new orientation of awareness aligned to the vertical axis of Transcendence and Immanence.*

The term "journey of return" is used in the study of mythological and religious symbolism to refer to the cycle of human existence which is said to begin in eternity and then descend into time, and from which we ascend back into divine Reality making our return.

Reciprocal feeding is a mystical term that is used in many traditions to describe the intimate exchange taking place between beings in mutual interdependence.

READINGS FOR INSIGHT

I

Taittriya Upanisad
3:10:5

I am Food, I am the Eater, I am the Eating.
I am the Firstborn of the world, prior to the gods,
I dwell in the eye of Deathlessness...

II

Teresa of Avila
The Interior Castle
Chapter II, 6

I have been thinking that God might be likened to a burning furnace from which a small spark flies into the soul that feels the heat of this great fire, which, however, is insufficient to consume it. The sensation is so delightful that the spirit lingers in the pain produced by its contact.

III

Jacob Boehme
Aurora
Chapter 11

The holy soul of a man and the spirit of an angel is and has one and the same substance and being, and there is no difference therein, but only in the quality itself, or their corporeal government; that which qualifies outwardly or from without in man...has an earthly quality, yet on the other side it has also a divine and heavenly quality hidden from the creatures.

IV

Fakhruddin Iraqi
Divine Flashes
120

Beloved, I sought You here and there,
Asked for news of You from all I met.
Then I saw You through myself,
And found we were identical.
Now I blush to think I ever searched for signs of You.
By day I praised You, but never knew it;
By night I slept with You without realizing it,
Fancying myself to be myself;
But no, I was You and never knew it.

V

Meister Eckhart

The human spirit scales the heavens to discover the spirit by which the heavens are driven....Even then...it presses on further into the vortex, the source in which the spirit originates. There the spirit in knowing has no use for number, for numbers are of use only in time, in this defective world. No one can strike his roots into eternity without being rid of the concept of number....God leads the human spirit into the desert, into his own unity which is pure One.

VI

Abulafia
Major Trends of Jewish Mysticism
131

All the inner forces and the hidden souls in man are distributed and differentiated in the bodies. It is however in the nature of all of them that when their knots are untied they return to their origin which is one without any duality and which comprises the multiplicity.

LOGION 12

Sapiential Themes

- *This is the second question Yeshua's students ask. It concerns their future and who their future leader should be. Leadership, however, is more about internal relationships than external authority.*
- *Yeshua's answer is historically interesting, for it focuses on Yeshua's brother, James—a Jewish visionary in his own right.*
- *Yeshua's prophetic awareness concerns the future and James's relationship to the unity of heaven and earth, of importance to all the followers of the Master.*

His students said,

We know that we cannot
hold on to you,
So who will lead us
then?

Yeshua said,

"Wherever it is that you find yourselves,
turn to James, one of the Just,
for whom heaven and earth
have come into being.

Parallel Texts

Acts 12:13-29, 21:18
I Corinthians 15:7
Galatians 1:19, 2:9
The Apocryphon of James found at Nag Hammadi, Egypt (a second century document said to have been originally transmitted by James).

Links

It may be that Yeshua's question in the last saying concerning the future ("What will you do?") is the impetus for his students' question in this Logion. Whatever it was, Yeshua's answer propels them into their future and into the life of one of the foremost leaders of early Christianity. In the Logion immediately following this one, three more leaders of the early movement are introduced.

FOCAL POINT

Something in the complex of sayings from the last Logion sparks a question in the students' minds about their future. Perhaps they are thinking that the world will end when Yeshua leaves them. They are certainly aware that their lives have changed and will change further. They live in a time of uncertainty, having staked their future on his leadership, therefore they are plagued with questions and perhaps doubts. Specifically they are worried about guidance. Perhaps they are aware of how adrift they would be without him, or how lost they could become. When that time comes Yeshua directs them to the leadership of James the Just—a focus of early Jewish Christianity.

Notes

James the brother of Yeshua, commonly known as James the Just, is familiar to those with a knowledge of Christian origins. He is crucial not only in answering a whole series of questions about the history of the early Church, he is also the missing link between the Judaism of his day and Christianity.

COMMENTARY

This dialogue gives evidence of the level of development his students have reached at this point in the text. It is clear that their primary focus remains on temporal concerns. They are dependent upon external support for their inner life. They seem not to have understood Yeshua's previous saying sufficiently, nor do they respond with a question that will take them beyond their immediate future. The previous Logion is aligned so differently from their present focus on personal history. They wonder, "What will we do when you leave us?" "When you are gone, what will happen to us?" instead of, "How do we move toward the inner experience that you bring?"

Like so many of his answers, Yeshua's response does (and does not) answer what they have asked. It extends their question in ways that, if they follow it, will lead them to a new understanding. Because their question is put in the context of time, Yeshua's answer can also be placed in history. "When the time comes (when you arrive at that place in time), you will be going to James the Just." On another level, however, his answer may focus on an inner state of development not in terms of chronological time (***chronos***) but in terms of developmental readiness (***kairos***). When they are at the place of readiness, they will be able to join James whose own relationship to heaven and earth is right or complete. When you are ready, then you will be going to the place where James already is. What is that place? It is the place where heaven and earth have come together in right-relationship, or perfect unity.

The name 'James' is a corruption of the Greek Jacobus which becomes Jacimus in Latin, from which we derive the English 'James.' Jacobus transliterates Jacob (or better, Yaakov or Yaqub) from the Hebrew.

The use of the name "James" in this Logion places this text at the heart of early Christianity. We know that James played a crucial role in the development of the Jerusalem community. He is said to have been its first bishop, leading the easily scattered flock of Yeshua's followers by virtue of his strength and wisdom. How he won that position is not perfectly clear, but it is known that the appellation "the Just One" is used early on and has great historical significance. Yeshua's perception of James' future might indeed be a prescient understanding of how history would unfold and the one to whom many of his students would look for external leadership. On a literal level, it may appear that Yeshua is honoring (or even flattering) his brother (whom many believe was not yet a student of Yeshua at this point in his ministry). After the resurrection, however, James becomes an ardent follower of Yeshua, and the reason seems to be more than mere blood-loyalty. The students who knew Yeshua best (even better in some respects than James) would not follow someone out of simple loyalty to their former spiritual Master if there was no other reason to do so. However, if Yeshua is aware of James' interior, spiritual state, that awareness becomes part of the underlying meaning of the text.

The mention of Zadok (the Just) is important, because the root on which this noun cluster is based, the three Hebrew letters Z-D-K, bears the meaning of 'Righteousness'. This is not only the basis for James' cognomen, 'the Righteous' or 'Just One', according to all early Church sources, but it is connected to the name of one of the (mystical) sects in Jesus' time. The word also transliterates into Greek, Sadducee or Zadduki/Zaddoki. In Hebrew, ee or i is a suffix referring to a person who is or does a thing, in this case, a Zadok'; or 'tzaddik', the latter meaning in English 'Righteous One.' (Eisenman 14-15).

Something of great importance happens to James. Heaven and earth are ultimately brought together (into being) in a new configuration of unity. In spiritual literature, this is called the "marriage of heaven and earth." It is to this "place" that his students must progress. As his brother, Yeshua may know that, like his ancestor and namesake, James (or Jacob) has "wrestled with the Angel" in the darkness of his own life to emerge into right-relationship with the cosmos. The use of the **Just** (***dikaios***—the Greek word used in the Coptic text) is spiritually significant, then, for it means that in James (the new Jacob), heaven and earth have been "wrestled" into a "right relationship." They are now in alignment as the precise coordinates of the Kingdom of God.

QUESTIONS FOR REFLECTION

1. Have you ever followed or been attached to someone whom you really did not want to lose, but were fearful that you might? What was your motivation for following that person? Why were you fearful about losing the relationship? What does this teach you about yourself?

For a good review of the various movements within early Christianity and their relationship to the final victory of "orthodoxy" as it is known in the West, see Bart Ehrman's ***Lost Christianities*** *(NY: Oxford University Press, 2003)*

2. How much do you know about early Christian history? You may want to read over the entire letter of James in the Christian Scriptures, but a portion has been included in this chapter. Read it carefully. What impression do you get about James from reading it? Would you be drawn to such a person as your leader? Why?

3. Do you think Yeshua was prescient about his brother in relationship to the future? How does a prophet foresee the future? What do you make of the final statement about heaven and earth coming into being for James? Think about the various ways this can be interpreted and try to make sense of each of those interpretations.

In the Abrahamic traditions, the role of the prophets is an honored one, not only because they are said to be prescient about the future, but because they can also see so clearly the nature of the present moment and what people are moving toward as a result.

EXERCISES AND MEDITATIONS

1. Imagine that you are one of Yeshua's first students. After hearing the list of sayings in the previous Logion (11), what would you like to ask him yourself? Write out that question and then, in a period of quietness, listen for the answer and journal what you hear.
2. This Logion suggests that the students of Yeshua are grasping or trying to hold tightly on to him. Perhaps they are in a relationship of total dependency. You have perhaps been in such a relationship with someone, even a spiritual leader. From your own learning, what advice would you give someone who was in this spot (include yourself in this instruction)? Journal your answer.
3. What would it be like for the two realms, heaven and earth, to co-exist and have rational people like yourself able to experience them together—not as separate and distinct entities? In your imagination, try to envision what this might be like. Many mystics have described this high state of awareness in exactly this way—as a unified field of consciousness where nothing is left out. Live one day with the sense that the two coordinates—heaven and earth—have come together. What happens?
4. If this saying is not just about James (for whom heaven and earth has come into being), but about any person who reaches a state where these two realms exist together as one, then what might it say about you? What would it take for you to enter and remain in this same state of consciousness and being?

READINGS FOR INSIGHT

I

Bahauddin
The Drowned Book
20

Ask for what you want, then dissolve like honey in milk.
The doors will open, and you will see
that you are already living inside the presence.

II

If any of you lacks wisdom, ask God and it will be given you, for God is a generous giver who imparts to all ungrudgingly and without reserve. But ask trustfully, with no hesitation, for … every good and complete gift is a generous descent from above, from the Father of Lights with whom there is no alteration nor play of passing shadow.

It is according to God's own purposes that we have been given birth through the word of truth to be a unique kind of firstfruit out of the whole creation. … Whoever, therefore, is wise or knowing among you, show it practically through the wisdom of gentleness and balanced living … For transcendent wisdom expresses itself first of all through impeccability, and then in straight-forward, considerate, open-mindedness. It is straight-forward, sincere, rich in compassion and in acts of goodness which are its fruits. Peace, then, becomes the seed-bed of righteousness, and peacemakers reap the harvest.

The Epistle of St. James
1:5, 17, 3:13, 17-18
Translation, L. Bauman

III

James was the leader of the Jerusalem Church, perhaps selected by the Apostles themselves after Yeshua's death, or alternatively appointed by Yeshua, after his resurrection. In either case he survived two decades before he was killed, and headed a movement of Jewish Christianity which today is known as "Ebionite" deriving from an original Hebrew word meaning "the Poor." Like the Essenes, Nazoraeans, Elchasaites, and other alternative Jewish movements that stem from the Hassidic traditions of the Maccabees, these early, first-century Jewish Christians were far more ascetic and Semitic in their orientation than they were Hellenic or Roman. Ultimately, it seems, James became the center of the alliance of those who opposed foreign rule in Palestine. His opposition to the Herodian Kings and their appointed priesthood is said to have led to the final uprising against the Romans which was crushed in the fall of Jerusalem in 70 C.E.

Notes from
Robert Eisenman's
James
the Brother of Jesus
4, 12

III

We are impoverished in our longing
and devoid of imagination when it comes to reaching out to others.
We need to be introduced to our longings,
because they guard our mystery.

Alan Jones

IV

The person who is always expecting consolation from without is like a swaying reed or a boat on a stormy sea. It seems as if in some uncanny way the surrounding world, the cosmic *maya*, senses this and loves to play with us—without malice to be sure, yet with a touch of mockery. To catch onto this trickery is a mark of sanctity.

Huston Smith
The Art of Pilgrimage
xiv

LOGION 13

Yeshua asked his students,

Tell me, then, who am I like? To whom will you compare me?

Simon Peter said,
"You are like a just angel."

Matthew said,
"You are a philosopher of wisdom."

Thomas said,
"Master, I cannot find words to express who you really are."

Yeshua said,
"Thomas, it is no longer necessary for me to be your Master for you are drinking from the gushing spring I have opened for you, and you have become intoxicated."

Then Yeshua took Thomas aside and spoke three sayings to him in private. When Thomas returned to the company of his companions they, of course, asked him, "What did Yeshua say to you?"

"If I were to tell you even one of the things he spoke to me," Thomas replied, "you would pick up these rocks and stone me, and then fire would blaze out of them and burn you."

Sapiential Themes

- *In the sapiential tradition of Socratic dialogue, Yeshua queries his students, drawing them into a deeper understanding of personal identity.*
- *Thomas moves to the source-point of his own wisdom.*
- *Secret dialogue begins between Thomas and the Master which should not be heard outside this relationship.*
- *Curiosity drives the ordinary mind, but to hear truth without inner preparation only creates fury and burning.*

Links

This saying follows naturally from the previous Logion as an extension of the continuing dialogue between Yeshua and his students.

Parallel Texts

Logion 61
Isaiah 46:5
Matthew 16:13-16
Mark 8:27-30
Luke 6:40, 9:18-21
John 4:14, 7:37-39

Notes

Though the answers from his students found in Thomas are somewhat different from the canonical Gospels, the evidence is clear that Yeshua questioned his disciples about their understanding of his identity. Unlike the canonical Gospels, there is no declaration here of Messiahship, which appears to be a somewhat later development within Christianity, giving evidence that this Logion is of an earlier origin.

FOCAL POINT

In form this Logion is a mirror image of the one preceding it. There the students question Yeshua and he answers. In this saying it is Yeshua who questions them, and they answer according to their personal perspectives. In the previous saying, the students of Yeshua have been interested in authority and hierarchy and who will lead them in the future. Yeshua continues a discussion related to this subject, but makes it personal, dependent upon the level of their understanding. The various answers given reflect the multiple points of view existing in the world of first-century Judaism.

COMMENTARY

Dialogue is an early form of sapiential teaching. Known in the West as "Socratic dialogue," it plays a very important role in all wisdom traditions where Master and student engage in conversation around some question, saying, parable (or ***koan***). In this Logion, Yeshua seeks out his students' understanding concerning his identity. This question has always been a watershed issue in historical Christianity (where in theological discourse it is commonly called "Christology"). Answers to this question typically take the Christian disciple far from the realm of wisdom and into issues of dogmatic theology where it has often been used as a means of enforcement and control. Through the power of his words and works, Yeshua has created a wellspring in Thomas where understanding about his identity (and what lies beyond it) flows from a deep inner source beyond dogma.

*For a review of the development of Christianity in the West see Richard Tarnas's important study, **The Passion of the Western Mind** (NY: Ballantine Books, 1991).*

In the world of his followers, Yeshua has become the center of religious and spiritual possibilities. How these followers relate to and understand him seems to clarify where they are in their spiritual progression. Yeshua pushes into their interior, questing and questioning. What emerges in response are three developmental levels across a wide spectrum concerning who he is and their relationship to him.

*For an understanding of the influence of the Greeks and the Persians upon Jewish theology, see Frederick Murphy's **The Religious World of Jesus** (Nashville: Abingdon, 1991), and Neil Fujita's, **A Crock in the Jar** (NY: Paulist Press, 1986).*

Simon Peter's is the first response from a viewpoint current in his day. His understanding is based in part on a theological perspective gained in exile among the Persians with their emphasis on Angels. It is combined, of course, with the conventional theology of the Hebrew people emphasizing righteousness (or right-relatedness). For Peter, Yeshua is a heavenly messenger bringing a message of righteousness. From his point of view, Yeshua confirms the revelation made to the Jews.

Philo of Alexandria, a contemporary of Jesus, was perhaps the greatest synthesizer of the Greco-Hebraic ideals.

Matthew's perspective reflects the Jewish Hellenism of his day, which combined the Hebrew and the Greek worldviews into a fresh understanding. For Matthew, Yeshua represents the realization of the synthesis of the Greco-Semitic ideal, specifically, the wise man—a lover of wisdom known among the ancients as a carrier of the sapiential tradition coming directly from Solomon and the Greek philosophers. Yeshua brings that ancient wisdom to bear upon the present conditions through a renewed message. Matthew's understanding is favorable to fresh interpretations as a result of the accommodation the Hebrew tradition has made with Greek culture. His perspective represents perhaps the broader viewpoint of Galilean Jewry.

Thomas, on the other hand, cannot articulate in concept or word what he sees and understands—in his mouth words are simply inadequate. Any category from his mind or culture will not suffice, for he cannot put into form who or what Yeshua is. Thomas thus avoids the tendency to categorize what is transcendent and thereby limit the mystery that ultimately escapes the realm of human language. It is this that Thomas knows but cannot say, for he knows beyond words. As a result, he appears to be in precisely that state of wonder and astonishment that Yeshua has spoken about earlier (Logion 2), and yet he forms the word "Master" which recognizes Yeshua as his mentor and teacher.

In this state of amazement, Thomas steps beyond the ordinary circle of the Master-student relationship. He himself has begun to "drink from the very source" which Yeshua knows and from which he draws. In truth he no longer needs the physical presence of the Master because that same stream of wisdom is bubbling up within him. This is a condition which Yeshua calls "inebriation," wherein living water is ultimately turned into intoxicating wine.

*Spiritual intoxication is widely recognized by many sacred traditions as a mystical state of ecstasy (**ekstasis**).*

Thomas' experience also illustrates perhaps the previous Logion's statement about going to the place where heaven and earth come together. Thomas knows something of the topography of that place now as the center where heaven and earth are one and the truth, like wine, pours forth as living water from a flowing spring. James will also know it, and later he will become for the followers of Yeshua another source from which they all can draw when the time is ripe.

It is at this precise point of intoxication that Yeshua draws Thomas into deeper solitude and takes him further by instructing him in three new sayings. Perhaps "in secret" he is directly demonstrating the work and relationship of an "interior" Master which is new to Thomas, but which will become the norm later. Such learning is a private matter. It is personally directed. It cannot be spoken to anyone that is not specifically where Thomas is in relationship to the Master.

The tradition of the "interior Master" seems to spring from Yeshua's teachings. John's Gospel is replete with it, as is the text in Revelation 3:20.

The final scene in this Logion is extremely provocative. Like Yeshua's first students, perhaps we too are spiritual voyeurs. When Thomas returns, we also want to know what Yeshua said to him. Who wouldn't? We want to know, but we cannot know until we too have touched our own inner springs. Such knowledge, spoken directly to one student alone for his (or her) ears only, is dangerous if disclosed publicly—dangerous both to the one who tells and the one who hears. Unprepared, we are opened to energies that could destroy us, for inevitably we would take issue with what is being said. We would act upon our fears and act out our prejudices. The results would set off a conflagration. In the end, though, perhaps this is the same fire which Yeshua is tending and which he intends to catch hold in the cosmos. Could both danger and purgation reside in such fire? Or is Thomas simply frightening his companions "off topic" to protect both himself and them?

QUESTIONS FOR REFLECTION

1. Which one of the three persons in this dialogue is most like you? What is the category of thought that you cling to concerning who Yeshua is? Have you considered that this might, in fact, be a projection and not the truth or the stunning awareness that Thomas eventually has?

The symbolism of wine is a powerful metaphor in the Abrahamic traditions. It is always an ambiguous image, however. Even in Thomas, at times it is a positive symbol (as it is here), but at other times it is used in a negative way (see Logion 28).

2. How do you understand the word **intoxicated**? Have you ever been intoxicated by something other than drinking or smoking? What was it and what was the effect that it had upon you?

3. If you were Thomas, what would Yeshua want to tell you in secret?

3. Why is truth often dangerous? Can you think of a truth that is?

4. What does Thomas know at the end about the nature of truth that he did not perceive at the beginning?

5. In religious terms, what would make you so angry that you might want to inflict harm or damage on yourself or someone else?

EXERCISES AND MEDITATIONS

1. Have you ever felt that some truth opened up to you like a gushing stream, and you could tap into its source? Perhaps it was a flood of insight, a flash of inspiration, a sudden seeing into something that heretofore had been closed and darkened for you. What have you seen in this way? Explore how it is different from the more academic ways of understanding that you have also experienced.
2. Suppose that the Master is working to instruct you from within—in solitude and secret. Imagine that this relationship either already exists or can grow inside you so that you too can be the recipient of fresh understanding not on a sporadic basis, but daily and continuously. What would you need to do to set the conditions for such instruction or for that relationship?
3. Thomas is exercising discretion (discrimination) in regards to truth. Knowing what you know about the students of Yeshua so far, what might inflame them? What might they not be ready to hear? What might you not be ready to hear?

READINGS FOR INSIGHT

I

He who knows himself
knows his Lord.

Hadith
of the Prophet
Muhammad

II

On the mystical path "knowing" and "being" are identical. We understand through our state of being, and the scope of our knowledge expands with the expansion of our being, with the unveiling of the veils which have covered our being. The non-ceremonial "widening of the horizons" through ***dhawq*** (tasting) is the true and only initiation on the path.

Sarah Sviri
The Taste of Hidden Things
41

III

Anger is hell's fire.
The moment it is lit,
we fall from our imagined height
into the flaming pit.

All heaven's glory is within
and so is hell's fierce burning…
You must yourself decide
in which direction
you are turning.

Angelus Silesius
Messenger of the Heart
87,83

IV

In what I have shown you, there is nothing secret
or hidden. If you reflect within yourself and
recognize your own face which was before the world,
the secret is within yourself.

Hui Neng

V

Before the visitor embarked upon discipleship, he wanted assurance from the Master.

"Can you teach me the goal of human life?"
"I cannot."
"Or at least its meaning?"
"I cannot."
"Can you indicate to me the nature of death and of life beyond the grave?"
"I cannot."

The visitor walked away in scorn. The disciples were dismayed that their Master had been shown in such a poor light. Said the Master soothingly,

"Of what is it to comprehend life's nature and life's meaning if you have never tasted it? I'd rather you ate your pudding than speculated on it."

Anthony de Mello
One Minute Wisdom
39

VI

My heart was pruned and its flower appeared, then grace sprang up in it,
and my heart produced fruits for the Lord.
For the Most High circumcised me by His Holy Spirit, then He uncovered my inward being towards Him, and filled me with His love.
And His circumcising became my salvation, and I ran in the Way, in His peace, in the way of truth.
From the beginning until the end I received His knowledge.
And I was established upon the rock of truth, where He had set me.
Speaking waters touched my lips from the generous fountain of the Lord.
And I drank and became intoxicated, from the living water that does not die.
And my intoxication gave me knowledge, and I abandoned vanity,
And turned toward my God, the Most High, and His bounty made me rich.
So I threw off the madness of the earth, and stripped it off and cast it away.
And the Lord renewed me with His garment, and held me in His light.
And from above He gave me immortal rest, and I became like the land that blossoms and rejoices in its fruits.
And the Lord was like the sun upon the face of the land.
My eyes were enlightened, and my face received the dew;
And my breath was refreshed by the pleasant fragrance of the Lord.

Odes of Solomon
11

Drink deeply from the living fountain of the Lord,
because it has been opened for you.
Come all you who are thirsty and drink, and rest beside the fountain of the Lord.
How beautiful and pure. It rests the soul.
For much sweeter is its water than honey,
and the honeycomb of bees are nothing beside it,
Because it flows from the lips of the Lord.
Its name is from the heart of the Lord.
It is invisible but has no borders,
and was unknown until it was wet in our midst.
Blessed are all who have drunk from it, and have refreshed themselves by it,
and now they rest.
Hallelujah.

Odes of Solomon
30

VII

"Why do you need a Master?" asked a visitor of one of the disciples.

"If water must be heated, it needs a vessel as an intermediary between the fire and itself," was the answer.

Anthony de Mello
One Minute Wisdom
42

LOGION 14

Yeshua says:

If you fast you will only be giving birth to sin in yourself.
If you pray your prayers will come back to haunt you.
If you give to charity, you will create evil in your own spirit.

If, however, you travel through a region and they welcome you,
eat whatever is put in front of you,
and heal their sick.
For it is not what goes into your mouth that contaminates you, but what comes out of it.

Sapiential Themes

- *The danger of external religious tradition is clearly identified in wisdom teaching.*
- *Traditional Jewish piety is under scrutiny in the original wisdom of Yeshua.*
- *A new form of inner practice supercedes outer ritual duty.*
- *The healing of others is a primary goal of sapiential practice.*
- *The inner sources of evil can be compounded through religious piety.*

Parallel Texts

Logia 6, 95, 104
Isaiah 58:6-9
Matthew 6:6
Mark 7:14-23
Luke 10:8-9
John 18:1

FOCAL POINT

To the ear turned to traditional Jewish practice, nothing could come more sharply than these inflammatory words from the lips of Yeshua. If taken at face value, his sayings here are nothing less than heresy and sacrilege spoken in contradiction to the religious values and traditions of his day. His own students would certainly be shocked to hear these words. Even today, this Logion is used as an argument that the Gospel of Thomas does not represent the authentic teachings of Yeshua because this example so clearly violates traditional religious thought. Surely Yeshua would never have uttered such words. If he did, in what context would they make any sense at all?

Links

Could it be that what Yeshua speaks in this Logion is precisely what he told Thomas in secret in the last saying? It is a possibility, or it may only be that Yeshua is commenting on the religious exoterism which appears to be the basis for Thomas' previous statements about fire. Regardless, it is clear that these words continue a topic that was already raised in Logion 6. It is here that Yeshua answers their questions, but only after he has demonstrated how dangerous religious duty can be for the soul and spirit of a human being when it is misguided.

Notes

As Logion 6 has already outlined, ritual Jewish piety consists primarily of proscribed prayer, fasting, the giving of alms, and prohibitions against certain foods considered unclean. Yeshua addresses his students' previous question concerning these practices, but in the process challenges the traditional answers given in regards to these.

COMMENTARY

If the testimony of his first students is truthful, Yeshua was a powerful and radical teacher of wisdom. Nothing could illustrate that better, perhaps, than this saying, which is provocative in the extreme, particularly to conventional religion. But then, Yeshua is not conventional. His values were often opposed to the religious standards set by local tradition, and so demonstrated the fire (and the violence) that wisdom will often create when cast into ordinary reality. To understand this saying, it must be juxtaposed with the two which precede it. It is likely that in the "logic" of the Gospel of Thomas it comes as a commentary on the potential "religious" violence about which Thomas speaks at the conclusion of Logion 13. There, if Thomas were to have uttered Yeshua's words, likely the students would have attempted to stone him and justified their action through Hebrew Scripture and tradition.

Deuteronomy 13:4-10
Leviticus 24:16

If, however, these are the sayings Yeshua was teaching Thomas (and given the opening words, it is possible that they were), then it is clear why they required a form of secrecy. It appears that Yeshua was already aware of the inner state (and intentionality) of his students. Yeshua's private teaching to Thomas would have been offensive to their conventional religious attitudes. To them, these would have been "fighting words." If indeed this was the inner state of his students, their religious values were both toxic to themselves and a danger to others. His words were not only a commentary on the interior state of his students, but also on the effects of external religion as it is practiced in that state. When it is performed within the narrow limits of intolerance and prejudice, religion can in fact contaminate the human spirit. It can cause harm to others (as it would have to Thomas) as well as to the wider social world, but more importantly it can damage the soul of the person who practices it. In and of themselves, fasting, prayer, alms giving, and eating "clean" (kosher) foods are not harmful practices, but done in a state of arrogance or bigotry, they become unsafe, injuring the human spirit.

This conclusion is supported by the opening words found in the original text: "Yeshua said this to them..." Normally the "to them" is missing from these opening words, indicating that Thomas at least sees this as a commentary on the action that would have unfolded in the final scene of the last Logion if he had disclosed Yeshua's teaching.

The students of Yeshua are being urged to "move" from external forms common to religion and "journey" into new territory. There they will ultimately be "walking about" in a new region. Rather than refusing the new condition, they are instructed to accept hospitality from it. Instead of fasting and refusing food due to the laws of ritual defilement, they are to eat whatever is provided, and, in that state, they are also to begin to heal others. Could the sickness that is the object of such healing be precisely that inner condition of "begetting sin, being judged by prayer, and creating evil in one's own spirit" outlined at the beginning of the Logion?

Interestingly, without the narrative context supplied in the canonical Gospels, the meaning of Yeshua's words could as easily speak to interior movement in "spiritual space" as they do to missionary activity in geographical space.

The image of the mouth is used in this and the previous saying. Here it has to do with both eating and speaking: the two primary functions of the mouth. In Logion 13, Thomas' mouth cannot form the words to speak his realization of who Yeshua is. In this saying, the issue of eating and fasting and speaking through language in prayer, as well as the ultimate contamination coming from within, are expressed. Such contamination cannot be anything other than words. This famous reversal, which is so counter-intuitive to the human (and Jewish) mind, puts the listener on notice that other reversals also apply. One would assume that prayer would never defile, but it does. Also, a pious Jew would be scrupulous about what entered the body because of the potential for ritual uncleanness, but as Yeshua teaches, unclean food does not ultimately corrupt anyone. Yeshua's wisdom, therefore, turns the religious world upside down and inside out. Once again, he puts the emphasis where it belongs: on the inside—the interior dimensions of a human being.

Here Yeshua is clearly going against both established tradition and the Bible itself.

QUESTIONS FOR REFLECTION

1. Has religion ever become toxic for you? How did this happen? In what state have you felt its positive attributes? How do you know the difference between toxic and positive effects?

2. Explore the damage done by external religion to the interior dimensions of an individual when practiced in a state of prejudice or narrow self-interest. What are the results to the individual? To others? To the cosmos?

3. What do the three negative possibilities suggested by this Logion—birthing sin, haunted by prayers, creating evil within, mean to you personally? What makes these three negative practice, and the final injunction positive practice?

Has injunction against these three negative conditions ever been a part of any spiritual teaching that you have known?

4. Imagine a pilgrimage in which these other possibilities apply: journeying forward into new territory, accepting hospitality, eating what is provided, and healing the sick. Is this pilgrimage literal or figurative? If it is the latter, what does it mean for you?

EXERCISES AND MEDITATIONS

1. Go through a day and allow yourself to be aware of how the words you speak affect the inner and outer environment. How does what comes from your mouth either help or contaminate you and those around you? Is contamination tied to what is actually said, or to something else?
2. When has some religious duty that you have felt obliged to undertake (knowing that you were doing it in the wrong spirit) harmed you? Has there been any previous religious experience where you preformed some religious duty unknowingly only to discover that in the end it made things worse? Describe that in a journal entry.
3. Think specifically about your prayer requests. Have your fervent prayers for some answer (which were perhaps granted) come back to haunt or judge you? Think of this in terms of being younger when you might have pestered your parents for some item or privilege, and which did not turn out the way you first expected. When have you experienced prayer in this same manner?
4. The life-style of a spiritual pilgrim is meaningful. In the Abrahamic traditions, spiritual life is never sedentary but nomadic, conducted in a state of openness and charity toward others. The picture expressed by this Logion puts the pilgrim in a place of deep receptivity and also gracious benevolence. Liberality and generosity of spirit flow both directions when religious experience is pursued outside the boundaries of the exoteric demands.

The Abrahamic traditions came into being largely in a desert environment where, in order to survive, pastoral peoples had to move constantly to find water and pasturage. Movement, therefore, was life. Staying put spelled death.

READINGS FOR INSIGHT

I

Anthony de Mello
One Minute Wisdom
120

"What does your Master teach?" asked a visitor.
"Nothing," said the disciple.
"Then why does he give discourses?"
"He only points the way—he teaches nothing."
The visitor couldn't make sense out of this, so the disciple made it clearer:
"If the Master were to teach, we would make beliefs out of his teachings. The Master is not concerned with what we believe—only with what we see."

II

Phil Cousineau
The Art of Pilgrimage
134

"For me," Eliade writes, "the sacred is always the revelation of the real, an encounter with that which saves us by giving us meaning to our existence." ... *Religion* originally meant "to bind back," in the sense of reconnecting to a fundamental reality. "Religion for me," reflects Huston Smith, "is the search for the Real, and the effort to approximate one's life to it."

For the pilgrim, the traveler with a deep purpose, this is the moment of truth, when the search for the *real* takes you to a place that pierces your heart.

III

Anthony de Mello
One Minute Wisdom
140

"What action shall I perform to attain God?"
"If you wish to attain God, there are two things you must know. The first is that all efforts to attain God are of no avail."
"And the second?"
"You must act as if you did not know the first."

IV

Wayne Teasdale
The Mystic Heart
165

The inner journey also grants us the ability to be genuinely *present* to others in all senses. When we are present, we meet them in the eternal now, where everything is continually arising. Through this incomparable gift of presence, we fashion and shape ourselves as a home for the divine within us, a place for ultimate realization of creation and all others. The present moment is thus sacramental because it is filled with the reality of the ultimate, with God...

V

Stephen Hirtenstein
The Unlimited Mercifier
160

Constant, endless traveling was once beautifully described by the fourth-century Cappadocian Christian master, Gregory of Nyssa, as ***epektasis*** (epectasy). This he callas an infinite progression "from beginning to beginning through beginnings that never end."

VI

Annonymous

There's nothing more confusing
than vested interest posing as moral or religious conviction.

LOGION 15

Sapiential Themes

- *Wisdom's journey is through temporality to its end-point: visionary seeing*
- *The possibility of vision and the necessity of adequate preparation constitute the "doctrine of* ***adequatio.****"*
- *The un-begotten (or un-Manifest) Godhead is the Source of all manifest reality.*
- *Wisdom tradition uses metaphors of both the divine Mother and the Father.*
- *Worship is at the heart of all human relationship with the divine Reality.*

Yeshua says,

When the time comes
and you are able to look
upon the Unborn One,
fall prostrate in worship,
for you have found your own true Father
(your Source and Origin at last).

Parallel Texts

Logion 101
Genesis 32:30
Exodus 32:11
Joshua 5:13-14
Job 42:5-6
Ezekiel 1:28
Daniel 10:5-11
Isaiah 6:1-8
Psalm 17:15, 24:3-6, 31:15-16
I Corinthians 13:12
Galatians 4:4-5
Ephesians 1:18, 5:17-21
Revelation 1:12-19, 22:1-5

Links

When you travel, your eyes see and take in the scenery. In the last saying, Yeshua invites his students to journey into new territory. If spiritual pilgrimage includes more than mere geography, then the territory through which one journeys and the destiny toward which one travels is nothing less than the divine Presence. In time, that journey will reach its destination before the divine face. There, one will not only taste with the mouth, one will see with the eye the Source of all Reality.

FOCAL POINT

As human beings, we have been specifically called into temporality in order to create the track (or history) of our own personal becoming through time. The endpoint of this journey is to finally come home and discover our origins there. A person cannot make that discovery, however, until he or she has become capable of seeing through and beyond creation and the realm of manifestation to the un-Manifest (or Unborn) as Source-of-All. To truly see in this way will effect perfect surrender in profound worship at the center—the heart— where all horizons and axes meet. There at that centerpoint, in the heart of all things, we will discover our true parentage, our Source: that which brought us into being.

Notes

*"The pure heart—whole, free, honest, good—is thus fit for worship (****tahor****), fit to be brought into God's presence....The clean heart, fit to worship, offers itself in sacrifice as a broken, humbled heart, a broken spirit (Psalm 51:18-19)"*

Harriet A. Luckman and Linda Kulzer
Purity of Heart
Liturgical Press, 1999

COMMENTARY

It may be said that up to this point in the Gospel of Thomas every saying is a step on the pathway of wisdom leading to the highpoint of vision. In the Sermon on the Mount, Yeshua says, "Blessed are the pure in heart for they shall *see God*." It is clear from the previous Logion that purity of heart, not probity of religious ritual, is the prerequisite for visionary seeing. Later to be known as the "Beatific Vision," the roots of ascent to the Divine Face are in the long prophetic tradition where Elijah, Ezekiel, Jeremiah, Daniel and Isaiah ascend to the Throne of God and behold the visage of their Lord. At a historical turning point two centuries before the appearance of Yeshua, the mystics of Judaism proposed that visionary ascent is also possible for extraordinary spiritual seekers. Yeshua steps into this same stream proclaiming that visionary seeing and ascent is available not only to the few, but to all whose hearts are purified by fire—without which no one can see the face of God and live.

Matthew 5:8

It is the destiny of the sons and daughters of humanity to behold the face of God, not as judge, but as beloved parent, and perhaps even as friend and lover. Yeshua does not say that this may happen ("**if** you should see God"), but that it will happen "**when** you see God." Our journey to the divine face appears to be certain. It is the time factor that remains unknown. If we are to behold God's face (the face of the Unborn One), experience in time is crucial, for we pass through time in order to become capable of seeing God. To see God is the end of all our searching in time.

Fatherhood appears to do with ultimate Source, and not gender. The Father is the "begetter" and in this Logion is said directly to be the Source from which we came and not just the "only" begotten Son's Source. According to Thomas, we too are "begotten ones," which suggests a different ontological perspective about humanity from the one taken by many early Christian writers. The gap between the only begotten One and the students of Yeshua is narrowed considerably by this Logion.

Such an understanding appears to be at the heart of the spiritual experience of Yeshua. At his baptism it is said that the heavens were rent asunder and the divine Father appeared, calling him beloved son and saturating him with Spirit. As a result, Yeshua becomes the Master of such seeing, and upon his path he initiates his students into a way of knowing which is also wisdom's way of seeing.

Every living thing (and each human being) can be thought of as having been "begotten from woman," or we might say today, from the "principle of the feminine." Two significant images, therefore, are in metaphoric play here: "Fatherhood," having not so much to do with gender as with Source, and "Motherhood," having to do with manifestation (or birthing) from that Source. These two metaphors are Semitic in every way, concretely imaging the more abstract idea of the Source of Being and the Manifestation of All Things. What we presently see is the realm of manifestation (that which exists within space-time). We are aware of created things. Indeed, this is all that most people know or believe to be "real." However, we are also capable of seeing more, beyond the realm of creation and the Manifest. The question, of course, is how that happens and where that will take us.

Interestingly, the phrase "the one not born of woman" is in contrast to the phrase that is used in the Creeds for Yeshua, as one who is "...born of a woman." The contrast between the begotten one (the Christ) and the Unbegotten One (the Father) is also the distinction that will be spelled out later in Christian theology as the Trinitarian contrast between Father and Son. Again, in the Nicene Creed, the Christ is said to be "eternally begotten" of the Father.

Other parts of this Gospel (and of Yeshua's teachings in the canonical tradition) answer the how and what questions specifically. Yeshua's words in Thomas extend the familiar phrase from the Sermon on the Mount ("Blessed are the pure in heart for they shall see God"). They also resonate to Yeshua's words found in John's Gospel where we not only see, but are united with God intimately. In this particular Logion, Yeshua is calling his student, however, to visionary seeing—a deep interiority that he describes as worship. One must again ask when in time when will this happen? The answer, perhaps, is the end result of all our searchings on this journey of spirit through time: when the heart is purified and made able to see.

QUESTIONS FOR REFLECTION

1. We often think of our personal history in terms of being here on earth in time. Suppose time (or temporality) is not just an aspect of space-time and earth history, but also exists in other dimensions as well. Suppose that our history extends into other times—back into the past before physical birth and into the future after death—well beyond our present earth experience. What might this mean for us? How would you explain this?

2. What might the possibility of history and time beyond earth have to do with this Logion?

3. How, by means of time, does one become adequate to see God? What would time have to do with creating this capacity?

EXERCISES AND MEDITATIONS

1. Suppose that, as the Sermon on the Mount says, seeing God (as Origin and Parent) comes through the instrument of a pure heart. Visionary experience (the sight of God) is directly proportional, then, to the ability of the "eye of the heart" to see. What does this say about your being and your life of spiritual practice? What might you need to do as a result?
2. Where in your experience have you made room for the recognition of the "holy Mother" and the "sacred Father?" Holy Mother may be your companion through time (as Christian tradition suggests), and sacred Father the goal reached beyond time, but each have their role to play in your becoming. Write a prayer to Holy Mother and Sacred Father.
3. Yeshua directs a profound act of surrender or worship: prostration before the Holy One. This ritual act is one that is well known in the ancient Hebrew tradition, and is continued on in Christian ritual as a profound bow or complete prostration before the divine Presence. Ritual prostration is an ancient mode of "body prayer." In addition to its obvious physical activity, it also has the capacity to create a spiritual dimension within you. Begin a practice of ritual prostration alone, before the Holy One as your Origin and Source. Some traditions perform such practice with multiple acts of bowing one's forehead on the ground (as in ritual Islamic prayer). Others perform this act of body prayer with a face-down, full prostration before God. Explore this act of prayer using it with such words as "My Mother, My Father, My Source," or "I bow before you, O Holy One." Continue this practice for a number of days until it no longer seems strange to you. Journal your experience. (For those who have difficulty bending down, kneeling, or performing a prostration, sit in a chair and bow forward with your head placed in your cupped hands).

The "eye of the heart" is a technical term for a real part of your larger being. In Greek it is called ***nous****, or (spiritual) Mind. It has the capacity to see into the Infinite, the Absolute and the Eternal.*

Prostration is ***proskynesis*** *in Greek (see Valantasis, 82) Ritual prostration is used as a part of traditional worship in Judaism, Christianity, and Islam, as well as in other sacred traditions.*

READINGS FOR INSIGHT

I

E.F. Schumacher
Guide for the Perplexed
39, 47

The understanding of the knower must be adequate to the thing to be known ("*Adaequatio rei et intellectus*"). The power of "the Eye of the Heart," which produces insight, is vastly superior to the power of thought, which produces opinion.

II

T.S. Eliot
The Four Quartets
"Little Gidding"

...We shall not cease from exploration
And the end of all our exploring
Will be to arrive where we started
And know the place for the first time.
Through the unknown, remembered gate
When the last of earth left to discover
Is that which was the beginning
At the source of the longest river...

III

***Suttanipata** IV*
Ix, 3

One cannot, I say, attain supreme knowledge all at once; only by a gradual training, a gradual action, a gradual unfolding, does one attain perfect knowledge. In what manner? A man comes, moved by confidence; having come, he joins; having joined, he listens; listening, he receives the doctrine; having received the doctrine, he remembers it; he examines the sense of the things remembered; from examining the sense, the things are approved of; having approved, desire is born; he ponders, pondering, he eagerly trains himself, and eagerly training himself, he mentally realizes the highest truth itself and, penetrating it by means of wisdom, *he sees*.

IV

Meister Eckhart
Love Poems From God
120

It is your destiny to see as God sees,
to know as God knows, to feel as God feels.
How is this possible? How?
Because divine love cannot defy its very self,
divine love will be eternally true to its own being,
and its being is giving all it can at the perfect moment.
And the greatest gift God can give is His own experience.
Every object, every creature, every man, woman and child
has a soul and it is the destiny of all,
to see as God sees, to know as God knows,
to feel as God feels, to be as God is.

V

Kabir Helminski
Living Presence
153

In worship we allow ourselves to be harmonized by something of the highest value. The regular and patterned exercise of consciousness, the energy of remembrance within worship, is a basic need. In worship we are more likely to experience a correspondence between body and soul, behavior and feeling, because we are calling on a harmonizing power.

LOGION 16

Yeshua says,

Some of you are thinking perhaps
that I have come into the cosmos to
bring it peace.

No!
You do not yet realize that I have come to
throw it into utter chaos
through burning, blade, and battle.

Five will be living in one household.
Three will face off against two,
and two against three.
Parents will rise up against children,
and children against their parents,
until at last they shall stand united
on their own feet.

FOCAL POINT

One of the highest of all human agendas is, of course, personal comfort. We want a life free from interference so that we can pursue pleasure and avoid pain unchallenged. Isn't that also the divine agenda? One might imagine that Yeshua, as God's Messiah, would come to bring peace to the earth, setting it free from disturbance and conflict so that we could live pain-free. But no—nothing is further from the truth. Yeshua says explicitly that his work is opposite the human agenda. The human cosmos will be disturbed, thrown into utter chaos, and the result will be conflict at every level. He images this through three disturbing metaphors—fire, sword and war—each a disaster that profoundly disrupts our comfort level. In this saying conflict appears close to home, even (perhaps especially) among friends and relatives. Ultimately the purpose of such conflict is not destruction, but unity. Conflict will continue until humanity unites against the internecine wars, standing up out of the chaos on two strong feet. Only then will it be possible to look upon the Unborn One.

Sapiential Themes

- *There are two kinds of peace: true and false.*
- *Yeshua sends holy war into the human **kosmos**.*
- *The households of humanity are divided by five degrees of separation.*
- *Yeshua's wisdom expresses the paradox of the way to unity by separation.*
- ***Monochos** is the integrated being—the **homo integer**.*

Links

*What prevents us from our destiny, which is to behold the divine Face? What, within time, propels us toward that ultimate vision? These are the natural questions raised by the assertions found in Logion 15. The answers unfold in this saying in an unsettling way which contradicts almost everything we commonly believe about Yeshua's message . This saying is also clearly linked to Logion 10, and describes what the effect of the presence of fire in the **kosmos** will be.*

Parallel Texts

Logia 10 , 58, 49, 75
Micah 7:6
Luke 12:49-53
Ephesians 6:10-18

Notes

Disunity and chaos mark the human condition. Why? Many answers are given, but in the end they all lead back to the way the world was created to be: with duality. It is absolutely clear that we live in a world of opposites, and that often these are at war with one another. Is this world, then, a "set up?" Wisdom's answer is "Yes, it is—this is the divine design for the world." This concept is contrary to our expectations; and therefore this disturbing saying flies in the face of our understanding of Yeshua as the bringer of peace. Although it has its equivalents in the canonical Gospels, the stark way this principle is stated here is troubling.

COMMENTARY

*The primary meaning of the Greek word **kosmos** (whose original spelling is used here to distinguish it from the English spelling and contemporary meaning of the universe) is that of an arrangement or order. Originally it was used by the pre-Socratic philosopher **Pythagoras** to designate the entire natural universe (as it is used today in the English word **cosmos**). Later, however, in common Greek (**koine**), it came to signify the conventionality or artificiality of a larger system of realities, powers, and authorities in the human world which are ultimately illusory (as in the word "cosmetic"). Human society as a system is embedded in this illusion, causing great distortion and deformity (see Luke 2:1, 4:5-6, 12:30-31).*

Yeshua has already shocked his students by saying that he will throw fire into the ***kosmos*** (Logion 10). In this new saying, that image is intensified. Yeshua now says that not only is he casting fire into the edifice of the ***kosmos***, but that he is also casting the instruments of conflict and war. These will shatter the peace of the ***kosmos*** and throw all its "orders" into chaos. Why? Does he wish to destroy the world and, in the process, do us irreparable harm? Is matter evil and to be annihilated? The answer lies deeper. It is the individual soul that must be freed from the hegemony of the ***kosmos*** by shattering through fire, sword and war.

Consider that Yeshua is speaking here about a "false peace," not a truly integrated state of reality. The premise which underlies the multi-layered world of human habitation is that we are on earth primarily to maximize pleasure and minimize pain. That premise grounds all human activity in a false peace. Whatever equilibrium we reach is only temporary. Yeshua comes to disturb this false peace through a process of elimination through fires, sword and war. This will render the individual free from the acquired characteristics that form an equally false self and fetter the soul. Yeshua's aims is to create a solitary being living in a unitary state (what Corbin has called **homo integer** in Avicenna 8, 11). As this saying suggests, the emergence of the Solitary involves an enigmatic process of struggle that fully integrates the powers of each realm into one's being, not as external forces, but now as interior realities.

Each individual soul has been cast into the ***kosmos***, where it appears we are prisoners in exile. However, this is so because we have not yet acquired consciousness of who, what, or where we are. We suffer inward disorientation. Unaware of our true nature or origin, we are lost and wandering because there is little light and no true direction. We move across the landscape of the ***kosmos*** in search, unaware that along the horizontal plane there are no answers and nothing but chaos. Only when we stand up out of the chaos and are reoriented vertically will we know our true nature. The horizontal world in which the soul lives must be broken apart. At the moment of dissolution, the soul is disoriented and bewildered in order that it might be reoriented to a different reality: the vertical axis of the kingdom.

*This sayings introduces the term **monachos** (the solitary being) which is described in two other Logia (49, 75). Here the meaning is placed on the creation of the Solitary One—how one becomes a **monachos**. What makes this solitary being is described as the Logion unfolds. It is one who has achieved "oneness" as an integration of duality.*

Yeshua describes the instruments of separation which disturb the peace as fire, sword, and war. These are the means by which the false peace is overcome in favor of individuation and integration along the vertical axis. Fire, which has been introduced into the ***kosmos***, burns in order to overcome the darkness and rid us of the false. With its powers of discrimination, the sword cuts the fetters that bind and rends the veil that keeps us from seeing the face of God. War shatters old boundaries, making way for new possibilities. No one, however, can complete this conquest for us. We ourselves must stand up on our own two feet.

The unified being is born out of the chaos of conflict, tragedy and alienation that is experienced in the "land of duality and opposites." Yeshua sees that the tragic history of humanity is a driving force that shall end in beings who are integrated. That is, these beings are able to stand and transcend duality on "two legs" (an image, perhaps, of the two axes), having united all dualities in a victory of overcoming. The one standing up out of the chaos is a soul whose integration, therefore, includes all souls and all conflicts. Such a conquest is not the destruction of "others," but union with the "other"—achieved slowly over time in a sequence, five to three, three to two, two to one.

QUESTIONS FOR REFLECTION

1. How do you personally respond to the idea of Yeshua as disturber of the peace and bringer of war? This is parallel to the ancient images of "holy war," a common metaphor to all Abrahamic traditions of the Middle East, and similar in some respects to the martial arts of the Far Eastern traditions. The way of the warrior and holy war are part of a complex set of sacred images. What is your personal understanding of these metaphors and your response to them?

2. The journey toward unitary knowledge and integrated being is a difficult path. It is far harder than the common one we usually take—the maximization of pleasure and minimization of pain. What have you experienced of this counter-intuitive path?

3. The image of a house or abode is used in this saying. From wisdom's point of view, what might that mean?

4. Suppose that the shattering and disorientation that Yeshua introduces into the ***kosmos*** is not about rejecting the material realm or the natural order. Imagine instead, that it is about disrupting our "safe" experience of the human world, leading us ultimately to reorientation, freedom, and reintegration. How have you experienced this?

EXERCISES AND MEDITATIONS

1. One moves through the layers (or abodes) of the ***kosmos*** out of exile and into freedom in a process of conquest that includes fire, sword, and combat. Each "victory" internalizes (and thus integrates) the powers of these various realms so that they no longer act upon us from without, but from within. Meditate, first, on how a child integrates the adult. Then, using that image, how the Solitary integrates the powers of the household, moving from house, family, and nation to earth, integrating these realms. How do all the dimensions and interconnections within the ***kosmos*** finally come to reside in one's soul so that their powers can now be utilized from within, rather than dictating to us from without?
2. Picture the positive nature of each of the instruments of conquest: fire ultimately produces light, the sword produces freedom, war produces victorious conquest (the eschatological overcoming of the Book of Revelation).
3. Rather than moving through the world on the warrior's path of individuation, we live by means of those unconscious "acquired characteristics" which dictate to us on their own terms. As an experiment, live throughout one day by consciously using light, freedom and eschatological overcoming as a means of freedom. Journal your experience.

Revelation 2:7, 11, 17, 26, 3:5, 12, 21

READINGS FOR INSIGHT

I

Eckhart Tolle
Stillness Speaks
34, 32

Built into the very structure of the egoic self is a need to oppose, resist, and exclude to maintain the sense of separateness on which its continued survival depends. So there is "me" against the "other," "us" against "them." ... The egoic sense of self needs conflict because its sense of a separate identity gets strengthened in fighting against this or that, and in demonstrating that this is "me" and that is not "me."

II

Henry Corbin
Avicenna and the Visionary Recital
8

It is through the integration of all its powers that the soul opens itself to the transconscious and anticipates its own totality. This totality—*homo integer*—can be expressed only in a symbol. The genuineness of this experience of spiritual maturity is attested in the measure to which a being attains the power to shape its own symbol.

III

Pema Chödrön
Comfortable with Uncertainty
145

As human beings, not only do we seek resolution, we feel that we deserve resolution. However, not only do we not deserve resolution, we suffer from resolution. We deserve something better than resolution: we deserve our birthright, which is ***prajna*** (unconditional wisdom), an open state of mind that can relax with paradox and ambiguity. ***Prajna*** is the unfiltered expression of the open ear, open eye, open mind that is found in every living being. It's a fluid process, not something definite and concrete that can be summed up or measured .... It is not regarded as a peaceful state of mind nor as a disturbed one. It is a state of basic intelligence that is open, questioning, and unbiased. Whether it comes in the form of curiosity, bewilderment, shock, or relaxation isn't really the issue. We train when we're caught off guard and when our life is up in the air.

IV

Kabir Helminski
Living Presence
51

We are slaves to a tyrant called "ego." Unless we are extremely astute we do not see the extent to which we are controlled by our habits, compulsions, and desires, because we are working so hard to satisfy their random expectations. ... A fixation on the false, compulsive self can distort our sense of reality, of justice, of balance. Again and again this false self can ruin things for the *whole* of oneself. The real possibility of the moment is destroyed from too much self-importance as well as from too little self-respect, from greed as well as from indifference, and from our disorderly desires as well as from inertia. Following the impulses of this false self, our essential Self is more and more eclipsed.

V

Jalaluddin Rumi
Mathnawi, II,
2443-2449

Save us from what our own hands might do, lift the veil, but do not tear it.
Save us from the ego; its knife has reached our hearts.
Who but You can break these chains?
Let us turn then from ourselves to You who are nearer to us than ourselves.
Even this prayer is Your gift to us.
How else could a rose garden grow from these ashes?

LOGION 17

Sapiential Themes

- *Sense-perception is the primary modality used in space-time, but not along the vertical axis.*
- *Other domains transcendent to, and perhaps "parallel" to, the horizontal axis exist, and we can have access to these.*
- *Wisdom's Master gives the gift of perception, as well as the instrument of perceiving.*

Yeshua says,

What your own eyes cannot see,
your human ears
do not hear,
your physical hands cannot touch,
and what is inconceivable to the human
mind—that I will give to you!

Parallel Texts

Isaiah 64:4
I Corinthians 2:9
II Corinthians 3:17-18, 4:17-18
Ephesians 1:18, 3:10-21

Links

Why would Yeshua place such burdens upon humanity as he did in the previous saying? What recompense is there for standing up vertically out of the chaos of the ***kosmos****? Logion 17 answers those questions with a new promise—the promise of transcendent knowing.*

FOCAL POINT

Just as there are waves on the electro-magnetic spectrum that we cannot hear, see, or feel, but which fill our universe nonetheless and remain hidden until we have the proper instruments to perceive them, so there are higher energies and realms of existence that we also do not know because they are not available to the senses or the rational mind. Truth received from reality beyond sensory perception and rational knowing is the focus of this Logion. Yeshua offers the gift of higher awareness and a way of knowing beyond the senses. Through this gift, that which is unknown because it exists beyond our normal perceptions becomes available to us and fills our hearts.

Notes

The issue of human knowing—how humans know or perceive anything, and how they come to understand what they know—is the philosophical issue of epistemology and hermeneutics. These issues are complex, especially in a world that tends to reduce everything down to physical laws and properties, or that believes there is no essential meaning in the universe because it and we are both the products of chance. Traditional wisdom believes otherwise, and bases its knowledge upon the existence of transcendent realities.

COMMENTARY

One of the important themes of the ancient Mediterranean world was the imprisonment (or exile) of the soul in the physical world. This idea appears both in Greek thought (in Plato's "Myth of the Cave," for example), as well as in the story of exile for the Hebrews in Egypt and Babylon. As spiritual symbolism, it may be entirely plausible to see our selves in this way. On the other hand, the wisdom tradition understands that our descent into space-time, far from being an exile, is the soul's spiritual journey undertaken by choice. From one perspective, we seem to be in exile. From another, we are making a sacred pilgrimage.

Human beings have been gifted with sense perception. Sensory awareness puts us in touch with the dimensions of space and time. Without the five senses we would be locked within ourselves, unable to communicate with the wider world around us. The teaching of traditional wisdom is clear, however, that while this is a great gift, if it is all we know, we are still confined to (some would say, imprisoned within) the horizontal axis. The five senses upon which we depend almost completely have no access to realities transcendent to the horizontal realm. We need other "senses," other apparatus for this, and if we are to become fully human, we also need input from domains that exist outside space and time along the vertical axis.

By original design, humans are said to be endowed with other cognitive capacities. To confine ourselves solely to the five ordinary senses not only limits our perceptions, it cuts us off from contact with the larger domains of macrocosmic reality. If we are to gain access to what lies beyond space-time, our cognitive capacities and perceptions must be expanded. The goal of raising each individual, solitary soul into the full realization and awareness of its celestial origins and its rank as a son or daughter of deity, will, however, make the common norms, rules, and collective precepts of the ***kosmos*** seem intolerable. The awakened soul cannot be satisfied by the ***kosmos*** alone, and, as the previous Logion states, finds itself in some sense at war with the ***kosmos***. As we have seen, it is precisely at the point when an individual stands up out of the chaos of the ***kosmos*** into the unitary state of a solitary being (***monachos***) that the gift of transcendent knowing can be given.

At the moment when the soul finds itself a stranger in a land which was formerly familiar, a new being emerges and differentiates from the false self, and the figure of the Guide, announcing itself to the soul, appears on its horizon. In truth, that same Guide already exists at the very core of the solitary soul. There is thus synchronicity between the soul's awakening and the appearance of the Guide (Corbin 20). It is this synchronicity which gives the newly emerged soul its unique structure, not as an autonomous being closed in upon itself, but as one who is now aware of the unified field held in the Presence of its Guide. In other words, the soul that was at war with the ***kosmos*** has come to know the truth about itself, its own transcendent counterpart, its original nature, and the wholeness that contains every opposite, every contrary or paradox. The small self is united with the large Self as one being that ultimately includes all selves. A larger knowing (Yeshua's promise) can thus come into this unitary state from every direction. What no natural eye has seen, ear heard, hand touched, or mind conceived is now available to the soul as gift.

The notion of the Guide who comes from without, but who also appears from within, has a venerable history. This particular theme has been ably explicated by Henry Corbin in his works, ***Spiritual Body and Celestial Earth*** *(1976),* ***The Man of Light in Iranian Sufism*** *(1978), and* ***The Voyage and the Messenger*** *(1998).*

Human beings who have at last discovered the truth of the unified Self are ready to receive the gift of all that lies beyond the senses. Having experienced exile within the ***kosmos*** (where it was given reasons for its existence and goals for living completely at odds with its own true nature), the previously fragmented soul becomes solitary (***monachos***), ready for ascent into transcendental wisdom. In such a state, Yeshua becomes both the Guide and the Giver of knowledge, and the soul begins the journey of vertical ascent and transcendental awareness of all that lies beyond the senses into the wisdom of the Kingdom of God.

QUESTIONS FOR REFLECTION

1. If this saying is ultimately about you, and what Yeshua intends to give you, then in what way might you prepare to receive the gift?

2. If, as the construction of the Gospel of Thomas suggests and the commentary explains, transcendental awareness is dependent upon the struggle for unitary being (the state of the ***monochos***), then what has already happened in your experience to create this state? Where are you in the process? What more needs to be done to facilitate this change?

3. What transcendental knowledge has already been given to you? What have you seen or perceived beyond the senses that is now a part of your store of wisdom?

EXERCISES AND MEDITATIONS

1. There are many examples of visionary seeing in the sacred literature of East and West. In the Gospels Yeshua himself sees "the heavens torn open and the Spirit descending like a dove." St. Paul and St. John have similar experiences, as do many of the prophets of the Hebrew Bible where there are many astounding visions of the transcendental world. (Among them are Ezekiel's, Daniel's and Isaiah's visions as well as John's in Revelation). Explore one of these. Imagine it in your mind's eye. Put yourself in the seer's place, undergoing the same vision. What do you see or feel? How might you respond to this strange experience? Would you be afraid? Does fear block your seeing or hearing in any way now?

Mark 1:9-10

Ezekiel 1
Daniel 7-10
Isaiah 6
Revelations 1:9-18

2. Other than these more extraordinary experiences, are there ones that we consider more normal, less overpowering? What are these communications from beyond ourselves? Have you ever dreamed something transcendent? How have you experienced this kind of communication in normal waking life?
3. At certain important moments, the native peoples of this continent went out deliberately to "seek a vision" (known as a vision quest). Is this something you should do? If it is, what preparations and precautions do you need to make?
4. We are told that wisdom is an active principle and that Yeshua is a living teacher, active and alive in our world. Suppose, then, that sources of wisdom are available to you now and that the only issue is whether you are listening or not. The capacity to receive the transmission of wisdom is dependent, of course, on many things. Among them is the ability to actively listen in the right context. Put yourself in a place that is quiet where you have enough time to listen. Write down a number of issues for which you are seeking wisdom. Gather some resources around you (reading materials and sacred literature that support this process). Go first into a time of silent listening and centering prayer. After a period of 15-20 minutes in silence, begin your reading in a slow, deliberate manner. Read passages from a number of your texts. Go back into a period of silent listening. Allow yourself to be aware of what forms in your mind and heart. Write this in your journal.

READINGS FOR INSIGHT

I

Bahauddin
The Drowned Book
49

The one who gave you senses to take in and absorb the world also gives ways of knowing the unseen.

II

Eckhart Tolle
Stillness Speaks
20

The next step in human evolution is to transcend thought. This is now our urgent task. It doesn't mean not to think anymore, but simply not to be completely identified with thought, possessed by thought.

III

Jalaluddin Rumi
The Rumi Collection
by Kabir Helminski
194

Is it possible for the bodily eye to see You?
Can thought comprehend your laughter or your grief?
Tell me now, can it possibly see you at all?
Such a heart has only borrowed things to live with,
But the garden of love is green without limit
And yields many fruits other than sorrow or joy.
Love is beyond either condition:
Without spring, without autumn, it is always fresh.

IV

Cynthia Bourgeault
The Wisdom Way of Knowing
49

Jesus taught that "the Kingdom of Heaven is within you" (Luke 17:21)—not later but *lighter*. To realize the Kingdom of Heaven here and now (which is what *enlightenment* means in virtually all the spiritual traditions) is really a matter of developing a kind of X-ray vision that can look right through the physical appearances of things and respond directly to their innermost aliveness and quality.

V

Jalaluddin Rumi
The Rumi Collection
by Kabir Helminski
183

Whenever Vision unfurls its ecstatic flag in you,
Or your mind blazes from a lightning flash of grace from heaven,
You are, in that moment, cold to "above" and "below,"
To all status and rank, mastery or leadership,
All man-made titles, praises, elevations, honors.
None of these things concern you:
You soar like a hawk in the cloudless sky of union.

VI

Willigis Jäger
Search for the Meaning of Life
29

Human consciousness can look behind the activities of its everyday mode. It can become one with the foundation out of which all things come into being. Human beings can go beyond their personal consciousness and become aware of a cosmic unity that in traditional religious language we call God, the Absolute, or the Numinous. This is evidently the Ground of Being for all humans. So long as we are cut off from this foundation, we can give our lives no meaning. This is the meaning of salvation or redemption: overcoming the illusory separateness that our ego-consciousness is always falling victim to.

LOGION 18

His students said to him,

"So, tell us, then, what our end and destiny will be?"

Yeshua answered,

"Have you already discovered your origin so that now you are free to seek after your end?

It is only at your source that you will find your destiny.

Blessed are those who come to stand in their place of origination, for it is there that they will know their end—never tasting death."

Sapiential Themes

- *The wisdom dialogues between Yeshua and his students are also between different developmental levels of being and consciousness.*
- *The focus of the students' question is themselves and their individual outcomes. Yeshua reverses their focus from the end to the beginning.*
- *The beginning point determines and gives meaning to the end.*
- *By understanding the beginning, one can know the end as the "place" where death has no taste.*
- *Wisdom's view of resurrection is taught through image and metaphor.*

Parallel Texts

Logia 4, 19
Genesis 1:1-2, 26-27, 2:4-7
Psalm 39:4, 139:1-18
John 1:1
I Corinthians 15:54-56

FOCAL POINT

It appears that his students are asking Yeshua about their end in death at the close of temporal life. If that is the case, their concerns are parochial and narrowly focused—what will happen to me? As is typical, Yeshua extends and expands their question in order to refocus it entirely. First, he changes the nature of the subject itself (their end at death) to encompass their entire life and destiny as a goal (their ***telos***). That destiny will be wherever their beginning is, for origination determines destiny and the end returns the individual to the place of beginnings. Yeshua redirects his students' attention, therefore, to the ***arche***—the place of origin. Only by knowing their true origination can they understand anything about their ultimate destiny. Second, he makes standing up in the ***arche*** a blessedness because, as a result, two things happen: one comes to know one's destiny; and in that place, one is no longer tasting death. It is where the Alpha and the Omega meet and are one that one gains the state of blessedness.

Links

It might be imagined that his students heard Logion 17 as referring to what occurs after death, and so they ask this question. It might also be that they are continuing to think about their future and the ending of their lives based on previous Logia. In any case, they are concerned about their destiny—how they and their lives will end. This is a serious question for all human beings, but once again Yeshua answers their question at a new level.

Notes

Logion 18 is semantically complex, and like other similar exchanges, the way Yeshua answers a question both changes the focus of the question and challenges the questioner. Structurally, the Logion is a dialogue in which Yeshua answers a question with a question followed by two declarative statements.

COMMENTARY

This shift of emphasis from the end to the beginning has occurred before in Logion 4. There, the person who is approaching the end of days seeks an answer from a child of seven days. Here, new reasons are given that bring the unified being (standing up in the ***kosmos****) to a new place of knowledge—the promise made in the Logion 17.*

This Logion makes it absolutely clear where the solitary one, who has emerged from the ***kosmos***, comes to stand. The unified being's feet are planted in the place of origins where the beginning and the end meet and are one. As the next Logion will describe, this is a place "out of time," prior to temporality.

The use of this complex imagery presupposes a particular cosmological structure as the context for Yeshua's teaching. The reader and seeker must therefore begin to comprehend this symbolic cosmology as the meta-system in which the words and metaphors of this and other sayings make sense. These mythological structures were widespread in ancient cultures and their religious traditions, providing a common context for the Logia of Thomas and the wisdom teachings of Yeshua.

To begin to understand this Logion, the soul has come to be "exiled" here from its place of origination. In the course of descent, ordinary human consciousness (operating in the ***kosmos*** as an autonomous egoic being) has lost touch with the larger Self. At the moment of true knowing, however, when the Self and self are united as one solitary being and receive wisdom from beyond the ***kosmos,*** there is a reversal. The soul gains new ground, but also comes to feel itself a "stranger" to the ***kosmos***—alien and in opposition. This is also why in its sojourn through time and space, individuation is required in order for the soul to know the truth about itself at the cost of this painfully won differentiation from the ***kosmos*** through combat and separation. It is ultimately only in this field of conflict, where inner freedom is slowly won, that there is sufficient room for the manifestation of the full image of the Self. Origin and destiny are united by completion, and the knowledge of both are fulfilled. At the end of our pilgrimage through time, the original design—the imprint of the divine Image (***imago dei***) set into the original creation—is fully discovered at the place of destination, so that the beginning and the end are one.

The second declarative statement in this Logion is a beatitude (sometimes called a ***macarism****, from the Greek word for blessed,* ***makarios****). It is the second beatitude used in this Gospel (7, 19, 49, 58, 68, and 103 being the others). This beatitude may stand independently, separate from the dialogue itself, summing up its teaching.*

Central to the realization of this beatific state are three actions: standing, knowing, and no longer tasting death. In essence, these actions define the true state of blessedness. If one is able to stand on two feet in the ***arche*** (the place of beginnings), and know there one's destiny, then one is no longer tasting death. In the wisdom tradition this constitutes the full image of resurrection. In this Logion, therefore, the ancient doctrine of the resurrection (learned more fully during the Persian exile) is being given a concrete form through image and metaphor.

The term ***arche*** *means the beginning point of something. It may (or may not) mean a beginning point in historical time, referring instead to other times or places outside of space-time.*

So we see, then, that to return to the place of one's beginning from out of the ***kosmos***, to emerge from the grip of death into new life, and to take one's stand in the ***arche*** (possessing full knowledge), is to be blessed with something new—resurrected life. It is possible to say that the sting and taste of death no longer apply. This is not, however, to say that one has escaped the experience of death. Indeed, the whole experience of battle in the ***kosmos*** has been to know death precisely through personal experience, but now one knows life in a similar way: by hard-won experience. It can be said, therefore, that the taste of death no longer lingers in the mouth. At the headwaters of existence there is no death, and no one there is any longer "eating death" as before. From that place and perspective, **all is life** because the taste of death no longer interferes.

QUESTIONS FOR REFLECTION

1. What is more important to you, how you began or how you will end? Why might it be more important for you to know your source than your destiny? Why do you imagine the wisdom tradition is so focused on origins?

2. Have you ever considered the fact that your origins may lie outside of space and time? Typically we imagine that we "got our start" at a certain time and place on earth. If this is not the case, what might this truth look like?

A multi-layered cosmos of many dimensions is believed to exist outside the physical universe. Your life is said to have begun in dimensions other than space-time, in a place called "paradise."

3. If you were to take your stand at the true place of your origination, what might that mean in real life? What does "stand" mean?

4. What have you already learned as a result of going through the struggles of individuation? Have your struggles ever transcended the need simply to be "yourself?"

EXERCISES AND MEDITATIONS

1. In the Socratic method of question and answer, wisdom teachers do not always answer a student's question directly. As often as not, they change the question itself. Could it be that the question(s) you are asking at this very moment need to be changed? This is difficult for us to imagine because questions can be so personal. Think about the nature of your most immediate questions: questions that are important to you personally and which, as the first students of Yeshua thought, have an impact on your life. Write a list of your own questions. Spend time listening for answers, but remember the answers may not be what you expect. They may change your questions.
2. Have you ever imagined that you might have existed before you came into space and time? For the sake of this meditation, imagine that you have an existence not here but elsewhere (wherever that "here" is). Report your findings. Write them in your journal.
3. If it is important for you to come to stand in your place of origination (and in that place come to know your end), then the quest to find your origins must become an important part of your practice. How might you continue the search to find origins?
4. How do you answer the questions that come not only out of your own searching, but also from those raised within the Gospel of Thomas? Yeshua seems to make his point here rather emphatically. In the course of this study, it might become very important for you to keep track of these questions and the answers you begin to receive about them.

It is interesting that something similar is taught in the Buddhist tradition where this search is described as the quest to find your "original face."

READINGS FOR INSIGHT

I

Hafez
Daniel Ladinsky
The Gift
207

All the talents of God are within you.
How could this be otherwise
when your soul derives from Divine Genes!

II

Carolyn Myss
Sacred Contracts
18-19

Like heroes in a mythic journey, we are meant to struggle to make the right choices. Our divine potential calls us to rise above the self's basic needs for survival in the physical world. We're called to grow beyond our self. But we can't grow spiritually only by using our intellect. Divine order and divine logic are different from earthly logic and reason and cannot always be perceived by our minds.

III

Jalaluddin Rumi
adapted from
The Glance
40

I am not this.
Your beauty closes my eyes, and I am falling into that.
You cut the umbilical cord with this love that's been with me since my birth.
My mother saw your mountain reflected in my face,
You that lifts coverings, You that brings death.
We agreed on this before creation.
I have been so hidden.
Ask my body who I am. It says, *solid ground.*
Ask my soul, *dizzy as the wind.*
Neither, I stand here facing your Sun.

IV

Henry Corbin
The Voyage and the Messenger
143-144

To orient oneself is to discover *where* one is. This orientation thus shows us the context in which it makes sense to speak of an *Orient* and an *Occident* of the cosmos. At this point, the question "Where?" may arise—but the only possible answer to this question must itself include a *sense* which situates this human existence, and by the same token reveals *who* the questioner is. The answer thus also orients the soul to its status as *stranger*. To *orient* oneself is to turn towards the *Orient*, to come out of the cosmic crypt, so as to rediscover the absolute "Orient" which is one's true and original home. It is this orientation ... where the poet is guided ... upon a "voyage towards the Light," a voyage towards the East.

V

Stephen Hirtenstein
The Unlimited Mercifer
161

It is the truth of this renewed creation that the gnostics realize. ... They have returned to the established point of their origin, "which is non-existence," and there find rest and repose, contemplating God in each of His manifestations. It is as if they have been propelled beyond the earthly gravity into the weightlessness of space—their hearts are in the heavens, while their feet rest upon earth. So they are simultaneously in the world but not of it. Outwardly they have to go through the changing states just like anyone else, but inwardly they have already returned to their unchanging starting-point.

LOGION 19

Sapiential Themes

- *In Yeshua's wisdom, the state of blessedness comes to those who not only know but live from their pre-existence.*
- *When a person is open to instruction, even stones in the material world can be a source of service.*
- *The enigma of the five trees of paradise provides a metaphoric key to paradise itself and the deathless state.*

Yeshua says,

Blessed are all who come to live
at the point of arising,
their "genesis," before they
came into temporality.

If you become my students,
listening deeply to my words,
even these stones will serve you.

And in paradise
five evergreen trees await you.
They do not change in summer nor shed
their leaves in winter.
If you come to know them, you will not
know the taste of death.

Parallel Texts

Logia 77, 84, 103
Genesis 2:9, 3:22-24
Psalm 1:3
Proverbs 3:18, 11:20, 13:12, 15:4
Ezekiel 47:7, 12
Luke 23:42
II Corinthians 12:4
Revelation 2:7, 22:2, 14

FOCAL POINT

Links

Logion 19 is related to a number of previous Logia: 4, 11, 13, 16, 18. Each has something to do with one's origins, the mystery of pre-existence, or the stones. This Logion is also linked to every other that mentions the "taste of death," as well as each of the beatitudes of the Gospel of Thomas.

Each of the three parts of this mysterious and enigmatic saying points toward mysteries that are normally outside human awareness, but meant to provoke further thought and questioning. Do humans exist before coming into space-time? If so, where? How could deeply listening to Yeshua's words make the most ordinary objects around us become servants to our learning? What are the five changeless trees of paradise? How does one come to know them and, in knowing, enter the deathless state? Each enigma is characteristic of the tradition of wisdom teaching in parables, of which Yeshua was a master. These, of course, can confuse us, but they can also induce wonder and amazement. Seeking to understand them will inevitably propel a student into a new search in unknown territory.

Notes

Logion 19 possesses a similar structure to Logion 18. It begins with a beatitude followed by two declarative statements. The collection of sayings in this Logion is part of the whole beatitude. Another similarity between this saying and Logion 18 is that they both deal with the beginning point, the place of origin, though the descriptions for each are different.

COMMENTARY

If indeed sapiential learning is about seeking and finding, being troubled and becoming amazed, moving towards sovereignty, and finally, ultimate rest, then this Logion marks the beginning of a steep new learning curve. Behind its various propositions there exists a larger metaphysical and mythological structure in common with several of the previous sayings and others which shall follow. It appears to be grounded on certain premises which are pre-conditions for making sense out of these Logia.

The vertical axis and the realms and dimensions that range along it suggest that time is experienced in multiple ways along this coordinate. If we think of the Ultimate Reality of the Infinite, Eternal, and the Absolute as one end of the spectrum where Eternal Time (known as the Eternal Present, Now), the other end is the fluid flow of passing time in the realm of sensible reality that we inhabit. Between these are dimensions with very different experiences of time inexperienced and therefore unknown to us. Nevertheless they are forms of time different from our own, in which duration and passing exist but in ways that cannot be easily calculated by us in the space-time continuum.

The first premise has to do with the pre-existence of the seeker. The second is that ordinary events and objects in time and space can come to be extraordinary means of service and epiphany. The third is the possibility of visionary cognition: seeing what lies beyond ordinary reality and into the "unseen." The fourth has to do with the objects of such awareness, which are extra-terrestrial realities transcendent to this dimension, but nevertheless potentially available to the seeker here who has access to paradise. Each of these remarkable premises needs further explication.

As has been noted, the term for "the beginning" used in the previous Logion is the Greek word **arche** (which I have translated as "origin"). Logion 19 uses a new term for a beginning that could be expressed as a genesis point when something actually emerges into existence in whatever dimension that may be. In this saying, then, Yeshua appears to be referring to the individual's particular point of emergence into existence in a dimension other than space-time, but within the framework of divine beginnings. Cosmologically, this implies that creation came into existence before humanity (either collectively or as individuals) had its own original starting point. In the case of the individual, that point, however, was not one's birth date in time, but at a point of "genesis" outside temporal, historical time.

An individual reaches a state of blessedness when he or she comes to know (participate or live in) that place before temporal existence. As difficult as this may be to understand, such a statement obviously suggests a far more complex cosmological framework than most of us are used to. Human existence, then, is more interesting than we ordinarily imagine (especially for citizens of the modern/post-modern scientific age). To benefit from Yeshua's wisdom in Thomas, we must accommodate ourselves to this wider understanding concerning who we are and where we came from. For example, ancient cosmological awareness described a larger world called "paradise" in which our temporal existence on earth is embedded. Paradise itself exists as a domain held within in an even larger realm which we today call "the Kingdom." In each of these higher domains there are many dimensions or worlds.

Many Jewish interpreters of the Genesis account place Eden (or paradise) not on earth, but in a domain beyond space-time. This interpretation is also supported by Yeshua's words from the cross, "This day you will be with me in paradise" (Luke 23:42).

If, therefore, we saw ourselves as originating not on earth or even in the physical cosmos, but in a realm that was ontologically higher—in this case "paradise"—then the meaning of this saying would be clearer. More typically, today we interpret the Genesis account of paradise as a place on earth, whereas, the paradise specified here (and elsewhere by first-century religious metaphors) is clearly extra-terrestrial. The blessed person, therefore, is one who, while existing in time, also becomes a resident of paradise. The rest of the Logion suggests that this is indeed the realm that marks the beginning point.

The second saying in this enigmatic Logion concerning the effects of authentic discipleship raises a number of important issues. The first has to do with the relationship between the student and the master. In the canonical tradition, Yeshua simply chooses his students. The construction of this saying suggests a more complex relationship. It implies that who is and who is not a student has less to with choice and more to do with Yeshua's sense about who has become a true student. This meaning is also conveyed by the literal words of the text, "if you should come to be to me a student."

The second issue has to do with listening. Clearly Yeshua's use of this word suggests something more than the simple hearing of an audible voice. It has to do with interior receptivity to the instruction: hearing it deeply, taking it into oneself, and living it. When that occurs, Yeshua speaks about the **service of stones**. This interesting phrase is in direct contrast to the earlier reference to stones which burn rather than serve the disciples. Could, however, these be the same stones? Their difference may only be in the "eye of the beholder." If they are the same stones, this may suggest that now they give light rather than fire, and that they represent the revelatory quality of the material world when it becomes illuminated from within and the student is able to receive it. Openness to Yeshua's words, therefore, allows creation to become an epiphany through which one can enter paradise sacramentally through the material gates of mystery.

This sentiment is in direct contrast to the view that the material world is opaque and evil—unable to give light; a view commonly held by some called "Gnostics."

The final enigma concerns the five trees of paradise, knowledge of which is said to deliver one from the condition of tasting death. There is much speculation about this statement, including the number five and the trees of paradise. What is the meaning of this complex picture? Are these metaphors for something else? Perhaps one way to begin to unravel the mystery is to remember that in the account in Genesis at the center of paradise stood the Tree of Life. The history of this image is long, but somewhere in Jewish tradition (perhaps much earlier than it is historically recorded), the Tree of Life is depicted in Kabalistic symbolism to have five central nodes: *Gevurah, Hesed, Tef'erat, Hod,* and *Netzakh*. Using the tree as a cosmological structure, some Jewish commentators place these five nodes (or living elements of the Tree of Life) at precisely the level of paradise—the World of Creation (***olam ha briah***). If we take this as a possible interpretative scheme, then the five trees are the living entities at the center of the Tree of Life which give manifestation to all created being. Their energies and qualities fill up creation, and combined, they are the source of all existence and of each human being in particular. To return to paradise and gain there a full knowledge of them, therefore, would mean that a person has come back to the wellspring of his or her being.

See Diagram 2 on the next page.

Many important studies of the Kabbalah and the Ten Sefirot (Tree of Life) exist. Among them are Daniel Matt's ***The Essential Kabbalah*** *(NY: HarperCollins, 1996), David Cooper's* ***God is a Verb*** *(NY: Riverhead Books, 1997), Moshe Idel's* ***Kabbalah: New Perspectives*** *(New Haven: Yale University Press, 1988), and David Sheinkin's* ***Path of Kabbalah*** *(NY: Paragon House, 1986).*

An Introduction to Diagram 2: The Tree of Life

The following diagram is a composite of many similar diagrams of the Jewish mystical Tree of Life. The ten spheres of the Sefiroth represent powers, energies, qualities, or living entities existing in the totality of created manifestation whose roots are ultimately in ***Ein Sof*** *as Source. English translations for the Hebrew terms vary depending upon the interpreter. The structure of the Tree is said to represent the totality of the cosmos in its multiple dimensions where it functions as cause of their many manifest forms. The lines separating the "worlds" of Manifestation can be drawn in various places, but this diagram generally represents the domains of existence as they are specified by the tradition. The origins of the Kabbalah are unknown. Although its full description emerged in the Middle Ages, its roots are said by many mystics to have come from King Solomon. Many scholars believe that Jewish mystical tradition began to flourish two centuries before the appearance of Yeshua, and his own exposure to this tradition and at least some of these ideas would have been likely.*

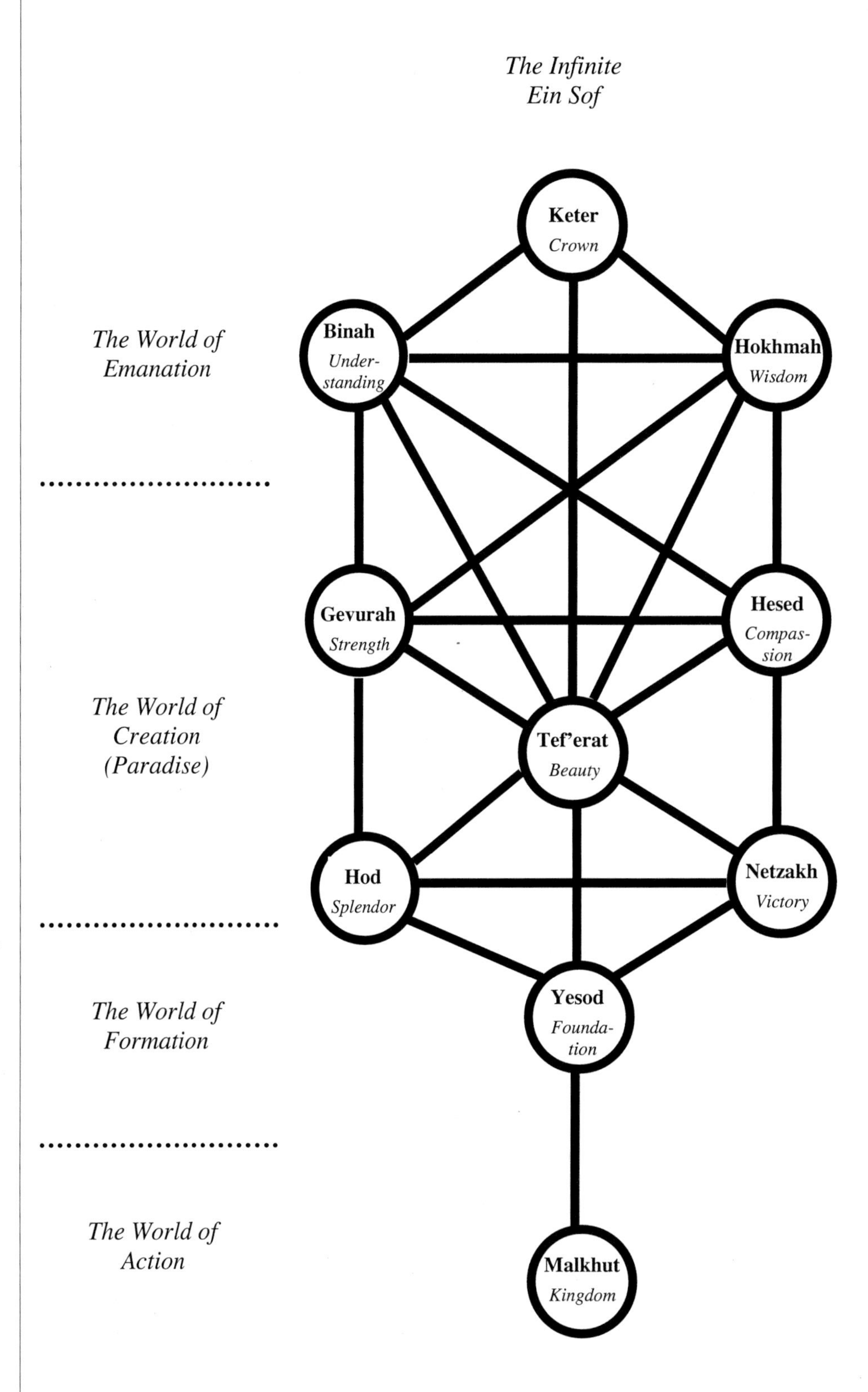

The Tree of Life
Diagram 2

QUESTIONS FOR REFLECTION

1. What might be waiting at your point of arising (your "genesis') that is so important to know? Why would such knowledge place you in a state of blessedness?

2. Have you had any intuition about an existence before coming into your personal history in time and space?

Notice that this teaching concerning pre-existence before coming into space-time is not describing reincarnation as it is typically understood today. This is about existing in another dimension before coming to this one, not about coming from a previous life on earth.

3. How is it possible to live at the "point of arising" when one is also moving through space-time?

4. What does deep listening really mean? Give an instance when you have listened deeply to a sacred teaching, text, or instruction.

5. When has some "ordinary stone" served you? Think of an instance when something ordinary became an extraordinary teaching for you. What state of mind or heart did you have to be in for this to happen?

EXERCISES AND MEDITATIONS

1. In your meditation, seek to connect the metaphors and statements of the various sayings that make up this Logion. One important connection has to do with listening deeply to the Master's words "these stones" as servants—and entering paradise in order to know the five trees. These seem like unrelated ideas, and yet apparently they are not. In a period of reflection, allow these ideas and themes to come together and to talk to each other, making their own internal connections. Use the "Readings for Insight" to help you do this. It may take awhile for these images and ideas to resonate with one another, but give them time. When they do, write out your insights in a journal. Notice that this meditation is itself a form of "listening deeply to my words." By doing this exercise you are engaged in deep listening.
2. Imagine the five evergreen trees in paradise. Using the interpretive structure of the Tree of Life in the diagram, seek to understand the meaning of each of the five trees (***sephiroth***) for you personally. What do these powers have to do with you? How are they life giving? How might you truly come to **know** them?
3. Do a study of the meaning of the five powers and qualities on the Tree of Life in the World of Creation as described by the diagram. You might start by writing your own definition for each, and then, if you have an opportunity, explore the many meanings of the Hebrew words from the tradition of Jewish mysticism.

There are many sites on the Internet that discuss the Tree of Life, the Kabbalah and Jewish mystical tradition. Not all of them are of equal value, but by exploring them, you will make some important discoveries about this tradition.

READINGS FOR INSIGHT

I

David A. Cooper
God is a Verb
293

Paradise is generally associated with the Garden of Eden, which is represented on two levels in Jewish mysticism. The lower garden is paradise on earth, while the upper garden is related to heaven. Descriptions rarely differentiate between the terrestrial and the celestial gardens. Because the mystical approach to all of creation is that everything below has its reflection above, there may be no clear difference between the two.

II

David Sheinkin
The Path of Kabbalah
116

Kabbalistically, the Tree of Life is a time-honored name for an arrangement of the Ten *Sefiroth*. Thus, the Tree of Life is viewed as a spiritual ladder: in the middle of the Garden of Eden was this spiritual ladder comprised of the Ten *Sefiroth*. They were arranged in such a manner as to form a ladder that one could use for spiritual growth.

III

Daniel Matt
The Essential Kabbalah
2

The kabbalists made the fantastic claim that their mystical teachings derived from the Garden of Eden. This suggests that Kabbalah conveys our original nature: the unbounded awareness of Adam and Eve. We have lost this nature, the most ancient tradition, as the inevitable consequence of tasting the fruit of knowledge, the price of maturity and culture. The kabbalist yearns to recover that primordial tradition, to regain cosmic consciousness, without renouncing the world.

IV

Emily Dickinson
The Poems of
Emily Dickinson
no. 466

I dwell in possibility,
A fairer house than prose.
More numerous of windows,
Superior for doors

Of chambers as the cedars,
Impregnable of eye.
And for an everlasting roof
The gambrels of the sky.

Of visitors, the fairest
For occupation, this:
The spreading wide my narrow hands
To gather paradise.

V

Pema Chödrön
Comfortable with
Uncertainty
187-188

"This very moment is the perfect teacher" is really a most profound instruction. Just seeing what's going on—that's the teaching right there. We can be with what's happening and not dissociate. Awakeness is found in our pleasure and our pain, our confusion and our wisdom. It's available in each moment of our weird, unfathomable, ordinary everyday lives.

LOGION 20

His students said to him,

"Tell us about this Kingdom of yours in the heavens. What is it like?"

Yeshua answered them,

"Let me compare it to a mustard seed,
the smallest of all seeds.
When it falls into prepared ground it
grows into a great tree capable of
sheltering the birds of the sky."

Sapiential Themes

- *The sapiential dialogue continues concerning Yeshua's teaching about the Kingdom in the heavens. The students have heard this and interpreted it as a reality that exists primarily beyond earth.*
- *Yeshua teaches by analogy, and gives Semitic expression to the theme of the Tree of Life.*
- *The cosmic tree has a universal function and purpose. It supports life beyond itself. This theme is found throughout all wisdom teachings.*

Parallel Texts

Logion 9
Psalm 1, 104
Matthew 13:31-32, 17:20
Luke 13:18-19
Mark 4:30-32

FOCAL POINT

The parable of the mustard seed is well known. In each of the places where it is recorded it appears to have the same purpose: to explain by analogy the dynamic nature of the Kingdom of Heaven, growing from the smallest of seeds to something far beyond its original magnitude. Any seed, of course, will do for this illustration, but the common mustard plant has a very small seed, and yet at maturity can grow into a very large tree-like plant. Unlike other plants of this kind that tend to stay small in that desert environment, it is proportionally much larger. Due to its small size, the mustard seed seems unlikely to produce such a plant; furthermore, it can grow quickly and become a habitation for nesting and seed-eating birds. It makes a good analogy, therefore, for the growth of heaven's own reality in whatever dimension it exists. As Yeshua will eventually say, however, that Kingdom does not exclusively exist in the heavens. It is everywhere and all-inclusive, becoming also a habitat for humanity.

Links

Images of planting and sowing are used throughout the Gospel of Thomas. This Logion relates to all these, but more directly perhaps to mention of the trees in paradise in the last Logion. Here the Tree of Life is singled out to illustrate the nature of the Kingdom.

Notes

It is of interest that the particular species of mustard grown in the Middle East has an extremely small seed, much smaller than the standard mustard seed we see in spice jars, or grown as a cover crop in the West. This particular seed is typically the size of a pencil point, or even smaller, and yet it grows into a substantially larger shrub, the size of a small tree. If, however, one were to take a small acorn that grows into an immense oak, it would be an equivalent analog.

*The Latin term **Axis Mundi** (Pole of the World or Cosmos) is the organizing principle of all manifest being. At the highest level, it is Unlimited Being (or Being relieved of all confines and conditions), understood as an expression of All-Possibility. At the lowest level, the Tree is something often called non-Being, absence, or the total limitation of being. Its roots, however, are in the Ultimate plane from which the vertical axis descends. Known as the Infinite, the Absolute, and the Eternal, that Reality is exempt from every mode of limitation or restriction.*

"From the pinnacle all lesser being derives. We can picture the vertical axis as a line which, tapping into the infinite reservoir of Being at its summit, transmits a portion of its store to the subordinate planes, which by dint of this transfusion 'materialize.' Each successively lower plane receives a smaller allotment, not because Being becomes progressively depleted--the reservoir, we recall is infinite--but because every grade of finitude must be actualized. Were any omitted, they would gape as holes, so to speak, depriving existence of the completeness the Infinite requires by name and possesses in fact."

*From Huston Smith's **Forgotten Truth**, 1976, 28-29.*

COMMENTARY

The students of Yeshua ask a good question related to his teachings. They ask for an explanation through similitude and metaphors about what the Kingdom is like "for them"—in relationship to human beings. Yeshua's answer is related to human interaction and relationship to that Kingdom. Instead of beginning with its ultimate and final reality, he gives an answer that relates first to earth and time—when the Kingdom in seed-form falls into prepared ground.

Yeshua's answer describes the organic quality of that kingdom through a developmental metaphor. It begins with something almost unseen, unnoticed, but alive in seed-form. The conjunction of this divine seed from the divine Reality with genetic material inside it, and the "ground" which is previously prepared, interacts to send out living branches which grow into the multiple dimensions of heaven.

This image of the mustard seed (and the "tree" that comes from it), is the Semitic analog of a universal theme found across cultures and history. Depending on the people who use it and the place it is being used, the image of the tree (or plant) differs by species, but the subject remains the same: at the heart of the cosmos is a living entity which, like a tree, has grown from something small, but then also spreads out nourishing and giving shelter to a far wider environment. Yeshua says that the Tree represents the Kingdom (the divine Realm), which is to be the habitat for all creatures. We too inhabit that Kingdom like a bird of the sky does a tree. We move into and out of its branches. We are sheltered under its canopy of living leaves. We build nests in its domain far from the ground. We are nourished by the fruits and food that it supplies. We are meant to flourish in just such an environment.

Yet in Yeshua's teaching, this vastness has grown out of something infinitesimally small. Small beginnings, however, do not mean small endings. Through this analogy we learn to treasure each potential seed-point in the Kingdom, knowing that its destiny will be different in form from its origin. In the wisdom tradition, growth in size typically equates to increase in quality. The seed will grow to maturity and become "qualified" to house the birds of the sky.

In whatever iconographic form the image of the Tree of Life is symbolized, it represents the ***axis mundi***—the immense, vertical, magnetic, and universal pole that is the center around which all cosmic reality forms. In its vertical orientation, it expresses both transcendence and immanence, experienced as the reality "beyond and above" the beings who reside in the "flatland" of the horizontal axis. It is also the deep interior mode of intimacy and presence—the epiphany that the divine Reality takes as the axial core of each individual being. As the Kingdom within, the tree is also planted in the "soil" of the human heart. So, it is both cosmic and personal, exterior and interior.

The function and purpose of the Tree as ***axis mundi*** is to establish the entire structure of being. The vertical axis, therefore, symbolically represents both scale and quality and the levels or degrees of manifestation as each thing is created outward from its core. The axis intersects, therefore, all the planes of existence, and spreads out branch-like from the trunk into each level or domain in the ontological hierarchy.

QUESTIONS FOR REFLECTION

*Found the world over, the "World Tree" (**axis mundi**) can be a stalk of maize in one culture, or a Yew, Bo, Oak or Pine tree in another.*

1. If you were going to explain to someone else Yeshua's purpose for using this metaphor with his students, what would you say?

2. Have you ever planted something from seed and watched it grow to maturity? What does that experience teach you about the nature of God's kingdom, the divine realm?

*The Coptic word **pe** can be translated both ways depending on context.*

3. It is interesting to remember that the word "sky" in Coptic is the same word for heaven. If we use this phrase as a metaphor for heaven, what might the "birds of the sky" be? If you thought of the Kingdom existing also within, how might that add to your description?

EXERCISES AND MEDITATIONS

1. This parable puts into focus not only the small size of the mustard seed, but also the beginning point—the point in time when the seed falls into prepared ground. As chaos theory has shown, the beginning point of anything is the most volatile of all—everything can be determined from tiny fluctuations there. Later these fluctuations have huge consequences, and it takes immense amounts of energy to shift things away from those consequences. However, at the beginning, with only minor adjustments, it quite easy to change the outcomes of everything. So, think of beginnings as critical points in time. Imagine that this very moment is the "beginning point" for outcomes in the rest of your life. What adjustments can be made at this moment that will affect your future, especially since you are a citizen of a Kingdom that includes all things?
2. Do you have anything to do with preparing the ground for the mustard seed? If this parable is about you, and your life is part of the whole picture (since you too are part of the Kingdom), then what kind of preparation is necessary inside you? What might that mean practically? In thinking about this, one cannot help but reflect back on Logion 9. These two sayings are directly linked because of this very issue: the prepared ground.
3. Imagine that in the future you might become an entire "environment," like a tree, and unlike a seed. A seed is nothing but itself. A tree includes far more than itself within its living system. If you were to imagine yourself as a future being with tree-like capacities, what would this mean? How might you envision it?
4. Most adults imagine that their growth processes are essentially over. Their body is no longer growing, and perhaps even their mental abilities are fairly well set. Suppose, though, that the most important part of you, the Spirit, is still in its infancy. What does that mean for your future and your work now?

Another way to think about exercise 4 is to ask yourself whether you have ever experienced yourself as expanding like a tree? Think of an example of how you might have experienced it and write it in your journal. Also, in what ways are you expanding or growing now?

READINGS FOR INSIGHT

I

Man is a Heavenly plant,
an inverted tree of which the roots tend Heavenward
and the branches downwards to earth.

Plato

II

I am the one who planted this tree for all the world to delight in. With it I spanned the All, calling it All, for all depends on it, all emanates from it, all need it, all gaze upon it and await it. From here souls fly forth in joy.

Alone I was when I made it. When I spread out my earth, in which I planted and rooted this tree—giving them joy in one another, rejoicing along with them—who was with me? To whom could I reveal this secret of mine?

Sefer ha-Bahir
The Essential Kabbalah
77

III

The tree is a riddle, a double-ended funnel. The riddle concerns the source and aim of its branching life. In the middle, the tree supports and is supported by an ecosystem. At one end, it draws material from the earth and extends the perimeter of organic life downward. At the other end, the tree's food originates on the sun.

David Applebaum
"Parabola," Fall 1989
15

IV

For behold! There grew
A tree whose leafage filled the living blue
With sacred singing, and so tall it rose,
A thousand grasses and a thousand snows
Could never raise it; but all trees together,
When warm rains come and it is growing weather
And every root and every seed believes,
Might dream of having such a world of leaves
So high in such a happiness of air.

It may be that some little root of the sacred tree still lives.
Nourish it then, that it may leaf and bloom and fill with singing birds.

Told to Black Elk
from the vision of
Sitanka
John Neihardt's
A Cycle of the West
1961

V

I thank Thee, Heavenly Father,
because Thou has put me at a source of running stream,
at a living spring in a land of drought, watering an eternal garden of wonders,
the Tree of Life, mystery of mysteries,
growing everlasting branches for eternal planting
to sink their roots into the stream of life for an eternal source.

And Thou, Heavenly Father,
protect their fruits with the angels of the day and of the night
and with flames of eternal Light burning every way.

A prayer from the
"Thanksgiving Psalms"
of the ***Dead Sea Scrolls***
VIII (viii, 4-12)

LOGION 21

Miriam said,

Then tell us, Master,
what your students are like?
How would you describe them?

He answered,

"They are like small children
living in a field not their own.
When the landlords return and demand,
'Give us back our field!'
the children return it
by simply stripping themselves
and standing naked before them.

"So then, I must also tell you this:
If a householder knows for sure that
thieves are coming to steal his goods,
he will keep careful watch before they
get there to prevent them from tunneling
in and taking his possessions.
You, too, from your beginnings,
must keep a watchful eye on the cosmos,
binding great power to yourselves
so that thieves cannot find a way
to get to you.
Pay attention then.
Any outside help you look for
they will try to seize first.
May there be someone among you
who truly understands this.

"So listen carefully,
if you have an ear for this!
When the fruit was ripe,
ready to burst,
the harvester came quickly,
sickle in hand, and took it."

Sapiential Themes

- *Miriam asks Yeshua to describe a serious student, and Yeshua gives three widely varying descriptions, each at the heart of wisdom learning.*
- *The image of the child is widely used in sapiential tradition as a central metaphor describing a precise state of readiness.*
- *It is crucial to understand who owns the "property" (real estate) of space-time.*
- *There are thieves in the cosmos whose actions must be taken seriously by the student of wisdom.*
- *Harvesters must know when a crop is ready and act immediately—no wasted time, no wasted product.*

Links

In the last Logion, Yeshua said that the growth of the Kingdom required "prepared ground." Could it be that Yeshua's answer to Miriam describes exactly what that inner state of readiness and preparation is (or is not). Many different forces are at work in the "field" of the Kingdom. Some are positive, and some are negative—but the goal of everything is the harvest. Agricultural themes continue the connection between this and previous Logia.

Parallel Texts

Logion 37, 50
Dialogues of the Dead, Dialogue 10 (Lucian of Samosata)
Genesis 2:25
Joel 3:13-15
Matthew 9:37-38, 24:43-44
Mark 4:29
Luke 10:2, 12:37-40
John 4:35
II Corinthians 5:1-3
I Thessalonians 5:5-7
Revelation 3: 5, 4:4, 6:11, 7:13-14, 14:2
Prayers Before Going to Sleep, #4 (St. Macarius the Great)

Notes

It is of interest that Miriam (thought to be none other than Mary Magdalene), a prominent student of Yeshua, asks a pertinent question of her own. What it reveals is that she is cognizant of her relationship to Yeshua as student—or at least of that possibility. She will continue this theme of the serious student in later sayings.

FOCAL POINT

*Early on in Christian teaching, the theme of watchfulness (**nepsis**) is developed by the monks of the Egyptian desert. Based upon Yeshua's teaching concerning staying awake and watching till the Master returns, this concept is clearly identified with the practice of wisdom.*

Again, a series of sayings are linked in this Logion which, at first glance, seem to be totally unrelated. What is common to all three is that they describe characteristics of the serious students of wisdom—wisdom seekers and wisdom learners. In each description the student must take action, or be ready for action. Watchfulness and attention seem to be the key. The child must be aware and ready to act when the landlords return. The householder must be alert and ready to act when thieves arrive. The harvester must be conscious of the crop's readiness and act with dispatch. Such watchfulness is crucial in the curriculum of wisdom and for the student who learns it.

COMMENTARY

The term "being" is used in philosophy to describe what comes into being and has existence. We might think of every object in existence as possessing "being."

Yeshua's answer to Miriam's question about the nature of a true student unfolds in three dramatic scenes. In addition, the actions in these scenes take place within two separate but embedded worlds or theaters (stages upon which the scene is played out). The first and largest stage is called "the field." Because the children are living in this field as human beings, we might think of it as the "field of physical existence" or perhaps of Being itself. Everything that is manifest lives in this vast field of creation—nothing that has been created exists outside of it. Embedded within the field, however, is a smaller realm, which the text calls "the cosmos." As we have seen previously, the way this term is used indicates that it is not the physical cosmos as such, but the human realm (***kosmos***)—the world of our own construction. This is the way the term is typically used in early Christian literature.

See Logia 4, 16

At the center of the first scene (in the largest field) are, of course, the children. This is not the first time the image of the child has been used. Here the theme of childhood is expanded, and future Logia will elaborate further. The children in this scene are gathered before the Lords of the creation, who own the field. All the while the children have been living on real estate that does not officially belong to them, but to beings who are obviously superior to them (perhaps wiser and older than the children). When the Lords return to their field and demand it be given back, the children release everything, including the clothes on their back. Nothing is withheld. In their willingness to let everything go, they appear to be wise beyond their years. Theirs is the correct relationship to physical existence in the field of creation. Truly they own nothing there, and show it by their nakedness. Though shocking, perhaps, their act seems to be a revelatory and not a demeaning act.

The mystico-metaphysical categories of "nakedness" and "clothedness" begin in the Genesis account and are encountered throughout the spiritual literature of both Christian and non-Christian sources. This theme illustrates both positive qualities (putting off the unnecessary, innocence) as well as negative qualities (absolute poverty).

This scene raises many issues, not least of which concerns the nature of the reality we each live within. To whom does it belong? Typically we view the environment we live in as "ours," to do with as we please. Life is ours. Our time is ours. Our field of consciousness is ours. But are they? Perhaps we live in a "borrowed" realm after all—even consciousness itself, and the energy of life which flows through us, as well as the ground upon which we stand (and in which our lives are played out) has never actually belonged to us at all. If we believe so, we have lived by false assumptions.

At some point in the future, for every individual, life as we have known it will be demanded back. We will be left with the naked form of our own being, stripped of everything external to it. Who will we be then without our many coverings and the ground upon which we have stood for so long? And these owners of the field, why do they want it all back from us? Do they have the right to demand it?

In the second scene, the individual is a householder who owns a house or even a homestead (or holding) which exists perhaps in this very same field. This domain, however, must be protected from robbers, for there are thieves in the cosmos, willing to steal away the householder's goods. They are nefarious beings who tunnel in, attempting to take possessions from the householder. Unless the householder knows this, and keeps careful watch on the surrounding cosmos right from the very beginning, the goods will be gone, and the owner will be bereft of his or her possessions.

The rest of wisdom's teaching is truly instructive. Watchfulness from the start is required, but watchfulness alone is not enough. One must possess power, power that is bound to one's being. This is an important assertion, for typically we seek for protection and security from the outside. Perhaps the local authorities or the law will assist us. What we discover, however, is that often those powers are themselves corrupted. Power that is not from within (or part of one's own being) is easily tainted—the cosmic thieves can seize and use it first. In the end, aren't most human beings susceptible to a fundamental desire to be rescued by a force (a Savior, perhaps) from without? Who are these thieves from which we must protect ourselves? The answer is not supplied here, but perhaps we will learn more later. In any case, the fact that the thieves tunnel in may picture their hidden and unseen nature.

*The idea of spiritual power possessed within (**dunamis** in Greek) is found throughout the writings of Scripture. See for example: Ephesians 1:19-21, 3:7-20, Philippians 3:10, Colossians 1:11, 29*

In the final scene, we may have returned to the larger field of the first scene. We are instructed to listen carefully! When fruit is ripe, ready to split open, that's the time to pick it. Harvesters knows this, and will not delay. The purpose of all farming—the soil preparation, the sowing, the tending and the growing—has been the harvest all along. So who are these harvesters? Are they the Lords of the creation? Or is it the lone watcher in the household who has homesteaded the field of life? Whoever it is, he or she moves at the right moment with precision-timing to reap the harvest—not a minute too soon, not a moment too late.

As we have seen in the parallel texts, the theme of harvest is used extensively by Yeshua in the canonical Gospels. It is also used by Paul in the Epistles. See for example: I Corinthians 3:6-9.

One might wonder in the first scene what the children have been doing with their time in the larger field of existence. Could they not have been farming and protecting the produce all along—the greater goods in the human household? Also in the end, could they not surrender it all back to the rightful owner, the Gardener of all existence who went forth, seed in hand, spreading fire in the cosmos in order to reap a harvest when the time comes? But other powers are also at work to steal everything away. So we are in a dynamic and fluid world, and in some sense, we live in a dangerous place. In such a place, watchful students gather their power, protect their goods, and wait expectantly for the time of harvest. When the end arrives, when the Lords return, they surrender it willingly, for everything is being gathered back to its Origins.

QUESTIONS FOR REFLECTION

1. Which of the scenes in this Logion most captures your imagination? Why?

This Logion is graphic, depicting many scenes. Use your capacity to imagine how each scene unfolds. If you want to extend the images into picture form, draw them either simply or in detail. Such an exercise will often help you to see new possibilities and meaning.

2. What do the Lords of Creation actually want from us? Why do they want the field they own back? In your view, who are they? Why is it a plurality of Lords?

3. Have you experienced something of value being stolen away from you in the cosmos? Why did it happen? Were you paying attention? What have you learned? Who or what are these thieves?

4. What is the difference between breaking in and tunneling in?

5. What is the power we can bind to ourselves? Where does it come from? Why is it easily corrupted (co-opted) if it is externalized?

EXERCISES AND MEDITATIONS

1. The image of the child is familiar in Yeshua's teaching. Today in psychological terms we talk about our "inner child" as that part of us that is most vulnerable and yet possesses power of its own. In this saying, the children seem wise to hold nothing back and yet, later in the Logion, to protect everything. Do you have an image of your own inner child? What is this part of you? Is it wise? In a period of meditation and reflection, you might go within, connect to the most vulnerable part of yourself—maybe that part you keep safely hidden away—and ask that child to teach you the technique of willing surrender. What do you learn from such an encounter ?
2. From the moment of your temporal beginning (either here or before entrance into space-time), thievery is said to be an issue. What is this Logion talking about that could be stolen away from you? What is so important about these goods or provisions that thieves would want to steal them? If you would imagine these to be immaterial, what would they be? In a period of meditation, reflect on what is most precious to you. What are your most precious possessions? Write these down. If these possessions are not material, then how could they be stolen?
3. There is a very interesting juxtapositioning in this Logion which appears to be paradoxical. It has to do with "holding on" to one's goods, letting go of everything. Meditate on these two actions which seems so opposite to one another. How can they both be true? In what context? Imagine yourself doing each of these. What is your emotional response to each? Is it fear? If so, why?

4. When do you feel most powerful? What is your power? Move through a day and pay attention to feelings of weakness and feelings of strength. When you notice strength, make a note to yourself, so that later you can take these observations into a period of meditation and reflect upon them. What you want to connect with is the power that keeps you "thief free."
5. Many people feel that "being centered" gives them great power. Stand in a spot by yourself. Close your eyes and feel your feet firmly planted on the ground, your body alert but relaxed, and your mind fully conscious of this present moment. Do not allow yourself to think about the past or move out into the future. Stay present, at attention for at least five minutes. Notice how this exercise centers you. What does "being centered" mean?
6. Acting at the right moment, when the time is "ripe" (not a little too soon, not too late), is a form of clarity and intuition that can be learned. Pay attention to your ability to act as a "harvester" in time. Can you detect when the right moment to act happens, or are you typically out of sync?

*The term **kairos** in Greek describes the right moment in time in distinction from **chronos**, the passage of time.*

READINGS FOR INSIGHT

I

We were born to be the companions of the angels.
Let us go there again, friend, for that is our country

Jalaluddin Rumi

II

It is the childlike nature...the need to love others and to be loved, the qualities of curiosity, inquisitiveness, thirst for knowledge, the need to learn, imagination, creativity, open-mindedness, experimental-mindedness, spontaneity, enthusiasm, sense of humor, playfulness, joy, optimism, honesty, resilience and compassionate intelligence, that constitute the spirit of the child. Together these traits add up to that innocence, that freshness, that characterize the child.

In other words, the spirit of the child is, in the profoundest sense, the spirit of humanity, an adaptive trait of the greatest biological value.

Ashley Montagu
Growing Young
95

II

People need to accept the spiritual freedom, life, and peace that they *already possess* because their true nature is rooted in the Good; the Savior admonishes his disciples to seek and find the child of true Humanity within. Knowing the truth about oneself and opposing the false powers that rule the world are foundational to achieving spiritual maturity and salvation.

Karen King
The Gospel of Mary Magdala
79

III

There is a knowledge and a practice of connecting ourselves with cosmic Life. It has nothing to do with belief; it is learned. It is increased by our consciousness of it, by our increasing awareness of the abundance of cosmic energy. Life is infinite, and this infinity can be tapped. The only limitation is one of awareness.

Life is not just this bioenergetic vitality, but a spiritual vitality that is eternal, and we *are* that. This lifespan that we know on earth is said to be one chapter in the story of Life. This Eternal Life reflects through us.

Kabir Helminski,
Living Presence
10

IV

David Appelbaum
"Parabola"
Volume 26, No. 1

Doesn't the gardener remember where control over conditions ends? That sun and storm are powers mightier than a human's? That watering and working the soil are means to an end? So a good gardener is well-practiced in sprouting seeds and getting them to grow, through agriculture, the "working of the fields." But what field is our human essence? For that is where the plowing and cultivating is needed—in the Garden of the heart …

V

Saint Athanasius
based on ***Life of Saint Anthony***

It is said that the great Saint Anthony used to tell his disciples:

"When you die and stand before the Judgment seat of God, you will not be asked whether you had become another Anthony, or Paul, or even the great Mary herself, but whether you had become truly yourself."

VI

Alan L. Miller
"Parabola"
Volume 17, No. 4

The experience of the sacred is fundamentally an encounter with power: that which is full of potential to act, do, and effect (or prevent) change, and which therefore represents both opportunity and threat. To the degree that sacred power can be channeled into useful actions, it is an opportunity for humans to participate in power and possibility far beyond anything that they might undertake merely by themselves. Insofar as the sacred cannot be controlled, it represents the direct threat to human life and property.

VII

William Congreve
Love for Love
1967

He that first cries out stop Thief,
Is often he that has stol'n the Treasure

VIII

Oscar Wilde
De Profundis
1976

Most people are other people.
Their thoughts are someone else's opinions,
Their lives a mimicry,
Their passions a quotation.

IX

Lynne McTaggart
The Field
xv

The world of the separate should have been laid waste once and for all by the discovery of quantum physics...As the pioneers of quantum physics peered into the very heart of matter, they were astounded by what they saw. The tiniest bits of matter weren't even matter, as we know it, not even a set *something*, but sometimes one thing, sometimes something quite different. And even stranger, they were often many possible things all at the same time. But most significantly, these subatomic particles had no meaning in isolation, but only in relationship with everything else. At its most elemental, matter couldn't be chopped up into self-contained little units, but was completely indivisible. You could only understand the universe as a dynamic web of interconnection. Things once in contact remained always in contact through all space and all time. Indeed, time and space themselves appeared as arbitrary constructs, no longer applicable at this level of the world. Time and space as we know them did not, in fact, exist. All that appeared, as far as the eye could see, was one long landscape of the here and now—*the field*.

LOGION 22

Sapiential Themes

- *Human experience of the divine in space-time is symbolized by the act of nursing children.*
- *Transformation through the transcendence of duality creates oneness.*
- *Non-duality or no-separation are keys to the kingdom.*
- *Singleness (wholeness) is described as the transcendence of duality.*
- *The original icons of one's being supercede their physical manifestation.*

Yeshua noticed infants nursing
and said to his students,
"These little ones taking milk
are like those on their way
into the kingdom."

So they asked him,
"If we too are 'little ones' are we on our
way into the kingdom?"

Yeshua replied,
"When you are able to make two
become one, the inside like the outside,
and the outside like the inside, the
higher like the lower, so that a man is
no longer male, and a woman, female,
but male and female become a single
whole; when you are able to fashion an
eye to replace an eye, and form a hand
in place of a hand, or a foot for a foot,
making one image supercede another—
then you will enter in."

Parallel Texts

Logion 106
Gospel of Philip 69
Odes of Solomon 34:5
Matthew 18:3, 10
John 10: 30, 17:11, 22-23
I Corinthians 12:12 14, 20
Galatians 3:28

Links

This Logion is a continuation of the themes concerning children and entry into the kingdom. It also concerns what it means to inherit the kingdom through oneness (or singleness) which was the subject of Logion 16, and which shall be expressed again in the following Logion (23). When Yeshua says that heaven and earth have come into being for James, this saying may also illustrate what that means for Yeshua.

FOCAL POINT

If one were to choose a key logion to summarize the wisdom of the Gospel of Thomas, this might be the strongest candidate. Through graphic wording and strong metaphor, and in concert with others before it (and many which shall follow), this Logion proclaims the vision of non-duality as the centerpoint of wisdom. True to its Semitic roots, however, the abstract concept of non-duality as a metaphysical principle is encoded in concrete images. The journey to the Kingdom requires transformation and transcendence depicted by the nursing infant and the androgyne. There is no other way forward into that realm that holds all realms, all creatures, objects, and elements of existence in unity. And the way forward is personal—no one can do it for you. You must bring oneness to realization within yourself. On the way into that Kingdom your task, says Yeshua, is to unite the "twins" of your being—the icons and the analogs—into one transcendent person. When the two are made one then you have reached your goal: oneness with the Kingdom.

Notes

The concept of oneness (or non-duality) versus twinness (or duality) is at the heart of this text. Semitic tradition tends to make the abstract concept concrete (or to use metaphors coming from the world of ordinary reality to illustrate the abstract). This saying combines the two approaches. As a metaphysical doctrine, however, non-duality is universal, a theme shared by all the world's great sacred traditions.

COMMENTARY

The image of nursing infants (taking in milk and, as a result, growing, changing and transforming into adults) is a central metaphor that graphically illustrates Yeshua's understanding of an individual's journey into the Kingdom. The nature of that process of maturation leading to unitive being will be like that of a nursing infant. But the child in this process is unusual, for the result of nursing creates the condition for transcendence and the possibility of reaching unity. It is only under the condition of unity that the child can be qualified to enter the divine Realm. Growth, therefore, is not simply change or transformation as we typically conceive of it—getting larger, older, or experiencing normal growing pains—it is seen instead as the process of replacing one set of "icons" with another. What can this mean?

Images of the divine feminine are typically secondary in Hebrew and Christian tradition. It is clear, however, that Yeshua changed the balance toward the feminine as a continuation of the feminine features of ***Sophia*** *in Hebrew wisdom.*

The images of children appear in several places in these sayings as well as in the canonical Gospels, representing the essential state of human life reoriented to the divine Realm (the Kingdom) that Yeshua seeks to create. Interestingly, in this saying transcendent Reality is portrayed in the mode of the divine feminine as the "divine Mother," who is the source of essential nourishment—the milk that feeds the spiritual life of humanity. This figure of the nursing infant at the Mother's breast triggers a series of enigmatic descriptions of unity which follow.

His students understand that perhaps they too are the "little ones" Yeshua is talking about, but what does that mean for them? So they ask: If indeed like these children they are "nursing infants" are they on the way into the kingdom? Yeshua does not answer their question with a simple response that "yes" they are on their way, or "no" they are not. Instead, he states the preconditions for entry into that realm. They must then decide and answer the question for themselves. If as nursing infants they are on their way, then they must also decode the paradoxes that appear in descriptions that follow.

In traditional thought there were seven heavens, and the heaven (or dimension) just above the physical universe held the templates (archetypes) for all of the diversity we find in space-time in perfect unity.

The complexity of this second part of the teaching, with its multiple references to spatial dimensions, genders, and parts of the body, reflects the multifaceted nature of a mature inhabitant of the Kingdom (the ultimate realm of divine Reality). Again, this series of metaphors centers around the crucial issue of unity: the uniting of two things (or multiple dimensions and images) into a fresh oneness. To understand the reference to image or archetype (icon, in the original) we must have some understanding of the cosmology which underlies these terms.

In that realm where all dimensions meet and are one, there exist the original archetypes (or templates) for the forms which appear in physical existence and which are analogs that re-present that higher reality. However, in the future, when the analog meets its archetypal twin, and the shadow-form is filled by its original reality, then all divisions and dualities will have been bridged and the One Reality will exist in fullness.

The wisdom traditions of the Far East speak in similar ways of beholding one's "original face" which existed before one was born. This is particularly true in the language of Zen Buddhism.

This higher Realm in which many dimensions are united, then, is the bedrock, the home ground fundamental to the existence of every human being on earth. It is also at the heart of the nature of the "single" (or whole) person who has emerged out of the chaos of space-time previously described in Logion 16. In the course of the process of transformation, therefore, an individual moves from relationship with the external dimensions alone (manifest in space-time) to other worlds which are at the core of his or her own reality. The ultimate image (as originally imprinted from the divine in the archetype) is the true source of our unique individuality on earth and one's true Self. Once we know the archetype and unite with it, we will at last know who we truly are. Only then, when one enters this Kingdom and comes to know their original reality does he or she come home. It is quite clear that such a journey of replacement will change everything, and Yeshua understands that transformation is the key.

The first of many transformations involves the uniting of the inner and outer realms along the horizontal axis, which is then balanced with the uniting of the higher and the lower realms along the vertical axis. These constitute the first fundamental shift in one's being. Though these concepts often seem altogether alien to the modern world, they were not strange in the world of the first century, especially among Jews who had lived and incorporated elements of the Hellenic tradition through such individuals as Philo of Alexandria. Basic to these mysteries (especially as they are expressed in the tradition of the **Corpus Hermeticum** where the axiom "As above so below, as below so above" is expressed in the *Emerald Table* within the Corpus) is the concept of worlds (or dimensions) in a hierarchy of relationships which are said to mirror each other: the above is reflected in that which is below, and what is below adds its energy and power to what is above.

Philo of Alexandria (30 BCE to 50 CE), a contemporary of Yeshua, was the great interpreter of the Hebrew tradition to the Greco-Roman world.

*The **Hermetica** is the ancient Greek and Latin writings which contain teachings ascribed to Hermes Trismegistus that combine the Greek and Egyptian wisdom traditions*

Modern understanding often fails to grasp that such a unity of being and an exchange between dimensions is possible. Until recently it has refused to believe that there are other dimensions outside space and time. And yet not only is this central to sacred tradition (and certainly to the essence of what Yeshua means by the Kingdom), it is becoming important to modern physics as well. The concept of the Kingdom includes all realms as a unity. It is not, then, simply a political reality, or primarily a future dominion established on earth. It exists in any place and time where heaven and earth are united and where interior and exterior worlds know themselves to be fully one.

The modern physicist, David Bohm, has pioneered the understanding that wholeness of the universe is contained in "implicate" and "explicate" orders.

In the common world of humanity we experience the duality of male and female forms. But in those dimensions transcendent to this one there exists a oneness which supersedes the split. This can be thought of as a sacred androgyny, but it does not mean the annihilation of either quality (masculine or feminine, male or female). Instead, it means their transcendence into a new and fruitful unity. Such a unity may also be perceived as the recognition (in each of the sexes) that the fullness of each is reached only when the opposite is also included and united into one's being. Modern psychology has understood that the acceptance of the **anima** or the **animus** (one's male or female counterpart) is necessary for the completion of each human being. That counterpart must be consciously harmonized if one is to reach full maturity (or individuation) within the psyche. This new level of conscious participation with one's gender opposite constitutes a greater fullness. Yeshua, however, may be moving far beyond even that unity into a new androgenic form of humanity where, as St. Paul described it, "there is neither male nor female" but one new creature made up of hands, feet, ears and eyes—all now reconfigured in unitive harmony.

It is through the pioneering efforts of the Swiss psychiatrist C.G. Jung that modern psychology has come to understand and accept this process of individuation.

*The ancient doctrine of the sacred androgyne is explicitly expressed in the **Corpus Hermeticum**, as well as in Chinese Taoism and Indian Tantrism.*

QUESTIONS FOR REFLECTION

1. If after asking a question of your own you had been given an answer like the one Yeshua gave, what would you think? What would be your reaction?

2. Is there any place in your life where you perceive you are making "two into one"? What does singleness (or wholeness) actually mean and what is the experience of it like? More importantly, how is it accomplished?

3. What does a single (solitary), whole being feel like from the inside? Have you ever felt any part of this form of androgyny in yourself?

4. Because there is an implied cosmology in this Logion where perhaps you exist simultaneously in multiple realms, how might you imagine your existence in the realm above and beyond space-time? Are you ever aware of that existence?

EXERCISES AND MEDITATIONS

1. There are multiple images and metaphors used in this Logion. A prominent one is often overlooked. It is the principle of the divine feminine nursing humanity at her breast. Western tradition has favored masculine imagery, but the two exist together, and in our day it is important to find a better balance. In a period of meditation imagine yourself nursing milk from the divine realm—the divine breast. What does such an image mean for you? What is it like for you to nurse from the divine Realm? In your own mind, picture how you take in milk. Write the results in your personal journal.
2. Imagine that in your lifetime you have the opportunity of uniting heaven and earth, the material with the spiritual, and that the laboratory of such work is your own being inside the experiences you have on a daily basis. As the site for such a possibility, how might you become an active participant, cooperating with and encouraging the process of unification? Think through your own experience. Make an inventory of areas that you feel are fragmented and that need to be brought together. Put them in an order of priority, and then begin to explore how they can be united in a new balance. Keep a journal of your "laboratory" experiments.
3. Suppose that there is a living template of your being that awaits your journey of completion through time and space. Imagine also that this template (your higher Self) needs the work of your life experience in space and time to become fully realized. If in your lifetime you can have some form of contact with this higher Self, receiving information and wisdom from it and returning the benefits of your experience here into it, what should you do now? Take time in your meditation to explore such a relationship. What happens when you do?

It is interesting that in the mystical poetry of both Christianity and Islam this image of the divine breast is used to express many forms of spiritual experience. For example, Rabi'a (the first woman Sufi saint) says in a poem:

I hear talk about the famous.
I hear talk about different cities....
All that can be said I have heard.
All that can be wanted I have seen.
My interest in this world has waned though, not because I am depressed.
As a fish in a bowl I was a bottom feeder, but now I nurse upon a breast in the sky.

In another poem, from St. Francis of Assisi, we hear lines which bring a new and almost shocking twist to the feminine image:

I asked for the most intimate experience with the Christ.
No one would believe what happened in a vision more true than this world:
The sacred chord pulsated light throughout the universe as I nursed my own Lord at my breast.

*(These two poems are found in Daniel Ladinsky's **Love Poems from God**, pages 25 and 55)*

READINGS FOR INSIGHT

I

God is unified oneness—one without two, inestimable. Genuine divine existence engenders the existence of all of creation. The sublime, inner essences secretly constitute a chain linking everything from the highest to the lowest, extending from the upper pool to the edge of the universe. There is nothing—not even the tiniest thing—that is not fastened to the links of this chain. Everything is catenated in its mystery, caught in its oneness. God is one, God's secret is one, all the worlds below and above are all mysteriously one. Divine existence is indivisible. The entire chain is one. Down to the last link, everything is linked with everything else; so divine essence is below as well as above, in heaven and on earth. There is nothing else.

Moses de Leon
Sefer ha-Rimmon
Book of the Pomegranate
181-182

II

Exalt the One over the dyad—the single over the dual—and free its nobility from all commerce with dualism, and you will consort immaterially with immaterial spirits; for you will yourself have become a noetic spirit, even though you appear to dwell bodily among other men.

Once you have brought the dyad into subjection to the dignity and nature of the One, you will have subjected the whole of creation to God, for you will have brought into unity what was divided and will have reconciled all things. So long as the nature of the powers within us is in a state of inner discord and is dispersed among many contrary things, we do not participate in God's supra-natural gifts. And if we do not participate in these gifts, we are also far from the mystical eucharist of the heavenly sanctuary. ...

Nikitas Stithatos
***The Philokalia**, Vol. 4,*
143

III

Each of us emerges from Ein Sof (the Infinite) and is included in it. We live through its dissemination. It is the perpetuation of existence. The fact that we sustain ourselves on vegetation and animal life does not mean that we are nourished on something outside of it. This process is like a revolving wheel, first descending, then ascending. It is all one and the same, nothing is separate from it. Though life branches out further and further, everything is joined to Ein Sof, included and abiding in it. Delve into this. Flashes of intuition will come and go, and you will discover a secret here. If you are deserving, you will understand the mystery of God on your own.

Moses Cordovero
Shi'ur Qomah
16d-17a

IV

Your spirit is mixing with my spirit
Just as wine is mixing with pure water.
And when something touches You, it touches me.
Now "you" are "me" in everything!

I have become the One I love
and the One I love has become me!
We are two spirits infused in a single body.
And to see me is to see Him.
And to see Him is to see us.

al-Hallaj
The Passion of al-Hallaj
41-43

V

God is no longer just the One who directs and rules everything. Rather, we use the word *God* to designate the totality of everything that exists. This Ultimate Authority, the Divine, has to be understood holistically. ...Theistic theology falsely calls this pantheism because it can't understand what esotericism is trying to express with not-twoness, namely the experience of conceptual terms as a unit of reality.

Sadly we can't make any statement without forming conceptual pairs. But in mystical experience we learn that such pairs are in reality, one. ...The Divine is a bipolar unity; it doesn't belong on the side of one pole or the other. It is what transcends both poles in oneness. ...

In the whole there is no polarity, no time, and no space. But this wholeness or totality is incomprehensible to our human consciousness, and that irritates reason. Mystical experience is the experience of this whole, and so it often comes into conflict with theology, which is anchored in the world of polarity. It's not as if mysticism were against theology; mysticism merely stresses the side of the whole that it experiences but that remains closed to reason. ...

People have to find their way back to the Whole. Wholeness embraces everything, there is nothing that could be outside it. In the Whole there is neither time nor space. Time and space are possible only within polarity. The Whole cannot be described concretely, only in paradoxes, parables and myths. The only way to illumine the Whole is to frame it in paradoxes.

When the One emerges into creation, it is polar. Creation means that unity crumbles into multiplicity. A popular image attempts to make this clear: light slants through a prism. Light stands for the unity, the colors are polarity. The prism breaks down the light into many different colors, but the light always remains what it is: light.

Willigis Jäger
Search for the Meaning of Life
57, 59, 61

VI

This world is viewed as the mirror of divine qualities, the site of their manifestation. The human heart is even more so a site of their manifestation. Recognizing these qualities in the heart is at the same time recognizing them in life. There is no separation in the field of Oneness (***tawhid***). There is, therefore, no antagonism between human life and the spiritual life. Only when human life has become shaped by the demands and illusions of the isolated ego is it reduced to a caricature, a particularized distortion of its wholeness. Otherwise, to be fully human is to fulfill our spiritual destiny.

Kabir Helminski
The Knowing Heart
22-23

VII

I am God's other self
He findeth but in me
His equal and His like
for all eternity.

No man shall ever know
what is true blessedness
Till oneness overwhelms
and swallows separateness.

Angelus Silesius
The Cherubinic Wanderer

LOGION 23

Yeshua says,

"I choose you,
one from a thousand,
two from ten thousand,
and you will stand to your own feet
having become single and whole."

Sapiential Themes

- *The work and presence of the Master is to awaken and cause individuals to stand up whole.*
- *The spiritual destiny of humanity and the goal of all human work is to become unified beings.*
- *Standing up is the metaphor for vertical alignment, awakening, and spiritual individuation.*
- *The mystery of the freedom of choice: the Master's and ours.*

Parallel Texts

Logia 16, 18, 28, 50, 75, 90
Deuteronomy 32:30
Ecclesiastes 7:27-28
Isaiah 66:4
Jeremiah 3:14
Luke 6:13
John 1:43, 15:16, 19
Romans 14:4
I Corinthians 1:27-28
Ephesians 1: 4, 6:11-14
II Thessalonians 2:13
I Peter 2:9

FOCAL POINT

Such a small text carries so much weight and the fragrance of many mysteries which lie just below the surface of human perception. At the heart of the mystery we hear the Master's passionate voice, his own desire for the student. We also begin to understand what the goal of all human existence actually is. This is the purpose for our life in the cosmos (and in the midst of it we receive Yeshua's assistance out of divine longing). This longing presides over the life of humanity and urges us to become whole human beings in proper relationship to the cosmos. The numbers, however, appear weighted on the side of those left out and "unchosen," but another mystery exists. In the end, we are pursued relentlessly despite the numbers. So at the moment, we cannot pay them much attention. It is only the way things appear at this juncture. We must look instead at the power which is pulling, attracting, and calling our hearts.

Links

Logion 23 follows naturally from the previous saying about unitive being: the process of becoming single or whole. The purpose of the Master's presence is to call individuals into such a state. The descriptions of this inner alignment have already been given (Logion 16), and will be discussed in a future saying (Logion 28) to which this saying is linked.

Notes

Free will has always had a prominent place in Christian thought. However, predestination (or determination) has also played a major theological role. Here the latter seems to be in focus. If there is only divine choice, however, then everything is determined. If, however, choices depend on perspective, then both are still in play.

COMMENTARY

In every sacred tradition there are Masters and prophetic voices that call out to humanity to awaken and arise from sleep. It is their longing to be heard, and for those who hear and respond it is as if they have been specifically chosen. They turn, and come to the Master's voice, and the Master says, "It is to you I have spoken. I choose you!" So the presence of the Masters, and the voice of prophetic proclamation, is crucial if ever there is to be awakening. From the Prophets' and the Master's point of view there is nothing but longing, and it is their love that speaks. From the viewpoint of the masses (the thousands and the ten thousands), there is no voice, and no presence, so it appears that no one hears—and yet out of the masses there arise those who do hear and respond. For them the presence of the Master is the essential gift, without which they could not come awake. And yes, it is as if they have been chosen, for they are dear to the Master who has loved and longed for them. At the first sign of their awakening, they have been called into personal relationship by name and onto wisdom's path of learning.

The visual picture implicit in this saying is of the horizontal landscape along which most human life survives at the surface level of existence. In that landscape, from a spiritual perspective, the vast majority of human beings are asleep, unaware, and unable to respond. As a metaphor, therefore, standing up means awakening, arising from the dead, and taking to one's feet against the flow of ordinary experience. It means aligning one's self to the vertical axis of being. Those individuals standing up (and standing out) from the rest become spiritually individuated beings who know themselves to be something more than the mere product of social conditioning. They take their stand against the social constructions of the ***kosmos*** and the programming which constitute the normative life of the ego in space-time.

It was C. G. Jung who developed the concept of individuation as a psychological process. Here we are using the term to designate a higher order of individuation distinct from the processes of the psyche.

So why do we pass through the horizontal axis? Why is space-time so crucial to our spiritual becoming? The first answer is contained in this and Logion 22. It is to become whole—one unified being who has united both axes. Through the chaos and struggle of living along the horizontal axis, a human takes to his or her feet and unites both within. From the divine perspective there is no other goal—though there are thousands and ten-thousands of other agendas which keep us perfectly aligned to horizontal reality. Once an individual hears the other voice calling, then bi-axial reality, united in one solitary being, is a new and unfathomable possibility. This is the Supreme Identity for which the Master longs. It is the goal of all human experience, the Omega point toward which all human beings inexorably move. The question is, when will we reach that goal? When will the choice to stand be made, and who will do the choosing?

The teaching of the Supreme Identity is central to the perennial wisdom we inherit. At its core is the concept that our true identity does not lie in the ego (which is illusory), but lies instead in a higher Self and ultimately in God. For an extensive introduction to this concept see Alan Watts' important text, ***The Supreme Identity*** *(NY: Random House, 1972).*

In this Logion we hear the mystery of our choosing from the Master's perspective. We are chosen, beloved, and longed for by Yeshua, the Master of Wisdom, through whom the divine Presence knew us before we knew ourselves. While we were still asleep we were understood, and now that we are awake we recognize the grace that has called us out of our sleep of death. But perhaps in hearing the voice we also chose to be awake—we chose to follow the voice; at least it appeared that way from our perspective on the horizon of existence. So the mystery remains, and each choice depends on the perspective of the one who is speaking.

QUESTIONS FOR REFLECTION

1. Think about your life and the choices you have made, especially on the spiritual path. From your perspective, who was doing the choosing?

2. Do you consider yourself to be "one in a thousand"? Is it possible that every single being is "one in a thousand, two in ten-thousand?" How could that be?

3. Have you ever wondered why you were attracted to the spiritual path and so many others were not? What is your answer to that question?

4. How can you detect whether in fact you have "stood to your feet?" Is becoming "single and whole" the precondition for such standing, or the other way around? How are the two ideas related?

EXERCISES AND MEDITATIONS

1. If you are in relationship to Yeshua as the Master of Wisdom, then, from his perspective at least, you have been chosen—and are beloved. You may not think you are "in relationship" to him at all, but if you are reading the Gospel of Thomas that may be the telltale sign that you already are. Could this Gospel have "found" you? At the right moment of readiness, could it have attracted you? Through it, could Yeshua, the Master, be speaking to you? Ponder this possibility. What happens if you imagine it to be so?
2. Is it only God's choice, or are there multiple choices and many possible points of awakening? Do we "choose" to wake up from normal slumber in the night? Is it our choice, or are there other forces at work? We awaken when we are ready, of course, but what does that mean? We often hear outside voices when we begin to arise from our deep slumber—and a strong enough voice will awaken us from a sound sleep, but is that preferable? So choice remains a mystery—the divine mystery and ours. Meditate on this mystery and on whether or not you share the moment as a choice when you are ready to come awake.
3. The unified being, discussed in the last Logion, appears in this saying as one who is standing up (out of the cosmos, as Logion 28 will tell us). So the purpose of the Master's call is threefold: 1) to stand up out of the cosmos, 2) to achieve vertical alignment, 3) to become a unified (whole) being. If this is the purpose and goal of our existence on earth, then the question is, how much of this goal have you reached? You might use the template of Yeshua's own life as a measure. Think about what each of these three conditions specifically means for you. These features also characterize the lives of saints in the various sacred traditions. Find a saint and explore these conditions as they are manifest in that person's life.

A good way to begin, perhaps, is to read the poetic work of a number of saints. Take, for example, the text, ***Love Poems from God*** *by Daniel Ladinsky, and find saints there that fulfill these conditions. You might seek to find it specifically in their poetry.*

READINGS FOR INSIGHT

I

At that moment his spirit grows wings and lifts.
His ego falls like a battered wall.
He unites with God, alive,
but emptied of *himself* (Nasuh). ...
Someone dead a hundred years
steps out strong and handsome
A broken stick breaks into bud.

Jalaluddin Rumi
Rumi the Book of Love
42

II

The creature has nothing else in its power but the free use of its will, and its free will hath no other power but that of concurring with, or resisting, the work of God in nature.

William Law
A Serious Call to a Devout and Holy Life

III

The choice is always ours. Then let me choose
The longest art, the hard Promethean way.
Cherishingly to tend and feed and fan
That toward fire, whose small precarious flame,
Kindled or quenched creates
The noble or the ignoble men we are,
The worlds we live in and the very fates,
Our bright or muddy star.

Aldous Huxley
The Cicadas

IV

For the most part, of course, the presence and action of the great spiritual universe surrounding us is no more noticed by us than the pressure of air on our bodies, or the action of light. Our field of attention is not wide enough for that; our spiritual senses are not sufficiently alert. Most people work so hard developing their correspondence with the visible world, that their power of corresponding with the invisible is left in a rudimentary state.

The moment in which, in one way or another, we become aware of this creative action of God and are therefore able to respond or resist, is the moment in which our conscious spiritual life begins. In all the talk of human progress, it is strange how very seldom we hear anything about this, the most momentous step forward that a human being can make: for it is the step that takes us beyond self-interest.

Evelyn Underhill
The Spiritual Life

V

We think we must climb to a certain height of goodness before we can reach God. But He says not "At the end of the end of the way you may find me"; He says "I am the Way' I am the road under your feet, the road that begins just as low down as you happen to be." If we are in a hole the Way begins in the hole. The moment we set our face in the same direction as His, we are walking with God.

Helen Wodehouse
"Inner Light" I

LOGION 24

Sapiential Themes

- *The light mysticism of the ancient Middle East, and especially among the Hebrews, permeates the Gospel of Thomas.*
- *Yeshua introduces the central teaching of light mysticism concerning the being of light.*
- *Inner light is also the source of illumination for the cosmos.*
- *The goal of a unified being is to become light.*
- *Darkness is defined in Yeshua's wisdom as an interior state.*

His students said to him,

Take us to the place where you are, since we are required to seek after it."

He answered them,

"Whoever has an ear for this should listen carefully!
Light shines out from the center of a being of light and illuminates the whole cosmos. Whoever fails to become light is a source of darkness."

Parallel Texts

Matthew 4:16, 5: 14- 16, 6:22-23, 17:2-5
Luke 11:34, 36, 16:8
John 1:4-9, 13:36
I Corinthians 15:39-49
II Corinthians 3:17-18, 4:6
Ephesians 5:8-14
Philippians 2:15
I John 1:5-7, 2:8-10
Revelations 18:1, 21:23, 22:5

Links

Each of the statements Yeshua has made before this saying continue to raise the stakes in his students' discipleship. They see clearly that Yeshua is in a different place than they are, and are aware of their need to be where he is, so they ask for help. Yeshua's answer takes them into the realm of light at the center of being, and this topic will be reflected throughout the next twelve logia. Later in Logion 50 Yeshua describes the specific realm of light from which humanity comes and to which it is returning.

FOCAL POINT

Logion 24 begins with a request from Yeshua's students. They want help in reaching the "place" where Yeshua is. Clearly their concern is not about the geography of Yeshua's residence or hometown, but about the spiritual place where he resides or, perhaps, his spiritual status in the Kingdom to which he constantly refers (and to which he has said they are moving). They see that place as superior to where they are now. Yeshua's answer, however, indicates not a physical place with a topography, but an interior state of being: an inner state from which light shines. This is "where" Yeshua is, and where they are also to come as human beings, without which they will remain in darkness. It is from this interior place that light shines to the exterior geography, illuminating both realms.

Notes

*The word **topos** in Greek is used here as well as in Logion 4. In both cases it refers more to a state (or a dimension) than to a geographical locale. It is easy to think of the Kingdom as an external place located either in the future, or in some locale in space-time. It is neither. The Kingdom is a place of light that is most associated with the dimensions within.*

COMMENTARY

The ancient monotheisms of the Middle East symbolized God as the manifestation of light and fire. Egyptian monotheism pictured God as the Sun of Light (Ra). The Zoroastrian tradition of the Mazdeans perceived Lord Wisdom (Ahura Mazda) to be the God of glorious light. Moses confronts God in a burning bush and, on the Mountain, in a blaze of light. The Psalms and the prophets all envision the heavenly glory as the divine Reality in which the Light of the divine Presence sets both heaven and earth alight with the divine fire.

Psalm 27, 67, 90, 97

Early Jewish mysticism two centuries before Yeshua speaks of the visionary light of the chariot which lifts humankind into the divine Presence, changing the very body of the one touched into a light-being. So it is not surprising that in his wisdom teaching, Yeshua will use similar words. These will pertain not just to God or the special emissaries of God—the prophets—but to the common person, and more particularly to the students of Yeshua. He, therefore, says to them, "Whoever (of you) fails to become light is a source of darkness."

From the Maccabean period of Jewish history two centuries prior to the advent of Yeshua, Merkavah and Hekhelot mysticism becomes a spiritual force that recognizes light, light beings, and transformation into light as primary mystical realities.

Light, inner enlightenment, illumination, and the shining forth of the divine glory are all in precise relationship to those human beings who have learned to live with light as inner fire. This "being of light" (***photeinos anthropos***)—or light-being—will also become a subject prominent in the canonical writings of Saints John and Paul. The Apostle John says that we are to be light's children, and the Apostle Paul speaks of a future destiny where we will obtain "celestial bodies" whose glory will reflect the light of other heavenly bodies, the stars.

John 12: 35-36, I John 1:7, 2:8-10, Ephesians 5:8, I Corinthians 15:39-49

It is common, however, to relegate the idea of light to a mere moral category without realizing that it holds ontological and epistemological significance. Not only are humans encouraged to manifest the "fruits" of light (goodness, righteousness, and truth) in their inner being and in their consciousness, they are to become sources (and carriers) of the divine light—to shine with the divine glory. This is a theme that runs throughout early Christianity, beginning with the Mount of Transfiguration into Pentecost, through the creation of celestial light in the writings of St. Paul, and finally to the visionary light seen at the end of human history by St. John. Light permeates everything. It is not merely goodness, but signifies the future taxonomy of humanity. Humans are made to become light-beings whose center, Yeshua says, will become its source.

The purpose of light, then, is to enlighten a human being from within (making them a causal agent of light) and then in turn to illuminate the cosmos on the outside, without which it will remain in darkness. Yeshua is the former (an enlightened being) and does the latter (brings light to the ***kosmos***). This is the "place" where he is (the state of his being), but it is not just a private state that belongs to him alone. It is to be shared by his students, and (St. Paul will say in his Epistle to the Romans) will eventually be shared by the whole creation. It is not kept as a personal privilege; it is his mission and the reason his voice speaks in the ***kosmos*** calling out to every human being. It is also the reason he pours fire upon the cosmos, without which darkness will remain the abiding habitation for humanity.

Romans 8:17-23

*One must continue to remember that the early Christian tradition used the word **kosmos** to signify the human world of imperfection and distortion.*

QUESTIONS FOR REFLECTION

1. The sense of inner darkness and light is not simply a concept. For most of us it is a very personal experience. We know both to be parts of ourselves. What has been your experience of inner light? What has been your experience of inner darkness? Describe them both.

2. Have you ever met someone that you felt was a light-being? What was your experience of them?

3. Have you ever met someone whom you felt was a source of darkness (a carrier of the absence of light)? What was that experience like?

4. How do you picture a light-being? Is that the description of an angel? What advantages would that person have over one whose body was made primarily of matter? Would there be any disadvantages for a light-being?

A further question is, if you were to ask yourself where Yeshua was from, what would you say? Would you emphasize his history (time) or his geography (space), or would you talk about his state of being? Most Christians talk less about any of these and more about their doctrines concerning him—he was the Son of God, for example. In your view, what should be emphasized and why?

EXERCISES AND MEDITATIONS

1. For the purposes of this meditation, imagine that one day you will move from being a "carbon-based" being to a "photon-based" being. Perhaps you have never thought of it this way, but something on this order is what St. Paul describes in I Corinthians 15:39-49. Read this passage and meditate upon it. Then in your own imagination, see yourself changing from one kind of being into the other. You might envision Yeshua on the Mount of Transfiguration as an example. Let your imagination explore what this might be like for you.
2. Go through a day and pay attention to the way you affect those around you. Don't make judgments about it, just observe. See when you appear to affect them with light, and when your effect creates some form of darkness or negativity. What happens in either of these cases? Next, watch the same interaction (perhaps on another day) and see if you can detect in yourself how a certain interaction is going to turn out based upon your own sense of yourself beforehand. Write about this experiment in your journal.
3. In reading about the saints in almost every tradition, there are stories of men and women who "shine with light" both literally and figuratively. Also, saints are usually depicted with a nimbus (halo of light) around their heads. This could be symbolic, but it could also express that they possess light from a higher dimension. Explore and mediate upon this phenomenon. How have you experienced it? How could you experience it in a greater way?

The history of the halo or nimbus is interesting. Its origins are in Egypt, where it represented the sun-disk behind a sacred person. That tradition carried over into the Fayyum portraits made by the Greeks in Egypt, which later gave rise to iconic images. More recently, the nimbus has symbolized the light-aura seen by some people around the bodies and faces of individuals.

READINGS FOR INSIGHT

I

Like a great starving beast
My being is quivering
Fixed
On the scent
Of Light

Hafez

II

I lost my world, my fame, my mind—
The Sun appeared, and all the shadows ran.
I ran after them, but vanished as I ran—
Light ran after me and hunted me down.

Jalauddin Rumi

III

We are all in mourning for the experience of our essence
we knew and now miss.
Light is the cure,
all else a placebo.

St. Francis of Assisi
Love Poems From God
45

IV

The power which issued from the Savior and which is now the man of light within us. ... My Lord! Not only does the man of light in me have ears but my soul has heard and understood all the words that thou hast spoken. ... The man of light in me has guided me; he has rejoiced and bubbled up in me as if wishing to emerge from me and pass into thee.

Mary Magdalene
in ***Pistis Sophia***
I:12, 1:30, 33

V

We can follow the presence of the idea of the "man of light." ... This doctrine refers ... to an anthropology from which the following idea of the man of light emerges: there is the earthly *Adam*, the outer man of flesh (***sarkinos anthropos***) subject to the Elements, to planetary influences, and to Fate .... And there is the man of light (***photeinos anthropos***), the hidden spiritual man (*Phos*), the opposite pole to corporeal man .... *Adam* is the archetype of carnal man; *Phos* is the archetype, not of humans in general, but of men of light, the ***photes***.

Henry Corbin
Man of Light in Iranian Sufism
15

VI

Abba Lot went to see Abba Joseph and said to him,

"Abba, as much as I am able to practice a small rule, a little fasting, some prayer and meditation, and remain quiet and as much as possible I keep my thoughts clean. What else should I do?"

Then the old man stood up and stretched his hands towards heaven, and his fingers became like ten torches of flame and he said to him,

"If you wish, you can become all flame."

Y. Nomura
Desert Wisdom
90

LOGION 25

Sapiential Themes

- *In the tradition of Yeshua's wisdom, love is perceived as the central sign of enlightenment—the evidence that divine light exists within.*
- *Authentic love focuses on the other and yet recognizes one's self (or psyche) as the ground upon which love is built.*
- *Love is practical, an act of protection and care.*
- *Love is instantaneous and immediate, a natural reflex for those who possess it.*

Yeshua says,

Love your brother and your sister as your very own being. Protect them as you would the pupil of your eye."

Parallel Texts

Deuteronomy 32:10
I Samuel 18:1
Psalm 17:8
Mark 12:33
John 13:34-35, 14:21,15:9, 13
I John 3:1, 16, 23

Links

If one imagines that each saying is the context for the next, then clearly this Logion reflects the light expressed in Logion 24 as the practical outcome of enlightenment from within. Light shine to the outside. It is not simply held within. The affect of light is love manifested as care of another, but as we shall see in the next Logion, a kind of caring that is also self-aware.

FOCAL POINT

Love is the sign of enlightenment, the manifestation of light. No other attribute will so assuredly predict the inner state of a human being as the quality of love expressed for those outside the circle of one's smaller self. Love is not simply an emotion, it is a sacred act of loving-kindness and care which guards and protects another as one would shield one's own eye from outside danger. One needs only to imagine the immediate and automatic reaction to blink or turn away to protect an eye from being hit by an incoming object to understand the force of this Logion. It occurs instantly, without thought, even before the conscious awareness of danger. One would most certainly protect one's children or family in such a manner, but to treat every other human being (as a brother or a sister) with this same sense of immediate protection and instantaneous response is the sure sign of the presence of another power—the divine light.

Notes

The word ***psyche*** *(in Greek) is used here and is often translated as the self or the soul. It is expressed in this translation as* ***your very own being****. The soul or psyche is central in both ancient and modern thought, where it expresses the unique configuration at the center of an individual's self-identity.*

COMMENTARY

Volumes have been written on the subject of love. It has a central and rightful place at the core of the human condition. Contemporary music, modern film and the present-day novel frequently center around the subject of love. We human beings are drawn to a great love story, and many songs are filled with its sentiment, either as a longing for love or as the travail of its absence or aberration. And yet, perhaps, there is no subject more easily misunderstood or more subject to the greatest distortions. In our common culture, the elegance of love has become the caricature of "luv"—a sweet sentimentality we mistake for the authentic attribute. Love has been reduced to a mere emotion: a flaring up of one's own egoic-wanting and the need to be satisfied by another. And so in the midst of a flood of language about love we live in its wasteland, devoid of its water, deprived of its life.

For the purpose of comprehending the qualitative difference between love and "luv" it is sometimes necessary to substitute the word **compassion**. Compassion is less contaminated, closer to the form of egoic detachment, and expresses the energetic concentration that authentic love requires. Imagine, then, that the divine qualities concentrated as light are transmitted to the human receiver, where it is transmuted into a new energetic form known as compassion. The human container acts like a transformer (as in the flow of electricity), taking one level of energy and adapting it to common conditions where it can be usefully applied.

The term the ***eye of the heart*** *is used once by in the Pauline corpus (Ephesians 1:18) and appears to be the Semitic equivalent of the Hellenic word* ***nous****, (Mind or consciousness at the deepest point of the heart within the soul).*

But the action taken in this Logion is not common or general. It is specifically targeted to the need for care and protection—knowing that danger is ever present to the soft vulnerability that is the eye of human seeing and knowing. If one were to interpret this text metaphorically (as should be done), then the deep subject matter is not the outer eye (though that too may be an object of our concern) but the inner eye-of-the-heart—the most vulnerable feature of human cognition and receptivity. We must protect this soft spot in ourselves and in our brothers and sisters. This is what we are here on earth to do—to learn to use the energy of love in this specific way. It is our earth-bound duty and a life-long process of learning. There can be no higher task than this.

In his important study, ***Avicenna and the Visionary Recital****, Henry Corbin has this to say about the dyadic image: "The substance of Light unceasingly engenders Friends* ***(awliya)****—that is, Angels—not by way of carnal generation but as light engenders light or as wisdom engenders sages. The substance of Darkness unceasingly engenders adversaries—that is, demons—as the stupid engender stupidity and vice versa" (51-52).*

There is also another interpretive layer to this well known and understandable text, one that points to the mystery of the dyadic or twinned relationships which remain central to the images of this Gospel. Imagine that the brother or sister represents one's own "self" (as Yeshua says about loving neighbor as one's self in the canonical Gospels). Imagine too, that this other "self" can be understood as the twinned nature of one's own person. Friendship and the protection of this "other" act as guardians for the light of the eye at the center of the heart, which is nothing less than, and none other than, one's own self. The "friend" (the brother or sister) that one protects is the Self that is also the object at the center of the eye of seeing. All outer persons (the brothers or sisters whom one protects) are analogs of one's inner being, and both inner and outer are twinned as a part of the deepest Self.

QUESTIONS FOR REFLECTION

1. How would you distinguish between compassion and love? Is there a difference? If there is, what are some examples?

2. Who do you consider to be your brothers or your sisters in friendship? How does blood relationship factor into this?

Native spirituality on this continent applied the terms brother and sister to include all living beings—four-footed, winged, finned, creeping and crawling. The same is true with St. Francis of Assisi in the western tradition, and other saints of the Celtic world and the Christian East.

3. What is your response when friendship is threatened, or when someone you love as a brother or a sister is in danger? Have you ever guarded someone's inner eye?

4. Have you ever defended another as you would protect your own eyes? What practical form did that action take for you?

5. What is the relationship between "selves" on the outside and the "self" inside?

EXERCISES AND MEDITATIONS

1. Meditate on your own sense of sight and the protectiveness you feel concerning your eyes. If you have ever had the experience of partial blindness, or of some damage to the eye, or of an object inside your eyelid rubbing against your eye over a prolonged period, you will recall your obsessive need to be rid of it and to see again. Could love exercised as an act of protection toward others be exactly the same—persistence in protecting others as the key to your own spiritual sight? In your meditation, imagine how this might be true.
2. Could it be, as the commentary suggests, that one's clear concern to protect another is an act of personal generosity towards the deepest aspects of one's own being? In order to find the answer, not as a theoretical concept, but as a living reality, you will need to experiment with this possibility through acts of compassion toward others. How does a protective response for others open your own inner sight? How does the opposite create interior darkness? Experiment and journal your findings. Share these findings with others.
3. If light is a divine form of energy—the highest, in fact—and love is its manifestation in the human context, then one can be attuned to light through love. In a period of meditation, accept an individual into your imagination to whom you could express this energy of light as love. Become the transmitter by focusing your energy, then sending it forward in time and through space to the heart of that individual. Find some practical way to show this (perhaps totally unknown to the individual) as a further expression of your guardianship.

*You might want to watch the film **Pay It Forward** as an example of these acts of compassion being played out in a modern context.*

READINGS FOR INSIGHT

I

It was easy to love God in all that was beautiful.
The lessons of deeper knowledge, though,
instructed me to embrace God in all things.

St. Francis of Assisi

II

Someone who does not run
toward the allure of love walks
a road where nothing lives.
But this dove here senses
the love-hawk floating above
and waits and will not be driven
or scared to safety.
My work is to carry this love
as comfort for those who long for you,
to go where you've walked
and gaze at the pressed-down dirt.

Jalaluddin Rumi
Rumi: the Book of Love
49, 51

III

I have come into this world to see this:
the sword drop from men's hands at the height of their arc of anger
because we have finally realized there is just one flesh to wound
and it is His—the Christ's, our Beloved's
I have come into this world to see this: all creatures hold hands as we pass through
this miraculous existence we share on the way to even a greater being of soul,
a being of just ecstatic light, forever entwined and at play with Him.
I have come into this world to hear this:
every song the earth has sung since it was conceived in the Divine's womb and
began spinning from His wish,
every song by wing and fin and hoof,
every song by hill and field and tree and woman and child,
every song of stream and rock,
every song of tool and lyre and flute,
every song of gold and emerald and fire,
every song the heart should cry with magnificent dignity to know itself as God;
for all other knowledge will leave us again in want and aching—
only imbibing the glorious Sun will complete us.
I have come into the world to experience this:
men so true to love
they would rather die before speaking an unkind word,
men so true their lives are His covenant—the promise of hope.
I have come into this world to see this:
the sword drop from men's hands
even at the height of their arc of rage
because we have finally realized there is just one flesh
we can wound.

Hafez
translated by
Daniel Ladinsky
Love Poems From God
159-160

LOGION 26

Yeshua says,

You detect a speck
in your brother's eye,
but fail to perceive the beam
sticking out of your own.
Remove the timber from your eye,
and you will see clearly enough
to extract the speck lodged
in the eye of your brother."

Sapiential Themes

- *There is a logical progression in any attempt to correct or ameliorate difficulties in the human world.*
- *Self-knowledge and correction in the inner world must manifest before any action can be safely taken in the outer world.*
- *The eye of inner vision often needs the removal of debris lodged there before it can exercise its extraordinary powers of sight.*
- *In the end, occluded vision is a form of ignorance, whereas clear-eyed self-knowledge is the foundation of wisdom.*

Parallel Texts

Proverbs 12:14, 20:6, 30:12
Lamentations 3:40
Matthew 7:1-5
Luke 6:37, 41-42
John 4:12
Romans 2:1, 14:4, 13
I Corinthians 4:3-5
II Corinthians 10:12
Galatians 6:1
James 4:8

FOCAL POINT

There are adages in many traditions which say something like the following, "Examine yourself before you attempt to judge another." Yeshua's wisdom agrees with this perennial adage but takes it to a new level of honest self-observation, inquiry, and action before attempting to work on the problems of others. He establishes a sequence (or sapiential logic) in the order of correction; first oneself, and then anyone outside the self. Any reversal of this progression will end in damage done to both persons, the one attempting to correct and the one who is perceived to be in danger.

Links

Based upon Logion 25, it is easy to jump to a conclusion and respond without the benefit of wisdom. The act of protecting another can so easily become an act of correction. The wisdom that Yeshua knows is how quickly protection becomes judgmental, and that judgmentalism is one of the greatest banes of human interaction and the destroyer of all clarity. There is an obvious link between this and the last saying through the metaphoric use of the eye and sight.

Notes

This saying is common both to Thomas and the canonical Gospels. In both cases the text appears in the religious tradition of Yeshua where judgments are so easily made about external behavior based upon legal prescriptions without due examination of one's own interior motivations.

COMMENTARY

Humanity has lived in (and become used to) a world of prejudice—that is, the preconceived and pre-judged notions which shape and distort our ordinary perceptions and actions. The lens of prejudice and preconception colors almost every human interaction and opinion. Prejudice—judging before examination—is the cause for most of the reactions we have and the actions we take in the world of human relationships. Prejudice is endemic and, like a virus, seems to affect the entire human organism as a social body.

*The term **prejudice** is used here as a philosophical category based in modern thought, where it refers to a judgment that is given before all the elements that determine a situation have been fully examined. Such preconceptions actually make understanding harder, in that they can go almost entirely unnoticed.*

Clarity of vision—a true seeing that perceives not just the outer form (or one's preconceived notions about that form), but the inner reality behind the form—is the key to wisdom. Sapiential knowing as a form of seeing is based upon self-knowledge and self-correction. Wisdom cannot exist without clarity. Because it is founded in ignorance, every action based upon prejudice damages not only one's inner eye, but brings harm to all other objects and persons in the attempt to take action. We cannot see our brother or sister for who they truly are if there are inner obstacles to our sight. Our lack of knowledge blinds us.

*In the ascent mysticism of Jewish thought, the mystic is taken up by the chariot (**merkavah**) into the heavens, where he or she sees the realities which are the origin of their earthly counterparts.*

If the wisdom Yeshua teaches is based on visionary awareness (the visionary experience of ascent to the archetypes), then everything depends upon such clear inner seeing. The eye of the heart must be cleared of any debris which occludes sight. In light of the last saying, the greatest obstacles to sight are those that block the flow of love between humans. The wisdom tradition of Yeshua, therefore, instructs us to remove any barrier to love that occurs within ourselves and distorts our actions, turning them into their opposite. The greatest obstacles to love are not located in others (their bad habits, their flawed characteristics, their warped personality structures, their false doctrines, their social ineptitudes) but within ourselves. These obstacles are blockages over which, or through which, we cannot see. They obstruct (or color) everything, contaminating any action we might wish to take, even if we deem it to be protective action.

Traditional spiritual counsel is provided by spiritual directors who act as mentors and guides, and support us in our temporal pilgrimage.

Self-knowledge and judicious self-correction are delicate processes for which we need guidance. Too often, the laser beam of judgment we have used as a weapon against others, is turned against ourselves. The wisdom tradition counsels patient and non-judgmental self-observation as the first step in obtaining clarity about ourselves. If we understand that such interior seeing comes from the eye of the heart, then it is our wisdom-work to remove any obstruction (veil over the heart, or distorting lens over the eye) before we can see clearly enough to act on behalf of our brother or our sister. Logion 25 enjoins us to act immediately, almost reflexively. Reflexive action, without full self-knowledge and interior clarity, however, will always pose an immense danger.

The crucial point for both ourselves and others is the exercise of discernment—a trait of the heart—versus the exercise of judgment (which is often only a tool of the egoic-mind). The question will always be, which eye are we using? Are we using the outer or the inner eye, and in what condition is this eye? For as we have seen, even the inner eye can be obstructed. When it is clear, then, we can exercise its powers carefully in our interactions with others.

QUESTIONS FOR REFLECTION

1. Think of an example in your life when you have been judged by someone unfairly. How did you feel? What was your reaction?

2. When has some form of criticism actually been of benefit to you? What made it beneficial instead of destructive?

3. What is the difference between judgment and discernment? Can you tell when you are doing one or the other? What are the telltale signs of this difference inside yourself?

4. Has it ever been true that those things about which you are most critical in others are what secretly bother you about yourself? What might they be?

In the field of psychology, this is called "projection."

EXERCISES AND MEDITATIONS

1. The injunction in this Logion is a problematic one for every one of us. It is difficult to see or acknowledge the beam in our own eye—someone else has to point it out, and when they do, we are often offended and act as if we are under attack. Notice your own responses and reactions to criticism (justified or unjustified, it makes no difference). We typically move into a fight-flight mode and become defensive and reactionary, or we try to escape entirely. In order to work gently with our own difficulties, it is important, first, simply to observe and take note of your inner responses when you feel under attack. Make notes about your discoveries in your journal.
2. Make a list of the "irritants" you experience which might prove to be obstacles to sight. You could define these as psychological factors in your personality, opinions you hold dearly, or social prejudices you hold that are likely to keep you from perceiving things clearly. For purposes of clarity, you might show this list to someone you love and trust who can give you objective feedback as a reality check. When you explore your experience through self-observation, use this list, and watch yourself in various situations where these elements factor in. What do you observe? What do you learn? What do you need to remove?
3. Removal of interior debris (obstacles to sight) is not something that one does easily. Often we need assistance (both divine and human). From the divine side, take your list of obstacles into a period of meditation and ask for guidance from the Transcendent—for insight and understanding about what steps you need to take. From the human side, these issues are important in spiritual direction. Seek guidance from a spiritual director who can give you clarity and understanding.

If you do not have a spiritual director it may be important to find one. Ask about this kind of person from your church. Roman Catholics and Episcopalians may be more likely to know who is available for this ministry in your area.

READINGS FOR INSIGHT

I

Bahauddin
The Drowned Book
78

The veil between worlds is the human incapacity to see. A single finger over each eye can keep you from taking in the world. What's depriving you of vision, of knowing spirit, is just that small and easy to remove.

II

Pema Chödrön
"The Wisdom of No Escape"
Comfortable with Uncertainty
7-8

The central question of a warrior's training is not how we avoid uncertainty and fear but how we relate to discomfort. How do we practice with difficulty, with our emotions, with the unpredictable encounters of an ordinary day? For those of us with a hunger to know the truth, painful emotions are like flags going up to say, "You're stuck!" We regard disappointment, embarrassment, irritation, jealousy, and fear as moments that show us where we're holding back, how we're shutting down. Such uncomfortable feelings are messages that tell us to perk up and lean into a situation when we'd rather cave in and back away.

When the flag goes up, we have an opportunity: we can stay with our painful emotion instead of spinning out. Staying is how we get the hang of gently catching ourselves when we're about to let resentment harden into blame, righteousness, or alienation. It's also how we keep from smoothing things over by talking ourselves into a sense of relief or inspiration. This is easier said than done.

III

B. Ward, trans.
The Sayings of the Desert Fathers
28

Abba Ammonas came one day to eat in a place where there was a monk of evil repute. Now it happened that a woman came and entered the cell of the brother of evil reputation. The dwellers in that place, having learnt this, were troubled and gathered together to chase the brother from his cell. Knowing that Bishop Ammonas was in the place, they asked him to join them. When the brother in question learnt this, he hid the woman in a large cask. The crowd of monks came to the place. Now Abba Ammonas saw the position clearly but for the sake of God he kept the secret; he entered, seated himself on the cask and commanded the cell to be searched. Then when the monks had searched everywhere without finding the woman, Abba Ammonas said,

"What is this? May God forgive you!"

After praying he made everyone go out, then taking the brother by the hand he said,

"Brother, be on your guard."

With these words, he withdrew.

IV

C. Luiheid, trans.
Pseudo Dionysius: The Complete Works
138

If only we lacked sight and knowledge so as to see, so as to know, unseeing and unknowing, that which lies beyond all vision and knowledge … We would be like sculptors who set out to carve a statue. They remove every obstacle to the pure view of the hidden image, and simply by this act of clearing aside they show up the beauty which is hidden.

LOGION 27

Yeshua says,

If you do not fast from the cosmos,
you will never grasp Reality.
If you cannot find rest
on the day of rest,
you will never feast
your eyes on God."

Sapiential Themes

- *Finding (or grasping) divine Reality as the Kingdom, and seeing God as Father (one's Beloved Source) are primary goals on the path of wisdom.*
- *To reach these goals, spiritual action is required. Yet, paradoxically, it is the action of non-action through Sabbath-rest that provides the method for reaching the goal.*
- *Detachment and rest are prerequisite for the visionary experience of transcendence.*
- *Fasting from the **kosmos** and resting on the Sabbath are calisthenics in the praxis of wisdom.*

Parallel Texts

Exodus 33:14
Psalm 116:7
Matthew 4:1-11, 11:28-29, 12:43
Luke 4:1-2
John 17:1
Acts 1:10
Hebrews 3:11, 4:3,9
Revelation 14:13

Links

How do you remove the beam from your own eye, and what might that beam be? Answers to the questions raised by Logion 26 are found here. Interaction with the human cosmos may create such an obstacle to spiritual seeing that only fasting and rest can remove it.

FOCAL POINT

On the pathway of wisdom, paradox and mystery replace reason and logic. This saying is full of both mystery and paradox, and suggests a depth of understanding concerning the play of complimentary opposites that belies the simplicity of the statements when taken at face value. Fasting and feasting are at the heart of finding and seeing, and the visionary experience of beholding the divine Face which is central to early Jewish mysticism. To find the Kingdom is to see the Father, so any loss of interior sight (the subject of the last saying) is a tragedy for all human beings whose destiny it is to enter transcendence and see. Remedy for loss is found in this saying, where we are enjoined, paradoxically, to act in a non-active way.

Notes

*In order to have a dynamic translation that is clear to the modern reader certain decisions were taken with this text. The word **Reality** translates the original word **Kingdom.** The phrase **day of rest** is literally the Sabbath. To **feast your eyes** is a contrasting metaphor for fasting which is literally the word **see**. **God** translates **Father**. A more literal translation would therefore read, "If you do not fast from the cosmos you will never find the Kingdom. If you do not make the Sabbath, Sabbath, you will never see the Father."*

COMMENTARY

We tend to speak of food only in terms of the physical body. However, each aspect of our being has its own kind of food that sustains it. We need food for the soul as well, which is why we crave human interaction, emotional support, love, beauty, art, intimate conversation, and many other nutritive elements that feed our entire life in the world. Without soul-food, we would starve to death.

The fundamental premise of this Logion is one familiar to the sages of all sacred traditions: one must detach and withdraw from a lower realm in order to enter and re-engage a higher one. Other important facets of wisdom are built upon this basic premise and transmitted by this saying. The first is that the ***kosmos*** (the realm of human convention and invention) provides its own kind of food for the human soul, but one which cannot sustain it for long, nor can it provide what we need to enter and know the fullness of Ultimate Reality. Second, abstaining from cosmic fare may allow us to feast in the realm of spirit where we may glimpse the face of God.

Fasting may be understood, then, as the letting go of one's normal attachment to sensory input as our primary source of sustenance, as well as the release of psychological dependence upon the human world. We could interpret the entire Logion, then, to say that fasting represents the "restriction of our normal intake" of food from the cosmos (to refrain from ingesting our typical "sensory-affective fare") in order to take in new food that will allow us entrance into the Sabbath rest.

For example, to rest in time means to enter Eternity.

The term **Sabbath** is rooted in the Hebrew tradition. As a Semitic symbol, it gives concrete expression to a deeper understanding of the relationship between time and eternity. Later in this Gospel, the term **rest**, which is linked to the Sabbath, will be contrasted with its complementary opposite, movement. Movement and action are required to sustain life in the ***kosmos***. In the Kingdom it is different. Life in the Kingdom is sustained by contemplative rest, so taking a Sabbath from the compulsive action, the norm for our life here, is the requirement for entry there.

It is important to understand that forces in the ***kosmos*** act as a kind of food to reinforce our false sense of self (the self that has been created or constructed out of the bits and pieces of our personal history in the social world). Imagine, then, that we cannot find our higher or greater self without refraining from eating the food that feeds the lower self. This idea, which is at the heart of wisdom teaching, is being directly expressed here by Yeshua using very Semitic metaphors.

In the sapiential tradition to which Yeshua belongs, the idea of entering **rest** (repose or Sabbath) becomes an important metaphor for a soul that takes up residence in the eternal Now transcendent to space-time and the human world. Our souls can be aligned to and absorbed by horizontal activity—the external traffic and exchanges that constantly move us here. Or they can find another rest-point at their center (T.S. Eliot's "still point of the turning world," where the vertical axis rests in Eternity. Without contemplative rest and interior alignment along the vertical axis, it is impossible to feast one's inner eyes on the Father, the Beloved Source of All. Yeshua's visionary proclamation in the canonical Gospels—that the pure in heart are blessed because they shall see God—points to the unobstructed eye of the heart as the condition that enables it to open out upon the Face of the Eternal.

The particular idea that spiritual life must be a balance between understanding and praxis as a form of athletic participation is expressed forcefully in the Pauline corpus. See I Corinthians 9:24, Galatians 5:7, Philippians 3:14, II Timothy 4:7-8, Hebrews 12:1

The preconditions, then, for entering this place of seeing, the "place where Yeshua is" (Logion 24), are detachment and repose. The students have asked him to tell them about these conditions. Yeshua has answered, but that answer entails the praxis or calisthenics of the Kingdom, which must be exercised as the precondition for entering the place where he dwells and attaining the vision that he sees.

QUESTIONS FOR REFLECTION

1. What does it mean for you to "fast from the ***kosmos***?" Practically, what would it look like? How would you know you were fasting and not simply taking a break?

There are many forms of fasting. One, of course, is from food over an extended period of time. Other forms have to do with fasting from the media, from noise or conversation, or from sensory or mental processes.

2. Have you ever fasted before? Is fasting from food different from "fasting from the cosmos?" If it is different, what is the difference? Is fasting from the cosmos the same as "withdrawing from the world?"

3. Have you ever had a visionary experience of God or of something transcendent? What happened?

Psalm 27:8

4. In the Psalms, we hear God say to the poet, "Seek my face." The psalmist replies, "Your face, God, I will seek." Have you ever looked for a face in a crowd? Have you ever looked to see the face of God? What did you see?

EXERCISES AND MEDITATIONS

1. Imagine that the human world around you is a kind of "set up"—it sets you up to act in a certain socially acceptable or expected way. This is called social conditioning, and it started well before you could understand the process. Now imagine that in your adulthood, and as a part of spiritual maturation, you could move against those social expectations and the various "sets" of pre-conditionings that make up the pattern of your life, and which you now know seriously limit you. What might you do to prepare yourself for the act of resisting these conditionings? To completely understand, this will perhaps take some thought, journaling, counseling, and spiritual direction. Now is a good time to reflect upon process. Take time to write what you are learning in your journal.
2. Suppose, then, that you do begin to fast from social expectations and past conditioning. What would need to happen? How could you withdraw? If these expectations and external conditions act as a kind of food or reinforcement to support a false sense of yourself, how then might you learn to let them go? You may not be able to do this alone or all at once. It may simply be too difficult, especially because there will be inevitable internal and external resistance to any changes you want to make. What kind of support system or community would you need around you that is different from your normal social world?

It might be important to establish a pattern of retreat days for yourself, and to visit places where you could get away from the busy environment of your life to find a quiet, spacious place of rest and renewal.

3. Resting and fasting have always been staple conditions in serious retreat work. Because we may have chosen to remain active in the human world, periods of physical withdrawal from it into retreat are very important. The ancient tradition wisely provided a day of rest (or retreat) called the Sabbath. How might you construct better "Sabbaths" for yourself?

READINGS FOR INSIGHT

I

Maria Jaoudi
Christian Mysticism East and West
101

Steeped in his usual biblical references and symbolism, Bonaventure speaks of the Sabbath as an interior contemplative state synonymous with union. Employing terms like *wayfarers* and *arrival*, he points to contemplation as truly a journey into God. When we do "arrive" in God, we find that we in ourselves have become the person of peace.

II

Dionysius the Areopagite
De mystica theologia
1

For transcending yourself and all things,
by the immeasurable and absolute ecstasy of a pure mind,
leaving behind all things
and freed from all things,
you will ascend
to the super essential ray
of the divine darkness.

III

Pema Chödrön
Comfortable with Uncertainty
8

Ordinarily we are swept away by habitual momentum. We don't interrupt our patterns even slightly. With practice, however, we learn to stay with a broken heart, with a nameless fear, with the desire for revenge. Sticking with uncertainty is how we learn to relax in the midst of chaos, how we learn to be cool when the ground beneath us suddenly disappears. We can bring ourselves back to the spiritual path countless times every day simply by exercising our willingness to rest in the uncertainty of the present moment—over and over again.

IV

Anthony de Mello
One Minute Nonsense
161

"What does it mean to be Enlightened?"
"To see."
"What?"
"The hollowness of success, the emptiness of achievements, the nothingness of human striving," said the Master.
The disciple was appalled. "But isn't that pessimism and despair?
"No. That's the excitement and freedom of the eagle gliding over a bottomless ravine."

V

Swami Abhishiktanada
Prayer
22

Truly speaking there is no outside and no inside, no without and no within, in the mystery of God and in the Divine Presence. Yet the mind is so much distracted through the senses that it needs first of all to be withdrawn from external things: hence the need of recollecting and gathering towards their center all thoughts and all desires. Then, after we have been inwardly fully illuminated by the glory of the Presence, we realize that there are no limits to that glory, no limits to that Presence.

LOGION 28

Yeshua says,

I stood to my feet
in the midst of the cosmos,
appearing outwardly in flesh.
I discovered that all were drunk
and none were thirsty,
and my soul ached
for the children of humanity.
For their hearts are blind
and they cannot see from within.
They have come into the cosmos empty,
and they are leaving it empty.

At the moment you are inebriated,
but free from the effects of wine,
you too may turn and stand."

Sapiential Themes

- *Nothing is as it appears in the human condition. The eye of wisdom sees humanity so differently from the way we typically see ourselves.*
- *The wine of the cosmos can so intoxicate us that we can neither see the vertical axis running through all things, nor can we stand alongside it.*
- *The metaphor of standing up, and the principle of enfleshment, have great spiritual significance in the original wisdom of Yeshua.*
- *The purpose of moving through space-time is, paradoxically, to leave us both full and empty.*

Parallel Texts

Psalm 60, 75, 146:8
Isaiah 42:7
Ecclesiastes 6:15
Luke 4:18
II Corinthians 4:4
Ephesians 4:18, 5:18
I John 2:11
Revelation 17:2

FOCAL POINT

There is probably no saying that is more personal, heartfelt, or that gives a better look into the motivations of Yeshua than this one. It is a cry from the depths of the cosmos, coming from one whose heart is broken by what he perceives in humanity all around him. There is no beam in his eye, so Yeshua sees clearly and precisely into the human condition. Using vivid imagery (drunkenness, blindness, emptiness, standing up, lying down), Yeshua says that we are inebriated by the wine of the cosmos. With these words he brings the biaxial universe (the horizontal and vertical axes of Reality) back into view. The Greek words retained in the original Coptic text reinforce his metaphors concerning what is to be the inner vertical orientation of humanity. The picture painted by Yeshua's words defines ***metanoia***—a key term that is normally translated as "repentance," but in his teaching is rich with multiple meanings.

Links

This Logion continues to answer the question: why would one need to fast from the cosmos? The answer is that the world's wine can make us so drunk we are unable to stand or see. If we are ever to be free from this condition, then we must fast from its heady, intoxicating effects.

Notes

The Semitic tradition, to which Yeshua belongs, tends to use vivid imagery as the metaphoric expression for complex abstractions. In the Wisdom Tradition of the Hebrew people, the Psalms are a perfect example. There, similar images of drunkenness and blindness are also found.

COMMENTARY

We are inveterate inquirers, curious about the interior life of famous people. Their public history may be open to us, but we want to know more: the way they think, their motivations, their inner secrets and struggles. All of this piques our interests. In the same way, in the contemporary world we have become fascinated by the personal life of Yeshua. We seek for personal (not just rational or theological) knowledge, distinct from what the Church thinks or teaches in official dogma. We want to know **him**, not just **about him**. In an interesting way this Logion gives us both personal insight and a truth-telling that takes us past history and dogma.

Because of its long use in western Christianity, the word repentance carries a heavy weight of baggage. It does not do justice to the original term. When repentance is used today, it echoes with homiletic harangues about evil inherent in the human heart and the terrible cost of original sin, which destroys its deeper significance. The original word ***metanoia*** *is not about morbid fascination with either original* or personal sin, *but about transcending (****meta...****) our normal awareness or consciousness (****noia*** *from* ***nous****--mind, or consciousness). By standing up out of the cosmos with Yeshua, we too can turn and stand alongside him as an act of courage and solidarity.*

As Yeshua faces the realities of the human world, we hear his words of compassion and see ourselves and our difficulties from his perspective. We also hear his solution to our dilemma, offering us a greater objectivity than we normally possess. Yeshua begins by speaking briefly about his own inner experience. He finds himself standing up in the cosmos, in vertical relationship to our horizontal realm. He also says that who he is has been manifested outwardly in flesh. The principle of enfleshment (or incarnation) is at work in him and there is no negative connotation to his material appearance in the cosmos. Flesh is not opposed to spirit. Spirit may manifest in flesh. The latter will not contaminate the former, but become its lens, a vehicle for its expression.

This principle (of incarnation or enfleshment), however, appears to be far larger than just the historical appearance of Yeshua. He is demonstrating not only the clarity and fullness of his own being, but a possibility—a necessity—that is the reason for our own existence in space-time. We may have forgotten why we are here. He has not. We may have gone to sleep along the horizontal axis. He is awake and aware that we have become drunk and have lost consciousness in the cosmos. We are no longer functioning according to the purpose for which we were designed. Far from being a mistake, however, his enfleshment (and ours) is a privilege, a sacred work to which we have been called. Yeshua summons us to stand up again in flesh, as we were meant to do, and continue our work through incarnation.

The doctrine of the incarnation is basic to the Christian mysteries. Although in later centuries it was turned into a dogma of orthodox belief, in reality it is a window to a mystery that must be experienced.

But what is that work? Why do we exist in flesh? What is our temporal and material vocation? From the perspective of Wisdom, the answer to this question is part of a great mystery that is being revealed. Far from a place of useless imprisonment, the material world is a land of possibility—a place where new forms of the divine life can come into existence and bless the creation. Each individual in his or her own uniqueness can act as a conduit for the divine energies, bringing new qualities into being that without enfleshment would never appear. We exist precisely to manifest the divine in energetic and qualitative form through matter in order to make its energies and qualities available to all. When we lose sight of this purpose, we lose our reason for being. Yeshua stands up in the cosmos to awaken us. He unites both heaven and earth—the horizontal and the vertical—as one unified field in which we can also live. We are asked to stand up in solidarity with him, bringing heaven and earth together in ourselves. This privilege is our work.

The Master sees all of this with a clarity that is unobstructed by the proverbial "beam in his own eye." He is aware of our present condition, but he does not judge us unfairly, for he observes through the lens of a broken heart. What he sees is that humanity is intoxicated by a wine that diminishes us. It is a heady mixture that drowns and floods the higher centers of consciousness until we are overwhelmed and unable to attend to the mysteries of our vertical origins. It is a drink that can satiate but never satisfy. In this world we compulsively seek for the satisfaction of our desires, but our deeper longings go unfulfilled. The world's wine is offered but is insufficient. It brings neither bliss nor insight, and in the end its effects are only soporific. We drink and drink and so are never thirsty. This temporal satiation becomes a curse without a blessing.

As this scene unfolds, complementary opposites are contrasted in paradoxical ways to illustrate its complexities. If we follow the theme of the twin set forth at the outset of this Gospel, this Logion continues the interplay of paired opposites. Sometimes one facet of the "twin" is presented in a positive light, but at another point its negative aspect is shown. Because this happens consistently, we must maintain a flexible approach in our interpretation. We cannot allow only one definition to exist. Each aspect of the pair must play out its meaning and significance.

*By themselves, the normal historical-critical strategies in interpretation theory (**hermeneutics**) are insufficient for understanding mystical and sapiential literature.*

One important example of this principle appears both here and earlier in the text when Yeshua congratulates Thomas for his state of intoxication. In that Logion, Yeshua says Thomas is drinking the wine that he has offered from the Source. In this Logion, however, the wine offered by the cosmos is equally intoxicating, but its effect is different, a kind of poisoning. In the end it proves to be a toxin that causes its victims to lose sight and vertical orientation. We see, therefore, that there are two opposite states of intoxication and sobriety. One state is positive and the other negative. To be intoxicated with the wine of the vertical axis is a blessed state, but to be stone sober in relationship to the same axis is a curse. To maintain a state of sobriety along the horizontal axis, however, is of great value, whereas horizontal inebriation leaves one in a spiritual stupor.

Logion 13

The other effect of the world's wine is to leave a human full (or satiated) and yet, at the same moment, empty. The state of fullness and emptiness have both negative and positive meanings in this text as well.

The subject matter of previous sayings, blindness and sight, also comes into view in this saying. Yeshua indicates that the inner eye of the heart is the instrument of seeing (or in this case the occasion for interior blindness). The emphasis that he puts upon seeing from within is crucial to this ability. As a cognitive organ, the heart lies at the deepest layers of one's being. It has the capacity to see, but it can also be blinded by the wine from the cosmos.

Realizing that we seek continual satisfaction from the wine offered by the world, what Yeshua says about both blindness and drunkenness becomes clear. The wine of the cosmos promises much—to satisfy our wants, needs, and longings—but it can do so only by appealing to our ego-centric demands. In drinking it, therefore, we become full of ourselves and empty of that which we most need: the divine fullness which allows us to see. Full of ourselves, we are empty of Self, needing a greater fullness which occludes our sight. Full of the divine Self, paradoxically, we are empty of our smaller self, and need nothing more. The relationship between these two selves is always in play in the world we inhabit.

The interpretation of this Logion highlights the teaching of the "twin" selves. There are many more aspects to the self than these, but an understanding of the twin self is basic.

Finally, addressing us, Yeshua says that we may throw off the effects of the world's wine and experience ***metanoia***. We, too, may turn and stand. This inward turning toward our "true North" (the axis of Ultimate Reality) is the crucial moment that he has been waiting for—the moment that ignites true vision.

QUESTIONS FOR REFLECTION

If you have ever been drunk before, you might think about your experience and the effects of alcohol on your consciousness. Has it been a positive or negative experience, and why?

1. How would you define the "wine of the cosmos?" What intoxicates you in this world? What are its negative side-effects? Are there any positive effects? What keeps you drinking this wine?

2. We use the idiom that we are intoxicated by love or beauty or joy. This state of inebriation adds a new dimension to our experience. What is it?

3. When have you experienced the shifting of your inner axis or orientation (a shift away from the horizontal and toward the vertical)? What has this experience been like for you? Has it been permanent?

4. What is the experience of spiritual emptiness like? How have you experienced its opposite, fullness?

EXERCISES AND MEDITATIONS

An important book that will help you in your practice of meditation is Cynthia Bourgeault's ***Centering Prayer and Inner Awakening*** *(Cambridge, Massachusetts: Cowley Press, 2004).*

1. The premise of this Logion is based upon the need for realignment in our inner orientation to the vertical axis of immanence and transcendence. We are either aligned inwardly to this axis, or in a state of horizontal sleep. Can you tell the difference in yourself? Explore this difference, and journal what you discover. As an exercise of inner alignment, begin your day by deliberately turning (and tuning) your heart to the vertical axis. You might do that through a practice of meditation using mantra, chant, meditative reading, or silence. Experiment with each of these and seek to discover how they effect this kind of fine tuning.
2. If inner blindness and sight are a state of the heart, then how do you exercise this interior function? There is a traditional designation for this inner perception, and it is called intuitive cognition. The heart has the capacity for intuition as a form of inner seeing. When we are in our "drunken" state this perception does not work well. When we are interiorly aligned to the vertical axis, the inner eye begins to open and work for us. As you live through a day, learn how you can use that eye to help you see from a spiritual point of view. Journal what you learn.
3. The goal of Yeshua's wisdom is to teach us how, through embodiment or material manifestation, to incarnate the qualities of heaven and make them available in space-time. You can bring forth divine qualities and make them available not only to yourself, but to others. In your own experience, can you see how this is done? Take, for example, the quality of peace and bring it down into your own heart. Now make that quality available to others by the way you embody it. Or, take the quality of loving-kindness, and through what you feel inwardly, manifest or reflect it back into the outer world.

READINGS FOR INSIGHT

I

Forgive them
for they see not what they look at.
How could they know
what they do?

Frederick Franck
Ode to the Human Face

II

Your conscious being, with what you've been given, should be like a beautifully laid-out park with wildflowers and cultivated wonders, a swift stream with secluded places to sit and rest beside it. When a grieving person sees you, he or she should recognize a refuge, refreshment, a generous house where one need not bring bread and cheese. There will be plenty.

Bahauddin
The Drowned Book
102

III

You say you grow restless
when you don't drink the dark world-drink,
but if you could see a living one for one moment,
you would draw out that thorn from your foot and walk with no limp.
Let the lamp of the Friend's face show you where to go.
Selflessness is your true self,
sword and shroud.
Whereas this is how most people live:
sleeping on the bank of a freshwater stream,
lips drying with thirst.
In the dream you're running toward a mirage.
As you run, you're proud of being the one who sees the oasis.
You brag to your friends,
"I have the heart-vision. Follow me to the water!"
This love of spying far-off satisfactions,
this traveling keeps you from tasting the real water of where you are, and
who. Nearer than the big vein on your neck,
with waves lapping against you: *here, here*.
The way is who and where you already are,
sleeping in your very being:
that which sleeps and wakes and sleep and dreams the sweet water
is the taste of God.

Jalaluddin Rumi
Rumi: the Book of Love
108-109

IV

"Where can I find God?"
"He's right in front of you."
"Then why do I fail to see him?"
"Why does the drunkard fail to see his home?"
Later the Master said, "Find out what it is that makes you drunk. To see you must be sober."

Anthony de Mello
One Minute Wisdom
52

V

Rabbi Ted Falcon
A Journey of Awakening
42

The universal seeks to express Itself in the material world. That Which Is Without Limit seeks to manifest through that which is always limited. And we who span both realities seek to remember which is which.

VI

Yehuda Berg
The Power of Kabbalah
128

We came to this world to create positive change within ourselves and the world around us. Positive change will encounter resistance, conflict, and obstacles. We must embrace these difficult situations. A man can live in a small town, in a modest house with a white picket fence and a wonderful garden that he tends all day long. It's a good life, a tranquil life. At age 95, he passes on peacefully in his sleep. On the surface, it appears to be an ideal existence. But was this really his purpose on this planet? Was there any internal change in this man's life? Is he a different, more evolved spiritual being at 95 than he was at 35 or 65?

VII

Bahauddin
The Drowned Book
17

I was wondering how any living thing can be familiar with the divine without having some of that within it. How do creatures rest and find their joy?

An answer came: Everything comes from me. I am in each compassion companion, each calamity, lust, any conversation among friends, secrets murmured, a spray of sweet basil, determination, the changing nature of what you want, prayer, love, everything flows from and returns *here*. Leaf, stem, calyx, any cause and effect, every sleep's return to waking.

VIII

Pema Chödrön
Comfortable with Uncertainty
39

Breathing in, breathing out, feeling resentful, feeling happy, being able to drop it, not being able to drop it, eating our food, brushing our teeth, walking, sitting—whatever we're doing could be done with one intention. That intention is that we want to wake up, we want to ripen our compassion, and we want to ripen our ability to let go, we want to realize our connection with all beings. Everything in our lives has the potential to wake us up or to put us to sleep. Allowing it to awaken us is up to us.

IX

Eckhart Tolle
The Power of Now
78

You are here to enable the divine
purpose of the universe to unfold.
That is how important you are!

To stay present in everyday life, it helps to be deeply rooted within yourself; otherwise, the mind, which has incredible momentum, will drag you along like a wild river. It means to inhabit your body fully. To always have some of your attention in the inner energy field of your body. To feel the body from within, so to speak. Body awareness keeps you present. It anchors you in the Now.

X

Sat Prem
Quoted in
The Biology of Transcendence
194

If you are thirsty, the river comes to you.
If you are not thirsty, the river does not exist.

LOGION 29

Yeshua says,

If flesh came into existence for the
sake of spirit,
it is a wonder,
but if spirit exists for the sake of flesh,
it is a wonder of wonders.
I am truly astonished how such richness
came to dwell in such poverty.

Sapiential Themes

- *Matter and spirit are in mutual relationship. They appear to be inextricably bound together through a principle of mutual arising.*
- *The question raised in these wisdom dialogues is: which element exists for which? Who is the servant, and who serves?*
- *There is a realm of wealth and there is a realm of poverty in the provenance of wisdom. They need not be separate, but often they are. When they dwell together each, perhaps, serves the other.*

Parallel Texts

Proverbs 10:15
Joel 2:28-29
John 16:12-15
Romans 8:1-12, 18-27
II Corinthians 8:2, 9
Galatians 5:16-26

FOCAL POINT

Yeshua asks the question about the relationship between matter and spirit, especially as it relates to human existence. Human beings are the "site" in which these two can come together into mutual relationship. The issue is, what is their relationship? Some feel that matter exists to serve spirit; that is the standard, theological explanation. If that should be the case, we would be in the presence of something wonderful. Here, however, Yeshua raises an even more tantalizing possibility: that spirit exists to serve matter (or flesh). Could this be true? Yeshua does not answer his own question directly, but he implies that when we consider this possibility we are in the midst of wonder—the mystery about which he spoke previously at the beginning of this Gospel. What seems to astonish Yeshua even more is that richness has come to dwell in poverty. Spirit does not disdain, and enriches matter, but when it does, it may come to serve matter as a new form of conscious awakening.

Links

In the last Logion we hear of Yeshua's appearance in flesh. In this saying, we hear why enfleshment is enacted—that, in the end, matter may be served by spirit. This reversal opens a window into the meaning of existence and the ultimate relationship between the many dimensions in the spiritual hierarchy.

Notes

In the first and second centuries of the common era the relationship between matter and spirit was hotly debated. For some, particularly those in many Christian, Gnostic, and related communities, matter was entirely suspect. Yeshua, however, sees something different. He speaks of an unexpected possibility, completely contrary to the Hellenistic dualism which so dominated the ancient thought world.

COMMENTARY

Throughout the sayings of Yeshua, we are faced with the mystery of our existence. Why am I here in physical form? Is this all of me? Is this it? What is the purpose for being here anyhow? These are only a few of the many questions which arise when we honestly confront the question of our presence in the cosmos. The Gospel of Thomas is a book about the mysteries which addresses these questions. In it, for all who are ready to listen, Yeshua pulls back the veil and, continuing the wisdom dialogues from previous centuries, probes deeply toward the answers.

Logion 62

Typically we do not have a coherent picture of the dimensions higher than material form. Ancient cosmology, however, pictured these realms in vivid and specific ways. They sometimes called the realm just higher than ours the lunar realm, and the one above that, the realm of Paradise.

Later Christian theology, following a more Hellenistic model, began to be very suspicious of the material order, creating a form of incipient dualism.

*Henry Corbin explains that Islamic tradition expresses the necessity of spiritual individuation as a matter of principle. Spirit must be hypostatized; that is, given individual expression in being. "Hence it (spirit) is ever after assailed by the desire, the love (**'ishq**) that carries it toward what is not yet realized in it, toward its principle of perfection. It is in order to attain to this that it will put in motion the body that is dependent on it. Its existence is necessary in the hierarchy of beings to explain this motion."* ***(Avicenna and the Visionary Recital,*** *73).*

Yet what Yeshua sees only intensifies the mysteries, and what he says collapses and inverts all our assumptions, expectations, and easy certainties. We assume that the material world is of lesser value than those worlds that are dimensionally higher. We imagine that matter may not be worthy of spirit, and that spirit is of higher value—to be honored at the expense of matter, perhaps. Traditional theology has tended to reinforce this view. But is it correct?

It is easy to feel that the body (or physical reality itself) exists only as the servant of spirit (perhaps it is even meant to become the spirit's foil). But is what we assume true? Was the body simply made to serve spirit? Suppose that our notions are wrong, and that reality is actually opposite to the way we think. The body and material existence were brought into being so that spirit might be their servant, ministering lovingly to the physical order.

Yeshua raises this possibility as a marvel that goes far beyond the first wonder, that materiality indeed does have the privilege of serving spirit. Perhaps in the end both situations are equally true: matter serves spirit and spirit serves matter. We have seldom, if ever, held both halves of this equation together.

Is spirit in love with matter, just as matter and material form is destined to fall in love with spirit? If so, this puts a higher priority or value on material existence and upon incarnation into physical form than we ever imagined. Also, if this be true, then spirit somehow propels material manifestation. The appearance of matter is an epiphany of spirit which spirit will serve in its best and most graceful way.

Yeshua's final astonishment is that the marriage of matter and spirit is between poverty and wealth. Perhaps we could say it is the marriage of the pauper and the king. It would be easy at this juncture, however, to return to the point of view that matter itself is in essence poverty stricken, and that the only wealth is spirit. This, however, would simply reinforce the view with which we began. However, once we understand that poverty is an absence of self-awareness (as Logion 3 explains), then spirit enters matter precisely to make it aware, or for the self housed in flesh to become fully aware of itself and its origins. It is only in this way (in this marriage) that matter becomes saturated with consciousness—aware of itself as Self. To see spirit take up residence in matter precisely for this purpose is an astonishing step of spiritual self-giving in which spirit donates itself freely to material form, and in which material form begins to give exquisite expression to spirit. The result is an unimaginable richness: the fullness toward which everything yearns.

QUESTIONS FOR REFLECTION

1. If you were going to describe your own questions about the mysteries of existence, particularly human existence, what would you say? What are the questions you have which would express your deepest inquiry about the meaning of life, your life, all human life, and existence itself?

2. We each know by personal experience what it means to be an embodied being. We are obviously intimately related to our physical form, its needs and vicissitudes, but obviously that is not **all** we are. How would you describe the sense that the physical form isn't everything?

3. When this text talks about spirit, what does it mean? How do you define spirit?

4. How could spirit best serve matter? How could spirit best serve you as an embodied being? What does matter look like when alive with spirit?

5. When you feel "poverty stricken" as an individual (and it has nothing to do with material wealth) what are you feeling? When you feel full and enriched, what makes that so?

EXERCISES AND MEDITATIONS

1. Imagine that spiritual energy awaits an invitation to do its work in you—a person in material form. Suppose also that it will not intrude unless invited to be of service. Take time to think about your invitation and how you might welcome spirit. What is the demeanor that one takes in relationship to someone or something that wants to serve, but is not pushy or demanding? Use, for example, the illustration of a mentor who wants to help you through a difficult subject, or a nurse who wants to help you heal as a patient. What is the relationship between these servers and the one in need of their services? Imagine how this relates to you, and how you might interact with spirit.
2. Go back and read Logion 3 and the definition it gives for poverty. If the opposite of that definition is wealth, then, in this context of spiritual service what might that mean for your daily practice? When are you most rich? When are you poor? Could those states change daily (or even more frequently)? Examine this not only from the viewpoint of psychological need, but from wisdom's perspective—that the truly wealthy are wise beings full of divine consciousness.
3. In your meditations take time to sit with these possibilities. Open yourself to spirit, and to spiritual service. What happens when you do?

*Rabbi Ted Falcon in **A Journey of Awakening** (57) suggests that we make this meditation a daily focus:*

"I become aware of any feelings of self-condemnation I carry. I know that I am a creative being, experiencing through my feelings the Greater Creative Presence Who lives in me and as me. When I accept my current experience, I allow an expansion of feelings. New forms emerge to express deeper levels of my own integrity. I welcome the fuller flow of Creative energies now."

READINGS FOR INSIGHT

I

When grapes turn to wine,
they long for our ability to change.
When stars wheel around the North Pole,
they are longing for our growing consciousness.
Wine got drunk with us, not the other way.
The body developed out of us, not we from it.
We are bees, and our body is a honeycomb.
We made the body, cell by cell we made it.

Jalaluddin Rumi
The Rumi Collection
155

II

Without the divine enhancement that arrives in the urgency of human desiring, people might look like mud-colored camels lying on bare ground. Basically people *are* donkeys concerned only with the straw and barley they're eating, until the presence of grace makes them otherwise (Qur'an 32:5). With faith a grandeur embellishes humanity, as when with a little work by you, God enters a dry seed and makes a fresh living plant. Every action becomes part of this gift. Look around at the sky and the earth. Don't be inert like a wooden bench. Watch the sky moving, and see how every motion in creation connects with the creator. Stars, these natural impulses, our very selves. ... Grief is better than happiness, because in grief a person draws close to God. Your wings open. A tent is set up in the desert where God can visit you. Wealth that arrives in grief is what we spend in joy. The soul is greater than anything you ever lost.

Bahauddin
The Drowned Book
79

III

O sea of bliss,
You have stored transcendental forms of consciousness in the heedless.
You have stored a wakefulness in sleep.
You have fastened dominion over the heart
to the state of one who has lost her heart.
You conceal riches in the lowliness of poverty.
You fasten the necklace of wealth to poverty's iron collar.
Opposite is secretly concealed in opposite:
fire is hidden within boiling water.
A delightful garden is hidden within Nimrod's fire.

Jalaluddin Rumi
The Rumi Collection
175

IV

Just sit there right now.
Don't do a thing. Just rest.
For your separation from God
is the hardest work in this world.
Let me bring you trays of food and something
that you like to drink.
You can use my soft words as a cushion
for your head.

Hafez
Love Poems from God
176

LOGION 30

Yeshua says,

Where there there are three divinities,
God is present.

Where one or two exist,
I am there.

Sapiential Themes

- *Consciousness inhabits the cosmos and becomes personally present to a unified being.*
- *Multiple forms of consciousness manifesting as divinities (gods) also exist in the cosmos.*
- *Wisdom lives in the interface between ordinary and higher forms of consciousness.*
- *The ancient Hebrew code of the I AM continues to be used in the tradition of Yeshua, and is carried over into other Christian Scripture such as the Gospel of John.*

Parallel Texts

Exodus 3:14
Psalm 82:1
Matthew 18:20, 28:20
John 6:35, 9:5, 10:7, 11:25, 14:6, 15:1, 16:32
Revelation 1:8, 17

Links

The previous two Logia express aspects of Yeshua's mission to the human world. One is to awaken and cause an individual to stand up out of the stupor of drunkenness. The other is to unite spirit to flesh in a new and fruitful union. When that happens, the divine consciousness is present, not in an abstract way but in a relational way—the way conscious beings interact with each other. This saying should be read in relationship to Logia 11, 16, 22, 23, 49, 75, and 106.

FOCAL POINT

From the standpoint of textual analysis, we have come to one of the most difficult sayings in the Gospel of Thomas. This Logion is not only thematically difficult; there are also concerns about the accuracy of both the Coptic and the Greek manuscripts. In each case, different readings of the text are possible, which makes definitive interpretation impossible. What is central to all of the readings, however, is presence: the divine presence in the ancient Hebrew form of the I AM which haunts the awareness of humanity. Conscious awareness of the I AM presence is available to all unified beings.

Notes

In a study of the Greek fragment of this text using ultra-violet light, one scholar, Harold W. Attridge, discovered what he believed to be an emendation to the original manuscript which changed the wording entirely. That, plus other readings based upon textual variations, are taken into consideration in this commentary.

COMMENTARY

There are multiple versions of this saying found in two editions, one preserved in the Coptic text, and the other found in a fragment called the Oxyrhynchus Papyrus 1:30 (which also includes Logion 77). In each case there is great ambiguity about both the exact wording of the text, and, consequently, its meaning. Scholars who do critical textual studies cannot agree about the outcome, so the student must look at the various possibilities and make a choice. This choice will, of course, affect any interpretive conclusion. Here are the possibilities as far as they can be determined from this distance and with very fragile documents:

Perhaps the ambiguity around the initial statement in this Logion attests to our own original confusion about the nature and definition of God. Trinitarian and non-Trinitarian definitions for divinity were debated in the early Christian communities. An individual could take one version of the saying to support either of these definitions. However, the notion that there is a Trinitarian aspect to the divine Reality is something that came to the fore in the final version of Christian orthodoxy. Could this statement allude to that process of understanding, as well as to a higher metaphysical principle that sees the divine Reality unfolding according to the "law of three?"

Coptic

[The printed version at the head of this Logion] or, *In the place where there are three divine beings (gods), they are gods (divine). In that place where there are two, or else one, I am there.*

Greek

Where there are (two) (or three) they are not without God, and where there is one, I say to you, I am with him. Raise the stone, and there you will find me, split the wood, I am even there. or (under ultra-violet light), *Where there are three, they are without God, and where there is but a single one, I say that I am with him. Lift up the stone, and you will find me there. Split the piece of wood, and I am there.*

Regardless of which version you choose, there is an obvious strangeness (and ambiguity) in the opening statement, and its meaning seems indeterminate. The final statement, however, concerning the I AM presence appears to be the kernel and key. The Greek version makes that final statement even more emphatic, tying it to previous statements about the single or united being (***monachos***).

If we take the opening statement about the presence of multiple divinities (divine beings) to be accurate, then its significance may lie not so much in a theological context as a philosophical one. For example, in the neo-platonic tradition of the Greeks there were important distinctions made between triads, dyads and monads. Each of these expressed principles of divine reality understood to impact human experience and the whole of existence. In this context one could understand that in a triad (where a trinity of deified beings exist), divinity is expressed in completion. Where duality exists, where there are dyads or twins (as for example, in flesh and spirit), there is a secondary order of divine Reality. However, where a monad exists, the I AM presence shows up and unites with it in order to assist it towards completion. This is, of course, only one such philosophical formulation, and may or may not represent the thought of this text.

Cynthia Bourgeault, a hermit monk, lecturer and scholar, expresses a metaphysical understanding of trinitarian relationships throughout all levels of being as the law of three which is rooted in Ultimate Divine Reality itself.

However, what has been clear from the beginning in this Gospel is that a unified being is one in which consciousness stands up alone and is assisted by the Presence of wisdom known in the Hebrew tradition as I AM (the capitalization being emphasis that is given in the Greek text). As a commentary on the previous saying, where spirit is said to come into being for the sake of flesh, Yeshua indicates his own work of spirit as a personal presence available and alongside those who come to unitive being.

QUESTIONS FOR REFLECTION

1. Do you have any place in your cosmos or theology for "gods?"

2. Suppose higher dimensional beings exist that appear to us to be god-like. What should our relationship be to them?

A divinity or god may be defined as a being who inhabits dimensionally higher realms.

3. Yeshua speaks about his own presence as a form of the highest consciousness described in the Hebrew tradition: the great I AM. Do you have any experience interacting with this Presence?

4. The state of being single, whole, or unified is given further expression in this Logion. Why do you think that I AM consciousness would be available to that state of being human, and not to another?

EXERCISES AND MEDITATIONS

1. You live in a multi-dimensional universe where humans are not the only inhabitants. In fact, despite our population, we may be a distinct minority. Suppose that we could come to know the other inhabitants of the greater cosmos, but that without proper preparation we might misunderstand them or what we were experiencing, and that the result would only damage our spirit or development. Imagine meeting a being of great strength and beauty who comes to our realm from one transcendent to it. In order to help you with this exercise, read C. S. Lewis' entire Space Trilogy, but in particular Chapter Sixteen of **Perelandra**, where the lead character, Ransom, encounters two of the great Eldila—angel-like beings from "deep heaven." Imagine yourself needing to prepare for such an encounter. What would it take for you to meet such a creature without fear or damage?

C. S. Lewis
Perelandra
Scribner, 2003

2. Suppose, though, that the Lord of the Cosmos comes to you gently and quietly, almost in a whisper (a still, small voice) that is barely recognizable as different from your own consciousness. Although this was not the first experience of I AM consciousness as told in the Torah, it becomes a part of that experience for later prophets. This same voice, according to the Gospel of Thomas, is also available to you—especially as you become a unified being. Enter a time of silent meditation as you await the I AM Presence. You might begin your period of meditation with the following chant (chanted a number of times at the beginning and end of your period of mediation on a single, low note):

   There is I Am
   Only I Am
   Fully I Am
   Simply I Am

Read over the following passages which speak about a human's encounter with the I AM Presence that has haunted Hebrew experience and history: Exodus 3:1-16, I Kings 19:9-15

READINGS FOR INSIGHT

I

Only
That Illumined
One
Who keeps
Seducing the formless into form
Had the charm to win my
Heart.
Only a Perfect One
Who is always
Laughing at the word
Two
Can make you know
Of Love.

Hafez
The Gift
84

II

Not from the beginning were we made god,
but first indeed humans, and then finally gods.

St. Irenaeus

III

Century by century God has guided nature up to the point of producing creatures which can (if they will) be taken right out of nature, and turned into "gods." Will they allow themselves to be taken? In a way, it is like the crisis of birth. Until we rise and follow Christ we are still parts of Nature, still in the womb of our great mother. Her pregnancy has been long and painful and anxious, but it has reached its climax. The great moment has come. Everything is ready. The Doctor has arrived. Will the birth "go off all right"? But of course it differs from ordinary birth in one important respect. In an ordinary birth the baby has not much choice: here it has. I wonder what an ordinary baby would do if it had the choice. I might prefer to stay in the dark and warmth and safety of the womb. For of course it would think the womb meant safety. That would be just where it was wrong: for if it stays there it will die.

C. S. Lewis
Mere Christianity
187

IV

The transformation that occurs within the individual is one that is directly being influenced by the *awareness* of God's presence. The more qualitative my awareness of that presence through my breath, my body, my daily encounters with grace, the more I will image God-likeness through the calmness of my breathing and the joy of experiencing a life centered in the stillness of the sacred. ... God as Being and Goodness enters reality as "self diffusive," that is "totally present everywhere and nowhere contained." Once we enter into the presence of the sacred in the magnificent image of Bonaventure as "the book written within and without," we enter into a continuous state of mystical ecstasy. The ecstasy experienced is partially caused by a constant underlying awareness that *God is presence*. When we consciously experience God within and without as One, we cannot help but be ecstatic...

Maria Joudi
Christian Mysticism
East and West
77, 100

LOGION 31

Yeshua says,

No prophet
is welcomed home.

No healer
cures acquaintances.

Sapiential Themes

- *The work of spirit is expressed through the prophetic voice and the healer's art.*
- *Spiritual work, however, is suppressed by over-familiarity.*
- *The prophet's voice is silenced in one's homeland*
- *Healing in the human community is highly prized, and yet to be acceptable its practitioners must be unknown or from the outside.*

Parallel Texts

Matthew 13:53-58
Mark 6:1-6
Luke 4:16-24
John 4:44

Links

The three previous Logia (28-30), where Yeshua explains his mission, the ministry of spirit to flesh, and his presence to a unified being, are linked to this saying. The question is, how would Yeshua minister? What would his mission of spirit be? Answers appear to be given in this text.

FOCAL POINT

If the previous Logion centers on Presence, this saying is aware of absence—the conditions under which spiritual Presence may disappear into a lack or a void. While this saying is a truism, observable from almost any perspective, it expresses circumstances under which wisdom's prophetic voice and healing touch may have no power to function. Two important tasks of wisdom (in two states of human affairs) are limited by an environment in which neither task is any longer effective.

Notes

Simple proverbs which express common sense observations about the nature of life and the human world are foundational to the wisdom tradition. The Hebrew Scriptures, for example, contain the book of Proverbs, which is entirely devoted to simple aphorism. In addition, every culture has its proverbial sayings which carry the folk wisdom of that society.

COMMENTARY

The Abrahamic traditions (Judaism, Christianity and Islam) are prophetic because they each accept the possibility of divine action to change outcomes, to warn of possible consequences, and to instruct human behavior. The prophetic voice has been central in the development of each of these traditions—and yet there is evidence that in each case that voice was resisted mightily.

When spirit is present in the human community, it often appears through a prophetic voice in the vocation of a prophet or a teacher. When it comes to its homeland, however, that voice cannot typically be heard. It is rejected or silenced because everyone "knows" that this is only a human speaking. "Haven't we heard that voice before in all kinds of ordinary ways? We have never before heard this voice speak prophecy."

In like manner, when spirit comes as a healing presence among acquaintances, no cure is easily effected. This is because there is no "mystery" about the practitioner; no mystery with its power to bolster confidence or conviction. The healer is a known commodity. "This is someone who could never heal before, so why now?" The healer, therefore, is rendered ineffective.

We, of course, notice similar difficulties in our own set of circumstances. The experience of powerlessness can be strangely disheartening. But it is often the way of things in the human world, and uncovers, perhaps, a fatal flaw or a deep prejudice that exists just below the surface in every human soul. We can be blind in response to familiarity. Often it is hard to see what is hidden in plain view all around us.

Social inertia is a widely recognized pattern of resistance to change. This pattern becomes more and more entrenched, hindering any fresh progress. The old pattern (the known) is simply more comfortable. The same pattern of inertia exists within us as individuals. We get used to a particular level of comfort, and any outside person or force that might alter that is seen as an enemy to be resisted at all costs.

On the other hand, it is easy for the world with which we are familiar, and the people we know as common acquaintances, to solidify into rigid social forms where thought and attitudes are encased in immovable ways of perception. From that perspective, there is no place for a voice from beyond (prophecy) or for healing energy (as cure to paralysis) because all the "space" has already been taken up. It is occupied by all the easy assumptions which have hardened into unchangeable patterns of perception. There is no room for spirit. The space is fully occupied.

Suppose, however, we were to "put the shoe on the other foot" and examine our own perceptions, or that of the experiences and journeys of prophets and healers. There are many individuals who are destined to carry spirit into this world. That is their calling, their vocation. Imagine, though, that what they experience as opposition is not simply rejection from the outside (those familiar forces from the homeland or acquaintances which challenge them). Imagine instead that the adversity is from the inside, from realities which are already at work within, projected into objectified forms.

In the process of spiritual work, a prophet or a healer may come up against his or her own rigid perceptions about the nature of reality. He or she, therefore, may need to leave familiar territory and friendly faces behind and meet the challenges of the unknown—all those potential obstacles which, in the end, enable the prophet or the healer to gain the necessary strength to do the work of spirit. It is not that the homeland or one's friends are inimical to spirit; it is that they represent what is known and familiar in the mind of the spiritual worker. And so the converse is true, and the work of spirit in the prophet and the healer is inhibited. It is no one's fault. It is simply a step of learning on the path of wisdom.

QUESTIONS FOR REFLECTION

1. Have you ever felt a sense of resistance or rejection from those most familiar to you, or from your home town or region? Why is this often true for so many people?

2. What is a prophet? Who is a healer? Define them. How have you experienced both?

3. Have your own gifts of spirit ever been rejected? What happened and what have you learned from that experience?

4. What spiritual voices or healing currently present in your life do you tend to ignore because you imagine that you already know the answers or are in no need of healing? Might you be dismissing the work of someone else as inconsequential or unimportant?

EXERCISES AND MEDITATIONS

1. Suppose that many of the resistances we feel from outside of ourselves are projections from within. We objectify our own inner challenges or obstacles—things that block or inhibit our spirit, and make the enemy someone or something on the outside. Have you ever noticed this? It is a blind spot, however, and not easily detected. In order to examine this phenomenon and get around the blind spot, it is important simply to observe who or what seems to be a barrier to us, blocking our progress. What (or whom) do we focus upon as the enemy? Using that information, examine instances where you feel this and ask yourself, what about my own interiority may have something to do with the effects I feel on the outside? Journal your reflections and discoveries. It may take you time to see anything, and you may want to consult with a spiritually mature individual who can help you with this exercise.
2. Explore your own gifts, spiritual gifts in particular. Where do you seem to affect the world around you most, moving it in a direction that is toward spirit? Make a list of the gifts you see in yourself. Ask others that you know to describe what they observe about your spiritual influences.
3. What is the work of prophecy in your life? (This, of course, depends upon your definition of the term). What is the work of healing? If Yeshua offers these gifts to you, what barriers does he have to get through that will allow you to receive his work? In a period of meditation (or perhaps in retreat) examine hurts and paralyses which need healing. Listen for a prophetic voice. How can you be healed? What do you hear?

You might want to use this affirmation in your daily practice:

"This day I honor the energies of Life which fill me. I am aware, first, of vital physical energy, but also revitalized by those energies which affect me from beyond myself. They bring insight, they heal wounds, and they assist me to work with the Life that infuses all things."

READINGS FOR INSIGHT

I

There is a glut of wealth in the city of Saba.
Everyone has more than enough...
Everyone is fat and satiated with all the extra. There are no robbers.
There is no energy for crime or for gratitude,
and no one wonders about the unseen world.
The people of Saba feel bored with just the mention of prophecy.
They have no desire of any kind.
Maybe some idle curiosity about miracles, but that's it.
This overrichness is a subtle disease.
Those who have it are blind to what's wrong
and deaf to anyone who points it out.
The city of Saba cannot be understood within itself;
but there is a cure, an individual medicine, not a social remedy:
Sit quietly, and listen for a voice within that will say, *Be...*
As that happens, your soul starts to revive.
Give up talking and your positions of power.
Give up the excessive money.
Turn toward teachers and prophets who don't live in Saba.
They can help you grow sweet again and fragrant
and wild and fresh and thankful for any small event.

Jalaluddin Rumi
The Soul of Rumi
64-65

II

All forms grow rigid. That is the nature of form.
All energies can overwhelm. That is the nature of force.

Rabbi Ted Falcon
A Journey of Awakening
62

III

These spiritual windowshoppers, who idly ask,
How much is that? Oh, I'm just looking.
They handle a hundred items and put them down, shadow with no capital.
What is spent is love and two eyes wet with weeping.
But these walk into a shop
and their whole lives pass suddenly in that moment, in that shop.
Where did you go? *Nowhere.*
What did you have to eat? *Nothing much.*
Even if you don't know what you want,
buy *something* to be part of the general exchange.
Start a huge, foolish project, like Noah.
It makes absolutely no difference what people think of you.

Jalaluddin Rumi
The Soul of Rumi
53

IV

If you do not give up the crowds, you won't find your way to Oneness.
If you do not drop your self, you won't find your true worth.
If you do not offer all you have to the Beloved, you will live this life free of that pain which makes it worth living.

Shaikh abil Kheir
Nobody, Son of Nobody
63

LOGION 32

Yeshua says,

A city built and fortified
on a mountain top cannot fall,
but neither can it be hidden.

FOCAL POINT

Using the metaphor of a city built on the summit of a hill (a "Tel," the most traditional of all sites for ancient cities) we are made to see that the structures of wisdom and spirit are similar in nature: they appear above the local landscape and are raised up like beacons on a hill. Their prominence makes them vulnerable to attack, but their inner strength can also make them invincible. At this elevation there is always a dynamic tension between vulnerability and invincibility. Know this: wherever wisdom builds her house, it too must be fortified and made impregnable.

Sapiential Themes

- *Wisdom is likened to a fortified city built in mountainous terrain.*
- *Structures of spirit built in transcendence are vulnerable but can be made impregnable.*
- *In such a state, visibility and vulnerability go hand in hand, but one may be protected by inner strength.*

Links

The immediate semantic context of this Logion is the previous saying, which describes the rejection of the prophet and the healer within his or her familiar territory. Certainly, in these cases, there may be a sense of vulnerability or even of attack. Because, as a person of spirit, the prophet and healer towers over the common landscape, he or she may draw fire. It is from that position, however, that wisdom's work must be carried forward.

Parallel Texts

Psalm 48:1-3
Proverbs 9:1-3, 14
Matthew 5:14
Acts 13:47
Ephesians 5:8
Philippians 2:15

Notes

To understand this mountain metaphor it is important to comprehend the social, historical, and cultural context in which such an image is used. Throughout the ancient Middle East it was common to build towns and villages on the tops of mountains as fortified keeps. Any community built in this manner was surrounded by a high wall with a single gate that gave entry into the complex. Such towns still exist today in many parts of the Middle East, particularly on the Arabian peninsula, where building practices from the ancient past continue into the present.

COMMENTARY

Standing alone, this simple proverb may suggest something political or military in nature, but is that the case? In the context of other logia surrounding it, is this city not a metaphor for a person of spirit—a prophet or a healer, perhaps, or of wisdom herself built upon a mountain high above the landscape? When wisdom (or persons of spirit) emerge onto the human scene, standing up along the vertical axis, they are like mountains, tall and imposing. Impossible to hide, and as a result, under threat of attack. In the end, however, if they are fortified from within they are unassailable. The fact of vulnerability hides the truth of invincibility. A person strengthened by spirit is ultimately indestructible.

This saying with its mountain imagery points, therefore, towards transcendence. In Semitic cultures, mountains have symbolized the high point of transcendental experience and reality. As individuals of spirit journey into the elevated terrain of the mountains, they are walking into transcendence. The issue is, what will happen there? Will the pilgrim simply be a visitor, sight-seeing the wondrous mountain terrain and then when the hike is over, go back to the flatlands again? Or does that individual take up residence in the mountains and build a dwelling there? Both are transcendental experiences, but the first is temporary, and the second is permanent.

The architecture of the ancient Middle East attests to the common use of this symbolism. Pyramids and ziggurats are the primary examples of mountain imagery built as signs of transcendence on flat, horizontal plains.

If one builds on the top of a mountain with the intention of making it a permanent residence certain conditions must be met because of its extreme exposure and vulnerability. One must build well, fortifying the structures, because there is always the possibility of attack. Safety at that height and in those elevations is dependent upon inner strength.

There are many advantages for a town built high off the plain and on a hill. The first is that because it is on the top of a hill, it spares more easily accessible land for farming. Hill tops are not agriculturally productive, valley land is. In addition, a town built well and in this manner is more easily protected because it is higher. The disadvantage is, of course, that it is also more visible to the enemy—but any enemy is also discernible from afar.

Suppose, then, that for any form of elevation—whether it be of higher truth, wisdom from above, or becoming a person of spirit—the same issues concerning vertical transcendence apply. Because wisdom exists at just such a transcendental vantage point, it is exposed and vulnerable. However, wisdom (or a person of wisdom) fortified from within can become invincible. Attacks from the horizontal axis may come, but a well fortified person, strengthened from within, can withstand those attacks.

From a very early period in the formation of Hebrew wisdom, references to building complexes of this sort, whether literally or metaphorically, are found throughout biblical texts. They also depict places of refuge to which one may flee for safety. The Psalms use this image over and over again. In most cases it is the Lord who is the keep, the high place of refuge, where the needy may find a hiding place. In other cases, it is the city of Jerusalem (or some other noted city of refuge). Or in some cases the refuge may be a righteous person who becomes the protector. In the Proverbs, it is Wisdom herself who builds a refuge on a hill occupying the high place of a city and bids seekers to come and find refuge there.

Psalms18, 31, 46, 71, and 144 use images of taking refuge, being a refugee, or finding safety in a mountain fortress.

It is not surprising, then, that Yeshua would continue to use this imagery as a part of the wisdom teachings expressed in this saying. The seeker of his wisdom, however, must carefully apply these truths to the interior levels of spiritual pilgrimage in the high places of wisdom.

QUESTIONS FOR REFLECTION

1. When you try to imagine transcendence, what do you see? What are your favorite images? Are mountains transcendental signifiers for you?

2. Have you ever visited a castle or a fortress that was built high over the surrounding landscape? What was your impression of such a keep?

3. If mountains and fortresses built on high hills are metaphors for places of transcendence within humans themselves, what are those high places? What do they describe?

4. How does one fortify transcendent territory within?

5. Who lives within the interior keep?

You might think of those higher truths you know which make you vulnerable to attack from the common culture.

6. Have you ever felt under attack as a result of having lived or expressed some higher awareness of truth or wisdom?

EXERCISES AND MEDITATIONS

1. Imagine how you strengthen and fortify your own physical body. Ask yourself, how do I remain strong, healthy, able to withstand the attacks of physical disease? How do I assure that my immune defense system is robust and working? Now by analogy, apply some of what you know about your physical well-being to your inner self and the sources of your spiritual strength. What practices and disciplines do you need to use continually in order to maintain an inner power or force able to withstand attack?
2. We often imagine attack as coming from some external object or force outside ourselves. Suppose the kind of attack that wisdom has in mind is not objectified in something external, but instead can be understood as assault from those peripheral forces, or from those less authentic parts of ourselves, outside the sensitive inner core of the heart. Suppose, for example, that we are continually assaulted from "without" by thoughts of our own unworthiness, stupidity, or inherent weaknesses. These thoughts continually assault the heart of our being, diminishing our strength, and undermining our spirit. What might those forces be that have shaped your life, coming from the horizontal realm of your own family upbringing, culture, or social conditions?

I affirm that there exists an inner high point which I can inhabit and strengthen. I will do what it takes to make that place within safe for refuge.

READINGS FOR INSIGHT

I

Listen to wisdom calling, pay attention to how understanding lifts up her voice to you. She takes her stand at the crossroads of your life, by the side of your path, at the crest of the hill you have just climbed, beside the gate you are about to enter, even at the entrance to the city you pass day after day. At each approach, by every threshold, at the doorway to every realm you enter she stands and cries aloud: "It is to you I am calling, to every human being I make my appeal." ...

See, wisdom has built you her house; she has hewn for you her seven pillars. She has prepared a feast, spiced her wine, and spread her table. At the highest points of the town she has sent her maidens to proclaim: "Come, eat my bread and drink my spiced wine. Abandon immaturity and live. Walk in the way of insight."

Proverbs 8:1-9:6
Trans. L. Bauman

II

1. Lord, you are for me a sacred rock
 a mighty mountain, great,
 a crag on which a fortress sits alone and unafraid.
2. You are also that same stronghold impregnable and secure,
 and the fierce-some warrior who lives within.
 You do battle with the world outside me,
 you shield me from my many foes.
3. But I ask you, God,
 who are we that you should notice or even care?
4. For our span of life is but a gust of wind,
 we are passing shadows in your night.

Psalm 144
Ancient Songs Sung Anew
Trans. L. Bauman

III

It takes two things to blow down a tree: a heavy wind outside and rot and decay inside. So it is with man. The winds of adversity may cause him to bend, but if he's strong and vigorous within, he will arise and grow to new heights after the storm passes.

Vern McLellan
Wise Words and Quotes
9

IV

The most painful troubles are not outside events but inside gnawings. ...

You were born with some weaknesses, you picked up others in the first months and years of your life.

Much of your life has been spent attempting to get rid of these natural weaknesses or lamenting over them. … "If only I was not so stubborn." "If only I were not so lazy." "If only" is a waste of time. Trying to rid yourself of your weak impulses is futile.

The impulse to indulge your weakness always presents an opportunity for growth. …

You are like a blade of a knife. When you were born your edge was sharp. But it did not stay sharp. With use it will dull and need to be resharpened. So at birth you were also given a whetstone. Your natural weakness is your whetstone. Through it you sharpen your edge. Without it you would remain dull.

Brother Tolbert McCarroll
Notes From the Song of Life
69, 75

LOGION 33

Yeshua says,

What you hear with one ear,
listen to with both,
and then proclaim
from the roof tops.
For no one lights a lamp
and then hides it away.
It is placed on a lamp-stand instead
where those who pass by
may see by its light.

Sapiential Themes

- *The voice and light of wisdom is both private and interior as well as public and exterior.*
- *Wisdom's work is characterized by deep listening and the transmission of what is heard.*
- *The purpose of listening and learning is to benefit others.*
- *Wisdom's work is also about enlightenment, both within and without.*
- *The purpose of light is to enlighten.*

Parallel Texts

Isaiah 9:2, 55:3, 60:3
Matthew 5:14-15, 10:27, 13:13-14
Mark 4:21
John 1:4, 8:12, 12:35
Acts 13:47
II Corinthians 4:6
Ephesians 5:8
Revelation 21:23

FOCAL POINT

It is often said that people hear but do not listen. They see but do not understand. This saying attempts to correct both of these inner conditions. It also seeks to produce deep listening and enlightened seeing so that these can bring benefit to the larger world. Wisdom's work involves both the eye and the ear. Its purpose is to help us listen deeply with both ears, and to radiate light. When we do both we can transmit good news from the roof-top and bring light to darkened pathways. Private speech or light has no benefit if it cannot be used to see or to live by, beginning with ourselves. This saying, then, is about the beneficial relationship between the immanent and the transcendent (the vertical and horizontal realities) working on personal and public levels. The play of these realities is necessary for the transmission of wisdom to the wider world.

Links

Logion 32 established the high point of the city on the hill as the dwelling place of wisdom, but the question is, what does one do there? The answer to what can happen as a result of its elevation is given in this saying. From its roof-tops news can be proclaimed. It can also be a place from which light shines forth. It is from this elevation that wisdom is received and transmitted. This saying also continues the flow of images describing the work of the wisdom teacher and healer giving voice to truth and bringing light.

Notes

As in Logion 32, there are cultural and historical references here that we might not completely grasp in the western world. The first is the flat-roofed dwellings built all over the desert region of the Middle East. People commonly use their roof-tops as living space. In the hot summer they sleep there at night, or gather before sleeping for conversation and refreshment. It is not uncommon for people to have conversation and share news from roof-top to roof-top.

The second image used in this Logion is also specific to this period of history—the use of oil lamps for lighting. An oil lamp is the equivalent of a flashlight or a light-bulb in our world.

In I Kings 19:11-13, Elijah the prophet has an encounter with the Lord in which he is progressively taken deeper into a place of inner listening to the "still small voice" of God. In these verses the divine Presence is not said to be in the spectacular outer events, but in the inner stillness of the heart..

*The Orthodox theologian, Gregory Palamas says, for example, "The divine Light is a prerequisite of mystical experience. He who shares the divine energy ... becomes himself in some sort light; he is joined to the Light and with the Light sees in full consciousness all that is hidden from those who have not received this grace." (**An Illustrated Encyclopaedia of Mysticism**, 106).*

COMMENTARY

It is common (and easy) for us to hear someone or something, but not really to listen. We may have the appearance of listening, but in truth we may be somewhere else, distracted by our own thoughts, not really hearing what is being said. Our ears catch many sounds around us, but most of them go unregistered as remembered auditory events. We constantly hear the sounds of birds, the noise of cars and machines, music or television programming, but unless we pay close attention, these sounds "go in one ear and out the other."

As it was for the prophet Elijah, if the voice of spirit is small and unassuming, then we have to learn to pay closer attention— to listen deeply with an inner ear tuned to another dimension beyond space-time. Typically wisdom's voice comes to us from within. It may even be more critical, therefore, that we learn to pay strict attention, especially if the stream of thoughts in our heads can so easily overwhelm any other, finer input. So a crucial condition for the public transmission of wisdom is called "deep listening" with both ears (the outer and the inner, perhaps). Learning to hear the "still small voice" of the Spirit is crucial if we are ever to communicate authentic wisdom to the world around us.

In a similar way, light has always signified the luminosity of transcendent truth and the stream of consciousness that flows from the divine Mind into every receptive being. In the language of the sacred, light is a universal symbol used to represent the divine radiance as it pours into the interior place of the heart. A burning oil lamp symbolizes the relationship of a human instrument lit and burning with the light of transcendence and being fed by oil from deep inner resources. It is a powerful image, and one that requires us to understand the mutual and necessary relationships between these three elements. In the end, though, the purpose of the three (oil, lamp and flame) is to provide illumination for a wider seeing. Light is not simply private; it is meant to be shared for the benefit of all.

What is clear in this saying and in previous images is that the public and exoteric work of wisdom is dependent upon certain inner conditions. What goes on inside the interior castle (the keep of Logion 32) must eventually find its way into the public domain on the plains below. The effectiveness of this work depends, however, on four things: interior strength, higher positioning in transcendence, inner listening and receptivity to interior light. These are the preconditions for the manifestation and transmission of wisdom to the exterior realm.

As in many of the logia of Thomas, here again the play of opposites (twins) continues. In this saying immanence and transcendence, inner and outer (esoteric and exoteric), vertical and horizontal, hidden and manifest, deafness and hearing, blindness and sight, darkness and light are partners in this play. Each side of the duality is in complementary (or oppositional) relationship to the other. As soon as one side of the complementarity is engaged, the other aspect comes into play, until there is equilibrium, or redress. In the unfolding of creation and in the revelation being made to us of Ultimate Reality, wisdom's work maintains a particular balance between these necessary forces.

QUESTIONS FOR REFLECTION

1. The skills of inner listening and seeing go beyond our normal mental processes and require that we pay attention with full consciousness at a deeper level. What has been your experience of either of these (hearing or seeing from within)?

2. What have you heard, or what have you seen, that you believe has come to you from this inner dimension? When you have tried to share your learning or experience, what has been the result?

3. What does it mean for you to be light for another person? Think of an example when this has happened.

4. What does light not based in the electro-magnetic spectrum look and feel like?

EXERCISES AND MEDITATIONS

1. Deep listening to the divine Voice within requires undistracted attention. This is often hard to achieve in a world of constant outer noise and activity. In order to learn to listen, it is important to spend time in seclusion and silence away from external distraction. Make time in a week for yourself to be alone and undisturbed for at least an hour. In that period of silence and quiet, begin by settling yourself into the spaciousness of the silence, and allowing yourself to turn inwardly to listen. You might begin with an invocation or prayer for assistance in this. Center yourself by chanting in monotone: *"Be still and know that I am God, Be still and know that I am. Be still and know. Be still. Be."* Do that several times. Sit in silence, going deeper within. In that depth read a short meditation, perhaps one of the Logion of Thomas. Read it slowly several times with silence between each reading. Open yourself, then, to listen to the divine Presence who may speak to your heart from out of the silence.
2. There is a famous "light verse" in the Qur'an which has much meaning and significance for this saying. Meditate on these words, pondering the relationship of the heart as lamp, the oil and the light:

   God is the light of Heaven and Earth. His light may be compared to a niche in which there is a lamp; the lamp is in a glass; the glass is as if it were a glittering star kindled from a blessed olive tree, which is neither Eastern nor Western, whose oil will almost glow though fire has never touched it. Light upon Light. God guides anyone He wishes to His light. God composes parables of humankind; God is aware of everything (Qur'an 24: 35-36).

My purpose is that my whole being becomes an ear of listening and an eye of seeing that I might be a gateway into this world for the flow of wisdom—giving voice from the roof-tops and bringing light from a light stand.

READINGS FOR INSIGHT

I

Bahauddin
The Drowned Book
126

There are beings who live because other beings have light,
And there are beings who die because someone let his lamp go out.

II

Pema Chödrön
Comfortable With Uncertainty
112, 120

Holding on to beliefs limits our experience of life. That doesn't mean that beliefs or opinions or ideas are a problem. It's the stubborn attitude of having to have things to be a particular way, grasping on to our beliefs and opinions, that causes the problems. Using your belief system this way creates a situation in which you choose to be blind instead of being able to see, to be deaf instead of being able to hear, to be dead rather than alive, asleep rather than awake. ... Our ancient habitual patterns will begin to soften, and we'll begin to see the faces and hear the words of people who are talking to us. As we learn to have compassion for ourselves, the circle of compassion—what and whom we can work with, and how—expands.

III

Jalaluddin Rumi

The lamps are different,
But the light is the same.
So many garish lamps in this dying brain's lamp shop, forget about them.
Concentrate on essence, concentrate on Light
In lucid bliss, calmly smoking off its own holy fire,
The light streams towards you from all things,
All people, all possible permutations of good, evil, thought, and passion.
The lamps are different,
But the Light is the same.
One matter, one energy, one Light, one Light-mind,
Endlessly emanating all things.
One turning and burning diamond.
One, one, one.
Ground yourself, strip yourself down to blind loving silence.
Stay there until you see you are gazing at the Light
With its own ageless eyes.

IV

J. K. Kadowaki SJ
Zen and the Bible
32, 34

When you have penetrated the Great Death, you will awaken to your Primal Face and realize the essential nature of the Self, which is the common root of all things. This is indeed the *prajna* wisdom which transcends reason and will. When the 'body' has been illumined, ordered, and unified by this wisdom, for the first time you are able to 'drop off the mind and body of self and others.' At the moment this happens, all traces of the illusive tendencies are completely extinguished. ...

There is a Neoplatonic principle that says the higher the ability, the broader and deeper its power to extend and penetrate. Accordingly, this wisdom can be integrated into every crevice of the 'body' disciplining and ordering it. Then, at last, the whole body will be an eye which radiates the light of wisdom and lights up the world. I believe this is the thorough purification of the 'body' that is aimed at in Zen.

LOGION 34

Yeshua says,

If the blind are leading the blind
they will topple together
into a pit.

Sapiential Themes

- *Blindness is both a physical and a spiritual condition.*
- *In the realm of spirit, blindness equates to a lack of inner light at the level of the heart, resulting in ignorance.*
- *Two people afflicted with spiritual blindness cannot assist one another. If they try, the results are disastrous.*

Parallel Texts

Deuteronomy 28:29
Proverbs 4:19
Isaiah 59:10
Matthew 6:23, 15:14, 23:19
II Corinthians 3:14, 4:4
Ephesians 4:18
I John 2:11

FOCAL POINT

The truth of this Logion seems so obvious that it is easy to overlook deeper aspects of its significance. This saying appears to reflect Yeshua's understanding of the human condition and the trap we find ourselves in. Anyone with the same condition of inner blindness attempting to assist someone else is sure to fail. All our attempts to get out of the pit created by blindness also fail. So there are an increasing number of difficulties in focus here: blindness itself as an inner condition, walking about blindly and trying to find the way, the attempt to assist others when we are plagued by this condition ourselves, and the inability to get out of the pit once we have all fallen in.

Links

It is clear that the previous saying has triggered the placement of this Logion in the series. Light in a dark place is necessary if we are not to stumble and fall into a hole, taking others with us. The "pit" may be, in fact, the rejection of light brought by the prophet and the healer into home territory. That rejection may be enough to create the hole which traps its victims in darkness and ignorance—the very state of inner blindness that Logion 28 talks about.

Notes

Ignorance, moral blindness, and lack of spiritual sight (or understanding) are descriptions given to the condition of blindness of otherwise "sighted" people by the world's great sacred traditions.

COMMENTARY

Blindness is a great tragedy. When it occurs naturally we know that for the individual who lives in a sighted world the incapacitation is great. When it occurs as a result of accident, a person may suffer losses which are both physically and emotionally debilitating. There is, however, another form of blindness. It is one we all experience again and again—the simple absence of light. We may awaken in the night and need to move, and without a light we stumble and sometimes fall. We may find ourselves in a situation where suddenly the lights go out, and we are instantly plunged into darkness. But this latter condition can be fixed. We can find a flashlight perhaps, turn on a light, light a match, or ask for light. This latter condition seems to be the context of this saying.

A powerful account of physical blindness and inner seeing is given by Jacques Lusseyran in his autobiography, ***And There Was Light*** *(NY: Parabola Books, 1998).*

Yeshua sees the world through the eyes of spiritual sight, and observes the tragedy of a world of spiritually blind men and women groping their way in the darkness. If you asked the average person, however, whether or not they can see spiritually, no doubt the answer will be, "Yes, of course, I can see." No one believes that they are spiritually blind. We seem to be completely unaware of our condition, ignorant of the loss of sight at the level of the heart. Like some flavor we have never tasted, we cannot imagine its existence or its absence. It simply does not appear on the landscape of our world. Because we have never experienced it, it does not exist for us. We are blind to that about which we are ignorant. The tragedy of such ignorance (and the absence of inner light) is that it compounds itself. Others are also affected. When, in our ignorance, we try to help those who feel as lost as we do, we end up by falling further into some unknown, unrecognized, or unexpected pit.

Each of the great sacred traditions has seen ignorance as a trap, and the light of wisdom (or truth) as the only means of escape. Plato's well known image of men and women living in a cave ignorant of the sun's light is an illustration of this state in the early western tradition. Yeshua's teachings about light, and John's explanation about the coming of light into a dark rejecting world, continue the theme.

The Greek philosopher Plato is most remembered for his analogy of the cave. In it people are living by firelight, not sunlight, imagining that it is all the light there is. They deny any greater light and ridicule anyone who seeks for it. To find sunlight, individuals must struggle against the accepted worldview of the cave, and ascend through the darkness into the light. Once they stand in the light, however, they, too, know the truth of Plato's Cave.
The Republic*, 7.514-5*

In this saying a specific difficulty is identified. Perhaps because we are altruistic beings, our condition is more dangerous. Philanthropy cannot overcome ignorance. Nothing will help us but the light which shines from within the heart as a result of transcendent wisdom. Without that light, we are lost and dangerous to ourselves and others. With that light, we can begin to see clearly enough to move in the right direction and perhaps to be of real assistance to others.

Wisdom's work is to bring light to the heart, to return people back into a sighted world and release them from the stumbling and groping which they have previously known. But the light specific to this task is not simply more of the same knowledge that has left us ignorant and in the dark in the first place. It must be a light brought to the organ of inner perception, the cognitive organ of the heart. It must provide true insight, sight from within. To grasp an understanding of that which was not previously known, such light must come from transcendent sources—the light from the vertical axis. Most, if not all, of our knowledge is horizontal in nature. It comes as a result of analysis, reason, data and information derived from space-time. From wisdom's perspective, this is not sufficient. The only light which will illuminate the heart from within comes through the inner aperture, the eye of the heart, flowing down from above. Only that light can banish the darkness of our ignorance.

QUESTIONS FOR REFLECTION

1. Have you ever been blind even for a short period of time? What was the effect upon you?

2. Describe your inner experience of stumbling around in the dark. Realize, however, that you **knew** you were stumbling and made blind by the absence of light.

3. Have you ever been led astray intellectually, emotionally, or spiritually? What was that experience like? Have you ever been the cause for others being led astray? How did that happen?

4. What is it like to be trapped in a hole of some kind and unable to get out? Describe your experience of this.

EXERCISES AND MEDITATIONS

1. It would be a good exercise to go out at night, and without hurting yourself, find your way around your yard without the use of light. Explore your feelings as you do so. You might also want to do this with a partner, and if you can, in a place that is unknown to you. See what you find out about yourself, and what you learn from this experience. Describe this in your journal.
2. Go back to a time in your life when you were more constricted in thought or spirit than you are now. In a period of meditation, try to re-enter that experience again and determine what it was like for you. Then re-examine it from the place you are now. Describe the difference between these two experiences and write what you learn in your journal.
3. Crucial to this saying is an understanding of the heart as an organ of inner perception. The fact that it can be blind leads, of course, to ignorance. The issue for all of us is whether or not we can see by means of the heart. Perhaps we can, or just think we can. Ponder this: how do you know whether or not this inner organ sees? If you detect that it cannot see or is myopic, how could it be opened and strengthened? Ask for guidance from above, or from another person with "kardial sight."
4. The readings for insight are full of wisdom, some of which may enlighten our ignorance (or lack of understanding). In this or in previous chapters, go to that section and determine which of those readings have given you the most light. What readings still seem unhelpful or confusing to you? Could this be a sign of the edge of your own blindness? You might want to mark those difficult readings and turn to them again, seeking greater light or clarity.

There are different ways of dealing with ignorance in yourself and in others. To overcome ignorance, the learner must be willing to receive instruction. What is the difference between trying to overcome ignorance in a willing recipient and in one who is unwilling? What happens in each case, in yourself and in others? What makes you willing to explore and learn? Can you detect where or in what way you are ignorant? How can that be remedied?

READINGS FOR INSIGHT

I

Jalaluddin Rumi
Love Poems From God
81

Magnetic fields draw us to Light;
They move our limbs and thoughts.
But it is still dark.
If our hearts do not hold a lantern,
We will stumble over each other,
Huddled beneath the sky as we are.

II

Shaidh Abu Saeed Abil Kheir
Nobody, Son of Nobody
30

O' Ever Present One,
Absent in the land of the blind.
O' Giver of All Wealth,
In whose Presence all pretense falls.
O' Singer of the Great Song,
Unheard in the land of the dumb deaf.
All this creation tosses and turns
To reach that gift beyond all understanding;
Consciously tasting Your Presence.

III

Yehuda Berg
The Power of Kabbalah
71

Although we stumble around in the darkness and turmoil of this physical world, we can take heart, for in reality, the Light is *still* here. Cover a lamp with many layers of cloth and eventually a room becomes dark. Yet the lamp is *still* shining as brightly as ever. The intensity of light never changed. What changed was the cloth covering the light. Kabbalah teaches us how to remove the layers of cloth one strip at a time—to reassemble the puzzle of Creation and bring more Light into our lives.

IV

Adapted from Anthony de Mello
One Minute Wisdom
119

The Master had quoted Aristotle: "In the quest of truth, it would seem better and indeed necessary to give up what is dearest to us." And he substituted the word "God" for "truth."

Later a disciple said to him, "I am ready, in the quest for God, to give up anything: wealth, friends, family, country, life itself. What else can a person give up?"

The Master calmly replied, "One's belief about God."

The student went away sad, for he clung to his convictions. In truth, he feared death more than ignorance.

V

A prayer from the Prophet Muhammad (Peace be upon him)

O God, give me light in my heart and light in my tongue and light in my hearing and light in my seeing and light in my feeling and light in every part of my body and light before me and light behind me. Give me, I beg you, light on my right hand and light on my left hand and light above me and light beneath me. O Lord, make light grow within me and give me light and illuminate me.

LOGION 35

Yeshua says,

You cannot take
a strong man's house by force
unless first you bind
his hands and remove him.

Sapiential Themes

- *There are powers in the universe which must be forcibly altered or removed, and at times these powers are invested in a "strong man" who has become enemy and tyrant.*
- *The active agency of evil is symbolized by hands which accomplish their work, but which can be bound, and the agent removed.*
- *Wisdom knows when such action is required.*

Parallel Texts

Isaiah 49:24-25
Matthew 12:24-29, 16:19, 18:13, 18; 22:13
Mark 3:27
Ephesians 4:8-11
Revelation 20:2

FOCAL POINT

At first glance, this Logion may seem out of place in the context of Yeshua's teachings. It appears that Yeshua is advocating violence, contravening his message of peace and non-violence. There are other sayings in the canonical Gospels, of course, that reflect these same sentiments, and they too appear to contradict what we know or normally expect from the lips of Yeshua. In all of these texts, the truth about overcoming another force, taking possession of enemy territory, or dwelling in a place of opposition is graphically described. It is clear that in certain cases something (or someone) must be overwhelmed and overcome in order for anything else to happen. In the end such action may have nothing to do with either physical or political advantage, but be entirely spiritual in nature. Sometimes strong, direct, unequivocal action must be taken, and a wise person knows when such a moment comes and how to act with precision and accuracy.

Links

This saying is in stark contrast to Logion 34 where individuals are said to be helpless against the debilitating effects of blindness. If such a condition signals an interior lack of sight and consequent ignorance, then such debilitation must be actively opposed. It is easy to wish that no one would fall into a pit, but if one were to witness such an event, it would be essential to do all in our power to prevent it. Our active agency would be called forth, and we would need to act quickly and decisively.

Notes

Both the canonical Gospels and the Gospel of Thomas contain what some have described as "the difficult sayings of Jesus." These are utterances that are difficult to reconcile with the other teachings of Yeshua, or with the standard interpretations about him. It is important to realize, however, that in the wisdom traditions, the voice of the Sage or the Prophet can often speak words that confound and stupefy the hearer. Much like Zen Koans, these are meant to awaken humanity out of its rational sleep.

COMMENTARY

This Logion may appear foreign to the message of Yeshua until we consider it in the entire context of the wisdom tradition. Is there ever a time in the progression of spiritual maturation that action defined in this strong and deliberate way is required and must be taken? Would wisdom herself, or the higher orders of transcendental reality, ever act to forcibly remove someone or something from the immediate environment? The answer has to be in the affirmative, but we must first construct a context in which a lower force might be overcome by a higher force; this, in the end, would be to the advantage of all.

There are many examples of Yeshua taking strong and definitive action. The following texts from the canonical Gospels show the power of such a force.

Matthew 8:22-34, 12:12-13, 22
Mark 5:1-20, 11:15-17
Luke 8:26-39, 19:45-46

It is fairly clear that in the realm of political reality, Yeshua would be unlikely to advocate the course suggested by this saying. Even in social and religious affairs his tactics were seldom violent (an apparent exception may be his driving out the money changers from the temple in Jerusalem). However, when it was necessary to deconstruct the forces of evil which held sway over individuals or societies, Yeshua was willing to take direct and immediate action, resulting in the power and force of goodness overcoming the oppressive powers which enslave and destroy. We need only to remember the times Yeshua took action against demonic force to know that he was very capable of "binding the strong man" in order to free a soul. There were also occasions when he would rebuke religious oppression and silence his critics in such a way as to render their power ineffective or to reveal their spiritual weakness. These instances may or may not have involved any physical force, but the effects were the same: the opposition's hands were tied, and the presence and power of evil was removed.

If we look at the larger context in which this particular saying is situated, these stark images suggest a profound meaning we might otherwise overlook. Previous to this saying, two blind individuals have helplessly fallen together into a pit. Earlier, in Yeshua's vision, he sees humanity intoxicated with a wine that has left it immobilized and unable to stand up. In both of these cases, the pattern of disability and ignorance is in focus. That pattern cannot be broken or the ignorance removed unless their power is bound and cast out of the "house" in which humanity resides. Something stronger than mere argument or gentle persuasion must be used. It is necessary that ignorance be bound and expelled if we are ever to be free. Sometimes one cannot speak gently to an overwhelming power. Only action can demonstrate force. Humanity appears to be impotent against the powers of darkness which blind and trap the soul. Those powers must be overcome, then, by that which is superior.

It is not mere action, but qualities in the actor which create force or power. In the ancient world, the Greeks saw the Good not merely as an abstraction, but as an active agency which permeates the cosmos, thus creating change.

The good news is, of course, that the active agency of the Good can bind the force of evil and loose those victims held in thrall. Wisdom has built her a house; humanity has been is invited to that house for the feast. Another power, however, has invaded it, filling it with ignorance and darkness. There is only one way to expel such an intruder. That power is at hand, and Yeshua is not afraid to use it. It is not action for action's sake, but action taken by the Good for the good of all. This is a distinguishing characteristic of wisdom's work.

QUESTIONS FOR REFLECTION

1. Have your hands ever been tied by a superior force? What happened to make this so? Can such constraint have a positive effect, even when you are fundamentally opposed to what may be happening and how?

2. Have you ever been an active agent for the forcible removal of some power against which you felt you had to move decisively? How did it happen and what was the effect? What were your "insides" telling you in this situation? Did you feel capable—that you had enough power to do what you were doing?

3. Under what circumstances would you think that action-with-force might be necessary (or that any lesser action would be ineffective)? Give several examples where such force was taken that you sensed was necessary.

4. If in this saying the words do not literally mean to handcuff or bind someone's hands physically, what would they symbolize? How does someone bind, loose, or free someone else?

EXERCISES AND MEDITATIONS

1. To understand the principle of force, two aspects must be distinguished. The first is the aspect of opposition which creates friction, and thus, energy. The second is the aspect of cooperation (or fusion) which also produces energy. The former (the aspect of opposition) is in focus in this saying, but the latter is central to the entire Gospel of Thomas. Union or oneness is a greater force than opposition, and yet sometimes opposition is necessary. Wisdom knows when each is appropriate. Go through a day, watching these principles at work. See when you are acting out of each aspect. What is your preferred mode of action? You might realize that you need to learn the other modality to complete your work as a lover of wisdom.
2. Wisdom tradition understands that though one can render an enemy impotent (unable to put plans into action), this, however, is not yet a victory. A deeper wisdom is to turn an enemy into a friend, wherein defeat does not simply overcome an enemy, but changes the whole relationship completely. This is true victory. Imagine, then, that the message of this saying is only the first step in the process. The second, more difficult step, is to change the relationship by transforming the enemy. Take an extreme difficulty of your own with another and imagine it in just this way. What would need to happen for this form of transformation to occur in you or someone else?

I affirm the power of love and compassion, which is a superior force. In the end, it is able to transform the power of evil into a force for good. I will seek to actualize this force as a possibility in my own being.

READINGS FOR INSIGHT

I

A. H. Almaas
Elements of the Real in Man
41

The unconscious fears and blocks which act as barriers to the experience of essence and the flow of physical and subtle energies, are seen in the body through the subtle senses as a certain kind of darkness, as a block in the energy flow. Many techniques have been developed through the years to get around these barriers, these dark spots—to let the energy move.

Some methods use exercises or postures to get around certain barriers. Some methods work to push through dark spots by sheer force of will or dedication...

II

Fra Giovanni
Letter to a friend at Christmas, 1513

I salute you. I am your friend, and my love for you goes deep. There is nothing I can give you which you have not got. But there is much, very much, that while I cannot give you, you can take. No heaven can come to us unless our hearts find rest in today. Take heaven! No peace lies in the future which is not hidden in this present instance. Take peace! The gloom of the world is but a shadow. Behind it, yet within our reach, is joy. Take joy! Life is so full of meaning and purpose, so full of beauty ... that you will find that earth but cloaks your heaven. Courage then to claim it, that is all! And so I greet you with profound esteem and with the prayer that for you, now and forever, the day breaks and the shadows flee away.

III

Yehuda Berg
The Power of Kabbalah
173

The Israelites did escape (from Egyptian slavery). And yes, the Red Sea (and *all* the waters of the earth) did part magnificently. *But God didn't do it.* When God asked Moses why he was calling upon Him, God was implying that Moses and the Israelites had the power to part the Red Sea on their own. God was revealing one of the Spiritual Laws of Life; *Overcome your own reactive nature and the heavens will respond and help you overcome the laws of Mother Nature, for the two are intimately connected.*

IV

Pema Chödrön
Comfortable with Uncertainty
119-120

It's daring not to shut anyone out of our hearts, not to make anyone an enemy. If we begin to live like this, we'll find that we actually can't define someone as completely right or completely wrong anymore. Life is more slippery and playful than that. ... Compassionate action, being there for others, being able to act and speak in a way that communicates, begins with noticing when we start to make ourselves, right or make ourselves wrong. ... This tender shaky place, if we can touch it, will help us train in opening further to whatever we feel, to open further rather than shut down more. ... Our ancient habitual patterns will begin to soften, and we'll begin to see the faces and hear the words of people who are talking to us. As we learn to have compassion for ourselves, the circle of compassion—what and whom we can work with, and how—expands.

LOGION 36

Yeshua says,

Do not spend your time from one day to the next worrying about your outer appearance, what you wear and what you look like.

Sapiential Themes

- *Worry over external conditions must not be the central focus of human consciousness.*
- *Our use of time is a payment we make to existence. How we spend time sets the conditions for our future becoming.*
- *Wisdom knows that external focus on the surface structures of existence is a waste of our time. The cost is that we are depleted, and that nothing of significance is added to our being.*

Parallel Texts

Matthew 6:25-34
Luke 12:22-32
Philippians 4:6
I Peter 3:3-4, 5:7
Dialogues of the Savior 51-52

FOCAL POINT

For most individuals, their primary focus in the temporal flow from one day to the next is upon external events and circumstances. We spend our time worrying about how we appear to those around us, and consequently how we should dress to be accepted or noticed. The fashion industry is driven by this concern. In the end, however, what we emphasize as we live in time determines who we are and what we will eventually become. This saying, therefore, places our attention on the use of time and its cost to us, and to what we pay out in terms of our worries and concerns. We expend energy on what we worry about, and if that energy is wasted because our worries are useless, then we have wasted more than our time. We have wasted life itself.

Links

If we take the previous saying as the context for Yeshua's teaching in this Logion, then the way we bind the "strong man" is by letting go—detaching from our worries over appearances. This approach to a contextual understanding of Thomas highlights a further question: who is the strong man, and what power does he have over us? This saying provides an answer.

Notes

In this translation of the original Coptic, the text is extended, putting emphasis on the exterior focus of this saying. A more literal translation would be: "Do not be anxious from morning to evening or from evening to morning about what you will wear." However, the Coptic is a simplification of an earlier, more extensive saying in Greek.

COMMENTARY

There is a Greek fragment of this Logion which is longer and closer to some of the canonical texts. It reads: "Jesus said, Do not be concerned from morning till evening and from evening till morning about your food, what you will eat, or about your clothing, what you will wear. You are far better than the lilies which neither card nor spin. As for you, when you have no garment, what will you put on? Who might add to your stature? It is He who will give you your cloak."

What do humans worry about most? Among our many worries, primary, perhaps, is how we appear to others in the external world. We want, of course, to be liked, approved of, and seen as strong and competent, The old adages, "Clothes makes the man," "Dressed to kill," and "Dressed fit for a queen" speak about our attempts to make ourselves look powerful or superior in the eyes of others. It is truly a human concern, and whole industries are built upon it.

It is also true that we are bound by our anxieties and cares. What we worry about most keeps us confined and focused (some would say imprisoned and bound as if by a "strong man") upon purely temporal concerns. When our focus is on the impressions we are making in the outer world and on the apprehension that we may not be making the right ones, we can become easily imprisoned as our locus of control is shifted from the inside to the outside. The approval of matters more to us than our own sense of integrity. It appears, therefore, that this very condition, along with the metaphors in the previous saying concerning binding the strong man's hands and removing him from the house, is what Yeshua's message in this saying is all about. The way to take the strong man prisoner, then, is by giving up the need for external approval, or giving up worry over how we appear in public. Attachment to these worries is as binding as being handcuffed. Detachment from them is as freeing as having a tyrant arrested and tossed out the door.

Over and over again, this Gospel shifts emphasis from external conditions and concerns to internal realities at the core of our being. Yeshua teaches that our inner condition can be spacious, blessed, and free when it is detached from powers on the outside, even when external circumstances are at their worst. Paradoxically, these interior realities are determined by how much power or control we give away to outside forces. Notice that the injunction against worry concerns the self in its most peripheral mode: the way we appear in the outer world. Not only that, the concern is how we appear to somebody else (and not simply to ourselves as seen from without). This places control even further away from the center of our being and into the hands of non-essential powers over which we have little or no control. In the end, perhaps, we will realize that these outer powers do not matter at all.

If one were to ask the average person about his or her personal freedom, it is likely that individual would emphatically deny that they were in any way enslaved. "Look, I am perfectly free to do what I want!" But are they? Are we? For most of us, the issue of our personal freedom has almost everything to do with external conditions, and very little to do with our internal state. This puts us far from understanding the concern of this saying; far from and the central viewpoint of wisdom and its focus on interior freedom which is more crucial than any exterior condition.

If we extend this image of dress and how we appear to others, and see it as a symbol signifying the ego's need to "dress up" for the sake of appearances, then this saying identifies who the strong man actually is: an aspect of ourselves. It addresses something far more critical than what we wear or how we appear to the world around us. The agenda of the ego (our peripheral self) is to manage our affairs in such a way that we make a good impression on others. This is often a hidden drive to which we give constant attention, whether we are aware of it or not. We want to appear acceptable and we use appearance as the means, but it is the ego's agenda which drives this behavior. From wisdom's perspective, this search for external approval takes so much time and vital energy, that our life is wasted and the essential self is neglected. No qualitative change can be made at the core of our being as long as our focus is on external approval and acceptance. Only a shift toward inner focus can guarantee full freedom. By moving focus from the outside to the inside, we discover a spaciousness that we would not have otherwise known. This is a form of wisdom we come slowly to understand; in the end, it is one we cannot live without.

QUESTIONS FOR REFLECTION

1. What do you worry about most? How important are your clothes to the impression you make on others?

2. Are there other ways you seek to make an impression (putting on appearances)?

3. How has this behavior shaped your personality and the focus of your life?

EXERCISES AND MEDITATIONS

1. Assume it is true that we learn to perceive ourselves when we are young as a result of the way people respond and react to us and the remarks they make about us. When, then, have you internalized that you now know to be false, or which detracts from your true self (maybe a part of you that you keep hidden)? In a time of personal reflection, think about the patterns of expectation and thought which may play the role of the "strong man" whose hands you need to bind. Whose expectations might you be living by? What are the cultural bindings that might keep you imprisoned?

Can you remember words and phrases that adults used to describe you when you were a child? These may give you important clues as to the patterns which hold for you now.

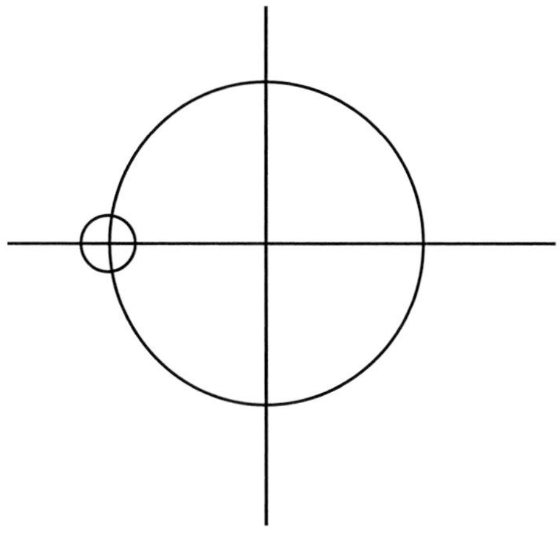

2. The human interior is complex. When sacred tradition uses such terms as the egoic self, peripheral self, central self, essential self, it recognizes that there are multiple dimensions and domains within us. The ego (that important aspect of ourselves which manages our affairs in daily life) is, in fact, at the periphery of our being. Deeper and more central is an essential core which contains the divine Image. We carry this image as treasure, but the treasure gets buried by all the surface material which hides it. This idea is clearly a part of Yeshua's own teaching in this and other texts. Look at the following diagram and label where these parts of your self might exist. Where and what is the "strong man" of the last Logion, and where is his house? Discuss your conclusions with others who are doing this same sort of study.

This diagram indicates that every human is a bi-axial being aligned along both a horizontal axis (depicting space-time) and a vertical axis (representing the range of transcendent dimensions). The human self lives along both axes and yet is most familiar with the horizontal domain.

READINGS FOR INSIGHT

I

Ralph Waldo Emerson

Self-control is coolness and the absence of heat and waste.

II

Pema Chödrön
Comfortable with Uncertainty
151

Cool loneliness allows us to look honestly and without aggression at our own minds. We can gradually drop our ideas of who we think we ought to be, or who we think we want to be, or who we think other people think we want to be or ought to be. We give up and just look directly with compassion and humor at who we are. Then loneliness is no threat and heartache, no punishment.

III

Eckhart Tolle
The Power of Now
37

Since the ego is a derived sense of self, it needs to identify with external things. It needs to be both defended and fed constantly. The most common ego identifications have to do with possessions, the work you do, social status and recognition, knowledge and education, physical appearance, special abilities, relationships, personal and family history, belief systems, and often also political, nationalistic, racial, religious, and other collective identifications. None of these is you.

IV

Mirabai
Love Poems From God
254

What if God asked you to give all your gold bangles
and fine cloths to the next beggar you see?
Giving God our clay (our being) to shape is one thing,
for this can excite us,
but when our jewelry and silk are at risk
surely it is time to seriously ask,
Is all this God stuff—
real?

V

A. H. Almaas
Elements of the Real in Man
29-30

As you grow up, because of your interactions with your environment and certain difficulties you encounter, you get cut off from certain parts of yourself at different times. Every time you get cut off from a certain part of you, a hole manifests. The holes then become full with the memory of the loss and the issues around the loss. After a while, you just fill in the holes. What you fill the holes with are the false feelings, ideas, beliefs about yourself, strategies for dealing with your environment. These fillers are collectively called the personality—the false personality, or what we call the false pearl.

VI

Kabir Edmund Helminski
Living Presence
51

We are slaves to a tyrant called "ego." Unless we are extremely astute we do not see the extent to which we are controlled by our habits, compulsions, and desires, because we are working so hard to satisfy their random expectations.

LOGION 37

Sapiential Themes

- *The students ask Yeshua for full self-disclosure, and he does not deny them, though he sets conditions.*
- *His conditions for disclosure go to the heart of their own process of self-revelation without coverings.*
- *Mutual self-disclosure is the way knowledge grows into intimacy.*
- *Shame and fear are egoic coverings which hide divine theophany and prevent personal knowing.*

His students asked him,

When will you manifest
yourself to us?
How long will it be
before we see you as you truly are?

Yeshua replied,

"On the day you strip yourselves naked
like those little children,
and take your clothes
and trample them on the ground
under your feet without shame,
then you will be able to look upon
the son of the Living One
without fear."

Parallel Texts

Genesis 2:25, 3:7-11, 14-15
Matthew 24:3
Mark 13:4
Luke 17:20, 21:7
Dialogues of the Savior 51-52, 84-85

Links

This saying is clearly linked to the previous Logion, where nakedness is contrasted with concern for the clothing one wears. This contrast appears to be an important context for interpreting its meaning. The earlier image of children stripping naked (Logion 21) provides a foundation for this saying to which it is linked by Yeshua himself.

FOCAL POINT

Yeshua's previous injunction about clothing may have spurred the students' questions about self-revelation. If clothing hides the real person, then the disciples may want to know more about who the Master is behind the clothes he wears, behind all appearances. They may also want a true seeing below the surface, beyond how individuals may ordinarily perceive him. Theirs is an important pursuit, for their questions go to the heart of their relationship with Yeshua and to the issue of knowing another human being deeply. Yeshua's response to their request clearly ties two sayings together. He directly refers to Logion 21 which indicates that, at least in the mind of Thomas, there is a continuity between sayings. Yeshua continues the stark image of nakedness without shame in order to set the conditions for self-disclosure.

Notes

The dialogical nature of the relationship and the learning of Yeshua's students is in focus here. Often the students' questions prompt a series of sayings in answer, continuing the dialogue. Such exchange is an important mode of learning known as the Socratic method, commonly used in the wisdom traditions of the ancient world. This form of learning, however, requires practice, and so Yeshua directs them in their next spiritual exercise.

COMMENTARY

Two ancient words summarize the students' request in this saying. They are asking for an ***epiphany***, that is, the manifestation (or appearance) of the true being whose exterior visage and presence they see before them. They are also asking for a ***theophany***, the divine self-revelation or disclosure of this being in his essence so that they may understand him more fully for themselves. In early Christian history, these two terms came to represent the revelatory nature of the Christian tradition. God appeared in flesh, making a powerful disclosure of the divine Self which would be otherwise hidden—humans have directly received the answer for which they have been asking.

Based perhaps on their earlier attraction to the person and teaching of the Master, his students now want to know more. What they have seen is not enough, or perhaps doubts linger and they want their faith strengthened and their reservations assuaged. How best can their request be granted? The question is, of course: are his students ready to receive that for which they ask? It would be easy for Yeshua to simply give them a description of who he is in the form of a discourse. Instead, what he gives them is a process which will bring them to the point of knowing him for themselves. That process has everything to do with what the previous Logion (36) has said, as well as the startling description given earlier (but repeated here) concerning the children in the field who must strip themselves before the Lords of the land.

Logion 21

In this Logion, the description of nakedness is even more graphic and puzzling. However, if we consider the previous metaphor of apparel as symbolic of the egoic self, we may be nearer to an understanding of Yeshua's shocking pronouncement. Beginning with the account in Genesis, humankind has used clothing as a kind of shield behind which to hide or cover shame. Nakedness is shameful to the human mind and so, in human society, we cover the body. Before the divine Mind, however, there is no such thing as covering. Everything is known for what it is. Using clothing to cover human shame or to project some image of the self is merely an egoic activity obligatory perhaps in human society, but not in the Kingdom. Divine "society" is different. In that realm, the old egoic coverings behind which we hide must be stripped away without shame in a full disclosure of our essence before the divine. When this occurs, the essence of the Master can then be fully revealed. Such acts of self-revelation or mutual self-disclosure are, of course, deeply personal. They can only be done without shame or fear between beings who know each other intimately.

Stripping and trampling are images used in the ancient Mediterranean world. Within the Orphic mystery tradition, these images suggest that to receive illumination one must strip off all external trappings and reject them. In the Semitic world, this image is used to express victory over someone by putting them "under one's feet."

The overarching issue for every follower of Yeshua concerns, then, the soul's inner state and condition. It may be that these are tainted by fear and shame, keeping us from revealing ourselves, and therefore from seeing the divine Reality as it is. Just as surely as clothes can hide us, shame and fear too can also veil our eyes, preventing us from perceiving the reality of the son of the Living One. These must be counterpoised with joy and love which represent the state of the soul when it is in complete openness before the divine mystery. In the end, the mystery of self-revelation is this: in the act of mutual self-disclosure (to deeply see the essence of the Master and to be seen for who one truly is), we come ultimately to know our selves, for the son (as the child of the ***Anthropos***) is the mirror of our true Self. When we can reveal ourselves without veils or armoring, we will be able at last to see the one who fully reflects us, because his is the final revelation of who we will ultimately be.

QUESTIONS FOR REFLECTION

1. What would you want to know about the Master? If you could ask anything, what would you want him to reveal to you about himself?

2. What coverings (veils or armor) do you typically use that could be discarded and trampled under your feet?

3. Reflect on the terms **shame** and **fear** in relationship to your own experience. How do they relate to you and how do you experience them?

4. What would "trampling" look like if you did it metaphorically? How would that happen? How would you or other people know that this kind of inner activity was going on?

EXERCISES AND MEDITATIONS

1. To whom is it safe for you to make full disclosure? Fear is clearly an issue in this regard, because we feel so vulnerable (naked) when we do so. Would you feel comfortable being "naked" in this way with God? What might that mean? Can you imagine it? Would God also be vulnerable (naked)?
2. What does it mean to be naked without shame, or to see without fear? If this is to be a condition in your relationship with God, how might that kind of intimacy and level of deep relationship evolve?
3. If the ego acts as a kind of covering (or clothing), what does it mean to be naked (without the ego as veil or covering)? Can you imagine this state? Have you ever experienced this state? What was it like for you? How might you continue to live in this state before God? In a period of reflection, imagine this way of being yourself.
4. Have you ever had a vision of or encounter with the son of the Living One? What was that like? You might take a Gospel passage in which there is personal interaction between a person and Yeshua, and imagine yourself in place of that person. For example: Mark 7:32-35, 8:22-26, Luke 11:38-42, John 4:1-30. Read the passage slowly twice. Stop after each reading and go through the story in your mind's eye, picturing yourself seeing Yeshua and hearing the conversation unfold. When you do this, what do you experience? After you are finished, write your reflections in a journal.

READINGS FOR INSIGHT

I

Cyril of Jerusalem
Mystagogical Catechesis 2:2

So then once you entered, you took off your garment, and this was an image of taking off the old person with its deeds. Having taken this off, you were naked. ... How marvelous! You were naked in the sight of all and were not ashamed. For truly you were bearing a copy of the first-formed Adam, who in paradise was naked and not ashamed.

II

Jalaluddin Rumi
Rumi: The Book of Love
65-66

If you want spiritual poverty and emptiness,
you must be friends with a teacher.
Talking about it, reading books, and doing practices don't help.
Soul receives that knowing from soul.
The mystery of absence may be living in your pilgrim heart
and yet the knowing of it may not yet be yours.
Wait for the illuminated openness,
as though your chest were filling with light
as when God said, *Did we not expand you?* (Qur'an 57:4).
Don't look for it outside yourself.
There is a fountain inside you.
Don't walk around with an empty bucket,
you have a channel into the ocean,
yet you ask for water from a little pool.
Beg for the love expansion.
Meditate only on THAT
The Qur'an says, *And he is with you.* (57:4).

III

Eckhart Tolle
Stillness Speaks
58-59

Most people's lives are run by desire and fear. Desire is the need to *add* something to yourself in order to *be* yourself more fully. All fear is the fear of *losing* something and thereby becoming diminished and *being* less. These two movements obscure the fact that Being cannot be given or taken away. Being in its fullness is already within you, now.

IV

Kabir Edmund Helminski
Living Presence
144

Love returns us to unity that is reality. Reality is not the isolation, suspicion, envy, selfishness, and fear of loss that we have come to take for granted; it is that we are all part of one life. The same Spirit moves in us all. You come to know this better when you realize that we all have the same kinds of feelings, the same wish to be known and respected, to share ourselves and let down our defenses.

V

Jalaluddin Rumi

Love comes sailing through and I scream
Love sits beside me like a private supply of itself.
Love puts away the instruments
and takes off the silk robes.
Our nakedness together changes me completely.

LOGION 38

Yeshua says,

On many occasions
you have longed
to hear such words as
the ones that I am speaking to you,
but you had no one to go to.
The day will come again
when you will seek for me
but will not be able to find me.

Sapiential Themes

- *Yeshua's wisdom focuses upon the spiritual history of his students and the flow of events in time.*
- *The temporal realm is a stream where there are waves and troughs in which things both appear and disappear.*
- *During the temporal flow, humans experience longing and desire in which the divine Presence is at times revealed and at other times hidden.*

Parallel Texts

Proverbs 1:28
Isaiah 26:9
Matthew 13:10-17
Luke 6: 21, 10:23-24, 17:22

FOCAL POINT

In this Logion Yeshua may be speaking of a premonition or an intuition he has had about the future, and history certainly bears witness to the truth of what he says. Before long, his students will live in a world where his physical presence has been removed. He knows too that in that moment their inner state will be one of loss and confusion, and so, perhaps, he is preparing them. However, in the context of his previous statements (and in what is to follow), his words suggest that there is more at stake here than emotional or psychological loss. He is not simply predicting the future for their benefit. He is talking, instead, about the various states of spiritual pilgrimage which they will not only experience, but which are necessary if they are to know him fully. Paradoxically, he must be physically removed if they are ever to experience him as he is—if there is ever to be complete mutual self-revelation and self-disclosure between them.

Links

At first glance, it may seem that there is little or no linkage between this and the previous sayings—that Yeshua introduces a new topic entirely. However, in both this and the previous saying, the subject of manifestation or appearance (or the lack of it) is central. Though the focus may indeed be upon past history or future possibilities, and on whether the Master will be present then, this and previous sayings also suggest a linkage to the level of spirit, to the inner dynamics of spiritual journey within the heart in the present.

Notes

We learn more about the spiritual biography of Yeshua's students and their motivations for coming into the circle of his work and teaching in this saying. The implication is that in their early history they had experienced spiritual hunger and thirst, and that this longing made them receptive to Yeshua's words and sayings.

COMMENTARY

It would be easy to imagine that Yeshua is not only describing a difficult human experience in this saying, but that his students must do everything in their power to avoid the negative experience of absence in their future lives. Searching and not finding, as well as longing without satisfaction, are facts of human life, but are they negative? One might assume so. Imagine, however, that such experience might not be either negative or positive, but both. From the human perspective, absence feels negative, and we resist it. However, from the divine point of view, it may be necessary in order to propel the human journey across the temporal landscape.

Later, this saying will be amended by the statement that anyone who seeks will ultimately find (Logion 94), but perhaps between the seeking and the finding there is a gap of not-finding, or a period when no discovery is made. Perhaps, also, seeking and finding is a continuous process, and there are interruptions in which a sense of the divine Presence is missing.

The truth appears to be that humans need periods in which they know longing without satisfaction, and searching without finding, in order to progress forward. Without those gaps, and the experience of thirst they create, humans might be tempted to settle down and never explore further. Yeshua says that in the past his students were looking for something they could not find, and so their longing drove them onto the path of Yeshua's teaching. Now, they have someone to whom they can turn with their questions, and they receive answers which bring satisfaction. In his presence they feel they have at last found what they were looking for, but that is not to be the end of their journey. Again, the time will come when they discover that his presence is missing and that they must continue to search. The question is, of course, why would the Master absent himself, and what does it mean when it happens?

The experience of Presence is a privileged state in the Abrahamic traditions. The divine Presence is said to haunt human history. It will not let us go, but there is also a counterpart to the experience of Presence: absence. The experience of absence is an important part of the story of the human relationship to the Divine. The Song of Songs expresses the image of the divine Lover hiding behind the lattice-work of history, just beyond sight or sense, watching and waiting for the right moment to disclose himself and for revelation to occur.

Song of Songs 2:9

The students' future experience may parallel this image used in the wisdom tradition of the Hebrews. As their journey continues, they may not only know longing for the familiar words of their Master, they may also experience absence and longing for his presence again. Their thirst will be compounded, and perhaps they will feel that because they have lost both his voice and his presence, there is nothing left for them. So, other than the need to keep searching, why does Yeshua draw attention to this possibility? Could it be that this state is a means not only to draw us forward, but for the very stripping away of the unnecessary ego trappings that he talked about in the previous Logion? Could their longing, unsatisfied thirst, and unfulfilled desire be a way to remove the "clothing" behind which they continue to hide? Until they know this sense of loss and the stripping, he will be hidden from view, his presence unknown and never experienced,

In the natural progression of spiritual pilgrimage, one seeks and then finds, but then the spiral turns. As Logion 2 suggests, there is confusion and trouble and one must continue to search. It is a never ending process because there are layers of egoic coverings that must be removed in order to enter the Presence anew and hear the words of divine self-disclosure. These can be more easily stripped away when one is in a state of lack and longing. Crazy with desire, we may be willing to do what we would otherwise resist.

QUESTIONS FOR REFLECTION

1. When in the past have you had such an experience where you were longing to hear, find, or know something that you simply could not? What did this state of longing create in you? Did you give up, or did you continue your search? Why?

2. Have you ever been deeply satisfied by some teaching, guide, or introduction to truth that seemed to assuage the thirst or longing that you had previously known? Tell what that was and how it happened?

3. When you have found answers for which you were seeking, and were in a state of satisfaction, have you ever had the sense that this was not going to last?

You have perhaps seen the bumper sticker, "I Found It!" What sentiment does this statement represent? How do you feel when you read such a statement or hear that level of certainty in another person?

4. What is it like to have the answers and, feeling fulfilled, believe that you no longer need to search or know anything further? How is it to be in that state? Is it a good state to be in?

EXERCISES AND MEDITATIONS

1. In many different places in Yeshua's teachings and instructions to his students he says that they will experience difficulty, persecution, loss, and suffering. He is very clear about that. Often, however, we hear the rhetoric that if you are doing God's will none of this will or ever should happen to you—and if it does, it must be a sign of God's displeasure or some form of punishment. How have you experienced these difficult realities? Has your theological understanding been strong or broad enough to accommodate the complexities that you have encountered in life? In the spiritual traditions, we learn that suffering and difficulty are the means for broadening our understanding. At this point in time, where do you experience fear, loss or abandonment by God, or a sense of absence? What is the remedy for such a condition?

For example, in Logia 68 and 69 Yeshua speaks of the blessed state that suffering and persecution bring.

2. If you know that in the future there will be days of not-knowing and even despair, that you will have a sense that God has disappeared out of your life, what is the way to prepare for it? In some of the sacred teachings, this particular difficulty is placed in the category of "warrior training"—the way a spiritual warrior or athlete trains for difficulty or greater challenge. We like "safe training" where all our needs are instantly met and we feel no undue pressure, but we know from experience that this does not produce the strengthening that we will ultimately need. We can, of course, know all this ahead of time, but in the middle of the experience, it is easy to lose heart. We might turn to the teachings of the great spiritual trainers to learn and keep up our spirits.

*One important text of this kind that is often used in the Readings for Reflection is Pema Chödrön's **Comfortable With Uncertainty** (Boston: Shambhala, 2003)*

READINGS FOR INSIGHT

I

Those who don't feel this Love pulling them like a river,
those who don't drink dawn like a cup of springwater
or take in sunsets like supper,
those who don't want to change,
let them sleep.
This Love is beyond the study of theology,
that old trickery and hypocrisy.
If you want to improve your mind that way,
sleep on.
I've given up on my brain.
I've torn the cloth to shreds and thrown it away.
If you're not completely naked,
wrap your beautiful robe of words around you,
and sleep.

Jalaluddin Rumi
Like This
314

II

There is a glut of wealth in the city of Saba.
Everyone has more than enough. Even servants wear gold belts.
Huge grape clusters hang down on every street and brush the faces of the citizens.
No one has to do *anything*. ...
Everyone is fat and satiated with all the extras, and there are no robbers.
There is no energy for crime … or, for gratitude,
And no one wonders about the unseen world.
The people of Saba feel bored just with the mention of prophecy and revelation.
They have no desire of any kind – O, maybe some idle curiosity about miracles,
But that's it. This overrichness is a subtle disease.
Those who have it are blind to what is wrong, and deaf to anyone who points it out.
The city of Saba cannot be understood within itself.
But there is a cure, an individual medicine, not a social remedy:
Sit quietly, and listen for a voice within that says, ***Be***.
As that happens, your soul will start to revive.
Give up talking and your positions of power. Give up excessive money.
Turn toward your teachers and the prophets who don't live in Saba.
They can help you grow sweet again and fragrant,
Wild and fresh again, and thankful for any small event.

Jalaluddin Rumi
The Soul of Rumi

III

In this dark night I have lost the path of the quest.
Come, then, O star that guides us.
Go where I may, my anguish does but grow—
Beware this desert, this endless road.

Hafez
The Green Sea of Heaven
22

IV

When your heart is consumed with longing and burned to ashes, the breeze of Love arises and sweeps up the ashes, and fills heaven and earth with the utterly burnt ones.

Kharaqani
Perfume in the Desert
131

LOGION 39

Sapiential Themes

- *Yeshua details a sophianic tragedy.*
- *Religion itself often becomes the barrier to sacred knowledge.*
- *Sacred knowledge is a key that unlocks doors to the inner dimensions of the sacred.*
- *Two animals (serpent and dove) are used as metaphors to correct the situation and help give access to sacred knowledge.*

Yeshua says,

Your scholars and religious leaders have taken the keys of knowledge and locked them away.
They have not used them
to enter in, nor have they allowed those desiring to do so.
You, therefore, must be as subtle as serpents and
as guileless as doves.

Parallel Texts

Logion 102
Matthew 5:20, 10:16, 23:13
Luke 11:52

Links

There is more than one cause for the absence of the sacred and the transcendent in human experience. Religions themselves can actively promote spiritual blindness. It is a danger, and sometimes a great sickness that overcomes a religious manifestation. Yeshua is also perhaps subtly warning about possibilities that lie ahead for those who carry his own message of recovery into the world.

FOCAL POINT

The natural question raised by Logion 38 is why, after knowing Yeshua, would some of his students seek him and not be able to find him? Some reasons have to do with the normative cycles of spiritual development on the sacred path. There are, however, other causes occurring in almost all religious histories. This saying posits just such causes as having to do with the degeneration of Spirit in the state of religious affairs in Yeshua's own world. He addresses the trouble that lies at the heart of the Hebrew faith tradition. The Jewish people were given a revelation and great insight, but their tendency was to hide it away and exclude others as unworthy of their sacred knowledge. Even the common Jewish worshipper was regarded in that manner—as unworthy of receiving from the treasury of sacred knowledge. Yeshua has come to use those same keys to open the door and bring its riches from the treasury into the life of everyday people. They are to receive what religion itself has kept hidden and guarded.

Notes

The term "the keys of knowledge" could just as easily be translated directly from the Coptic text as, "the keys of gnosis." Modern men and women have been made aware that in later Church history this tem ***gnosis*** *was given heretical connotations. Thereafter, wherever it appeared it became suspect. Here, however, it is used in a neutral manner.*

COMMENTARY

Some would say that the use of the term ***gnosis*** *is evidence of at least an incipient form of Gnosticism in this text. The word, however, appears elsewhere in both the writings of the Christian Scriptures and in early Patristic texts in exactly the way it is used here: to mean simply a form of knowing available from and about the sacred.*

There are unique moments when a prophet, a seer, or some enlightened being rises on the horizon of human history and throws open the doors to Reality. Obstructions are destroyed and even common folk are invited onto the pathway of sacred knowing. The way seems so clear at those time, but how quickly those passageways often disappear, blocked by those who follow in the conventional religious tradition. The state of religious affairs in any given period of history can be problematic. More often than not, religion becomes its own worst enemy, preventing the very thing it was designed to promote: an understanding of the sacred mysteries. The gift of religion in its purest form, can bind humanity to Ultimate Reality. But instead, it may all too often bind our freedom, not allowing us to see and know Truth. The very organization which declares itself to be a way into divine Reality, often becomes a barrier to that way.

This, as well as other texts, shows how great a gap existed between Yeshua's understanding and those within his own tradition whose minds were firmly fixed within rigid doctrinal limits and the received interpretations of the tradition. Perhaps out of good intention to protect the truth from corruption (or else out of some deep distrust or fear), individuals who have been given gifts from that treasury attempt to hide away the keys that would make it available to all. Later, the danger becomes clear: the same individuals who threaten him now will later take his life.

Logion 62
Matthew 13:11
Mark 4:11
Luke 8:10
I Corinthians 2:7
Ephesians 1:9, 3:3-4, 9

This Logion, however, offers us a key to opening the door to the mysteries of knowledge, and a way of understanding Yeshua's own work and vision using that knowledge. In the very details of his denunciation, new ways of seeing the truth appear. First, it is clear that an important form of knowing is indeed involved on Yeshua's path. Second (as he says later in this Gospel as well as in the canonical texts), his concern is to offer knowledge about the mysteries. But what are these mysteries to which he refers? One way of understanding them (supported also by such texts as the Letter to the Ephesians) is to say that there is a "deep structure" (or hidden purpose) behind all of existence which determines not only its outer form, but where it is going: its destiny. The key to understanding that purpose now exists, but access is being blocked.

These mysteries and inner dimensions are explicitly spelled out throughout the entire Gospel of Thomas.

The question is, how is the truth blocked? One possible answer is provided by the text itself. Yeshua says that the scholars and religious leaders who hold the keys will not go inside, nor will they allow anyone else in. This image suggests that there is both an outside and an inside dimension to religious phenomena. The exterior (or exoteric) forms of religion are what hide the interior (esoteric) dimensions and realities. It is this interior dimension that Yeshua is bringing to his own Jewish tradition. He is concerned with the "inside of things" and the revelation of the mysteries held by Jewish tradition. However, those concerned only with the exoteric forms will not allow anyone access to the inner dimensions, nor do they avail themselves of that knowledge. So to gain access one must use certain strategies—illustrated metaphorically by doves and snakes—images which carry traditional and historical meanings for the Jewish peoples. In their native habitat, snakes are quiet. Though dangerous, they are also cunning, wise, and capable of subterfuge. In the face of exoteric opposition, these characteristics in a seeker are crucial. On the other hand, a dove is harmless and non-violent, and yet capable of transcendent travel or flight. These images speak directly to the tactics which a sincere seeker must use as well.

QUESTIONS FOR REFLECTION

1. Have you ever experienced the outer form of religion not as an invitation, but as a barrier? What has been your experience? Have you ever yourself been a barrier to sacred knowledge for others?

2. What are the inner dimensions of sacred knowledge to which you have access now?

3. Is there such a thing as "false esoterism?" How can you tell the difference between true and false esoterism?

4. How have you ever acted as a serpent or a dove, or observed those positive qualities in someone else? Describe what you have done or observed.

There are many teachings today that claim to be the true inner dimension of an external religious tradition. Some of these may prove to be inauthentic or only partial.

EXERCISES AND MEDITATIONS

1. If religion represents a genuine revelation from above, holding keys which unlock the doors of knowledge, how does one use the key to gain access? If religions themselves (and religious leaders entrusted with a tradition's riches) become obstacles to spiritual progression, preventing further growth in themselves and in others, how can you determine that? To circumvent these barriers, and to find and use the keys again, you must develop skills and strategies illustrated by doves and serpents in the animal kingdom. It might be useful to take these metaphors seriously and study the behaviors of these creatures in the wild, and then apply what you learn to your own behavior. Take time to observe, read about, study, or do an on-line search to help define these characteristic features. Write out what you learn. Take what you learn into a period of meditation and reflect on how they might apply to your own experience.
2. Yeshua uses these animal metaphors because they are familiar creatures not only to his geographic region, but also to the sacred texts of the Hebrew Scriptures. Do a search of the Hebrew Bible, and find out about the positive use of these metaphors as sacred images.
3. Explore the inner, spiritual, or mystical dimension of another tradition held in some traditional form that seems alien or strange to you, and see what you can find about that tradition. For example, you might explore Kabbalistic Judaism, Sufism within Islam, or the Vedanta within Hinduism. There are many texts available on these traditions. An on-line search over the Internet is also a fruitful place to begin.

READINGS FOR INSIGHT

I

Things fall apart; the centre cannot hold;
mere anarchy is loosed upon the world. ...
The best lack all conviction, while the worst
are full of passionate intensity.
Surely some revelation is at hand;
surely the Second Coming is at hand. ...
And what rough beast, its hour come round at last
Slouches toward Bethlehem to be born?

William Butler Yeats

II

All will come again into its strength:
the fields undivided, the water undammed,
the trees towering and the walls built low.
And in the valleys, people as strong
and varied as the land.

And no churches where God
is imprisoned and lamented
like a trapped and wounded animal.
The houses welcoming all who knock
and a sense of boundless offering
in all relations, and in you and me.

Rainer Maria Rilke
Book of Hours
Love Poems to God
121

III

Those who have faith in the envoys according to inner vision are Muslims, people who have surrendered themselves and do not allow themselves to enter into interpretations. They are of two kinds: either someone who has faith, and has surrendered and relinquished any knowledge of this to Him until he dies—he is called to follow of another's authority. Or it is someone who acts through what he knows of the details of the revealed law and who has firm faith in what the envoys and sacred books have brought. Then God lifts the veil from his inner vision and makes him a possessor of inner vision in his affairs, just as He did with His Prophet and Messenger and the people to whom He was solicitous. He gave them unveiling and inner vision, and they called to God "according to inner vision," just as God said about His Prophet, giving news concerning him: "I call to God according to inner vision, I and those who follow me," Those who follow him are the knowers of God, the gnostics, though they are neither messengers nor prophets. They follow clear proof from their Lord in their knowledge of Him and what has come from Him.

Ibn al-'Arabi
Futuhat al-Makkiyya
I:218

IV

I find nothing more destructive to the well-being of life
than to support a god that makes you feel unworthy and in debt to it.
I imagine erecting churches to such a strange god will assure
endless wars that commerce loves.
A god that could frighten is not a god—but an insidious idol
and weapon in the hands of the insane.

Meister Eckhart
Love Poems From God
115

LOGION 40

Yeshua says,

A grapevine was planted away from its Source where it remains unprotected. It will be torn out by its roots and destroyed.

Sapiential Themes

- *The grapevine is one of the images used by Yeshua referring to the organic nature of spiritual reality as the living plant meant for the good of humanity.*
- *Transcendence through the inner dimension, is the native soil for the metaphoric vine.*
- *Religion planted firmly in the exoteric lives in "foreign soil," in a place where it cannot thrive.*
- *The natural consequence of unprotected living is eventual destruction*

Parallel Texts

Psalm 1
Matthew 15:10-20
John 15:1-17

FOCAL POINT

A religion maintained and protected only by external forms and expressed as a rigid orthodoxy, though it may seem strong, is actually quite vulnerable. Yeshua's religious world was held captive in such rigidity, kept from the life-giving nurturance of its original Source. As a revelatory tradition Jewish religion assumed that in all its proclamations it was manifesting the Source. Yeshua saw differently—that the religious leaders of his day were deluded and making false assumptions. That religious vine, though apparently viable, was nonetheless vulnerable, for Yeshua knew its inner dimensions were missing. This message was at the forefront of Yeshua's teachings. He focused attention on the fact that the religious tradition which existed all around him was disconnected from its true Source, and would therefore suffer destruction.

Links

The dire warning given in this Logion appears to be in direct response to the previous saying about the negative consequences of the religious tradition to which Yeshua belonged. In this Logion and the one before it Yeshua is deliberately shifting the emphasis away from the exoteric norms, toward the One Source at the Center—the wellspring of the sacred—and criticizing the over-emphasis on exoterism.

Notes

The text does not say that God will uproot the unprotected vine not planted in the Source, but that it will be uprooted and destroyed. Perhaps this is a natural consequence of its unprotected state—an inevitability for anything that lives away from its true cause.

COMMENTARY

The Gospel of Thomas: The Wisdom of the Twin. *Lynn C. Bauman, (White Cloud, 2004), 89*

To better understand this saying we must use the academic version to help us see certain nuances in the text more clearly. *They have planted a grapevine outside the Father and have not protected it. It will be pulled up by its roots and destroyed.* If the sayings collected in the Gospel of Thomas are indeed juxtaposed to one another as a means of interpretation, then the "they" referred to in this saying are the same religious leaders and scholars of the last Logion, and the grapevine is a reference to the living plant symbolic of the spiritual body which sacred traditions are designed to protect. But those whose responsibility it is to protect such a living entity have planted it in a place **outside** the Source (in the domain of the exoteric), where, like all temporal entities, it will be destroyed. Rather than drawing its life from the heart of Reality, religious authorities had maintained that religious identity through strict adherence to external forms.

Within religious orthodoxy the case is often made that the only truth available to humanity comes explicitly through the symbols and revelation of that particular tradition of which it is the guarantee. The Jewish religious leaders of Yeshua's day certainly felt this way. Their proscriptions for truth excluded anyone but themselves. Their favored interpretations of the sacred texts were the only explanations allowed. The sources of their authority were the exoteric propositions set out by the tradition over time and the privilege of their power to enforce them. For them, anything outside these norms failed the test of true religion.

It is clear that Yeshua experienced the religious norms of his day as a shell devoid of Spirit and the Presence of the One who is the Source of All. As an empty shell Jewish tradition maintained its outer appearance through rigid forms perpetuated by power and authority. The truth was, however, that it had become disconnected from its original ground, and could not bring its members into living contact with the eternal sap which is the spiritual life-stream of humanity. The very thing that religion was designed to do—unite humanity to its Source—was no longer possible. It was playing a false role as channel for the sacred, but the actual function was missing.

In contrast to the emphasis on external control, Yeshua offered direct access to the Source—***Abba***—the life force which binds all things into a perfect, organic unity. It was this greening power, the Spirit of wisdom and compassion flowing through him and all things and holding all things in consubstantial relationship, that Yeshua knew. To illustrate his teaching he used living plants (trees, vines, grain, and bushes) as metaphors to demonstrate its life-giving power (the principle and force of "greening") which flows through all things. Metaphorically this same power to make alive is the life-force of renewal that is needed to sustain religion itself. Coming from Transcendence outside of space-time and human control, this greening power is able to create life, bring things into being, and reanimate them even if they die. Humans also have the potential of uniting to this "vine" and becoming channels for its energy, helping to shape and bring renewal to the world. However, by making the outer reality its primary Source, religion loses its true Center at the expense of the living "plant" it was designed to protect.

There are indeed counterfeit manifestations of religion as a living entity which appear to be alive and yet are unable to access Transcendence. Like the individual whose peripheral self becomes the (self) center of its own small world and becomes paralyzed by egoism, religion too becomes self-centered, protecting only its power, self-interests, and the perimeters of its external forms.

Elsewhere Yeshua has said that as a living vine he is connected to the Source. Anyone united to him receives the power of greening. Anything not connected to and drawing its existence from the Infinite and Eternal Source as he does, dwells only in impermanence and change, and so will pass out of existence. Like a whirlpool it appears as an eddy in the current of time and then passes away. Conversely, all things coming from the Source and returning to the Source (as Father or Origin), take their existence from the stability of the Eternal and the Absolute. So religious orthodoxy cannot be protected by carefully managing its external forms, but only by fortifying itself from within. Like taking vitamins and strengthening the immune defense system, true health and vitality comes only when the interior is balanced and inwardly fortified. Yeshua's message is quite clear, only by being rooted in its original soil will humanity survive the vicissitudes of

QUESTIONS FOR REFLECTION

1. Have you ever planted something in a particular kind of soil that is not conducive to a plant's growth, for example, cactus in peat moss? What happens when you do?

Suppose by analogy that you are like a plant. What does this saying mean in relationship to your life?

2. How do you discern the difference between a religious manifestation deeply rooted in its Source from one that is not? What is the difference?

EXERCISES AND MEDITATIONS

1. Imagine that within yourself there exist different "soil types" in which some things grow better and other do not. Yeshua's own parable about the seeds which fell on four kinds of soils suggests this. If you were to do a topographical mapping of your own soul, what kinds of soils and climates might you find there—for example, you could imagine the cultural soil in which your social system grows as one variety. Now suppose that some plantings of Spirit do not do well in cultural soil, but need something else entirely. How might you envision this and what might you do to ensure that these soils are available?

See Logion 9
Matthew 8:4-8, 11-15, 13:3-9
Mark 4:2-9, 4:13-20

2. Read the following Psalm (1) in light of this Logion. How could it be interpreted as a commentary on Yeshua's words? Notice, too, the images it uses about humans.

Blessed, O blessed, I say are those who walk upon a path
whose steps are firmly planted on your eternal law,
For in that word they find their joy, their meditation day and night,
and do not wander far to take the counsels of the worldly wise.
These "wise-of-word" speak guile, their scorn of you is made from prideful
seats above the masses far below.
But the blessed ones grow strong as living trees,
their roots sink deep and hidden
Beside the flowing streams which come from you.
And through life's passing seasons
They do not cease to bear a plenitude of fruit,
nor do they fade from giving shade of leaf that covers all with good.
While on the other path there is no shade or water near,
and all life withers quickly in the winds that blow across the grass.
So when the sad results of wickedness give witness to their lives
they fall away and have no place in your eternal circle of the wise.
You guard and guide the path that leads to life
and those who walk in right-relationship to all.
But those who choose the other path?
Their steps lead surely into doom.

Lynn C. Bauman
Ancient Songs Sung Anew
(Praxis 2000), 1

READINGS FOR INSIGHT

I

When your actions and thoughts strike that living spark in you,
Engendering your soul,
You work from that subterranean flow of joy
That runs like a laughing torrent in you.
All other origins bring only dried fruit, no love,
No energy sinews your emotive being.
Be not made hollow by the nose of others,
Lead by the nose by blind and devious men.
There's one way which leads to the spring,
One rope to use for the bucket to scoop up clean water
—the trackless way of selflessness.

Raficq Abdulla
Words of Paradise
90

II

The Water of Life which flows from the Source of All Being becomes manifested *concretely* in the living teacher. If ***Khidr*** (in Arabic ***khadir*** is green, and hence ***al-Khidr*** is the Green Man—the force of life) is the archetypal life force behind the spiritual journey, then the contemporary, living teacher is the earthly manifestation of this life force. Without a link with a teacher, real transformation may not come about easily. Or if it does come about, it might dwindle after a while. But when one becomes connected to a living teacher, life cannot continue along its former routes. Things start changing. All those who have been seriously interested in spiritual life know this from their own experience. Most difficulties on the path arise because, although the seeker craves change, he does not really want to give up anything. The teacher, like ***Khidr***, has therefore a twofold aspect: he comes across as a merciful, nourishing benefactor; but he can also appear as a ruthless, uncompromising demolisher of habits and thought-forms. *He first seduces, then executes, then revives.* ... The contact with a teacher according to all mystical traditions, assures that the seeker does not fall back into the sleep of unconsciousness and mechanical existence. The teacher, like ***Khidr***, is both the reviver of dead souls and the destroyer of illusions. Like ***Khidr***, he too stands at the meeting point of the opposites within oneself.

Sara Sviri
The Taste of Hidden Things
93-94

III

Like all gardens, the gardens are temporal rather than spatial organisms. They must be cultivated in time, living time. All depends upon the right gesture at the right moment, and each moment is alive and drawn beyond itself by the whole in which it participates. Living time is immanent in the seasons, in the daily, hourly rhythms of climate, weather, and the moon, sun, and stars. Such time is fecund and enclosed, like the garden itself is. It seems to flow backward and forward, and round about, continuously circulating, teleological, connecting seed and fruit. Throughout the garden, fruit calls to seed and seed calls to fruit, and through the stages between seed and fruit, time nurtures and proliferates the infinite, harmonious infolding of the vitality, the regenerative power, the freshness of nature. Hildegard of Bingen calls the invisible sap *viriditas*, "greenness"—"the greenness of a paradise that knows no fall."

Christopher Bamford
An Endless Trace
275

LOGION 41

Yeshua says,

To the one who has
something in hand,
more will be given.
To the one whose hands hold nothing
even that "nothing" will be taken away.

Sapiential Themes

- *Contraries and the coincidence of opposites are modes of sapiential teaching.*
- *To possess and not possess are states each human being experiences on the path of wisdom. What these states mean in reality must be lived.*
- *In this saying conflicting interpretations play against each other.*

Parallel Texts

Logion 70
Matthew 13:10-13, 25:14-30
Mark 4:24-25
Luke 8:18, 19:11-27

FOCAL POINT

The focus of this Logion is upon the contraries, gain and loss. Are these what they seem? In traditional wisdom discourse, paradoxes, parables, contraries and opposites go hand in hand. This saying is a prime example of such opposites or contraries expressed throughout this Gospel text. Here, Yeshua is using the tension created by a contrast not only to illustrate wisdom's message but to push his students into living with and beyond the tension. The questions are, what do we possess, and what is being stripped away? Are they what they seem, or is it a matter of false perception? Is having "more" a positive, or a negative. Is the second state of "nothingness" a loss or, in the end, an advantage? It is hard to determine the answer from the outside. One must live these paradoxes to know.

Links

If one perceives the condition that Yeshua has just described in the last Logion as a kind of lack or emptiness in the state of religious affairs, then clearly this saying is a commentary on what happens to religion devoid of contact with its Source. This is also a follow-on from Logion 39 which describes both the absence of knowledge and the protection of spiritual knowledge exhibited by the religious authorities of Yeshua's day.

Notes

Paradoxes and contraries are native to the wisdom traditions because they see the nature of reality as a web of competing and sometimes conflicting forces. One cannot be wise and disregard the coincidence of opposites. Wisdom teaches humanity how to recognize and live with these contraries. Using them Yeshua is a supreme wisdom teacher.

COMMENTARY

A paradox occurs when one side of a contrary is not only an opposite, but violates the law of non-contradiction—if something is true, then logically, its opposite cannot be true.

At its core, the transmission of traditional wisdom engages complementary opposites (contraries)—nothing and something, giving more and taking something away. In the end (and as a result), on an intellectual level, wisdom teaching becomes profoundly difficult to the rational mind. Paradox, however, expresses the nature of reality as we experience it in the midst of contrasting forces and the clash of our own competing desires. As a part of the corpus of wisdom, these sayings also help to form a more complete metaphysic which says that opposites occur on many different levels of Reality and must therefore be held in complementarity. In this saying surplus and poverty, emptiness and fullness constitute polarities and contraries which can themselves be understood as opposites—in either a positive or negative way. Thus the contraries and paradoxes increase exponentially.

In truth this saying may point in two different hermeneutical directions. One interpretive possibility points in the direction of the last saying concerning religious exoterism, and the other toward the next saying on interior spiritual praxis. Each interpretation appears to contradict the other, but both are part of a whole which makes up the domain of wisdom.

Religion as an empty cipher means that it is devoid of the esoteric dimensions, spirituality, or interiority.

In this Logion Yeshua probes the relationship between a certain kind of possession and its absence as a form of nothingness. After reading the last saying, one can certainly see this Logion as an explanation of what happens when the tree of religious tradition is planted away from its Source. The result is nothingness. If one possesses (is planted in) the Source, then indeed there will be "more," perhaps in abundance. If, however, one holds nothing from the Source, and in fact becomes the cause of emptiness, even that little bit (religion as an empty cipher) will itself be taken away (uprooted and destroyed, as the last saying indicates). So on the one hand, possessing even a little from the Source will result in a growing custody, on the other, becoming a guardian of "nothing" strips one of guardianship.

We often assume that because we have so little in hand, our relative poverty means that nothing more can or should be expected. Since we feel that the divine owes us nothing, we expect nothing. This attitude fails to see what the potential energies of even the little that we do hold actually are. If we feel that because of our religious or social status (guaranteed by external authority), we possess much (when in fact may we possess little or nothing of value), we will lose even that, for in the end religious dogmatism fails and is a false claim. Both attitudes are often at the center of religious and spiritual life. Humans think in these ways, but Wisdom knows differently.

The way to this fullness through emptiness will be explored more fully in the next Logion.

Suppose, then, that there is another entirely different way to understand this saying—one that is rooted in another insight—that poverty (nothingness and emptiness) is a state of ultimate blessedness. In this case the absence (in terms of religious exoterism) would mean an eventual fullness of spirit, but one that was known only in the state of complete emptiness. Any "fullness of self" and the "more" it promised (for example, the abundance of material goods) would mitigate against the nothingness of poverty. In our ordinary consciousness we imagine that having our "nothingness" taken away is the ultimate destruction, but as Yeshua says elsewhere, "Blessed are the poor in Spirit for theirs is the kingdom of God." Here nothingness leads to something greater—fullness-through-emptiness.

QUESTIONS FOR REFLECTION

1. When faced with contraries (for example, gain and loss), what is your typical response?

2. There are two possible interpretations suggested in the commentary. Which one is more convincing or appeals to you? Why is this so?

3. When have you experienced a "little bit" becoming more? When have you experienced that "little bit of nothing" being taken away? Is the latter experience always a negative? When or how have you experienced it as a positive?

Explore those losses in the past that later became gains, and those gains which turned out in the end to be empty.

EXERCISES AND MEDITATIONS

1. Many times we doubt ourselves or that what we hold is precious or of value. The thinking sometimes is, "If it was of value, I wouldn't be in possession of it!" That thought denigrates the treasure with which each person has been gifted from the Transcendent Source. What is it that you hold inside yourself to which more may be added? What do you carry as treasure from the Source? You may never have thought about this, but it is worth consideration. In a time of meditation, ask the divine Guide, to make this "something" clearer to you.
2. In light of the meditation above, read the two stories that Yeshua told in the canonical Gospels concerning the talents (Matthew 25:14-30, and Luke 19:11-27). How do these illustrate this saying, or clarify the gift you may have been given?
3. Often we hold on to what turns out in the end to be an illusion. We discover that it has been empty (nothing but our fantasy) all along. The truth is we must be stripped of such illusory objects to which we often cling. Think about what you hold onto that may be a "nothing," but with which you have invested a part of yourself. Sometimes we use such objects to support a sense of who we are—our identity. Are you holding on to some illusion which you feel that if you lost would diminish you? The exercise of finding out the answer to this question can be quite frightening because it deeply touches our sense of who we are (or at least, think ourselves to be). Take time to reflect on this question. Journal your discoveries over a period of time (days, weeks, even months) until you have further clarity. Talk about this exercise with a trusted friend.
4. How can your own experience of emptiness become a kind of divine gift? If what turned out ultimately to be "nothing" was stripped away from you, how would you respond? In the end, how might you come to accept that you are enhanced by this experience?

One important definition for the ego is precisely our self-identity that is often attached to objects and material goods to which we tie our personal image and sense of self worth.

READINGS FOR INSIGHT

I

Human intelligence contains knowledge of the Divine Being who embodies the Absolute Reality and the Universal Good. Intelligence thus envisioned leads to a profound desire and a deep aspiration on the part of humanity to partake of that knowledge and internalize it within as a defining truth. The natural consequence of the knowledge of God is the desire to achieve the promises of that knowledge, to realize the full potential of that reality, and to be good in view of the principial Good. When the state of mind and heart achieves a consciousness of these universal possibilities, "the kingdom of God" will then indeed be "within you" (Luke 17:21).

John Herlihy
Borderlands of the Spirit
62-63

II

All theologies are straws His Sun burns to dust;
Knowing takes you to the Threshold, but not through the Door.
Nothing can teach you if you don't unlearn everything.
How learned I was before Revelation made me dumb.
You are a sea of gnosis hidden in a drop of dew,
You are a whole universe hidden in a sack of blood.
What are all this world's pleasures and joys
That you keep grasping at them to make you alive?
Does the sun borrow light from a mote of dust?
Does Venus look for wine from a cracked jug?

Raficq Abdulla
Words of Paradise
90

III

Love is the flame which, when it blazes,
consumes everything other than the Beloved.
The lover wields the sword of *Nothingness* in order to dispatch all but God:
consider what remains after *Nothing*.
There remains *but God*: all the rest is gone.
Praise to you, O might Love, destroyer of all other "gods."

Kabir Helminski
The Rumi Collection
162

IV

Abundance is seeking the beggars and the poor, just as beauty seeks a mirror.
beggars, then, are the mirrors of God's bounty,
and they that are with God are united with Absolute Abundance.

Kabir Helminski
The Rumi Collection
168

V

... the meaning of having "something in hand" has nothing to do with material wealth, but instead concerns the capacity to give of ourselves. It also means having love and self-knowledge, or gnosis. Without this gnosis, any possibility of understanding the world will be denied to us ... If we cannot give love, even the little we have will be taken from us.

Jean-Yves Leloup
The Gospel of Thomas
128

VI

You must be emptied of that with which are full,
so you may be filled with that whereof you are empty.

St. Augustine

LOGION 42

Yeshua says,

Come into being
as you pass
away

Sapiential Themes

- *This aphorism concentrates wisdom's powerful injunction, expressing opposite modes of action.*
- *Simplicity of phraseology masks interpretive complexity in this Logion.*
- *Multiple possibilities in translation mark differing interpretations.*
- *Detachment and letting go are crucial practices in the processes of human becoming.*

Parallel Texts

Matthew 10:1-23
John 16:28
I Corinthians 7:31
II Corinthians 4:16
Hebrews 11:9
I John 2:17

FOCAL POINT

In the original Coptic, this saying is made up of two simple phrases or worlds and is the shortest and most cryptic of all the collected Logia in the Gospel of Thomas. Interpretive emphasis can be placed on either of the two words or phrases, shifting the meaning of this text in important ways. The first word is "become." The second phrase is "as you pass away." Depending, of course, on how you translate these words into English, the stress in the meaning will fall on either of the phrases. The possibility is that Yeshua intends emphasis on both meanings which (continuing the method of using contraries) appear to contradict to one another. In other translations the two ideas are often combined to form a more neutral meaning, such as, "become passersby."

Links

If we understand that the final phrase in Logion 41 could be interpreted positively—that having even a little bit stripped away—is ultimately a great gain, then this saying is a further reflection on the process of letting go what small amount one may have in hand.

Notes

Such a short statement gives rise to multiple translations. In addition to the one chosen above, others might be: "Come to be as you are passing away," "become yourself as you pass away," or simply, "Become (or be) passersby."

COMMENTARY

By definitions aphorisms and proverbs are short, pithy sayings that deliver wisdom condensed or concentrated into a few words or phrases. This saying, the shortest of all of Thomas' collection, expresses just such power in a few, short words. Underneath the syntactical simplicity, however, there appears to be a great hermeneutical complexity. The conventional translations have tended to objectify these phrases translating them similarly to, "become passersby." The original Coptic, however, is more active. Movement and action are clearly expressed in this Logion, and in some sense appear to be opposite from each other—coming into being (becoming), and passing away (or passing out of existence). However, it may be possible to understand these movements as a form of "mutual arising:" one comes into being as one passes away. Though they may be together they express a double action that is mutually interdependent; as one action occurs so does its opposite.

The concept and term "mutual arising" is drawn from Buddhism which sees the universe-in-flux and ourselves within it in a constant state of interdependent creation.

If emphasis is placed on the first word then something is indeed emerging into existence at the very moment that existence itself appears to be passing away. The object which arises out of impermanence is a subject who is becoming. If as we see that impermanence is the state of the universe all around us, then nothing is fixed—all is in flux. The only permanent feature of the universe is change itself. This is the nature of reality as we experience it, and yet this background of constant flux is the stage upon which humans come to be, becoming who they are truly destined to be.

Impermanence and flow are primary ways that the Eastern traditions, in particular, Hinduism, Buddhism and Taoism, understand the universe to manifest.

What the wisdom of Yeshua wants us to see concerns the nature of reality as it is (in a state of constant fluctuation), and how to use that very fact as a means of coming fully into being as a human self. Typically, we experience impermanence as a challenge to who we are (in particular to the ego). This in fact may be the point. The ego itself is an ever-changing, impermanent feature of ourselves, but in traditional teaching there is a more permanent Self, a higher Self that must arise and be recognized for what it is—the true Self. It is this Self that comes into being as the egoic-self passes away. This interpretation is in line with Yeshua's other teachings found in the canonical Gospels about the loss of the self (or ***psuche***) in order to find (or gain) the true Self.

Matthew 10:39, 16:25, Mark 8:35, Luke 9:24

A further aspect of this powerful text is on the praxis of detachment—the letting go that is the basis for the mutual arising of the true Self. Not only is the reality around us impermanent and passing away, we must actively practice letting it go when all our instincts in our impermanent world are to cling to what can never stay. The practice of letting go (and remaining in a state of non-attachment) is also a wisdom at the center of traditional spiritual teaching.

Ecclesiastes 3:1-11

To be a "passerby" is to become a wise being who allows things to arrive and then lets them go in the natural flow of impermanence, never clinging, never attempting to make the world secure for our own egoic purposes. Traditional Hebrew wisdom saw this clearly, and the writings of the Hebrew sages are in agreement (that there is a "time for everything") but that these ebb and flow in the passage of time. To become a "passerby" means, then, that one acknowledges the impermanence and then one actively releases it from one's grasp. To participate in the stripping away into "nothingness" (a possible interpretation of the last Logion) is an act of interior spiritual discipline, and the condition in which the state of "blessedness" can ultimately appear. Rationally this may make no sense, and our impulse is just the opposite. It takes spiritual courage and strength to pass by the world of beautiful

QUESTIONS FOR REFLECTION

1. It is important to know that the process of our own becoming is something in which we ourselves participate. Our attitudes and ways of being in this world either help to solidify a limited image of ourselves, or allow a new form of being to emerge. It is not always clear what the new form will be—but in the Christian tradition it is modeled after the pattern of Yeshua's own nature. The question is, how are you participating in this unfolding? What can you do?

2. Have you noticed your own attachments to things, ideas, and images of yourself? What are your primary attachments? What happens when you try to let them go?

EXERCISES AND MEDITATIONS

1. Though it is the shortest Logion, in practice it may be the most difficult. First, we must understand its meaning, and then we must begin to experience that meaning in daily life. Wisdom demands that we not only know the meaning intellectually, but put it into practice in our normal living—becoming the meaning. Having read the commentary, choose one of the exercises below to begin your work of practice.
2. Notice how quickly things change around and inside yourself. You will see that not only do your circumstances change constantly, but you yourself are changing from moment to moment (your moods, emotions and thoughts). How do you react to this river-flow of change? Most people pick something (a thought, an image, an idea, an object) and make that their focus. For example, they may decide that they are conservatives or liberals, or that they must have a new car or house, find a new mate, or get a new job. None of these are in themselves harmful, unless we use them to define who we are and become something external to our true essence. As things, events, and you yourself quickly pass through and then out of existence, who are you becoming? Are you the objects you attach yourself to, or something else entirely? If you are not the things around you, then who are you? Meditate and journal your insights to these questions.
3. If this Logion is translated, "Be passersby," this is similar to other Semiticisms for "not holding onto anything." In spiritual literature this is also called detachment, or non-attachment from things. In an act of non-possession, "letting things go" is also known as "spiritual poverty," understood to be the ideal spiritual state in which one can receive inner abundance and wisdom. We tend to hold onto positive moods and good feelings, or in other cases, resentments and bad feelings. We could simply let these go when they arise and fall away in the stream of events and experiences. Experiment and allow things to be what they are and then pass away without attempting to attach yourself or your image to any of them. Especially practice letting resentments go. Journal what you experience through this exercise. Share your findings with others.

In the section which follows, Readings for Insight, it is clear that this same idea and idiom is used in Middle Eastern culture in many different periods of history.

READINGS FOR INSIGHT

I

Phil Cousineau
The Art of Pilgrimage
126

Pilgrim,
pass by that which you cannot love.

II

Inscribed over the gateway to the city of Fateh-pur-Sikri in India By Moghul emperor, Akbar

The prophet Isa [Yeshua], peace be upon him, said this:
The world is a bridge.
Pass over it,
but do not make your home there.

III

Al-Kalabadhi
quoted in Sara Sviri
The Taste of Hidden Things
153

The mystic passes away from what belongs to himself, and persists through what belongs to God … When "centered" he is also "dispersed," … He is "absent" and "intoxicated" because his power of discrimination has passed away, and in this sense all things become one to him.

IV

A Hadith of the Prophet Muhammad

Be in this world as if you are a traveler, a passerby, with your clothes and shoes full of dust. Sometimes you will sit under the shade of a tree, sometimes you will walk in the desert. Be a passerby always, for this world is not your home.

V

Maria Jaoudi
Christian Mysticism East and West
19

Mere emotional reactions have the capability to engulf us in their virulence of anger, hatred, and judgmental narrow-mindedness. Indeed, we often become so attached to our emotional blocks that the reaction itself becomes reality to us. Here is where the wisdom of detachment, guarding one's thoughts, and spiritual warfare become obvious. If strong, violent emotions are internally identified, we can halt them at the gate of our hearts, dismantle them, and choose to comprehend the why of our reaction. Herein lies freedom from our own reactions and a new grounding in transformative calm.

VI

Willigis Jäger
Search for the Meaning of Life
143

In the course of time the hunger for new impressions subsides, and the addictive need to busy ourselves internally lessens. When desiring stops, contemplative seeing becomes possible. Once we have reached this stage, we also realize that nothing lasts. There's nothing we can cling to. The only constant is the flow. Permanence lies in flux, not in any status quo. Attentiveness awakens in us the capacity to experience this flow and yet to know tranquility amid all the hustle and bustle.

LOGION 43

His Students said to him,

"Who are you
to be saying
such things to us?"

Yeshua replied,

"Do you not realize who I am
from everything I have said to you?
Have you come to be like the Judeans
who either accept the tree,
but reject its fruit,
or welcome the fruit
and despise the tree?"

Sapiential Themes

- *Polemic (serious questioning and response) is a step in the advancement of wisdom.*
- *His students express concern about Yeshua's person, and doubt about his message. Yeshua offers objectivity from the "whole tree" rather than its parts.*
- *Cause and effect, source and manifestation, belong together if we are to gain wisdom's vantage point.*

Parallel Texts

Logion 21
Mathew 7:15-20, 12:33, 42
Mark 6:2-3
Luke 6:43-45

FOCAL POINT

The religious world of Yeshua's students was unstable. Yeshua points out that the religious traditions of his day had an either/or mentality—either one side or the other was true, but not both. Whichever they championed in the endless religious disputes between communities and their diverse interpretations, their seeing was limited and their understanding fragmented. They could not embrace the whole, only the part, but the part without the whole is unstable. Yeshua offers a wider wisdom that is inclusive of "both/and"—multiple perspectives must be included in their considerations, for wisdom knows that the whole is greater than the sum of its parts.

Links

From all that has been previously said, perhaps there is fear and uncertainty in the hearts of his students and it is this that provokes their apparently hostile polemic. They are shaken and uncertain. Doubts have been raised instead of quelled. They want certainty based, it seems, on the very limitations that Yeshua has targeted in the previous sayings. Yeshua is moving them toward a higher understanding where parts and wholes are connected.

Notes

Throughout the ages philosophers and theologians have discussed the relationship between parts and wholes, manifestations and their causes. It is easy to privilege one side of an equation and dismiss the other. However, the part cannot be known without the whole, and the whole is incomplete without the parts. Manifestations point to causes, and in turn, sources are revealed through manifestations.

COMMENTARY

Once again, Yeshua sees through the question raised by his students to deeper issues below the surface. He is aware of their internal conflicts riled perhaps by his insight and teaching—a teaching that transcends all the parts of which they are aware, and reaching out beyond them to include everything within a larger whole. Like the combatants in the religious and theological debates raging throughout Judea, his students are not only divided among themselves, they experience interior conflict as well. They see only one dimension of the picture, and as is typical for all human beings, they mistake that dimension for the whole. It is the typical condition for those in this particular state of being and knowing: where some aspect of truth is mistaken for (and held at the expense of) the totality. When one aspect of the truth is affirmed without the web of its constituent parts, then fractures and divisions are created throughout the fabric of existence. The result is incoherence and chaos.

First century Judea in Yeshua's time was a hotbed of controversy and competing forces. There was no consensus in the Jewish community about religious matters, and so division rather than unity was the rule.

Yeshua's teachings have raised the bar. His wisdom is holistic and inclusive. Perhaps in the minds of his students he has gone too far. More than likely his teachings have touched the core of their fears and uncertainties. Throughout his ministry (and over the preceding Logia), Yeshua has spoken out against the religious milieu of his day and its limiting perspectives. More importantly, he has addressed the inner condition of many on the religious path. His words trouble the sensibilities of the "sensibly" pious and their leaders. They challenge the barriers raised by the religious authorities which prevent the people of his day and even his own students from assimilating the wisdom he teaches. He pushes toward a wholeness that is unacceptable. He belongs to none of the factions, and yet embraces a larger totality.

Philosophically, the coherence theory of truth maintains that in the fabric of truth there must ultimately be a seamless weaving rather than separation and contradiction.

So they question him. Who are you, really? What gives you the authority to say such things to us? Where do your teachings come from? And perhaps, what is the lineage and pedigree of your teaching? If he casts doubt on the recognized religious structures of his day, then who can authenticate his truth claims? Is what he teaches wisdom after all, or an affront to the traditions of wisdom? Either they are deeply disturbed by the new dimensions of his wisdom, or they are being pushed to some new relationship with it. In a state of discomfort, they question him. As is typical, he answers their questions with a question of his own. Perhaps it is rhetorical, perhaps not. They may now be in doubt about answers to any questions they have previously asked. Yeshua's teaching and aphorisms claim to be wisdom, but much of it is unfamiliar and difficult to comprehend. So, again, where does he get all this?

Mark 6:2-3

Their unknowing, doubts, and lack of trust led to an inner state much like that of the religious peoples of Judea, where the debate was ongoing between those who supported the authority of Jerusalem and the Temple (the Sadducees), and those who rejected and denied it (the Essenes). The battle raged over religious sources and manifestations among multiple religious authorities. There was no conclusion to the controversy. In the end, the students would have to decide the source of Yeshua's words, and whether they were authentic. Once again, we are drawn back to the issue of the previous Logion which speaks of the tree being planted away from its Source. If Yeshua's words were rooted in the deep and eternal Source of wisdom, then they would live. If they were not, they would fail and perhaps destroy even those who accepted them. The students seem aware of this. Their questions are legitimate, but no direct answer that Yeshua gives will suffice in the end. They must come to find answers for themselves.

QUESTIONS FOR REFLECTION

1. In your spiritual pilgrimage, when have your doubts surfaced into serious questioning? What has been the cause of your concerns, or the circumstances which have raised those doubts?

2. Have you had doubts yourself concerning the veracity of the teachings of Yeshua? What were they? Why have you questioned?

3. How is Yeshua's response in this Logion an answer perhaps to both his students' and your own concerns?

4. What partial knowledge may have been resolved for you when it was set into a larger, more holistic seeing?

EXERCISES AND MEDITATIONS

1. The egoic tendency is toward separateness—to divide one thing from another so that they remain isolated and often in hostile relationship. Entities often appear as opposites, but they need not be in opposition. Notice that the tendency we find within ourselves towards separateness and division is an illusion produced by the ego because we like one thing and dislike another. It is wisdom's role to overcome egoic illusion, and unite that which has been separated into false dichotomies. In a period of reflection, take note of what you reject or distance from yourself. Is this an attempt to choose one dimension (or aspect) at the expense of the whole? Allow yourself several periods of reflection so that you gradually see the realities you separate. Journal what you discover.
2. There is an in-between state of ambiguity that we must learn to tolerate if we are to become wise beings. Typically we dislike ambiguity, and move as quickly as possible toward some resolution that aligns us with an either/or position where one side is accepted and its opposite is rejected. Wisdom requires that we learn to live in a state of "both/and," where we feel the ambiguous nature which constitutes much of reality because it includes what appear to be contradictions that must be held together in tension. It is this ability, this skill—to be able to stand in the middle (in the in-between state)—by which we become practitioners of wisdom. Therefore, we must use opportunities where we experience opposites and extremes, and hold them in tension. We can practice this skill on a daily basis if we pay attention. As you live through your day, note your tendency to privilege one side over the other (for example, joy-sorrow, success-failure, loss-gain). Can you experience both with equanimity? See what happens when you hold both together without judgment.

In logic there is the law of non-contradiction—if something is true then its opposite cannot be true. This makes sense to us. However, paradoxically, in wisdom tradition this law often does not apply. Opposites may exist in complementary opposition.

READINGS FOR INSIGHT

I

Once a group of thieves stole a rare diamond
larger than two goose eggs.
Its value could have easily bought three thousand horses
and three thousand acres of the most fertile land in Shiraz.

The thieves got drunk that night to celebrate their great haul,
but during the course of the evening the effects of the liquor,
and their mistrust of each other grew to such an extent
they decided to divide the stone into pieces.
Of course then the Priceless became lost.

Most everyone is lousy at math and does that to God—
dissects the Indivisible One by thinking, by saying,
"This is my Beloved, he looks like this and acts like that.
How could that moron over there really be God?"

Hafez
Love Poems From God
157

II

God is greater than Wisdom and encompasses Wisdom. God's greatness is not "other than" but "inclusive of." If God were "other than," there would be a place where God was not. God could not be infinite if God did not include you. God includes all. Nothing is "other than" to God. Nothing is outside of God. This is what God wants Job to know, and what Wisdom wishes to teach you. ... And who is God? Your truest Self.

Rabbi Rami Shapiro
The Divine Feminine in Biblical Wisdom Literature
106

III

Imagine how it would be, to have the beginning and the end and all that passes in-between existing within our beings as a principal reality? What would it really mean to fully realize the Quranic truth that "wherever you turn, there is the Face of God" (2:115)? The imagination begins in the mind as a modality of creative inquiry and ends by becoming a threshold in the spiritual realities, so that we can be shown and see things as they are and become the true beings that we were intended to be.

John Herlihy
Borderlands of the Spirit
87

IV

There was a dervish once who entered the presence of a king. The king started to pay him tribute and said, "O ascetic."

The dervish quickly interrupted, "*You* are the ascetic."

"Me?" the king gasped, astonished, "How am I an ascetic, seeing that the whole earth is mine?"

The dervish smiled, "You see things the opposite of how they really are. This world and the next one, and everything in both, belongs to me. I have taken into my possession all the worlds. What you have become satisfied with is a handful of dust and rags."

Jalaluddin Rumi
Light Upon Light
15

LOGION 44

Sapiential Themes

- *The primacy of spirit over image or concept.*
- *Relationship to spirit determines relationship to the eternal and temporal orders.*
- *Spirit understood as an energetic force is in a different category from that of father and son.*

Yeshua says,

You may speak against the Father
and it will be forgotten.
You may speak against the son
and it will be dropped.
But if you speak opposing
the sacred Spirit,
that is irrevocable
both in heaven and on earth.

Parallel Texts

Matthew 12:31-32
Mark 3:28-29
Luke 12:10

Links

Where does the line fall between religious bickering and argumentation, and the stifling of the sacred altogether? This is a question that has to be raised in the context of the Jewish community in first century Palestine. Controversies and disputations dominated the scene. Does that have an effect upon the human or the divine Spirit? The answer will be given in this Logion.

FOCAL POINT

It is easy to imagine that Yeshua is suggesting here that the students' seemingly hostile questioning from the previous Logion constitutes a form of blasphemy (you disciples better watch out! The tone of your questioning suggests you are getting close to the line of blasphemy). Could it be just the opposite—their controversies and theological debates do not constitute blasphemy, nor does their harsh questioning about religious manifestations and their sources? The only thing that can put one in jeopardy is to limit the force or drive of the Spirit. When, by words and actions, we oppose the sacred Spirit from within, we change our relationship to heaven and earth—and nothing can change it back until we adjust our fundamental relationship with Spirit, realigning our souls once again to the Spirit's central role in maintaining life in its relationship to heaven and earth.

Notes

The Coptic translation of the Greek text shows a high degree of sensitivity to this saying and expresses a nuanced understanding of the Greek meanings. The word "blasphemy" is expressed as saying "something against" and in the Coptic text the traditional term "forgive" is expressed as to "leave alone."

COMMENTARY

To begin to understand and interpret this saying sensitively, we must place it within the context of the sayings of Thomas, and then look at alternative possibilities of meaning which the Coptic version gives us. In addition, we may be able to follow alternative lines that the wisdom tradition makes available to us, rather than the typical theological approaches we have inherited.

There is perhaps no other saying in the canonical Gospels (and in Thomas' corollary) that has created more consternation and turmoil than Yeshua's words concerning "blasphemy against the Holy Spirit" (as it is traditionally translated into English). The interpretive history of this saying is long with much theological baggage and heated rhetoric. The implication is that once the line of blasphemy has been crossed (whatever that means), nothing more can be done—damnation is sure and inevitable. Over the centuries, this interpretive approach to the saying has traumatized multitudes of sincere followers of Yeshua, and the institutional church has turned these words into a weapon of coercion. Does the Gospel of Thomas shed any different light on this saying and its traditional interpretations? Is there any alternative but to return to the traditional viewpoint and repeat that Yeshua is simply laying down the harshest of all condemnations: that anyone caught in the blasphemous net is doomed?

In the last Logion Yeshua addressed his students and fellow religionists alike over their tendency to take sides in the interminable religious debates and internecine theological wars within first century Judaism. He identifies it as the tension between the fruit and the root (accepting one and rejecting the other), and implies that these two clearly belong together as a part of the whole tree. Illustratively, this image points toward the greater issue of source and manifestation and their interdependent relationship. In this saying, Yeshua goes beyond that dichotomy (illustrated here, it seems, through the traditional images of father and son) to the primacy of Spirit. One can certainly put emphasis on either the root or the fruit (the father or the son), but there exists something deeper, connecting both—the sap that flows through the entire tree. In religious controversies, one might take the side of the father or the son, but in truth these are only images and manifestations. They are exterior, and the life that energizes the entire domain of the sacred is not image per se, but the flow of Spirit which courses beneath its surface. Controversies over images (fruit or root, father or son) are of little consequence in comparison to the presence of Spirit which signifies a deeper reality.

*In his extraordinary commentary, Jean-Yves Leloup highlights a similar understanding when he writes, "We may be blocked from the insight that would enable us to see through the variety and multiplicity of creation toward the One who is its Source. This is a denial that does not recognize the Father. Or we might be blocked in our heart center, so that we are unable to see the beauty of human beingness or to feel awe at the divine compassion that can manifest in a human being. This is a denial that does not recognize the Son. But to be cut off from the Spirit, the very Breath, that is the source of our life, is far more serious. It is a denial of our most intimate being (**The Gospel of Thomas**, 132).*

One's own relationship to spirit is, therefore, crucial. Essentially it determines the nature of one's entire relationship to heaven and earth. In other words, a microcosmic (personal) relationship to Spirit conditions relationship to the macrocosm. What that relationship is at any moment is irrevocable—it is the template which determines everything else. But can one change the template? It seems so, but you cannot do so simply by changing images concerning it. You have to change your relationship to Spirit (and not simply your ideas about Spirit). This is another possible approach to understanding this text.

The way we perceive the terms "father" and "son," are by means of conceptual definitions amenable to the human mind. The term spirit, however, refers to an energetic force rather than to an image. In fact, it is difficult to make an image of spirit at all. As Yeshua says, it is more like the unseen wind. So the mind has difficulty describing or grasping spirit, Nonetheless, we are receptive to its force. The work and energy of Spirit is the reality underlying and animating all things. These things (sacred or otherwise) are imaged, and humans give them temporary forms that appear and disappear throughout history. Though we argue about them as if they were the most real thing, they are only provisional. It is only Spirit, difficult to define, that remains constant.

QUESTIONS FOR REFLECTION

1. Have you ever been warned by someone about your behavior who thought you were possibly blaspheming the Spirt? Have you ever worried perhaps that you had somehow transgressed its injunctions? What were the circumstances?

2. What would be your response now to someone who accused you of blasphemy against the Holy Spirit?

3. Have you ever spoken out against an image or a concept accepted in religious tradition with the thought that it was wrong?

4. When have you felt yourself realign with the universal Spirit? What were the circumstances and what has been the result?

*The terms father, son, and spirit are usually interpreted as a Christian formula for the Trinity. These terms, however, need first to be seen within a more traditional Hebrew context where they do not carry that same meaning. There they are related not to dogma, but to wisdom. In the wisdom tradition, the term "father" relates to origin and source, and not even to God as a theological proposition. The term "son" relates to the image of manifestation (that which is birthed) from the source. It may also be seen as a term for primordial humanity springing whole from the Source. Spirit is the sacred force which exists in all things as divine breath (**ruach**), animating all things and present to everything from within.*

EXERCISES AND MEDITATIONS

1. If, as we have interpreted this saying to mean, one's relationship to heaven and earth is a spiritual one—determined by the intimate relationship we have to the sacred force of spirit within us—then it is crucial to know what that relationship actually is. Because you cannot see this force as such, but only its effects outside you (or feel the flow of spirit within you), then knowledge of the spirit comes either by its "fruits," or, perhaps, by feeling their inner force. If indeed these two criteria give us an understanding of our relationship to Spirit, take the time to examine what your relationship is both externally and internally in your daily life. Keep a journal of your observations and findings. Because the Spirit is active rather than passive, the implication is that you can ask for guidance and also for signs of the Spirit's presence and relationship to you and then receive them.
2. One of the oldest methods of contemplative prayer is called the **Breath Prayer**. The word for Spirit in Hebrew and in Greek carry both meanings—breathing and spirit. So these words and ideas have been connected from the beginning. One could make the case that prayer is built right into the physical structure of a human being. God breathed (prayed) and we came into existence. We breathe and the Spirit exists within us, and our gentle inward and outward breathing is a sign of something greater that breathes us. Sit in meditation breathing slowly, watching your breath passing in and out. Remembering that this comes from the primordial breath of God. Another method for the Breath Prayer is to imagine your breathing to be like the waves of the sea. On the in-breath the waves roll up onto the shore. On the out-breath they recede back into the ocean. Picture this as you breathe. It is customary to allow the pause at the end of the out-breath to be sustained for a longer period of time.

READINGS FOR INSIGHT

I

Picasso

We are all born artists.
What do adults do to children to kill that spirit?

II

Sara Sviri
The Taste of Hidden Things
98-99

The Sufi tradition has distinguished a special group of seekers: those whose *sole* link with the teaching is through ***Khidr*** (the Green Man) himself. There are those rare Sufis who do not have a teacher in the flesh. Their only teacher, as in Moses' case, is ***Khidr***. They have been given a special name: ***uwasiyyun***. They are named after Uways al-Qarani, a contemporary of the Prophet Muhammad, who lived in Yemen and, due to his mother's illness, could not make the journey to Medina to join the companions of the Prophet. And yet he had a direct link with Muhammad. The Prophet said that the sweet scent of Uways wafted all the way from Yemen to Medina, and thus their spirits had been at all times together. Such meeting in the spirit takes place also in the case of seekers and teachers whose link with the mystical tradition is via ***Khidr***.

III

Bro. Tolbert McCarroll
Notes From the Song of Life
31

In every corner of your world there blows a gentle wind that sings a silent song. You must listen for that song.

IV

Pema Chödrön
Comfortable With Uncertainty
139-40

The more we connect with a bigger perspective, the more we connect with energetic joy. Exertion is connecting with our appetite for enlightenment. It allows us to act, to give, to work appreciatively with whatever comes our way. If we really knew how unhappy it was making this whole planet that we all try to avoid pain and seek pleasure—how that is making us so miserable and cutting us off from our basic goodness—then we would practice as if our hair were on fire. There wouldn't be any question of thinking we have a lot of time and we can do this later.

Yet when we begin to practice exertion, we see that sometimes we can do it and sometimes we can't. The question becomes: How do we connect with inspiration? How do we connect with the spark and joy that's available in every moment?

V

John Herlihy
Borderlands of the Spirit
91

The God of the mind is one experience of the Divinity; the God of the heart is another. They meet in the soul where human selfhood finds it fullest and most complete expression. It is the human spirit in the form of a soul that lays ultimate claim to the accomplishments of a human life. Human beings have had no part in the arrival of the animating spirit: but with its coming, *Homo sapiens*, the ethical animal, found within a light that no other animal ever had before, a light that modern science simply cannot account for and will never classify on its own terms. Traced back through the history of time, the human soul simply disappears into the antediluvian woods with the traces of its footsteps.

LOGION 45

Sapiential Themes

- *The congruence between root and fruit is the critical issue of evil and its source.*
- *The heart is the metaphor for the core human repository of both goodness and evil—the storehouse of virtue or vice.*
- *Evil speech is a primary cause of great suffering in the world. Its source is the human heart.*

Yeshua says,

Grapes are not
harvested from thorns,
nor are figs gathered from
thistles—neither produce fruit.

Good people
bring goodness out of
a storehouse of inner treasure,
while evil ones bring wickedness
out of the repository of evil
collected in the heart.
It is from there that they speak.
For from the heart's overflow evil enters
the world.

Parallel Texts

Genesis 3:17-19
Isaiah 5:1-4
I Samuel 24:13
Matthew 7:15-20, 12:33-37
Luke 6:43-45
James 3:5-8

Links

If, as is said in the last Logion, resistance to spirit cuts one off from the flow of life, then the question naturally arises, where does such resistance come from? What is its source? This saying confirms a truth that has already been identified in Logion 14—resistance and contamination comes from within. They are not imposed from without. We have control over the inner treasury of our own being.

FOCAL POINT

What is the origin of evil? This question, and the presence of evil in the universe, is one of the most troubling of all human problems. Throughout the religious history of humanity sages, saints, theologians, metaphysicians and philosophers have attempted to answer this persistent question: if God is good, why does evil, suffering and pain exist? Using another agricultural metaphor, Yeshua gives his answer, pinpointing the presence of evil in the human world. Evil exists and its source is not the devil, or other demonic forces external to human beings. Its source is located in an inner dimension, from a repository that collects over time in the heart. From out of that "treasury" we speak and our words carry the influence of good and ill into the world around us. This, Yeshua says, is the source of the evil and the good that we know.

Notes

At the center of the heart is something which the Greeks called the ***nous*** *(the highest point of Intelligence a human being possesses. It may be this word that the Coptic is translating as Mind—understood as the Intelligence at the heart's core.*

COMMENTARY

One of the concerns of Hebrew wisdom was the use of the tongue and how calamitous the consequences could be when language and speech were allowed to run wild, harming the outside world.

We often imagine that evil—at least moral evil in the way that religion understands and expresses it—has something either to do with an external threat posed by evil forces greater than ourselves, or is a result of corrupt or bad behavior which we enact because of wrongly held beliefs that influence our behavior. A theological case can be made for any of these, and they all seem accurate, but does Yeshua agree? His analysis is based upon personal observation and uses a homespun example of fruit production in the agricultural world of his day. The obvious fact is that thorns and thistles produce no edible fruit. So, too, at the core of a human being, a repository of resistance can build and produce no real fruit, but only a storehouse of malice from which evil flows, typically in the form of speech.

Yeshua's observation answers, perhaps, an unspoken question raised in the last saying, "How does one blaspheme (or go against) the spirit?" How does one go out of proper relationship to heaven and earth? Does it have to do with right or wrong belief? Yeshua's answer is that it does not have to do with external forces but with the condition of the heart.

An important study of this research and its implications for each of us in common life is the work of Joseph Chilton Pearce, ***The Biology of Transcendence*** *(Park Street Press, 2002). In this work he reviews not only the scientific literature in regards to the heart's neuronal capacities, but its connection to the wider cosmos and to human consciousness. Once again, the heart is seen not only as a physical, but also a spiritual center of great significance.*

The heart is key in traditional wisdom, Semitic spirituality, and for Yeshua's way of seeing. Certainly it is a metaphor for the central spiritual organ of a human being, tied, metaphorically, to the central role that the physical heart plays in body—but it may be more than that. Recent studies have suggested that neuron cells existing in the physical heart exercise a separate form of intelligence with ancillary linkage to the brain. Ancient wisdom intuited not only the deeper significance of the heart as metaphor, but seemed to be aware also of this finer, more subtle intelligence that plays a key role in spiritual consciousness. The term "kardial awareness" is a way of indicating that we possess a form of consciousness that exceeds and is superior to our normal rational consciousness located in the brain. We think with our brain, but we appear to intuit with our kardial center.

It is this center, Yeshua says, which becomes the storehouse collecting into itself materials which are transmuted by human will into both goodness and evil—the primary motivating source of the actions and language we use in the world around us. In the modern day we know little and have been taught less about this center, nor about its "alchemical" properties which take the raw material of our world and create new, useful, or destructive substances. But in ancient understanding and in traditional wisdom, the heart played a strong role in personal knowing and in the language of instruction and direction.

The implication for what is being said here is that the external world is neutral. We collect from the events, attitudes, mores, and values of the world around us. Even those that are contaminated by previous systemic distortion need not contaminate us. It all depends on what we do and how we connect these materials within.

In the modern world we speak of "core values." Could these actually reside in a place within us that we can now think of as their kardial carrier or repository? No doubt Yeshua has this possibility in mind when he speaks this well-remembered saying. Implicitly we act out of our core values, and these are created and hidden within, unseen to the physical eye, but manifest externally by our actions and through our speech. These also are the ground for the produce (the "fruits") whose roots are planted in the heart. Do we have any control over what is stored there at the core, or what is planted in that ground? Again, obviously we must or there would be no moral accountability in the larger cosmos. We each carry treasure which can be made available to the world, or which we have buried so deeply that our land lies fallow only producing thistles and thorns.

QUESTIONS FOR REFLECTION

1. What have been your conclusions about the origins of good and evil? Are they similar or different from what is presented in this Logion?

2. How does Yeshua's statement in this Logion change any of your thinking?

3. Imagining this storehouse deep within a human being, what is the mixture of ingredients there?

4. How can you come to know the inner treasury of your own heart? What is the process by which you also begin to draw material out of that repository?

5. What do you feel is your most precious inner treasure—that which you can give as a form of good fruit to the world?

EXERCISES AND MEDITATIONS

1. Self-knowledge and the discovery of the true nature of the self is an essential part of wisdom learning. Nothing can proceed very far unless we know ourselves deeply and intimately. This, however, involves reflection, analysis, and questioning. Sometimes we can accomplish that process through a form of self-revelation alone or by ourselves. At other times we need the assistance of a neutral party—a friend, counselor, spiritual director or mentor. First, in a period of meditation and reflection, get to know the storehouse of your own heart. It is best to open yourself to that inner domain and ask for guidance and clarity to aid in your discovery. Second, you want to explore both the treasures of goodness which produce fruit, and the repositories of evil that produce thistles and thorns. This may be a painful exploration, and so courage is needed. Do not judge, simply observe. In both cases write what you have discovered.
2. Take the discoveries that you have made to a trusted friend or counselor, mentor or spiritual director and ask him or her to help you clarify what you have found, and to uncover material that might be obscured, or from which you could be hiding.
3. For a day pay special attention to your speech and how it affects others. Can you observe when it bears fruit? Can you detect when it is harmful, producing thistles and thorns? Make these observations a part of your journal. You might also want to review these with a mentor or spiritual director as well.

Read the story where Yeshua comes to a fig tree with no fruit which he then makes to wither as an illustration of this saying. What meaning do these two sayings and acts of Yeshua point toward? (Matthew 21:18-19)

READINGS FOR INSIGHT

I

Your conscious being, with what you've been given, should be like a beautifully laid-out park with wildflowers and cultivated wonders, a swift stream with secluded places to sit and rest beside it.

When a grieving person sees you, he or she should recognize a refuge, refreshment, a generous house where one need not bring bread and cheese. There will be plenty.

Bahauddin
The Drowned Book
102

II

By their fruits you shall know them.

Yeshua

III

The Master became a legend in his lifetime. It was said that God once sought his advice:

"I want to play a game of hide-and-seek with humankind. I've asked my Angels what the best place is to hide in. Some say the depths of the ocean. Others the top of the highest mountain. Others still the far side of the moon or a distant star. What do you suggest?"

Said the Master, "Hide in the human heart. That's the last place they will think of!"

Anthony de Mello
One Minute Wisdom
44

IV

The Compassionate One wants the heart.

The Talmud

V

There was a treasure in the earth which the lord loved. I was astonished and considered what it could be; and I was answered in my understanding: It is a food which is delicious and pleasing to the lord. For I saw the lord sitting like a man, and I saw neither food nor drink with which to serve him. ... I watched, wondering what kind of labor it could be that the servant was to do. And then I understood that he was to do the greatest labor and the hardest work there is. He was to be a gardener, digging and ditching and sweating and turning the soil over and over, and to dig deep down, and to water the plants at the proper time. And he was to persevere to his work, and make sweet streams to run, and fine and plenteous fruit to grow, which he was to bring before the lord and serve him with to his like.

Julian of Norwich
Showings
273-274

VI

Awake, O north wind,
And come, O south wind!
Blow upon my garden that its fragrance
May be wafted abroad.
Let my beloved come to his garden,
And eat its choicest fruits.

Song of Solomon
4:16-17

LOGION 46

Yeshua says,

Among those born on earth
beginning from Adam to
John the Baptist,
no one has reached a higher state
than John — and you should bow
in honor before him.

Yet, I tell you this,
whoever of you becomes "a little child"
will not only know the kingdom,
but will be raised to a state
higher than John's.

Sapiential Themes

- *There are lineages of wise beings who undergo spiritual transformation through the ages, of which Yeshua and his students are a part.* '
- *John the Baptist is to be honored for his place in that lineage and for his role in the spiritual evolution of Yeshua.*
- *John, however, is not a final point, but perhaps only a way-station in the longer journey of wisdom.*

Parallel Texts

Logion 4, 21, 22
Matthew 3:1-17, 11:7-15, 18:3
Mark 1:5-8, 10:15
Luke 3:2-17, 7:24-30, 18:17
John 1:6-8, 18-28

FOCAL POINT

To this day, John the Baptist remains an enigmatic and haunting figure in human imagination. Who was this "Voice" crying out in the wilderness of the first century? Why did crowds come out to hear to him? What compelled Yeshua to submit to his baptism in the river Jordan? In the arc of ancient figures from Adam through Abraham, Isaac, Joseph, Moses, David, and the Prophets all the way through to John the Baptist, for Yeshua, at least, no one is greater than John. It is perhaps because he completes the arc and in this way prepares for a new progression on wisdom's perennial journey across time.

Links

In Logion 45 the source of grapes and figs is seen to be their parent stock in the same way that goodness comes for an inner treasure of like quality and evil from its own repository. Both are said to exist in the heart. So what is this state of the heart that can produce good fruit? In this Logion that state is described, first, in the consciousness and being of John, but beyond that in the state of a little child. This image links to Logia 4, 21, and 22, as well as 50.

Notes

John the Baptist may have historically been a member of one of the first-century communities of the Essenes along the Dead Sea, or at least he was in sympathy with their point of view. He was clearly a Jewish ascetic who eschewed the trappings of religious and political power in the halls of the Judean state. He may also have been an independent and prophetic thinker with the spiritual power of initiation.

COMMENTARY

The Essene communities were gatherings of devout Jews in opposition to the religious and spiritual authorities in Jerusalem. They practiced strict asceticism which they believed made them ready to become warriors of light in the battle between good and evil.

All indications are that John, Yeshua's senior, was also in some sense his teacher, and perhaps initiated him into the spiritual world. Yeshua certainly submits to his rite of purification and ***metanoia*** *(spiritual turning), and it is at the very moment of surrender to John in baptism when Yeshua is called forth by the realm of Transcendence and anointed with Spirit. It is also a turning point in first century Judaism. Yeshua is likewise propelled into John's desert, undergoing significant spiritual transformation, and returns out of it as one of Wisdom's greatest sages and a Healer of humanity who attracts multitudes, pointing them toward heaven's realm.*

The state of the child is discussed throughout this text as a preferred point of departure for spiritual transformation. In many traditions, including Thomas', it is seen as the primordial state of humanity out of which one comes and to which one returns perhaps to grow again.

Yeshua's strong statement of positive regard for John the Baptist indicates, perhaps, something more than personal or familial affinity. It is understood that John was Yeshua's first cousin on his mother's side, and perhaps they had grown up together, or at least had been in touch through their years of physical and spiritual maturation. John's proclivities were toward the South and the movement of Jewish asceticism which seemed to collect around the Dead Sea. The Qumran community is reputed to have been the headquarters of the Essene movement, a separatist enclave holding out against the compromises of establishment Judaism centered in Jerusalem. It was the epicenter of spiritual resistance in the war between good and evil as it was perceived in the first-century, and John may have been associated with or at least in favor of that point of view. If, by the standards of the Essenes, Judea and the religion of the Temple were compromised through affiliation with Roman authority, then Galilee by comparison was beyond the pale entirely. Yet there is affinity between the Galilean Yeshua and the Judean Baptist.

In this Logion Yeshua honors his spiritual lineage, his teacher, the inner seeing and the prophetic voice of the ascetic John. In his view, none have any reached a higher state of being and consciousness that John's. It is interesting, however, that Yeshua does not focus upon his teaching, his doctrinal or religious purity, his piety, or even his rite of baptism, but on his inner state, and it is this state which he lifts up as the ideal, a stepping stone to an even higher state of being and consciousness—that of the "little child."

If one were to meet John he would no doubt exemplify the image of the prophetic tradition where a human seized by Spirit cries out what he sees and compels action and response. John's proclamation was a crisis point, providing a place of choice and so those who heard either had to return home from that brink or move across it as Yeshua did in his turn toward Spirit.

The waters of John's baptism may be seen, then, as birth waters and on the other side is a realm where one enters and has little choice but to begin again as a little child. Implied in this image is the "second birth" from above, declared in the other John's Gospel. One is first born of woman, but beyond that is another birth into a new realm, the kingdom, where one must begin again as a little child. But the question needs to be raised immediately, is one meant to stay always a child? The answer appears to be "no," for the image of the child itself implies growth—a child grows from that state of being which is only a starting point. From there it must be that there are even higher states commensurate with the magnitude of the divine Realm itself, far beyond anything John attained or perhaps even imagined.

So what is this new beginning point beyond John? Metaphorically it means, like a child to become open and free to grow again—eager and ready to learn, unafraid of the new, asking questions that are innocent of personal agenda and artifice, staying wide open to a greater world full of wonder. All that reflects the child's mind, the state of consciousness that is characteristic of a child, is a precious state. Perhaps it was because John's consciousness had settled down into some familiar track (no matter how good), from which he could not easily change course or move higher, that Yeshua makes this declaration. Yeshua's challenge to the very best of first-century religious consciousness is that it must move forward even from there.

QUESTIONS FOR REFLECTION

1. In the long lineage of Semitic men and women described in the Hebrew scriptures, who for you is the greatest example of early spiritual pilgrimage and power? Who inspires you the most?

2. If John the Baptist was Yeshua's initiator and master, what kind of a person would he have to be? What would his inner state need to be like?

3. Have you experienced the power of a Master of Initiation? Has Yeshua ever expressed himself to you in that way?

4. What does it mean to "know the Kingdom?" Is this a theological proposition to which one assents? If not, then, what is it?

EXERCISES AND MEDITATIONS

1. If within the spiritual tradition of Thomas, the waters of baptism symbolize "birth waters," then Yeshua's experience of baptism and what happened beyond it in the wilderness exemplifies a new beginning as a child. If this is so, then what does the temptation in the wilderness describe? Where in Yeshua do you find the manifestation of the child's mind?
2. Imagine starting a path of learning in some new field heretofore unknown to you. Imagine being a novice and knowing virtually nothing. How would the "child's mind" be a symbol for what you would need to do, or the attitude you would need to take? Imagine something else; you feel you are fairly accomplished in a particular field, but someone wants to teach you something they believe you do not know. How might this affect you and the experience of being a "little child" again? In a period of meditation move through both of these scenarios, letting yourself experience each inner state you encounter.
3. It is easy to imagine that what Yeshua is calling here for leads to an implicit form of ignorance—that becoming a little child again means becoming childish or blissfully ignorant of the wider world. If this is not what Yeshua is asking, then imagine what this state actually is? Could you give examples of childlikeness which are not ignorance, but wisdom? In or outside of meditation have you ever entered such a state? Can this same state be carried into the world? What does the ego have to do with it all?

READINGS FOR INSIGHT

I

Yeshua
Mark 10:15

Truly, I say to you,
whoever does not receive the kingdom of God like a child shall not enter it.

II

The way to the kingdom of God that Jesus teaches is the way of a child. In the quotation above the word "receive" is the most important one for an understanding of what that way is. In the Greek manuscript it is the indefinite form of the verb ***dexomai***, which means to take something which has been held out, to accept, to receive warmly, to welcome cordially. Thus this sentence is telling us how important it is to welcome from our hearts and docilely accept the "kingdom of God" that been offered to us by God the Father. "Like a child" means to accept someone's kindness docilely, impartially and promptly, without the least bit of doubt or suspicion. If, in addition, we consider the meaning of childlikeness against the background of the good news which Jesus proclaimed, it seems to have an even deeper meaning. As the Scripture scholar J. Jeremias says, it is only a child who, knowing he is safe in God's protection and conscious of his boundless love, can call God ***Abba*** (dear Father) with childlike confidence.

J.K. Kadowaki, SJ
Zen and the Bible
85

III

He who is in harmony with the Tao
is like a newborn child.
Its bones are soft, its muscles are weak,
but its grip is powerful.
It doesn't know about the union of male and female
yet it can be aroused.
So intense is its vital power
it can scream all day,
yet it never becomes hoarse,
so complete is its harmony.

The Master's power is like this.
He lets all things come and go
effortlessly, without desire.
He never expects results;
thus he is never disappointed.
He is never disappointed;
thus his spirit never grows old.

Tao Te Ching
55

IV

The great fault of Iblis (Satan) was to imagine
"I am greater than Adam!"
And this illness lives in each human soul
However humble you imagine you are.

Jalaluddin Rumi
Light Upon Light
116

LOGION 47

Sapiential Themes

- *We experience duality in the midst of the world as we know it. Oneness, however, is the ground of existence and forms the background against which duality unfolds.*
- *Wisdom requires that we learn to work with duality using the background of oneness as our template.*
- *There are multiple states and stages in the progression of sapiential learning that engage the paradox of duality in the midst of oneness.*
- *Yeshua illustrates two important steps in the progression of learning wisdom.*

Yeshua says,

No one can mount two horses,
or draw two bows at once,
and you cannot serve
two masters at the same time.
If you honor one,
the other will be offended.

No one drinks a vintage wine
and immediately wants
to taste wine freshly bottled.
New wine is not put into
old containers lest it be ruined,
nor is aged wine put into
new barrels lest it spoil.

Also old cloth is not sewn
onto new garments because
it only makes the tear worse.

Parallel Texts

Matthew 6:24, 9:14-17
Mark 2:18-22
Luke 5:33-39, 16:10-13

Links

What does one gain in the higher states of consciousness and being? How would the state of the child manage the fierce dualities in our world? What wisdom would this particular state attain as it passed through the struggle between opposites? These are some of the questions which are addressed by Yeshua in this Logion.

FOCAL POINT

We live in a world of duality where extremes, opposites, disparities and contrasts exist. This is the nature of reality as we experience it, believing often that this is all there is and that it is an immutable state of affairs. In this Logion Yeshua illustrates the conditions in which we find ourselves by providing multiple and contrasting images. At issue is how we are to be guided by wisdom in the midst of these conditions. Horseback riding, archery, service to a master, wine tasting, wine making and tailoring all provide examples of how one must wisely choose between the disparities and contrasts in this world of duality. It is not easy to learn wisdom in such a world, but we must. Some attempts will work and some will fail. Some choices we make are better than others, and some are poor and lead to disaster.

Notes

Yeshua's grasp of complex philosophical ideas is clear, but what he does as a master of wisdom is to make them available and practical through common illustrations which can become the basis for the practice of essential wisdom. This particular translation, using dynamic equivalents, changes some of the images into modern illustrations. Skins in the original, for example, are wine bottles in this text.

COMMENTARY

The central theme of this Logion is the contrast between twoness and oneness, and yet the applications vary. In the first set of doubles, oneness is clearly in view—only one correct choice will suffice. In the second set there are alternatives, but each of these has a specific application to a particular set of conditions. One set is not necessarily preferred over another, they are simply different, but one can only make one choice at a time and so one must choose which actions are to be correctly applied—this complexity is at the heart of our experience of duality. Twoness and oneness, therefore, are realities. Each has its own domain. One cannot be confused with the other, but in the end the state of oneness supersedes the state of twoness.

Many scholars have noted that the order of sayings about the patch and the garment and the wine and wineskins is reversed in Thomas from the way they appear in the synoptic Gospels. The synoptic version appears to have undergone a Christian transformation , because the new has now been equated with the new movement around Yeshua, whereas the concern in Thomas is for the mature wine. Comparing these the argument is made that the form of Thomas is more original, staying within the limits of these proverbs as they would have been before they were incorporated by into the synoptic texts through the "Q" redaction.

The Five Gospels,
499-500

Let us place the first set of doubles in a definition of oneness we may call "singularity." We often speak of "having our cake and eating it too." This is what we could call the "both/and syndrome" where one refuses to choose, keeping all options open. In the end this strategy proves to be an impossibility and before it does it creates a state of mind that the wisdom tradition was very wary of: the instability of double-mindedness. Two horses, two bows, two masters to choose between, and one cannot proceed forward without choosing between the two and then acting. This leaves the other alternative, of course, unfulfilled, but the benefit of such a choice is both commitment to a particular course of action and its ultimate fulfillment. Unable to choose between the two (or being stuck in the middle), leaves all alternatives unfulfilled and the state of the human mind in an unstable condition. Wisdom's first teaching concerning duality points toward the practice of a form of "oneness" through the love of and commitment to some particular object or individual. In fact love cannot exist without particularity and choice—one chooses to love a particular being or thing and leaves all others aside. This is the first state of oneness called singularity to which wisdom leads.

The second state involves the next set of contrasts in which distinctions are discerned between possibilities—each of which is a necessary part of reality in a world of contrasts. There exists both new wine and old, and both are necessary for the whole process of winemaking. There are new and old kegs. There is new clothing and old, and ways of working with each that will maintain the integrity of the particular set of conditions intrinsic to each. So again one must discern and make choices, but each choice is for the good of the particular conditions with which one is presented. This is the second step in wisdom teaching—learning to discern for the good of each particular set and acting with discretion and integrity.

In wisdom's progression, however, these are only the first steps in learning oneness in a dualistic world. Other steps will need to be taken which build upon these that include reaching a state of detachment from all exigencies. Another teaches active self-emptying as a choice so that new possibilities may emerge. And then, there is the state of "no distinction" where oneness ultimately transcends all alternatives to include both at some higher level of reality. All of these are taught most effectively through our difficult engagement with duality—the condition without which we can never learn wisdom at all.

QUESTIONS FOR REFLECTION

1. In the first set of three contrasts, it is only the third and last in which the outcome of trying such a feat is expressed. How would you describe the outcome of the first two?

2. What is the point of the first statement of the second paragraph about not immediately wanting to taste wine freshly bottled? What are the implications of this statement?

3. The final two illustrations (the one about wine being bottled, and the other about patching clothes), are similar in nature. Since these illustrate wisdom teachings, what is being taught?

4. The choices that are made in the latter descriptions illustrate discernment. In your judgment how does one learn the skill of such discrimination?

EXERCISES AND MEDITATIONS

1. Review your own history and determine when you have had to make choices of particularity and commitment that affirmed one path and made you surrender up others. What was the result of this? How did it feel? When have you refused to make a choice between two possibilities? What were the results?
2. If you were the teacher of these principles to people you know and care about, what illustrations might you use that would be different from Yeshua's? Write out your illustrations and tell them to friends and cohorts in a group and see how they work.
3. Reflect on the wisdom of commitment to (and love for) particularity. Why is this such an important first step in learning the principle of oneness? Write your reflections in a journal. Reflect also on the wisdom of discernment. This appears to be an "older" wisdom and not gained easily. In your own experience how have you learned to discern? In what areas do you find that you are more proficient and in what do you still need practice?
4. Choose a realm where you feel you need practice in the wisdom of discernment and write out both what the difficulties are and what you have experienced so far. What kind of learning (or experience) would it take to help you make the right choices in that area? You might discuss your reflections with a group of trusted individuals to help you gain perspective, determine missing elements or points of view, and discover further steps in the learning process.

READINGS FOR INSIGHT

I

Robert Bolton
The Order of the Ages
38

... Besides being the causes underlying the relative reality of the world, Form and Matter are also the archetypes of all the endless dualities, polarities, and complementarisms in which natural life so largely consists. Some of these are body and soul, subject and object, male and female, cause and effect, quality and quantity, acid and alkali, light and dark, positive and negative, active and passive, interior and exterior, substance and attribute.

II

Kabir
Love Poems From God
224

You are sitting in a wagon
being drawn by a horse
whose reins
you hold.
There are two inside of you
who can steer.
Though most never hand the reins to Me
so they go from place to place
the best they can,
though rarely happy.
And rarely does their whole body laugh
feeling God's poke in the ribs.
If you feel tired, dear,
my shoulder is soft,
I'd be glad
to steer a while.

III

Bahauddin
The Drowned Book
41-42

One man works for several different people who are continuously disagreeing. Another works for one man only. Compare the quality of their lives. I might put it this way. You overload your boat so much that it rests firmly on the bottom of the dock. It won't be going anywhere. You have so many projects that you have to lie down and rest. You are taking careful inventory of a cargo with no destination. The difficulty of your work is ridiculous.

You say, *But I'm doing this for my beautiful children and their children, for this culture of shops and villages, for civilization.* Grand purposes. Those are like pictures on embroidered screens that you set up to keep from seeing the landscape itself. Remove the images, as they will surely be removed someday. Look *through* your prestigious position and your progeny.

So here we sit, buried in detail, concerned about winning some game, fearful we're about to die. These are trivia and cheap magic tricks. Do you remember the story of Solomon loading provisions in a boat to go out on the ocean to feed a whale? He was helping us see how unnecessary our *planning* is, this proposed agenda we argue the dimensions of.

LOGION 48

Yeshua says,

Should two make peace
in one house,
they could speak the word,
"Move!" to a mountain,
and it would obey them.

Sapiential Themes

- *The power of oneness comes through the peace achieved in unity and not through the subjugation of one over another.*
- *One's own "house" is the domain in which one has a larger degree of autonomy.*
- *A mountain is a metaphor signifying both transcendence and an unmovable object which challenges one's pathway.*
- *The power of voice is not in the command itself, but in the authority behind the command.*

Parallel Texts

Logion 106
Matt 17:19-21, 21:18-22
Mark 11:20-25
Luke 17:5-6
I Corinthians 13:2

FOCAL POINT

In this terse and compelling saying Yeshua declares the power and superiority of oneness over duality. In one's dwelling place, wherever two live together, there can be either chaos and strife or peace and harmony. If there is conflict, then there is no serenity. However, should peace triumph over conflict and harmony be restored, there is the condition for the possibility of a greater power—the power to move mountains. This power, used with authority, has great effect. Nothing, in fact, may be able to withstand it.

Links

The achievement of oneness, which was the focus of the last saying, is clarified here so that we are able to understand what can be accomplished when conflicting people or positions attain peace and unity. Power is available to overcome the obstacles which were inherent in the descriptions found in Logion 47.

Notes

One's own house or dwelling place may be the literal domicile in which one lives, but figuratively it may be the domain of one's own inner existence where one is often at war between conflicting desires, demands, drives and priorities.

COMMENTARY

It is historically clear that correct belief, especially about the person or nature of Jesus, became a central issue in early Christianity. This focus seems to have supplanted Yeshua's earlier concerns about the discontinuity between outer religious form and inner spiritual reality.

This saying is already familiar to us, for versions of it are found in the canonical Gospels. There, it is said that if one has faith enough, one can move mountains. Though this may have been the original context for Yeshua's teaching, it appears to show a development in early Christianity where true versus false faith becomes a concern in the Christian communities. In this more primitive Gospel, the original context for Yeshua's teaching does not focus upon the matter of right belief, but instead on the ability to overcome twoness or duality (and the problem of double mindedness) in order to achieve peace in the interior and an exponential potential for spiritual power.

We can more fully grasp the meaning of the two becoming one in this text by using various formulations to help us understand different relationships. We are, of course, familiar with the mathematical formula, $1 + 1 = 2$. In this equation numbers are added together to make a greater quantity, but as this saying suggests, the simple increase of quantity is not a solution. In fact it may become the very basis of further difficulty. In the formulation $2 - 1 = 1$, the subtraction of one entity from another results in only one being left. The problem has been removed, but the result is perhaps a diminishment rather than an increase of power. However, by combining their separate energies in a new unity, the power of action is multiplied as in $1 \times 1 = 1$. This text suggests something of the latter formulation, which we might then call the power of intensification or the concentration of energies.

Philosophically and metaphysically, the principle and manifestation of the doctrine of Eternal Return (descent and ascent) appears to be at the heart of many sacred traditions. In his classic study of the world mythic traditions, ***Hero With A Thousand Faces****, Joseph Campbell explores the many representations of this universal symbol. This topic will be discussed in greater depth in the next Logion.*

If we think cosmologically about the unfolding of reality in the grand cosmic scheme, we must begin with the divine Unity out of which all multiplicity comes. Downward causation, or the descent of reality in an unfolding of being, follows the principle of plenitude and a pattern of multiplicity. The desire of the Infinite is to accomplish a form of realization through expansion into the fullness of being. This is followed by the contrary movement of return as a mode of upward causation (or ascent), where the multiple forms and energies which have been brought into being unite through the principle of unification or harmonization. This brings about an intensification and concentration of power which is able, then, to "move mountains."

Using these fundamental images to illustrate the great cosmic cycle of descent and ascent (or manifestation and return), it becomes clear that in each instance of manifestation the Infinite finds concrete expression. But it is in the arc of ascent where the realization of unification is most needed at the interior level—in the "house" where we dwell, living and moving and having our being. It is here in the interior where our own internal divisions weaken and tear apart the cosmos that the first steps in the new unity-after-diversity must be achieved. Should peace descend there—two becoming one—then any word spoken is not simply a command, it is an act accomplished because a new form of being has been realized.

The realization of a new form of being opens up new possibilities that were never available before. In this image, being precedes action, and action reflects the realities and qualities of being.

The world of duality is indeed filled with "mountains," challenges to any progression. Mountains suggest barriers, and if a barrier is allowed to stand unchallenged it becomes the sign of inertia. Little or nothing is ever achieved and no journey made. However, the journey to ascend—climbing the mountain—is one thing. The possibility of its ultimate removal is quite another. This can only be accomplished through the transcendent principle of unification. This unification releases the power of intensification, where, at the end of the great cosmic cycle, the higher has power to include and transcend the lower.

QUESTIONS FOR REFLECTION

1. We each know the truth underlying this saying. We have been in close proximity to conflict, and we may have also experienced the restoration of peace. Give an example in your own life of both peace and conflict "under the same roof."

2. This saying does not explain how peace between opposing parties is restored. It only says that peace is preferable and more powerful than conflict. How would you explain the power of peace over conflict?

3. In our world we obviously think that conflict is more powerful than peace. What is the basis of our justification for war and conflict?

4. Being a peacemaker is a critical skill in a world where discord abounds. If you were going to teach "peacemaking" what would be its principles? Outline those.

5. Have you ever "removed a mountain?" What was that mountain , and how did you overcome it? What mountains need to be removed in your life at this moment?

An extraordinary example of peace-making is illustrated by the life and work of a woman who was called "the Peace Pilgrim." For a description of her 28 year pilgrimage to promote peace see: ***Peace Pilgrim: Her Life and Work in Her Own Words*** *(1992).*

EXERCISES AND MEDITATIONS

1. You may be in some form of conflict at the moment. In a period of prayerful reflection imagine its opposite, peace. If peace is not capitulation or the subjugation of one party over another, then what is it? How have you experienced this balance, and how did you lose it in the conflict you may currently be experiencing? Can desire for the restoration of peace simply be wishful thinking?
2. Conflict resolution, negotiation, peacemaking and mediation are skills that can be taught. Go online and find out the basic principles underlying each of them. They are not the same, however. Look for how they can be different.
3. The modern experience of making peace in South Africa without tearing the country apart in a bloody civil war has the status of a modern miracle. What was required for this to have happened? How did the power of speech contribute to this accomplishment? What made that voice so powerful? Again, you may wish to go to the Internet and do some historical research. It would be important to share what you find.

In addition to the events in South Africa, survivors of the holocaust have many important things to say about peacemaking in the face of extreme conflict and injury. An important text on this issue and the great conflict of the holocaust is by Tzvetan Todorov, ***Facing The Extreme*** *(NY: Henry Holt, 1996).*

READINGS FOR INSIGHT

I

In the world of things as they are,
there is no self, no non-self.
If you want to describe its essence,
the best you can say is "Not-two."
In this "not-two" nothing is separate,
and nothing in the world is excluded.
The enlightened of all times and places
have entered into this truth.

Seng-Ts'an
The Enlightened Heart
27

II

Our intellectual and moral development is lagging behind the rapidly changing conditions of our existence, and we are finding it difficult to adjust psychologically to the pace of change. Only by renouncing selfishness and attempts to outsmart one another to gain an advantage at the expense of others can we hope to ensure the survival of humankind and the further development of our civilization.

Mikhail Gorbachev
2001

III

Everything can be taken from a man but one thing,
the last of the human freedoms,
to choose one's attitude in any given set of circumstances,
to choose one's own way.

Viktor Frankl
Man's Search for Meaning
104

IV

The well-known paradox holds true:
the more she gave of herself,
the more she found she had to give.

Tzvetan Todorov
Facing the Extreme
88

V

Hasan of Basra was given to extreme ascetic practices. Through these, he won certain occult powers which he took great pride in flaunting.

One day he saw Rabia on the bank of the river. He threw his prayer rug onto the water and shouted to her, "Rabia, come! Let's pray together!"

Rabia replied, "Is it really necessary for you to sell yourself like this? If it is, it is because you are weak."

Then, Rabia ascended into the air on her prayer rug and called down, "Hasan, come up here! Everyone will see us!" Hasan, who was not as advanced as she, stayed silent.

Rabia said to him, "What you did a fish can do. What I did a fly can do. The real work is beyond either of our tricks. The only thing necessary is to do the real work."

Rabia
Perfume in the Desert
121

LOGION 49

Yeshua says,

Blessed are those
unified and chosen.
The Realm of
the Kingdom is theirs.
For out of her you have come,
and back to her you are returning.

Sapiential Themes

- *The continuation of the theme of blessing or beatitude (**makarios**) is extended into the cycle of Eternal Return.*
- *The solitary one participates in an eternal movement coming from beyond space-time and returning to the Realm of transcendence.*
- *Being a Chosen One has in this teaching everything to do with singularity and little or nothing to do with ethnicity.*

Parallel Texts

Logia 16, 23, 75, 106
John 16:28
Plotinus,
***The Enneads** 1.6.8*

FOCAL POINT

In the cycles of blessing which flow through the universe, Yeshua says, the chosen and unified ones are the receivers, for they participate in something far greater than the temporal realm. They come to know the Realm of the Kingdom, for it is theirs. Using the image found universally throughout the sacred traditions across the face of the earth—the circle of Eternal Return—he expresses why it belongs to them. The flow of manifestation and return is the source of the blessing, the unification, the choosing, and the divine Realm in this cycle of Eternal Return. All of these lie at the heart of Yeshua's way of wisdom. He is tuned to these universal principles that are available to (but commonly ignored by) his co-religionists. Their focus instead is upon the precise enactments of external religious form. They choose to make the exoteric faith the heart of their spiritual energy. Another choice must be made.

Links

If unity has been achieved in the preceding Logion, then this saying indicates on what basis the power to move mountains is grounded. The entities (or individuals) in conflict who were the subject of the previous saying, having been unified, are in the flow of blessing which is the movement from and back into the Kingdom.

Notes

This translation returns to the original order of the Coptic text: unified and then chosen. While it perhaps makes logical sense to us the other way, the spiritual semantics may require that we hear it counter to our normal understanding of the order.

COMMENTARY

At the outset it appears that Yeshua espouses a form of exclusivism in this saying—there are those who are chosen and those who are not, and apparently God (or some other transcendent agency) does the choosing—perhaps Yeshua himself. But this interpretation does not solve the problem of who actually does the choosing. Is it we ourselves, and the sum total of all of our choices, which seems larger than any one of them, and looks, then, as though the hand of fate itself has chosen? Is that the ultimate decision maker? Or is it (at least to our eyes) an arbitrary choice made by the Creator who chooses one person over another for whatever reason? Nothing in this saying resolves the question. Perhaps it should be left open-ended. Perhaps it is a mutual decision determined by joint cooperation and participation in the process of unification itself.

The one, however, who chooses (or is chosen) is already the one unified, for, in the original text, the unification comes before the choosing. Here then may be the key. Anyone who moves from fragmentation toward unity—toward the overcoming of opposites (as it has been expressed in the preceding Logia)—becomes a "Chosen One." Unification and choosing, then, may in fact be the same thing. A unified being (a ***monochos***) is a chosen one—chosen for new purposes that have heretofore been unavailable both to the person and for use as divine agency. Perhaps these are two sides of one coin, and anyone living in a state where opposites have been reconciled, by definition, also dwells within the Realm that both transcends and includes all opposites. That realm is **theirs**. It is not simply that they have come to dwell there, but in some fundamental way it now "belongs" to them and they belong to it.

There is a flow out of and back to that Realm. As this saying suggests, it is a primordial flow inherent in the destiny of each being. The Realm of Heaven "belongs" to all of us, for out of her we have come into existence, and to her we are returning, having passed through the difficult initiatory passageway of "this world." So it is here, in this world, then, that one is unified (or not). And it is here that one becomes "chosen."

Joseph Campbell's important text is A Hero With A Thousand Faces (Princeton University Press, 1973).

The myth of Eternal Return, as it has been recounted by Joseph Campbell, is what he calls a **nucleating monomyth**. That is, it is the basic plot line around which all mythological stories from across societies and civilizations are told. According to this Great Myth, a form of God descends from the original home in Light and is caught up in the travails of space-time, which is a kind of shadowland of the Real and Ultimate Reality. After great struggle the hero or heroine breaks through, back into the Light, and ascends toward the homeland once again. This appears to be the image that Yeshua is using here, which is also the plotline of the quintessential story of the Prodigal Son.

__Katabasis__ (descent) and __anabasis__ (ascent) are the words used in Greek for these two great arcs or movements.

The possibility of returning home out of this world, then, is premised upon becoming a unified being. Unification means implicitly that a state of greater wholeness has been achieved from the fragmented parts and pieces that have no cohesion—the common state of humanity. Overcoming fragmentation to attain unity is the prerequisite for participation in the divine Realm that is the motherland, the origin and destiny of all human beings. Only in this condition of unity can it be said that one both dwells in the divine Realm and belongs there because one has become that condition.

QUESTIONS FOR REFLECTION

1. If the basis for being a Chosen One who is useful to the work of the Kingdom is singularity (becoming a unitary being), then what for you is unity? How would you describe it personally?

2. What, for you, is fragmentation? Where do you experience it? How is fragmentation overcome?

3. What is your sense of being an active participant in the Realm of the Kingdom? Do you have any sense that it "belongs" to you?

4. What sense do you have of being in the cycle of Eternal Return, either having come from somewhere else to planet Earth, or being on a trajectory out of it back toward some future destiny?

EXERCISES AND MEDITATIONS

1. Reflect on your sense of being chosen or not chosen for something. You may have experienced this as a child—being chosen for or left out of some game or activity that you wanted to participate in very much. What was this like for you? What are the psychological and emotional results of such choosing?
2. Your parents may have reminded you about your choices and that you ultimately reflect your choices. Or you yourself may have said this to your own children. As you reflect on your own life, how do the choices you have made either include you in certain possibilities, or exclude you from them?
3. Have you ever been ready for something and then excluded from it because you were overlooked or your skills or abilities went unrecognized? Can this happen in regards to the divine Reality, God, or the Kingdom? Reflect on this and write your reflections and how your conclusions may affect your future actions.
4. In a time of meditation read through Yeshua's story of the Prodigal Son, placing yourself within its plotline and framework. Using that story and your imagination, see yourself both leaving your homeland and, after difficulty, returning to it. If this is what your earth-bound experience is like, then how is your personal experience both similar to and different from this story?

READINGS FOR INSIGHT

I

Luke 11:15-24

There was a man who had two sons. The younger of them said to his father, "Father, give me the share of your estate that will belong to me." So the Father divided his property between his two sons. A few days later the younger son gathered all his belongings and set off to a distant country. There he squandered his inheritance on a life of decadence. When he had freely spent everything he had, a severe famine struck the country, and he found himself in desperate need. So he hired himself out to one of the people of that country, who sent him into the fields to feed the pigs. And there he longed to eat his fill of the husks upon which the pigs were fed, and yet no one gave him anything. Finally he came to himself and said ,"How many of my father's hired hands have more than enough bread to eat, but here I am dying of hunger! I will arise and go to my father, and I will say to him, 'Father, I have sinned against heaven and before you; I no longer deserve to be called your son; treat me as one of your hired hands.'" So he set off returning back to his father, who while he was still far off, saw him and was filled with compassion. He ran out to his son, put his arms around him and kissed him. But the son said to him, "Father, I have sinned against heaven and before you; I am no longer worthy to be called your son." But the father ordered his servants, "Quickly, bring out a robe--the best one--and put it on him; put a ring on his finger and sandals on his feet. Then get the fatted calf and kill it, and let us eat and celebrate; for this son of mine was dead and is alive again; he was lost and is found!" And they began to celebrate.

II

C.S. Lewis
Mere Christianity
86-87

... every time you make a choice you are turning the central part of you, the part of you that chooses, into something a little different from what it was before. And taking your life as a whole, with all your innumerable choices, all your life long you are slowly turning this central thing either into a heavenly creature or into a hellish creature: either into a creature that is in harmony with God, and with other creatures, and with itself, or else into one that is in a state of war and hatred with God, and with its fellow-creatures, and with itself. To be the one kind of creature is heaven: that is, it is joy and peace and knowledge and power. To be the other means madness, horror, idiocy, rage, impotence, and eternal loneliness. Each of us at each moment is progressing to the one state or the other.

III

Lao Tzu
Tao Te Ching
16

Each separate being in the universe
returns to the common source.
Returning to the source is serenity.
If you don't realize the source,
you stumble in confusion and sorrow.
When you realize where you come from,
you naturally become tolerant,
disinterested, amused, kindhearted as a grandmother,
dignified as a king.
Immersed in the wonder of the Tao,
you can deal with whatever life brings you,
and when death comes, you are ready.

LOGION 50

Sapiential Themes

- *The Light-Source of humanity is one of the key doctrines of sapiential tradition. Human origins are not found here on earth, but elsewhere.*
- *According to many wisdom cosmologies, archetypal images and icons precede physical manifestation.*
- *Human beings have a living relationship to the Father of Light.*
- *The paradox of movement and rest is a formulation of complementary opposites held together in unity.*

Yeshua says,

Suppose you are asked,
"Where have you come from?"
say, "We have come from
the Light at its source,
from the place where it came forth and
was manifest as Image and Icon."

If you are asked,
"Are you that Light?"
say, "We are its children,
and chosen by the Source,
the Living Father."

If you are questioned,
"But what is the sign of
the Source within you?"
say, "It is movement and it is rest."

Parallel Texts

Logia 2, 51, 60, 83, 84, 90
Luke 16:8
John 12:36
James 1:17

FOCAL POINT

Links

In the previous Logion (49) we entered the movement of descent and ascent. Within this circle of Eternal Return, there is much complexity and many questions about the process. In this saying, Yeshua begins to give instructions on how to work within the framework of those two arcs.

Yeshua introduces a dialogue with a strange set of questions and answers to an inquiry whose context is unknown to us. In the previous Logion (49), Yeshua speaks of descent and ascent, the two arcs of manifestation and return which constitute the pilgrim's passageway through existence. It is a great cosmological vision, one that is shared by many of the ancient sacred traditions. Humanity is on a journey of manifestation from and return to the Source, and in that passageway there are questions and concerns, some raised perhaps by authorities who have dominion over realms through which we must pass. Could this saying, then, relate to that journey and the many stages one enters either in descent or ascent? Yeshua very directly and simply expresses the truths found here which situate the wisdom tradition in an important sacred context. This Logion conveys an entire sapiential theology of its own.

Notes

The metaphysical and cosmological implications of this text are significant. Among them is the concept that Light itself has a transcendent Source which gives itself into energies (Light) and beings (Images, icons and the human children of Light). Manifest reality comes in a great multiplicity, reflecting the infinitude of the great Unmanifest beyond being.

COMMENTARY

*Chariot mysticism (or **Merkavah**) is the early precursor to later mystical traditions within Judaism that we now call the Kabbalah.*

*April DeConick's masterful work is the source for much of the commentary in this Logion. Her text, **Seek to See Him: Ascent and Vision Mysticism in the Gospel of Thomas** (Leiden: E.J. Brill, 1996), examines the entire cosmological framework which grounds this interpretation as a part of the visionary tradition of ascent mysticism explored in early Jewish mystical traditions.*

A number of important scholars of this text consider Logion 50 to be a pivotal saying, crucial to understanding the thought-form behind this entire Gospel. This passage can only be understood if one is familiar with the images and concepts of the Jewish mystical tradition of ascent mysticism (known also as **Merkavah** or chariot mysticism) in which a chariot descends for a human subject and then ascends to the throne and presence of God. The image of this began, of course, in the Hebrew scriptures where Elijah and Ezekiel were said to have been carried aloft in a chariot which descended from above to receive them.

Beginning around the time of Alexander the Great's conquest of Palestine, these images grew into a tradition of spirituality that made the chariot available not only to an elite few, but also for the ordinary human being. A person of intense spiritual devotion could also ascend to the throne of God. According to the ascent mysticism of Judaism it was possible, and many men and women of the first century believed this, including, apparently, Yeshua.

There is also a tradition of mystery teaching that gives instructions and "pass-words" to those who undertake the journey of return or ascent. Yeshua himself, it seems, imparts the mysteries, giving such instruction in what appears to be three stages of the journey.

In the first stage, the true origin of the sons and daughters of humanity is made known. Human origin is not on the horizontal plane as we normally conceive of it. We are not merely physical beings by human birth, but sons and daughters of Light by divine birth. We have descended from the highest point along the vertical axis and became manifested in that descent, perhaps on multiple planes. We have been given imagistic and iconic form in the realm of Paradise, our true birthplace: the place of our primary spiritual manifestation.

At the second stage of the journey a question is asked concerning human essence. Are we the Light or its source? Did we not create light? This may be an examination directed at the hubris of humanity, or it may indicate a query that tests ignorance or proficiency. All who are examined must know, then, that they are not Light's origin, says Yeshua, but were birthed by Light as its children, having been chosen to come into manifestation by Light's living Source, the ***Abba***. It may be that manifestation itself is the sign of being "chosen," which answers the issue in the previous Logion concerning its implied elitism or exclusivism.

At the third and final stage, when questioned about the manifestation of the Source of Light within, Yeshua says that one is to speak this paradoxical formula as proof: "It is movement and it is rest." Movement and rest are at the root of things. This is the state of dynamic equilibrium that holds steady in the midst of change. In Yeshua's teaching, this might be thought of as the Taoism of the West with its Yin and Yang principle. Now the question is, does the simple reiteration of the formula suffice, or is there something more involved? Remember, it is a "sign," and the signification is that it can be observed either by the person who is making the inquiry, or most certainly by the individual who speaks the formula. The sign will not work if there is no evidence, no manifestation of the equilibrium. It is just an empty cipher.

QUESTIONS FOR REFLECTION

1. In the wisdom traditions, human beings are understood to be complex and multidimensional. How many dimensions, realms, or domains are implied in this particular saying?

2. Have you ever experienced the kind of questioning expressed here by either forces outside yourself, or by some inner experience with possible other domains? What were those like?

3. If you were to describe the wisdom theology of this text, what would you say? How would you explain it to someone unaware of it?

4. What is your sense of the realms in the heavens through which you will pass on your way home to the Light and its Source?

EXERCISES AND MEDITATIONS

1. You may not have experienced anything like what this saying portrays. It may lie somewhere in your future, and so Yeshua is preparing you. Imagine that you must know these answers not by rote, but by experience. What would you need to come to learn? How would you learn it? What experiences of learning must you have before making this passageway?
2. In a period of reflection and meditation, imagine yourself confronted by superior beings who question you along the pathway of your journey. What is your sense as you approach these thresholds of inquiry? Do you fear them, or look forward to them? Can you imagine other questions that might be asked that relate either to your life-experience, or to the teachings found in the Gospel of Thomas?
3. There are many interesting examples of movement and rest within our experience. Some of these are known as either movement or rest, which cannot be held together but only experienced sequentially. For example, water is either at rest, as in a quiet pond, or in movement as in a quickly flowing stream. It cannot be both at the same time. Other examples, however, convey the complementary nature of these two states held together in some extraordinary way. For example, you might imagine riding a bicycle, or flying in a glider where the two states are held together. How do you see that both movement and rest can exist at the same moment? What does this mean about the spiritual state that a human can experience within? Have you experienced this state? How can it be made a central part of your inner experience?
4. As you go about your day, practice this inner state of complementarity where movement and rest are held together in balance.

Henry Corbin calls us to the struggle of engaging the ascent into light by turning inward to access the Angels of Earth and Humanity. There we enter multiple realms of light which were envisioned in the Neoplatonic hierarchies and Avicennan recitals. Henry Corbin's ***Avicenna and the Visionary Recital (University of Dallas: Spring Publications, 1980).***

READINGS FOR INSIGHT

I

Jalaluddin Rumi
Light Upon Light
11

We are in darkness and God is Light.
This house receives all its splendor from that Sun.
But here, the Light is mingled with shadow.
Do you want your light totally pure?
Leave the house and climb out onto the roof.

II

Pema Chödrön
Comfortable with Uncertainty
184

As long as we believe that there is something that will permanently satisfy our hunger for security, suffering is inevitable. The truth is that things are always in transition. "Nothing to hold on to" is the root of happiness. If we allow ourselves to rest here, we find that it is a tender, nonagressive, open-ended state of affairs. This is where the path of fearlessness lies.

III

Jalaluddin Rumi
The Book of Love
170

Love is an ocean.
This wide sky, a bit of foam on that.
Restless ... sky-changes move across day and night.
If there were no love, everything would freeze and be still.
Instead, inorganic grains are entering plants.
Plants enter animals, animals enter spirit,
and spirit sacrifices itself for one breath
of that which made Mary with child.
Each sapling lifts, and the universe winds,
like a locust swarm,
its wing-rush toward perfection.
Each article purified
in a song of praise for motion.

IV

Bahauddin
The Drowned Book
36

My soul has two conditions, of motion and of stillness. The moving fills with the energy of love and tenderness actively overflowing and approaching God. The still condition is for resting when I am tired. There I fill with peace, content and contained within non-activity, settling in, loving the quiet.

V

Najm ad-Din Kubra

There are lights which ascend and lights which descend. The ascending lights are the lights of the heart; the descending lights are those of the Throne. Creatural being is the veil between the Throne and the heart. When this veil is rent and a door to the Throne opens in the heart, like springs toward like. Light rises toward light and light comes down upon light, "*and it is light upon light*" (Qur'an 24:35).... Each time the heart sighs for the Throne, the Throne sighs for the heart, so that they come to meet....Each time a light rises up from you, a light comes down toward you, and each time a flame rises from you, a corresponding flame comes down toward you.

LOGION 51

Sapiential Themes

- *Apocalyptic ideas share space with the sapiential tradition, but wisdom trumps the ideas of apocalypse.*
- *The category of* ***rest*** *is one that transcends life and death.*
- *The Realm of Heaven exists in the here-and-now if it can be recognized.*
- *The ability to perceive at a level deeper than sensory or rational knowing is crucial for contemplative wisdom.*

His students asked him,

When does 'rest"
for the dead begin,
and when will the new
cosmos arrive?

Yeshua replied,

"What you are looking for
is already here. You simply have not
recognized it."

Parallel Texts

Logia 3, 113
Matthew 17:9-13, 24:23-28
Mark 9:9-13, 13:21-23
Luke 17:20-25

FOCAL POINT

Links

This conversation is clearly linked to Logion 50, where he also speaks of rest in his final instruction. What this means to the students, however, appears to be very different from the way Yeshua is using the word "rest." Yeshua's answer forces them to attempt a different definition of the word in relationship to themselves.

This section of the Gospel of Thomas contains a series of sayings in which his students ask Yeshua questions and his reply become the core teaching of the logion. In this saying the students' concerns are about their future. They want some explanation of their Teacher's understanding of what the future might be. Their own implicit beliefs are, of course, revealed by the questions, and, as is typical, Yeshua's answer directly challenges those beliefs in order to assert other possibilities that they may have not considered. It appears that they do not fully comprehend the wisdom contained in Yeshua's teaching, remaining often just as puzzled by his answer as they were before they asked, and so they ask another question. Just as often, Yeshua's answers directly contradict not only their beliefs but ours as well, forcing our awareness past the norms of our own contemporary thought.

Notes

The genre of wisdom dialogues is central to sapiential discourse. The format of question and answer is formative for learning. Without a real question, no answer will appear, but a question is always in danger of being challenged and changed by the answer itself.

Early apocalyptic Judaism and Christianity are focused upon future outcomes and political structures. The Kingdom that is to come is imagined as replacing the Roman world's tyranny with a world of justice. The longing for that world underlies much of the dynamic of social and theological thought that is the matrix of the writings from that era and Yeshua's own speaking.

The roots of Jewish apocalyptic thought go back to the Persian period and may be seen in some of the later writings of the Hebrew scriptures, especially Ezekiel and Isaiah 56-66. Among other things, these writings look forward to the return of the theocratic rule in Judea as a kind of new "golden age." Persian influences may also be seen in the sharpening of lines between good and evil forces. Known as "dualism," this idea has often been traced to Zoroastrianism, the dominant religious tradition of Persia after the sixth century. Even so, none of these elements alone constitutes full-blown apocalyptic as such. Instead, the rise of apocalyptic thinking in Judaism may be traced to the latter half of the third century BCE, while Judea was still under Ptolemaic control. It combined elements of new astronomical investigations from (continued...)

COMMENTARY

In the minds of his students, "rest" is a state beyond this life, the purview of the dead. One dies physically to achieve rest, and only then—after death—will one know its reality. Likewise, the new world is a future event. It comes not now, but later, when other events have taken place (and—in the view of most apocalypticists—when the Messiah returns, ushering in a new kingdom on the earth). These are the eschatological coordinates for much of first century Judaism and Christianity, and they remain so today.

In the popular mind of the first century there was no rest here in this world, but only in the hereafter. And the new world could only begin later—at the second coming, for example—when the old world was replaced with a new heaven and earth.

Yeshua seems not to agree with these deferments, nor with the propositions which hold that the here-and-now can never be the site for ultimate realities. Though there is evidence that the future will contain these realities in a fullness that is perhaps greater than what we may experience now, Yeshua plainly teaches a form of "realized eschatology"—that what is in the future can be realized in the present moment in a state we might also call the Eternal Now.

The problem is one of recognition, rather than of not waiting for temporal unfolding or the sequence of certain events which must proceed one after the other. Do we possess the power of conscious perception that will allow us to see that these states and realities are already present in the here-and-now? Or are we are blinded by outer appearances, which seem only to contradict our greatest hopes?

Perception is the key, and has everything to do with the inner states of consciousness and being. Perception is wisdom's answer to human ignorance, and the only answer that the Teacher of Wisdom can give his students who are confused by this troubled world. The Reality that Yeshua sees is here-and-now and he is acting upon it. There is, of course, struggle, and as we shall see in later Logia, deep conflict, which appears to contradict all that Yeshua asserts. His students will experience no rest in this world, at least outwardly, and the kingdom they enter in their immediate future will harass and persecute them. And yet, Yeshua sees that another Reality is indeed present and working now, and it is with that Reality he aligns himself and towards which he assists his students.

Can one know his rest before he dies? It all depends on perception. Rest is not primarily an outer state, but an inner reality of equilibrium and balance, a form of repose or serenity even in the midst of chaos. Is the outer world the only dimension and the exclusive domain of humanity? Yeshua sees that the vertical dimensions of Transcendence and Immanence, an axis which pierces this world, is present as an active agency. In its ultimate unfolding, that Kingdom will have full sovereignty. In truth, one can know that sovereignty now. It is, however, an inner form of knowing, a true ***gnosis*** which contemplates the multi-dimensionality of existence as opposed to its "flatland" appearances. Two eyes, the eye of sensory awareness and the eye of contemplative knowing, can give a human being full dimensional awareness, bringing peace in a world of dis-ease.

QUESTIONS FOR REFLECTION

1. If you had opportunity to ask the Teacher questions about your future, what would you want to know? Is it possible to get answers to these questions now? How?

2. What are your beliefs about the coming world? Do you see breakdown and chaos or breakthrough as the likely outcome?

3. What does inner "rest" mean in a troubled world? How do you actually come to experience it?

4. How do you develop the "recognition software" within your heart that appears to be critical if you are ever going to perceive the world in depth? What would make it possible to develop this way of seeing? What is the practice (or practices) necessary for this to happen?

5. What would be the characteristics of a new world (or the Kingdom) showing through the chaos we experience now? Are there any signs of it? Where do you see those signs? Where do you look for them?

Greek science, the legacy of Persian and Egyptian influences, and basic Jewish theological convictions about the unity and power of the creator God of Israel .... The result was a new kind of cosmological reflection on the nature of the universe that looked back to biblical traditions to understand both present and future conditions. In turn, these new ideas were expressed in a new genre of literature which came to be known as the apocalypse.

L. Michael White
From Jesus to Christianity
69-70

EXERCISES AND MEDITATIONS

1. Inner peace or rest seems to be exactly the state Yeshua is describing. Is "inner peace" actually already within, and you have not recognized it? Is the problem of inner peace a problem of recognition, or is it a state of being related to something else? You cannot know the answer without testing these questions in your own experience. You should explore when it is that you are at rest inwardly and when you are in turmoil. The most vivid image of this is the Gospels' description of storms on the Sea of Galilee and Yeshua walking across the water and speaking peace to the sea. Read the following passages as a part of your meditation and allow them to teach you (Matt. 14:23-36, Mark 6:45-56, John 6:15-21). What can you learn?
2. You have perhaps had some inner sense of knowing that did not come from analyzing the external world and reaching a conclusion about it. This inner awareness is sometimes called **intuitive cognition**. Developing a capacity for intuitive awareness is crucial if we are ever to fully know reality. You might want to spend a day being aware of when things come to consciousness through analysis, and when they seem to "appear" without going through a rational process. Take notes on what you discover about intuitive ability in yourself.

The great Zen master Rinzai, in order to take his students' attention away from the time, would often raise his finger and slowly ask: "What, at this moment, is lacking? A powerful question that does not require an answer on the level of the mind. It is designed to take your attention deeply into the Now. A similar question in the Zen tradition is this: "If not now, when?"

Eckhart Tolle
The Power of Now
43

READINGS FOR INSIGHT

I

Daniel Pinchbeck
2012: The Return of Quetzalcoatl
1, 3-4

Our civilization is on a path of ever-increasing acceleration, but what are we rushing toward? Anxieties are multiplying. The environment is disintegrating. The heat is rising as the ozone layer thins. Jihad faces off against McWorld in senseless wars and televised atrocities. Populations are displaced as cities disappear beneath toxic flood tides. Rogue nations stockpile nuclear arsenals ... These days, an approaching or imminent "End of the World" has taken on the Styrofoam ambience of a cultural cliché. ...the Apocalypse refused to release its grip on the profane imagination of our culture. Movies and television shows spray the message of cataclysmic world destruction, by polar shift, alien attack, flood, flame, comet, or nuclear wipeout. On the level of the collective imagination, W. B. Yeats's famous poem "The Second Coming" is perpetually rephrased.

Things fall apart; the center cannot hold;
Mere anarchy is loosed upon the world,
The blood-dimmed tide is loosed, and everywhere
The ceremony of innocence is drowned;
The best lack all conviction, while the words
Are full of passionate intensity.

II

Eckhart Tolle
The Power of Now
43

Since ancient times, spiritual masters of all traditions have pointed to the Now as the key to the spiritual dimension. Despite this, it seems to have remained a secret. It is certainly not taught in churches and temples. If you go to a church, you may hear readings from the Gospels such as "Take no thought for the morrow; for the morrow shall take thought for the things of itself," or "Nobody who puts his hand to the plow and looks back is fit for the Kingdom of God." Or you might hear the passage about the beautiful flowers that are not anxious about tomorrow but live with ease in the timeless Now and are provided for abundantly by God. The depth and radical nature of these teachings are not recognized. No one seems to realize that they are meant to be lived and so bring about a profound inner transformation.

III

C. G. Jung

The dread and resistance which every natural human being experiences when it comes to delving too deeply into himself is at bottom, the fear of the journey to Hades.

IV

Eckhart Tolle
The Power of Now
43

The whole essence of Zen consists in walking along the razor's edge of Now—to be so utterly, so completely *present* that no problem, no suffering, nothing that is not *who you are* in your essence, can survive in you. In the Now, in the absence of time, all your problems dissolve. Suffering needs time; it cannot survive in the Now.

LOGION 52

His students asked him,

"Each of Israel's twenty-four prophets spoke about you."

Yeshua said,

"You ignore the one living in your presence and talk only about the dead."

Sapiential Themes

- *Tradition, a critical focus in religious faiths, can be both a gift and a hindrance. In this saying Yeshua points out its negative aspects when it prohibits attention in the present moment.*
- *Spiritual presence in the present is also the key to knowing the past.*
- *Yeshua's ability to teach his students depends upon their willingness to give him attention in the present without the pre-conditioning of the past.*

Parallel Texts

Logion 5, 59
Revelation 4:4, 10, 5:8, 14, 11:16, 19:4

FOCAL POINT

If in the last question the students were concerned about their future, in this one their focus is upon the past. Israel has a history of honoring (and sometimes dishonoring) the patriarchs and prophets. In what may be a form of flattery, his students say to him that "the twenty-four prophetic elders recognized in Jewish tradition all spoke about "you, the Messiah." Their comment suggests awareness that there is a continuity of wisdom which they understand to be leading toward the one whom they now accept as the Messiah. Yeshua's response, however, is not encouraging. In fact, he discourages their line of thinking because it cuts them off from the present moment. Just as their focus on the future blinded them to reality now, so their attention on the past prevents them from seeing what is already present before them.

Links

The line of questioning continues, and though perhaps there is no direct link to the subject matter of the last saying, in this Logion the students of Yeshua continue their inquiry and shift the focus from the future to the past, which is the locus of Jewish tradition and practical concern.

Notes

The number twenty-four, a multiple of twelve, is significant in both the Jewish and Christian traditions. This number may stand for the full complement of patriarchs and prophets accepted by convention in Yeshua's day. Comparatively, then, Yeshua is seen to be connected to the prophetic line and its focus upon the Messiah.

COMMENTARY

Past and future are favorite playgrounds for human consciousness. The present moment can be avoided by wandering into speculations about the future, or loitering in the certitudes of prior tradition. It is not that either of these are forbidden realms, it is simply that they tend to capture and hold human attention, helping us avoid what is actively available in the present moment.

We are conditioned by the past. The positive value of tradition is that it provides a context by which we may assess objects and events in the present. Our current thinking and understanding, however, is often "pre-judged" (prejudiced) by the parameters which past thinking and understanding have put around us, like a barrier that prevents us from seeing other possibilities. In the case of his students, Yeshua is aware that their focus upon traditional understanding is keeping them from knowing and engaging the very one to whom they claim the past points. They must come to know him, not about him. They discuss the dead and avoid the living one in their midst, or they know him only in terms of the values tradition has already imposed on them.

Today in philosophical circles, tradition is seen to be the condition under which human beings "read," pre-understand (or make assumptions about), and judge the present. This pre-understanding is the anticipatory structure which determines the way we see reality. It is a kind of prejudice which often keeps us from perceiving its essential reality in any other way.

What Yeshua brings has continuity with the past, of course, but it is also a fresh eruption of wisdom into time. Because it is not a codified wisdom from a traditional perspective, it must be lived out in the real world they inhabit to be fully known. The students' understanding can only grow as they encounter, not the dead traditions of the past, but the one who is living the tradition they honor in the midst of the world they know.

The great line of Jewish patriarchs and prophets is surely in the minds of his students as they question Yeshua. While he too honors the patriarchs and prophets, Yeshua's wisdom is to "live them"—that is, live out their vision, their light, their faith and power in this world. He is the embodiment of the light which falls within their angle of vision. He, too, sees what they saw, but to invoke them as one's primary authority may in fact mask the very light they provide. How often in our world do we hear folk invoking an honorable name in order to strengthen a weak position, hide the truth, or even obfuscate what is real. That person's own actions belie the qualities of the person they have named. Yeshua will have none of it.

Yeshua's students may be expressing their acceptance of Yeshua as the Messiah in this saying. If the prophets pointed toward a coming Messianic figure, then, in their inquiry at least, are they questioning how he might respond to that focus?

Yeshua's answer to his students is a call for them to come out of the future and the past into the present moment, where he works *for* them and *in* them in the Eternal Now. Being present to him as a wisdom Teacher (and as the embodiment of traditional wisdom), they can learn all they have come to honor in name from their past. He is calling them out of duality and double-mindedness (past and present, tradition and originality) into unitary being. Here, the emphasis is not only upon the present moment as the original source of their own becoming, but both past and future have a new living force within the life they experience now. He is inviting them into a living relationship with the transformative Presence standing before them. Tradition will (and has) shaped them, but it will not transform them. This is a truth we have been slow to learn, and while honoring tradition and traditional wisdom, Yeshua knows and teaches that wisdom itself is a form of personal and contemplative encounter which cannot be grounded solely in the past, or for that matter, in the future. Instead, it must be engaged in the present, within lived reality, where it becomes embodied and enfleshed and is not simply invoked through approved names and traditional words.

QUESTIONS FOR REFLECTION

1. The past as tradition can become an idol, especially in a religious environment. When so enshrined, there is very little breathing room for what is happening in the present. The past simply overwhelms the present. How have you experienced religion like this?

2. If you were to identify those traditions, figures from your past (or from history), that influence the patterns of your life at the present moment, what would you choose? Have any of these become barriers to forward progress?

3. Imagine that the Living One as a personal presence is actually within your field of awareness now, and yet you remain unaware because that presence is not available to the outer senses. How might you come to know it without sensory input?

4. Is Yeshua active in your field of awareness for you? How?

EXERCISES AND MEDITATIONS

1. Religion often focuses upon the past, upon tradition with its terms, understandings and regulations. This focus can easily veil or even obfuscate the needs, demands, and difficulties of the present moment, in which case the past can become an escape. In our memory we often think of the "golden" past where difficulties fade into the glow of treasured remembrances. What for you might be such an escape? When, where, and how do you avoid the present moment by living in the past? Is this an ongoing problem, or simply an experience that you know? How has the past become a focus into which you escape from the present moment? Think about this carefully, and give some thought to whether or not this may occur without your even being fully aware of it.
2. In a period of creative imagination, image the person of Yeshua as standing before or alongside of you, wanting contact. In your mind's eye, how might such contact be made? What is the process of getting to know something (or someone) that is far more subtle than the objects of physical reality?
3. Knowledge by Presence is considered to be one of the fundamental ways of coming to know both yourself and another human being. You can learn of someone, but until you are in their presence you can never fully know them, and, in some interesting way, deeper knowledge depends upon how well you know and are aware of yourself. Reflect back on Logia 3 and 5, where the message is similar. Journal your understanding of how Yeshua's abrupt injunction might shake you loose from the past into the present and what that might mean for you.

Balancing the rich treasury of the past with the equally rich flow of events and insights in time is crucial to spiritual practice. As the adage says, "One who forgets the past is doomed to repeat it." Remembrance, therefore, is important, but so too is flexibility and freedom. Mastering such dexterity is serious spiritual work.

READINGS FOR INSIGHT

I

A modern quip

It is often said that religions prefer their mystics dead
rather than alive.

II

Irma Zaleski

In order to find the truth,
we must learn to let go of the lies.

III

William Segal

A master carries the responsibility of refining the capacities of the disciple so that he can begin to realize his true nature.

IV

Doug Thorp commenting on the ***Brothers Karamazov*** *"Parabola" (Vol 25, No. 3, Fall 2000) 28, 30*

In seeking to settle a family dispute in which one brother, Dimitri, is singled out as the scapegoat by a negligent father and his other sons, the elder and guide Zosima stops the "trial for justice" in an unexpected way:

The elder suddenly rose from his place and stepped towards Dmitri Fyodorovich and, having come close to him, knelt before him ... Kneeling in front of Dimitri Fyodorovich, the elder bowed down at his feet with a full, distinct, conscious bow, and even touched the floor with his forehead ... A weak smile barely glimmered on his lips.

"Forgive me! Forgive me, all of you!" he said, bowing then on all sides to all his guests. ...

What is there to say about such a moment? The elder Zosima bows to the ground before Dimitri—before the suffering one. He does not judge, for he knows from within himself this pettiness and arrogance. He sees himself darkly in Dimitri, and knows that this seeing is a gift. His bow and words simply return the gift purified.

V

Peterson Zah

Traditional living is inside a person,
not outside of the person.

VI

Jalaluddin Rumi ***Mathnawi*** *III:1251*

The mention of Moses' name is sufficient to shackle our thoughts, for we tend to assume that what we are reading is a retelling of events that happened in the past. The name 'Moses' acts as a mask, concealing from us the 'Light of Moses' which should be our real concern. In fact, the names 'Moses' and 'Pharaoh' refer to aspects of our own being, so when we read of the enmity between them we should look for these two adversaries within ourselves. The Light of Moses has been passed down from generation to generation, and is with us until the Resurrection.

LOGION 53

His students asked,

"Is circumcision of any help to us?"

Yeshua replied,

"If it were, your fathers would have been born fully circumcised from their mother's womb. The only circumcision that will benefit you at all is spiritual."

Sapiential Themes

- *Physical rites and religious obligations may point toward transcendent reality, but they themselves do not guarantee access to that reality.*
- *If circumcision is accepted as a rite of initiation, its only effectiveness would be interior.*
- *There are aspects of spiritual reality that must come "under the knife," so to speak.*

Parallel Texts

Genesis 17:10-27
Deuteronomy 10:16, 30:6
Jeremiah 4:4
John 7:22-23
Acts 7:8, 15:1, 24
Romans 2:25-29, 3:1
I Corinthians 7:19
Galatians 6:15
Ephesians 2:11
Colossians 2:11

FOCAL POINT

As in the last Logion, the students of Yeshua have tradition and its practice on their minds—in particular, the central act of the Jewish covenant, circumcision. As a physical, social, and religious rite, it is a sign for the Jewish nation of their difference from others and their special status as God's chosen people. It is something to be honored because it singles out the Jewish people as particular and unique, and in their minds at least, special to God. Due in part to the fact that Yeshua is pushing at the boundaries of the tradition, seeking either to extend or even break them down, this question arises perhaps naturally. The students are curious about his attitude toward this venerable tradition. Perhaps he has said nothing about it up till now, all the while making himself available to the "uncircumcised." Are Jews special or not? Is their chosen status in peril if one follows Yeshua's teachings?

Links

The line of questioning from the previous Logia continues, and reaches the point where Jewish uniqueness is involved. Are Yeshua's teachings a threat to national and religious identity? Obviously he has threatened other aspects of Jewish thought and their personal ideals, but now he moves to the core of their personal identity. It is a bold move.

Notes

The notion of the Covenant between God and the nation of Israel is not written in stone, but in flesh—in this case, the literal flesh of Jewish males. This tradition has been sacrosanct for generations, and is now a part of national and religious identity. It seems bedrock, and yet it too will be shaken by Yeshua.

COMMENTARY

For further information on the rite of circumcision, see David L. Gollaher's ***Circumcision: A History of the World's Most Controversial Surgery****.*

There is perhaps no better known rite than the act of circumcision as defining the Jewish tradition. Ancient in origin, it has survived through the millennia into the present day, where its practice no longer has a mythological or theological basis within sacred tradition, but now has solid backing from the medical community on the basis of health. Does it have benefit or not? The majority in the medical profession assert that it does, at least from the point of view of preventing certain illnesses among both males and females.

In ancient Egypt, an intellectually and technically advanced society, circumcision was a ritual that transformed the young into manhood, allowing them admittance into the mysteries. Some scholars suggest that circumcision was, therefore, limited to the elite: priests and pharaohs—but others disagree. For the Egyptians, circumcision was a method of purification—the body's openings were considered portals through which impure and malignant spirits might penetrate.

What has been termed "the world's most controversial surgery" has been in existence from at least the time of the ancient Egyptians. There are Egyptian reliefs that portray this ritual act from the tomb of Ankhmabor in Saqqara dating from around 2400 B.C. According to some scholars, the Jewish people borrowed the practice of circumcision from the Egyptians, who considered it to be rooted in wisdom. Jewish tradition, however, ascribes the act directly to divine revelation made to Abraham, and so roots it in the covenant made between the people and the Lord (YHWH).

Whatever its provenance, the practice of circumcision was of central concern to Jews everywhere, and a mark to distinguish them from the Hellenic culture which rejected it. It is perhaps in that context that his students want to know Yeshua's teaching on the matter. As is so typical of his reply when questioned, Yeshua subverts the common understanding of the tradition, and moves the discussion from external and historical concerns to his central focus: the inner tradition of the heart. It appears that Yeshua even questions whether or not it was an act given by direct revelation. If it were so important to divine Reality, would not humans have been born circumcised? This is at least an interesting deconstruction of Jewish tradition.

What Yeshua sees as priority over tradition and culture is spirit. When he speaks of circumcision "in spirit" or as a spiritual practice, he is referring, without question, to the sense that the outer sign reflects some inner "cutting away" from the organ of the heart. The most sensitive and exquisite organ possessed by a human is the heart with all of its capacities. Yet that core, sensitive organ is often unreceptive because it is covered or veiled from without. That covering or veil must be cut or stripped away. Could it be, then, that the very concerns of his students about the traditional rites are in fact the coverings that must be removed before there can be clear and unmediated receptivity to the divine Reality at the level of the heart?

Nothing in the outer religious tradition gives us the same direct inner access to Spirit that the heart has. If we imagine that some outer religious authority or tradition will give us greater access than the inner organ of the heart, we are wrong. Yet the heart veiled is also a barrier, and so the unveiling (or to use the metaphor of this Logion, the cutting away) of any excessive or extraneous material will be crucial. These coverings may be egoic and self-imposed, or they may be the impositions of culture, social convention, or religious tradition. In either case, we "cannot see from within" (Logion 28), and the resulting blindness cripples the spirit and prevents us from reaching the goal of realized humanity.

QUESTIONS FOR REFLECTION

1. There are many ancient rites that are still practiced in the modern world today. Some of these have lost their original meaning and sacred character, circumcision in particular. How do you feel about such rites and ceremonies?

2. Many people today are reviving ancient rites, some from the Celtic and pagan worlds, to strengthen their ties not simply to the past, but to Spirit. What is your attitude toward this tendency? Do these rites have validity?

3. Is Yeshua's response positive or negative? Why did he respond as he did?

4. If you could ask Yeshua something similar today, what would you ask? Is there something about your own religious tradition you would ask him to comment upon?

EXERCISES AND MEDITATIONS

1. The emphasis that Yeshua puts upon the spiritual observance and symbolism of circumcision is a classic move within wisdom tradition. It represents an emphasis that some call "interiorized Judaism" in Yeshua's teaching. Yeshua continually pointed toward the heart at the core of our being. Its eye can be occluded, its sensitivities clouded. We are put on notice by his response to know the condition of our hearts. In a time of reflection, imagine what could cover the heart and keep it from seeing or being receptive. Make a list of things you notice that diminish its capacities. Write them in a journal and share that list with a trusted friend who, perhaps, does the same exercise with you.
2. It is almost impossible to be aware of that which you are unaware. It's like having a blind spot. You only know something by its absence, not its presence. Suppose that the heart's capacities are like that. If you do not have them, you never notice. However, when they do begin to operate, but are occluded in some way, you notice it. An exercise in inner awareness would be to stay very present in an encounter with someone, and while noticing the outer signs, pay strict attention to the "signs" that you are receiving inwardly and adjust your interaction accordingly. Over time this exercise in discernment can be tuned more finely as your capacities strengthen. Note, however, that inner awareness and the discernment of the heart is something that can not only be covered over, but can also be skewed or distorted by your ego structure. Learning the exercise of ego-detachment, therefore, is critical.
3. An exercise in ego-detachment is allowing external circumstances that are bothersome, irritating, or a challenge to ego-identity to have full play without pushing them away. Respond by dropping the ego's demand for protection and allow the painful encounter to challenge and perhaps diminish egoic demand.

READINGS FOR INSIGHT

I

Too many people are living in a prison
that they themselves have manufactured.

Michael Beckwith

II

For the sake of the Lord, be circumcised,
remove the foreskins of your hearts,
O men of Judah and citizens of Jerusalem;
lest my anger break out like fire
and burn till none can quench it,
because of your evil deeds.
Your conduct, your misdeeds, have done this to you.
How bitter is this disaster of yours.
How it reaches to your very heart.

Jeremiah 4:4, 18

III

My heart was cloven and there appeared a flower,
and grace sprang up from the midst bearing fruit to the Lord,
for the Highest One split me open with the sacred Spirit,
exposing my love for him and filling me with his.

His splitting of my heart restored me,
so now I followed the way of his peace, the way of truth.
I received his knowledge from its beginning to its end,
and now I sit, resting on the rock of truth where he has placed me.

Odes of Solomon 11

IV

Male circumcision was, of course, a custom already widely practiced in the ancient world. In pagan societies, circumcision, performed at the time of puberty, was part of a male rite of passage (it may have served symbolically as an act of human sacrifice to the gods). A mark on his maleness, circumcision was a sign not only of the youth's new sexual potency but also of his initiation into the male role and male society (putting an end to his primary attachment to his mother and the household, to the society of women and children). But in the new way of ancient Israel, the special obligation of the covenant gives the practice of circumcision a new and nearly opposite meaning. An initiation rite of passage of young males into adult masculinity is transformed into a paternal duty regarding the male newborn. Israel's covenant with God begins by transforming the meaning of male sexuality and of manliness altogether.

Covenantal circumcision emphasizes and sanctifies man's natural generative power, even as it also restricts and transcends it. To be performed on children only eight days old, it celebrates no sexual potency but procreation and (especially) perpetuation. Though it is the child who bears the mark, the obligation falls rather on the parents; it is a perfect symbol of the relation between the generations, for the deeds of parents are always inscribed, often heritably, into the lives of their children.

Leon R. Kass
The Beginning of Wisdom
313

LOGION 54

Sapiential Themes

- *Material wealth and spiritual abundance are worlds apart.*
- *The experience of poverty opens the way into the reality of heaven.*
- *Blessedness is an inner state having little to do with external coordinates.*

Yeshua says,

You poor are blessed,
for the realm of heaven
is already yours.

Parallel Texts

Psalm 35:10, 40:17, 72:12-13, 109:22
Matthew 5:3
Luke 6:20
James 2:5-7

FOCAL POINT

Ask most people what they would want to happen to them in their wildest dreams, and the answer for many would be winning the lottery and having no financial worries for the rest of their lives. What could be better than to be rich? In our minds those who are truly blessed are the rich of the earth, and the cursed are those who live in poverty. Yeshua does not agree. His perceptions and values of this world are completely different. This saying, which is central to what has traditionally been called the Sermon on the Mount, is at the heart of his seeing and teaching. The question is: why would he see it this way, and what is the meaning of this teaching? If this is not just another form of piety that encourages thrift, frugality and prudence as a moral category for a "righteous person," then what is it? How is it a principle of divine Reality and not simply another ethical admonition?

Links

The question which his students ask about circumcision and whether or not it is of any benefit, in the semiotics of this text, is perhaps what determines the position of this next Logion. If the external marks of circumcision are of little benefit, then what is? In a surprising move, Yeshua introduces the benefits of poverty—another form of "taking away" or "removal" of what is extraneous.

Notes

Wealth and riches are often perceived only in terms of external accumulations and obvious signs of abundance. Hidden abundance or wealth is another matter. Only a true spiritual Master can perceive the difference. Throughout his early sojourn Yeshua demonstrates his capacity to see past the surface to the inner states of wealth or poverty.

COMMENTARY

Greed used to assure a steady growth in economic development at the expense of the future of humanity, the environment, our health and the health of the planet. It is a mind-set that is touted as being the cold, hard reality of the "real world." But the evidence all around us is clear: it is not reality at all, but an illusion that is destroying us.

Contrary to popular opinion and the dominance of the social values and expectations all around us in the contemporary world, the current direction we are headed is not only wrong, but in the end, bound to fail. The emphasis we put in the West on the economic bottom line for almost every activity and enterprise we undertake is a poison which has the potential of destroying us, not only individually, but collectively, and the planet as well.

Think about it this way: the systems of our world are built upon the foundations of money and finance. Having it, making it, having enough, securing it for ourselves until we die—all this becomes the central focus of human life in the contemporary world . It is perhaps not the only value. But for many, if not most folk, the value of economic gain is very high indeed. The economy is what drives the engines of contemporary thought, politics, industry, commerce, power and politics. Even religion has succumbed to this powerful force, creating "prosperity theologies" which insist that being rich is a sure sign of divine blessing, while financial failure, want, and loss are a mark of divine displeasure. Wealth, then, becomes the driving force behind our social conventions, and society's richest individuals become cultural icons.

Like bliss in the East, blessedness is an inner dimension of interior fullness that has nothing to do with external wealth.

The Masters of spiritual wisdom and human transformation see this clearly. They do not accept the world's evaluation that what is important, crucial, valuable, or worthy of our energies is economic value only. On the contrary, they assert that it is the poor, not the rich, who possess another value that is truly blessed, thought this may be an absurd assertion for many of us. One could make the case, of course, that greed of any kind not only eventually destroys the external world, but has serious deleterious effects upon the human spirit as well. This seems to be more of a moral principle in people's minds than a spiritual reality. The issue of blessedness and what it actually means becomes critical here. If blessedness is not a commodity, but rather a state which one enters from within, then it may not have any physical coordinates whatsoever. In fact, if we are to understand Yeshua's teaching, external wealth may inhibit or even exclude the state of interior blessedness. The question, again, is why? The answer appears to be that because the maintenance of wealth is an external (horizontal) focus or even obsession, it cuts us off from openness to the wealth and flow of interior vertical reality.

Being poor may in fact open up the inner domain of a human being in a way that wealth never can. Perhaps also the experience of external poverty creates the condition for the possibility of inner wealth that material prosperity obstructs. It makes no rational sense to us that this should be true, but experientially we often find that it is the case.

Might any experience of poverty, for example, a lack of beauty, silence, or social contact, create an inner condition of sensitive awareness that the full satisfaction of these needs and desires could never do? Might that longing (not necessarily the lack of these things, just the longing) be the very state which is called blessed, because in that privation an inner dimension of sensitive awareness is opened that we would not experience otherwise? It is not poverty per se, then, that is blessed, but rather the inner condition—which creates a new state of the heart that is receptive, open, and sensitive. That receptivity and openness is what constitutes the condition of blessedness. Yeshua is not focusing upon outer conditions but upon inner states and possibilities. Anything that might awaken an inner awareness of the vertical axis and its dimensions is ultimately blessedness—a state into which we are invited by the Master of Transformation.

QUESTIONS FOR REFLECTION

1. Have you ever been poor? What was it like? Was there any benefit to being poor that you noticed?

2. How do you view the universe: as full and plentiful, or as a world of scarcity where abundance is in short supply? What is the result of your viewpoint?

3. How do you view your relationship to wealth and poverty? Do you actively seek one versus the other? What form of activity does that take?

4. What benefits have come to you from any kind of lack or true need?

EXERCISES AND MEDITATIONS

1. Experiment with satiation and emptiness and journal the results. One way to do this is to overeat or over drink and then to observe what happens when your senses are on overload and satiated. What happens when the opposite is the case and your external needs are unfulfilled?
2. Another experiment would be to envision what happens when there are no challenges, no rough edges to life experience, no pain, no threat—nothing but largesse and security, and then, when things get rough, to examine your inner life again. How does the experience of pain or threat change the nature of your spirit, your inner sense of reality, or your relationship to God?
3. Fasting has always been one methodology for creating a spirit of inner need and openness. Many traditions have extended periods of fasting as a part of the spiritual discipline that a student undergoes. In Christianity this is a regular practice during the Lenten season, and in traditional Catholic Christianity, a form of fasting was observed on Friday. In Islam, the whole month of Ramadan is devoted to a special form of fasting where food and water are not ingested while it is daylight. Some native traditions in North America practice extreme forms of fasting from food and water for up to four days as a part of a cleansing ritual or a vision quest. You might choose a period of retreat for one or several days to refrain from eating. Observe what it does to consciousness and your inner awareness of spirit.
4. Examine what happens to you when the external indicators of abundance, security, plenty, or fullness of any kind are stripped away. What part of you reacts negatively? What part of you may respond with greater sensitivity? No one likes the feeling of pain, but clearly pain itself can bring opportunity.

READINGS FOR INSIGHT

I

There is a glut of wealth in the city of Saba.
Everyone has more than enough.
Even servants wear gold belts.
Huge grape clusters hang down on every street and brush the faces of the citizens.
No one has to do *anything*.
You can balance a basket on your head and walk through an orchard,
And it fills by itself with ripe fruit dropping into it.
Stray dogs meander down lanes full of thrown-out bone scraps
With barely a notice.
The lean desert wolf gets indigestion from all the rich food.
Everyone is fat and satiated with all the extras, and there are no robbers.
There is no energy for crime....or, for gratitude,
And no one wonders about the unseen world.
The people of Saba feel bored just with the mention of prophecy and revelation.
They have no desire of any kind – O, maybe some idle curiosity about miracles,
But that's it.
This overrichness is a subtle disease.
Those who have it are blind to what is wrong, and deaf to anyone who points it out.
The city of Saba cannot be understood within itself.
But there is a cure, an individual medicine,
Not a social remedy:
Sit quietly, and listen for a voice within that says, ***Be***.
As that happens, your soul will start to revive.
Give up talking and your positions of power.
Give up excessive money.
Turn toward your teachers and the prophets who don't live in Saba.
They can help you grow sweet again and fragrant,
Wild and fresh again, and thankful for any small event.

Jalaluddin Rumi
The Soul of Rumi
64

II

People generally eat up the teachings, but when it comes to doing ***tonglen***, they say, "Oh, it sounds good, but I didn't realize you actually meant it." In its essence, this practice is: when anything is painful or undesirable, breathe it in. In other words, you don't resist it. You surrender to yourself, you acknowledge who you are, you honor yourself. As unwanted feelings and emotions arise, you actually breathe them in and connect with what all humans feel. We all know what it is to feel pain in its many guises.

You breathe in for yourself, in the sense that pain is a personal and real experience, but simultaneously there's no doubt that you're developing your kinship with all beings. If you can know it in yourself, you can know it in everyone.

Pema Chödrön
Comfortable with Uncertainty
85

III

If you want to learn how to govern, avoid being clever or rich. The simplest pattern is the clearest. Content with an ordinary life, you can show all people the way back to their own true nature.

Tao Te Ching
65
Translated by
Stephen Mitchell

LOGION 55

Yeshua says,

Whoever does not
refuse father and mother
cannot become my student.
Whoever does not reject
brother and sister
accepting the cross as I do,
is not ready for me.

Sapiential Themes

- *Symbolically, one's family stands for the root identity of the personal self.*
- *Personal identity as defined by the social order or family systems theory may be one of the most debilitating definitions for ultimate identity.*
- *Being made ready for the Master's instruction is always an issue of spiritual direction and developmental progression. Spiritual pilgrimage is dependent on readiness or "adequation."*

Parallel Texts

Logion 101
Matthew 10:34-39, 16:24-25
Mark 8:34-35
Luke 9:23-24, 14:25-33

FOCAL POINT

The image of the cross is a vivid and even lurid symbol in the culture and times of Yeshua. Upon it hung criminals and malcontents, particularly those who had been judged to have agitated against the "law and order" of the Roman empire. As a warning to others, Roman authorities often crucified men and women in an attempt to subdue the rebellions smoldering just beneath the political and social surfaces of the Empire. Is this the cross to which Yeshua is pointing? Or, rather, is the suffering of the cross he knows a self-induced rejection of the rigid family structures to which the Jewish world was traditionally bound? Does Yeshua deliberately set himself against the tradition of family—his own parents and siblings—in order to follow his heart and his mission? It appears from this Logion that he has some personal experience of this excruciating choice of breaking his family ties.

Links

Yeshua speaks about the blessings of impoverishment in the previous saying. Counter to our understanding of modern (or western) life, his statements point toward another state in which some new opening and possibility occurs when there is diminishment. One of the forms of impoverishment and letting go may be as close to home as our own family and parentage.

Notes

*The terms **refuse** and **reject** used in this translation express the word that is traditionally translated as "hate" in other early texts. The fact that it can be translated in other ways is shown by how it is used in Logion 43.*

COMMENTARY

In this saying, one authority pits itself against another. Yeshua sets aside the normative influences of family, social programming, and the influences of our native home-world for a higher authority—heaven itself. Yeshua asserts that such a choice must be made if one is to be his student. It is a hard and difficult choice. It is a form of crucifixion. Many troubling issues are raised by this saying and by the traditional ways of translating it that make the statement of Yeshua appear even harsher. Traditionally, the phrases have been translated to read that one must "hate" one's parents and siblings in order to follow Yeshua. This goes clearly against the fundamental tenets of Jewish law as set out in the Ten Commandments, where one is enjoined to honor one's father and mother. Could this be the correct interpretive approach to this saying, or is the wisdom of Yeshua directed at something entirely different? It is highly unlikely that Yeshua is setting aside the requirement of honoring one's parents for a hateful dismissal of their rightful parental claim. So how do we approach Yeshua's stark proclamation as a decisive form of wisdom crucial for the realm of heaven?

One of the crucial insights in the modern age is that the structure of the personal self is, in fact, a "social construct;" that is, it is made up of the stuff of our social environment. In essence, the "I" has been constructed out of the building materials of the social world around us. One of the most crucial sites from which the materials that make up the "self" comes from is, of course, the family structure and heritage to which we belong. It is easy to see that the external world in large part defines who most individuals are. It is natural that this be so, for without it, we cannot live within the societies into which we have been born.

Someone born into a Chinese family and into the social world of China will develop a personality that reflects the mores, belief systems, behavior patterns, and ways of seeing the world that are the result of that social structure. This pattern connects us to the human world around us.

The wisdom tradition sees, however, that the "self" we imagine ourselves to be is, in fact, not the ultimate form of our being, but a temporal and transitional entity which is evolving toward its ultimate shape and destiny. The Ultimate Self is far different from the temporal self born out of human culture. It transcends what we know as ourselves, for it moves in the direction of a destiny that includes far more than the human realm. To awaken to this possibility will mean, inevitably, that we must forsake the tightly limiting definitions of the self as seen from the perspective of our culture and society in favor of another, higher perspective that includes, but is not limited to, the purely human temporal form. In order to move forward, then, we must in some sense refuse to accept the belief system concerning who we are as perpetuated by our fathers, mothers, brothers and sisters. If we are not prepared to do this, and simply hold onto the human (parental and societal) definition of who we are, then we will remain developmentally arrested in infantile patterns when the greater adulthood of our heavenly paternity and maternity awaits us.

It is easy to imagine that the reference to the cross used here is the one Yeshua will experience at the end of his life. Perhaps, though, it is a mistake to see the cross as only an external reality, and that the cross meant here is the burden of suffering that is born as one is "nailed" by the social systems all around us, putting pressure and pain upon the spiritual pilgrim.

To refuse to believe the definitions of the self perpetuated by social conditioning is not a dishonor to our parents and siblings, but it does require an act of courage that may, in some respects, be as difficult as physical crucifixion. For to leave behind the carefully defined self is to run counter to the expectations of who we are that are maintained around us. To step outside those boundaries can be, for many, a form of excruciating pain, especially when the familiar world then becomes hostile to the new definitions we begin to express. This can be a daunting task, but the courage it takes to undergo this evolutionary transformation readies one for the teachings and ministrations of wisdom's Master.

QUESTIONS FOR REFLECTION

1. If you are an adult, undoubtedly at some point in your young adulthood you left home and family to establish yourself independently of them. What did this feel like? Did your parents perceive it as a rejection of them?

2. Many teenagers go through a period of rebellion where they totally reject the mores and patterns of their parents in order to establish individual difference. Did you have to go through this? What was it like to do so?

3. Have you ever had to "crucify" something dear to yourself in order to move forward? What happened and what was the result?

4. Is there something that needs to be rejected that you have not been able to do up till now, but which holds you back in your spiritual pilgrimage?

EXERCISES AND MEDITATIONS

1. Reflect on your own identity. How much are you your mother's or father's child (or product)? How much are you the creation of your family-of-origin and the society from which you come? How have you evolved to become different from these? How has your own spiritual evolution come about? Reflect on what role rejection of accepted definitions of who you are (or should be) has played in your life. Consider the projections of your siblings (your social soul-mates). Consider the pressure your peers have put upon you. Consider the social conditioning that this represents, and how it has shaped your life. After these reflections, make an inventory of those aspects that might in fact cripple you. You might want to talk to a trusted friend or spiritual advisor and get his or her honest evaluation of your findings as a kind of cross-check.
2. If the criteria for becoming a student of Yeshua is outlined in this saying, how close are you to being one of his students—that is, taught and guided by him? What would it mean to "get ready" for the teaching of this Master of wisdom? How would suffering (the sense of crucifixion in some way) support the learning and make you ready for the teaching? In a period of reflection, consider the role that suffering has already had in making you either ready for or resistant to Yeshua's teaching. Could it be that your relationship to him has not been sufficiently tempered by human experience—especially the experience of pain?
3. If you were going to help someone else understand the principles of this saying, how would you teach this wisdom? What illustrations would you use to do so?

READINGS FOR INSIGHT

I

In contemplating Paul's spirituality of "the cross," finally, we must never forget the meaning of crucifixion during the *pax Romana*. Crucifixion was first-century Rome's most insidious and intimidating instrument of power and political control—"the most miserable [or pitiable] of deaths," "the worst extreme of the tortures inflicted upon slaves," an "accursed thing" or "plague" (Josephus). It was Rome's torturous, violent method of handling those who were perceived to threaten the empire's "peace and security"; everyone in the empire knew of the "terror of the cross" (Cicero). To suffer crucifixion was to suffer the most shameful death possible. Moreover, for Jews a crucified person was a person cursed, since "anyone hung on a tree is under God's curse" (Deut. 21:23). It was therefore an inherently absurd and offensive move on the part of early Christians, Paul included, to make a crucified political criminal and his cross—"the most nonreligious and horrendous feature of the gospel"—the focus of devotion and the paradigm for life in this world. Since this world was indeed the world of the *pax Romana*, centering on the cross was also an inherently anti-imperial posture that unashamedly challenged the priorities and values of the political, social, and religious status quo. The modern interpreter of Paul, who has no firsthand experience of either the horrors or the political function of crucifixion, is obligated to recall this reality deliberately and frequently while reading Paul's letters.

Michael J. Gorman
Cruciformity: Paul's Narrative Spirituality of the Cross
5

II

When Moses saw the Light from the (burning) bush, he said, "My search is over, for I have been granted this gift.'
God said, 'O Moses, cease your wandering! *Throw down thy staff'* [Q 28:31].
Moses straightaway cast from his heart kinfolk, friends, and companions.
This is the meaning of *Put off thy shoes!* [Q 20:12]
'Sever thy love from the two worlds!'
The house of the heart has room for none but God …

Jalaluddin Rumi
Mathnawi I: 1239-40

III

The opposite of samsara is when all the walls fall down, when the cocoon completely disappears and we are totally open to whatever may happen, with no withdrawing, no centralizing into ourselves. That is what we aspire to, the warrior's journey. That is what stirs us: leaping, being thrown out of the nest, going through the initiation rites, growing up, stepping into something that's uncertain and unknown.

What do you do when you find yourself anxious because your world is falling apart? How do you react when you're not measuring up to your image of yourself, everybody is irritating you because no one is doing what you want, and your whole life is fraught with emotional misery and confusion and conflict? At these times it helps to remember that you're going through an emotional upheaval because your coziness has just been, in some small or large way, addressed.

Pema Chödrön
Comfortable with Uncertainty
65

LOGION 56

Yeshua says,

Those who make knowledge
of the cosmos their specialty
have made friends with a corpse,
but the cosmos is not worthy
of those who know it to be so.

Sapiential Themes

- *Traditional wisdom understands the world we live in (the worldly cosmos) to be an outer form hiding its essence.*
- *Wisdom's insight is that the current form of the world is lifeless—without its inner essence.*
- *Knowing the true nature of the world is the understanding of the sage who transcends it, whose worth is inestimable.*

Parallel Texts

Psalm 1
Matthew 16:26, 24:38-39
I Corinthians 7:31
Ephesians 2:2
Colossians 3:2
II Timothy 2:4
James 4:4
I John 2:15

FOCAL POINT

At the center of this Logion is the vivid image of a corpse or a cadaver. Few of us are unaffected by the sight of a dead body either at a funeral, or one discovered suddenly in an unexpected place. No one wants to be confronted unexpectedly by a corpse. Horror stories abound with this theme, often beginning with just such a scenario. Yeshua points out a corpse he sees lying just in front of us. Through his eyes, the conventional world of human experience is a kind of horror story in which we each are busily making friends with the dead. Stated in this way, we begin to feel the repulsive power of this metaphor. It is shocking, but if we will not turn away, we may learn a new depth of wisdom from this hard saying.

Links

In the last Logion, giving up the familial foundations of the human self as a fleeting aspect of one's being and replacing it by an eternal essence is said to be a cross that one must bear. This saying expands the notion of the familial by taking it from the family to the cosmos, the world of human invention. To know the truth about this world and these relationships determines the extraordinary nature of the person who possesses such knowledge.

Notes

*The phrase "made friends with" is a translation of the Coptic term meaning **seize** or **take hold of** which is used in the first and other Logia to indicate finding or grasping something.*

COMMENTARY

The term ***cosmos*** *(kosmos) is one which stands in this text (as well as in the early writings of the Apostle Paul), for the world of human construction, riddled with distortion and structural evil.*

The esoteric understanding for the imbalances of the modern world is explained by Tom Cheetham in this manner: "On the one hand, the truths of Nature are taken literally—those Abstractions of the Will to Power the inflationary effects of which on the soul are wholly destructive. ... On the other hand, are the whims of the ego, *unconstrained, fantastic: the result of an Eros disoriented, grasping and desperate for Presence, abandoned and alone.* ***The World Turned Inside Out****, 129.*

Interestingly, the word ***cosmetic*** *is derived from the word* ***kosmos*** *in Greek, which associates the external manifestation of the world as a face made to look better than it is.*

Within Sufism there is the concept of a human being who has attained a heightened state of wisdom and transformation, and as such has become the ***pole*** *around which the world revolves unknowingly and without which it could not survive physically.*

A corpse is, of course, a body with no animating power or life to sustain it. It is, therefore, in a state of degeneration and decomposition. A decomposing body is abhorrent to us. The only safe thing to do with it is to bury it. This harsh evaluation of the world-as-corpse is a theme that Yeshua often uses in this text to describe the normative life of humankind along the horizontal axis; that is, we live in a world engineered by human motivations cut off from transcendent reality. This defines the way the word "cosmos" is used in this and other early Christian texts, particularly in the Gospel of Thomas. It is not the starry heaven that the speaker has in mind, but the manufactured world of human creation that often inflicts horrible pain upon its members, marginalizing the majority of humanity in favor of a privileged few.

This is the world of the Roman empire in an occupied land—the land in which Yeshua ministered, and was born and reared. It was **that** world which appeared to Yeshua to be a corrupt and decomposing corpse. To the naked eye it appears to be "alive," but it is not. The lifelikeness is illusory. In fact, the world as we know it is a hollow shell—a form without its essence. Yet we mistake it to be the essence—the be-all-end-all—and thus have grasped a corpse.

To embrace the world in this way, to be its spokesperson, a person of expertise on how to explain the world and make it work, is to befriend its lifeless body—a body that might look alive, but is in fact devoid of spirit. A human body without its animating and life-giving spirit is a great sorrow and tragedy. Human society without access to the flow of divine Spirit is the same, and the result is more often than not a horror. It is no different today. The twentieth and twenty-first centuries bear witness to that fact and its terror. In fact, terrorism has become its watchword.

To become a connoisseur of this particular social configuration of human-making is, again, to grasp hold of a corpse. Imagine hanging on to a dead body. Knowingly, it is something we would not want to do, and yet we do it unknowingly. Wisdom teaches us the truth because it sees past the surface of the world and its cosmetic appearances to the reality (or lack thereof). It is exactly here that we encounter the crucial point of this saying. True knowledge—sapiential knowing—is the key. The sage knows the truth of things and can discern the surface structure of the beautified cadaver from the Reality behind forms. The sage also knows whether something lives or is only made to look alive.

Someone who possesses or has grasped this form of knowledge transcends the world of the corpse and all of the enormous efforts to make it appear real. That person is a treasure to this world, and in terms of worth and value, far beyond anything this world knows and counts as valuable. In truth, the human world is not worthy of such a person of wisdom and will probably reject and expel this person from its precincts along with his or her wisdom. Still, such wisdom exists, but normally goes unrecognized and unacknowledged in our midst. Two evaluations of conventional human culture, two attitudes toward its relative importance, and two kinds of knowledge which one may possess—the divide between them runs like a fissure inside human experience between those who see and those who do not. There are those with sapiential sight and those who are "born blind."

QUESTIONS FOR REFLECTION

1. How did this saying strike you originally?

2. What has been your experience of contact with the body of a dead person? Have you ever come upon a dead body unexpectedly?

3. Have you ever experienced that something was dead and gone (perhaps figuratively), when everyone else imagined that there was no change and treated it as fully alive? This might be a relationship or some institutional entity. Explain your experience.

4. The opposite experience is not to see something that someone else sees deeply, and to feel either that that person is imagining something, or that you are somehow inadequate and left out for not seeing what they see. Describe this kind of experience.

Most of us have a fear of death. We quite naturally resist that passageway, and do everything in our power to avoid it. We resist what we do not know. Folk who have undergone Near Death Experience in some form report a lessening of this fear. You might want to explore NDE (Near Death Experience) literature, of which there is now quite a lot.

EXERCISES AND MEDITATIONS

1. There is a Buddhist practice that asks monks to go into a cemetery and meditate there on the transient nature of human life in the cosmos. To reflect upon this saying is similar, for it focuses our attention upon the illusory nature of the way we view the world and our life within it. In a kind of adaptation of Buddhist practice, find a family photo of one of your relatives that has passed from this world. Set it up so that you can quietly gaze at this picture of a loved one. Allow your mind to focus on the fact of that person's life—how they have passed through this world in all of its details, and are now so quickly gone from it. Spend time with this image. Experience how this kind of meditation upon the transience of life affects you. Journal your experience and your observations.
2. Saints and sages were the wise beings who knew the world for what it was and responded so differently to it from the normal expectations about human behavior. Iconic images are tools that may assist in knowing the truths of these wise beings. Find one of these icons. In a time of silent meditation, gaze at the image and allow your awareness of this individual's life to teach you about the treasury of wisdom available to you.
3. We have experts in this world's affairs all around us. One immediate source is to watch a news channel on television and experience the response of individuals who are questioned about their expertise. Notice the certitude that is expressed about the solidity and importance of the world. Notice how little of this knowledge is expressed in light of something transcendent to their narrow field of expertise. Take one example and outline what you find. Share your findings with others of like mind.

READINGS FOR INSIGHT

I

To realize my original nature
and to do good is my religion.

Daisetz T. Suzuki

II

There are two complementary ways of effecting an irreparable scission between the sensory and the spiritual, between the exoteric and the esoteric: namely, by an exclusive attachment to one or the other; the catastrophe is the same in either case. Esoterism degenerates into a purely abstract knowledge, that of the forces of nature, for example, or else succumbs to spiritual libertinage ... the exoteric, deprived of its theophanic function, degenerates into a covering, a hollow cortex, something like the corpse of what might have been an angelic appearance, if this would be conceivable. Everything, then, becomes institutionalized; dogmas are formulated, legalistic religion triumphs; the science of Nature becomes the conquest and possession of Nature ...

Henry Corbin
Swedenborg and Esoteric Islam
107

III

We must not disparage the body, nor sacrifice the spirit. The body is the discipline, the pattern, the law; the spirit is inner development, spontaneity, freedom. A body without a spirit is a corpse and a spirit without a body is a ghost.

Abraham Heschel
God in Search of Man
341

IV

I search for what is truly alive, wanting to be clear with discernment there. I read in the Qur'an 17:110, "Call on God the most merciful, the most compassionate, or use any of the gracious names." When you move into those qualities, vitality and intelligence increase. The energy that builds a city, minaret, and archway colonnade comes as a gift from the qualities of god, the same that holds the sky in its motions and the mountains in their stillness (51:47). When you cannot sense this being held, nothing interests; nothing delights or makes you wonder. Human aliveness fades as vision fails to see the source that makes and moves through form, shaping events.

Bahauddin
The Drowned Book
108

V

"When will I be Enlightened?"
"When you *see*," the Master said.
"See what?"
"Trees and flowers and moon and stars."
"But I see these every day."
"No. What you see is paper trees, paper flowers, paper moons and paper stars. For you live not in reality but in your words and thoughts."
And for good measure, he added gently, "You live a paper life, alas, and will die a paper death."

Anthony de Mello
One Minute Wisdom
37

LOGION 57

Yeshua says,

God's realm is like this:
A farmer planted good
seed in his field,
but at night enemies came
and sowed it with weeds.
When he found out
he did not allow them to be
pulled up, saying
"No, you might uproot the grain
along with the weeds.
Wait till harvest.
It will be perfectly apparent then
which ones are the weeds,
and you may pull them out easily
and burn them."

Sapiential Themes

- *In Yeshua's wisdom, the activity of the divine Realm is likened to the world as being a field under cultivation.*
- *The farming is done by the Master of Wisdom who knows how to treat unwanted produce in the fields of existence.*
- *The Eschaton is the place of definitive discernment and ultimate decision.*
- *Patient waiting is required in the work of cultivating the world.*

Parallel Texts

Logion 9
Job 4:8
Psalm 126
Proverbs 6:14, 16:28, 22:8
Hosea 8:7
Matthew 13:24-30, 13:36-43
Luke 8:5
Galatians 6:8

FOCAL POINT

God's realm is a world under cultivation. In fact, one could say that God is farming the human world, producing for a future harvest. We judge the outcome in the middle of time. God discerns the outcome at the end of time. This is a difference in perspective that determines whether or not we will seek to control the results now by disturbing the process in the middle, rather than waiting till the end. The sapiential concept of letting be till the *Eschaton*—the summation at the end of temporality—is one that is difficult for people possessed of common sense, especially men and women of the western world where instant results and immediate gratification are so valued. It is difficult to take the long-term view, but in this saying Yeshua's understanding spans the whole history of human time and sees from that perspective.

Links

Like previous sayings, this Logion is also a commentary on the ambiguous nature of the world in which we live. Here opposing forces in the world are seen to actively sow harm in the field of human endeavor. Whoever the enemy is, it acts with intelligence, and yet wisdom's response is different from what one would imagine.

Notes

The term ***Eschaton*** *is Greek and refers to the end or consummation of time as a historical process. History will meet its End in a sorting-out process. The Jewish tradition seems to have received its ideas about eschatological time not only from its prophets but also from its encounter with the Zoroastrians.*

COMMENTARY

As in other Logia before and after it, in this saying Yeshua uses the metaphor of farming, planting and harvesting to illustrate the nature and processes that characterize the divine Realm. Simple metaphors point toward eternal truths, and this particular illustration is one which is experienced by any farmer or gardener: weeds appearing among the carefully tended plants, sometimes overwhelming the entire garden or field. It is a common frustration. What is one to do about it? The labor of keeping a field or garden weed-free is intensive and never-ending.

So what about life? Life is messy. It is full of weeds, enemies, and unwanted intrusions sprouting in all our carefully-tended plans of perfect development. The unexpected and the unintended interferes with our agendas and expectations. Spiritually speaking, there is no pristine field. If we are honest, we recognize "weeds" in our lives. If not, we pretend otherwise. So, what are we to do about it? Seen from the perspective of our ambitions, there are "enemies" all around—perceived threats to our security. But are our perceptions correct? We cannot believe otherwise. Ambiguity abounds. Paranoia is with us, and no one is weed-free. This is clear evidence of the presence of evil and its hateful intent. How do we deal with evil? The first impulse is to get out and pull up everything that does not fit our perceptions, but the fact is, our perceptions may be wrong and such action often tears up the tender plantings right along with the weeds. In some circumstances the wiser course is to let it be, and let be what is, letting things take their course.

It is normal to assume that the Enemy mentioned in this Logion is the Devil. In the canonical Gospels Yeshua is said to give this interpretation. There are other alternative interpretations, however, not least of which is the possibility we are projecting our own perceptions.

So how are we to understand this strange wisdom of "letting things be"—not seeking to interfere in outcomes, but allowing the processes which have been set in motion in the world to unfold and come to fruition? This non-interventionist view is counter-intuitive, and yet not unlike the Taoist tradition's counsel. In the Hebrew world it is said that there is a time for planting and a time for reaping. This is the time for planting. There are always unexpected results from the planting. Things lying fallow suddenly come to life under the new circumstances of intensive and intended cultivation. In the spiritual realm, one cultivates some new element or facet of being and consciousness, but there are unintended consequences. What was unknown or latent appears. Wisdom says, "Let it be till the harvest at the end of time." Can that be the right answer? Suppose that, as in another saying of Yeshua's, these "weeds" simply suffocate the crop. Could the same answer apply there?

*The primary text of the Taoist tradition is the **Tao Te Ching** by Lao Tzu, an ancient seer from the dawn of Chinese history. This text, which many see as rooted in nature-mysticism, perceives the underlying force of physical existence as being something like the understanding of the **Logos** which acts as the unknown Source of all manifestation.*

Often we judge too quickly. We assume that something is evil, when it is merely inconvenient. Or we see evil intent and enemies all around, when what we come to see later is that it was nothing but pure projection. The divine discerns differently, allowing rain to fall on the just and unjust alike, and letting things grow to completion as a result of that rain. Who knows what the harvest will produce—only then will one know. "Judge not," says Yeshua elsewhere. We often apply this to our perspectives about people, but suppose it could be applied to our judgment of events as well.

Judgment is often seen as punitive: God's justice bringing redress to the injustices of history. While this is one aspect, another is allowing the law of cause and effect to take its course, in which case the outcome is the final judgment and the justice.

Only at the end of time, when the harvest occurs, will we have the perspective (the hindsight) to know what was weed and what was wheat. Till then it takes discipline and patience to wait. With the advantage of hindsight discernment will be perfect, and what needs burning can be burnt away. That is the Apocalyptic answer of unveiling at the end of time. It lies at the heart of Yeshua's wisdom, which sees the true outcome of things.

QUESTIONS FOR REFLECTION

1. You may have gardened yourself and had to fight the "weed problem." Describe what "weeds in the garden" means.

2. Have you ever felt as though some carefully tended aspect of your life has suddenly come under attack—planted with weeds that some known or unknown enemy has seeded? What has that experience been like?

3. What is the practice of "letting be" in actual experience? How would you describe it to someone who is having difficulty with the practice and wanting to act immediately?

4. In any condition you are trying to fix, what are some of the results of letting things take their own course versus trying to find an immediate solution?

EXERCISES AND MEDITATIONS

1. Reflect on your own experience. Are you more likely to try to fix a problem, or to let it be and see what happens and where it goes? If it is the former, how could you move to a more neutral position? If it is the latter, is there any chance of falling into lethargy, allowing things to fall apart because you are not willing to take responsibility? What is the proper balance between these two states of being, and how could you discern where that balance is? Discuss this with others who have reflected on this same issue. See what wisdom emerges from your discussion together.
2. There may be a problem in your life at this moment that feels somewhat like the image Yeshua is using. Take the image of the field (the desired crop and the unwanted weeds), and work through the condition or issue you are dealing with. Who or what would be the "enemy?" Could this be a false projection on your part? What might happen if you took your hands off the desire to control, and instead let the situation take its course?
3. One of the most important texts that explicates a "let it be" approach to life is expressed in the **Tao Te Ching**. You might want to get that text and read through it carefully, allowing the principles that it advocates to sink into your understanding. You may not agree with every principle it suggests, but it may help to clarify what that particular practice of wisdom actually is. Read the text in a period of meditation and reflection (as a form of ***Lectio Divina***), rather than simply for rational information. Give yourself time to absorb the truth of it at the level of the heart and not simply the level of the mind.

*A contemporary reading and translation of this ancient text is Steven Mitchell's **Tao Te Ching** (NY: Harper and Row, 1988).*

READINGS FOR INSIGHT

I

St. John of the Cross
Love Poems From God
312

Some seeds beneath the earth are dormant.
They fell the last time the cool air turned the leaves gold.
Those seeds have different needs than we do;
let them go about their life completely unharmed by your views.
We have cracked open,
we sensed even beneath the earth—the holy was near,
and are reaching up to know and claim light as our self.

II

The Gospel of Philip
Analogue Four

Those who sow in winter, reap in the summer. Winter symbolizes the world-system (the ***kosmos***), and summer, the Great Age (the ***Aion***), the realm of transcendence. Let us sow, therefore, in this world that we may reap in the summertime. For this reason, we are not asked to pray for harvest in the wintertime, but for the summer, which comes from winter. If one tries to reap in the wintertime it only uproots the field, and there is no harvest. This approach is fruitless since nothing emerges in the winter, and, as a result, in that other realm—the true Sabbath—the fields become barren.

III

Lao Tzu
Tao Te Ching
48

In the pursuit of knowledge,
every day something is added.
In the practice of the Tao,
every day something is dropped.
Less and less do you need to force things,
until finally you arrive at non-action.
When nothing is done,
nothing is left undone.

True mastery can be gained
by letting things go their own way.
It can't be gained by interfering.

IV

St. Catherine of Siena
Love Poems From God
188

I talk about it sometimes with Him, all the suffering in the world.
"Dear God," I have prayed, "how is it possible
All the horrors I have seen, all the atrocities you allow man
To commit when you—God—are ever standing
So near and could help us?
Could we not hear your voice say 'No"
with such love and power never again would we harm?"

And my Lord replied, "Who would understand if I said that I cannot bear
to confine a wing, and not let it learn from the course it chooses?"

LOGION 58

Sapiential Themes

- *Humans are designed to live in a state of blessedness or beatitude.*
- *The counter-intuitive precepts of traditional wisdom introduce trouble as the precursor to life.*
- *Life, not death, is a prize to be gained by conscious evolution, not simply through biological inheritance.*
- *Humans are brought into a realm in which pain and misery are part of the human condition, but that condition, if used, becomes a gift.*

Yeshua says,

Blessed are the troubled ones.
They have seized
hold of life.

Parallel Texts

Logia 54, 68, 69
Matthew 5:10-12
James 1:12
I Peter 3:14

FOCAL POINT

As students of wisdom, we have stumbled into a world of trouble and confusion for the human mind. Contrary to our expectations about the way the world ought to work, we are surrounded by pain and trouble. This surprising stage of confusion and perplexity was introduce in the second Logion, which said that the discovery of wisdom would lead through a state of confusion to something greater. We might accept this notion as an option, but we would not easily choose or volunteer for it. In this saying we are told that from the perspective of transcendence—Yeshua's Realm of Heaven—it is an essential state, the necessary path that leads ultimately to life. Life, of course, is understood in this text in a wholly different way from simple physical existence. In the Gospel of Thomas life is a state of fullness that includes everything: pain, trouble, confusion, perplexity, and of course, wonder.

Links

The previous two sayings (Logia 56 and 57) tell us of the true nature of the world we inhabit. On one level it is devoid of life. On another, it is populated by undesirable and unplanned-for elements: weeds. There is trouble in space-time. We dwell not in safety but in danger. Yet, that very quality of insecurity is the basis for advancement in wisdom—a knowledge that brings life.

Notes

*The term **troubled** points toward a condition of inner distress due to the fact that the conditions of human life (from our perspective at least) are unfavorable. To **seize hold of life** is exactly the term that is used in the first and subsequent Logia to indicate active involvement in the pursuit of something.*

COMMENTARY

In exactly the same way that the Beatitudes strike us as perplexing and counter-intuitive in the canonical Gospels, this additional Beatitude from the Gospel of Thomas presents us with a profound paradox. How can it be that those in this world who are troubled are, in fact, the Blessed Ones—those who exist in a state of blessedness? How is it that such a state of trouble can move the individual to seize hold of life? Wisdom is routinely counter-intuitive to normal perception. And so, in this Logion, yet another of the long line of Beatitudes which defy our commonsense view of the world, Yeshua, the Master of Wisdom, challenges our normal worldview.

In a previous saying (Logion 56) we are introduced to the image of the world-as-corpse, a troubling image indeed. In Logion 57 there is trouble in the carefully planned garden of human affairs—weeds have appeared among the wheat. At the heart of these two Logia is a form of conscious awakening that brings an awareness of the realities and difficulties existing all around us. We come fully awake to the fact that the world is not an easy or simple place—there is trouble here, and only those asleep would believe otherwise.

Although it spells difficulty, such an awakening is paradoxically the means by which one grasps life. To stay asleep is to be entrapped in a crypt of death. To come awake, as troubling as the state may be, is in fact to begin to know reality: to know true life in contrast to phantoms, fantasies, and rosy projections. The awareness that life in its fullness does not conform to our easy perceptions is a step in the direction of wisdom. Knowledge of that sort gives advantage to those who possess it in the world of the dead and the dying—in a field full of weeds.

*In an important book, **The Wisdom of Insecurity** (Vintage Books, 1951), Alan Watts explores the critical condition of the world in which we live and looks at the question of how we are to live in a world in which we can never be secure.*

We are aware that our own children must leave the safety and security of the family in order to become mature, individuated adults. In the divine household, is there any other means for attaining spiritual adulthood? Apparently not, and to gain life—life defined from heaven's perspective—there is the complex path through space-time as an awakened being aware of pain and trouble. This is the difficult path, the narrow way, wisdom's journey not often or easily taken. This is especially true in a society convinced that security and comfort (life, liberty and the pursuit of happiness) are human, if not divine, rights of passage.

*Another crucial text on this same topic is Pema Chödrön's **Comfortable With Uncertainty** (Shambhala, 2002). The author, coming from a Tibetan Buddhist perspective, guides the reader toward higher qualities of compassion and awareness in the midst of a troubled world.*

Typically we suppress such knowledge, and do almost anything to avoid the catalysts of painful awakening. Echoing many of the themes in the Beatitudes of Matthew's Gospel, this saying reflects the same conviction that persecution and sorrow, far from being curses, are heaven's gifts. To become a "troubled one," one awakened by trouble out of sleep is, from wisdom's perspective, a state of blessedness. Our task in this world, counter to the propaganda of contemporary culture, is not to secure unassailable comfort behind gated walls, but to stay open to the world of flux and insecurity. This is difficult practice, but it is the only means by which humans grow and evolve.

This experience is also the traditional definition of spiritual poverty, where one is driven by the pain of the world out of the narrow limits of the small self into Life and the fullness of the Supreme Self. Only there can one taste Life as an ultimate Reality, and not simply as a biological necessity.

QUESTIONS FOR REFLECTION

1. Typically we avoid any troubled state, looking for comfort and security. When has trouble entered your life unavoidably?

2. How has that experience of trouble moved you out of your normal comfort zone into some new state, or toward some new goal?

3. How can the experience of trouble be a form of blessedness? What is the exact relationship between trouble and blessedness your experience?

4. How might trouble lead to a better grasp of life for you?

EXERCISES AND MEDITATIONS

1. At opposite poles are two states in the human condition. One is a state of wretchedness and the other, a state of blessedness. In the Far Eastern traditions this latter state is called "bliss," for it concerns the aspect of human consciousness which knows the highest felicity. Its opposite is the knowledge of the depths of human despair. These two states are not out of reach for any of us. Every human has tasted something real at both ends of this spectrum. The notion that trouble in the affairs of our world can lead to a state of blessedness (and that the state of security and comfort can lead to its opposite, wretchedness) is, however, difficult for the ordinary mind to comprehend. But it is not contrary to the precepts of wisdom. In a period of reflection, take time with these two concepts. In your life, how could one state lead to the other in both cases?
2. We live, but often we have no clear idea what "real life" is actually all about. We just take it for granted. Is life simply existing without death? Is it being in a state of happiness? What is true life? If it is not incompatible with trouble (and degrees of discomfort and insecurity), then how should we define life? If eternal life, or divine life, is also not incompatible with these things, then how must we define that form of life? In this saying it is clear that Yeshua does not believe most folk actually have life. Take some time to meditate on this issue for yourself. Share your reflections with others doing this same kind of work.
3. As you move through your life, you inevitably experience trouble. If, by the practice of acceptance (or the acknowledgement of its role in your life) you allow this experience to change your inner awareness into the state of blessedness, you are reaching out for a greater quality of life. Quality, and not quantity (or even intensity), is central to your journey toward divine life. Can you, by a new form of spiritual practice, "taste" the change in quality, and thereby know a state of blessedness? Journal what happens as you practice this.

READINGS FOR INSIGHT

I

It costs so much to be a full human being that there are very few who have the enlightenment or the courage to pay the price. One has to abandon altogether the search for security and reach out to the risk of living with both arms open. One has to embrace the world like a lover. One has to accept pain as a condition of existence. One has to court doubt and darkness as the cost of knowing. One needs a will stubborn in conflict, but apt always to total acceptance of every consequence of living and dying.

Morris West

II

This being human is a guest house.
Every morning a new arrival.
A joy, a depression, a meanness, some momentary awareness
comes as an unexpected visitor.
Welcome and entertain them all!
Even if they're a crowd of sorrows,
who violently sweep your house empty of its furniture,
still, treat each guest honorably.
He may be clearing you out for some new delight.
The dark thought, the shame, the malice, meet them at the door laughing,
and invite them in.
Be grateful for whoever comes,
because each has been sent as a guide from beyond.

Jalaluddin Rumi
The Essential Rumi
109

III

... Then I recalled the qualities of God: compassion, generosity, elegant intricacy, luminous wisdom, mercy, beauty. I became grateful that I know the taste of some of these qualities according to my limited capacity, and even beyond it.

I see a long table spread with a tablecloth. On it are the powers and qualities and creations, the seven stars from which flow our pleasure here. Even in my unconsciousness, God enters my desire and my soul with the *taste* of those qualities.

I feel myself *becoming* one of the ways God tastes.

Bahauddin
The Drowned Book
4

IV

Disappointment, embarrassment, and all the places where we cannot feel good are a sort of death. We've just lost our ground completely; we are unable to hold it together and feel that we're on top of things. Rather than realizing that it takes death for there to be birth, we just fight against the fear of death.

When we practice generating compassion, we can expect to experience our fear of pain. Compassion practice is daring. It involves learning to relax and allowing ourselves to move gently toward what scares us. The trick to doing this is to stay with emotional distress without tightening into aversion; to let fear soften us rather than harden into resistance. ... An analogy for bodhichitta is the rawness of a broken heart. This is our link with all those who have ever loved. The genuine heart of sadness can teach us great compassion. It can humble us when we're arrogant and soften us when we are unkind. It awakens us when we prefer to sleep and pierces through our indifference. This continual ache of the heart broken open is a blessing that when accepted fully can be shared with all.

Pema Chödrön
Comfortable With Uncertainty
93, 71-72, 117

LOGION 59

Yeshua says,

Give attention to
the Living Presence
while you are alive
so that when you die and have
the desire to do so,
you may have the power to attend.

Sapiential Themes

- *Yeshua clearly asserts the reality of life after death and instructs us as to the relationship between the two.*
- *Conscious attention is a state of awareness to be developed in this world. Its use, however, extends beyond space-time.*
- *Presence, the hidden reality pervading all of existence, is something (someone) we can come to know as surely as we know other individuals in space-time.*
- *The practice of* ***remembrance*** *is central to the Abrahamic faiths.*

Parallel Texts

Logia 5, 52
Mathew 6:22
Luke 11:34
John 7:33-34, 8:21, 13:33, 14:8-11

FOCAL POINT

This saying is divided into the two halves that make up human experience: life in this world, and the passageway through death into what lies beyond. The two are inseparable and constitute the totality of human experience. It is clear that Yeshua is describing the existence of life after death and the journey we will take following our physical demise in this world. In this saying he clearly asserts a critical relationship between the two—that our practice of life here will have a direct effect on the life to come, since these two are inseparably related. The relationship between them is built upon conscious attention to the Living Presence which (as Logion 5 has stated) is right before our own face in the present moment and which shall be available to us after we pass into the next world.

Links

When one seizes hold of life, as is taught in the previous saying, what is one to do? This saying answers that question. Seizing life is coming to know Presence, and one may have to be "shocked" into that awareness, so that the focus of life is not simply on the surface, but upon its depths.

Notes

The term ***give attention to*** *translates the familiar Gospel theme of watchfulness. Many of Yeshua's teachings center on this theme of being ready to look or watch for that which is present or coming. Here it is used as an inner state of being that is to characterize his students.*

COMMENTARY

At the heart of this practice is the Presence of the Living One who is the axis and source of all conscious awareness. Yeshua asserts that this Living Presence is to become the focus of our attention while we live, in preparation for our passage into the next world. As we make our way into and through the next world, it will become absolutely crucial to have known and become related to that Presence.

Consciousness is often understood to be "ours." We think it belongs to us. But suppose this is only the way it appears because we are experiencing it. Suppose consciousness is an energy-state that is shared and flows through all sentient beings.

The "living Presence" is a state of the heart, while "death" is a state of mind or body. When you live in the first you can see the Presence; when you are in the other you cannot. The injunction is to stay in the heart.

The practice of attention inside the divine Presence is also called ***remembrance*** *or* ***invocation*** *and often includes a mantra-like invocation of the Divine Name.*

In this saying, we come a step closer, perhaps, to Yeshua's own spiritual experience and to his understanding of practice from the standpoint of traditional wisdom. At multiple points throughout this text Yeshua's personal knowledge through direct experience shines through the words. What he knows and what he has experienced is summed up in ways that convey not only his inner reality but also his personal practice. This saying, therefore, provides his followers an opportunity to learn a form of practical teaching allowing them direct access to Yeshua's own experience.

What Yeshua proposes is the practice of attention now in order that consciousness itself may become an instrument capable of focusing upon a reality greater than individual and personal identities. Normally, the landscape of human awareness is filled with the objects of our immediate concerns, needs, self-identity, and desires. Typically we attend only to what meets our immediate needs, so our focus becomes easily scattered across the landscape of our wants and demands, or it is consumed with meeting some single desire that has captured our full attention. If we limit our awareness simply to our own immediate gratifiers, we fail to use the instrument of conscious awareness to its maximum nor will we raise our consciousness to that transcendent Presence which has the potential of filling it.

The Living Presence which surrounds and holds us is worthy of our attention, for from it we originate, and toward it we inexorably return. Failure to attend to the Presence now limits the scope of our future awareness. We have the possibility in this present world of strengthening the power of conscious attention so that in a crucial future phase of our evolution, when we desire to do so (when we have the "desire to see," as the original Coptic text states), we may use the power already gained.

The tradition of Hebrew wisdom makes it clear that humans are destined to see the Face of God. The question is, however, in what condition and through what means will this be done? Is it through a power and potentiality that has already been learned by personal practice in the journey in space-time, or is it a lost power that is only possible when forced by fear or by an "emergency state" provoked by the divine Presence itself? It is possible, however, that such divine force is never actually used, and that one becomes lost and disoriented. Or could it be that the struggle to find that power on the other side of life in this world is far more problematic? The answer to these questions is not given here, but the solemn instruction to learn the power of attention now (attention to transcendent presence) is emphasized by Yeshua. This is something he knows, and as a Messenger of heaven he brings that critical message to us.

The crucial practice, therefore, is learning to stay attentive to Presence in all of the vicissitudes of life. In the Abrahamic faiths, attending to the divine Presence has been known as practice which entails some form of invocatory methodology; for example, the invocation of the divine Name or Names. Simple repetition of words, however, is not the concern. Invocation is a means whereby one might stand at attention at the level of the heart. There, and only there, is it possible to detect the divine Presence, for that Presence "knocks" at the heart's door, so that it is the heart which knows and sees what is there before it, closer than we can ever imagine by logic or reason. The heart knows. It detects Presence—the Presence standing before it, calling out to us "heart to heart."

QUESTIONS FOR REFLECTION

1. When you think about death, your death, what are your personal thoughts and feelings?

Material on Near Death experience that has accumulated in journals and studies over the last number of decades makes it appear more and more likely that divine Presence, as well as the presence of friends, plays a major role in welcoming us to the "other side."

2. Why would you imagine that attention now to the Living Presence is essential for what is to follow this life on the other side of death?

3. What is your experience of the "practice of attention?" What does it mean specifically? How would you describe it to another human being who, like you, is a seeker?

4. What do you expect to find at the gateway of death?

EXERCISES AND MEDITATIONS

1. In many traditions it is not uncommon for the student-seeker to be given the assignment of a "meditation on death." In some cases this meditation actually takes place in a graveyard. Following this tradition, it might be good for you to go into a nearby cemetery and enter a meditative state there. Find a place where you can sit quietly and observe the graveyard. Allow your mind and heart to be guided by what it tells you. If such a place is not available to you, still you can practice a meditation upon death in a quiet spot by yourself. In your mind's eye, imagine all those who have passed from this world, particularly those you know. Think about the fabric of their lives and that now they are gone from the earth. What does their previous presence and now their absence tell you? In another session perhaps, meditate on your own passage from this world into the next.

Both Islamic Sufism and Tibetan Buddhism suggest and prescribe this practice to their disciples. Christianity may have practiced it in the days of the Desert Fathers and Mothers.

2. The power of attention is a contemplative skill. It is not gained by practicing concentration, even in meditation, but by moving contemplatively and in the state of contemplative prayer from mind-awareness to awareness at the level of the heart. This may be hard to understand, and even harder to define, but it is a learned experience and also "felt" as a movement or journey from attention held in the mind to awareness experienced in the heart—it is a form of deepening. To practice attention at this ***kardial*** (heart) level means that we must drop down in our awareness from thoughts and thinking to simple awareness held deep within. It is the same type of awareness one feels inwardly when one has been moved by a beautiful piece of music and is in the state of awareness it brings as the sound fades. It may or may not be accompanied by any particular emotion, but it is not tied to any of them. Instead the power of attention is the ability to remain deeply aware, without thought for a period of time, and, if possible, to carry it out into daily activity in what we call "normal life."

READINGS FOR INSIGHT

I

Stephen Hirtenstein
The Unlimited Mercifier
100-102

Ibn 'Arabi describes the true knowledge of the **private face**. ... A Divine gift, such contemplations are described as "descending" from the realm of purity and sanctity upon the one who is needy. ... This Presence strips away all plurality. There is no "we" when facing Him through the private face. All appearances, aspects and attachments are left behind. Even if a person does not realize it in this life, this is the face that will be made evident after death. It is a "one-on-one" situation, which no-one else knows about. ... The degree to which this private face is realized is the measure of our true reality, the extent to which we have accepted our own Divine specialness.

II

Jalaluddin Rumi
The Essential Rumi
138

On the night when you cross the street
from your shop and your house to the cemetery,
you'll hear me hailing you from inside
the open grave, and you'll realize
how we've always been together.
I am the clear consciousness-core
of your being, the same in
ecstasy as in self-hating fatigue.
That night, when you escape the fear of snakebite
and all irritation with the ants, you'll hear
my familiar voice, see the candle being lit,
smell the incense, the surprise meal fixed
by the lover inside all your other lovers.
This heart-tumult is my signal
to you igniting in the tomb.
So don't fuss with the shroud
and the graveyard road dust.
Those get ripped open and washed away
in the music of our finally meeting.
And don't look for me in a human shape.
I am inside your looking. No room
for form with love this strong. ...
Now, what shall we call this new sort of gazing-house
that has opened in our town where people sit
quietly and pour out their glancing
like light, like answering?

III

Maria Jaoudi
Christian Mysticism East and West
15

Through contemplation one is able to live life fully, because one has emptied oneself of all the obstacles of the mind and entered the realm of one's God-likeness. Then and only then is one able to live, breathe, eat, and make a cup of tea, and work in tune with the Spirit present in reality. To come into contact with the real means to let go, as Mary did, of all the busyness and demands and to take the time to truly enter the presence of God. When one returns to the activities of life after contemplation, God's presence is carried through the very pores of our body-emotions-mind.

LOGION 60

Sapiential Themes

- *The line between what we call "life" and what we understand to be "death" is a difficult one. Yeshua draws it.*
- *Misperception of what living and dying actually are often hides a deeper spiritual perception.*
- *Dying now, in the midst of life, and finding Eternal Rest is a spiritual exercise we are called upon to practice.*

They saw a Samaritan
on his way to Judea
carrying a lamb.

Yeshua said, "Notice the Samaritan
with the lamb."

His disciples said, "He must be carrying
it in order to kill and eat it."

Yeshua responded, "As long as it is
alive he cannot eat it. Only after he has
killed it and it is dead will it be eaten."

They replied, "What other way is
there?"

Yeshua said, "You must be careful
to find a place for yourselves
in that realm of eternal rest,
lest you too be killed and eaten."

Parallel Texts

Logion 7, 56, 112
Romans 7:14-25
Galatians 2:20

Links

Paying attention to the divine Presence in life, before one dies, is crucial preparation for the afterlife, but it is just as important for life now so that it does not become a "living death." This appears to be the direct link between this and the previous saying, and the approach of death in Logion 61 which follows.

FOCAL POINT

Logion 60 is one of the finest examples of a true parable. It not only gives us a window on the way in which Yeshua worked with his students using the flow of events around him, it also makes use of the paradox and mystery which are at the very heart of what a parable is. This saying is culturally and spiritually complex. It contains images of first century Palestine that contrast binary opposites. It is, therefore, a parable that is easily misunderstood. Perhaps that is why it was not included in the narratives of the canonical Gospels. It simply was not understood by the average student, and what one does not understand is often conveniently dropped from the record. Nevertheless, Thomas records it in the context of other sayings, which makes him remarkable.

Notes

As an historical note, some commentators have suggested that it is not the Samaritan who is on his way into Judea (which may be problematic), but rather Yeshua who is traveling there, and on his way into Judea he witnesses this scene in the region of Samaria.

COMMENTARY

Samaria was the troubled middle region of Palestine. After the return of the exiled Jews from Persia, the remnant who had stayed in Palestine were seen as "compromised" and not truly Jewish. Conflict between these two groups began some three hundred years before Yeshua, and continued on till the Roman destruction of Jerusalem in 70 AD. The disputes were both political and theological.

The setting for this Logion appears to be a scene observed by Yeshua and his students in Samaria. According to many canonical accounts, this middle region of Palestine was a frequent route in Yeshua's travels between Judea and Galilee. Unlike many of his contemporaries, Yeshua would often travel through Samaria rather than go around it to avoid the people of that region. There was bad blood between the Samaritans, who were considered contaminated and "half-breeds;" and the "pure Jews" of Judea and perhaps Galilee. Yeshua, however, seemed to have an affinity for this people and its region.

In their journey, this band of travelers observes a man who may also be on his way into Judea, carrying a lamb on his shoulders. Perhaps he is going with the intention of sacrificing it in Jerusalem. Or perhaps, as some have suggested, because Samaritans are not easily welcomed in Judea, the man has to carry his own provisions, and at some point he intends to kill and eat what he has brought into the land of Judea to the South in order to sustain himself. The exact circumstances cannot be determined from this small story, but the intent is clear. The live lamb he is carrying will at some point be killed and eaten, something very common in the pastoral cultures of the Middle East.

The students of Yeshua make an obvious inference from the observation that the Samaritan is carrying the lamb in order to kill it. Yeshua takes that observation and extends it further to include the state of the lamb now and in the future. As long as the lamb lives it cannot be eaten. Only when it is dead is that possible. That is obvious to the students as well, but the spiritual implications are not.

From all appearances, every human being around us is alive. But are they? Yeshua appears to see it differently. He perceives that most souls actually exist in a state of death—spiritual death. To escape this state they must come alive, and it is precisely here that he introduces the greatest paradox.

Yeshua counter-intuitively sees that to be a truly living being—spiritually alive—an individual must enter the very state that most folk describe as the death-state, the place of eternal rest. However, far from being a death-like state, this state called "rest" is very much alive, perhaps the most alive state one can ever imagine. From a normal human point of view, to be in the state of "rest" appears to be in a place of "suspension" (suspended from normal activity), and yet inwardly, it is a place of fullness, a "productive state" where everything lives and is fully alive. According to wisdom teaching it is the state from which all other things that we see around us emerge, for the state of rest is Paradise, and Paradise exists now.

Logion 11

Yeshua has referred to this state in earlier sayings. He has made it clear that this transcendent state is not necessarily something in the future, but exists at a higher level of reality right in the present moment. To enter this state of rest now, to know it by experience and to begin to live there even while navigating space and time, appears to be exactly what Yeshua is expressing. If one lives outside that state of eternal rest in the normal death-like state we are so typically used to, then all indications are that we can be "killed and eaten" in some sense by the ravenous world around us. No doubt this notion is ultimately metaphorical, but it indicates that we can be overcome by forces that consume us and in that process, kill the human spirit. It is about this possibility that Yeshua is warning his students. His message to us is that we must find and enter eternal rest now in the midst of time, for it is now that we are truly to find life. We can live now, therefore, as it says in the first Logion, continuously eating death.

A corpse is obviously a difficult object regardless of the Jewish questions about ritual purity. Carrying a corpse about is not something anyone wants to do, and thus there are two levels here: the personal or social, and the legal.

QUESTIONS FOR REFLECTION

1. Have you ever had to kill something in order to eat it? What difference did (or does) that make to your diet and to your feelings about life and food?

2. What does it mean to survive physically in this world? Can that skill on the physical level be transferred to the spiritual, or are other skills required?

3. What does the term "eternal rest" mean to you?

4. How can you make contact with the realm of eternal rest now?

EXERCISES AND MEDITATIONS

1. Staying alive (or the biological survival reflex) is very much what all creatures spend time doing. Eating is a primary way to stay alive on the physical plane, but in the human community, preoccupation with eating to stay alive to the exclusion of anything else may in fact be an obstacle to finding (or knowing) a higher form of life. Exclusive pursuit of physical survival may block out other spiritual pursuits. Look at your life realistically. Look at the time spent on "staying alive" versus other pursuits (artistic, creative, recreational, spiritual, and educational). What is the focus of your life? What is the priority? Are focus and priority different? Why? You might make a graph or pie chart of some sort. Share your insights and discoveries with a group of trusted friends.
2. Let's suppose that, as Yeshua says, you can enter the realm of eternal rest now, in the present moment. Let's imagine that that place lies deep inside of you, at the level of the heart, beyond the thinking mind or the normal pursuit of thoughts, plans, ideas, and images, etc. To go there, you must drop down below that level of mentation and reach a state of inner awareness that is free from the "external" activities that normally occupy the mind. You may want to use music, a mantra, an icon, or a rosary of some kind as a prelude to getting to this place—as a way of withdrawing from normal thought patterns in order to descend more deeply into the space of heart-awareness.
3. The spiritual instruction "Die before you die" which is at the heart of much Sufi teaching applies to Yeshua's insight. There is a form of living which is involved with dying—a recognition of mortality and living its consequence in the midst of life. Spiritual pilgrims have experienced this state in many ways through myriad of circumstances. Coming to live in this state of "death" is a form of eternal rest. It cannot be adequately described, but it can be lived. Life provides us with opportunities for living there. Meditate on the experience of your life and on what circumstances may have led, or be leading you to, this state. Journal your insights.

*Being at peace and finding a place of rest transcends temporality. That "place" (**topos**) can be known now as a special topography.*

READINGS FOR INSIGHT

I

A Hadith or traditional saying in Islam

Die before you die.

II

In Tolstoy's great novella **The Death of Ivan Ilych**, he describes how Ivan, down to the final days of his life, screaming and struggling against going into what he perceives to be the "black sack" of his death, suddenly experiences a shift …

To a few of the truly spiritually courageous it has seemed, then, that the real trick would be to end the resistance—go through that inner shift of direction—*before* the end of one's actual physical life. The practice is called "dying before you die," and it represents the highest aspiration of all the spiritual paths. "For the mystery of 'Die before you die' is this," explains the great Sufi poet Jalaluddin Rumi: 'that the gifts come after you die and not before." Only after the terror of one's own diminishment and annihilation, after the last scraps of clinging to life at any cost have been left behind forever, is it possible to truly live in hope.

Cynthia Bourgeault ***Mystical Hope*** *68-69*

III

In addition, there is the accumulated emotional pain from the past that you and each human being carries within, both from your personal past as well as the collective pain of humanity that goes back a long, long time. This "pain-body" is an energy field within you that sporadically takes you over because it needs to experience more emotional pain for it to feed on and replenish itself. It will try to control your thinking and make it deeply negative. It loves your negative thoughts, since it resonates with their frequency and so can feed on them. It will also provoke negative emotional reactions in people close to you, especially your partner, in order to feed on the ensuing drama and emotional pain. How can you free yourself from this deep-seated unconscious identification with pain that creates so much misery in your life?

Become aware of it. Realize that it is not who you are, and recognize it for what it is: past pain. Witness it as it happens in your partner or in yourself. When your unconscious identification with it is broken, when you are able to observe it within yourself, you don't feed it anymore, and it will gradually lose its energy charge.

Eckhart Tolle ***Stillness Speaks*** *96-97*

IV

In the middle of winter I discovered in myself
an invincible summer.

Albert Camus

V

Do not seek death.
Death will find you.
But seek the road which makes death a fulfillment.

Dag Hammarskjöld ***Markings***

LOGION 61

Yeshua says,

Two will be resting on a bed.
One will die,
the other will live.

Salome said,
"Then how is it, Sir, that you,
coming from the one Source,
have rested on my couch
and eaten at my table?"

Yeshua said to her,
"I am he who has appeared to you
out of the Realm of Unity,
having been granted that which belongs
to my Father, its Source."

"I will be your student!" she exclaimed.

"Then I say this to you,
If you become whole
you will be full of Light.
If you remain fragmented
darkness will fill you."

Sapiential Themes

- *Two states of existence are actually two states of rest—one in life and one in death. These exist both now and in the future.*
- *Transcendent Unity is at the heart of Yeshua's wisdom and knowing. To become a student of his is to learn and receive from the Realm of Unity as a condition for one's own being.*
- *Enlightenment is a subject of early Christianity where it has to do with unfragmented wholeness.*

Parallel Texts

Matthew 11:25-27, 24:37-44
Luke 10:21-22, 17:26-35
John 13:1-4

FOCAL POINT

We come to a scene in the Gospel of Thomas which is so rich with possibility and insight that it almost defies words. Textually this saying is rich but also problematic, presenting interpretive challenges for the reader-listener who witnesses this exchange between Salome and the Master. Here a woman understands and experiences a breakthrough into seeing that seems to elude most of the other students. Salome breaks through to a place of insight that marks a turning point in her life, and what she see is at the heart of this Gospel: the good news of oneness, wholeness, equilibrium, and unity. So Yeshua instructs her further, and his instructions describe the state of Enlightenment.

Links

The subject of the previous saying is eternal rest, but here Yeshua takes a further step, making a distinction—rest as the experience of physical pleasure on a couch, or as an experience of something eternal that takes one beyond the death-like state into Life itself. What lies buried in this life is raised to the state of Rest.

Notes

*As a female figure, Salome appears in the canonical Gospels of Mark, Matthew, and John at the time of the crucifixion, burial and resurrection. Her name is perhaps a Hellenized version of the Hebrew **Shulamit**. She also appears in non-canonical Gospels such as Thomas, the Secret Gospel of Mark and the Gospel to the Hebrews as one of Yeshua's primary students along with Mary Magdalene.*

COMMENTARY

In this gathering of students and teacher, we are privy to a conversation between one of Yeshua's female students, perhaps one who is hosting the gathering at a supper in which, in the Middle Eastern style of the day, the Master engages her. They are reclining around a common table to partake of traditional delicacies. Relaxed and at ease, Yeshua makes a provocative statement. It concerns the state of rest, and contrasts two individuals who appear to be at opposite ends of a spiritual spectrum.

Salome immediately wants to know why it is that if indeed Yeshua is from the state of Eternal Rest he would come to her humble couch to receive her hospitality. Yeshua's answer is simply to say that his inner reality takes its condition from the realm which can only be described as Unity and Equilibrium—that place where opposites meet and are reconciled. Who he is and what he knows manifests from that Reality, and so he comes to her, not from out of himself as something autonomous, but as a gift from the Source, who is for him ***Abba***.

The Realm of Unity can also be translated as "the Equilibrium," or perhaps, the place of balance. In any case, whatever is opposite here is unified there and is maintained in balance.

Salome's first awareness of this reality, coupled with Yeshua's affirmation of it as the ground of his reality, fills her with the expressed desire to partake as well. She affirms that she will be his student and his follower. By implication, she will, if it be granted, participate with him in that same ground of being, the Source of Unity, the realm of Equilibrium where all forces meet and are in balance. She dedicates herself to this path and to his teaching. She is not shy or reticent. She joins in solidarity with the divine Unity and he who proclaims it and makes it available.

It has been a characteristic of the western Abrahamic traditions to think of enlightenment as something that is eastern, and therefore alien to the western understanding of spirituality. Clearly this is not the case. Perhaps now we can begin to see its full implications for the followers of Yeshua.

Yeshua's first words of instruction to his "new" student is to acknowledge that his knowing and experience of the unified field of Ultimate Reality comes not through proposition or dogmatic creed, but through the creation of an inner state of being which resembles that Reality. Wholeness, not fragmentation, is the condition for the possibility of being flooded with Light. A light-flooded being (an in-lightened being) is one in which the lens through which the light pours, or the mirror which reflects it, is no longer in a state of fragmentation, but has become unifed or whole. Unity of being which exists in a Realm transcendent to but including us must be also known and experienced within. Without inner unity, human experience is perpetually dark without the powerful effects of light. There is perhaps biological life, but there is no seeing, no light to bring illumination from the outside, no vision of Ultimate Reality.

When Yeshua says, "if you become whole..." the word ***whole*** *in the original is one letter different from the first word* ***Unity*** *used in the text, but the word literally means* ***destroyed****. This would appear to be a contradiction. But if it is not a scribal error, then the sentence should read: "If you become destroyed you will be full of light," which appears incongruent with the meaning of the rest of the text.*

At this juncture there must be a caveat to this interpretation that takes into account an interesting possibility that accepts the Coptic text as it is: that, far from being corrupted, this Logion actually states a deeper complexity of understanding that knows how the state of unfragmented wholeness can be achieved. If, as the text in its present form expresses, the Coptic word which we have translated as "whole" is as some scholars believe, the word "destroyed," and that this is not a scribal error, then perhaps our understanding should be that the "deconstruction of the ego" is, in fact, the way to unfragmented wholeness. The reading would then be: "If your egoic self becomes destroyed, you will be filled with light." This would be, then, a further seeing that supports (and does not distort) the ultimate meaning of the text and Yeshua's primary teaching concerning becoming whole and one and "solitary" (***monachos***) as is everywhere expressed throughout the Gospel.

QUESTIONS FOR REFLECTION

1. What is it like for binaries to be in balance, or for opposites to be unified? You have certainly experienced this. Describe it and the difference in experience between being in balance and out of balance.

2. Have you ever felt fragmented? How have you eventually achieved unity or a balanced state?

3. What do you think Yeshua means when he says he has come from the one Source? Does it have the same meaning as the phrase in the Nicene creed, "He came down from heaven?"

4. Enlightenment is typically understood to be an Eastern tradition. Here it is part of Yeshua's teaching. What does it mean to be a light-filled being?

EXERCISES AND MEDITATIONS

1. Imagine yourself at the same gathering as Salome and Yeshua's other students. Listen as Yeshua makes his provocative statement at the beginning. If you were in the place of Salome, what would you say? What question might you ask, or how might you respond? In your imagination, follow through on Yeshua's response to you. In a period of meditation and reflection, imagine what he would say to you. Write down your answers.
2. What parts of you are fragmented—not unified, but "left hanging" somehow? Reflect on that experience and your growth to become whole. Adolescence is typically the time when an individual feels most fragmented and pulled between inner divisions and loyalties. Later, these divisions are either healed or suppressed. If they are suppressed they can easily resurface to create a sense of division or fragmentation. Allow yourself to reflect honestly on this issue as it pertains to your own inner sense of wholeness.
3. There is a chant that reflects profound unity (non-duality) as it is expressed in the Abrahamic faiths: *There is nothing but God, there is only God. There is no one but God, there is only God.* A more personal and intimate way of saying it is: *There is nothing but You, there is only You. There is no one but You, there is only You.* Chant these lines every day for at least ten minutes using a monotone, or speak them mantra-like to yourself for the same period. What happens? How do you understand what happens as a result?
4. Has Yeshua ever appeared to you out of the Realm of Unity, or some other Realm? What has that appearance (called **Epiphany**) been like for you? In your view does Yeshua make such appearances? Consider whether or not it would be good for him to do so in your present condition. Would you be ready for it?

READINGS FOR INSIGHT

I

Indeed, our angels were put forth in unity, they say, being one, because they came forth from one. Now since we were divided, for this reason Jesus was baptized, that the undivided might be divided, until he unites us with them in the Fullness, so that we, the many who have become one, may all be mingled with the One that was divided for us.

Theodotus 36:1-2

II

I want to unfold.
I don't want to stay folded anywhere,
because where I am folded,
there I am untrue.

Rainer Maria Rilke

III

Is there even one soul, however materialistic,
that does not wish to unfold?
There cannot be.
It is in the unfoldment of the soul
that the purpose of life is fulfilled.

Hazrat Inayat Khan

IV

Our path in life evolves through a process of unfolding, which gives rise to an emerging flow of new discoveries, as what was hidden becomes revealed and what was obscure becomes accessible and clear. At least two different kinds of unfolding operate in human development: a gradual or "horizontal" unfolding, in which new discoveries and developments appear progressively, each one building on those that preceded it; and beyond that, a more sudden and surprising kind of "vertical" emergence, in which a larger, deeper kind of awareness unexpectedly breaks through into consciousness, allowing us to see things in a radically new light. The organic process of unfolding reveals the creative, emergent nature of human experience. It also sheds light on how change happens in psychotherapy and how therapeutic change, creativity, and more radical kinds of spiritual awakening are related to one another.

John Welwood
Toward a Psychology of Awakening
87

V

We were green:
we ripened and grew golden
The Sea terrified us:
we learned how to drown.
Squat and earthbound:
we unfolded huge wings.
We started out sober:
now we're love's startled drunkards.

Jalaluddin Rumi

LOGION 62

Yeshua says,

I disclose my mysteries
to those ready for Mystery
—so keep secret from your left hand
what your right hand is doing.

Sapiential Themes

- *There are mysteries of truth that can be disclosed under certain conditions.*
- *Readiness, or adequacy, for knowledge is a crucial element in spiritual work.*
- *The metaphor of the right hand and the left describes truth at different levels at their function in human knowing.*

Parallel Texts

Logion 5
Isaiah 45:3
Matthew 6:2-4, 13:10-17
Mark 4:10-12
Luke 8:9-10

FOCAL POINT

Salome's breakthrough into an understanding of Yeshua and his origins prompts him to speak of inner revelation and disclosure. Yeshua is speaking the mysteries—truth in Mystery form not easily known or understood—and only disclosed when the student is ready. Such disclosure is rare because the instrument necessary for knowing Mystery is also rare. As such, the mysteries cannot be grasped at the surface level. There is a difference between knowing things at the surface and knowing things at the level of deep-truth. Qualitatively they are different. These distinctions can only be understood when the function of the right hand and the left are discerned. Such discernment is also a mystery, because in this case, it is not one of concept, but of practice.

Links

Salome is the subject of both this and the previous Logion. To her has been given keys to the mysteries of which Yeshua is the locus and source. He brings a level of insight that only those prepared for it can receive. Such preparation is also what he does by keeping back what cannot be said, and moving forward what must be said.

Notes

*There are important technical elements to the Coptic version of this text. The first is that the word **ready** (or worthy) fills in a missing word in the text itself. This is considered to be a credible reconstruction. The word **hand** is also not in the text, but implied. Finally, **keep secret** could also be rendered "do not let the left realize..."*

COMMENTARY

In the previous Logion, Yeshua is teaching one of his women students, Salome. She appears to have broken through to a place of understanding not only about who Yeshua is and where he comes from, but more importantly, about who she is. In Logion 61 Yeshua instructs her concerning the state of human wholeness and fragmentation. In this Logion he very clearly describes what he is doing: disclosing something called "my mysteries," but only to the one who is ready to receive them, and thus, worthy of their value and meaning. He ends his statement with a very enigmatic proverb concerning action and secrecy between the right and left hands. The topics in these two Logia combine to describe the content and purpose of Yeshua's mystery-teaching.

Among the Hebrews, the term "mystery" appears to have been added to their theological vocabulary at the time of the Persian exile. The Persian word "raz" is borrowed into the Hebrew language.

In traditional wisdom, the term "mystery" relates to the inner tradition (the esoterism) of a particular teaching. There is public teaching meant for the many, and there is private, esoteric teaching for those ready to hear it. Yeshua's teaching clearly falls within both categories. He speaks to the crowds, but he also privately instructs the students who walk with him. The corpus of his teaching accommodates a wide range of human capacities for understanding, but is directed especially to those made ready (or adequate) for his teachings—what will later be termed ***adaequatio*** in the tradition. He ministers to all, but discerns the differences between what is right-handed and what is left.

The truth of becoming adequate for knowledge takes its origins from Plotinus (died 270 CE.), who said that "Knowing demands the organ fitted to the object." E.F. Schumacher suggests that "Nothing can be known without there being an appropriate "instrument" in the makeup of the knower. This is the Great Truth of "adaequatio" (adequateness), which defines knowledge as adaequatio rei et intellectus—the understanding of the knower must be ***adequate*** *to the thing to be known."*
A Guide for the Perplexed
39

What Yeshua calls "my mysteries" seems to refer to the previous saying concerning his disclosures to Salome about his origins and the necessary inner state. It is easily seen that the state of becoming whole or remaining fragmented that he describes there has everything to do with readiness for the mysteries. Because of our egalitarian tendencies in the West, we imagine that everyone is equally ready if they would only listen. Readiness, however, is far more than simply hearing. It is ontological—having to do with one's state of being. One kind of being can receive these mysteries. For another it may prove fruitless or, perhaps, even toxic.

The proper mode of being appears related to the statement which follows "... so keep secret from your left hand what your right hand is doing." The right hand is preferred in the Middle East. It is also a public hand—the one that is used to present things in public view, while the left hand is used for private functions. If this cultural identity is used, the case could be made that the right hand works in public at the surface, and the left hand signifies the esoteric depths that are hidden from the right hand. This is counter-intuitive, perhaps, since the right hand appears to be preferred in most cultures. However, because the left hand stays out of sight and is less visible, its interior, hidden function becomes the focus. This symmetry, the discernment of the two functions, the two levels of reality, and the two relationships possible to the teaching is crucial. Can an individual know and practice this form of discernment between the two? This is a criteria for readiness. If not, then perhaps the original mysteries of Yeshua and the mysteries of his origin cannot be revealed and must remain unknown until such a time of readiness.

The use of the image of the right and left hand also signifies action and practice. Hands are for use and action, which suggests that knowledge of the mysteries is not simply conceptual, but can only be realized by practice. This form of knowing by experience is implicitly "left-handed" in that it takes you below surface knowing to personal and experiential knowledge deep within.

QUESTIONS FOR REFLECTION

1. Are there "mysteries" that you feel you have received, or that the inner Teacher has disclosed to you?

2. Readiness (or adequacy) is a central topic in this Logion. The question for each follower of Yeshua is how ready are we to receive the truth of his teaching? Have we missed things because we are not ready for them? Is there a way to know your level of readiness?

3. Have you ever felt excluded from some kind of teaching, or from some level of understanding? What was that experience like?

4. How would you interpret the meaning of the proverb about the right and left hand? Do you have any sense of how this works from your experience, or what the principles of public and private truth or disclosure are?

Further questions concerning the mysteries you might want to consider are: What for you remains a mystery? Are there mysteries in your life or in your thinking? How would you know that some domain or subject is a mystery?

EXERCISES AND MEDITATIONS

1. Inner readiness for a particular truth or level of understanding implies a progression of preparation over time. Let's suppose that the Divine Mind or the inner Teacher (Yeshua as the Master of one's life) desires to disclose deeper and fuller understanding to you. Let's also imagine that this requires that you prepare for it. What form would such preparation take? It is easy to imagine that it might involve expanding our current thinking to include new insights. How might you do that (or assist in the possibility of that)? However, this saying suggests that intellectual groundwork is not the only, or even the most important, aspect of preparation. Spiritual practice is. What forms of spiritual practice that you currently use might expand your capacities?
2. It is important to know those forms of spiritual practice that have traditionally been seen to be critical for such inner preparation and expansion. If truth is not simply known at the level of the mind (rational or conceptual thought), then other forms of practice must involve something more than the mind; they must involve the deeper instrument of cognition, the heart. Traditionally, the heart has been understood to be the seat of the spiritual intellect (***nous***) which operates beyond space and time. The heart can be exercised and used in many ways, most of which involve meditation and contemplative experience. Enter a period of silent, alert awareness. Move your conscious awareness from the head to the heart. Sense that you are aware at this deeper level of the heart. Remain there without thought for as long as you can (10-20 minutes). Simply be conscious, alert, awake and aware. This tunes and readies the heart.

READINGS FOR INSIGHT

I

Thomas Aquinas

Knowledge comes about
insofar as the object is within the knower.

II

Pistis Sophia 133

Jesus said, "I have brought the keys of the mysteries of the kingdom of heaven, otherwise no flesh in the world would be saved. For without the mysteries no one enters into the kingdom of Light, be that person righteous or a sinner. For this cause, therefore, have I brought the keys of the mysteries into the world, so that I may release the sinners who believe in me and harken unto me."

III

The encounter with Shah Firuz as told by Emir Hanza (died in 1710)
Idris Shah
Caravan of Dreams

"Teach me," I said.

He answered, "What do I sing, and what does my lute sing? You and I are not in harmony, although I understand your thoughts. What have you already taught yourself? What have others taught you? You are uneasy because you have come so far and at the end of your journey have found someone who can read your thoughts. And you feel that perhaps you could learn this power, and then use it to your heart's content. I seem acceptable to you, as people sometimes think of doctrines as being acceptable to them. But are you acceptable to me? People never bother to think that the doctrine may not accept them."

IV

Frederick J. Murphy
The Religious World of Jesus
164

Because right action depends on right knowledge, wisdom terminology ("wisdom," "the wise," "knowledge," "understanding") abounds in apocalypses. ... Apocalyptic wisdom is available only through revelation. Because of its esoteric nature, the revelation is often called a "mystery" or a "secret." The means of revelation point to the mysteriousness of the knowledge. The seer travels to where others have gone, or sees visions others have not seen. He or she does not understand what is seen. Someone from the supernatural world must explain the vision. God is mysterious and remote.

V

Rainer Maria Rilke
Ahead of All Knowing
169

As once the winged energy of delight
carried you over childhood's dark abysses,
now beyond your own life build the great
arch of unimagined bridges.

To work *with* Things in the indescribable
relationship is not too hard for us;
the pattern grows more intricate and subtle,
and being swept along is not enough.

Take your practiced powers and stretch them out
until they span the chasm between two
contradictions ... For the god
wants to know himself in you.

LOGION 63

Yeshua says,

There was a rich man
who had expendable wealth.
He said to himself,
"I will take my money
and use it to plant, sow and harvest,
filling my barns with produce,
then I'll have everything"
— these were the thoughts
occupying his mind.
That night he died.
Listen, if you are paying attention!

Sapiential Themes

- *The lure of wealth, and abandonment of everything for it, is a subject of literature from fairy tales to wisdom dialogues.*
- *Can a rich person come awake, or are riches the ultimate soporific? This question is at the center of Yeshua's teaching in this Logion.*
- *The swiftly flowing stream of time catches us off guard. We imagine ourselves impervious, but we are soon swept away.*
- *Our thought-life is at the core of the values we hold in this world. Paying attention to something higher is of maximum value.*

Parallel Texts

Logion 36, 59
Luke 12:31-21

FOCAL POINT

The conundrum of living on this earth with a spiritual rather than simply a material focus is the subject of this Logion. Previously Yeshua has said that whoever makes this world their specialty has in fact made friends with a corpse (Logion 56). A corpse, possessing no life, is of extreme temporality. It will disappear quickly, leaving behind its previous form. A person who lives entirely for this world has invested in such temporality. Life passes quickly, and is gone. That is a fact of existence in space-time. The question always is, then, what is worth doing? Yeshua uses the man of temporal means to illustrate the contrast between focus on the surface structure of temporal reality and its eternal depths.

Links

Earlier, Yeshua states to whom the mysteries will be disclosed. In contrast, in this Logion he illustrates those to whom nothing can be disclosed and why this is so. We might call this and the next two Logia an example of inadequacy or lack of readiness for the mysteries. In these Logia none of the individuals are ready because their lives are devoted to the exoteric, and so they cannot receive what Yeshua has to give.

Notes

There are two interesting details in the original text that bear on both the meaning and translation of this text. The word ***barn*** *is literally "treasure house," meaning this was the place he stored his "treasure." The phrase* ***I will have everything*** *translates "so that I do not need anything." Needs and possessions are very closely linked here.*

COMMENTARY

This saying may have connection to another in the ancient wisdom of the Hebrews:
A man may become rich through a miser's life, and this is his allotted reward; when he says "I have found rest, now I will feast on my possessions," he does not know how long it will be till he dies and leaves them to others.
The Book of Sirach
(Ecclesiasticus)
11:18-19

In this saying, a rich man who has money and the power to use it is in focus. His expendable wealth gives him the luxury of following his desires however he chooses. In terms of earth's history and the continuum of human experience, this individual is in the top fraction of a percent of the population. Most men and women do not have such luxury, but he does. His wealth is discretionary, and so the question is how will he use his holdings, money, and power? His decision, like most who are possessed of wealth, is astute in the ways of this world. He will use his money to make more money—as capital to produce more goods. It is a wise business decision. His desire is to have everything—everything he wants, everything he needs, everything he desires—to lack nothing. These were his inner thoughts, and the processes he was going through as he made his decisions about his material wealth and what to do with it. This is what occupied his attention in this world. These thoughts were his "friends." He was at home with them.

When we are advised in money matters, we receive the same advice: use your money to make more money. Turn your profits into assets. Use your assets to build security. It is the way our world works. It is, in essence, the foundation of capitalism which has served useful to so many in the West, though its ultimate outcome may be the utter depletion of the earth's resources as the practice goes unchecked by any other value.

This individual has not taken into consideration one other contingency: the temporality of life. He has gambled on longevity. All his plans will pay off if he lives long enough to see them through. He is counting on that. In fact, there does not seem to be the slightest doubt in his mind that he will live to see success. But that night he dies! Much to his surprise, certainly, and the surprise of others—perhaps his business empire—he passes from the scene and his plans vanish. His fortunes begin, like the corpse he now is, to disappear.

It is common for human beings to be focused on a future that takes as its sole coordinates the dimensions of space and time. We know of so little else, for it is what constitutes our world. The sacred traditions, however (and wisdom in particular), continue to teach us to raise our sights above this immediate horizon and begin to focus on a wider perspective beyond space and time. Even while passing through the world, this perspective is crucial. In truth it may save us from the myopic fate of the individual in this Logion, who gambled on temporal longevity, and missed the perspective of Eternity. Had he done so, his treasury may have not been stored in barns, but in that realm to which he was now so swiftly removed.

Modern physics speaks not only of the explicate order of space-time, but also of the implicate order made up of many dimensions upon which rides the surface of the temporal and the material-like foam on the sea.

The emphasis in this saying is put upon the interior ruminations of this individual as he walks through life. The trouble is not precisely in his actions, but in his thoughts. Thinking precedes action, and in this particular case he is obsessed with his wealth—apparently nothing else occupies his mind. The end result is a loss. Yes, loss of wealth, and eventually, loss of life, but not just physical life—spiritual life and spiritual wealth as well. Yeshua teaches a lesson in divine economics. He grounds the understanding of wealth beyond its temporal coordinates in a dimension that is not affected by the swiftly shifting patterns of space and time.

QUESTIONS FOR REFLECTION

1. How do you feel about temporal wealth? Do you have "enough" money, or do you feel that you need more?

2. When you become focused on the temporal world, what are the things that typically occupy the center of your attention?

3. What do you think about most? If you were to give a percentage to the main topics that occupy your mind, what would they be?

4. When you think about your own death and how it will occur, what images and ideas come to mind?

EXERCISES AND MEDITATIONS

1. It would not be untrue to say that we *are* our thoughts—at least our inner being is constituted and flavored by the quality of our thought life. Eckhart Tolle has truly stated that within each individual there is a dimension of consciousness far deeper than thought. It is the essence of who we actually are. That deeper reality, he says, is what the ancient teachings mean by our "Buddha nature," or the "Mind of Christ." So, obviously, there are two levels at least to our interior life: the surface level of consciousness constituted by the stream of our thoughts upon which we are carried day after day, and the deeper current below the surface that touches the unconditioned consciousness of the divine Presence. To know these two levels and the difference between them is a part of our spiritual work. Take a day and keep remembering to observe where your focus and attention is. Notice how quickly you are carried down the stream of swiftly flowing thoughts. Notice also that you could "get out of the boat," so to speak, and either plunge within to some deeper place of awareness that is more central, or you could stand on the bank and observe the thought process itself flowing by. Try this over a period of several days. Journal what you discover.

Eckhart Tolle ***Stillness Speaks*** *13*

2. In a period of reflective meditation, take time to move "below the surface of thoughts" and stay in the depths of your own heart. This is a place of quietness and peace—a place of centeredness, where you are not unconscious, but more fully alert and aware than you were when the thought-stream was carrying you "down-river." Stay in the quiet inner spot, awake and aware.

An important form of this practice is called Centering Prayer as it is taught by Tom Keating and Cynthia Bourgeault. If you have an opportunity, read C. Bourgeault's crucial text, ***Centering Prayer and Inner Awakening*** *on this topic.*

3. It would be good to evaluate the degree to which you have assumed the values of contemporary culture concerning money and material possessions. Society puts tremendous pressure on us to own things, to consume goods, to comfort ourselves with wealth. In the end it is ephemeral. What is your relationship to wealth now?

READINGS FOR INSIGHT

I

Eckhart Tolle
Stillness Speaks
13

The human condition:
lost in thought.

II

Kabir
Love Poems From God
221

I don't think there is such a thing
as an intelligent mega-rich
person.

For who with a fine mind
can look out upon this world
and hoard
what can nourish
a thousand
souls.

III

Eckhart Tolle
Stillness Speaks
13

Most people spend their entire life imprisoned within the confines of their own thoughts. They never go beyond a narrow, mind-made, personalized sense that is conditioned by the past.

IV

Cicero

To be content with what we possess is the greatest and most secure of riches.

V

Anthony de Mello
Taking Flight
98

Two monks were on their travels. One of them practiced the spirituality of acquisition, the other believed in renunciation. All day long they discussed their respective spiritualities till toward evening they came to the bank of a river.

Now the believer in renunciation had no money with him. He said, "We cannot pay the boatman to take us across, but why bother about the body? We shall spend the night here chanting God's praises, and tomorrow we are sure to find some kind soul who will pay our passage."

The other said, "There is no village on this side of the river, no hamlet, no hut, no shelter. We shall be devoured by wild beasts or bitten by snakes or killed by the cold. On the other side of the river, we shall be able to spend the night in safety and comfort. I have the money to pay the boatman."

Once they were safely on the other bank, he remonstrated with his companion, "Do you see the value of keeping money? I was able to save your life and mine. What would have happened to us if I had been a man of renunciation like you?"

The other replied, "It was your renunciation that brought us across to safety, for you did part with your money to pay the boatman, didn't you? Moreover, I had no money in my pocket, but your pocket became mine. I have observed that I never suffer; I am always provided for."

LOGION 64

Yeshua says,

A man was throwing a dinner party and when everything was prepared, he sent his servant out to call the guests.

The servant went to the first and said, "My master invites you." But he replied, "I have set aside some funds for merchants who are coming this evening, and I will be placing orders. I beg to be excused from dinner."

So he went to the second and said, "My master has invited you." But he said, "I have bought a house which requires a day of my time. I am too busy to come."

He went to another and said to him, "My master invites you now." He replied to the servant, "My friend is getting married and I am to prepare the wedding banquet. I simply cannot come. I beg to be excused."

He went to another and said, "My master calls you." In reply he said to the servant, "I have just bought a farm and am about to pay taxes. I cannot come. Please excuse me. I must be off."

The servant returned to his master and said, "The ones you invited to the dinner have all excused themselves." The master said to the servant, "Then go to outsiders and strangers on the roads. Find folk there and bring them here to eat."

Those busy buying and selling cannot get into my Father's realm.

Sapiential Themes

- *This longest of the parables in the Gospel of Thomas gives us wisdom's view of life lived along the horizontal axis.*
- *There is a world of mundane activities which keeps humanity busily engaged, and there is another world, transcendent to that one, described as a feast. The invitation is offered us to join it.*
- *One's focus determines one's capacity for spiritual knowledge, as well as the ability to respond to the invitation to move beyond the mundane world. Interior focus is the key to the quality of spiritual life.*

Links

This Logion is the second in the series illustrating the issue of readiness for the mysteries (Logion 62). The question in each saying is about the state of one's inner life. Does it exist, or is one's sole focus on the outer exoteric world? In this saying we have four examples of a life that is entirely externalized with little or no room for the inner dimensions necessary to receive the mysteries.

Parallel Texts

Deuteronomy 20:5-7
Matthew 22:1-14
Luke 14:15-24

Notes

The literary features most prominent in this saying are, first, its universality, and, second, its seemingly contemporary nature. Little has changed in human culture for the last 2,000 years since this parable was uttered. It reads like a modern description of life as we know it. It also has universal application for all times and cultures.

FOCAL POINT

Yeshua throws wisdom's light upon what we today call "the real world." It is a world of insubstantiality, but one nevertheless in which we invest most everything we have. As was clear from the previous Logion, it easily captivates our thoughts, and becomes the sole focus of our attention. Yet, no matter the world that we live in, no matter its depth or substantiality, inevitably there comes a messenger with an invitation to a gathering beyond it called a Feast—a "dinner party" prepared by the Master host.

This parable expresses a common theme told in multiple wisdom traditions throughout the centuries. It is a perennial tale of opportunities lost by some and then offered to others.

COMMENTARY

The divine invitation offered in this parable is to come out of the mundane world of our preoccupations and small agendas into a larger world prepared for us where a form of feasting is at the center. One cannot imagine refusing such an invitation or of resisting it in any way, but the truth—the incontrovertible truth—is that humankind (and each individual within it) does refuse and resist constantly.

In a series of exchanges—small scenes that condense down the various preoccupations into a brief conversation between the messenger and the invited guest—we get a glimpse into the human world with its primary agendas. It is a world of intense focus upon transactions taking place along the horizontal axis—the normal business world of human interests and affairs. These transactions, as in the previous Logion, occupy our minds and thoughts. What is described, however, seems entirely normal. We could call it "business as usual" in a world where such transactions fill our time from morning to night. Yet in each scene, the preoccupation becomes an excuse to turn away from an invitation to a higher reality, but one that apparently does not fulfill the immediate desire of that individual.

One would think that the possibility of a feast prepared and an invitation to it freely given would surpass any possible mundane activity, but it does not. What occupies the normal human mind is a sense of obligation so immediate and so compelling, either personally or socially, that one is forced to refuse the invitation, however politely.

In the first scene we meet a business man who is engaged in normal business transactions. These he cannot stop for any reason. In the second, the messenger encounters a real estate investor who is preoccupied with his investments and cannot spare a day of his time for anything else. In the third, an individual, perhaps a woman, is socially obliged to get ready for another feast, a wedding banquet, and there is, again, simply no time to spare. Finally, the last individual has bought property and now taxes must be paid. Regardless of when or how quickly these obligations can be fulfilled, they become the excuse to refuse the invitation. In each case, these are considered to be serious obligations and the excuses (to that individual at least), appear to be warranted.

From wisdom's perspective, however (and from the viewpoint of the one preparing the feast), the excuses are all obstructions to a reality beyond immediate human concerns. Yet, the feasting will go on and guests will be present. So, strangely, the Master invites individuals unknown to the community and strangers to the household who do not refuse the invitation. The final comment summarizes wisdom's critique of the human world—the world of exchange along the horizontal axis—and its sole focus. Personal agendas, and the constant attention to the obligations that keep us occupied, bind the human will so that little or nothing remains free to respond to transcendence. By refusing to let go of our immediate concerns, the soul is caught within space-time, and so in the end its eternal essence cannot be nourished.

QUESTIONS FOR REFLECTION

1. Role play. Put yourself in the place of the individuals who receive but refuse the invitation. In each case, what is the inner motivation that obliges the excuse? What is that person "really" thinking beyond the words of excuse?

2. Have you ever made an excuse for some invitation offered to a party or a dinner, and you didn't really want to go? What were your feelings? What were your motivations? Give an example of how you backed out of the invitation so as to appear as polite as possible.

3. This being a parable, what do the various figures represent? On how many levels can this parable be interpreted? What is the symbolic value of each person (or persons) represented, and the states and activities to which they refer?

4. Who do you think the "worthy others" are who accepted the invitation? Why are they so different from the rest? Could you identify them in the world you currently live in?

EXERCISES AND MEDITATIONS

1. This parable gives each one of us an opportunity for serious self-examination: to explore the personal agendas that occupy our attention, and that perhaps block our access to the Transcendent. It is hard to imagine that any of those who offered an excuse thought that what they were turning down was more important than what they were doing. That is the key. What do you think is important in life and why? Think of folk around you who occupy their time with things that you feel are frivolous (perhaps sports, or shopping, or some hobby that appears to you to be inane). By contrast, your agenda seem to be worthwhile and important—just as, we can suppose, theirs does to them. Is there a difference? What might it be?
2. This parable suggests two important things. First, that the Divine sends messages and invitations into our lives that we often refuse. Can you imagine this for yourself? When might this have happened? Second, this parable suggests that there is a kind of feeding or feasting that is being offered us that we cannot see as being more important than what we are doing. What might that form of feasting be (not theoretically, but actually), which you need but cannot currently use? How might you stay alert now to wisdom's invitation? How might you begin to choose differently, assuming, of course, that this is an ongoing invitation and not merely offered once and for all? Is it possible for you to choose differently? How?

You might also want to think of the various sacred messengers that have come to offer humanity a taste of Transcendence. What has their message been? What have they offered us? How have they often been treated?

READINGS FOR INSIGHT

I

If God
invited you to a party and said,
"Everyone in the ballroom tonight will
be my special guest."
How would you then treat them when you arrived?
Indeed, indeed!
and Hafez knows that there is no one in
this world who is not standing upon
His jeweled dance
floor.

Hafez
Love Poems From God
158

II

What is your relationship with the world of objects, the countless things that surround you and that you handle every day? The chair you sit on, the pen, the car, the cup? Are they to you merely a means to an end, or do you occasionally acknowledge their existence, their being, no matter how briefly, by noticing them and giving them your attention?

When you get attached to objects, when you are using them to enhance your worth in your own eyes and in the eyes of others, concern about things can easily take over your whole life. When there is self-identification with things, you don't appreciate them for what they are because you are looking for yourself in them.

Eckhart Tolle
Stillness Speaks
98-99

III

The Master once referred to the Hindu notion that all creation is "leela"—God's play—and the universe is His playground. The aim of spirituality, he claimed, is to make all life play. This seemed too frivolous for a puritanical visitor. "Is there no room then for work?"

"Of course there is. But work becomes spiritual only when it is transformed into play."

Anthony de Mello
One Minute Nonsense
96

IV

What are we doing here, and what should we be doing here? What most of us are doing here in this world is living in a daydream called ordinary life, in the state of forgetting what Christ called the one thing necessary, that is, the Divine Reality. And we are in such a state because we have forgotten who we are. All we need to do is to wake up and realize our primordial nature, which is always there although buried deeply within many layers of the dross of forgetfulness. The Prophet said, "Man is asleep and when he dies he awakens." Sufism is meant for those who want to wake up, who accept dying to the ego here and now in order to discover the Self of all selves and to be consumed in the process in the fire of Divine Love.

Seyyed Hossein Nasr
The Garden of Truth
22

V

Security is mostly a superstition. It does not exist in nature, nor do the children of men as a whole experience it. Avoiding danger is no safer in the long run than outright exposure. Life is either a daring adventure or nothing.

Helen Keller,
Wabi Sabi,
by Diane Durston
61

LOGION 65

Sapiential Themes

- *Human beings resist the divine invitation, or any direct challenge from the divine realm perceived as a threat, either passively or actively.*
- *Such resistance can lead to violence, done of course out of a misguided sense of self-righteousness.*
- *Displays of resistance are evident throughout human history in general and religious history in particular.*
- *Wisdom challenges us: To whom do you belong, and what belongs to you?*

Yeshua says,

A good and fair-minded man had a vineyard that he gave over to tenants to work and make productive.
When he sent a servant to collect profit from the vineyard, the tenants took him and nearly beat him to death.
When the servant returned he told his master who said, "Perhaps they did not know him."
So he sent another servant and they beat him as well.
Then the master said, "I'll send my son.
Maybe that will shame them."
But those tenants, because they knew him to be heir to the vineyard, seized and killed him.
Whoever can hear this, listen!

Parallel Texts

Logion 21, 81, 88
Psalm 118:22-23
Isaiah 5:1-5
Wisdom 7:27
Matthew 21:33-46, 23:37
Luke 13:34, 20:9-19
Mark 12:1-12

Links

This third in the series describing those who are not ready to receive the mysteries adds another layer of resistance and provocation. Until this point, perhaps, we can see how one could inadvertently deny the divine offer of life or truth. It is excusable. But in this parable there appears to be no excuse. However, the intent of this saying is to describe the nature of the human condition. We could certainly remonstrate, this is not me! But is it?

FOCAL POINT

Just as there are levels of readiness, so are there levels of resistance to the wisdom and the mysteries that Yeshua is teaching. All sorts of responses are possible, and during his ministry he experiences each of them in some way. Resistance can be passive and even unconscious; it can be passive-aggressive and only partly available to the conscious mind; or it can be entirely conscious and aggressive in nature in the way it is expressed in this Logion. In the last two Logia and now in this one, Yeshua is progressively illustrating the ever-increasing forms of resistance to the wisdom he speaks. Perhaps no one is exempt from this list. Perhaps we all experience each of these levels of resistance in a lifetime, and perhaps, some even appear to be our permanent relationship to higher realities that we resist.

Notes

There is a strange phrase in the original Coptic text which may either be intended or a scribal error. It seems to contradict what we would expect. The actual phrase in response to the rejection of the first servant says, "Perhaps he did not know them," meaning that the servant was a stranger and did not know how to act toward the tenants and that was the reason for their reaction. A more usual understanding expresses it the way it is translated here.

COMMENTARY

If Logion 65 is the culminating point of human resistance—the ultimate extreme to which we will go to keep ourselves from responding to the divine invitation—then Yeshua "ups the ante" here. Not only is the response from ordinary human beings extreme, but over the course of this and the last two sayings, the direct encounter from the transcendent realm has escalated as well. In the first instance, what is illustrated is the simple pressure of life passing unnoticed and human agendas taking up the whole territory of life, leaving the individual forgetful of possible outcomes. In the second, a messenger, a servant of the Master, arrives with an invitation to four individuals. Excuses are given and he goes away. In this final Logion, the first messenger, a servant, is badly treated, as is the second who suffers similar abuse. In the end, a son is sent, and he is abruptly killed. It is an extreme, not an excuse, but an ultimate, violent rejection. Humans will go that far to protect what they consider theirs: their rights, their property, their self-determination. We are often a violent people in our response to that which is beyond us. This is a cautionary tale.

Even if the theology of Thomas does not support the notion of the Son of God from heaven, this saying implies that Heaven sends its own "kind" as envoy to earth in a final act of self-giving.

The swift reaction to the messages delivered by the servants from the Master of the field raises critical issues about the nature of existence and our response to the divine Realm. We are capable of extreme resistance—resistance unto death. We can become vicious in our resistance to the divine Will, not only refusing and rejecting the message, but killing the messenger as well—and thereby putting all our resources and our very existence in jeopardy.

The concept of masters or landlords of the field has been discussed earlier in Logion 21.

In the canonical Gospels, Yeshua makes mention of the Hebrew ancestors who not only rejected the message but killed the messengers, the prophets in Matthew 23:37, and Luke 13:34.

The opening lines say that this demand on the part of the owner of the vineyard was properly motivated by someone who was both good and fair-minded. Nothing about his request is out of line. He is not demanding more than was normal for a legal owner who allows tenants in to tend his vineyard. It is understood that a tenant farmer will work for food, housing, and perhaps for a cut of the profits. That is normal, but these tenants see otherwise, and they become aggressive in their resistance to the owner's attempt to collect from the vineyard. The question is, of course, why would they act in this manner? Only one real conclusion can be reached: they began to see all the profits and benefits as rightfully theirs. In our own realm we actively protect what we conclude to be ours, despite the legal definitions. After all, had they not done "all the work" to make the profits possible? Why should they give anything back?

One cannot but assume, then, that in the view of Yeshua, this behavior reflects the standard way in which we treat the activities and gains we make from the "field of existence" we call life. We assume, of course, that everything we do and own and make for ourselves belongs to us alone. We imagine that life (our life, our body, our resources) are all our own—they "belong" to us. But do they? Is anything we possess truly ours? Does anything we have gained from life, in fact, belong to us? Or have we been living on borrowed time in a land we do not own, using the resources that actually come from somewhere and someone else who has allowed us to be "tenant farmers?" Are we, in fact, like the tenants in this parable, misinformed about the true nature of reality at best, and delusional at worst—crazy with the desire to protect "our property" and "our rights," none of which, in truth, belong to us? It is a sobering assessment that Yeshua makes. This is a wisdom perspective shared by other Logia in this text.

QUESTIONS FOR REFLECTION

1. According to Logion 65, what is our reason for being in this world?

2. Put yourself in the place of the tenants. Would you ever respond in this manner? Under what circumstances? What do you consider "rightfully yours," belonging to you and no one else?

3. We are a people who highly value human rights. We also put great emphasis upon the individual. Does this parable address that issue either explicitly or implicitly?

4. What belongs to you? What do you own? What would you fight to keep as your own?

5. What is the symbolic difference between the servants and the son in your view?

EXERCISES AND MEDITATIONS

1. Would you (or can you) release your rights to yourself – your identity—your stuff? Whose "land" is this? Whose property are we on? Who has rights to the use of what we possess, or think we possess? Who, in fact, are we? These questions go to a profound rethinking of what it means to live in the field of existence and to understand why we are actually here. According to the wisdom tradition, the image we have of who we are and what we own is an illusion, and so we are trapped in a false picture of the world. Move into a period of meditation and reflect on this wisdom way of seeing. Enter that viewpoint and stay there, looking at your own life from that perspective. What do you see? Journal your insights and share them with like-minded friends.
2. One of the most instructive ways to engage the Gospel of Thomas is to work with the "twin image" of whatever is being presented—its opposite. In this and the last two logia we have images of resistance in one form or another. Now imagine their opposite (their twin). What are the levels of readiness or acceptance that would mirror the images presented here? Take each Logion (63-65) and in your own words write out an opposite scenario using the template of that saying. Put yourself in each scene and reconstruct it to show what the opposite of resistance might be, and how it might affect the outcomes.

READINGS FOR INSIGHT

I

A Sufi parable

A bumptious man dismissed a wandering sage by shouting at him,
"Be off, nobody knows you here."
"But I know myself," said the sage.
"How sad it would be if the reverse were true."

II

The Buddha

The right time to show your good character
Is when you are pestered by someone weaker than you.

III

Brother, why do you strut about, so full of yourself?
How come you've forgotten those ten months
when you were suspended upside down inside the womb?
When the body's cremated, it turns to ashes;
When its buried, it's eaten by armies of worms.
The body's a jar of unbaked clay containing water—
that's its greatest claim to fame.
As a honeybee accumulates its honey, so a man accumulates his wealth.
But when he's dead, the others say, *Take him away, take him away! Why have we let this corpse lie here so long?*
His wife accompanies his bier from the inner rooms to the threshold; beyond that, his friends bear him away.
The folks in his family go as far as the cremation ground.
Beyond that, the swan's all alone.
Kabir says, listen, O creatures, those who fall into the well of death ensnare themselves in make-believe Maya,
like parrots who delude themselves and fall into a bird-catcher's trap.

Kabir
The Weaver's Songs
112-113

IV

Most of us live caught up in prereflective identification most of the time, imagining that our thoughts, feelings, attitudes and viewpoints are an accurate portrayal of reality. But when awareness is clouded by prereflective identification, we do not yet fully *have* our experience. Rather, *it has us:* we are swept along by crosscurrents of thought and feeling in which we are unconsciously immersed. Driven by these unconscious identifications—self-images, conflicting emotions, superego commands, object relations, recurring thought patterns—we remain asleep to the deeper import of our experience. We remain angry without even knowing we are angry, anxious without understanding why we are anxious, and hungry without realizing what we are truly hungry for. This is the condition that Gurdjieff called "the machine."

John Welwood
Toward a Psychology of Awakening
126

LOGION 66

Yeshua says,

Bring me the stone
the builders discarded.
That one will be the key.

Sapiential Themes

- *There are two wisdom principles in action: rejection and integration. Understanding them is a key to wisdom.*
- *The students of Yeshua are asked to perform the task of finding what is rejected and bringing it to him, for he is building something important.*
- *How Yeshua uses the keystone will perhaps be the subject of the next in the series of sayings.*

Parallel Texts

Psalms 118:22
Matthew 21:33-46
Mark 12:1-12
Luke 20:9-19
Acts 4:11
I Corinthians 3:11-17
Ephesians 1:20
I Peter 2:4, 7

FOCAL POINT

Traditional Christian theology interprets this saying (and its cognates in the canonical Gospels) as being about the rejection of Jesus as the Messiah. Yeshua is seen here to be accusing the people of his day of rejecting him and his ministry. This interpretation was the one most favored by his early followers. Their accusation was that his own people had refused to accept him and here he acknowledges it. Is this, however, a correct understanding of this text, or does Yeshua see something entirely different here? Does he see that it is the deeper essences which are the keys to the spiritual world, and that have been blindly discarded by humanity in general? If we accept this interpretation, then they must bring back to him what has been thrown away, and he will use it perhaps to construct a new temple: a new building worthy of its interior content.

Links

This Logion is clearly linked to the three before it by bringing into focus what has been previously rejected. Here Yeshua is inviting it back in, saying that it is a key to his work, and perhaps the work of wisdom in any individual's life.

Notes

In both ancient and modern building practices, the "key stone" locks other stones in place or provides a gauge for the rest of the building structure.

COMMENTARY

This Logion highlights two principles critical to the tradition of wisdom: rejection and integration. In the three previous Logia, Yeshua focused upon the characteristics of rejection, but now he turns to its opposite: the integration of that which has been previously rejected. Yeshua asks his students to find and bring him the rejected stone. That, he says, will become the key. His request, of course, raises crucial questions both for them and for us. Do we know what has been rejected? Have we ourselves rejected something that is key? What is it that cannot be tolerated within our circle of comfort? Can we discern what we may have cast away from ourselves, and can we find it again and bring it to the Master of integration?

Stones and minerals have traditionally symbolized essences—core realities and fundamental principles that are the foundation for any other building process.

If we use the examples of the last three Logia to help us understand the nature of spiritual rejection (what it is that resists Spirit and its force within wisdom), then we can gain insight into the various forms of rejection. In Logion 63, what is rejected is a state of spiritual wakefulness to the wider world beyond narrow human self-interest. Nothing concerns this individual except what affects his personal bottom line. Anything that does not serve his immediate needs or financial gain is of little value. This individual is not aware or awake to any other reality than his own. In some sense, his is the widest rejection, encompassing almost everything but himself.

Logion 64 includes four instances illustrating the rejection of transcendence itself (the invitation to go beyond ordinary concerns) in favor of the mundane activity of the immediate moment. These folk are aware of a higher reality (the gathering at the dinner party), but are swept along in the ordinary world which trumps anything higher. They, therefore, cannot rise into transcendence. In effect, they have rejected it.

In the final illustration of spiritual rejection, Logion 65, the tenants are certainly aware of their higher responsibility to someone other than themselves, but they abandon that responsibility (which they surely agreed to earlier) for a violent confrontation with the rightful owner. What they have soundly rejected is servanthood, or service to their Lord. By analogy, they have been called into service, to give up something of themselves to a higher authority, but they refuse it. All of these—forgetfulness, narrow focus, self-centered service—all must be brought to the Master of integration. Surrendered up, these will become the key so that something new can begin to be built. What has been rejected can now become fully integrated and turned into wakefulness, transcendent focus, and self-giving—these are the keys. From them a new temple of Spirit can be built.

In traditional architecture, particularly in the Middle East where arches are a dominant feature, the wedge-shaped stone at the top of the arch is called the keystone. It holds the arch together, for the weight of the arch ultimately comes to rest upon it.

On another level, if we use the building metaphor exactly as it is used here, we can see that both in his day and in ours the "arches" of the religious and political temples may have collapsed. What has been so carefully constructed by humanity is tumbling down. Why? Because, from his spiritual perspective at least, the keystone is missing. Religious systems that try to build without this key (the keystone at the head of the arch) are doomed to failure. The whole structure will not hold. The very thing that is crucial in the construction is missing. Yeshua sees this and asks them to bring him that stone. Can they do it? Do they know what this missing piece actually is? Do they know why it has been rejected? As participants in this same tradition, we must ask our current religious systems the same questions.

QUESTIONS FOR REFLECTION

1. It is easier, perhaps, to understand what it is that we accept than what we reject. If it is rejected then it is "out of sight," and also "out of mind." So then we do not have to deal with it or think about it. What is it of a spiritual or theological nature that you have definitively rejected? Do you have any doubt now about that earlier decision?

2. Have you ever changed your mind theologically or spiritually, at one point denying the importance or legitimacy of some particular point of view, and later coming to see its truth? What has your experience been?

3. Are there things about you or within you that you have rejected, putting them outside yourself because you felt that in some way they were not "you?" If they are a part of who you are, can they then be received back? How might you be able to integrate those rejected parts of yourself?

Another important question is to determine what you fear, and therefore, what you might reject or push away from yourself. The premise is that we reject what we fear (See Readings for Insight). If this is the case, then what we fear may be the clue to what we have hidden away from ourselves. This could become both a serious question for inquiry, but also a subject for deep meditation. Confronting our fears is an important part of spiritual practice.

EXERCISES AND MEDITATIONS

1. Imagine that Yeshua came to you and said, "Go find and bring back to me that which all the builders of religion have rejected." What would you do? How would you respond? If you agreed, how would you accomplish that task? There are multiple and competing ideologies within religious traditions. This is certainly true within Christianity. Should one ideology or theological perspective "win?" This would mean that others lose and are rejected. Church history is replete with such battles. It would be instructive to review some part of that history and examine objectively what has been rejected from the viewpoint of standard western Orthodoxy. This would include early Jewish Christianity, the Arians, the Nestorians, the Celtic church and the Pelagians. Pick one of these (or some other controversy) and explore this form of rejection. Try to determine if there was something important that might have been lost and need rehabilitation. Journal what you find.
2. Finding a key (something that will open new doors) is critical in any form of spiritual exploration. If we stick to what we already know, never exploring what is new for us (and perhaps, what is frightening territory), we will not possess the key that will open new doors. Choose a topic of interest. Something that you have never explored. It might be, for example, another religious tradition, or a theological perspective or a discipline which heretofore you have avoided. Enter that territory with a sense of curiosity. Pick up a text that will help you explore it. Talk to individuals who are in that world. Visit places that represent that point of view. All the while, look for keys that will unlock previously closed doors. Again, journal what you discover.
3. In a period of quiet reflection and meditation, ask the Master of Integration to show you what has been rejected. Listen for his answer.

Two informative texts on the issue of rejection and integration are: John Welwood's ***Toward a Psychology of Awakening*** *(Shambhala, 2002), and A. H. Almaas's* ***Diamond Heart,*** *Books 1-3 (Diamond Books 1987-1990)*

READINGS FOR INSIGHT

I

John Welwood
Toward a Psychology of Awakening
141

The only way to promote healing is by reversing the condition of rejection that creates dis-ease in the first place.

II

J. Jelinek

We learn more by welcoming criticism than by rendering judgment.

II

W.M. Pepper

I claim no superior intellect, but do subscribe to a gut feeling which says, "I am not afraid to intellectually test any idea contradictory to my own because from that direction, truth will surely come if I do not now possess it."

III

Anonymous

You fear what you do not understand.

IV

John Marks Templeton
Worldwide Laws of Life
21

During World War II, Allied soldiers referred to the Germans as "Jerrys." During the Korean and Vietnam conflicts, the Red Chinese, North Koreans, and Vietnamese were called "Gooks." These names served to dehumanize the enemy and create a sense of superiority and loathing (which is a form of fear) in the troops that had to fight them. If the name callers had understood that the troops on the other side were also fighting for what they believed in, killing them would have become an infinitely more difficult task. An old Moorish proverb brings to mind a great truth: "He who is afraid of a thing gives it power over him."

V

Pema Chödrön
Quoted in ***Toward a Psychology of Awakening***
137

If your everyday practice is to open to all your emotions, to all the people you meet, to all the situations you encounter, without closing down, trusting that you can do that—then that will take you as far as you can go. And then you'll understand all the teachings that anyone has ever taught.

VII

Albert Einstein

A day without learning is a day wasted.

VIII

Rabindranath Tagore

My eyes have seen much,
but they are not weary.
My ears have heard much,
but they thirst for more.

LOGION 67

Yeshua says,

If you come to know all,
and yet you yourself are lacking,
you have missed everything.

Sapiential Themes

- *Yeshua changes our perception about what is crucial for spiritual knowing.*
- *In the wisdom tradition, ontology precedes epistemology—being comes before knowing, or being is the key to knowing.*
- *True knowledge is not about information or facts, but concerns a quality of being that is the key to wisdom.*
- *One's being is the lens (the aperture) that allows the Light of knowledge in.*

Parallel Texts

Logion 2, 70, 77
Luke 10:41
Book of Thomas the Contender 138:16-18

FOCAL POINT

In the previous saying, Yeshua asks his students to bring him the stone that has been rejected by the builders. "That one," he says, "will become the key" to everything (or "the All"). This is a critical step in the building of the living structure of wisdom, which appears to be Yeshua's task. So the question is, of course: what is the rejected keystone that they must bring? This saying appears to give us our first clue. That which is neglected and rejected is not something outside and apart from ourselves, something far off that we must go out, search for and find, but is rather, as this Logion suggestions, something intimately related to who and what we already are or, at least, could become.

Links

Logion 66 (as well as the illustrations in the Logia leading up to it) sets the stage for this saying and the Logia which shall follow it. We move to the heart of the matter: how to open ourselves, and not reject wisdom. Everything comes down to the nature of the individual. Ours is not simply a collective journey, but an individual one that contributes to the whole.

Notes

Similar phraseology to this saying that has been preserved in the Thomas tradition is found in an ancient text, ***Book of Thomas the Contender****: "For one who has not known oneself has not known anything, but one who has known oneself has already acquired knowledge about the depth of the universe" (138:16-18).*

COMMENTARY

Gnosticism is a problematic word. It has been used as both a way of denigrating early movements within Christianity, as well as to loosely describe any viewpoint that contradicted nascent orthodoxy. That said, there were Gnostics who were extreme dualists, and who felt that they possessed the "secret keys" to which no one else had access.

We often imagine that if we could find that one last missing piece of information, or read the next important breakthrough book, or have a vision of that final truth, then all of our questions would be resolved and we would possess the key that we need for the spiritual journey ahead. But is that correct? Is that the answer that we need? Yeshua appears not to agree.

For him, the key is something else entirely that is missing. It is not more information, another book or author, or even adding to the store of knowledge. Instead, it is the inner, personal qualities of an individual being. As he suggests, being is more important than knowing. At first this may seem to contradict our sense of this very Gospel. It does indeed contradict the tenets of some of the early Christian Gnostics who appeared to advocate "lost knowledge" as the key to entering the heavenly kingdom. But Yeshua says it is the missing part of ourselves (the lacuna within), that determines the outcome. What is missing must be found and brought forward. We may, as St. Paul says in his first Corinthian letter, possess all external knowledge. We may have a wealth of theological understanding, but if we lack the critical inner quality of love, then we have missed the one thing necessary.

I Corinthians 13: 2, 12

The key to building the structure of wisdom is the growth, evolution and transformation of one's being, and not the addition of further knowledge as we typically understand it. Another way to say this is to recognize that we must not simply know the truth, but, more importantly, we must become the truth we know. Truth must be built into the very structure of our own being. That is the key. We must live in our personal life the truth we know in the mind and heart. It is clear that this is also the missing ingredient in much of what we recognize to be religious and spiritual life.

A further way to understand this essential issue is to say that we can only truly know reality by perceiving it (contacting it) through the lens of our own being. Who we are and have become is the aperture through which we see and know the truth of things. If the lens is weak, covered with a film, or missing essential inner, structural dimensions, then it cannot pick up the light that is coming to it, or see what would otherwise be available to it. A strong inner being operates as the lens of seeing and knowing. That is the missing key to the acquisition of wisdom which Yeshua has come to offer. Nothing else will suffice. Without it, everything else is a loss.

So what is it that can be absent from one's being or added to it that will change its nature? Sacred tradition is insistent that the quality of (or qualities in) one's being can change either by addition or subtraction. The quality of who we are can be added through the virtues, or subtracted by the vices. These terms are suggestive of those divine qualities that either enhance or detract from human nature. The quality of a piece of fruit can be increased by ripening. Similarly, the quality of an individual can be amplified as a person matures (or ripens) in wisdom. Something of substance changes, but if it is missing altogether, then the lack of it is an absence that has consequences, contributing to even greater want. In the way that the original Coptic text is worded, there is the suggestion that knowing the All, but having this inner lack, means that there is no place for the All to reside or come to be. This way of reading the text emphasizes the spiritual being (not intellectual knowing) as the proper residence for the fullness that is known as the All.

The Greek term "the All," which is a code for the fullness of everything that exists, is used twice in this text. It is not a term that is easily understood in English if translated directly, but in Greek it stands for the entire cosmos of existence—all that is.

QUESTIONS FOR REFLECTION

1. Everyone, at some time or another, has felt inadequate—felt that something essential was missing. When have you felt that way, and what has been its effect on you?

2. Imagine there is some essential ingredient that makes a recipe really good, and without which it will only be so-so. Imagine this also applies to a human being. What essential ingredient (quality or value) makes a human a person of "high quality?"

3. Have you ever "missed something" that everyone else around "got," or felt that everyone else knew something you did not? What was the reason? Later, perhaps, you did get it. What made the difference?

EXERCISES AND MEDITATIONS

1. Ripening, spiritual maturity, growth, AND transformation are keys to the acquisition of wisdom. Wisdom is an ingredient that makes a person of high value and quality. Think through your own experience. When have you met such a person? How did you detect high quality in that individual? What did you see and experience? It is impossible for the eye to see itself (except, of course, mirrored in something else). What do you detect about yourself that is mirrored in others? Do you see any of those same qualities you value in others reflected in yourself?
2. What might you be lacking? Usually disruption, disharmony, and lack of equilibrium are signs that something is missing. This is not always true, for this is a disordered world, but the fact is, we create our own order or disorder around us. So look at your environment critically. In the wake of your moving through the world, is there further order and harmony, or is there disorder and disequilibrium? You might choose a week to explore this idea. Imagine the world that you experience around yourself is your mirror.
3. In a period of reflection and meditation, sit with these issues. Allow the Inner Teacher resident within you to reveal those things that need to be seen. We require input from the sacred realm, and a Teacher intelligent beyond our knowing. For several days in a row, sit quietly for a period of time and allow teaching to "arrive" — that inner seeing which will alert you to those "keystones" that need to be brought into the core of your being to complete the building, or strengthen the structure of your being.
4. Imagine fruit ripening into "sweet perfection" and of the highest quality. List the things that make that happen. What might you learn from this process that you do not already know? What do you need to apply to your own experience?

In his book, ***The Garden of Truth****, Seyyed Hossein Nasr points out that "Harmony is the result of the reflection of the One in the manifold, and therefore it is closely related to beauty. Objects of beauty possess qualitative harmony associated with such realities as colors. They can also possess not only qualitative but also quantitative harmony. This can be found, for example, in music, which in addition to the quality of sounds, is related quantitatively to measurement and mathematics, disciplines studied in the science of harmonics." (75)*

READINGS FOR INSIGHT

I

Jalaluddin Rumi
The Rumi Collection
194

Suppose you know the definitions of all substances and their products, what good is this to you? Know the true definition of yourself, that is essential.Then, when you know your own definition, flee from it, that you may attain to the One who cannot be defined, O sifter of the dust.

II

J. W. von Goethe

Only by joy and sorrow does a person know anything
about themselves and their destiny.
They learn what to do and what to avoid.

III

Pema Chödrön
Comfortable with Uncertainty
109-110

Start where you are. This is very important. ...You may be the most violent person in the world—that's a fine place to start. That's a very rich place to start—juicy, smelly. You might be the most depressed person in the world, the most addicted person in the world, the most jealous person in the world. You might think that there are no others on the planet who hate themselves as much as you do. All of that is a good place to start. Just where you are—that's the place to start.

What you do for yourself, any gesture of kindness, any gesture of gentleness, any gesture of honesty and clear seeing toward yourself, will affect how you experience your world. What you do for yourself, you're doing for others, and what you do for others, you're doing for yourself. When you exchange yourself for others ... it becomes increasingly uncertain what is out there and what is in here.

III

Rainer Maria Rilke
Duino Elegies
The Seventh Elegy

Nowhere, Beloved, will the world be but within us. Our life passes in transformation. And the external shrinks into less and less. Where once an enduring house was, now a cerebral structure crosses our path, completely belonging to the realm of concepts, as though it still stood in the brain. Our age has built itself vast reservoirs of power, formless as the straining energy that it wrests from the earth.

Temples are no longer known. It is we who secretly save up these extravagances of the heart. Where one of them still survives, a Thing that was formerly prayed to, worshipped, known before—just as it is, it passes into the invisible world.

Many no longer perceive it, yet miss the chance to build it *inside* themselves now, with pillars and statues: greater.

IV

Seyyed Hossein Nasr
The Garden of Truth
85

We are beings who know, love, and act, and there is an interplay between our being and our knowing, loving, and acting. Ontologically our being comes before everything else, but existentially our knowing, loving, and acting are the realities that fill the moments of our lives and of which we are aware. Our soul knows, loves, and acts—the latter primarily through the body. Moreover, knowing and loving both affect our actions and are often expressed through them. Furthermore, all three affect our mode of being while our mode of being and level of consciousness determine what we know and can know, what we love and can love, and how we act.

LOGION 68

Sapiential Themes

- *Blessedness is the original and foundational state proper to the life of a human being.*
- *Contrary to our common perspective, the human experience of pain and suffering is the precondition for a positive change in relationship to the self.*
- *Ego-consciousness is absent at the core of our being.*
- *Finding freedom from the ego allows an individual to gain access to the state of blessedness.*

Yeshua says,

Blessed are you who
in the midst of persecution,
when they hate
and pursue you
even to the core of your being,
cannot find "you" anywhere.

Parallel Texts

Job 5:17, 23:10
Psalms 66:10, 119:67
Isaiah 48:10
Matthew 5:10-12
Luke 6:22-23
II Corinthians 4:17
I Peter 1:6-7, 4:12-19

Links

In the previous Logion, Yeshua speaks about a human who is lacking some crucial element in his or her being. That individual, Yeshua says, has missed everything despite perhaps having superior knowledge. This being the case, the question is: what might be lacking that is essential? This saying directs us to a paradoxical and unexpected answer. It concerns the state of blessedness that is lacking nothing essential.

FOCAL POINT

In this and the next Logion (69), Yeshua directly challenges the common understanding of the nature and states of blessedness (what the Buddhist tradition would call ***ananda***, or bliss). His triple description is far from what we would imagine such states to be. They are not normative for us, nor do they fall into what we would ordinarily describe as either blessing or human happiness. Nothing could be further from our understanding of what constitutes pleasure or contentment than these three states of blessedness, and yet, as is suggested by the previous saying, they appear to be essential keys for the building of wisdom. Without them nothing substantial or lasting is ever or finally built.

Notes

In the original Coptic text, the individual pursued and persecuted is the one who cannot be found (or "seize") even at the core of his or her being. This term "seize" is the one that has been used previously to describe forms of acquisition, either positive or negative, that have had an impact on the search triggered by this Gospel.

COMMENTARY

in the last saying (Logion 67), Yeshua has instructed us that if in our own being we are lacking, though we perhaps know everything else, then we have missed the whole point entirely and cannot participate in the fullness of the All. One would assume, then, that whatever is missing is an addition—that qualification and virtue must be added to one's being. Though this is true, the condition for the possibility that this might ever occur happens to be a paradox; there must be no "you" present. In that state of being, there must be emptiness in order for anything else (especially the virtues) to fill the space that "you" formerly occupied.

There is a truer you (the blessed you) that fills the space when there is not a "you" (the "you" that can no longer be found anywhere anymore). It is confusing—this you/not you paradox. Students of spirituality are aware of the fundamental teaching about the nature of the false self, the "you" that is, in fact, a social construct, a temporary entity made up out of the human contingencies of family history, upbringing, cultural background and education. That "you" is not the eternal You which preceded your entry into space-time and will survive it. This larger, transcendent You is something that must replace the smaller "you" when it finally "goes missing" or disappears entirely. When that happens, Yeshua says, you exist in a state of blessedness.

Teaching concerning the false self (or "the flesh" as St. Paul will express it) begin with Yeshua's own instruction about giving up the self. Great spiritual teachers throughout history have described this reality in their teaching. More recently, Father Thomas Keating has based his work in Centering Prayer on the doctrine of the false self.

The actual context and precondition for this change in the state of being, however, is not something we welcome or easily understand. It involves the violation of what we believe to be our survival, safety, security, and "comfort zones." Persecution, hatred, and pursuit are said to be involved in what we might term the "hounding of the ego." The result is that one is forced to move beyond its boundaries to the core of one's being, or to the limits of one's ego. It is necessary to escape in the only way possible: by breaking free from the contours of the ego and moving to the core—the center and the origin of one's being. There, there is no "you" present. There is only presence—the Presence of that Self which is beyond the "self" as we have known it. There is no ego there, no inflated self, no illusory being. That, the persecutions have destroyed, or at least shown for what it is: a provisional and impermanent entity.

The twin selves (self/ Self) come into focus as part of the meaning of the opening emphasis upon twoness. Each person is twinned , and it is the recognition of this twoness that makes possible the growth of the soul.

So what are these events through which one may be forced to flee? Are these the early persecutions of the Church, or is this something else entirely? Certainly one should never exclude anything that challenges the self, but if we understand this direct challenge to the small self to be the central agency, then any event, any set of circumstances which can do this (anything which persecutes, hates and pursues the accepted image of ourselves) will work. There are no specifics here, and no particular set of circumstances which must come into play. There are only the circumstances peculiar to us that will have their own unique and powerful effect: purging, purifying, and compelling us to move beyond our safe edifices. The self (the "you") that you have known as "yourself" is always provisional and temporary. It will not last. In the fires of persecution and destruction it will collapse, and the consciousness that is eternal will escape it to move toward the larger Presence resident at the center of one's being. To enter the fire of persecution is to enter the state of blessedness and bliss. This is the keystone that will ultimately bridge heaven and earth in the building of the arch of eternal wisdom.

QUESTIONS FOR REFLECTION

1. If someone were to ask you to describe the state of blessedness and/or bliss, what would you say?

2. What is the nature of persecution? Describe the experience of hatred. Have you ever felt either of these? How has that experience affected you?

3. How would you describe yourself—the person you know to be "you?"

4. What does "core of your being" mean to you? Do you know that place? Have you ever gone there, deliberately or otherwise? What happened? How did it change you (if it did)?

5. How does a spiritual Master (such as Yeshua) move students toward the place of freedom using the conditions of persecution, pursuit, and hatred?

EXERCISES AND MEDITATIONS

1. The experience of being more than simply troubled, but harassed and hounded by forces of hatred and persecution, is one that has been known by humans throughout history. Think about an example of this historically, and then imagine it occurring in your own life. How is this experience different from simply being bothered or inconvenienced? What is being described here? Could the "fires of persecution," as they are often called, be similar to the "fiery trials" described by other writers of the Christian Scriptures (such as is found in I Peter 1:7)? How could this experience in fact be a state of blessedness, and not a curse? Would you perceive it as such? Reflect on this difficulty and paradox as a possibility in your own life. Have you experienced it? What has been the effect? Journal your answers.
2. The nature of the "self" is a complex mystery. The "you" that you know, and the you that you could become, are quite different. If you met this second you before your own spiritual evolution, would you recognize it? Imagine, then, that the first "you" (the one you know now) has somehow to disappear or fade from sight, so that the true you, the real Self, can emerge. Imagine, also, that this first you, though it resists, has somehow to be "annihilated" (to experience ***fana',*** as the Sufis will say) before the true Self can arise, and that it will take persecution (or hounding) of some sort for that to occur. Now think about the "you" you know, and the you that is becoming. What is the sequence of events that are occurring in your world to challenge the first and bring forth the second? How would you (and what "you" is that), work with this process?

Many manuals of spiritual life discuss this complexity—the mystery of the self. You might want to use some of the more contemporary spiritual texts to explore the process of the growth of the true Self. I recommend that you look at some of the following: Michael A. Singer's ***The Untethered Soul*** *(New Harbinger Publ., 2007); Eckhart Tolle's* ***Stillness Speaks*** *(New World Library, 2003); Cynthia Bourgeault's* ***Centering Prayer and Inner Awakening.*** *(Cowley Publ., 2004); and Kabir Helminski's* ***Living Presence.*** *(Jeremy P. Tarcher/ Perigee, 1992).*

READINGS FOR INSIGHT

I

John Welwood
Toward a Psychology of Awakening
152

We fabricate our notion of who we are out of "self-representations"—images of ourselves internalized from our early interactions with our parents and social environment. Our consciousness comes to identify itself with various objects of consciousness—ideas about ourselves and the world, the work we do, the things we own, our personal history, dramas, and achievements, the intimate relationships we hold most dear. We hold on to all of these things because they are supports for our identity, because they make us feel that we exist, that we are real.

II

Pema Chödrön
Comfortable with Uncertainty
111

A woman is running from tigers. She runs and she runs, and the tigers are getting closer and closer. She comes to the edge of a cliff. She sees a vine there, so she climbs down and holds on to it. Then she looks down and sees that there are tigers below her as well. At the same time, she notices a little mouse gnawing away at the vine to which she is clinging. She also sees a beautiful little bunch of strawberries emerging from a nearby clump of grass. She looks up, she looks down, and she looks at the mouse. Then she picks a strawberry, pops it in her mouth, and enjoys it thoroughly.

Tigers above, tigers below. This is the predicament we are always in. We are born and sooner or later we die. Each moment is just what it is. Resentment, bitterness, and holding a grudge prevent us from seeing and hearing and tasting and delighting. This might be the only moment of our life, this might be the only strawberry we'll ever eat. We could feel depressed about this or we could finally appreciate it. We could delight in the preciousness of every single moment.

III

Bahauddin
The Drowned Book
95

Having anxieties and feeling sad about being alive is like piling black mud and garbage on your head. ... Try to stop doing it. Let your eyes get clear enough to see the beauty around you. *Say*... "O giver of worriedness and grief, remove me from my being. Give me the peace of not-being."

IV

Pema Chödrön
Comfortable with Uncertainty
165-166

Obstacles occur at the outer and inner levels. At the outer levels the sense is that something or somebody has harmed us, interfering with the harmony and peace we thought was ours. Some rascal has ruined it all. This particular sense of obstacle occurs in relationships and in many other situations; we feel disappointed, harmed, confused, and attached in a variety of ways. People have felt this way from the beginning of time.

As for the inner level of obstacle, perhaps nothing ever really attacks us except our own confusion. Perhaps there is no solid obstacle except our own need to protect ourselves from being touched. Maybe the only enemy is that we don't like the way reality is *now* and therefore wish it would go away fast. But what we find as practitioners is that nothing ever goes away until it has taught us what we need to know. ... It keeps returning with new names, forms, and manifestations until we learn whatever it has to teach us: Where are we separating ourselves from reality? How are we pulling back instead of opening up? How are we closing down instead of allowing ourselves to experience fully whatever we encounter?

LOGION 69

Yeshua says,

Blessed are all those persecuted into the depths of their heart. Only there will they come to know their true Father and Source. Blessed are the hungry ones. Their inner longings will be satisfied.

Sapiential Themes

- *Every human being experiences the "mystery of suffering" whether or not we have the knowledge of why we experience it.*
- *Trouble in this world has a purpose, a role to play in the spiritual evolution of a human being. It is not a wasted experience.*
- *The spiritual heart is the core of a human being, and a place of residence and refuge for those who have found it. Finding it, however, may include trouble, which drives us to that interior place.*

Parallel Texts

Logion 15, 40, 50
Matthew 5: 6, 10-12
Luke 6:21-23

FOCAL POINT

It is clear that Yeshua saw what many mystics and seers throughout the ages have seen and known: the mystery of suffering, the purpose of earthly existence, and meaning for the human self. Why on earth must we pass through such a world? Why must we experience the "hounding of the soul" across space and time, a hounding that can drive a person into the depths of despair and strip the self of the "self?" Why this harrowing on earth? Why the suffering we know personally and as a collective body? For much of humanity, the experience of pain appears to be immense and unrelenting. Yet, as this Logion teaches us, life is purposeful. Yeshua knows that secret, and so we come to his understanding at the heart of the mystery.

Links

This Logion is part of a longer series beginning with Logion 66, but is related directly to the last saying concerning the state of blessedness. The theme of persecution or pursuit from the outside is once again emphasized, mirroring an inner state of hunger and longing. The difficult combination of the inner and outer realities results in an unexpected experience of blessedness.

Notes

The final phrase in the text translated as "their inner longing" is idiomatically expressed in Coptic as "their womb of longing." This beautiful phrase expresses both the depth and the fecundity of that state of deep longing that defines the core of human experience. It is only in that same interior place that ultimate satisfaction can be known.

COMMENTARY

The question raised by the last saying (Logion 68) is, what survives the death of the ego? Is there anything on the other side after the loss of the self? This question is at the heart of Yeshua's teaching in this Logion, and certainly at the heart of the Gospel of Thomas itself. Yeshua teaches a form of unitive wisdom that takes us past the surface structure of our lives and the world and to its depth. In this saying, we reach some greater fullness—the state of blessedness which is the highest form of being known in Abrahamic traditions..

After fleeing from the surface structure of ourselves (the provisional self) by persecution, we are driven to the Source—the living Father (and Mother, as we shall see later) of all selves, to the very center of consciousness which is the Self. Beyond the emptiness that we have experienced—through self-emptying—comes the fullness. This is Yeshua's Good News. But the Self that knows itself to come from the Source (and the experience of the fullness after hunger) is not the same self.

Marvin Meyer writes that Clement of Alexandria said: "... the most difficult persecution is from within, from pleasures and passions: The one being persecuted cannot escape it, for he carries the enemy around within himself everywhere."
The Gospel of Thomas: The Hidden Sayings of Jesus
96

Persecution and suffering move us toward a state of blessedness because we are driven out of the surface structure of our being into our own depths. The deepest part of a human being is not the mind, not the emotions, nor is it the storyline that narrates who we are and what we have become. It is the heart. It is that deepest place that was spoken about in the last saying, which is the foundational and fundamental aspect of what it means to be a human being. It is the crucible carrying within it the divine image (***imago dei***)—the gift made to us from the Source. The source of ourselves is not located in the world of historical and human contingency. We have only imagined this world to be our original home. Our true origin, however, lies at the heart of divinity itself. And at the center of our being in our deepest core (at the level of the heart) we are in constant contact with the true Heart-Source of Reality.

Some will say that the divine image has been "downloaded" into our human existence from our ancient beginning-point outside space and time.

In modern physics, at the sub-atomic level, a similar idea to this has come to be known as "entanglement." Elements that were in relationship at their beginning point, though separated by time and space, never lose contact. They are always "together." The action in one is immediately reflected in the action of the other, instantly. Suppose, then, that there is such a reality in the spiritual universe that could also be called "metaphysical entanglement." The Heart-Source and the heart of a human being are one (or are forever entangled), never to be separated by either time or space. But it is only when we go to that place within, and come there to know the self to be other than we imagined ourselves to be, that we know the true state of blessedness. That state of bliss fills and satisfies the insatiable longing that we have known incessantly from the beginning of our earthly pilgrimage where we experience the sense of separation. Nothing external can fill that longing. Only the Source can, because that is our true Self. To find that Self again and the truth about ourselves is to have our deepest questions about suffering answered, and our longings satisfied.

Contrary to our ordinary perceptions, however, the precondition for such a state of blessedness is just this experience of suffering, of separation, and of the gnawing, insatiable hunger. To allow that state to exist without trying to change it is terribly difficult. Yet, despite whatever else we might imagine, Yeshua calls that groundless state blessedness, for he knows the deeper truth that answers the mystery of our existence in this transitory and transitional world. This is the wisdom he offers us. We can seize hold of it and allow it to become our wisdom as well.

QUESTIONS FOR REFLECTION

1. Have you ever experienced being driven into the core of your own being, the depths of the heart? What happened to you and what was the outcome?

2. What advice would you give to an individual who was going through such an experience?

3. How do you understand God to be both Father and true Source? Theologically and spiritually, what do these terms mean to you?

4. What is it like to be really hungry and then to eat a delicious meal? How and why is spiritual hunger, then, a precondition for satisfaction?

EXERCISES AND MEDITATIONS

1. Let's imagine that there are multiple levels within ourselves, but that typically we stay at the surface in our thoughts and in the flow of immediate events rather than going to the depths. Going to the depths of the heart requires that there be a "letting go" of our attention to what is at the surface (thoughts, images, plans), and a movement of descent (some would say, perhaps, ascending) to the core of our being and into the Presence that dwells there. This Logion calls that place "the heart," and says that we meet the Father (the Source) there. It is critical that we have this whole experience of letting go, descent, and encounter. Give yourself a space in which you can explore this interior movement. Centering Prayer is a powerful way to begin. When the time comes and your attention turns toward the heart, go there and step into the Presence which is your Source. In periods of meditation, do this exercise for a week. Write in a journal what you experience and how it affects you.
2. How do you know when you have encountered (or experienced) the Source at the level of the heart? This is an important question to answer. Is it possible that one could mistake one's own egoic projections for such an encounter? Knowing the difference between these two kinds of experiences would, of course, be a critical form of discernment. The question is, of course, how can one discern that difference? Discuss this important topic with a group devoted to the work you are doing, or with a spiritual director.
3. The theme of constant human longing and its opposite, deep satisfaction, fill pages of poetry and the airwaves with song. Each one of us seems to have a fundamental sense of this dichotomy. It appears to run right through what we know as human beings. What is this inner experience and the rhythm of it like for you? Why would this be part of who we are? Explore these questions up close on a daily basis.

READINGS FOR INSIGHT

I

Anthony de Mello
One Minute Wisdom
44

The Master became a legend in his lifetime.
It was said that God once sought his advice:
"I want to play a game of hide-and-seek with humankind.
I've asked my Angels what the best place is to hide in.
Some say the depths of the ocean.
Others the top of the highest mountain.
Others still the far side of the moon or a distant star.
What do you suggest?"
Said the Master, "Hide in the human heart. That's the last place they will think of!"

II

John Welwood
Toward a Psychology of Awakening
155

If we can stay present and not recoil from the emptiness we encounter when our familiar sense of self breaks down, we eventually discover not just a meaningless void but a fresher quality of presence that feels awake, alive, and liberating.

III

Bahauddin
The Drowned Book
48

A great depth comes when one gets separated from the Friend. Only then is a human being tragically alive. If there is no Joseph, Jacob is never really Jacob. Unless you have spent some time in a garden with your beloved and then been pulled apart, your life will not have passion or vivid depth like a story told in scripture.

Everything has an opposite. When you love one thing, you hate the reverse. Another truth is that with any situation there is always a better one just above it. This proceeds upward until it reaches the divine, which is all around you but you do not see it. Expand your vision and you will. Live inside the story of Joseph and Jacob. Sit and beg to see God. Plead like the prophets. It is your birthright to be shown and *see* the divine.

IV

Gretel Ehrlich

To know something, then, we must be scrubbed raw,
the fasting heart exposed.

V

Pema Chödrön
Comfortable with Uncertainty
158

There's a discrepancy between our inspiration and the situation as it presents itself. It's the rub between those two things—the squeeze between reality and vision—that causes us to grow up, to wake up to be 100 percent decent, alive, and compassionate. The big squeeze is one of the most productive places on the spiritual path and in particular on this journey of awakening the heart.

VI

Phil Cousineau
The Art of Pilgrimage
13

Uncover what you long for,
and you will discover who you are.

LOGION 70

Yeshua says,

When you give birth to that which is within yourself, what you bring forth will save you.

If you possess nothing within, that absence will destroy you.

Sapiential Themes

- *The eternal Source is within and exists inside like a womb ready to give birth to a new form of our humanity.*
- *Our future "salvation" does not depend on the Church, or on a Savior from without. It depends on a restoration to fullness of being from within.*
- *The absence of such a birth is our undoing—our ultimate "unmaking."*
- *We are destroyed by absence, not the Presence of an external judge.*

Parallel Texts

Song of Solomon 3:4
Logion 4, 41, 42, 67
John 3:1-12
Gospel of Philip
Analogues: 16, 22, 51, 52, 57, 62, 71

FOCAL POINT

This text from the Gospel of Thomas has a certain resonance with the passage on new birth from the Gospel of John (John 3:1-12). There Yeshua converses with Nichodemus, the religious leader, who comes to speak with him after dark. His teaching in John is about the crucial issue of being born anew (or from Above). The distinction here, perhaps, is that Yeshua speaks of a birth from within rather than from without. There may, in fact, be no real distinction, for the interior of a human being is directly connected to the vertical axis of transcendence Above. In both texts, a new birth is crucial. The result of not passing through such a birth experience, however, is dramatic and consequential to spiritual life. Its absence has a destructive power.

Links

The previous saying speaks of being driven into the interior of one's being and, there, knowing hunger. It is perhaps out of such an experience that one becomes ready for a new form of birth from the very place into which one has been driven. In this saying we begin to realize what the divine strategy actually is capable of bringing about in the alchemy of new birth.

Notes

Note that the temporal element "when" sets the action of this Logion as an event either now or in the future. It is not if, but when. Absence, however, is destructive both now and in the future. The word "save," of course, is a term used extensively in the Pauline corpus. Its original meaning in Greek has to do with restoration to fullness of being, and not merely salvation from sin.

COMMENTARY

Logion 3

This Logion expresses a crucial "key" that opens a doorway into the Kingdom of Heaven. That Realm, Yeshua says, is found primarily within, though it never excludes the external world. Its wealth, however, can never simply come from without. Only by seeking its sources within can we find true treasure.

John 3: 1-12

The action expressed here entails a birthing process. Births, of course, require wombs, and acts of procreation, pregnancy, and a period of gestation. All these images are part of a larger process that is unfolding within the divine Realm. Elsewhere, in the Gospel of John, Yeshua speaks about a new form of birth—being born from above, beyond the natural patterns of birth. We know that physical birth is a normative event taking place along the horizontal axis in space and time. It is familiar as a this-world experience. In this Logion it appears to be quite different. This is an inner-world birthing; a process leading to a new form of human being. To use another metaphor familiar in the teachings of Yeshua, this new kind of life begins in seed-form and is planted within the soil of the outer person.

These questions need to be examined carefully and answered. The Gospel of Thomas provides answers for many of them. Some may be left for us to answer later in our sojourn on earth.

Many questions are raised by this saying and these images. They open new doors of exploration for spiritual practice and experience. What is entailed in this birthing process? What are its consequences? What happens if such a birth does not take place? What is life like on the other side of such a birth? What kind of new being emerges out of this womb? How do you care for the infant?

The True Human Being is the fullness or completion of what it means to be human when understood as a divine template already in existence.

Answering these questions is the work of a wisdom seeker. Direct answers can theoretically be given, but they remain conceptual (residing only in the mind) until they are experienced and lived in the totality of one's being. One key principle, however, remains at the heart of this Logion. It is this: only through this form of birth can there be the restoration of humanity to the form of the True Human Being. Its absence means that there is a hole in one's being, an emptiness, a form of poverty within that will eventually implode upon itself, taking the whole house down with it. This is what Yeshua sees.

*This term **noetic** is used to speak about the Greek term **nous**, which is used extensively to denote the central core of a human being that opens out on the transcendent aligned to the vertical axis.*

There is some place within us out of which we can emerge restored to fullness of being. This inner womb can be variously described as the core, the heart, or the *noetic* center which has open access to the Source from which we come. To be born out of that center into the realities of space and time, and to live from that place, is the sapiential secret which Yeshua is teaching. To never know that center, and to have in one's being nothing coming forward from that center, means that we are an empty shell made up of the stuff of the temporal and cultural orders only—the ***kosmos*** of illusion. This is the emptiness and impoverishment that Yeshua has already described in Thomas (Logia 3, 28). It is a deficiency from which we can recover.

To connect with the deeper force within—the genuine power of Life and Love itself streaming from the Source—is the goal. There is a holy longing inside each of us to give birth to this truer Self, to discover its inner fire, and to give way to its force. Losing access to the higher "qualities of heaven" means that we are unable to respond creatively to the challenging nature of our sojourn in space and time. Without integrating and embodying these higher, missing qualities (wisdom, compassion, love, clarity, patience, flexibility, confidence, strength, trust and generosity), the egoic self simply implodes from the force of external pressure. One must have access to a countervailing pressure and the force from Above.

QUESTIONS FOR REFLECTION

1. Read John 3:1-12 and reflect on the conversation that the religious leader has with Yeshua who comes to discuss spiritual matters with him at night. Are the teachings of this Logion and John's description similar, complementary, or opposed in any way?

2. What is "new birth" about in your view? How is it explained in conventional Christianity? Is this Logion a new teaching, or does it confirm what you already perceive about the doctrine of the new birth?

3. What is added in this Logion that is not in the passage in John's Gospel?

4. Compare this saying with Logion 3. How are they a commentary on one another?

EXERCISES AND MEDITATIONS

1. What is there within that needs to be born inside of you? Reflect on the issues of impregnation, pregnancy, gestation, and birth. How might each of these have been a part of your own experience in some way? What kind of urgency or state of awareness do you have about this saying at this point in your experience?
2. Do you have any awareness of your own birth? Some people have gone through some kind of prenatal regression and discovered things. Have you ever witnessed the birth of a child? What does that process tell you about how spiritual birth takes place? If you have not experienced a human birth, have a mother describe her experience. Apply that experience to this passage.
3. Meditate on the destructive nature of absence. We often define destructive acts as the intrusion of something hostile into another otherwise peaceful environment. Suppose, though, that the lack of something is also destructive. Think of some examples in human health or the environment where this might be entirely true. What elements missing from one's own being might ultimately prove to be the undoing of that being?
4. This is serious teaching. How concerned do you think we should be about fulfilling its requirements? How, in fact, do we bring to birth something from within? What is there within us already that might be the key element?
5. If you were to diagram how spiritual birth takes place, what kind of symbolic image or picture might you draw?
6. Write a prayer that expresses something of your own concern about this teaching and pray it over a period of several weeks. Share your insights, your findings, your images and your prayer with others who are on a similar path of exploration to your own. In addition, read and pray Psalm 139. What do you discover there?

There is a beautiful chant created by Ward Bauman that says,

Beloved One,
You are my being,
born from my
mother's womb.
I praise, revere and
adore you,
your mysteries fill me
with wonder.

You might at least say this chant as a prayer form in your own daily practice, and then, if you can, learn to chant it.

READINGS FOR INSIGHT

I

Rumi
Light Upon Light
187

I and Eternal Love were born into this Universe from one Light-Womb.
I may seem like a new Lover, but I am older than the two worlds.

II

Rumi
The Book of Love
29, 89

You that come to birth and bring the mysteries,
your voice-thunder makes us very happy.
Roar, lion of the heart and tear me open!
Love is the way messengers
from the mystery tell us things.
Love is the mother.
We are her children.
She shines inside us, visible-invisible,
as we lose trust or feel it start to grow again.

III

John Welwood
Toward a Psychology of Awakening
221, 220

In the secular humanistic perspective, individual development is an end in itself. In the view I am proposing here, individuation is not an end but a path of means that can help us give birth to our true form by clearing up the distortions of our old false self. As we learn to be true to our deepest individual imperatives, rather than enslaved to past conditioning, our character structure no longer poses such an obstacle to recognizing absolute true nature or embodying it. Our individuated nature becomes a window opening onto all that is beyond and greater than ourselves.

... the more we cultivate the full range of human qualities latent in our absolute true nature, the richer our quality of personal presence can become, as we begin to embody our true nature in an individuated way. ... it involves forging a vessel—our capacity for personal presence, nourished by its rootedness in a full spectrum of human qualities—through which we can bring absolute true nature into form: the "form" of our person.

IV

Anaïs Nin

Life is a process of becoming, a combination of states we go through. Where people fail is that they wish to elect a state and remain in it. This is a kind of death.

V

Meister Eckhart
Two Suns Rising
by Jonathan Star

God gives birth to the Son as you, as me, as each one of us. As many beings—as many gods in God. In my soul, God not only gives birth to me as his son, he gives birth to me as himself, and himself as me. I find in this divine birth that God and I are the same: I am what I was and what I shall always remain, now and forever. I am transported above the highest angels; I neither decrease nor increase, for in this birth I have become the motionless cause of all that moves. I have won back what has always been mine. Here, in my own soul, the greatest of all miracles has taken place—God has returned to God!

VI

Angelus Silesius

I must be the Virgin and give birth to God
Should I ever be graced divine beatitude.

LOGION 71

Yeshua says,

I will destroy this house and no one will ever be able to rebuild it.

Sapiential Themes

- *Destruction as well as construction is part of the spiritual force that Yeshua brings.*
- *The context for understanding this saying may be personal or historical, but in either case it illustrates a principle of spiritual unfolding.*
- *We must each consider how and why the destructive energy that Yeshua unleashes must often be applied to our own experience.*

Parallel Texts

Logion 10, 11, 16
Matthew 26: 59-68, 27:39-40,
Mark 13:1-4, 14:55-65, 15:29-30
John 2:13-22
Acts 6:12-14
I Corinthians 3:11-17
I Peter 1:7, 4:12-13

FOCAL POINT

It is common in eastern sacred traditions to consider the aspect of divine destruction. In Hinduism, for example, Kali expresses a divine destructive force. This is not perceived negatively, but as a necessity in the divine unfolding. Creation and destruction are complementary opposites. Things must pass out of existence in order for new things to emerge. Creation and destruction co-exist together. In the Gospel of Thomas there is, likewise, a corresponding juxtaposition between construction and destruction—a building up and a taking down. One aspect is not rejected in favor of the other. Yeshua's work is both to build up and to take down—it is both constructive and chaotic.

Links

Logion 70 talks about destruction coming from within, as a result of not giving birth to what lies at the core of one's being. In the end, lack of birth is destructive. Here the theme of destruction continues, but understood perhaps as occurring not within, but coming from without, at the hands of the Master himself. In both cases it is destruction. In this case it is perceived perhaps as a positive force, whereas in the previous Logion destruction is a negative force.

Notes

Hinduism honors Kali, a goddess of fearsome appearance who is the consort of Shiva. In the tradition of the Hebrew prophets, YHWH speaks of being both the Creator of darkness and light, and of good and evil (Isaiah 45:7). In the Wisdom tradition, Job experiences the utter destruction of what he has known as his safe household, and all this is sanctioned by the Lord.

COMMENTARY

We must use our active imaginations to grasp the meaning of this saying in some kind of original context in which it may have been spoken. Suppose that Yeshua is speaking and using his hand to point away from himself at some object. Or imagine, instead, that he is pointing toward his own body. If it is outward, we might imagine that he is pointing toward buildings that constitute the cities of his time and place. Or perhaps, even more pointedly, as some canonical texts suggest, he is pointing toward the Temple in Jerusalem itself. Any of these are possible, and perhaps also none of them, but it gives us a range of possibilities to contextualize the meaning.

We may hear these words as a direct threat and perhaps with a sense of terrible foreboding. On one level this statement may be a sentence of doom, and if so, we are rightly made afraid. But on another level, it is also possible to hear these words as a statement of promise and liberation concerning our ultimate state of freedom from the prison-house of the world of human making (the ***kosmos***) and our bondage within it.

This is a favorite theme in the poetry of the Sufi, Jalaluddin Rumi.

Imagine yourself at some period of history as a slave bound to a horror from which you cannot get free. If you heard these words in that context, what would you think? With what joy and promise might you understand their meaning? Suppose you were held enthralled to powers you became so used to that you didn't even notice any longer, and yet they remained a huge, crushing burden nonetheless. Later poets will call this world "a cage" from which, like a bird, we are released by God into the freedom of transcendent flight. In such a context this saying would mean liberation for all of us.

If you have a stake in maintaining the safety and security of any temporal or impermanent "house," you will see the undoing of its construct as the "end of the world" (at least as you know it). And it is! But just as the visionaries and prophets did, you have to see beyond the constructs of this world (either our human creations or the construction of our own being) to what replaces it. Our egoic self is a house far too small for the spirit. It must be taken down, but we are not strong enough to do it alone. We need the Master's force. Let's imagine, then, that as much as we hang on to it, the system of the world around us is a prison-house of indifference, injustice, oppression, and greed that not only contaminates the human spirit, but destroys the balances of the world. To destroy "that" house would be a welcome relief, especially if the Kingdom of Heaven replaced it.

See also Logion 16

Elsewhere in this Gospel, Yeshua has indicated that the fire he brings will create a kind of chaos that wreaks havoc until human beings are able to stand up out of the ***kosmos*** on their own two feet. These powerful images indicate that indeed something is being destroyed in order that something greater may come into being. Whatever that "house" may be—our egoic selves, the constructs of our own making, the human constructions we have built throughout history, or some false notion we have constructed out of which we have built everything else—that house cannot stand permanently. It will be taken down and never rebuilt.

This is in line with St. Paul's statements about the destruction of death itself (I Cor. 15:54-57).

Another possibility created by the juxtaposition of this saying to the previous Logion (70), is that the destruction Yeshua is bringing is directed against the very destructive force that a lack of true spiritual birth has caused us. Yeshua comes to destroy the destruction we visit upon ourselves. This is his act of restoration through destruction.

QUESTIONS FOR REFLECTION

1. Have you ever created something (perhaps in writing) that you later felt you needed to destroy? Have you ever built something that in time you needed to tear down? What were the circumstances?

2. How comfortable are you with the idea of Yeshua as a destroyer and not simply a healer or builder?

3. Is there any part of your life that you might be glad to experience Yeshua's destructive force?

4. Have you ever seen something destroyed that you felt sure was the result of some divine action?

EXERCISES AND MEDITATIONS

1. There are many spiritual themes in the tradition of early Christianity that focus on loss, destruction, letting go, abandoning, leave taking, and the crumbling away of the world as we know it. These form as a constellation of truths that mirror one another. Look at these themes more closely. See what you can find about this group of teachings in this Gospel as well as in the canonical Gospels. How do they relate to one another? After exploring, write some notes to yourself that you can share with others who are studying these same teachings.
2. Meditate on the power of destruction. When is that power a negative force? When can it be perceived to be something positive and necessary? When have these forces been at work in your life? What has been their effect upon you? Can you always tell immediately when a destructive force is negative or positive? Can they be both? Write out your reflections on these questions.
3. In a period of prayer and meditation work with the interior Master on this difficult issue. You might express your concerns both in prayer and in journal entries. Is it possible to offer yourself to the de-constructive force of a superior being, who knows what must be taken away and what should be left? Ask: what "building" or "house" that I "live in" metaphorically needs to be taken down? Can you offer up that process?
4. Read the prayer spoken by Rabindranath Tagore from the "Readings for Insight." What does he mean by this prayer? How does this prayer relate to the discussion about destruction? Over a period of time, as you are able, offer this prayer on a daily basis. You might also rewrite this prayer to fit your own experience or needs.

You might also want to create an anthology of such prayers. Make your own personal "prayer book" that contains a timeline of the experiences you have had on your journey. Consider keeping a personal prayer journal (or anthology) of this kind over a lifetime.

READINGS FOR INSIGHT

I

Jalaluddin Rumi

O Bringer of the sweetest wine,
And Enemy of the sober,
You have laid waste to
Every house I ever built!

III

Rabindranath Tagore
1861-1941

Time after time
I came to your gate with raised hands,
Asking for more and yet more.
You gave and gave, now in slow measure,
Now in sudden excess.
I took some, and some things I let drop;
Some lay heavy on my hands;
Some I made into playthings and broke them when tired.
Till the wrecks and the hoard of your gifts grew immense, hiding you,
And the ceaseless expectation wore my heart out.
Take, oh take—has now become my cry.
Shatter all from this beggar's bowl:
Put out this lamp of the importunate watcher.
Hold my hands, raise me from the still-gathering heap of your gifts
Into the bare infinity of your uncrowded presence.

III

Kamo Nno Chomei
Wabi Sabi,
44

The flow of the river is ceaseless;
And its water is never the same.
The foam that floats in the pools
Now gathering, now vanishing
Never lasts long.
So it is with man
And all his dwelling places on this earth.

IV

Juan Ramón Jiménez

A permanent state of transition is man's most noble condition.

V

Anthony de Mello
One Minute Wisdom
117

To a distressed person who came to him for help the Master said, "Do you really want a cure?"

"If I did not, would I bother to come to you?"

"Oh yes. Most people do."

"What for?"

"Not for a cure. That's painful. For relief."

To his disciples the Master said, "People who want a cure, provided they can have it without pain, are like those who favor progress, provided they can have it without change."

LOGION 72

A man said to Yeshua,

"Speak to my brothers
so that they will divide my father's
belongings with me."

Yeshua replied to him,
"Sir, who has made me the divider?"

He turned to his students and asked,
"Am I here to divide?"

Sapiential Themes

- *Yeshua is drawn into the mundane world of financial disputes and family arguments.*
- *He responds by asking two questions about his authority to act and his role as a divider.*
- *Division is a pen-ultimate, rather than an ultimate, goal for Yeshua as a wisdom teacher.*
- *Division may indeed precede unification.*

Parallel Texts

Logion 16
Luke 12:13-14
Ephesians 6:17
Hebrews 4:12

FOCAL POINT

In this Logion we are thrust into a first century scene that undoubtedly takes place among Yeshua's countrymen and neighbors in which the counsel of an important teacher or scholar of Torah is welcomed. The Logion opens on a dispute between brothers involving an issue of inheritance. One of the brothers in this family wants Yeshua to decide just how their father's possessions should be divided. The brothers are not in agreement, but perhaps a neutral person can resolve the dispute fairly. The Logion does not say whether Yeshua agrees to their request or not. At least he does not do so until he asks both the disputant and his students a question first. His questions have to do with authority and the role that he plays among them. Has the one coming to Yeshua for help understood (or misunderstood) why he is there? Have his students understood this matter clearly? Do we currently understand? As a master of wisdom, is it Yeshua's role to settle quarrels, make contracts, divide wealth, and adjudicate disagreement? Or is he here for some other purpose entirely?

Links

In the previous saying, Logion 71, Yeshua speaks about destroying "this house." Whatever sort of house that is, Yeshua's aim is to take it down. Could this saying indicate the very household that Yeshua has in mind for demolition? It is a provocative possibility. The question is, of course: how would one go about tearing down and perhaps, then, rebuilding just such a house?

Notes

The issue of dividing and uniting is at stake throughout this text, and so the term "divider" instead of "arbitrator" or "apportioner," is used to describe what Yeshua calls himself. Any of these translations, however, would be entirely appropriate.

COMMENTARY

It is not uncommon in the Middle East for a highly esteemed spiritual leader to be put in the role of judge to arbitrate civil disputes. That role of a judge is often left to tribal elders, heads of state, and religious leaders of various kinds.

Obviously disputes between parties (even family members), especially over possessions inherited from parents, are common in every age. Our courts are filled with just such litigation. Nothing much has changed. In the Middle East it is common to ask someone whom the community respects to adjudicate disputes or even make a final arbitration. Tribal elders and chiefs often play that role, and town authorities do the same all over that part of the world. There need be no formal court, but there has to be a respected mediator. So Yeshua is asked to step into the role. It is not clear that he refuses, but what he does do is raise the question whether this is the role that he has come to play and by whose authority.

But the questions he raises are even more pointed. Is he here to be a divider? First, he asks this of the feuding family member, then he turns to his students with a similar question. In fact they are not the same question. To the disputant he wants to know how he has determined that Yeshua possesses such authority to become a "divider." Perhaps his question is simply to protect himself lest his answer cause further disagreement in the end, or he is questioning this man's deeper commitment to him in the first place. It may be a question that gets to the heart of the spirit of this individual—as a kind of questioning typical of Yeshua. Perhaps Yeshua sees a deeper issue inside this individual and strikes at the spot. We will never know, of course, but the exchange raises very interesting possibilities of meaning, from the mundane to the sacred.

We know more, however, about his students and their attitudes. All through this text it has been clear that they are having some amount of difficulty deciding who he actually is. So based upon the request made of him, Yeshua asks them a simple question about their view of his role on earth. He asks whether they perceive that he has come among the people of his time to play the role of a divider. So what is the answer?

It is clear in Logion 16 that the unified being Yeshua is talking about is born out of the very chaos and conflict, tragedy, and alienation that Yeshua's fire has ignited (Logion 10).

It would seem at first, perhaps, that the obvious answer would be "No, of course not, you're not here to divide." But before we reach that conclusion, we should remember that he has already said that he **has** come for just that purpose. In Logion 16 Yeshua tells his students that he has not, in fact, come to bring peace but division in the same household—that is, until they are able to stand alone at last on their own two feet. Perhaps, then, his question of them should be answered with both "yes" and "no."

Ultimately, it is clear that he is not here to divide, but to unite. But in order to bring things together in unity, he must first divide (or detach) from whatever cannot be united. If we think back to the household that Yeshua had in mind when he uttered his declaration of division in Logion 16, then it is possible that it is just this kind of household he has come to demolish—the kind that is always at loggerheads over the wrong things: money, possessions, acquisitions, and ownership. Isn't that often what families come to be about? In the end, could it not also be that it is this very divisive way of being that Yeshua has come to destroy, and the only possible destruction for divisiveness is ultimately through union. Unitive seeing that leads to unitive being is the only possible alternative that overcomes division and the desire to divide. The family quarreling over possessions and acquisitions can never find reconciliation unless they are united at a higher level, one beyond their divisions and acquisitiveness. So has Yeshua come to unite or divide? The answer, of course, depends on the level of spiritual evolution. The answer that his students both see and give will be determined by their level of growth and understanding, as will ours.

QUESTIONS FOR REFLECTION

1. Have you ever had what seemed to you like an irresolvable family dispute? Have finances, inheritance matters, or possessions ever become a subject of controversy in your family? How have you resolved these issues?

2. Would you ask a spiritual leader to arbitrate in a family dispute of your own? If you did have such a dispute over possessions, who would you go to help in resolving the issue? What role would religion play?

3. How would you have immediately answered Yeshua's question before reading the commentary? How would you answer it now, after reading the commentary?

4. What is Yeshua's role in this world? Was he sent into the world to save us from our sins, or for some other purpose?

EXERCISES AND MEDITATIONS

1. Because the narrative context for the various sayings of Yeshua has not been supplied in this Gospel in the way that it is for the canonical Gospels, the reader is required to supply that context out of the experience of his or her life and culture. If this scene were playing itself out in our world, what sort of scenario would you create for it? You might want to write (and even act out) a script around this saying that supplied the various contexts as to what is going on in the minds of the speakers or those being questioned. What answer would you have the original speaker make to Yeshua's inquiry? How would you, and various other students of Yeshua, answer the question he asks of them? What would they be thinking at this moment? How would the scene eventually play itself out? This exercise encourages you to use your imagination in a creative way to explore possible meanings and outcomes.
2. Divisiveness and differences of opinion between people which create social and familial divisions are a deeply rooted aspect of every society. Each culture has strategies for dealing with such divisions. Some societies use social constraint, others use various legal structures, while others simply battle (or argue) things out till there is a winner. How do you deal with divisiveness? Is there a "wisdom way" of dealing with this issue?
3. If unity is an ultimate goal for spiritual growth and progression, then what sort of practice is involved? If the answer is not to use a powerful external force to achieve or maintain unity, then what other alternatives are there? What is the practice of unity, and how does it affect the individual who follows such a practice?

Is unity always preferred over division? In the wisdom tradition there is clearly room for division and detachment. Examine the text found in Hebrews 4:12. What is the role and instrument of division specified here?

READINGS FOR INSIGHT

I

Kabir

When I calmed my mind
And entered my heart,
The Love of the Lord
Leapt like a flame within me.
All my old ideas and beliefs
Just blew away like chaff in the wind.

II

Pema Chödrön
Start Where You Are
101

It all starts with loving-kindness for oneself, which in turn becomes loving-kindness for others. As the barriers come down around our hearts, we are less afraid of other people. We are more able to hear what is being said, see what is in front of our eyes, and work in accord with what happens rather than struggle against it.

III

Tao Te Ching
Section 6

The ....spirit never dies;
It is the woman, primal mother.
Her gateway is the root of heaven and earth.
It is like a veil barely seen.

IV

Lin Yutang
The Wisdom of Laotse

The Tao person dwells in peace:
Reaching out
In a community of heart,
Regarding all that lives
As one family.

V

St. Symeon
the New Theologian
Hymns 23

God whose providence
extends to all details,
How is God not in everything?
How is God not in everyone?
Yes, God is in the middle of everything.
Yes, God is also outside everything.

VI

A traditional
Sufi saying

Whoever has the outer law without the inner reality
has abandoned the True Way.
Whoever has the inner reality without the outer law
is nothing but a heretic.
Unite the two, and you will be realized.

LOGION 73

Yeshua says,

The harvest is abundant.
The reapers are few.
Implore the Master of the Harvest
to send out workers.

Sapiential Themes

- *From a wisdom perspective, the cosmos/kosmos is a great garden and God is its gardener.*
- *From the divine perspective a harvest of great abundance is expected but it is dependent also on human participation. .*
- *Something in the present moment (and not just the future) can be gathered in, but few can see this, and fewer still have the ability to bring about this realized form of abundance.*
- *Prayer by and on behalf of humanity is part of the work of harvesting.*
- *Prayer produces harvesters.*

Parallel Texts

Psalm 52, 80, 104, 107,128
Matthew 9:35-38
Luke 10:1-16
John 4:31-38
I Corinthians 3:5-9

FOCAL POINT

Throughout the Gospel of Thomas, as well as in the canonical Gospels, the image of the world as garden (or farmland) is used to illustrate the purpose of both human and divine activity in space-time. In this image, God is the gardener (or farmer) who is cultivating the world, and humanity is a crop being cultivated. Individual human beings are "planted" like seeds in the ***kosmos***, and from that planting the Gardener-Farmer is expecting an abundant harvest. When the crop is ready (when the fruit is ripe and mature), it is time for harvest. The question is, of course, who will do the harvesting? You would imagine that it would be the Farmer-Gardener, but strangely that appears not to be the case. The Farmer will not harvest alone or without help. In this saying, Yeshua instructs his students to pray to the "Master of the Harvest" (the Lord of the fields and the harvest) and implore that workers be made available at this final, critical moment in this long planned-for, last crucial step in the process. The saying ends simply with this declaration of a need for prayer at a critical moment in history.

Links

If Yeshua is not here to divide, but to unite, as the previous Logion says, then the goal of such work is clearly stated in this next saying—it is, at the end of all things, to produce a harvest. However, in this and the next two Logia problems arise. There are not harvesters, there is no water, there are those at the door who do not enter. All of these images are observations about the true nature of religious and spiritual reality around Yeshua. His commentary is a critique.

Notes

There is an implied hierarchy expressed in this saying. There is the field of ripening plants itself. There are reapers in the field, but not enough. There is an observer of the situation who is able to assess from an objective point of view (Yeshua). There are those who are asked to pray, also, it seems observers. Finally, there is the Master of the Harvest who appears able to assuage the difficulty.

COMMENTARY

This, and the next two Logia, express Yeshua's critique of the religious and spiritual condition in the human world through vivid images—a harvest with few harvesters, an empty well, and crowds gathered at the door who do not or will not enter the inner world. Each is a sign of the times, and an indicator of what is now needed, and what, it is assumed, Yeshua is here to do.

When the process has been completed, there is a destiny that awaits humanity. It is a time of harvest—the moment of intense activity and rejoicing at the end of the long season of growth. All great seers have known this and there is nothing like it in all human history—this consummation. But getting there and being there is the issue. This Logion, as well as the next three, are constructed in a similar manner. In each case a contrast is set up between possibilities (oppositionary twins). The way things are and the way things could be are examined. These three appear to be a set of sayings based upon the observation that in the current state of human affairs, one essential thing is missing and it must be rectified. Yeshua sees deeply into the issues at hand.

To rectify the condition, human concern and prayer are essential. Yeshua, perceives the issue and asks that his students enter his concern for prayer that there will be an increase of essential workers at the critical moment of harvest. On the one hand Yeshua sees abundance and the harvest, on the other there is scarcity. The harvest is ripe and waiting, but little attention seems to be paid to the act of harvest. The confluence between readiness of the harvests, the prayer of entreaty and petition to the Source for labor, and the final act of harvesting are brought together in this saying. Harvest is never automatic, nor is it a singular act of only one party. It is a communal act where different agencies interact to bring into being this moment of accomplishment. Without this confluence there is the possibility of failure.

In this saying, for whatever reason, religious tradition has not been attentive to the ripening and to the final act at the end. What has it been doing otherwise? Nothing is said, but the implication is a lack of attention to the final, critical outcome—and perhaps attention only to temporary and transitional details.

Why will the Master of the Harvest not act without human involvement? Obviously the product cannot harvest itself—some agency of a higher order must be involved. In addition there must be awareness by someone (we're not told who, but perhaps by some intermediate being), who, conscious of the time and the process of maturation and ripening, signals heaven that a message must be sent to the Source of the activity.

So why do we pray? Do we do it to "get things from God"—to get our prayers answered and our needs met by handouts from heaven, or, is it possible that we pray to be changed by our prayers? If it is the latter, though this possibility does not exclude the former, then the changes that we ask for (and we are always talking about change in the present circumstances) may begin with changes first in the one who prays. Imagine, then, that the prayer for harvesters is in fact to create harvesters—that is, by praying, those who pray are actually turned into harvesters, cooperating with the goals and plans of heaven, whose main purpose in all crop cultivation in the end is abundance and harvest. But it will not be a solitary act on the part of the Divine, it will be a collective and cooperative act in which many levels of being are involved.

All of these suggest very mysterious prospects beyond the realm of normal religious thinking it seems, but nonetheless essential to the outcome of farming the ***kosmos***. To be a part of the unfolding at the end of time (which is the planting and growing season), there must be these actors, states of awareness, and harvesters in the field of time and space before the final harvest is possible. It is not automatic, but progressive, and there are those with the capacity to both recognize the need, implore the Lord of the Harvest, and perhaps, in the end, enter the field as harvesters. There are those whose knowledge gives them the right to take up these essential, final acts in that season of growth and maturation.

QUESTIONS FOR REFLECTION

1. Have you ever raised a garden—flowers or vegetables? Why did you do it? What was your goal and your purpose?

2. Could you raise a garden without a purpose?

3. Can you imagine the neglect of a garden at the very end? Why would this happen?

4. What do you think is Yeshua's purpose in telling us this saying?

5. How does this apply to your religious or spiritual experience in our world today?

EXERCISES AND MEDITATIONS

1. Imagine yourself raising a garden. What is in your mind and heart as you do so? What is it about the end that is so all-consuming? What are the difficulties that you have experienced at the end of the season when the crop is in and ready to pick? What have you experienced about the joy and the disappointment of this season?
2. Prayer, prayer for more laborers, is an interesting solution that Yeshua offers here. It is an appeal to the Master beyond the garden or the farm. In what cultural setting does this make sense? In that setting, then, imagine the ability of the Master of Harvest to do something about it, and your job to bring it to his or her attention. What does that say about you and your relationship to the Master? Put yourself not only the cultural setting where this applies, but also imagine some meaningful relationship to your own experience of such things.
3. Imagine some outcome, some important final destiny that you deeply long for—some kind of expected or unexpected harvest that is not now clearly visible. Compose a prayer for that outcome. Keep it near at hand. Pray it several times daily. Change it as you change, or your thoughts change, or your awareness of the outcome changes. This kind of participation in outcomes through the active imagination, in some sense, has an effecton reality itself. Perhaps, as some say, it "programs" into it new possibilities, or sets into motion new patterns that will eventually bring about a completely different outcome. Pay attention to this process. Notice any changes in you or the world around you as you move through time. Journal your findings.

READINGS FOR INSIGHT

I

The sea is full of pearls,
but the number of pearl-divers is few.

The world is full of music,
but the number of dancers is few.

Now I'm afraid that no prayer will be answered—
since those who pray truly
are really quite few.

Imad al-Din Faqih Kirmani

II

A growing number of concerned people voice a common sentiment: the world needs nothing less than a new vision for the future, based on a new set of values. This new vision needs to include a worldwide respect for the earth and a reliance on sustainable resources. Such a vision also needs to consider the plight of billions of people suffering from poverty, disease, and dislocation in underdeveloped countries. The new values need to be more inner-directed than outer-directed. Responsibility for the planet and its people needs to take precedence over economic advantage and unlimited expansion.

Edmund J. Bourne
Global Shift
15

III

Learning is only the outer wrapping
of the letter,
the dry husk that covers the nut—
not the kernel concealed within.
Yet the husk must exist
to ripen the kernel.
So from learning
comes the sweet knowledge of faith ...

Begin to till your field
for next year's harvest.
Knowledge is your heritage.
Be adorned with the principle
of all virtues.

Mahmud Shabistari
The Secret Rose Garden
72

IV

There are beautiful wild forces
spiraling within us.
Let them turn the mills and fill the sacks
that will feed even the heavens.

St Francis of Assisi

LOGION 74

Yeshua says,

O Lord,
many have gathered around the fountain,
but there is nothing in the well.

FOCAL POINT

The image is clear. A fountain (or a well) exists which is meant to be a source of water. Many have come there to draw from it and quench their thirst, but when they get there they find that the well (or fountain) is empty. The water has disappeared. It has dried up and now holds nothing—no water, no refreshment, no life. Drought, perhaps, has taken it away, and the people around the well are left bereft and wondering, so Yeshua prays,

"O Adonai, look!
What needs to be done?"

Sapiential Themes

- *There are places, deep wells and fountains that are meant to be sources of water.*
- *Yeshua observes that these have gone dry, nevertheless people are gathered around empty wells waiting.*
- *Yeshua addresses his observation as a prayer to God.*

Links

In the last saying, Logion 73, Yeshua implores that we pray to the Master of the Harvest. In this saying, Yeshua himself prays, recognizing the crisis occurring in the human condition. Just as he has in the last Logion, Yeshua critiques the spiritual conditions around him in his world. It is not unlike our world—drought and emptiness where there is meant to be refreshment and fullness are a part of the human condition.

Parallel Texts

II Peter 2:17

Notes

Both words well and fountain (or even Spring) are used in the Coptic version. It appears that the text is trying to translate an idea from the Greek which indicates a living source of Water fed by underground streams.

COMMENTARY

In this saying, Yeshua is, of course, using the metaphor of the lack of water to illustrate another kind of shortage which is just as critical in the human world. Having physical water, the source of life, is essential, especially in a desert climate. Without it humans die quickly in a parched climate. Metaphorically speaking this whole world is a desert and the wells that are meant to provide sustenance have dried up. The spiritual water of life within the well of religion itself has vanished, and there is a human crisis. The sole purpose of religion is to be a source of life. Often, however, it is not. In his own day, Yeshua's sense was that the Spirit had disappeared from traditional religion, and instead of bringing life and refreshment, it was only an empty well with nothing to give its people. When the well has gone dry due to damage or neglect, then what was once available is gone, and this is tragic.

In a conversation with the woman of Samaria who had come to draw water from a well at which Yeshua was sitting, the subject inevitably turns towards religion and things of Spirit. In the course of their conversation, Yeshua speaks about the presence (or absence) of Spirit in the wells of religion in his day, using similar images to direct the woman at the well in Samaria away from drawing water from conventional religion sources to seek for a deeper source of life. He talks about how the wells normally available to her are no longer sufficient—perhaps already dry. So he offers her water from a deeper layer of the aquifer, from much further down, and perhaps much deeper in. Waters of Spirit from deep underground aquifers are meant to flow into those sources.

This is the diagnostic that Yeshua makes concerning the current religious conditions of his day. The question is, of course, what is to be done about it? This particular Logion offers no immediate solution. It only highlights the problem, but the subsequent sayings offer insights into possibilities and what action must be taken given the current conditions.

Before we move in that direction, however, perhaps it is instructive to realize that in the Beatitudes Yeshua makes the case that "emptiness" is actually a favorable condition, and a precondition for ultimate fullness. Far from being fatal or avoided, emptiness may in fact be the condition for the possibility of finding what one so desperately needs—fresh, new sources of water. One is driven by emptiness and the consequence of hunger and thirst to go beyond what one had come to rely on as the source. When the source goes dry, the search for new sources is an act of survival driven by these very conditions.

Yeshua said, "Those who are lowly of spirit (empty in spirit) live in a state of blessedness, for out of their very being the Reign of the Heavens arrives.

Blessed are all those who are hungering and thirsty to be in right-relationship, for they shall be fed to overflowing.
Matthew 5:3, 6

We avoid and sometimes despise the state of emptiness. But in the end it provides the motivation that will push us past the ordinary, beyond the conventional, deeper still, to where new sources of water truly exist. Yeshua knows this and, in his day, he is proposing a way out of the dilemma—an answer to an empty well. The observation about the well and people around it is meant to stimulate a new search and help us find a way forward. It is not simply an indictment. There is no reason to linger where water no longer exists. In speaking this Logion, Yeshua's motivation is to prompt us to leave our parched condition in search of more—more water, more refreshment, and a deeper aquifer of life.

QUESTIONS FOR REFLECTION

1. When have you experienced something that was once full of life for you going dry or becoming empty?

2. What did you do in response to this experience?

3. What is your sense about the well of religion? Does it hold water for you?

4. What is water for you? When do you feel refreshed, rejuvenated and revived? What is it like to go thirsty?

5. Yeshua addresses his observation about the lack of water to God as a short prayer. What might this mean?

EXERCISES AND MEDITATIONS

1. To find water, real inner water that refreshes, is one of the most amazing experiences, especially after a dry spell. If someone were to come to you and say that everything for them is dry and empty; that they cannot find water (or spiritual life) anywhere, what would you tell them? How would you advise them? Is there a ready solution to this problem? Examine your own experience. What changed for you and how might that guide your sense for another human soul in that same condition?
2. Examine your own experience at this moment. What and where are the refreshing springs of life for you? If this world is a desert, where and what are the oases? Do you know how to "find water" like many desert peoples do? They seem to have a "sixth sense" about this survival technique. They are "water trackers." They can detect where and even when water is going to be, perhaps in rains or showers. They know where the secret springs are, the out-of-the-way cisterns that hold water for those who know. How could you become a better "water tracker?"
3. Ponder the condition of emptiness. Only an empty glass can be filled, and only a soul empty of clutter can perceive the perceive the clear water of heaven. We know, in some sense, that this is true, but what does it mean to be "empty?" How can we stand it? What is the experience of emptiness? Could it be (should it be) a permanent state? Are the cycles of hunger and thirst the pattern of spiritual life? How long can you stand the feeling of emptiness? Is the experience of fasting this same experience? Fasting certainly creates a state of emptiness, which after time can be tolerated, though it changes the state of the mind in some way. Fast for a day or two. Journal your observations about emptiness.

Examine the two Beatitudes on the previous page in the sidebar. What is Yeshua teaching? How does it apply here?

READINGS FOR INSIGHT

I

Heinrich Zimmer
Divine Sparks

Limitless and immortal,
the waters are the beginning
and ending of all things on earth.

II

Jalaluddin Rumi

Let Love's Water of Life flow through my veins.
Let the mirror of dawn reflect in my nights.
O Father of this new delight, flow through my soul,
as I become the universe's cup and leave both worlds behind.

III

Enes Karic
"Words About Water"
Parabola, Summer 2009
39

... water, colorless, tasteless and odorless, enables the desert regions to burgeon and bloom with all kinds of colorful and sweetly fragrant flowers and plants. In classical treatises on color in general ... it is said that water likes to conceal itself, to retreat. It is without color itself, but makes color possible. It has no taste, but makes taste possible. It has no fragrance, but makes fragrance possible. Islamic esoteric thought, like the thinking of the Latin Church Fathers, has generally seen in material things and their diversity the multiform signs of God. ... Water is seen in particular as the most amazing sign of God, colorless, tasteless, formless, odorless ... Transcendental. Water is therefore used ... as a symbol of God's oneness, of ***tawhid***.

IV

Mira
Daniel Ladinsky,
Love Poems from God
264-265

In my travels, I came upon a village that had a new temple built over a big well, but no one could draw water from it without paying a price. I asked about this, and this story was told:

One hundred years ago, there was a group of boys that would go to the well to swim, that is, all but one would dive from the top, for one was crippled and could only watch. With all his heart he would wish he was like his friends, that his one arm and leg had not been limp since he was born.

One day, when it was especially hot, and he was watching his friends cut up and laugh at the bottom of the well, they all turned to him and stared in awe as if seeing something miraculous. The crippled boy turned around and Krishna was standing there smiling wonderfully and said, "It sure is hot today, climb on my back—we will dive in." And they did. Krishna never came up from the bottom of the well, it is said, and when the child who had been on the back of Krishna came up, he was no longer crippled and remained healed the rest of his life.

The fame of the well spread and many legends and rumors naturally evolved and began to circulate. But the water remained free, and hundreds would travel to drink it and camp there at night and tell the different stories they had heard: the point being, they would be thinking of the Lord and participating in the stories, in a way that helped them most.

...A scholar, a lawyer, and a priest arrived one day and all pissed in the water, so to speak. What the priest and the scholar wanted the people to believe got printed in books, which they also sold along with the water, and of course the lawyer made their insanity legal. The water I tasted was sour. I think Krishna left. In this sorrowful world why tamper with anything that lifts our spirits.

LOGION 75

Yeshua says,

Many are standing at the door,
but only the single
or solitary
will enter the place of union.

FOCAL POINT

This is the third Logion in a series that describes something missing (or of a state of spiritual deprivation). In the first in the series, Logion 73, there is an abundant harvest, but not enough harvesters. In the second, there is a fountain or well around which many have gathered, but it is empty of the one thing necessary—water. In this final Logion, many have gathered around the door, but no one is moving from the outside in because there is, in fact, a precondition for entrance into the inner chamber, and few have been able to fulfill it. It is clear that the inner chamber is an intimate place. In this context it seems that one must be "married" (or united) to be allowed in.

Sapiential Themes

- *The journey from the door to the interior of things is a spiritual pilgrimage.*
- *An ultimate image of spiritual intimacy is used to describe oneness and union with the divine.*
- *Interior oneness is the key to union with God.*
- *Celibacy becomes a false image foreign to Semitic spirituality in general, and to Islam and Sufism in particular.*

Links

As in each of the two previous Logia, there is a potentiality expressed that is not fulfilled, and a need, therefore, for action or a change of plans or of agenda. The realities of this world and the realm of the divine Sovereignty force us to make choices—new choices that will also change the way we relate to both.

Parallel Texts

Thomas 23, 49, 106
Matthew 25:1-13

Notes

The phraseology of "the place of union" translates the more metaphoric, and perhaps more graphic, "bridal chamber." Though not as well understood in the West, in Semitic culture it is the place of marital consummation after nuptial union. This reference to the most private of intimacies is a difficult, but descriptive metaphor for ultimate relationship and union with Divine Reality.

COMMENTARY

The two previous Logia and this, the third, do not, of course, describe the same conditions. Nonetheless in each case, they tell us that something vital is lacking. The three Logia appear to describe separate conditions, illustrating three different states of spiritual reality. The first reality concerns the condition of the harvest going on in the world now or perhaps at a future gathering point of history at the end of time. The second concerns the state of conventional religion both now (and perhaps universally), which understands the lack of life-giving water at its deepest point. The third goes directly to the heart of Yeshua's own teaching. It concerns interiority illustrated by the inner chamber, the place of meeting and union, at the level of the heart.

The metaphor of the bridal chamber appears in the canonical Gospels and is clearly original to the Semitic culture of Yeshua. It becomes the main subject in the Gospel of Philip, which takes this imagery to its most extended limits and equates it to the inner state of a union which can be achieved with the Divine in both this world and the next.

This saying suggests that the secret, innermost chamber (using the vivid image of the Bridal Chamber) can only be accessed when the one seeking it has become adequate (or ready) for entry, and not simply because one knows where the door might be (or "who" the door might be), or even because one has a casual desire to enter it. The realities are much more stringent than that. There is a demand for a state of being that must be achieved, or one will remain on the outside, on the margin of things.

The picture created by this saying, however, is culturally accurate. Many dwellings in the Middle East, especially those in villages, open right out onto the front walkway or road. There, people can gather in front of a doorway in what is a public space. It is not uncommon for there to be an inner courtyard just off the main entry way, or, further in, a living space that is the interior of the house, which might also be used for sleeping. This is the picture, and it fits into the cultural milieu of Yeshua's own time, especially at Capernaum where he lived for an extensive part of his ministry.

One might wonder from the canonical Gospels if this central idea was ever really important to the four Gospels of the western canon. Clearly oneness and unity is talked about, for it shapes the central teaching of Judaism concerning God. The clearest example where such oneness or union is at the center of Yeshua's teaching and understanding is expressed in the prayer of John 17 where Yeshua prays that his students might know oneness in the same way that he knows such union and unity with the Father. This is a critical commentary on Yeshua's meaning here in Logion 75.

The crucial and central part of this saying focuses on the state of being that we might call "singularity" (the word in Aramaic is ***ihidaya***, that is a state of undivided wholeness and therefore union within oneself and with Ultimate Reality). One is no longer in a state of twoness, but oneness, which is the condition of being that is a most important aspect of the teaching of Yeshua in the Gospel of Thomas.

It is a large historical mistake to equate the term "singleness" used here with an unmarried, celibate state, though this mistake was made very early. Celibacy appears to be far from its meaning in Thomas. Yeshua is not advocating celibacy, he is pointing us toward becoming whole (or unfragmented) beings. Currently, most human beings live in a state of fragmentation and inner division. Our hearts are divided from our minds. Our egos are uncontrollable and separate from our own deepest nature. Our multiple desires tear us apart—first one desire appears, and then another which may be its opposite. We can become very fragmented beings and our inner divisions splinter us into pieces.

Inner wholeness, completion, or singularity—where the disparate parts of ourselves have been healed and brought together into some higher unity—is the inner state that is the precondition for "marital union" of the human with the Divine. The inner chamber is the place of such intimacy—described here in frankly sexual terms. Unity within ourselves leads ultimately to union (marriage and intimacy) with God. Fragmentation leads to separation where we stay at the margin of things outside of intimate union. It is a graphic and powerful picture.

QUESTIONS FOR REFLECTION

1. Have you ever felt yourself drawn to something but unable to "step through the door" and fully commit? What was the cause? Were you afraid, unready, or it was not yet time? Was there some other reason?

2. What does spiritual readiness mean to you? In order to meet the conditions for entry suggested by this saying of Yeshua, what would you imagine one would need to do?

3. The image used here as "inner chamber" and, more particularly, "bed chamber" can best be understood perhaps as the bridal suite. How does this image of sexual intimacy strike you?

4. Could you think of this image in any way as describing your relationship with God?

5. Where do you think you are in your own intimacy with God?

EXERCISES AND MEDITATIONS

1. Intimacy with God is described in Semitic terms as being like the experience of nuptial union and the first night together after being married. If you have been married, or had your first sexual experience as an indicator for such a level of union, what does your own experience tell you about this? Think this through experientially, and then the description of those who are still hanging to the outside of the door, and never going in. In a time of meditation, put yourself in both positions and imagine the realities in both experiences. What do you learn imaginatively from such a meditation?
2. A precedent for this kind of language is found in the ancient Hebrew poetry of the Song of Songs attributed to Solomon. It is a love poem describing the ups and downs in a relationship of intimacy between two lovers. The descriptions are complex. Imagine that the images of the following poetic passage are related to the words of Yeshua. How does this change your perception of Yeshua's words?

Through the ages the images of eros, longing for and union with God described in sexual terms, have become more and more common.

Kiss me, make me drunk with your kisses!
Your sweet loving is better than wine.
Take me by the hand, draw me after you.
My lover, my king, has brought me into his chambers.
We will laugh, you and I, and count each kiss, better than wine.

Song of Songs 1:2, 4 from a translation by Ariel and Channa Bloch

READINGS FOR INSIGHT

I

I was asleep, but my heart stayed awake.
Listen! My lover is knocking.
"Open, my sister, my friend, my dove, my perfect one!
My hair is wet, drenched with the dew of night."
...My love reached in for the latch and my heart beat wild.
I rose to open to my love,
my fingers wet with myrrh,
sweet flowing myrrh on the doorbolt.
I opened to my love, but he had slipped away.
How I wanted him when he spoke.
I sought him everywhere, but could not find him.
I called his name, but he did not answer.
...Swear to me, daughters of Jerusalem!
If you find him now,
You must tell him I am in the fever of love.

The Song of Songs 5:2-8
from a translation by
Ariel and Channa Bloch

II

Knowledge always deceives.
It always limits the Truth,
every concept and image does that.
From cage to cage our caravan moves,
but I give thanks,
for at each divine juncture my wings expand
and I touch God more intimately.

Meister Eckhart
Daniel Ladinsky
Love Poems from God
101

III

Excerpts from
the Gospel of Philip,
Luminous Gospels,
Analogues 41, 45, 72, 52

It is in the iconic Bridal Chamber, where the bride is united with the bridegroom that … balance is attained.

The Master says: "My Father dwells in secret, so go into the hidden chamber and shut the door and commune there with the One who is in this hidden place within you." The Father is there in your innermost being, and there is no other place transcendent to this, which is the Fullness beyond all "place."

Anyone who is born a child from the Bridal Chamber shall receive the Light, for if one does not receive it there, there is nowhere else to receive it. Those who welcome the Light are hidden from the world and cannot, therefore, be controlled or troubled by it.

No one can be granted this grace, however, unless they are clothed in perfected Light, saturating their being. Clad in Light, they can move forth into the cosmos as a Completed Being from out of the Bridal Chamber.

LOGION 76

Yeshua says,

The Father's Realm can be compared to a merchant who discovered a pearl hidden in a consignment of goods. Wisely, he returned the goods and bought the single pearl instead.

You too must seek out for yourselves an enduring treasure in that realm where moths cannot get in to eat or insects come in to destroy.

Sapiential Themes

- *The Pearl and the Treasure are important metaphors that speak about what is of greatest spiritual value while living upon the earth.*
- *These elements are metaphorically accurate for understanding what lies hidden or buried to us.*
- *The true task of the seeker on earth is to discover (or find) these elements of highest value.*
- *The spiritual symbolism of a pearl is as a form of "embodied light."*

Parallel Texts

Thomas 76, 93
Matthew 6:20-22, 7:6, 12:35 14:44-46, 52, 19:21,
Mark 10:21
Luke 6:45, 12:21-34, 18:22.
Gospel of Philip 30
The Hymn of the Pearl

FOCAL POINT

The twin images of the pearl and the treasure play central roles in the teachings of Yeshua. Each of these images also appears later as key metaphors in the spiritual transmissions within Oriental Christianity and the Islamic tradition of Sufism. The Pearl is the treasure (or jewel) found in the depths of the warm waters of the Gulf symbolizing the divine element of light found in the dark depths of the human soul. This luminescent pearl worth more than its weight in gold, is buried in soft flesh, surrounded by a hard shell, and lying at the bottom of the sea. Another form of treasure is also hidden or buried on earth (but at other times it is not here in space-time at all, but found in another realm where thieves and destruction do not exist nor have they any power to steal it away or diminish its worth or value).

Links

The question was left open in the last saying as to what constitutes a "single" or a "solitary" being. The answer may have to do with the "single Pearl" that has been found or the buried treasure that has been discovered. They allow access into the bridal chamber. Their finding and the discovery give entry into the place of union.

Notes

Pearls are found in the warm waters of the Persian Gulf in particular and much sought after in the ancient and modern worlds. They embody wealth. Their worth has not only to do with their size and luster, but also with the risk that is taken in finding them. Gemstones and precious metals are rare elements not commonly available. They may have been found and buried and used as exchange over and over again.

COMMENTARY

This saying in the Gospel of Thomas holds two key elements, the single Pearl and the Treasure together in a close relationship. Perhaps they are different sorts of riches altogether of parallel value, but which need to be considered side by side. Following the three Logia concerning various forms of diminishment and lack, the metaphor of the pearl and the treasure present opposite images of the "one thing necessary" that has been lacking so far. To find and obtain these singular elements is to realize what has been missing, buried, or undiscovered, but which may be found at considerable cost to the seeker. To discover them in this temporal world is of inestimable value. Human beings are always in search of treasure, but often in all the wrong places. Though they ceaselessly look for bargains, they miss the one necessary element which is of highest value. It is easy to be distracted, or for the eye to miss the singular element that must be found. It is common also to store treasure in places where there is no security at all and we are in danger of grave loss.

*In the Oriental stream of Christianity there is a tradition called: **The Wisdom of the Pearlers**. In it various teachers through the centuries have taken this theme of the Pearl, in particular, and conveyed teaching that is both metaphorical and allegorical. There is an anthology of this teaching with that same name by Brian E. Colless from Cistercian Press (2007).*

The bazaar is a place of endless fascination—a place of high energy, but also of danger for the unwary consumer. Like a bazaar, the impermanent and insecure ground of this world cannot keep its secrets easily or secure permanent value in a place of continuous haggling and debate or of relative supply. We feel this world to be substantial and permanent. We imagine that it is secure (or that we can secure things here), but we cannot. Its temporary nature will not hold what is permanent easily.

Though the merchant's bazaar (the "field" of business and commerce in this world) may indeed be a place to find treasures and the single Pearl, but it is not a place to leave them. They each must be secured from the relative "safety" of this world and transferred to a Realm that cannot be touched, which is both higher and more interior. They must be lifted out of the relative into the Eternal. They must be taken from the general field and placed in the inner storehouse of the heart—where true treasure belongs.

*A key text on these same themes is preserved in **The Hymn of the Pearl**, found in the **Acts of Thomas**—a Syriac text. This particular hymn (or poem) falls under the category or genre of literature that is often called "visionary recital," which is a narrative of transformation that involves both ascent and descent.*

The key questions concerning this saying are these: What is the Pearl and the Treasure? Are they the same? How can they be found? Throughout the centuries these questions have been pursued, of course, by way of exegesis and interpretation theory. But, more importantly, answers to these questions have been pursued through practice. Academic answers are certainly important, but to engage them as a form of existential commitment and spiritual practice is to begin to find answers that move away from the head and ground themselves in life and the heart. What can be said, however, is that there are many clues both in the words themselves and in the teachings of the saints and sages concerning the symbolic wisdom of the Pearl and the metaphor of the buried Treasure. Yeshua himself highlights these themes in his own teaching, and through the ages so do the great spiritual teachers, particularly in the Oriental traditions.

The Pearl is a luminous substance involving not only physical materials, but also light. Treasure is of unknown value until it is discovered and used. Neither lose their value, but they can be underestimated and even misused. The Pearl symbolizes embodied light made through a transformative process that is biological in nature, whereas the Treasure is made in a place that is out of the reach of human ingenuity, in fiery processes in the depths of earth or even space (as we now know). These insights help us understand essential wisdom features—they lead us to breakthroughs of understanding.

QUESTIONS FOR REFLECTION

1. Have you ever felt that your own life is in some way a "treasure hunt" for the rarest of elements? When? What is it like to be on a treasure hunt?

2. What have you found, discovered, or uncovered in your searching that is now priceless to you? What are those elements that without search or taking great risk would not now be yours?

3. Do you feel you now possess this treasure (or a single Pearl) that this saying is speaking about?

4. If you were going to explain to yourself or to someone else what these images are about or symbolize, how would you describe them? How are they spiritual in nature?

EXERCISES AND MEDITATIONS

1. If you can, find for yourself a strand of pearls and use them as a visual object for meditation. Do the same with a gemstone or a piece of gold of some kind. If you have a single item without adornment or setting it may even be more effective? Next to these place plastic jewelry, rhinestones and an ordinary pebble of some kind that contrast with these more valuable things. Using these objects for meditation, answer the questions: what is their natures and what is the essential difference between them? What does this meditation teach you?
2. If, as is clear by looking at a pearl, the essential feature is its luminescence, then in some spiritual way a pearl symbolizes "embodied light." It is as if the pearl picks up light and reflects it in such a way that it glows almost unnaturally. Imagine that something in the heart and soul of a human being is like that. Meditate on how that is created and embodied using what you might discover of the natural process of "pearl-making" in an oyster applied spiritually to your very own being. Working interpretively, write your own commentary on the spiritual meanings you may have discovered. More importantly, what does this teach you about inner, spiritual realities and processes? How are you embodying light? Where and what is that "light-body" inside of you? Journal your findings.
3. There is a chant that uses this traditional imagery. Here are the words.

Do an online exploration of pearls and pearl creation.

Seek the Treasure
Seek the Light
Seek the Pearl
In the Ocean of Night

You might want to call someone on the list of contacts from the website (www.theooow.com) and learn how it is chanted.

READINGS FOR INSIGHT

I

Blessed is the one who has compared the Kingdom of the Most High to a pearl.

On a certain day, my brothers and sister, heirs of that Kingdom, I picked up a Pearl and saw in it symbols, images and types of the divine Majesty, and it became a well of water from which I drank symbols of the Son. I placed the pearl in the palm of my hand to contemplate it. I looked at it from all sides and saw that it was covered with faces, and so it is with examining the Son, both are unsearchable, being all light.

O Pearl, in your smallness you are uniquely great. Though you are diminutive in size, small in measurement and weight, in your splendor you are great, for on the diadem beyond price you have been set. Anyone who is unable to perceive your greatness because of your smallness, who despises you or loses you will be reproached for their ignorance. But seeing you on a king's crown, they will inevitably be drawn to you.

*Ephrem the Syrian Taken from his **Hymns on Faith**.*

II

In sleep we lose the essence and worship the husk.
But who wants the shell without knowing the Pearl inside?
Seduced by external forms we're not yet really alive,
but awake, our inner essence becomes life itself.

Sana'i

III

Your heart is the mirror of the essence most high.
Of the great royal treasure, your heart is the prize.
Your heart is a vast ocean—but only holds a single pearl.
If you want such a treasure, it is your heart you must find.

Shah Ni'matallah Wali

IV

O my friend,
leave aside everything else and speak now of yourself.
Say what you possess, what treasures you have found.
Speak about the Pearl you have drawn up out of the deep,
so that when your senses fall into the darkness, as they will,
your heart will be a trustworthy flame.
When the dust fills your eyes at last, still your grave will be bright.
When your hands and your feet fail you, as they must,
you will rise then on great silent wings
lifting out into the light.

from Jalauddin Rumi

V

The passionate and all-consuming love of God is the Immortal Element within us, and with its courage and skill we can find the Pearl. Without it, we may find and own everything else. But what are other jewels to the Pearl? All worlds and heavens together are worth far less than it, being just passing shadows of its Eternal Luster.

from Jalauddin Rumi

LOGION 77

Yeshua says,

I am the light shining upon all things. I am the sum of everything, for everything has come forth from me, and towards me everything unfolds.

Split a piece of wood, and there I am. Pick up a stone and you will find me there.

Sapiential Themes

- *The I AM Presence is the origin of creation streaming from and returning to the Source.*
- *This Presence is the voice speaking through Yeshua.*
- *The journey of Eternal Return is the cosmological foundation for human experience in space-time.*
- *Divine Presence is everywhere. Nothing excludes it.*

Parallel Texts

Thomas 11, 24, 50, 61, 83
Matthew 13:43, 18:20
John 1:1-5. 8:12-20
I Corinthians 8:4-6
Ephesians 5:8-14
James 1:16-18

FOCAL POINT

Perhaps no other saying evokes the sense of Oriental thought and tradition more than this Logion. Centered on light or the radiance of consciousness itself, the divine Presence (understood in the Hebrew world as the great I AM), claims to be both origin and source out of which all existence unfolds and to which it returns. In this saying light-consciousness precedes matter and is the founding principle of the universe. There is no place that consciousness light does not extend including the very being of Yeshua himself. This I AM consciousness proclaims its Presence as the center of all things from the earliest and greatest to the smallest and simplest of elements. It pervades everything as both origin and destiny.

Links

Linked to the Pearl and the Treasure in the previous saying, the light streaming from the divine Presence is at the core of all spiritual experience of finding what has been hidden or buried. Where do you find the Pearl? Where do you find the treasure? Are they not at the heart of all things, pervading the whole universe? Are they not in the field at the center of one's own being? Do they not reside within the interstices of nature?

Notes

The Abrahamic faiths speak with a unanimous voice concerning the divine Presence as consciously available and in relationship to all things. Presence (not absence) is the hallmark of these traditions. In Christianity this same voice is said to speak through Yeshua, the Messiah. He is the site for the I AM speaking, just as the burning bush was for Moses. Later in Islam this same word will be spoken through Gabriel and encoded in the Qur'an.

COMMENTARY

Perhaps the most cosmic of all the sayings of Thomas, this Logion points toward cosmological realities that held at the heart of Yeshua's teachings. Whether spoken by him, or extrapolated by his later disciples, this saying encompasses a metaphysic that has become universal in almost all wisdom teaching. Traditional Christianity gives expression to these teachings, and in this saying they fall from the lips of the Master himself.

Could this text reflect influences from the far East—from Buddhism and Hinduism which share similar wording and sentiment? While nothing can be proven, perhaps, the similarities in thought and speech are remarkable. At the very least the world's sacred traditions share a common understanding of light streaming from the divine Source.

In almost a Zen-like way this saying points to what is clearly beyond the normal understanding of space-time, and to realities and presences that issue from Realms transcendent to this one. These realms clearly have impact and effect here however. Reminiscent of the Hebrew understanding of the I AM Presence first encountered by Moses in the desert, Yeshua speaks as the mouthpiece for the divine Presence. Through him streams a form of consciousness that is clearly universal in nature, calling to the whole universe.

Two words define that consciousness—light and sum (or totality—the All). The I AM Presence as consciousness streams out as a form of light. Consciousness and light are often synonymous in spiritual writing and wisdom texts. The totality of all things (their summarization and coordination—known as the All) is held in that light—in that consciousness from which there is both a streaming forth and an ultimate return. Nothing is excluded.

The Journey of Eternal Return has been called the "nucleating mono-myth" which holds all the great mythic traditions together as representative of one great story concerning humanity's purpose on earth. In this text, at least, Yeshua share's that cosmological perspective.

Descent (from) and return (to) the Source have been at the heart of all ancient cosmological and sapiential understandings. What is manifest comes from the Unmanifest Source expressed through the I AM Presence and is ultimately drawn back into that same Source. This is the divine Breath of mercy and compassion in its widest sense breathing the universe into being and drawing it back into its origins.

The second part of the saying makes it abundantly clear that that I AM Presence not only breathes the universe, but also pervades it. Down to the smallest detail, the most mundane activity (splitting wood), the most common element (a simple stone)—there you can find the Presence of the divine. Presence (consciousness) is everywhere. Nothing excludes it, and nothing can barricade itself against it. It simply is—present. Woven into (perhaps it is best to say, saturating) the nature of the reality that we know in space-time, is the divine Presence of consciousness itself.

The divine Logos in the Gospel of John is said to share the same characteristics concerning light.

The question is, of course, how does this Presence relate to the historical person of Yeshua? Is he claiming here that he is God-incarnate, or is it more subtle than that? This and similar statements make it seem that the traditional doctrine of God-in-flesh uniquely manifest in Jesus of Nazareth is the only correct interpretation. Another, perhaps more nuanced interpretation is that, like other manifestations of the I AM Presence beginning in the Hebrew Scriptures, this text expresses the fact that the divine Logos (understood as the direct manifestation or Word of God) is speaking out through a human being submitted to its Spirit and flow. This interpretation also accords with the opening lines of the Gospel of John. In this interpretation, Yeshua is not claiming special status, he is simply speaking as a fully open instrument of Spirit—it is the voice of the Logos which is speaking here, and we are given ears to hear it, so that in the long run we too may express the I AM Presence with the same clarity.

QUESTIONS FOR REFLECTION

1. What is your image of cosmological reality? Is it similar to or different from the one portrayed in this saying?

2. If, as this saying suggests, light and presence stream into this world from beyond it, what have you experienced yourself of this reality?

3. What is your experience of consciousness—your own personal inner experience? How is it like light?

4. How have you experienced yourself to be part of a larger story or manifestation flowing from and returning to the Source?

5. How have you detected the divine Presence in the natural world or in ordinary human affairs?

EXERCISES AND MEDITATIONS

1. There is a "grand unified theory" of what human beings are doing here on the earth. It is the story of descent from and return to the Source of all being. It is also called the Myth of Eternal Return. If you have the opportunity find and read the book **Hero With a Thousand Faces** by Joseph Campbell. It explains the larger story of humanity's purpose on the earth, and the journey that we are making in space-time as a great mythological story. After you have read this text, it would be helpful for you to make a "map" of this journey using the diagram below. Place on it as much of the material from this Logion and Campbell's text as you can. Make a new drawing.

Joseph Campbell ***Hero With A Thousand Faces*** *New World Library, 3rd Ed. 2008*

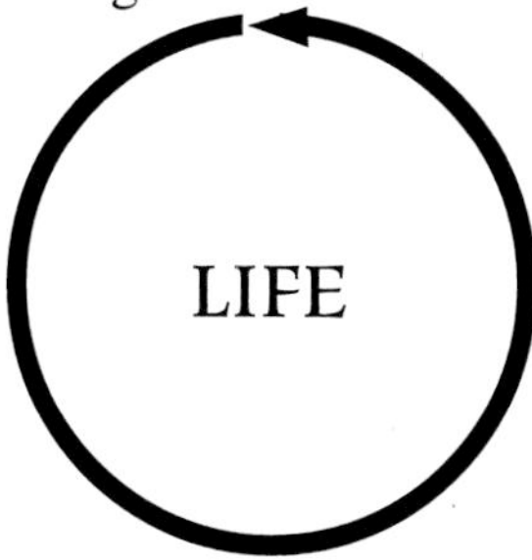

2. In a prayerful act of meditation and contemplation go out into the natural world and split a piece of wood. Lift up a stone. Find the I AM Presence that Yeshua is talking about here.

READINGS FOR INSIGHT

I

from Jalauddin Rumi

I and Eternal Love were born into this Universe from one Light-Womb.
I may seem like a new Lover, but I am older than all worlds.

II

Kaivalya Upanishad

In me alone originates the All, in me the All is established,
in me all things come to rest.
I am that Brahman [God] without a second.

III

Tom Cheetham

So long as we are opaque to ourselves
we will be unable to see the light shining through all things.

IV

Maria Jaoudi
Christian Mysticism East and West
100

God as Being and Goodness enters reality as "self diffusive," that is, "totally present everywhere and nowhere contained." Once we enter into the presence of the sacred in the magnificent image of Bonaventure as "the book written within and without," we enter into a continuous state of mystical ecstasy. The ecstasy experienced is partially caused by a constant underlying awareness that *God is presence*. When we consciously experience God within and without as One, we cannot help but be ecstatic because, as Bonaventure quotes Augustine, we will honor "the course of being, the basis of understanding, and the order of living."

V

Layman P'ang

My daily affairs are quite ordinary; but I'm in total harmony with them.
I don't hold on to anything, don't reject anything; nowhere an obstacle or conflict.
Who cares about wealth and honor? Even the poorest thing shines.
My miraculous power and spiritual activity:
Drawing water and carrying wood.

VI

Valentin Tomberg
Meditations on the Tarot
314

The law of terrestrial gravitation, evolution and earthly life in general is *enfoldment*, i.e., the coagulation of mental, psychic and physical stuff around relative centres of gravitation, such as the earth, the nation, the individual, the organisms—whilst the law of celestial gravitation, evolution, and spiritual life in general is *radiation*, i.e. the extension of mental, psychic and physical stuff rising up to an absolute center of gravitation. "Then the righteous will shine like the sun in the kingdom of their Father" (Matthew xiii, 43)—this is a precise and comprehensive characterization of the law of celestial gravitation.

VI

from St. Teresa of Avila

Light baptizes life wherever it falls,
and every religion and everything upon the earth is but a shadow
made from that light.

LOGION 78

Sapiential Themes

- *The subject of this saying could either be John the Baptist or Yeshua. Both minister from the desert.*
- *The contrast is between the spiritual dweller in the desert and the conventional religious leader who has succumbed to power and comfort.*
- *Discerning the truth is perhaps the antidote to being seduced by power and influence.*

Yeshua says,

Why did you come out into the wilderness? To see a reed blown about by the wind? A man dressed in soft raiment like your rulers and the powerful?

Yes, indeed they are clothed in fine, luxurious garments, but what they lack is the ability to discern truth.

Parallel Texts

Thomas 39, 46
Matthew 11:7-15
Luke 7:24-30

Links

In light of the previous saying, the question is, how does Light streaming from the Source act as it takes shape in the world of material and temporal reality? How does divine Presence affect the world? How is it different from other manifestations that claim to be representations of Spirit and Light? Like many other sayings, sharp contrasts are drawn here.

FOCAL POINT

Who inhabits the wilderness of Judea? Is it Yeshua, or is it John the Baptist? Whoever it is, the one living there is very unlike those found in the courts of human power perpetuating their own comfort and self-aggrandizement. The one in the desert is not to be sought because of power, but because he has the ability to discern truth. Truth here is juxtaposed with political influence and power. However, they are not simple, equivalents because the power of this world (the *kosmos* of human civilization) is blind to the truth and can only bend with the winds that blow it first this way, then that.

Notes

It is well known that both Yeshua and John the Baptist were in many respects counter-cultural figures. They represented challenges to existing religious conventions and authority. Particularly they drew attention to the constructs of the human world around them, confronting the accepted norms as expressed by the ***kosmos*** *(Greek spelling) of human affairs.*

COMMENTARY

Today John the Baptist is thought to have belonged to the Essenes or an Essene-like sect that considered the religious bureaucracy of Jerusalem to be horribly compromised. He certainly represented a more ascetical branch of first century Judaism.

The context of this saying has traditionally been assigned to a description of Yeshua's own cousin, John the Baptizer. In the canonical Gospels it expresses John's unconventional religious mission to the people of Israel—and the controversy he created by setting himself against the religious establishment of his day. Nothing in the Gospel of Thomas would contradict this same interpretive setting, except that John is not directly mentioned here. Juxtaposed with the last saying concerning the I AM Presence, a new context could also be imagined referring to Yeshua.

It is clear that Yeshua also spent time in the wilderness, traveling through it and teaching there. The expectations about him (as well as his cousin) were fluid and, at times, hostile. In the context of this Gospel, following the previous saying about the I Am Presence, this Logion may express the condition in which that Presence fills and manifests itself through him, not just in the cosmos (as was the case in the previous saying), but in history and in space-time. The difficulties this manifestation causes all who go against the conventions of their own day will become evident.

The lives of both Yeshua and John (and their way of being in the world) clearly go against common expectations. Their understanding of power and status fly in the face of the norms. What the general public often wants is simply a passing fad—"a reed swayed by the wind," or smoke on the wind that quickly dissipates and is replaced by another tantalizing possibility which will also soon fade in the public imagination. John and Yeshua, however, are not reeds which bend with every social and public whim. Yeshua and his cousin represent an alternative to the religious conventions that court entrenched powers, displaying themselves as well clothed and acceptable to the powers that be and the norms of first-century society. They are very different kinds of "reeds"—not shaken by wind, but **filled** with wind or Spirit. This is the image that later spiritual teachers like Rumi will use to described a Spirit-filled being—an Anointed One.

It is interesting that the Aramaic word is ***suf*** *which perhaps refigures the Sufi figure filled like a reed with divine longing and the Spirit-breath that makes its complaint.*

This saying juxtaposes of the use of public power and the private discernment of truth. Conventional religion is drawn almost inexorably to the first—to the instruments and the means of power. The solitary one—the one who dwells in the desert, at the margins of human civilization—is drawn to something entirely different, to the sources of truth and the means of knowing it. Perhaps it is only in the desert, without the trappings of power and comfort, that truth can be known. Knowing in this way is not so much through direct access to truth as it is the testing of things which constitutes the act of discernment.

The question is, of course, what is the judgment called discernment. Do we do it through testing?

To discern is to distinguish between things, to make choices perhaps between common "goods." It is to differentiate, discriminate, and determine what is real. This inevitably involves what one modern author has provocatively called "crap detection"—being able to detect when something is empty or false.

This particular phrase was coined by Neil Postman in ***Teaching as a Subversive Activity*** *(Delta, 1971).*

In all spiritual pursuit, as well as in the realm of religion in general, can we detect what is real and what is false? The wisdom Master in the wilderness says that conventional religion is unable to make these distinctions. It does not possess this ability to discern because it is already caught up in the maintenance of power, as well as in the perpetuation of comfort. These tendencies cloud the ability to see inwardly or to make distinctions. In such cases it becomes impossible to perceive illusion from reality.

QUESTIONS FOR REFLECTION

1. How do most leaders (including religious leaders) seem to you? Politicians, in particular, are known for expediency (saying the things that people most want to hear) and then, perhaps, changing it all later. What is your reaction to this?

2. Is the ability to change your mind (or stance toward something) a necessary part of spiritual maturation and evolution? How do you discern the difference between that and "bending in the wind?"

3. How would you define the term discernment? How does it work in your own life or in experience?

4. Defining truth is often very slippery. We realize that typically there is no real "black" or "white," but mainly grays. So what is truth? How do you know it when you see it?

EXERCISES AND MEDITATIONS

1. One way of understanding what our ego wants or believes it needs is to say that our normal agenda is "the maximization of pleasure and the minimization of pain." We want to increase whatever gives us most pleasure and diminish what causes us pain. This might be a definition of "soft raiment," or keeping ourselves feeling comfortable and secure. Also we feel happy, it seems, when we feel in control of our lives and the world around us. So power and comfort are two top priorities in normal living, and we will often "bend" with whatever wind to get them. Reflect on this. Applied to your own life, is this what Yeshua is talking about? Instead of the application being about someone else out there (a person of power and status), perhaps this understanding comes home to us where we live on a daily basis. With this interpretation as a possibility, spend the next couple of days watching yourself and your agenda. Where do you seek power and safety? Where do you bend with the winds of opportunity?
2. Here is a thought experiment: Two people who you really care about tell you opposite things—believing they are the truth. Let's suppose that what they tell you does not concern "hard facts," but is their subjective feelings about someone else. Let's imagine that they say that another person who all three of you know and love, is "out to get you," or its opposite, "is in your corner and has your back" Who is right? How would you discern the truth of things? Imagine that they each say something about you—one statement contradicting the other. Because it's about you, how do you discern the truth?

In a group you might want to discuss these examples and use concrete examples. You might also want to be specific about a particular characteristic concerning yourself that people either do or do not agree upon. Ask someone to rate you on reliability or ingenuity or your capacity to problem solve (1 to 10, for example). If you get opposite answers, or different numbers, who is right?

READINGS FOR INSIGHT

I

Yeshua
John 8:32

You shall know the truth
and the truth will set you free

II

Anthony de Mello
One Minute Wisdom
8

"Don't look for God," the Master said.
"Just look—and all will be revealed."
"But how is one to look?"
"Each time you look at anything, see only what is there and nothing else."
The disciples were bewildered, so the Master made it simpler: "For instance: When you look at the moon, see the moon and nothing else."
"What else could one see except the moon when one looks at the moon?" they exclaimed.
"A hungry person could see a ball of cheese. A lover, the face of his beloved."

III

Jalaluddin Rumi

Out beyond ideas of wrongdoing
and right-doing
there is a field.
I'll meet you there.
When the soul lies down in that grass,
the world is too full to talk about.
Ideas, language, even the phrase *each other*
doesn't make any sense.

IV

Dante

"The love of God, unutterable and perfect,
flows into a pure soul the way that light
rushes into a transparent object.
The more love that it finds, the more it gives itself;
so that, as we grow clear and open,
the more complete the joy of heaven is.
And the more souls who resonate together,
the greater the intensity of their love,
and, mirror-like, each soul reflects the other."

V

W. R Beattie

We should be the truth;
truth, through and through.
Truth is not just a thing of words.
It is a thing of life and being.

LOGION 79

A woman in the crowd said to him, "Fortunate is the womb which bore you, and the breasts which nourished you."

Yeshua turned to her and said,

"The ones who hear the Father's Word and guard its truth are truly fortunate. But the days are coming when you will say, 'Lucky is the womb that never bore, and the breasts that never gave milk!'"

Sapiential Themes

- *Fame and fortune are uppermost in ordinary minds. Wisdom does not worship the famous, but the truth.*
- *Deeper than bloodlines is an inner loyalty and vigilance that understands the priority of truth.*
- *Apocalyptic vision is an undercurrent in the sapiential tradition providing prophetic unveilings of the future.*

Parallel Texts

Thomas 10, 99
Luke 11:27-29, 23:29

FOCAL POINT

A brief conversation is sparked by a woman's comment about fortune and blessing. Who is more fortunate, the mother of Yeshua or any person known or unknown who hears truth from the Source and cherishes it? In the future history of world events that are about to unfold, it is the latter, not the former that will be of crucial importance. This world is an unstable and unsafe place. The only true stability is this deep wisdom arriving from its Source in the Absolute. Everything else fails or is only a temporary example of blind luck.

Links

This and the previous Logion suggest that there were many interactions between Yeshua and his students in the wilderness where his is teaching spills over into lively conversation. The earlier statement about the ability to discern truth is perhaps the immediate context for this saying, which points both toward the woman who has made a first step in discernment, but, more pointedly, toward the one who hears and guards the truth of the Father's Word. Such a practice, in Yeshua's thinking, leads to discernment.

Notes

It is important to note that the word "fortunate" which is sometimes translated as blessed is different here from the term ***makarios*** *which designates a particular state of blessendess. The term here signifies luck or fortune that creates happiness. The Father's Word is literally the* ***Logos*** *of the Father, which is protected in the same way that Yeshua protects the cosmos in Logion 10.*

COMMENTARY

If the historical scenes suggested by this and the last saying constitute an environment of interaction and dialogue between the Master of Wisdom and wisdom seekers then we are introduced here to a mother's simple human longing. The awareness of this one individual in the crowd (acknowledging the state of the teacher of wisdom) expresses perhaps a nascent form of curiosity about the "solitary ones" (the desert dwellers) that she and others have come into the wilderness to see.

The woman who cries out speaks of human origins understood best, perhaps, from a mother's point of view. She recognizes that any woman who could give birth to such a person as Yeshua would be the mother of a blessed lineage. Perhaps she is projecting her own need or history here. Nonetheless, in contrast to the individuals mentioned in the previous Logion, she has begun to discern the truth of things. Yeshua, however, will not allow a simple birth-narrative to define his lineage or the larger truth. This kind of matrilineal thinking, so common to humankind, which privileges bloodlines over anything else, in the end becomes a trap.

Within religious traditions, bloodlines have been used to assert power or as a means of establishing institutional authority. This approach to religious tradition, however, limits the truth. It excludes those not privileged to share it. The Jewish bloodlines of the first century (and throughout later Jewish and Christian history) have been privileged as something both sacred and special—a divine right or dispensation, but in the process, excluding whole populations from the "fortune" (blessing) of the tradition.

Contrary to the original covenant made with Abraham and Sarah whose lineage, in the end, was to carry fortune to all the families of the earth, exclusion according to bloodlines became a norm in many aspects of the Abrahamic faiths. In this saying, Yeshua sets himself against this understanding of religious and spiritual privilege, and establishes a new inner norm.

Greater than any bloodline, of course, is the voluntary respect for (and submission to) the original Word of the Father—the Source. To carefully guard (or protect) that Word as Truth is to become a truly blessed being. Truth from its source blesses, not because of some special biological, social, or cultural privilege which we humans so prize. Truth conveys blessings because in the end it liberates us from the limitations put upon us by the social fabric around us or the environment we grew up in. This form of truth takes us to the "original blessedness" of the Father which is our birthright—a true knowledge about our origins in the Source.

Our experience in time, however, is a mixed blessing—clearly ambiguous. Yeshua acknowledges this, and in a visionary way, perhaps, sees that in the unfolding of history, there will be states and times when anything but blessing (or blessedness) is the reality of our experience. This is the way of the world. This is perhaps also the necessary condition for the unfolding and spiritual evolution of humanity in the environment of time and space. Yeshua does not say whether this state in which blessing appears to be absent is good or bad. He simply acknowledges that it will be the case and our experience in time.

QUESTIONS FOR REFLECTION

1. Have you ever witnessed "idol worship"—that is the adoration from his or her fans that comes to someone with fame or fortune? What have you observed?

2. Have you ever idolized someone yourself? What has that experience been like? What does that cause you to do? How have you responded to that person? How has that person responded to you?

3. What does it mean to keep (or guard) a truth? Can you think of any examples of this in your experience? What truth have you guarded?

4. Have you ever kept a secret? How would you describe this experience?

5. Yeshua seems to speak about a coming time of tribulation or apocalypse? What is your view of that possibility either then or now?

EXERCISES AND MEDITATIONS

1. Imagine yourself in a crowd listening to the words of Yeshua. What would it be like to be part of the gatherings that crowded around him? Where would you be in that crowd? What would you be wanting from him? What would you want to know, to ask, or want to hear? During a time of reflection, put yourself in that place. Ask Yeshua a question, or make some comment. Listen for an answer or a response. What do you hear? Journal and share what you have written.
2. At various times in your life you may have been asked to keep a secret, or guard a secret truth for someone. Or you may have stumbled upon some truth that no one else seems to believe or understand—that sets you apart from your peers or the society around you. Explain what you have experienced in a journal entry, and then share that with a spiritual friend. Imagine that this truth is about some "word" from God—your Source. What might that word be? How might it best be kept? Are you now keeping some word that has been directed to you from the Source? Can it be shared?
3. Being prepared for the future is something that our parents teach us. Often as we grew up we were warned to be prepared for various happenings, or to avoid danger. What might be in our future (or in the larger future of the world), that needs careful attention? How do we prepare for an uncertain future? Why is it important? What does that do to our security? Should we be worried about it. Does living in the moment preclude such preparation?

READINGS FOR INSIGHT

I

Flattery makes friends,
and truth makes enemies.

A Spanish Proverb

II

All that matters is to be at one with the living God
to be a creature in the house of the God of life.

Like a cat asleep on a chair
at peace, in peace
and at one with the master of the house, with the mistress,
at home, at home in the house of the living,
sleeping on the hearth, and yawning before the fire.

Sleeping on the hearth of the living world
yawning at home before the fire of life
feeling the presence of the living God
like a great reassurance
a deep calm in the heart
a presence
as of the master sitting at the board
in his own and greater being
in the house of life.

D. H. Lawrence

III

The Master set out on a journey with one of his disciples. At the outskirts of the village they ran into the governor, who mistakenly thought they had come to welcome him to the village and said, "You really didn't have to go to all this trouble to welcome me."

"You are mistaken, your highness," said the disciple. "We're also on a journey, but had we known you were coming too we would have gone to even greater pains to welcome you."

The Master did not say a word. Toward evening he said, "Did you have to tell him that we had not come to welcome him? Did you see how foolish he felt?"

"But had we not told him the truth, would we not have been guilty of deceiving him?"

"We would not have deceived him at all," said the Master. "He would have deceived himself."

Anthony de Mello
One Minute Wisdom
53

IV

There is only one thing that will really train the human mind and that is the voluntary use of the mind by the man himself. You may aid him, you may guide him, you may suggest to him and, above all else, you may inspire him. But the only thing worth having is that which he gets by his own exertions, and what he gets is in direct proportion to what he puts into it.

Albert Lowell

LOGION 80

Sapiential Themes

- *The particular wisdom of embodiment is a sapiential teaching that considers space-time experience a precious commodity.*
- *To experience the human condition is to know the body intimately, and to come to know the purpose of the body through embodiment is a value beyond price.*
- *The knowing that constitutes ordinary human understanding rarely arrives at this insight, and when it does it meets resistance.*

Yeshua says,

Whoever knows the cosmos discovers the body, but the cosmos does not deserve the one who makes that discovery.

Parallel Texts

Thomas 56, 111
Matthew 24:28
Luke 17:37
I Corinthians 1:20-28, 2: 12

Links

The question raised in the previous Logion concerns the nature of truth and the one who hears and guards the Father's Word. The nature of what this truth entails is perhaps very subtle. It is not propositional, but existential. It involves the learning that we do in this world—through the body, and how we relate to the world (cosmos) of human affairs. It is not easy to put this kind of learning into propositional statements. It is not a creed, but a form of knowing that is inevitably sapiential.

FOCAL POINT

In the world of human affairs, what one comes to know most intimately is one's own physical existence—one's body. Most human beings protect the body zealously and often at the expense of everything else. But the body is only an instrument useful in physical reality. It has no other purpose but to put us into contact with space and time. The one who discovers what the body's true purpose is and how it is to be used has made an immense discovery that will lead to a transcendence beyond the known *kosmos* in which this discovery has been made.

Notes

In spiritual tradition the body usually gets a bad rap. Typically it is either suppressed, subjugated or ignored. This is built into the dualistic approach of many forms of first-century spiritual teaching. Yeshua appears to contradict it by making the body an instrument of knowing in the kosmos (that is the world of human affairs). As we have seen elsewhere ***kosmos*** *is a technical term for human civilization where emphasis is upon the "cosmetic nature" of human culture.*

COMMENTARY

This Logion focuses on the mystery of embodiment—what does it mean to be an embodied being, living inside a material form (or frame of flesh)? What does it mean to be incarnate? What is this great mystery? What is its purpose? It is clear that we are here for a reason, and though our passageway through space-time may be a difficult and often problematic journey, it is clear that if it were not meant to be so, and if it were not important (and even precious to the divine Mind), we can assume we would not be here. So what are we to learn now that we're here? What does this saying teach us?

One of the great sapiential themes is understanding fully what earth-experience is designed to create inside a human being. According to great mythologies encoded in the traditions, we have been sent into space-time on a mission, with the purpose of gaining great benefit not only for ourselves, but for the greater well-being of humanity in its highest collective form. Every human being is an emissary sent into this domain on a mission for the collective body, and the task is both difficult and critical for the for the outcome of humanity.

Alchemy has typically been described as a pseudo-science in our day—the quest to turn lead into gold, for example. However, the subject is more complex than that. Alchemy is a "sign system" that points toward inner and not just outer realities. Or it uses outer realities as signs of inner processes. Both are then related to a higher order that concerns the transformation of the soul and not simply physical properties or forms.

We are here to learn. This school-like experience on earth has a very steep learning-curve. We make many mistakes—as any new learner does, and that is in itself part of the experience. So to become embodied is the necessary means and environment for this learning. This is, after all, a material universe and we must become material beings. But more important than the form of the body is what must occur when we engage the human body. It is precisely into the crucible of flesh that we are meant to make real ("download" or realize) certain qualities that must be held and embodied here by being built into us through temporal and corporeal experience.

This is what has been called "divine alchemy," and only the interaction of this mixture—matter with spirit—can catalyze the process and bring about the "new forms" that the universe and the future form of humanity will need to become its true Self. Just as a child cannot become an adult without leaving the safe confines of home, and "mixing it up" in the outer world of chaos, difficulty, pain and confusion, so it is in the realm of Spirit.

As an inner alchemical reaction it is said that "The constant heat of love's fire allows a soul to fully ripen. It allows an individual who is "raw" or immature to attain a "cooked" or even "burnt" state. Most important, the power of love allows the individual to surrender the false self of the isolated ego for the sake of the Beloved and receive a deeper vision of reality—a vision that is no longer self-centered."

—David Fideler
Love's Alchemy
xix

To discover this truth and, more importantly, to act on it, is to make a discovery that is truly remarkable—so remarkable, in fact, that the cosmos of human affairs around us (unaware of these facts and realities), is not "worthy" of the discovery. In all likelihood it will both resist and try to suppress this discovery—and when it becomes manifest (as it must through a realized human being), then it will at best deny the truth, and at worst attempt to destroy it. This is the normative reaction to higher truth lived out in human history and in the midst of human affairs. With its own particular agenda for power, self-aggrandizement, and pursuit of pure pleasure, everything else is seen as a threat and is actively resisted by those who, as of yet, are unable to see.

But no matter the reaction to it, this discovery of the relative relationship of a human being to temporality, and yes, to the transient body, and the ability through embodiment to implant divine Quality in the material realm, is precious beyond imagining. It is, in effect, the proverbial "pearl of great price," of unimaginable worth. The world around us may never know this, and in its current state, cannot realize it. But it makes no difference. In the end, it is that realization which will raise the whole body of humanity to a higher, future state of being.

QUESTIONS FOR REFLECTION

1. What is your relationship to your own body? Do you enjoy it or fear it? Is it peaceful or adversarial? Describe it.

2. Do you have a personal sense of mission on the earth? What is it?

3. What has being embodied taught you so far? What are the lessons that you could only come to know by being in a body?

4. What do you make of the term "divine Alchemy?" What does it mean to you?

5. Do you have any experience where lower truth resists and even seeks to destroy higher truth? Do you even have such resistances within you?

EXERCISES AND MEDITATIONS

1. Examine your life and experience here on earth as a kind of spiritual classroom. But rather than making a good grade, you are actually here to become something—not only well-educated, but also the master of certain abilities and skills. These will be useful to you in your eternal future, as well as, of course, now in time. In a period of reflection, re-evaluate the purpose of your life in light of this saying and the commentary. How might this change the way you are living and the way you see yourself and what is going on around you? Journal your insights. Share these with a trusted friend, or with someone who also shares your spiritual journey. Explain to that person what you are seeing, and the new viewpoint this may have given you.
2. Imagine, then, that new, divine qualities are being built into your being. Imagine what those might be. Look at a list of the Names and Qualities of God. You might want to see such a list of the Ninety-nine names of God that Islam uses to express these qualities. Think about your experience and how these qualities are being made yours, and not just as ideas, but truly built into your being. Record what you have found.
3. Spend a day contemplating and reflecting on one of the divine Qualities—for example, humility, patience, or compassion. Watch what happens when you seek to live that quality. Watch your own resistance to it—or your difficulty in living it. Watch how the outer world might challenge you in seeking to live it. This challenge may intensify your efforts—making them more poignant.

The Names of God are qualities that live in the core of our being. There are numerous online internet sites which list and record the 99 beautiful names of God. www.arabacademy.com and www.physiciansoftheheart.com are two that give extensive exposure to the tradition.

READINGS FOR INSIGHT

I

L. Bauman

The awareness, the knowing, the discovery that is involved in that part of ourselves that realizes of the impermanence of life and that we will die, but live through death, is a fragrance that burns within us. This, perhaps, is at the core of the Knowing Heart which can see beyond the limits of space-time. It produces a profound gladness that fills us when we get to know that part of our self that does not die. The dying of the body gives the soul more range. It allows it to perch on a cliff in the wind of Spirit with an awareness that is deeper than love and lift off into the chasm of the eternal Abyss.

II

Charles Upton
Knowings
140

...I can only realize I am not the body if I know what the body is, and I can only know what the body is when its own particular energy is fully deployed, which requires that it not be confused with the energy of any other center.

III

inspired by Rumi

Lovers experience divine inner fire and the circling stars.
But then the sun comes up and all the stars disappear,
and on some days we cannot even see the face of the sun.
All our wanderings seem not to be worth much.
Every morning we hear some call
and we go toward it and are scattered into a myriad pieces,
drowning in our own embryo-blood,
ground down fine by the mill of experience.
There seem to be no real rules here
in this vale of human darkness,
no real mind—but madness,
madness inside of madness, and chaos everywhere.
But all of this—all of it is held within tender-Love,
and where, O where is that love moving?

III

Charles Upton
Knowings
121

The mystical life has first to do with Being, and only secondarily with experience. Our duty is to come into a real, viable, relationship with Absolute Truth, a relationship which holds true *whether or not we presently experience it.* As Beat Generation poet Lew Welch wrote, "I seek union with what goes on whether I look at it or not"—not with the subjective experience of the thing, but with the very thing itself. In the words of St. Paul *faith* is 'the presence of things hoped for, the evidence of things not seen.' In the mystical life, experience is the product of faith, not faith of experience.

There is no mystical life, of course, without experience because God is generous, because the Absolute Truth, by Its Infinite Self-manifesting Radiance, must communicate Itself. We ourselves, in fact, are actual instances of that communication. Experience, however, is inseparable from the subjectivity whereby it is experienced—that is, from our ego—while the entire *raison d'être* of the mystical life is to transcend the ego.

LOGION 81

Sapiential Themes

- *The contrast between outer riches and inner poverty, and the converse, inner riches and outer poverty has been a perennial subject of sapiential teaching.*
- *Yeshua introduces the element of power into the discussion of wealth.*
- *Surrendering power is one of the most provocative of human acts.*
- *Self-surrender is crucial to spiritual progression.*

Yeshua says,

Let whoever becomes rich be king, but let whoever holds power surrender it.

Parallel Texts

Thomas 21, 110
Matthew 19:23-24
Mark 10:23-25
Luke 6:24, 18:24
I Corinthians 4:8
II Corinthians 6:10, 8:9
James 2:5-6

Links

In the previous saying, Yeshua observes that to come to know the ***kosmos*** *is also to discover the physical form called the body. That discovery is an advancement that exceeds the worth of the kosmos itself. So what effect does that discovery have on the person who makes it? What is the result? This saying provides us with the answer. Transcending the* ***kosmos*** *means going beyond its norms and principles. This Logion provides us with a sapiential understanding of such transcendence and its effects.*

FOCAL POINT

Power (or the use of power and its riches) is central to all human interests in the world. Acquiring riches and the power to use them is the central purpose of human life in the world for almost all individuals. Let, then, the ones who play this game and amass riches, also take up the role of authority (or king). But if, in the end, power is at stake or in play, then true wisdom concerning power is to surrender it. This is a counter-intuitive point-of-view taken by the Master of Wisdom, who knows that self-surrender is ultimately the most powerful force of all.

Notes

Wealth and power are linked since wealth gives a person power. The translation of the word surrender could equally be "abandon" or even "abdicate"—which is what one must do if one gives up sovereignty in the cosmos. Elsewhere Yeshua talks about wealth and the giving away of riches. Here the focus is upon the power that riches bring. This becomes an act of self-surrender.

COMMENTARY

In our own day, more and more on the political stage, wealth seems to be the key to power. Candidates vie for office, and the ones that have the most financial resources tend to win. Those without wealth tend to lose. So, perhaps, it has ever been—wealth lends human beings privilege and power, and from that power they gain political influence and with influence they accede to supremacy—in effect, they become "king." This is the way of the world. Yeshua acknowledges this inevitability. Does he agree with it? Clearly by understanding the second aphorism in the context of the first he does not.

There is another step, another evolution to be taken. For those on the path of wisdom, let those who find they have power release it—do not hold on to it. Let it go. This is, of course, counter-intuitive. It goes against every norm of our society and social conditioning. Everything within us, within our culture says—hold on to power, desperately. Whatever it takes hold on! Do **not** let it go for any reason.

Yeshua knows another way. He lives by another insight. He lives by rules and laws that apply to a higher Kingdom which says that the way to true authority is to release power. It's crazy to us here in space-time. It does not seem at all like the right thing to do. It does not make for good, human politics—but it is the politics of wisdom.

Sapiential seeing knows that the path of true leadership is the path of the servant—the one who serves, the one who gives away everything for the benefit of another—for the benefit of All. This is the only power that lasts, because it transcends the ego and survives the many traps that lay in wait for human political stratagems.

It may seem to us that the powerful and rich "win." But in the long run, they lose—they lose everything because nothing is permanent, and everything returns to its Source. We, in fact, cannot hold on to anything. In the end we must let everything go—surrendering our own life back into the cosmos. So what is the purpose of holding on to it now? Why amass power and wealth for a short-term temporal goal that has no staying power and no ability to accrue true wealth judged by a different measure than the typical monetary standards.

True wealth is something entirely different from amassing material prosperity. True power transcends the normal political desire to control masses of people or to exercise dominant control over institutions and material resources. To accumulate whatever amounts we deem as wealth in this world, is from an eternal point of view insignificant. But it is difficult to see from that perspective or to tell our "brains" that. Our reasoning in this world does not agree. We have to be led almost kicking and screaming away from the point of view that says "more is better," and even then the allure of the human viewpoint persists, down into the very fabric of our being. We want more, but there is another way—a wisdom path.

This is what Yeshua knows. This is at the heart of his wisdom teaching. This is sapiential politics in its highest form, all held within the confines of this small, seemingly insignificant Logion. But through it we are led to a new edge, to the entryway into the realm of the Kingdom of God, where other laws, other mandates apply that trump the politics of earth.

QUESTIONS FOR REFLECTION

We might be tempted to shrug off this saying as inapplicable to us since most of us are not considered "wealthy" by the standards of our society. To opt out of this saying, however, is to ignore that Yeshua's disciples took this saying to refer to them, who if not poor for their day, had hardly any possessions as compared to most of us today in the developed world.

1. How wealthy would you consider yourself to be?
2. Wealth gives a person a degree of power—how seductive have you found that to be?
3. What is your own experience of power and powerlessness? The desire to control one's environment is normal. How much power is too much power?
4. What does it mean to surrender? What is it like to "surrender power?"
5. If you are in charge, is delegating power or responsibility the same as surrendering power?

EXERCISES AND MEDITATIONS

1. The desire to exercise some degree of power and control over our environment is normal. To be totally helpless is to be enslaved. Freedom, in part, means the ability to control one's destiny. But the question always arises then where are the limits of power? The tragic history of humanity testifies to the destruction that occurs when an individual (or a totalitarian regime) out of total self-interest (or a narrow national-interest) accumulates more and more power at the expense of the liberty of others. Only when one is able to transcend and surrender self-interest in favor of the profit of all, do we understand both the limits of power and the nature of true power. To profit the whole is, in the end, to profit oneself. So this becomes, then, an issue of practice. How do you balance legitimate control over your immediate world, and the letting go of personal power? Can you think of a difficult edge in your own experience right now where this issue is in play? Outline the difficulty as you see it. Share that with others. Where is the balance? How is Yeshua's insight to be applied to your experience?
2. Imagine making an act of self-surrender so profound that it seems like a kind of death—the giving up of one's own identity, which in our world is precious. Under what conditions would this be possible? Ponder the ultimate surrender of power that Yeshua talks about in his words, *Whoever would find his life must lose it, but whoever loses his life shall find it* (remember the word "life" in the original language is the word for one's psyche). Journal your reflections.

Matthew 10:39

READINGS FOR INSIGHT

I

The major task of the American way of life is to keep on repeating to people that they are free, while teaching them to be utterly docile. The chief means of doing this is the system of rewards. The more you accept the assumptions of the system (the more, for example, you accept the principle of competition) the more likely your advancement will be. Moreover, the easiest way to end complaints about the system is to raise people's salary by a thousand dollars or so a year. It is not necessary to use a Gestapo to attain conformity; one may just as easily attain it by paying good rewards. In place of bread and circuses, modern technology pacifies our people with cars and color television.

Michael Novak
A Theology for Radical Politics
53

II

As the Beloved One
I want no lordship, no mastery.
I want astonishment and devastation.
But like monks,
you hide away in your cloisters of security.
I want you to give up everything
and roam the world like a dervish.

—Attar

III

Calamity has befallen the western world. The modern technological system has swallowed us up, enslaved our spirits, restricted our options, and narrowed our perspectives. The system has demanded a heavy price for its rich material rewards; the total capitulation of whole societies and the individuals within to its own valuation of time, wealth, natural and human resources. We are no longer free to choose between alternatives. We are virtually forced to conform to the world's system of values in order to keep the vast western technological machine functioning. And so we serve the twin gods, "Progress and Efficiency," and to these we give our time, energy, and allegiance.

L. Bauman

IV

Reason said,
"We live in a world of only six directions, and that's it!"
But Love replied,
"There is a field beyond all of that,
and I have traveled its path many times."
Reason saw a marketplace in this world
and immediately set up shop.
But Love trades in another kind of currency altogether
—a consciousness that flows through the arteries of the universe.

—Jalaluddin Rumi

V

Pass away—even from yourself, then you'll find the infinite and eternal shore.
To reach the Friend, you have to go beyond yourself.

—Fekr-e Khurasani

LOGION 82

Sapiential Themes

- *Fire and light are themes which speak of the energetic nature of Ultimate Reality.*
- *Nearness to the Master puts one in relationship not only with the Kingdom with the divine energies.*
- *Relationship is the key. This expresses the tradition of knowledge by presence or proximity.*

Yeshua says,

Whoever comes close to me dwells near the fire.

Whoever moves away from me remains far from the kingdom.

Parallel Texts

Mark 9:49, 12:34
I Corinthians 3:10-13
I Peter 1:6-7

Links

Two questions arise out of the last saying that appear to be the context for this Logion. The first is, why would you abandon power in the first place? And the second is, what kind of power or reality does Yeshua possess that the kosmos around us does not possess? This saying answers those questions. You abandon human power in order to encounter divine power, and draw near to the Kingdom. Yeshua's Kingdom has a different kind of energy, one that both enlightens and burns.

FOCAL POINT

Light comes from fire and fire is the source of light—this is the reality of things in the ancient world. But to come near to the light of Wisdom's Master is to be near a blazing fire. Who would want "nearness" in such a burning? Would it not pose a grave danger? Might it not be safest to keep one's distance from such a blaze? That determination, however, will itself create a greater threat—distance from the fire is also distance from the Kingdom (or the Realm of divine Reality). One either chooses the cold, dark reaches of remoteness from the fire, or nearness to the eternal blaze of Light. What is wisdom's choice?

Notes

Nearness and distance are aspects of relationship. Essentially Yeshua is speaking of those aspects of relationship that draw us closer or put us at distance. The nature of the Kingdom of God is not one of power, but one of relationship described as nearness. Human power often marginalizes and keeps things from the center of power. Yeshua's task is to draw men and women into relationship with the Center—the heart of the Kingdom.

COMMENTARY

In what can only be called a prophetic voice (not unlike that which is heard in Logion 77), Yeshua is speaking in a manner that must be described as either cosmic (or alternatively what appears to be as a megalomaniac). Such speaking is found throughout the early texts of Christianity. At the very least it sounds to our ears strange, and for many, very troubling.

How can Yeshua describe himself in this way? Traditional theology assigns such words to Jesus as the Son of God incarnate speaking. That is a common understanding throughout Christianity, but it is not the only possible way to interpret this and other similar texts. Like many other mystics, Yeshua appears to be giving voice to that form of Consciousness which fills the entire universe—the I AM consciousness which lends itself to every sentient being. So, again, it is not the egoic being of the Palestinian Yeshua who is uttering this, it is the Spirit that fills him as an open vessel and which speaks through him. The "me" here is not the small ego-identity of Yeshua, but the Consciousness which is the divine Self (what the Hindus would call ***Atman***) that is the inside all things, and here it is speaking larger, prophetic and cosmic truth.

Knowledge by Presence.

Credence is lent to this interpretation by the contrast between the "me" of the saying and the "kingdom." The Voice speaking is out of that Realm, and to draw away from the Voice is to find oneself distant from that Realm because the two, in some way, are coterminous. The opposite relationship is nearness (closeness), immanence, and ultimately, perhaps, friendship. Entry into that Realm requires such a relationship—and its converse is alienation, the state we so often find ourselves in.

But closeness to the One speaking involves something that for us is formidable—fire. Is this a warning? Or is this a new understanding so that we might prepare ourselves for what lies ahead? In either case, fire is always an ambiguous word and experience. To hear the exclamation, FIRE! FIRE! is to put us on high alert. Fire is destructive, it burns, it is dangerous, but also a fire-place and a campfire are place of extreme comfort and attraction. So which is it? To dwell near the Voice that is speaking through Yeshua will be to dwell near danger, or will it be comfort? Will it be light or will it be burning? Or will it be both?

In any case, for people in the ancient world fire was the most intense energetic form that they knew (except, perhaps, for lightning, which was another kind of fire). Fire is a higher energy. Yeshua is offering access to a source of energy that is greater than ordinary human energy. More energy means more potentiality, more possibility, a more powerful outcome.

But what does it mean to have access to divine fire? Perhaps in this case it is to be near the same fire that Yeshua has elsewhere cast into the cosmos. To be a part of that fire is to be kindled into flame—both to be burned as a purifying element, and to be enlightened through inner illumination. Both are possible, and later in the tradition they become the norm of spiritual teaching. Purification is the process that will enable the dross (or impurities) to be burned away to leave the purest concentrated elements. Illumination is a form of seeing that allows us to penetrate the darkness and see the reality of things.

QUESTIONS FOR REFLECTION

1. Yeshua raises the issue of relationship to the Master, but proximity to him is to live near the fire. So what is your knowledge of this fiery Master?

2. What does friendship, nearness or intimacy to someone involve? Who is your closest friend? What is the nature of nearness?

3. Why is knowledge of the Master a fire? What is divine fire? What is Yeshua actually talking about?

4. How do you handle higher and higher levels of divine energy?

5. What is your experience of distance, alienation and absence? What would you say you have experienced most, nearness or distance from the Kingdom of Heaven?

EXERCISES AND MEDITATIONS

1. To know someone or something intimately is a great responsibility—it often puts one into situations where otherwise "ignorance would be bliss." Meditate on your relationships of nearness and those of simple acquaintance. Why is one fiery and the other not?

2. When have you experienced fire as light and fire as burning? Describe that experience and the difference. Journal it, and tell another individual about that experience. What have you learned from both experiences with light?

3. Journal your thoughts and perceptions concerning the Realm of the Kingdom. Why does Yeshua call it that? Why is it not a democracy? How do you imagine fire and the Kingdom to be related? These two metaphors have been juxtaposed in this saying, in your mind what makes that significant.

4. You may have heard the phrase, "Never play with fire." This saying suggests that we entertain the possibility that we should entertain that thought as a possibility. How does this strike you? Does it make you afraid? Ponder these questions in light of the passage from the Gospel of Matthew.

Matthew 10:39

READINGS FOR INSIGHT

I

If you stay away from fire,
you will remain sour, doughy, numb, and raw.
You may lovely, unbaked loaves all around you,
but those friends cannot help.
You have to feel the oven's fire.

—Rumi

II

When does gold ore become gold? When it is put through a process of fire. So the human being during the training becomes as pure as gold through suffering. It is the burning away of dross. Suffering has great redeeming quality. As a drop of water falling in the desert sand is sucked up immediately, so we must become nothing and nowhere ... and disappear.

—Bhai Sahib

III

From the beginning,
the Kingdom of Union with You
was always and forever the true home of my being:
How long will you leave my tortured heart in exile?
I have no only lost you;
I no longer know myself.
Who am I?
I keep turning and turning around myself, asking,
"What is your name? Are you in love? With whom?
Are you loved? By whom?
A flame keeps leaping in my heart,
a vast, immeasurable flame
which has charred my entire being to ashes.
Do I still know where I live? Can I still taste what I eat?
I am lost in my own desert ... I am pulled towards death;
Death lives within me.
But when your heart is consumed with such longing
and burned to ashes, the breeze of love arises
and sweeps up the ashes,
and fills heaven and earth with the utterly burnt ones.

—arranged from Kharaqani, Nizami, and Rumi

IV

The way towards God always involves an inversion: from outwardness one must pass to inwardness, from multiplicity to unity, from dispersion to concentration, from egoism to detachment, from passion to serenity.

When we withdraw towards the heart, we will find therein all the beauties perceived outwardly; not as forms, but in their quintessential possibilities. In turning towards God, *we* can never lose anything.

—Frithjof Schuon

LOGION 83

Sapiential Themes

- *Light as source, streaming and embodied, becomes the manifest world.*
- *Levels of manifestation each hiding a form of light veiled behind it is the secret core of existence.*
- *The light of the Father is the Source from which all things and all light comes, and yet that Light hides the "image of God."*
- *Human beings are the image of God made manifest.*

Yeshua says,

Images are revealed to humanity while the light within them is hidden by the brilliance of the Father's light. It is God who is being revealed, but the image of God remains concealed by the blaze of light.

Parallel Texts

Thomas 24, 50, 77
I Corinthians 15
II Corinthians 3:18, 4:4-6
Ephesians 5:8-14
Colossians 1:15, 3:4
I Timothy 6:15-16
I John 1:5-6, 3:2

Links

To dwell near the fire, as was expressed in the previous Logion, is also to dwell with and in light. Light in all its manifestations is the human habitat, though it may be veiled from the senses. Layers of Light issue at last into the manifest world where the sources remain hidden from view.

FOCAL POINT

Levels of light; light upon light; light within light; blinded by light so that only an after-image remains—all of these are ways of describing this saying. The true nature of light is both to reveal and at times to conceal. In this saying, both roles are in focus, both realities exist side by side, or one inside the other. All objects in the created order around us are images or manifestations of light, but in their uniqueness (and their radiance) they hide the deeper, more interior light of their one, true Source.

Notes

There is ambiguity in the original Coptic version. The word "image" (or ***ikon*** *in the original) is translated as "brilliance" in the phrase that speaks of the "Light of the Father." This is done in order to clarify what seems to be the relationship of light and its image and the reason that some images remain hidden in the brilliance of light, much like blindness caused by a camera flash.*

COMMENTARY

Throughout the ages and across sacred traditions, the image of light remains a potent metaphor for God and for the divine energies that pour from Ultimate Reality. The universe is flooded with Light. Light-energy in its many electro-magnetic forms permeates everything we know to the very core of human being itself. The Source of All is an uncreated "light-energy" at its highest calibration. Only now are we coming to understand the nature of the universe, and we have discovered, at last, that physical matter itself is not discreet packets of substance, but energetic waves in a field containing it. We are also beginning to understand that the universe is also saturated with consciousness as a form of light. All that we know, in fact, is based upon this light streaming through everything including ourselves.

Light has been a perennial metaphor for conscious awareness. Much material is now available concerning multiple levels of consciousness which are part of a wisdom understanding of knowledge and perception. Ken Wilber's exploration of the evolution of human consciousness is of particular importance. See especially ***Up From Eden*** *(Quest, 2007), an important overview of this subject.*

From the time of Euclidean geometry through the establishment of Einsteinian physics, the nature of reality has become increasingly more mysterious and difficult to pin down. No longer is it even possible to speak of material reality as something entirely discrete. Everything is a manifestation of energy, and energy itself has been found to be indeterminate and uncertain—everything appearing as an "image" of something higher (behind the images or manifestations). Modern physics also posits other unknown realities that are virtually undetectable in the ordinary way.

This Logion suggests just such a complexity—a metaphysical reality of rich diversity lying behind the appearances that we call "the real world." We are accustomed to thinking of material reality (the result of the Big Bang), as the essence of things. We imagine that if we can discern and uncover the mysteries of physics and the physical universe, we can know the true nature of reality. But even physical reality is proving to be much more elusive and far more mysterious. Physical reality (the known universe detectable through our senses and their extensions (the instruments that speak to our senses) may only be one surface layering. Contemporary physicists discuss multiple dimensions, strings of vibrating energies, the Zero-Point Field—all of which indicate a layering of energy (or light) that is suggested by this Logion.

Several books on modern physics and the Zero-Point Field might help to clarify what is being discussed today concerning the underlying nature of the universe. Lynn McTaggart's ***The Field*** *(HarperCollins, 2008) is a general introduction to the topic. A more in-depth analysis of contemporary thought in physics is* ***The Purpose Guided Universe*** *by Bernard Haisch (New Pages Books, 2010).*

So if we start at the lower end of the spectrum of light (as this saying does), where images appear to our senses, we are told that these images reveal (or reflect) an inner light, but that this inner light is itself overwhelmed by a greater, deeper Light still—the Light streaming from the Source. That Light trumps all and is the Source of All. In reality everything that is manifest—seen or unseen, revealed or hidden—is God, but who God is, what that Ultimate Reality or Image is, is itself hidden in a blaze of Light.

So, a careful reading of this Logion seems to suggest five levels of metaphysical reality in manifestation. First, humans who, with their senses, are able to see. Second, the images they perceive. Third, the inner light of those images that remain hidden to the senses. Fourth, the brilliance of Divine Manifestation—expressed perhaps by the words "God is Light." Finally, the inner "image" or essence of God which is hidden behind or within the divine Light itself. As Logion 77 says, Light and its expressions stream forth unfolding into manifestation. A unity of being links all reality in a golden chain of light. We stand at one end of that chain of divine self-disclosure observing the beauties of divine manifestations. Ultimate Reality stands at the other, as the Source of this Beauty and as Light itself expressing itself and holding all. This is the nature of reality both hidden and revealed, and Yeshua sees this continuum as the background for everything in his visionary understanding. His purpose is so that we might not only see manifest reality, but know of the unmanifest realms behind it.

QUESTIONS FOR REFLECTION

1. How is conscious awareness like light—like turning the light on in a dark room, or the sun coming up over the horizon? How do you experience your own consciousness?

2. Have you ever had your normal, ordinary consciousness flood with some kind of higher light (or level of consciousness)? What has this experience been like for you? Or have you read of such events in the lives of others, for example the Buddha, who claimed that this experience altered their lives entirely?

The "Enlightenment Tradition" does not exclusively belong to Buddhism. It is known and expressed in every mystical tradition worldwide and sometimes also called "illumination." Many consider the roots of this tradition as beginning in the Axial Age around 500 BCE.

3. If you are carrier of the divine Light in the form of an "image" (an "after-image") from the divine Source, what do you imagine that Ultimate Image to be like? How would you then describe the unique features of the image that is you?

4. What, for example, have you been able to detect that lies behind appearances? This is an exercise in ***kardial seeing*** (seeing from the level of the heart). Human beings can see in this way. They have to learn how to do it through practice, however.

The term "kardial comes from the Greek term ***kardia*** *from where we get English words like "cardiac." Kardial seeing is a form of intuitive cognition that transcends rational awareness in human beings.*

EXERCISES AND MEDITATIONS

1. You might go through a day "detecting light," and the "iconic" images that a revealed by that light. You have a "light-detector" and it is your own heart—that organ of subtle perception that is at the core of your being. The heart's way of knowing and detection, however, is not through logic or analysis, but by a kind of inner seeing that is intuitive in nature. Using this organ (or in your spiritual practice intending to "open" it to the world around you), find out what you can see. Make notes on your experience in a journal. Sometimes we need corroboration from others to help us learn to use *kardial perception*. You might want to have a thorough discussion of this issue in a group studying this or other spiritually related texts and topics. Discuss what *kardial seeing* means to each of you.
2. Reflect on the image in the sidebar. Use it as an icon or an object of meditation. There are multiple layers of meaning possible in understanding it. There is a "wisdom light" that shines behind and within it. Allow yourself time to let this image speak deeply to you. Each day sit with the image and let it teach you. As insights come, write them in a journal. Compare your reflections with others who may be studying the same material with you.
3. Create a prayer of your own that will express the many meanings you have discovered. As you meditate and move through the day, pray your prayer as an expression of your own spirit.

READINGS FOR INSIGHT

I

You cast us
like sunlight upon the earth
and your Light,
passing through the body
as if it were an open window to its Source
returns, purified to you.

Jalaluddin Rumi

II

... the Light, the great penetrating, searching, unveiling, unmanifesting, and healing light of God [*is*] now breaking over the world. The breaking of that Light is eternal. It is at the core of every moment. The end of the world lies hidden in every moment. The termination of the cycle, the dissolution of all things, the passing away of heaven and earth, the dawning of the new heaven and the new earth, is always there, in time-present pregnant with time-future, where the whole creation groans to be delivered—until *now*.

Charles Upton
***Knowings**, 223*

III

I had such a hopeless
desire for
YOU
till I saw how
YOUR LIGHT
yearned for me too.
I pushed and I pushed
till I saw it was you who had
ALREADY
drawn me
to every good
that I knew.

Michael Green
*in **One Song***

IV

Know the cosmos to be the light of God's light.
God is hidden in the world because He is [so] evident,
His obviousness has caused Him to remain hidden.

Mahmud Shabistari
The Secret Rose Garden

V

We are in darkness and God is Light; this house
Receives all splendor from that Sun.
But here, the Light is mingled with shadow.
Do you want your light totally pure?
Then leave the house and climb out onto the roof.

Jalaluddin Rumi

LOGION 84

Sapiential Themes

- *Wisdom tradition embraces the concept of humankind's pre-temporal existence in Eternity.*
- *Within Semitic tradition human beginnings take place in Paradise.*
- *Human beings have "twin" existences both in and outside of time.*
- *Individuals are brought into time for a purpose, to fulfill a destiny which will include a future meeting of our original template..*

Yeshua says,

When you see your own likeness projected into time, it makes you happy. But when the time comes that you are able to look upon the icon of your own being, which came into existence at the beginning, and neither dies nor has been fully revealed, will you be able to stand it?

Parallel Texts

Thomas 24
Genesis 1:26-28
I Corinthians 15:54
II Corinthians 3:17, 4:7, 5:1-5

Links

We are the "image of God" projected into time by the divine Light. You might say that we are the shadow of a higher image that falls into physical existence as analogue. This saying builds on the last Logion and relates the shadowy analogue on earth to its higher archetype beyond space-time. This revelation is the answer to a previous question about the nature of images cast by the divine Light.

FOCAL POINT

The experience of living in time as an embodied being who has come to earth and the temporal order from elsewhere is directly expressed in this saying. Who and what we are (or were) in those other dimensions of our being that is not apparent to us now in space-time is the focus of Yeshua's wisdom. A contrast is made between the limitations of our present experience, and the possibility of awakening to a higher, fuller aspect of ourselves about which we are not currently aware. The question is, are we ready (or preparing) for such an encounter? Have we grown sufficiently in our understanding that when we do meet our own iconic nature in the future we will be prepared for it?

Notes

*In the Coptic language **image** and **likeness** are contrasted in this saying. We could say that image is the foundational form and likeness is the projected analogue. This latter form is projected into temporality (expressed) as days. When image and likeness finally meet, the question is raised of the ability to "bear" the weight of that meeting.*

COMMENTARY

This is a profoundly mysterious saying. It suggests an underlying cosmology and a world of understanding that has almost been entirely forgotten in the traditions of western Christianity. Implied in this saying is the existence of a higher self before coming into time. Knowledge of this possibility was common in the ancient world, but it has become lost to modern awareness. Theological discussions today do not include it, but in the great telling of "the Myth of Eternal Return" (which is known in every sacred tradition), individuals leave the "homeland of Light" in the East and travel to the temporal lands of the West where they reside for a time before returning home again. This is a universal story and stands, perhaps, behind this saying as a narrative background.

The work of anthropologists Mircea Eliade and Joseph Campbell is critical in understanding the underlying mythic structure of all traditional teaching concerning our eternal return to our origins. Campbell's ***Hero With A Thousand Faces*** *is a crucial text explaining the structure of this mythology.*

So how do we understand who are we on earth? According to this saying we are "likenesses projected into time." There is a higher template and we currently are its analogue. We mirror or reflect a higher image of ourselves which remains in the original homeland of human creation. In ancient cosmology, this land, called "paradise," is a garden which does not exist in space-time. It is the place from which we came into physical existence. There, our original image continues its existence, and that image is the template (or "icon") of our being, as this saying literally expresses it.

In modern terminology, this higher icon of the true self could, perhaps, also be called the archetypal self—that is the self, which holds the entire template of our being past, present and future which we are in the process of "realizing" or embodying while living in space and time. This "icon" comes into existence "at the beginning" – meaning the ***arche*** (beginning point, or point of creation) when all original forms were brought into manifestation. We imagine our "beginning" to be our birth in time, but this saying sets the date of the beginning of our existence well into the past before temporal birth.

Readiness to encounter or reengage the original icon or template of our being is not something we have talked about in our western spiritual traditions for a long time, but it is clearly a subject of concern in the tradition of Thomas and in this Gospel. Who we will be when we discover our origins and gaze upon the icon of our being is something that awaits us, but should be of concern now. We are being made aware that we might not be ready (or we could become ready), to bear up under the weight of this experience. So what does this mean? We often say the beauty of something was "almost too much to bear." Suppose that this is the intent of this question, and not the suggestion that such a meeting will in any way be negative. Our preparation for it, however, is critical.

It is important to point out one further proposition that this saying clearly supports; the icon or image of our being is indestructible—it does not die. Nor has it yet, and perhaps it will never be "fully revealed." This, again, is not a negative, but a clarity about the infinite evolution of an "image of God" into the Infinity of God. This teaching was called the "doctrine of ***epektasis****" (or Infinite Growth) and became part of patristic Tradition under Gregory of Nyssa..*

Questions may be asked of this saying and of the entire text of the Gospel: how do we prepare, and do we bring anything to this meeting that is of importance for our future existence? Clearly this text, and Yeshua in this saying, is asking us to reflect on a possibility now that has perhaps been almost unimaginable to the ordinary human mind. Readiness is critical, and if it is, then we can perhaps prepare now. The next series of sayings may be critical in answering these questions. For now, however, (and for the purposes of our commentary on this saying), it is important to realize that our future is in play in the present moment, and what we do with the present moment is not to be wasted. At the very least we are to be awake, as Yeshua has clearly indicated throughout his teachings.

QUESTIONS FOR REFLECTION

1. If you knew that you had lived a previous existence before coming to this world, would it make a difference? How would it change the way you live now? Would you do anything differently than you are doing now?

2. What would be the purpose of coming to earth instead of staying elsewhere (in Paradise, as many traditions suggest)? Does this saying give us any clues in answering that question?

3. Why does seeing our own "likeness" make us happy in time? What is that pleasure about?

4. What would you believe to be the preparation necessary to be able to gaze on the original icon of your being? If you were not prepared, how might it trouble you?

EXERCISES AND MEDITATIONS

1. In a time of meditation try to put yourself in touch with the archetype of your being that pre-existed before your coming to earth, and which continues to exist in a realm beyond it. This archetypal Self is sometimes called your "Higher Self" or, as this Gospel understands it, your Twin. If this Twin exists, then it continues to influence you, perhaps on a daily basis. As you continue to imagine this figure and understand its influence upon your life, allow a new perception of it to open at the level of the heart. Ask to be taught. Ask what you need to know. Wait for an answer, perhaps over a period of time. See what arrives. Journal what you learn. Share your experiences with others studying this same material.
2. Inner preparation is a crucial part of the sapiential tradition—perhaps the major part. In wisdom teaching it is claimed that one leaves this world with nothing more (and nothing less) than the amount of wisdom one has gained through life-experience, the divine qualities that one has built into the character of one's being over time, and the degree of freedom that one has gained from the egoic programming that is clearly part of the social-construction of the self while on earth. Imagine these three as the "work of preparation" that you are here to do. Allow these three to be a major part of your practice—practice accumulating wisdom, working with the virtues that make a person real and beautiful, and transcending the normal limitations that the ego imposes on the self. How do you practice this? What is that practice like? How does your practice differ from someone else's practice?

READINGS FOR INSIGHT

I

God the Omnipotent, the Glorious, has set a very high price on each one of you, for in His Book He says, "God has purchased their selves and possessions from the believers, and given in their stead the gift of Paradise."

The poet says:

You are more valuable than both heaven and earth.
What else can I say? You don't know your own worth.
Do not sell yourself at a ridiculous price,
You who are so valuable in God's eyes.

God is always saying to you, "Look, I have purchased you—each moment of your life, each breath, all of your possessions and lives. And if you spend all of them on me, if you offer them to me, I will give you in exchange—Paradise. Realize how infinitely I value you."

—Rumi
Light upon Light
by Andrew Harvey
19

II

The image in question is not one that results from some previous external perception; it is an Image that precedes all perception, an a priori expressing the deepest being of the person, what depth psychology calls an Imago. Each of us carries within himself an Image of his own world, his *Imago mundi*, and projects it into a more or less coherent universe, which becomes the stage on which his destiny is played out. He may not be conscious of it, and to that extent he will experience it as imposed upon himself and on others in this world that in fact he himself or others impose on themselves.

—Henry Corbin
Avicenna
7-8

III

By making conscious this Image of the soul, one steps "beyond the system of the cosmos" that rational thought has erected, and this cosmos is revealed as coming from the soul, as the soul's own, and now consciously integrated with it. The recitals are the record of an "exodus from this world." ... This momentous Event, this spiritual birth, frees the soul from its entrapment in and subordination to an alien and external world. It marks an escape from the world of impersonal knowledge, that Absence in which only objects can appear. There can be no more objects, for with this exodus there arises the Soul of the World, the *anima mundi*, and all creation comes alive through the encounter with the *imago mundi*.

—Tom Cheetham
The World Turned Inside Out
57

IV

Neither you nor I know the secrets of pre-eternity.
Neither you nor I have grasped its deepest mysteries.
For now we are speaking behind the veil,
but once that curtain is lifted
neither you nor I will exist.

—Abu al-Hasan Kharaqani

LOGION 85

Sapiential Themes

- *Themes from Genesis and its meaning for humanity run consistently throughout this text and the wisdom tradition.*
- *The creation of Adam and Eve is both a mythology and a wisdom tale of deep sapiential significance.*
- *The goal of all such telling and the goal of the journey forward from the original garden to the final New Jerusalem is the trajectory of human being.*
- *The completion of humankind, and not its failure, is the focus of the sapiential teaching.*

Yeshua says,

Adam came into being out of a great power and fullness, and yet he is not superior to you. Had he been prepared for it, he would not have tasted death.

Parallel Texts

Thomas 1, 18, 19, 111
Genesis 1:26-28, 3:17-19
John 8:51-52
Romans 5:12-14
I Corinthians 15:21-22. 42-50

FOCAL POINT

In the Hebrew tradition, the progenitors of the human race are said to be Adam and Eve—the first parents, and now the great-great grandparents of humanity. In the book of Genesis these earliest ancestors set the template for humankind at the beginning of time in Paradise, prior to their exile. It is very clear that this saying points to that beginning point, which, according to the previous saying, existed not in time at all, but in a place before being projected into time. It is this intriguing mythology to which we are directed. One of the great images, therefore, revealed by the Light of the previous saying, concerns the First Human, or Adam of Earth who is the Earthling. He was brought into being from a great power and a great fullness, but was not yet ready for immortality. Paradoxically, to be prepared, he had to forgo immortality and taste death. To pass beyond this state and to taste the food of eternal life, however, is the ultimate goal of this Gospel and of the teachings of Yeshua.

Links

Who am I? How did I get here? When and where was my beginning point? What am I doing here? Where am I going? All these constitute the great questions addressed by the wisdom tradition. From wisdom's perspective, the answers are found at the beginning point and our projection from that beginning. Related to the last Logion, this saying makes the point that our journey through time from the unfolding at our beginning, is the pathway to reach a state of immortality.

Notes

The superiority of Adam and Eve is assumed because of their privileged position as the first-born of humankind. Yeshua contrasts superiority with readiness (or adequacy) which is emphasized in the Coptic text.

COMMENTARY

In the vision of this Gospel, humanity fell out of Paradise into time—into historical reality on earth. The Fall did not take place on earth in time, but before time in the homeland of Paradise. Adam, therefore, came into being in a place of great power and fullness—the Edenic garden. His beginnings, and that of Eve, were auspicious and fulsome, and yet even then they were not ready for the conquest of death. Despite coming from the place of power and fullness, Adam was in no way superior to a human being born into time—he had no clear advantage because he was not yet ready. Human beings born into time may be in an "inferior place" in regards to origins, but where they are now (in time) does not preclude that they can receive what Adam and Eve were not yet ready to receive. In fact, the opposite may be the case—human beings may now be ready to enter the deathless state when Adam and Eve could not.

***Pardesh** is the original Persian word for garden, from which we get the word paradise.*

The question is, of course, what is readiness? What makes a person ready to taste eternal life instead of death? The term "taste of death" has been used in Thomas right from the beginning of the text, and it expresses symbolically the state of mortality in which human beings exist—humans are, in fact, "eating death" as we pass away from our existence in time. We also consider our death here to be a curse. But the hope is not simply to gain a new life after death, but to reverse the curse of exile from Paradise, and restore humanity to a full, deathless existence. This is a major focus of this (and all) sapiential texts. Again, the key is to become adequate (or be made ready) for such a state. Readiness is the precondition for the possibility of immortality.

Another way of understanding what has traditionally been called "the Fall" (from grace, or out of Paradise) is to understand it not in a moral sense, as Adam and Eve "sinned" and were thus driven from the garden, but that they had to leave because they were not yet (but had to become) "sufficient." Original insufficiency of being, as in any child, has to be overcome, and the only way forward is the pathway of maturation into the difficult world of human becoming.

Accordingly, we are being prepared here for a higher form of life. The key questions are, what was it that brought death to humanity, and what brings life? What makes us ready for the latter? These questions are obviously related. If Adam and Eve were forced from the garden because they were not ready for immortality, then what must they or any other human being do to prepare to reenter paradise? In wisdom teaching three critical elements are said to be absolutely essential for what lies ahead for humanity. These three are also the reason that human beings inhabit space and time—in fact, it is this environment of space-time that makes it possible for humans to gain the "three great treasures" (as they are called)—wisdom, virtue and freedom.

Wisdom is that fundamental form of knowing that is achieved through hard-won experience which makes it possible to know anything deeply.

At the beginning of existence humans had yet to gain wisdom. Human beings as of yet were also without the necessary qualities that make a person real and full—possessing "moral weight." This vital missing element has for centuries been called "virtue." Virtue signifies the value and worth that is realized because someone embodies divine qualities which are the eternal elements of heaven. These must be built into one's being element by element through personal participation. Finally there is a freedom to be won. Because of their existence in the world, human beings are socially-conditioned—limited by the viewpoints and prejudices that cause us to conform to societal norms and values. The ego is, therefore, a "social construct" reflecting the norms and values of family and society imposed upon it. To become free is to win liberation from the limitations of this social construction and move into a state of self-transcendence. These three key elements prepare a human being for another kind of existence. They are the entryway into the deathless state. They make us adequate for and trusted to take up the responsibilities of immortality, without which we would otherwise fail ourselves as Adam did, and fall short of the high demands of transcendent existence.

QUESTIONS FOR REFLECTION

1. What is your understanding of the accounts of Genesis in the Bible? Is it literal and historical or is it metaphoric and mythological? If it is mythology, then what is the meaning and purpose of the mythology? What is the point of it all?

2. Each one of us carries the spiritual archaeology of human history within us. We are all affected by that history in some way. How do you experience that influence? Can you detect aspects of human history within yourself?

3. Given the discussion concerning preparedness and adequacy in the commentary, what is the sense of your own readiness for immortality?

4. What does immortality mean? Does it mean living in time forever? If not in time, then where?

Jalaluddin Rumi said that we are like sea-birds that plunge down into an ocean of mystery, and that that ocean becomes the turning center of our being. And then he said:

More and more
concentric heavens
appear with the heart as
their center.
You call for us to start
out, and we do.
So this is the path Adam
left paradise
to walk upon.
The ocean of love roils
with praise for you,
and that sound increases
now as I end this and
wait for your deep inner
discourse to begin.

It would be good to use this poem as a part of a practice of meditation.

EXERCISES AND MEDITATIONS

1. It is important to remember and connect to our ancestors. Suppose that rather than this being simply an exercise of the imagination, there is a way to establish a living relationship with our ancestors. We are not talking about a séance, but about a connection through the heart to the heart of another. It is said that our ancestors wish for our best. Imagine a great-grandmother or grand-father figure who exists to assist you in becoming able to taste immortality. Somehow they lend their weight to the process, and you can receive this in time. In a time of reflection, see if you can establish this connection. Journal your experience and share it with others if there is occasion to do so.
2. Of the three critical elements of preparedness (or adequacy)—wisdom, virtue, freedom—which one seems most critical in your life at this moment? Which one needs your attention? They all are critical, but you need to begin somewhere. If you begin with **wisdom**, then the question in daily life is, what knowledge are you integrating that is larger than your normal sphere? If you begin with **virtue**, then begin to look at the deficiencies you experience—the lapses in virtue—and choose one that needs your attention. Make a study of it and journal your findings, but more importantly watch your daily life for ways of intentionally working with that virtue. Notice the opportunities and the resistances you experience. Finally, if you choose **freedom**, then you may want to explore your egoic programming and its limitations. Explore where it binds you and keeps you from experiencing freedom from the social construct of your being. Again, pay close attention to daily life. Watch how the ego responds to being challenged. How do you break free?

*You might want to explore traditional material on the **virtues** and how they are described in sacred teaching. Do an internet search, for example, on the "four cardinal virtues" to begin.*

READINGS FOR INSIGHT

I

The Lord God planted a garden in the East in Eden. The myth of the Garden of Eden is one of the most beautiful and significant in the Bible and indeed in all human history. It has all the elements of an archetypal myth, the garden and the tree, the serpent and the man and the woman. The significance of this myth is inexhaustible. ... We can now begin to see the original structure of human nature, its state of original justice, as it has been called. First of all, man, that is the human being, is created in harmony with nature, as an element in the vast system of energies which stretches from this dearth to the farthest stars. But at the same time man has in him the breath of the Spirit of God, a capacity for reason and free will, a specifically human consciousness, which raises him above the whole material world, and gives him the capacity to know himself and the world in which he lives. It is this capacity which makes man an image of God with the ability to become 'like God.' ... Both man and nature are evolving in time and space, and the purpose of the whole evolutionary process is that both man and nature should come to participate in the infinite and eternal being of the one Supreme Spirit or God.

Bede Griffiths
The Marriage of East and West
117, 122-123

II

Adam was a light carrier for you.
Eve acted as Eve on your behalf.
But Adam and Ever weren't really the ones doing these things alone.
It was the Creator acting through them.
The four rivers of paradise are now flowing into your chalice.
But their majesty does not come from
the five senses or the six directions found here.
Having tasted the water of life in that cup
your love affair with this world is over.
In this new world of love you are the hidden treasure,
you are the owner of eternity.
The living word of pure Consciousness is inside you now.
The mirror reflecting the divine Face lies in your heart.
There is nothing really outside yourself, so look within.
Everything you want is already present, so move into it.
In a single upward movement, scatter your whole being
so that your cries of confirmation can fill the heavens.

Jalaluddin Rumi

III

The ancestors possess this in-between quality of the flown soul and the hovering presence. They seem to have a kind of materiality and exalted awareness; they also display an immateriality, a repose and introspective serenity that suggest they inhabit a timeless dimension ... How would we have survived had we not been carried on the shoulders of the ancestors? How would we have found our way had we not been guided by the psychic deposits they have left us as signs? By what means would we hold in balance the worlds of natural and supernatural if not for their occult meditation? The ancestors arrive at the threshold of consciousness in the sheaths of dreams and imagination to ask questions, impart knowledge and to peel away the multiple skins of our identity. They visit us in familiar patterns of behavior as well as inexplicable phenomena, inviting our curiosity and engagement.

Armi Ronnberg, Editor
The Book of Symbols
790

LOGION 86

Yeshua says,

Foxes have dens and birds have nests, but the son of humanity has no place to lay his head and rest.

Sapiential Themes

- *In the wisdom tradition the idea of a wandering sage is one in which placelessness (or no permanent abode) is a sign of the very nature of this world.*
- *A wisdom teacher has no continuing residence in the* ***kosmos*** *(the world of human impermanence and change).*
- *The animal kingdom, however, is not afflicted with a sense of impermanence—they know their "place" and are at home in it.*
- *Wisdom teaches us the value of impermanence in contrast to the ultimate state of humanity as the* ***Anthropos****.*

Parallel Texts

Thomas 51, 52, 90
Daniel 7:13
Matthew 9:19-20, 11:28-29
Luke 9:57-58
Hebrews 4:1-11

FOCAL POINT

On the surface, this Logion appears to be a simple, straight forward saying that can easily be interpreted. At that level Yeshua is making a historical statement of fact about his life, and one should take it literally. If this is all there is, there would be no teaching here, no wisdom content—just a direct reference to the circumstances of his life when he spoke those words. But is this all there is to the simple statement and the metaphors he uses, or is there something more, something which transmits wisdom? As we have seen, the trajectory of the Son of Humanity is to pass through temporality not only as one particular expression of human manifestation, but also as a paradigmatic figure guiding toward some ultimate goal. Because this is only a temporary passage, it can never offer us a final resting point. This is in the very nature of human existence upon the earth. On the way to a greater fullness, there is no ultimate point of rest in this world. Rest lies elsewhere.

Links

What is the superior condition that human beings can achieve even though they are exiled from Paradise? What is it that will make a human being immortal (without having to continually experience death)? Where is Yeshua taking his students? Is it to paradise on earth?

Notes

It is interesting how this saying in Thomas emphasizes the aspect of rest (the term is ***anapausis*** *in the Greek text). This is a key phrase throughout this Gospel and it is also found in the letter to the Hebrews.*

Given its apparent simplicity, this Logion provides an opportunity for us to test various hermeneutical (interpretive) approaches to understanding a simple declarative statement. The question is, how is this text a carrier of sapience with real wisdom content?

COMMENTARY

Traditionally, sacred texts (especially Scripture) were treated on four fundamental levels by the early interpreters: literal, moral, typological, and anagogical. We might apply a more contemporary, amended version of this hierarchy and see how it applies. First, there is a literal level, second, the mytho-metaphoric or traditional level of religious (or sacred) symbolism, third, the sapiential-mystical and praxiological level, and fourth, the metaphysical or principial level. This is a somewhat different but related hierarchy to the traditional, early interpretive structure.

To begin on the literal level, Yeshua would be making a statement about the contrast between the normal resting places for any creature who has a home to go to, in contrast to his more mendicant life-style with no real home to which he can return to rest. It seems clear that Yeshua was not a home-owner, but an intinerate teacher. He might, in that declaration, help people to understand both his circumstances, and, perhaps, the nature of his work. This gives us some basic information and understanding.

At the symbolic and mythological levels, Yeshua seems to be aware of the fact that traditionally almost all sages, like himself, experienced the alienation that comes from a message and teaching that runs counter to normal social discourse. This puts the teaching and the teacher outside the comfort zones that are typical of conventional society. In the religious tradition of the Hebrew people, a prophetic voice put one at odds with normal religious conventions. No prophet had a "home" there any longer.

The translation here, Son of Humanity, could as easily be "Child of the Anthropos" which is typically designated as Son of Man in the Gospel tradition

At the third level, we enter the realm of wisdom itself—the realm of perennial wisdom and ***theosophia*** (divine wisdom or wisdom from Above). Yeshua sees something that perennial wisdom has known, but he adds insight that is critical to our understanding. At this level, a key term is *Son of Humanity*. In sapiential literature, the Son of Man is the ***Adam Kadmon***—the prototypical human that incorporates all of humanity into one, great organic whole. In Aramaic it is also known as the ***bar Enash*** (or the ***Anthropos*** in Greek). Yeshua, then, is speaking about himself not simply as one human person, but as a revealer and channel for archetypal humanity. The homeland of that form of humanity is **not** in time, but outside the temporal world. There is no place for that form of humanity to finally come to rest in time. Its resting place is outside of time.

In perennial wisdom teaching, time is considered to be the place (or state) of impermanence and temporality—everything is passing away. There is nowhere to rest, for rest (used metaphorically) is a state beyond impermanence. As Yeshua indicated earlier, there is *movement* and there is *rest*, and together they constitute reality in all its aspects. Yeshua is saying, then, that temporality and impermanence is not a place of ultimate *rest*. This is also, of course, a critical teaching in Buddhist tradition. Finally, at the fourth level of metaphysical or principial knowledge the meaning points to the significance of "placelessness" (or no-place) in Ultimate Reality. This aphorism signifies that the homeland of the Anthropos (the ultimate form of humanity) is outside of time and space where "place" does not exist. Yeshua rests in that no-place, or placelessness, metaphysically, which is the true ultimate residence of humanity—the realm beyond being (or place).

QUESTIONS FOR REFLECTION

1. Have you ever interpreted a simple text in this four-fold way? Give an example of another text with multiple levels of interpretation (something you remember, perhaps, from this Gospel or from a text in the canonical Gospels).

2. Which level of interpretation in the commentary is especially meaningful for you? Why do you think this is so? Reflect on what it teaches you about your own experience.

3. Have you ever had "no resting place," either literally or figuratively—you felt homeless, or rootless, or that you were a stranger in a strange, strange land (Heinlein)?

4. How do you experience the equilibrium (and the oscillation) between movement and rest? How do those conditions manifest themselves in your life?

EXERCISES AND MEDITATIONS

1. Let's imagine a mobius strip in which there is oscillation between two extremes. These may be any set of opposites that you encounter in your daily life—for example, focus on serious work as one extreme, and a focus on play and recreation as its opposite. If we said that this movement between these extremes or differences was what Yeshua meant by the term **movement**, then at the center, at a point between the oscillations there might be something called **rest**. To be at rest, then, would not necessarily mean there is no activity, but that there is a place of equilibrium, where they are in balance. Using this diagram, reflect on your inner life and your outer life and the movement between them. What is the place of "rest" in your life? Use another example to explore this "resting place." Then reflect that if rest is not to be found, in this world, then where is it? What is it?
2. Move through a day finding **rest**, not as a category of comfort or freedom from labor, but as an inner condition. What do you discover about this practice? What do you experience? Describe it for yourself. Journal it. Share it with others.
3. Read Psalm 23 using the version in the Readings for Insight. What does it teach you about the meaning of this saying? Where are the resonances with Yeshua's teaching and its various interpretations? Spend time with this Psalm in quiet and contemplative prayer.

A Mobius Strip is a surface with only one side and one boundary. If an ant were to crawl along the length of the strip it would return to its starting point having traversed every part of the strip. Make one for yourself by cutting a strip of paper, giving it a half twist and taping the ends together.

READINGS FOR INSIGHT

I

1. O God, you are my shepherd,
   nothing needful shall I lack or want
2. For in the meadows where you make me lie to rest,
   or on the paths you lead beside still waters,
3. My soul revives, refreshed again,
   to follow further the pathways of your name.
4. Even though the way that I must take leads through the deepest shadows
   I shall not fear the lurking evil there, nor death.
   Your presence is my rod and staff,
   my comfort and my guide.
5. And in those places where my foes rise up to trouble me
   you spread a table and make a feast;
   Anoint my head,
   and fill my cup to overflowing.
6. So now I know, O Lord, that all my life-long through
   your goodness and mercy flows and follows after me,
   And at the last when journey's done
   your dwelling place shall be my home forever.

—Psalm 23
Ancient Songs Sung Anew
trs. L. Bauman

II

God is pure no-thing,
concealed in now and here:
the less you reach for him,
the more he will appear.

Angelus Silesius

III

Between the conscious and the unconscious,
the mind has put up a swing:
all earth creatures, even the supernovas,
sway between these two trees,
and it never winds down.
Angels, animals, humans, insects by the millions,
also the wheeling sun and moon;
ages go by, and it goes on.
Everything is swinging: heaven, earth, water, fire,
and the secret one slowly growing a body.
Kabir saw that for fifteen seconds,
and it made him a servant for life.

—Kabir

IV

Your task? To work with all the passion of your being to acquire an inner light, so you escape and are safe from the fires of madness, illusion, and confusion that are, and always will be, the world.

—Rumi

LOGION 87

Sapiential Themes

- *Sacred psychology and soul development is at the heart of sapiential teaching concerning the soul and the body in temporal experience.*
- *In wisdom tradition, the connection of body and soul must be related to the transcendence of Spirit.*
- *Wisdom understands the inevitable suffering and pain caused when human beings substitute the higher for the lower order.*
- *There are higher and lower dependencies in an interdependent world.*

Parallel Texts

Yeshua says,

Miserable is the body that depends upon a body, and the soul that depends upon both.

FOCAL POINT

In the popular mind we are either a body and/or a soul. This is what constitutes a human being—the physical and the psychological dimensions. In either case, the issue is, on what do you depend for your life? Where do you stake your future? Where do you put your life's emphasis? Or metaphorically, perhaps, *Where do you lay your head to rest?* Where is the center point of your being? Dependence, independence, liberation, and freedom from suffering are the focus of this saying. How does one escape suffering? Conventional wisdom says we are to make a concerted effort to protect the body at all costs, and to use any physical means to keep the body safe from misery and harm. Or we are to make psychological happiness the goal of life and do everything in our power to secure it. In truth souls suffer, no matter what. Suffering is in the nature of reality here in space-time. For souls and their bodies to have only one recourse (or resource)—physical reality as a means to escape suffering becomes a double form of misery.

Links

The previous saying expresses the impermanence and temporality of the world—things change, and so there is no-where to rest. The question remains, where does one place one's head? To what does one give one's focus and attention? Where is the center? It is typical to place one's whole security on either the body or the soul. These become the focus, but again, they are not sufficient. Misery is the result of making your only "rest-point" here.

Notes

The word ***misery*** *is one that expresses pain and suffering in this world. Wretchedness is opposite the state of blessedness, and is the hardship or calamity that human beings experience when their security rests in impermanent structures.*

COMMENTARY

If your focus is upon the body alone, then health and wealth and physical comfort become paramount. How to pleasure the body and to keep it healthy and strong is life's primary task. There is nothing better to be done in life than to make sure that the body's needs are well taken care of. Living revolves around exercise and play, proper feeding, and keeping any weaknesses and discomforts at bay. If, on the other hand, the soul is emphasized above all else and becomes the focus of one's life, then to be happy, powerful, in-control, to be seen as competent and successful, and to enjoy a rich inner life of experience is the goal. To enjoy life is to have rich experiences, and to be able to engage mentally and socially with others, to enter the world of culture, the fine arts, science, and technology, and to be as competent as possible in all those realms.

In some combination unique perhaps only to ourselves, these do become the center of human existence for most everyone on earth. In large measure this is what defines who we are, our interests, and the trajectory of our life-path. If you find your center in the body and/or in the soul—then life is defined by these dimensions almost entirely.

This is not to say that most individuals do not have some taste of or longing for that which transcends these two fundamental domains, but that the latter takes up the work of their lives almost entirely. Yeshua, however, calls that condition miserable. One has fallen, perhaps, below the actual greatness of what it means to be fully human. One has aimed too low. In the end, only misery accompanies that limitation—it does not deliver ultimate value, worth, or profit (if one can even speak in these terms).

So what is life, and what is a human being? Are we just body and soul, or are we more? Obviously Yeshua believes we are, and thus we are introduced to the transcendent realm of Spirit and to the vertical axis of consciousness and being. He points away from our exclusive attachment to the horizontal axis and the human constructions of the civilized world that we imagine to be ultimate.

A human being is a physio-psycho-spiritual complexity. Body, soul **and** spirit, make up the full compliment of human being and consciousness. Only when we attend to these in balance or in some kind of equilibrium will we know bliss—misery's opposite (or as he names it **blessedness**, ***makarios***).

Blessedness, not misery, is to be the ultimate state of humankind. But that condition cannot be found or achieved through attention to the body or the soul alone, as important as these may be to us. In this text and in his wisdom teaching, Yeshua offers us another way, a path of inclusion that involves all the dimensions of one's being, and full access to the domains of reality that we have described as both horizontal and vertical.

When "dependency" (or perhaps in this case co-dependency) upon one or the other or both of the first two (body and soul) sets in, then we have restricted our possibilities and limited our future becoming. We were made for more, for far more. This is what Yeshua knows and understands. It is his desire to lead us on a path beyond these. It is his pathway forward (through his teaching and its practice) that will bring us to the fullness of being that can be described as a "true human being" in a state of blessedness.

QUESTIONS FOR REFLECTION

1. Have either your body or your soul let you down? Have you ever been miserable because of over-dependence on either one or both?

2. When does the body fail you? How? Has the personality structure of your soul ever failed you?

3. How is it possible to be overly dependent upon the soul? What does that mean?

4. In your life has there ever been a time when you have transcended both the physical realm and the psychological realm and entered another domain (the domain of spirit) entirely?

5. Describe this other domain? How do you maintain contact with it?

EXERCISES AND MEDITATIONS

1. There is nothing wrong, of course, with having a healthy body and a well-balanced soul. They are essential to life here in space and time. Think about how much time you spend maintaining these—keeping them in balance. Make a list of the ways you do that. Now think about what lies beyond both body and soul. Think about how you create a sense of the Spirit's importance in your life. Compare the time you spend on maintaining spiritual health in contrast to physical and psychological well-being. How are these related? Take an inventory of your daily life and see how much time goes into each category. Do you want to change the equation somehow? What would you change? Talk this over with a close friend, or with a group that is studying this material with you.
2. Have you ever taken a break from the physical and the psychological demands, and given yourself a kind of "holiday" (holy day) in a realm outside these? Going on retreat is one way to do this. Can you think of other ways to accomplish this kind of break for yourself? Give yourself a retreat. A retreat can be several hours (even one). Take a day or several days, or if you can manage it, a week or more. Plan so that you feel entirely free. Go away from your normal surroundings. Find a quiet place. Change your dependence on the physical and the psychological dimensions—though you still want to maintain health.
3. One important practice related to all of this is fasting. We immediately think of food fasts, but there are many more forms (from the media, from sound, from constant talking). Experiment with one of these for a day. What are the results? What changes for you?

READINGS FOR INSIGHT

I

One of the first fruits of a solitary life is the sharp awareness that what I assumed to be "me" is not singular. Being alone is like living in a large family that is never quite at peace with itself. It is just like some of the dreams we have, peopled with all kinds of characters, more than we can count, and each with their own personalities, playing out their dream roles. One is wise, another foolish; one is compassionate, and another vicious and dangerous; one compliant and happy and carefree, while others are vulnerable, wounded, or depressed. Our inner family, what we call ourselves, is made up of opposites that aren't quite at ease together.

Gregory Mayers
Listen to the Desert
10

II

Today I feel trapped,
tightly bound
in the cage of existence.
I need the scent of you—
beyond Being
to set me free.
Just for a moment
lend me the polish of your grace
to scour the rust of being
from the mirror
of my true Reality.

—Shihab al-Din Yahya Suhrawardi

III

Abba Sisoes the Theban said to his disciple: Tell me what you see in me and in turn I will tell you what I see in you. His disciple said to him: You are good in soul, but a little harsh. The old man said to him: You are good but your soul is not tough.

—Y. Nomura
Desert Wisdom
97

IV

Within your nature lives
every element,
so listen to Wisdom's voice.
You are demon
and wild beast
Angel and human—
Whatever you cultivate
that you will become.

—Baba Afdal Kashani

V

Pain pushes you, sometimes gently, sometimes forcefully, but always in the direction of healing and growth.

—Amy Dean

LOGION 88

Yeshua says,

The angels and the prophets will Come and bring you what already belongs to you, and you will give to them what you have to give.

But ask yourself this: When may they come and receive back from you what already belongs to them?

Sapiential Themes

- *Sapiential cosmology, ancient and traditional, is complex and full of promise for the seeker.*
- *Human beings are linked and webbed to higher orders of reality and the intelligences that inhabit them.*
- *There is reciprocal exchange (or feeding) between realms and the beings within those realms.*
- *The communion (or community) of the saints is real. Without we are impoverished.*

Parallel Texts

Thomas 31, 50
Matthew 13:17, 41
Luke 10:24, 12:20
John 1:51

FOCAL POINT

It is in the western psyche to believe that "Every man is an island," and that on this "island" we are left to fend for ourselves—for no one else will do it for us. This fierce streak of independence, while admirable in some ways, leads inevitably to isolation and alienation from the web of interconnectedness which holds all things in being. In the end, rigid self-dependence, is not a stance of truth, but simply the mirror of an egoic mind. Traditional cosmology says that there is a great hierarchy of transcendental beings, inhabited by angels and prophets who play a significant and crucial role, especially for the welfare of human beings in temporal existence. Here on earth we are not without our interlocutors. The question is, what is the reason and role for these interactions within the divine hierarchy? What is the purpose for being in relationship to these beings who inhabit the hierarchy? As this saying suggests, there is something both to be received and, eventually, to be given back. The exchange is momentous for both sides.

Links

If dependency upon lower levels of being in oneself and in the world around us creates misery, then dependence and reliance upon higher orders of reality and the vast community of spirit (beings and entities) which surrounds us is a source of deep satisfaction. It is the essential blessing with which we are imbued. It is the community to which we turn to find both solace and rest.

Notes

*The word **Angel** simply means messenger (or message bearer) between realms and beings. These beings both carry and are the message sent. Prophets are likewise messengers of the proclamation, and often the spokespersons for angelic proclamations. Their role is as a mouth-piece to make the message heard in ways that can be received by the ordinary person unable to hear.*

COMMENTARY

According to traditional wisdom, we belong to a cosmic community of many dimensions, full of intelligence at every level. Not only is the universe alive with Presence, it is radically responsive to everything within it, including ourselves. Each human being is a focus for the beneficent forces of Good which seek to shape the whole universe into a greater reality in its evolutionary trajectory.

There are midwives of Spirit everywhere—Awakened Ones who shepherd and guard our becoming. Among them are Angels and the Prophets who have come before us, as well as saints, sages, poets and visionaries. They gather to guide us on our way forward. They minister to our needs and so there is nurture, care, and feeding provided for us. But the great mystery is that it is reciprocal. Reciprocal feeding is a hidden truth held perhaps in secret until we are ready to know it, or equipped to act for the good of heaven and earth.

The angel (our guardian angel in particular) comes to feed us, and we are nourished. The prophets come to light the way and we awaken and begin following one particular "light" that has chosen us. And so the journey and the transformation begins—but then, a new and surprising question arises out of this cosmological clarity. When may our guides (our angel and the prophets we follow) come to us and claim what actually belongs to them? When may we feed them as we have been fed and give back new food which will gift the universe with those unique provisions that have emerged out of the treasury of our own wisdom and the alchemy of our own becoming? Like bees, we have to gather honey for the good and nourishment of the whole. When will we be ready to selflessly serve the universe?

It is easy to imagine ourselves to always be on the receiving end of the divine grace. If we are to grow, the divine comes to offer us the beneficence that is necessary from infancy into maturity. But as with our own children, we do not assume that the years of selfless labor which are the gift that a parent makes to his or her child are all there is. In the end, what the parent wants is the gift of reciprocity—a relationship that is mutual and in some sense the appearance of a whole new kind of bond between peers (even equals). We do not imagine having that relationship as children, but when it comes, there is something transcendent about it—something unspeakably strong and good. Can we imagine that heaven wants that as well? Are we able to see that from the parenting that once the gift has been given, the moment of exchange will come and new gifts are given and received? Is it possible to imagine that heaven is diminished without the gift that we have to bring?

None of these thoughts may ever have occurred to us. We have been so busy on the receiving end of the equation, we have never wondered what we had to offer that is lasting and eternal. Yeshua introduces a whole new dynamic to the issue of our destiny and the purpose in the universe. There has been exchange all along, as the saying suggests, but then something happens and the exchange is elevated to an adult responsibility that puts us, perhaps, on par with the prophets and the angels. Have we ever imagined such a status? Yeshua suggests that it is not only possible, but that we possess something that, in the end, we don't own, but must give away . Perhaps it is borrowed, or perhaps we have simply been custodians, or perhaps we created something that is not "ours" in the first place—it belongs to all, and so the angels and prophets take from us and give it away in a universal exchange for which they have been the merchants all along.

QUESTIONS FOR REFLECTION

1. This saying presents the modern mind with myriad challenges to our common perceptions. We basically have lived in a "flat-earth" universe that sees it as devoid of life—but is that so? How does this saying challenge your current worldview and cosmology?

The "flat-earth" point of view collapses multiple dimensions into a single uni-dimensional view.

2. Are you ready to accept your responsibility toward the wider world of multiple beings and intelligences which both guide and require something from you?

3. Have you ever pondered what it is that you, perhaps uniquely, have to give to the universe of intelligent beings? What would that be?

4. What is your relationship to angels and to prophets? Could you name any that you are particularly attached to? What are your relationships are?

EXERCISES AND MEDITATIONS

1. The doctrine of the Twin concerns many things, but among them is the possibility that you yourself are twinned to a higher-order being that has traditionally been called your "guardian angel." It is the archetypal form of your higher Self which exists as a part of yourself, but in a dimension transcendent to this one. Now imagine that this Angel both gives you guidance, and can also receive from you. Imagine that you are not alone; that you have been guided all along your pilgrimage in time by this being, quietly, unobtrusively, but effectively. In a period of reflection seek to establish contact with your Angel-archetype. What do you discover? Journal your experience. If you wanted a more specific understanding of what that relationship is, and what you have to give and receive, what would you ask from the Angel?
2. Images (icons) of Angels abound in the Christian tradition, and in other of the world's faiths. Some of these (especially in the West) are of the quality of cupids and valentines—but others are substantial and deeply authentic. Do a search on the Internet for images of Angels in the various traditions. Look specifically at Greek and Russian icons. Find one that stands out to you. If possible, print an image and use it as a focus of meditation.
3. Prophetic guidance is offered us as well. Broadly speaking, in the Abrahamic faiths, Moses is the prophet of Judaism, Jesus is the prophet of Christianity, and Muhammad is the prophet of Islam. Getting to know these prophets is one of the privileges of belonging to any of the branches of the Abrahamic traditions. You might take it as your task to find a relationship with each of these prophets.

Seeing the meaning and significance of each of the Prophets from the perspective of that faith tradition is very important. A sympathetic reading of each prophetic tradition is essential if we are to be on "speaking terms" with a particular Prophet and the tradition.

READINGS FOR INSIGHT

I

Tom Cheetham
The World Truned Inside Out
85

This limitless cosmos is full of Presences, full of Persons—full of Angels. We have to discard all our trivialized and anthropocentric conceptions of the nature of such beings. They are personified metaphysical presences, the movers of worlds, and they provide the connection between ourselves and divinity. There is no question of anthropomorphism. The personality of these beings is not derived from ours; ours is only a dim reflection of theirs. The charge of anthropomorphism has a certain force while the world is "wrong side out." But it is only by turning the world right side out again that we can see this.

II

Jalaluddin Rumi

Let go this world that you may become sovereign of all worlds.
Toss away your handfuls of sugar and become a whole cane field.
Leap like a flame toward the sky.
Scatter the dark spirits and become a pillar of heaven,
so that when Noah sails forth upon the flooding waters
you may be his ark.
When Moses goes forth as a shepherd before the people,
you will be his staff.
When the Prophets ascend into the heavens,
you may be their chariot.
When Jesus walks among the weary souls of earth
you will be his healing breath.

III

Henry Corbin
Avicanna
20-22

[T]he idea of the integration of the *ego* with its Self becomes the recital of an Event that … is real to the highest degree. … The Self … is, "in person," the heavenly counterpart of a pair or a syzygy made up of a fallen angel, or an angel appointed to govern a body, and of an angel retaining his abode in heaven. … [This syzygy] individualizes the Holy Spirit into an individual Spirit, who is the celestial *paredros* of human being, its guardian angel, guide and companion, helper and savior.

IV

Gulzar Isfahani

Any heart who resides in the Beloved's alleyway
Becomes a confidant in the great Court of Secrets.
So polish off the alien rust from the heart's mirror;
Only then will it deserve to receive the splendor of the Friend's face.

V

Martin Lings
Symbol and Archetype
47-48

… all those who pass through the gates of Heaven incur thereby a tremendous responsibility; it is henceforth the function of each to be, himself or herself, an integral feature of the celestial Garden, a source of felicity for all the other inmates, a vehicle of the Divine Presence.

LOGION 89

Sapiential Themes

- *Emphasis upon the interior state of the soul is at the heart of the wisdom tradition.*
- *Exoteric faith and exoteric reality are two aspects of the larger vessel of religion.*
- *Yeshua reestablishes the core values of an interiorized Judaism which was lost in the details of external observance.*
- *Remembrance of the Creator of all inner and outer forms is the practice that maintains the balance.*

Yeshua says,

For what reason would you only wash the outside of a cup?
Do you not realize that the creator of the outside is the one who made the inside as well?

Parallel Texts

Thomas 22
Matthew 5:8, 6:22-23, 23:25-28
Luke 11:39-41

FOCAL POINT

The practices of ritual purity in Jewish law are central to the understanding of this saying. In the exoteric religious practice of first century Judaism, priority was often given to the correct performance of rites related to purity laws—what was clean and unclean. Individuals focused on the fulfillment of external forms. Yeshua reverses this emphasis. Central to his message is an interiority that moved attention from the outside to the inside, from the exoteric to the esoteric. This is often called "interiorized Judaism." Yeshua was always concerned about the inside of things. Fastidious focus on the proper care and cleaning of the outside (as was obsessively done by some proponents of the external law) missed the inner dimension of that same Law—the inner Torah of the heart that had been the central concern of the prophets and in the earlier wisdom tradition.

Links

The transition from the cosmic vision of the last saying to this one puts the locus where it belongs. It is not on the outside, at the public level, that the angels and the prophets interact with us, but on the inside (of the cup) where we live, where consciousness resides. If that interior place is not clear and empty, then no exchange can be made.

Notes

*The word **realize** that is used here is not the common word for know, but a term that has to do with awareness through the **nous**—the interior Intellect, or Eye of the Heart. To come to know something there must be a deep form of knowing beyond mere belief or attachment to external religious observance.*

COMMENTARY

The turn toward the interior state of an individual as the key to spiritual practice began well before Jesus. One can see evidence of that in the Psalms and the Prophets, but a sharp turn took place with the advent of Alexander the Great, who conquered Palestine 200 years before Christ. This shock pushed many Jews toward a deeper interiority, which Yeshua continues and deepens in his own life and practice. The term "interiorized Judaism" simply refers to its most esoteric aspects.

Yeshua knew that spirituality based upon adherence to external form alone is fruitless. He knew that purity defined simply in terms of the rules of ritual behavior, applying cleanliness only to the external world, in the end, creates a deeper impurity. He was aware that exoteric religion finally fails us because it cannot address the core values of the soul, and only rearranges surface structures and social customs. Yeshua's wisdom urges humanity inward, toward the interior. In the world of his own day he proclaimed a religion we might call today "interiorized Judaism."

It is in this Logion, perhaps, that we come closest to the core value of Yeshua's teaching: purity of heart. The religious establishment of his day stressed purity on the outside—in external behavior. The purity codes of his religious tradition put strict conformity to the exoteric practices at the center of religious life. Yeshua reverses it. It was not the outside which needed attention most. It was the inside. This is the basis for Yeshua's "interiorized Judaism" which returned religion and practice to a spirituality that made one's inner relationship to the divine Reality the key. Everything else was secondary. Who could dispute the simple culinary practice that it was the cleanness on the inside of the vessel that was most important in any kitchen?

Rules about what was pure and impure, especially in regards to clean and unclean foods, have dominated Jewish thought from earliest times. Yeshua clearly followed custom and was an observant Jew, but he also distinguished external purity from the more critical inner purity of heart. This made his teaching a challenge for much of religious authority.

In Yeshua's day washing and cleanliness were central to the purity codes of his religious community. It was customary that an individual observe the conventional requirements that kept strict observance regarding cleanliness and separation from what was commonly understood to be unclean. What one was on the inside was not as important as what one did to conform to those rules and laws. But Yeshua overturns the order of importance. He changes the focus from the outside to the inside. Washing and cleanliness are at the center of every working kitchen, and in a kitchen one would, of course, never simply clean the outside of a vessel. For practical use it is the inside which is far more critical. To state the principle broadly, Yeshua is practicing "interiorized Judaism." He shifts religious tradition from its blind adherence to exoteric practice to its central core—its inner values.

We make many assumptions because of our typical perspective on the outside of things. We assume that the objective observations we make on the external world are the best and most that can be said. When we do, however, we forget many things. The surface structure of something may be entirely different from its inner form—in fact they may hide the inner reality completely. There is often far more going on below the surface than we might imagine. It is to the interiority that we must turn and it is that which has the attention of the Creator of both realities—outer and inner.

Interiorized Judaism is not so much a religious or metaphysical doctrine as it is a stance toward life—in particular the life of spirit within one's self. It is not so much what one does or even thinks, but more fundamentally what one is. Interiorized Judaism is the gift of an open-emptiness to the Spirit and the waters of life to fill the cup. What one offers back to the world depends deeply on that gift received there, remembering that the Source of the water of life is both the Maker of the cup and the Giver of life. Yeshua's great summation of the Torah was an expression of love for God and one's neighbor, and clearly love is an inner condition reflected in external action. In order for the cup to receive the water of life, it must be empty and clean, and in order to offer the same water to others (one's neighbor) in this parched land—the cup must be free from the impurities that would contaminate the gift.

QUESTIONS FOR REFLECTION

1. What is your experience of exoteric religion? How is that different from a tradition of spirituality (or from mystical experience)?

2. Congruence between the inner and the outer is essential to a well-balanced life, and certainly for spiritual life in particular. When have you experienced being out-of-balance? What is your experience of equilibrium between the two?

3. If you were to define religion as the balance between the exoteric and the esoteric (and if you are a practicing Christian, for example), how would you describe interiorized Christianity? (Or, you might want to use another religious tradition).

4. This saying looks for a deep form of knowing as opposed to ritual or conventional beliefs. What would you say you know deeply, from being on the inside of things?

EXERCISES AND MEDITATIONS

1. The whole force of Yeshua's work was to drive his students to the interiority of the heart. To focus only on the performance of correct ritual behavior on the outside is to miss everything—for it is not on the outside (but the inside) that real relationship with the divine Presence begins. In this inner chamber one encounters the Presence of God in a state of intimacy. Every person has such a place and can know the same intimacy that Yeshua knew with the One he called ***Abba***. Leave your external focus for awhile and in a time of inner reflection come to know this place. Find your way to the level of the heart. Begin an inner conversation there between your soul and the Heart of God that you were always meant to have. Begin by finding a place of quiet. Sit or kneel quietly there. Then leave the outer world of your personal concerns and journey inward. Go to the "cave of your own heart" and rest there. Attend to the divine Presence that is already awaiting you there.
2. If we think of purity in terms of clarity and not simply as a state of uncontamination, then we might better understand Yeshua's statement about purity of heart. He may not be speaking as much about purification as he is clarification. If knowing your true Self is such an important part of wisdom's teaching about clarity (purity of vision), then the clearing away of what occludes your inner seeing is critical. What is clarity of heart in your experience? How do you polish the mirror of the heart for this kind of seeing? As an exercise in intuitive cognition, while in a conversation with someone, avoid using your sensory or analytical capacities exclusively. Use instead something deeper inside yourself to give you insight and clarity. What do you find when you do this?

When Yeshua says, "do you not realize," he brings realization in as a part of the underlying meaning of this saying. Remembrance, remembering, awakening from the slumber of forgetfulness—these are the practices of interior realization. Yeshua is instructing his students in such practices. Behind the aphorism, then, is a way of life, the path of inner realization.

READINGS FOR INSIGHT

I

Jalaluddin Rumi

Friend calls friend to the secret cave.

II

How is ... Spirit to be found? If it is everywhere, it should not be too difficult to find. But where is it most concentrated? Firstly, the Spirit is most concentrated in the human heart, when the human turns toward it and realizes it within. By turning toward our own [inner] experience, by cultivating a vigilance regarding our own [inner] states, we can come to know ourselves and therefore know the Spirit we reflect.

... we are reflectors of this greater Spirit. All intelligence, all beauty, all strength, all compassion, all forgiveness, all patience, and all trust are gifts, and attributes of this Spirit. As the awareness of our connection with Spirit increases, these attributes are reflected more perfectly through us. To the extent that we polish the mirror of the heart, we become reflective and bright. We become lovers of this pure Spirit.

Kabir Helminski
Living Presence
14

III

Within this body
are enchanted fields and woods,
the seven seas and innumerable stars.
Within this body
are the touchstone and the jeweler.
Within this body
the Eternal keeps singing
and its spring goes on and on flowing.
Kabir says, "Listen, my friend, listen—
my beloved Lord is within."

Kabir
Perfume in the Desert
46

IV

"Life" means a kind of seething in which a thing ferments and first pours itself into itself, and all that it is into all that it is, before spilling over and pouring itself outside.

Meishter Eckhart
Maria Jaoudi
Christian Myasticism East and West
8

V

The gateway to the spiritual path is you. Look inside if you want to find the wisdom to grow. Everything you need is waiting for you. As you truly become yourself you become less conscious of yourself. You simply are who you are. All of the great conversions in history have meant simply a person discovering his own nature. Behind the self-centered brat is a divine flame. It may take many years of the flame to be liberated, but it is there. No matter how hard it is to accept, you must understand that the only difference between you and any religious person you admire is that your hero has discovered his own nature. Many may die without knowing about this treasure within them. Most discover it only a few hours or days before their last breath. Some do it much earlier.

Brother Tolbert McCarrol
Notes from the Song of Life
35-36

LOGION 90

Yeshua says,

Come to me for justice is my yoke,
and gentleness my rule,
and you will discover
the state of rest.

FOCAL POINT

This aphorism, similar to one repeated in the Gospel of Matthew, is expressed as an invitation to a way of life and a relationship with the Master that requires attention and responsibility. Here Yeshua is both offering an inner state (the discovery of his inner state), but also the means by which it is realized. At the heart of the invitation is the acceptance of a yoke and a rule. Translated in this way, other aspects of the traditional understanding from the canonical texts emerge. Through this Coptic version one has access to levels of insight that have heretofore, perhaps, been unavailable.

Sapiential Themes

- *The relationship between the Teacher and the student, the Master of Wisdom and the seeker of wisdom, is a crucial one in the transmission of wisdom.*
- *Yeshua is offering humanity a way into the interiority of the Kingdom and its divine life, which is at odds with the world's way of being.*
- *Justice, gentleness, and rest are qualities of heaven, not often found on earth, but can be known in the intimacy of the relationship to which Yeshua invites us.*

Links

What is the experience of the "inside of the cup" that Yeshua has expressed in the previous logion? Why must there be clarity? What kind of clearness is he talking about? This appears to be a hermeneutical link between these two sayings and continues the theme of interiority and, now, intimacy established between Master and student.

Parallel Texts

Thomas 2, 50, 51, 60
Sirach 51: 26-27
Isaiah 42:3
Matthew 5:5, 11:25-30
I Peter 4:14
Revelation 6:11, 14:13

Notes

The many terms related to the authority of the Master typically translated as "Lordship" imply something quite different from the qualities that Yeshua is describing here. If his authority is gentle and free from coercion, then exercise of his authority is not a "Lordship" at all, but one that describes perhaps a yoke of equality.

COMMENTARY

If we imagine that to make a link of discipleship with the Master of Wisdom is to become harnessed to a yoke where Master and student pull together, then that relationship need not be an undue burden, or make the relationship one of inequality. It does mean, however, that the student must step out of the margins and come to the center of the work itself. Likewise, if we allow the Master to act as Master (if we allow his "Lordship" to have authority in our lives), we must understand that he is speaking about the quality and kind of authority he has in one's life and how it is exercised. His students had clearly come under some form of education and discipline in which he played the central role of teacher. Here Yeshua expresses his way of exercising that form of authority.

The relationship between a Master and a student is key in the transmission of traditional wisdom. Was Yeshua a guru-like figure, or was he collaborative? This saying suggests the latter as does his interaction with Thomas in Logion 13.

The word justice (or fairness) forms the root of the word righteousness, and one must note that righteousness is a relationship of right-relatedness to something. To be in right relationship to things is, in the end, the yoke or bond of justice. We are bound to earth, one another, and to God in such a way that there must be fairness and equanimity, or the bond is one of imbalance and disparity which advantages one party and disadvantages the other. But Yeshua offers the bond of mutual beneficence—a relationship of reciprocal caring in which whatever authority he may hold (whatever laws or principles may apply), they are applied with gentleness and without coercion or force. This is a voluntary relationship of moral courage that exists in a state of rest.

So much of this Gospel has as its backdrop the images of early Genesis in the Garden of Eden, and the state and human condition described there.

The word rest has appeared before (Logia 2, 50, 51, 60), and in each case it points back to the creation Sabbath when the work had been finished, and now all things alive were in an Edenic state of perfect balance and mutual benefit to all within the whole. This state existed in the past, and it will again be the state of humanity in the future—all things are leading to the restoration of what has been lost. Is this state to be found in time? Or does it exist outside of time? We could say, perhaps, that both are true. For if we follow the sapiential direction of the sayings, we discover that the previous saying point toward the interior state known and lived by Yeshua as the place of rest. And now he is offering us a drink from that same cup.

But once again, that interior state is not imposed from without. It is to be discovered within oneself in right-relationship to all and with gentleness toward everything. This is a very different way of being in the world from what we find in conventional society where the opposite is so often the rule. Injustice, cruelty, prejudice and ruthlessness are more typically the mode by which authority is exercised, leaving the world in turmoil, not in peace or rest.

The nature of the Kingdom of God is entirely different. The rules and principles that apply to the state of Eden are a way of being that has been absent from human society far too long. In order to access that world, and for that reality to come to "earth as it is in heaven," something must change, not simply in the way external authority is exercised, but in the state of our own interior experience ("inside the cup"). If, as Yeshua has said in the previous saying, the interior of the vessel must be pure or clear (free from the contamination of normal human attitudes) in order to receive what he has to offer, then from this saying we know why. The qualities of the Kingdom do not mix easily with the conventions of earth. Also if we try to impose the conventions of earth on the qualities of heaven, the contamination from the one to the other becomes apparent—the life-giving waters are muddied and no interior rest can be found.

QUESTIONS FOR REFLECTION

1. Of the teachers who have had most impact upon you and the unfolding of your life, what was it about the manner in which those teachers or mentors exercised authority that affected you the most? What were those crucial qualities or characteristics used by or resident within your mentors? Is your experience congruent with anything that is being taught in this logion?

2. How is gentleness a factor in human affairs? How often do you experience it in the public arena? When you do, what is the effect?

3. Right-relationship to things is essential in the human community. Without it we live in an unjust society of disequilibrium and chaos. Describe how you know you have established a right-relationship. Describe when you have not and the consequences.

4. How yoked are you to the work of the Master, Yeshua?

EXERCISES AND MEDITATIONS

1. Gentleness and loving-kindness are aspects of a single movement toward the world and the people around us. In the prophecies of Isaiah, it says that when the Messiah comes he will not break a bruised reed or snuff out a smoldering candle. These are images of gentleness and a stance toward the world which is tender in the face of a culture of ferocious violence in the first-century world. Cultivating this inner attitude is something that we can practice in any historical context. Rabbi Rami Shapiro calls it the practice of an art form. Imagine that in your daily life it takes practice to shift into this perspective and attitude. It takes deliberate attention and intention. There are many ways to respond to life's challenges, and choosing to respond with gentleness and with loving care means that we must be strategic in regards to ourselves, and in relationship to others. Pick a situation you know that demands this. What is your strategic plan of action?
2. The question concerning who is your Master of Wisdom is crucial to the processes of learning and practice. If you do not have an inner/outer teacher of any sort, or a traditional wisdom path, then at this point it might be good to begin to settle that issue.
3. Being yoked to the spiritual authority of an inner teacher seems to be the crucial. If Yeshua is to be your inner teacher (by invitation and choice), then it is important to establish that relationship in the inner chamber of your own heart. To do so you need to consciously go there and listen in silence. Don't go with a set of pre-determined expectations. Enter it with openness. After a period of quiet adjustment, let go of your thinking processes as much as possible. Wait quietly for 20 minutes. Read a short text of his teaching. Continue to listen.

Isaiah 42:3

Rami M Shapiro
The Sacred Art of Lovingkindness
Skylight Paths (2006)

READINGS FOR INSIGHT

I

Norvene Vest
"Ear of the Heart"
The Inner Journey
133

There is no more precious thing in the world than each individual soul, created by God and called forth into wholeness of being without which the universe is somehow diminished. ... The seeker has heard the call to be received into God's very life and has accepted it as a promise. Based on a trust in this invitation to relationship, a hope arises for fullness of life. In that hope, a commitment is made.

II

Rabbi Rami Shapiro
The Sacred Art of Lovingkindness

We express kindness through right speech. The Baal Shem Tov, the founder of Hasidim, taught that each of us is born with a fixed number of words to speak and when we have spoken the last of our quota, we die. Before uttering words of condemnation, frustration, or gossip, we should question whether they are worth dying for.

III

Jalauddin Rumi
Mathnaw I
2195-98

Help me with this ego of mine
that is seeking help from You;
I seek justice from no one
but this justice-seeking self.
I shall not get justice from anyone
except Him who is nearer to me than myself;
for this I-ness comes moment by moment from Him.

IV

Andrew Harvey
Perfume of the Desert
33

As the seeker deepens her experience of the nature of God and of the soul, an astounding secret starts to derange her—she realizes that what she has read in the great mystical books of every tradition is not poetry, or enthusiastic exaggeration, but a literal, and all-shattering truth: that she and the Beloved are not separate, but one and that the One she is looking for is also looking for her. This inner secret of identity with the Absolute has many sides to it, and slowly, miraculously, each one of these sides is lit up for the seeker, in the light of the heart, until she realizes, with a certainty beyond "faith" or any possible formulation in words, that the entire creation is one with the Creator, that everything is held together by the force of love, that every atom is drunk on this love, and that the universe that before seemed so orderly is in fact always reeling in drunken, ecstatic dance. She comes to know what Shabistari means when he says, "Under the veil of every atom is hidden the ravishing face of the Beauty of the Beloved!"

As the implications of this secret start to expand in the seeker's heart and mind—through a constant practice of prayer, meditation, and service and through revelation after revelation—the seeker's own passion for the quest grows more and more ardent.

V

Proverbs 11:17

Your own soul is nourished when you are kind,
but you destroy yourself when you are cruel.

LOGION 91

Sapiential Themes

- *Beliefs in or about a person are not the core of the wisdom tradition. The practice of Presence is.*
- *Wisdom teaching turns human attention from outer affairs to affairs of the heart and inner attention.*
- *According to Thomas, inner attention and affairs of the heart (as a sacred practice in the present moment), are rooted in the teachings of Yeshua.*

They said to him,

"Tell us who you
really are so we
may believe in you."

He said to them,
"You have learned to read
the face of earth and sky,
but you do not yet recognize
the one standing in your presence,
nor can you make sense of
the present moment."

Parallel Texts

Thomas 5, 13, 24, 61
John 1:23, 4:46-48
Acts 3:19
Ephesians 1:10, 5:16
I Timothy 2:19, 5:1
II Timothy 1:9, 2:6
Jude 24
Revelation 14:10

Links

Yeshua offers an invitation in the last saying, which prompts an immediate response in some. The exchanges in this saying appear to be the result of the questions Yeshua's invitation raised. He must move them, however, from simple questioning to a deeper reflection on their inner awareness and the ability to attend.

FOCAL POINT

In our world (and in the world of conventional religion), emphasis is given to correct belief. Early in the historical unfolding of the Christian tradition, the question posed to Yeshua was, "Who are you?" The question was answered in later Christianity by statements of beliefs "about him." These became litmus tests for true orthodoxy. Yeshua's own answer to this same question, however, was entirely different. He turned it from a "reading of the outer forms or signs of religious orthodoxy" (which perhaps they were looking for as a confirmation before they were ready to believe him) to an inner experience (or realization) of Presence in the present moment. Beliefs without Presence are of little consequence. The practice of Presence, and not belief, is the principle work and appears to be at the heart of Yeshua's own experience.

Notes

*A contrast is made between **read** and **recognize** (or know). The first is an interpretation, the second is a form of direct knowledge. The important word used for the **present moment** is **kairos**, which is understood to be the "right time" for something to happen. Knowing it is a form of discernment.*

COMMENTARY

When one is offered an invitation in a relationship by anyone it is cause, perhaps, to question both the motives and the character of the person who is asking. One might wonder—who are you really, before I accept? Who are you that can offer such an invitation in the first place? And is this real or is it a fantasy of your own mind? How are we to believe you? Can we trust you?

Yeshua's answer is not some further explanation or justification for such belief. It is a declarative statement offering an observation about those who are questioning him. By the way he speaks, one might infer that questions about his identity were also about his integrity (or authenticity). There was perhaps an implied critique. Yeshua's response goes to the heart of the inner state of those who questioned him and do not already know the answer.

Weather patterns on the "face of the sky" are, of course weather reports—the subject of much ordinary human discussion. We devote whole segments of our daily news to a determination of the outcome of those patterns. Some patterns can be read easily. Some are entirely enigmatic to us and unfold contrary to our expectations.

To clarify this teaching it would be of benefit to familiarize yourself with Brother Lawrence's ***Practicing the Presence of God****, and Eckhart Tolle's* ***The Power of Now****.*

Yeshua's "face" apparently is not a pattern that can easily be read. They see an outer countenance or images, perhaps, and they make a judgment and determination, but they have missed something—the "one standing in that presence" (the presence behind the face). That is the "one" they do not recognize. Again, it is an inner recognition of something that has been obscured by external forms and they have missed it. They know the outer form, but they do not yet know who or what inner presence stands behind the outer form of Yeshua. Why? The answer goes to the heart of something vital. It has to do with the practice of Presence in the present moment—the Now. They do not know this practice and so they cannot recognize what is really going on.

They are not yet ready for a right-relationship to him because they are not living in the present moment—they are reading the signs of future weather patterns, but are unable to attend to what is in the here and now. They cannot know him in any other way but at the surface level—they cannot determine who he is inwardly because they are fixated on ever-changing exterior patterns.

This introduces us, once again, to the teaching of knowledge-by-presence. If one reads a biography about a person, or even better, an autobiography—one gets to know something about another individual. It is a fair level of knowledge, but only when one comes into the presence of someone and attends (or gives focused attention that person) can there be a true knowing of the individual by personal experience. This appears to be what Yeshua is talking about. Reading only the horizons of history, or the face of the external sky, rather than attending to what is in the present moment and the Presence who inhabits it, is an inferior form of knowing.

Yeshua is leading his students into a deeper form of knowing, a knowledge by presence that can only be practiced in the present moment. Thus, this teaching is not about knowledge per se, but about ***praxis***—the spiritual exercise that has been traditionally known as the "practice of the Presence of God." This practice is often sustained through remembrance or invocation in the Abrahamic traditions. This Logion is one example of the roots of this wisdom in the teachings of Yeshua.

QUESTIONS FOR REFLECTION

1. Have you ever received an invitation to join a spiritual community led by a teacher or listened to a teaching? Have you ever questioned such an invitation or teacher? What was your motivation?

2. If you were Yeshua, how would you answer the question that is raised in this logion?

3. Talking about the weather is a common human occupation. Why do we do that? Does it hide or detract from some other observation in some way?

4. When you get to know a person who was once a stranger or an acquaintance more intimately, what does a person's presence have to do with that change in relationship?

EXERCISES AND MEDITATIONS

1. This Logion indicates that it is common for spiritual seekers to have questions about a teacher or a teaching and to raise them. How these questions get answered is, of course, another matter. The answers are determined perhaps as much by the reflective depth of the questioner as by the one who answers. Imagine that at this very moment you have questions you would like to ask the Master of Wisdom. What would they be? This is an important exercise, and it is equally important to wait and listen for answers. Remember, pay attention! Answers might come from any direction, some of them very unexpected.
2. As is often the case, Yeshua turns his students from intellectual questions (or those that are mere curiosity) to focus upon the inner life and spiritual practice of the one who raises the question. He makes an observation that suggests most people pay little attention to anything deeper than the surface of things. They are so busy paying attention to surface detail that they cannot (or do not) recognize the inner dimensions. Yeshua is calling for an act of attention. He is also rooting attention in being aware of the present moment as an act of conscious attention. As you move through a day notice when your attention is in the present moment and when it has wandered away and you are not truly attending to what is in that moment.
3. To practice the Presence of God in many spiritual lineages is done by invocation—to speak or pray the Divine Names with attention. The calling out to the divine as a way of attending to God's presence is considered a priceless means of practicing attention. Choose a Divine Name, and invoke that Name quietly in your heart and mind throughout your day.

Names such as: Holy One, All Light, Compassionate One, Beloved, Master of All, Lord of the Cosmos might be important as invocatory names, as would the Jesus Prayer for many Christians.

READINGS FOR INSIGHT

I

Jalauddin Rumi

Existence is exuberant, time is a husk.
When the moment cracks open,
ecstasy leaps out and devours space; love goes mad with blessing.
So why lay yourself on the torturer's rack of time-past and time-future?
The mind that tries to shape tomorrow beyond its capacities
will find no rest.

II

Seyyed Hossein Nasr
The Garden of Truth
140

As long as we are in the human state, we remain inseparable from here and now no matter where we are and when we live. Here and now are connected to human consciousness by an unbreakable bond. Wherever we are we can be here, and whenever we come to our senses we find ourselves in the present moment, or now. God is always near to us, the here and the now being the ever-present gateway to Him. And yet fallen humanity, whose soul is dispersed and whose attention is turned to the world of multiplicity, does everything possible to escape from here and now. Most of our lives are constituted of daydreaming, whereby we seek not to be here but somewhere else and not to be in the present but either in the past or the future. The goal of the spiritual path is to bring us to the here and now, to the Center, which is also the eternal present moment.

III

Anthony de Mello
One Minute Wisdom
18

"How shall I attain Eternal Life?"
"Eternal life is now. Come into the present."
"But I *am* in the present now, am I not?"
"No."
"Why not?"
"Because you haven't dropped your past."
"Why should I drop my past? Not all of it is bad."
"The past is to be dropped not because it is bad,
but because it is dead."

IV

Rabbi Rami Shapiro
Divine Feminine
98

Inquiring into the past in order to understand the present reduces the present to a by-product of the past. What is simply reflects the inevitable culmination of what was. This is karma: The past determines the present. Inquiring into the present reveals each moment to be the ripening of the conditions of the past, and your engagement with this ripening can be fresh and karma free.

The present moment is the field on which you engage reality. The field is the result of conditions established in the past. If you are a compulsive liar, in time your lies will catch up with you and the field on which you find yourself will reflect the lies you have told in the past. Yet how you play out the moment is not predetermined. ... If you choose to stop lying, then the new field will reflect the new conditions and things will change. You cannot change what is; you can only choose how to engage it, and in this way influence what will be.

LOGION 92

Sapiential Themes

- *Seeking and finding, are the two initial and necessary conditions in the sapiential tradition.*
- *Passivity is not possible in a search for wisdom.*
- *Readiness is always a pre-condition for both searching and finding.*
- *There is general inertia in the human condition which has, in other sayings, been compared to sleep.*

Yeshua says,

Seek now, I say,
and you will find
that for which you search.
You see, I am ready to tell you
everything you were asking earlier
and did not explain,
but at the moment
no one is searching out anything.

Parallel Texts

Thomas 2, 94
Psalm 27:8, 63:1
Proverbs 8:17
Ecclesiastes 7:25
Jeremiah 29:13
Matthew 6:33, 7:7
Luke 11:9

Links

In the previous Logion, his followers ask him questions, but in Yeshua's judgment, perhaps, they are inane inquiries, and the questioners are unprepared to "read" what is actually present before them. Still, Yeshua encourages them to keep seeking, and now, at an even deeper level—for he is ready to be their teacher and guide, even if they are not yet prepared for this venture. The Presence is always able to speak. It only awaits the condition of "seeking."

FOCAL POINT

Seeking, finding, and readiness of heart have been at the core of this Gospel from its beginning. They are the critical practices and the inner states of being in which pure Presence can be fully manifested and known. But that Presence who is "in the midst" is not passive to the seeker. It is an active agent participating in the positive outcome of the quest for wisdom and understanding. In this world, however, the sad truth is that there are few who are ready to seek out such wisdom from the Master. Human affairs are almost totally focused on other agendas, which in the end cut us off from the wisdom quest.

Notes

The phrase, "I am ready" translates a condition of positive regard. It is also possible to say "it pleases me," or "it is my desire" to do so. Whatever has happened, Yeshua's discernment is that it is time—the "right moment" has arrived, though it requires two parties in order to realize the finding.

COMMENTARY

The six states of wisdom that Yeshua teaches may, in fact, be an important way of perceiving the semiotics of this text. It may be divisible into these six areas, and the Logia associated with these states of wisdom explain and express the complexity of the human experience.

Spiraling has been understood in the ancient world as the normal means of growth according to a pattern called ***helikos tropon****—in the manner of a spiral.*

Hearing this Logion, it is as if we have returned again to the beginning point of the Gospel—but in the process perhaps we have taken another turn of the spiral. This spiraling and turning may be the ultimate structure of the text—a spiraling movement that touches the six states of wisdom over and over again which have been outlined by Yeshua in Logion 2. At the beginning of the Gospel, after being introduced as the Master of Wisdom, we hear his instruction to search and not stop until we find. Here, once again, we return to this initial instruction, the entry point of wisdom, after he has just instructed his students about how to search in the present moment from within the Presence that is before them. Yeshua says, however, that there is no doubt about it, in their searching they **will** find, though still there may be few who are willing (or ready) to make that journey of discovery. As the Master of Wisdom, he offers himself to those who pursue the path of wisdom. He is willing to teach, guide, instruct, and tell them now what he was unable to explain earlier—now is the right moment. They have reached a new stage of the journey.

So, we might ask, what is seeking and what is finding in this new context as we come to it in this part of the Gospel of Thomas? If we examine what has come just before this Logion, there have been a series of instructions and insights, most of which have focused on Yeshua's message of interiorized Judaism. As we have seen, his path is not simply practiced at the level of conventional religion. The center of Yeshua's attention is on an interior pilgrimage at the level of the heart. Developmentally, perhaps, there is the growing recognition that the "inside of the cup" is far superior to any form of exterior display meant to win social approval (Logion 89). When an individual reaches this level of understanding one recognizes that one is webbed to a world larger than simply the historical and cultural context in which we live (Logion 88). In that context the Master issues an invitation to become yoked in a bond of relationship which, again, is interior. The student is asked to live in that relationship with both the difficulties and benefits that it will mean (Logion 90). And as the previous saying suggests, it is a lived experience before that Presence in the present moment (Logion 91).

Wisdom, in Thomas, is mediated through the Teacher who guides the student on a path, but it is far deeper than simply a change of paths—even from external religious practice to inner spirituality. It is about relationship.

All these are preludes, then, to a renewed and deeper search and to a new finding at a new level that will require discernment (as the next Logion will detail), once the inner world has been detected and replaced as the central axis of orientation. The outer forms, the duties, the correctness, the pride of having acceptably met all the requirements of the outer practice of religion, and the arguments over details and doctrines—all these are replaced when wisdom appears.

In that Presence, in that new knowing—when the student is ready—there is friendship and love that trumps everything else. There is beauty and the Reality toward which it points. If you are ready for it, the knowing that occurs inside that Presence—the look of recognition and the friendship, all these take place in the light of the Beloved's face. There is now no figuring of profit and loss, but surrender to the gentle yoke of the Master. There is no more talk of correctness or right belief, but praise for the light inside all things, and the qualities of God pouring through them. All this the student begins to perceive in that Presence, and it instigates a new searching and finding, a new knowing with its own confusions and wonders, a new sovereignty and a new form of rest. It is this that, in deep relationship with him, Yeshua is willing to reveal.

QUESTIONS FOR REFLECTION

1. Think about your own experience: When have you been ready or willing to search and find, and when have you been resistive to the whole process? What makes the difference between these two responses?

2. Have you ever sensed that you were being guided specifically to a particular understanding? When you were ready for it, what is it that has come most forcefully to you?

3. Do you have this sort of relationship with an inner Master? Is Yeshua that kind of figure for you? What has been your experience of him in this way?

4. What kind of relationship might be the condition for the possibility of this deeper form of learning?

EXERCISES AND MEDITATIONS

1. Try to teach someone something that you know (cooking a recipe, for example, or a technique in sewing or building, or understanding a business principle that they might not otherwise know). Explore what this experience is like from the side of the teacher. Reverse roles, then, and see how this might apply to your own learning experience under divine guidance. Journal your observations and what you may have learned.
2. Ask yourself, what am I seeking for this moment? What is it that I want or need to know right now? Write this specifically. Share it with someone who is spiritually connected to you. Do they understand what you are seeking? Or do they not understand? Clarify it for them until they can understand you. Be as specific as you can. Take this clarification, then, into a time of silent reflection. Sit with it as a part of your intention before the Presence who is constantly there in your midst. Ask for instruction. Wait for guidance.
3. It seems quite clear in this saying that friendship with the inner teacher is critical to the learning of wisdom. It is not merely about gaining insight that is abstract, but understanding that comes "in relationship to" personal guidance from a teacher who dwells within. We often think that we learn just because we want to, but suppose that not only do we have to be ready to learn, but also the teacher also must be ready and willing to teach. So what might this mean in practical terms? Examine other such relationships you have had in your own life. What has made someone ready to teach you? When have they been willing and when have they resisted you? Reflect on how that might apply to your own inner learning experience in the context of wisdom. Journal your reflections.

READINGS FOR INSIGHT

I

A Sufi Tale

A holy man arrived at a village far from his own home and found that his reputation as a great teacher had preceded him. The villagers assembled and their spokesman said:

"Teach us your wisdom, Sir."

"Very well," replied the saint, "but first of all let me suggest something useful to you. Would you like that unsightly hill opposite the village removed, so that you might enjoy the cool breezes which it now prevents?" The villagers were delighted with the proposal.

"Now," said the saint, "bring me a rope long enough to encircle the hill, with some left over." After months of weaving the villagers produced the rope.

"Just put the rope around the hill, then lift it onto my back, and I shall carry it away," said the saint.

"This is ridiculous said the villagers, how can we lift a hill?"

"How can I carry it away unless you do?" asked the saint. "It is the same problem when you ask me to teach you wisdom."

II

A Sufi Tale

A certain teacher of the highest rank was also a farmer, although he had written many books and given many lectures. One day a man who had read them all, and imagined himself to be a Seeker, called to discuss higher matters with him. "I have read all your books," said the visitor, "and I agree with some and not with others. In some, again, I agree with some parts, and do not understand other parts. Some books I like better than others."

The farmer-sage took his guest into the farmyard, where plants and animals grew in abundance. Then he said, "I am a farmer, a producer of food. Do you see those carrots and apples? Some people like the one, some the other. Do you see the animals? Some like hens, others like goats. Liking or disliking is of no importance to me, only the quality of the food."

III

Brother Tolbert McCarroll
Notes from the Song of Life
43-44

There will be times when you will use a spiritual guide. Your attitude will limit your teacher's ability to help you. He [she] can only talk to you about the things you are ready to hear.

You will often be disappointed in him [her]. You have gone in search of a great spiritual master and all you find is a rather mundane and very human person. Soon you realize that he [she] is no better than you! ... The true teacher will not attempt to encounter you except where you are. He [she] will often appear a little foolish. If underneath your mask you are babbling on, then your teacher will babble. As he [she] walks along your path he [she] will try to point out a few things that will help you slow down a little, but he [she] can only talk about what interests you.

... A teacher is only a mirror. He [she] helps you see yourself. He [she] is a medium for the true guide residing within you. The teacher gives your inner guide a voice. And when you and this ever-present guide engage in a flowing conversation your teacher will quietly leave. Then if you want to find your teacher you must look on his [her] path. There the teacher will be walking and talking to the guide within.

LOGION 93

Sapiential Themes

- *There are states of readiness and consciousness which either exclude or include understanding.*
- *One must await developmental readiness and discern in him or herself when that has been achieved.*
- *Keeping secret higher mysteries until readiness is achieved is what parents do with their children. Wisdom teaches the same.*
- *Truth, beauty, and goodness are sacred things easily damaged by what is not prepared to receive them.*

Yeshua says,

Do not give what is sacred to dogs who will only discard it on a manure pile.
Do not cast pearls in front of pigs who will only trample and ruin them.

Parallel Texts

Thomas 5, 17, 18, 21, 26, 27, 51, 62
Matthew 7:6, 8:30-32, 15:26, 22:8, 24:4
Mark 5: 11-16, 7:27-28, 14:38
Luke 16:21, 17:8

FOCAL POINT

The condition of unreadiness, and the inability to perceive the true nature and value of wisdom's teaching, is not unlike being an animal that has no innate notion of what is true, beautiful, or good. These higher perceptions and qualities are of no real value in the animal kingdom (at least as we perceive it from the human perspective). So, then, the consciousness of the seeker must be higher than that of animal awareness—total occupation with its ordinary surroundings and survival, and unaware of anything else. On this wisdom path what can and cannot be fruitfully shared with others from among the treasures that one has found must always be kept in mind.

Links

Yeshua is ready to impart wisdom, but when you receive it you must treat it with care. Understanding the necessary care (and discerning when wisdom should be transmitted fruitfully), is all in the art of sapiential mastery. What happens when you are not ready to receive higher wisdom is concretely illustrated in this saying.

Notes

There is some physical difficulty with this text. Words are missing, but implied by the context and by other canonical texts which confirm that these were the words used by Yeshua. ***Trample*** *and* ***ruin*** *are implied but not present in the text.*

COMMENTARY

One could imagine that the impetus of this saying comes from actual, lived experience in Yeshua's life. If it is autobiographical, then clearly he knew that what he counted precious and sacred had been discarded or disregarded by others. What he knew was beautiful had been trampled on by common unconcern, or perhaps by institutional hostility. We know that the official antagonism of conventional religion against the work and teaching of Yeshua ended in his execution by the authorities—the ultimate rejection—so clearly during his ministry the animosity was building, and Yeshua had real reason to be concerned for his own life.

This saying raises the issue of spiritual elitism—that some individuals may be more spiritually advanced than others and should act accordingly. If one were to use the analogy of children in school, it would be clear that there are more advanced students who are further along in their studies, than those who are, perhaps, just beginning their work. This does not mean that the newer students are less important or inferior to the more advanced students, but that they have not been in the process long enough to understand certain things. We do not judge the worth or merit of an individual when we make that discrimination. We simply acknowledge the developmental levels and needs of each student who is then worthy of help and encouragement based on their individual development.

But suppose it is more than autobiography, and Yeshua is teaching a wisdom principle. Imagine that humans have the proclivity for simple disregard of the sacred no matter the reason. It is quite easy for the average human being to discard, disregard, or throw aside what is sacred, because it has no real use or utilitarian value to them. Imagine that we take what is beautiful and rare and walk all over it, ruining what is both beautiful and good.

There is, then, the need to protect one's inner searching and finding from social and institutional disregard. There is even better reason to guard and defend those who are new to the path from such ridicule and disdain. When an individual is ready for the discovery of wisdom, then safety and protection may need to be offered. This may be one of the central tasks of any community gathered around what is sacred and what is beautiful. It is certainly true that wisdom is precious and easily contaminated by conventional beliefs that miss its thrust and subtlety. One can easily see this in the development of early Christianity where doctrine and dogma supplanted Yeshua's wisdom.

So, in keeping with his instructions to search and find, Yeshua gives a caveat that concerns discernment about sacred things, and perhaps the journey of seeking and finding itself. He issues a warning to those who are seeking, that they turn their search from a public affair into one that is private and not subject, perhaps, to public scrutiny.

There is evidence in the Gospels that there were levels of orders of secrecy involving Yeshua's own wisdom teaching. To some, it is said, he talked in parables. To others he spoke more directly. Again, this had nothing to do with whether they were good persons or not, but with the level of capability to receive what Yeshua was saying, and at what potential benefit for their own lives.

In Jewish law there are classes of animals—clean and unclean. Swine and dogs are considered to be unclean, and cannot be eaten. These serve as metaphors for kinds of individuals perhaps, not clean and unclean per se, but those whose sensitivities toward sacred things are animal-like because they have no sapiential knowledge and cannot distinguish between higher truths and realities and lesser orders. In some sense it is in the nature of pigs and dogs not to be able to detect or recognize what is sacred or beautiful. They are developmentally (or perhaps, evolutionarily) incapable of making those distinctions. Could it be that developmentally (and in terms of spiritual evolution), this also applies to human beings as well? It is evident that at least in Yeshua's mind it does.

Some human beings, it seems, cannot detect the sacred or respond appropriately to what is beautiful. If they do encounter it, they totally disregard it, treating it as though it were of little value. Yeshua is making a judgment here, but it is a discernable pattern in human affairs, and one is wise to heed his warning, especially on a wisdom path. Truth needs to be both shared and guarded. Knowing how or when to do both is the task of a practiced wisdom teacher.

QUESTIONS FOR REFLECTION

1. This saying raises the issue of levels of consciousness in human beings illustrated by animal consciousness. Can you detect multiple layers within yourself?

2. How have you experienced swine-like or dog-like consciousness in yourself that pays no attention to higher qualities or values? When have you valued something of higher quality that those around you simply cannot recognize? Give examples.

3. So if there are levels of consciousness within individuals, how should we distinguish them? As we discern these differences, what should our attitude or approach be? Should we withhold certain truths from some individuals?

Another question to consider is whether or not all truth is egalitarian—everyone has equal access to everything. Is this true in the world of science, business, art, or medicine?

4. How might you help someone who is new to the spiritual path so that they are not subjected to swine-like or dog-like consciousness?

5. When have you ruined something that was beautiful or good by neglect or ignorance?

EXERCISES AND MEDITATIONS

1. It is always easy to rush to judgment concerning another individual's state of consciousness. Someone else may be at a lower level, therefore I am somehow superior. But the truth is we all have the whole gamut of consciousness within ourselves, and furthermore it is also true that one state in us can devastate or subjugate another. Let's imagine, then, that there are deeply embedded levels of consciousness and being that are dog-like or swine-like in their disregard for what is truly precious, sacred, or of eternal value. These are trampled and ruined by our mindless consciousness whose only value is survival. In a time of meditation, use these two images (the dog and the swine) to explore that state of disregard and its corollary, the insistence on its own narrow self-interests. How do the figures in the sidebar illustrate it?

2. While it is true that most individuals have a longing for that which is greater than themselves, it is also true that we often feel we are ready for more than we are. Sometimes something else needs to be accomplished first before we can take that next step, but because we are not there yet we do not see it. Can you imagine a state of unreadiness in yourself that even now is not recognized? One test is to pay attention to what your longing actually is and the reasons for it, and then to explore those frustrations where you are seeking to achieve something, and you cannot, and ask yourself if this might be a sign of being yet unprepared for something. In a time of reflection (and group discussion), focus on this issue. Use concrete examples in your own experience when you do.

READINGS FOR INSIGHT

I

Return! Return!
No matter who you think you are,
a skeptic, an unbeliever, a worshiper of idols,
Return!
No one leaves these gates hopeless or empty-handed.
If you have broken your vows ten thousand times,
Return!

Abu Sa'id Abil Kheir

II

Remember that it is far easier to love enemies whom we have never seen, who live hundreds of miles away, than our next-door neighbor whose dog or radio irritates us. The borders that separate nations are easier to cross than the fences that separate neighbors in the same city; the fences between those of different races, class, and religion are sometimes the strongest. But when we have learned to recognize the spark of God's Spirit in the least lovable of our neighbors, then we find a gate, a passage, a crack in the fence. And then begins our work for that justice which must underlie the making of peace.

Muriel Lester
Baptist Wisdom for Contemplative Prayer
135

III

Don't reveal secrets to those who don't believe.
Don't tell the Beloved's story to an impostor.
Don't speak to strangers who cannot understand.
Don't talk to a thorn-eating camel about anything but thorns.

Jalaluddin Rumi

IV

A pious person with a hundred prayers,
or a drunkard in a tavern,
Any gift you bring the Beloved will be accepted
as long as you come in longing.
It is this pain,
this bleeding wound of separation
which will guide you to the Heart of Hearts.

Abu Sa'id Abil Kheir

IV

Polish your heart and you'll soar above all color and perfume;
You will contemplate Beauty ceaselessly;
You will abandon the form and rind of consciousness,
And unfurl the flag of Certainty.

Jalaluddin Rumi

LOGION 94

Sapiential Themes

- *Wisdom's instruction is to seek in order to find. This is the basic pattern and fundamental principle.*
- *Wisdom's assertion is that the search—any search—will be rewarded. Doors will open for the serious seeker who persists.*
- *The universe is radically responsive, but the heart and intention of the seeker must be questing and open to change.*

Yeshua says,

Those seeking will find
what they are looking for.
Doors will swing open
for the ones who knock.

Parallel Texts

Thomas 2, 92
Mathew 7:7-11, 21:18-22
Mark 11:20-25
Luke 11:9-13
John 14:12-14, 15:16-17, 16:20-28

Links

On the one hand, it is easy to squander true treasure—to waste it needlessly. On the other hand, the universe is truly generous and everything will be provided. These two ideas are juxtaposed in Logia 93 and 94. Be frugal (or discriminating) with what you have and know, but never stop seeking and moving forward on a path—if you have a path. Spend that form of energy. The universe will respond abundantly and is never sparing in its response.

FOCAL POINT

In the modern world we are familiar with the word synchronicity. It has something to do with the meaningful juxtapositioning of apparently random events. One notices that things are happening together in a particular way that does not seem, in the end, to be random at all. Yeshua may or may not be referring to this phenomenon, but the notion that the universe is responsive to the seeker, and that finding is also an active force that coincides with one's own basic intentions—these possibilities were noticed in the ancient world, and commented upon in the stream of traditional wisdom.

Notes

There is a break in the text where the traditional word "knock" would be found in the canonical texts. It is implied here. It is clear that in both the canonical and Thomas texts persistence matters and is rewarded regardless of how this text may be translated.

COMMENTARY

In an important book, ***A Sense of the Cosmos*** *(1975), Jacob Needleman makes a strong case that the universe in which we live is not passive and unaware of our thoughts and intentions, but is profoundly, if not radically, responsive to who we are, what we desire, and what we are becoming.*

For every human being there are days when all the doors seem shut—locked up tight. And then there are days when they appear to swing open of their own accord. What one actually experiences or perceives all depends, it seems, on the state of consciousness that one has attained (animal-like or higher). For the individual who is prepared (ripe or ready), the universe itself is a door standing open, ready to assist. Such assistance is in the form of active agency. The universe is prepared and radically responsive to an equally far-reaching commitment and receptivity from the human side. It is a state of mutual arising into wisdom's realm that is, in the end, a profound act of divine generosity.

This saying expresses something of that experience and is, of course, the positive affirmation (following the instructions of Logia 2 and 92) that universal wisdom expresses itself indeed in this way. The sapiential tradition encourages an active pursuit of wisdom. Passivity will not produce what an active intention will, and the promise is that active intention will be reciprocated with an equally active response because the divine Realm and the universe are in league with the seeker.

Seeking and finding are, to be sure, inward conditions. What one seeks, and the answers one finds, all depend upon the unique sense of the individual and his or her ability to ask questions and discern when an answer has come. If the search is for wisdom, and wisdom is about integral knowledge (that is, the ability to integrate all knowing into one's being as lived practice), then, in the end, nothing is simply theoretical. Everything becomes practical, a part of lived experience.

We must always keep the possibility in mind that what we want at one level may be countermanded at another, and that what was once of interest to us at a particular moment in time may become entirely unimportant later as we grow. As Yeshua indicated in Logion 2, finding is often followed by confusion. This may be caused by the challenge that the Master makes to our questions, raising the stakes and upping the ante in our search. Or confusion may result from the fact that the answers we sought in the tranformational process of finding may no longer be sufficient. We must go deeper, we must search for more, past what we initially thought was the right answer.

We often think of seeking in terms of theories and finding answers to our speculations, but the search for wisdom has greater depth than that. It will entail our deepest questions, and even our deepest longings, but (as is clear in this text), what the students asked for and wanted to receive was constantly challenged and expanded. Their questions and the answers Yeshua gave in response dared them to think differently or desire something entirely new. Seeking and finding are not only extensions of our particular wonderings, they are shaped into something larger by the responses that we make to Wisdom's demands of us. The search for wisdom is dialogical.

We are required, then, to examine more deeply the interactive nature of this quest as a dialogical exchange with something much larger than ourselves. What is going on? First, there is the active searching that is demanded in the opening Logion to this text. It is insistent and, we might say, even demanding in that the full force of our intention be brought to bear. But this is only the beginning. Second, what is required next is true inner work. We not only search the world outside ourselves, but we search within, and our findings demand that we attend to the inner dimensions of ourselves. We work, then, from the inside-out to apply what we are learning not only to our own souls, but to our lives. This requires that we stay receptive as life responds to what we are practicing. It is in this context that we begin to detect lines of divine grace and opening that appear, and direct manifestations that have traditionally been called, ***theophany***. The divine shows up in direct ways that encounter us and pass through us as we stay open to the Presence in whom, in the end, everything is being done. All of these are part of the balanced life that is the interactive play between Wisdom and her seekers.

QUESTIONS FOR REFLECTION

1. Do you have any confirming evidence that this saying is true? What has happened in your experience that reflects the truth or wisdom of this saying?

2. In your experience, when has the door seemed shut and the universe entirely unresponsive? When has it responded to you—doors opening at the moment you knocked?

3. What has your searching been about? When have you felt most inclined to seek and knock on new doors?

4. Would you agree that there is an active agency in the universe that is responsive to humankind? What excites that responsiveness? What seems to shut it down?

EXERCISES AND MEDITATIONS

1. At the headwaters of the wisdom tradition is the injunction to search and find. The active pursuit is essential for spiritual pilgrimage. And Yeshua says that it is reciprocated with a response in kind. This claim can be tested. It is within our abilities to see whether or not this assertion actually works or is true. We need only to set our intentions and to begin a serious search in pursuit of a deep understanding of some question or concern that has vexed us or been uppermost in our minds. As a test, make a list of a number of different concerns and questions you have had. Choose one to begin. Set your intention and ask questions. Actively seek for answers. Remember seeking is a form of awareness, and the answers may come unexpectedly. So only when we are awake and aware will we begin to notice what arrives. Keep a journal of what occurs as you do this.
2. It is often good to read an autobiography of someone who has searched and how they describe the process and what they have found. There may be some individual that you would like to know better who has expressed their journey of discovery autobiographically. See if you can find such a text and read it for insight.
3. Another genre of important literature concerns the "journey of eternal return" (as Joseph Campbell and others have described it)—the journey across the horizons of human experience from out of and back to Eternity. The mythological writings which describe this are sometimes works of fiction. For example, Ursala LeGuin's **The Wizard of Earthsea** is a tale told expressing the eternal truths of seeking and finding. If you are so inclined, find this literary work and allow it to teach you about the journey. Share your insights with others.

Examples are:

***The Way of the Pilgrim**, Reshad Field's **The Last Barrier**, Irina Tweedie's **Daughter of Fire**, R. M. Pirsig's **Zen and the Art of Motorcycle Maintenance**.*

READINGS FOR INSIGHT

I

In the end,
everyone reaps what they have sown.
And each person, whether sober or drunk,
seeks the Beloved One.
And every place is love's home,
whether here or there,
whether synagogue or mosque.

Hafez

II

The great journey of the soul to Union begins with the soul's awakening in wonder to its divine nature and its response to the summons of love that is always sounding to it from all sides of the cosmos. One of Rumi's greatest odes begins:

Each moment the summons to Love
rushes to us from all sides.
Do you want to come with us?
This is not the time to stay at home,
but to go out and give yourself to the garden...

Andrew Harvey
Perfume of the Desert
3

III

The first necessary thing is to acquire real sight. How can you do this except through devotion, surrender, and hard work? Then you have to look. And even when you *do* look you may not be able to see. Not everything is meant to be visible. There are many advanced saints in this world, who live in union with God; and then there are those even further on who are named the Veiled Ones of God. Those who live in union are always praying: "Please, God, show me one of your Veiled Ones!" As long as their whole being is not one fire of longing, or as long as God intends, however hard they look they will not be able to see anything. ... The most holy are nearly always hidden, hidden in a cloud of humility and Divine Protection.

Andrew Harvey
Light upon Light: Inspirations from Rumi
224

IV

There is a way that consists entirely of asking questions, and not giving up. For what did the Buddha sit under the Bhodi tree? He said, 'I am not going to get up from this place until this question is answered.' That is not everyone's way. But it does not mean that it is not everyone's business to ask this question and to return to it. You must keep it in front of you. We have to assimilate it, so that it has become part of our nature, so that it is truly within us, in our very breathing. That is how this question has to be answered. There has to be the real conviction in us, that this state of existence is not enough. And that does not mean that I want more. When I said 'not enough,' I realize that I made a faulty use of language. Obviously I did not mean by that that we must have more existence than we have got now. I simply meant that we have to have this way of living. It is part of man's nature.

J.G. Bennett
Intimations
88

LOGION 95

Sapiential Themes

- *The right use of wealth (and money) is a subject of importance not only in the Jewish Torah tradition, but also in the tradition of Jewish wisdom.*
- *Wisdom tradition integrates the inner with the outer and makes them a single whole including the way an individual thinks about money.*
- *Abundance, and not scarcity, is a signal feature in wisdom's worldview. Generosity of spirit and wealth spent without fear or worry is a sign of spiritual maturity.*

Yeshua says,

If you have money,
do not lend it at interest.
Give it instead
to those from whom you
cannot take it back.

Parallel Texts

Exodus 22:24
Leviticus 25:36-37
Deuteronomy 23: 20-21
Ezekiel 18:13, 17
Matthew 5:38-42
Luke 6:27-36

Links

An obvious interpretive link between the previous logion and this one is that if you are seeking and searching for yourself, then a sign will be your responsiveness to the world around you and your sense of openness and compassion to the needs of others. For the search to be successful, the searcher must also be a compassionate being. The two go hand in hand. Otherwise all our seeking is just a form of narcissism.

FOCAL POINT

Imagine that the pursuit of wisdom is not just a private inquiry, but an engagement with the whole world in such a way that involves even financial transactions. We often imagine the "real world" of finance to have nothing really to do with spiritual pursuits or with wisdom. But suppose they are intimately connected—that is, the way we treat the world works according to some fundamental law of cause and effect that either enhances our inner wisdom pursuits, or obstructs them. We cannot separate them into unrelated domains—the inner and outer worlds are interwoven.

Notes

An interesting semantic aspect of this saying has to do with the opening conditional clause beginning with "if..." The implication is that many who hear this saying will not have any money at all, but those who do must learn to use it radically for the greater good of others. This use is not only as interest free loans, but also with no expectations about the ultimate repayment.

An understanding of Jewish law that encompasses the standards of usury (the charging of interest) is very complex. To charge interest to other Jews was considered to be a sin. To charge Gentiles interest, however, was possible. By this injunction, Yeshua appears to be expanding the limits of usury beyond the Jewish world.

COMMENTARY

In today's society, it is customary to keep many things separate from each other—the private from the public, the sacred from the secular, for example. In a pluralistic society where tolerance is of high value, that strategy is a very good idea indeed. But for the individual, it is often a form of fragmentation. Inner integration is critical. We have a public life and a private life, but they must be intimately related. . We have our own inner experiences and we enjoy the multiplicity of outer experiences which we constantly pursue through recreation and the seeking of new adventures. However, these are all part of one larger whole. They are woven together like a fabric and they affect each other. In us there should be no separation between the two.

Wisdom principles apply to the outer world and the world of public finance as well as to the wisdom path of seeking and finding and have everything to do with this seemingly counter-intuitive logion. Yeshua's saying would never be acceptable in the normal world of finance or in day-to-day business transactions, or would it? Maybe this principle is a key to finding and understanding a higher truth. To practice this form of generosity might trigger the very forms of knowing and finding that Yeshua has been talking about in the Logia before it.

Try to imagine what would happen if you **did** lend money without interest, and never actually expected to receive either the interest or, for that matter, anything back in return. How might that act of generosity affect the lender as well as the person in need of a loan? How might it change the world as a whole? Could it alter the nature of the world's interactions and the levels of consciousness affecting this world? This goes counter to everything that we understand about normal financial transactions. It flies in the face of common sense, but imagine a world in which wealth is shared in just this way.

Such practice, however, is not meant to encourage irresponsibility, or to let the person who has been entrusted with funds feel that he or she has no responsibility to the agreement. But suppose the world changes, and unforeseen events occur, and it is not possible to repay the money—the letting go of those expectations creates something extraordinary in the lender, as well as gratitude and humility in the one who is required to pay back the loan. It remakes the relationships and the inner condition of the world.

It is a fact that many traditional peoples and societies have operated in just this way. Wealth was shared generously and without strings attached. We find this in gift-giving cultures among aboriginal peoples around the world. In today's society, we often experience it among neighbors and friends who simply give things away without thought that they will be repaid. When we ourselves are the recipient of such amazing generosity, it is experienced as a form of unconditional grace—exactly the kind that Yeshua speaks about in regards to his knowledge of the kingdom of the Father. This practice is the sign of the divine generosity. In human beings who experience such generosity, it creates an atmosphere of "paying it forward" that changes the whole dynamic of human society. In the end this practice lays the foundations of a true "wisdom culture" that is not transactional at all, nor does it depend for its generosity on quid-pro-quo or the establishment of external conditions and rules. This may be the exact definition of grace as it has been understood in the biblical tradition in its most practical sense.

QUESTIONS FOR REFLECTION

1. Yeshua challenges us to think about our use of money. How is this statement a challenge for you? Do you agree with it? Do you think we should build monetary policy based upon it or not?

2. Recall a time of unexpected generosity in your own experience where, quite suddenly, you were the recipient of an act of compassion or kindness that you neither expected or perhaps deserved. How did you feel? How did you respond? Imagine the opposite—an act of uncommon greed or a tight-fist that limited your world in some way.

3. Suppose that Yeshua is talking about the way one could work with the world out of a position of abundance instead of from one where scarcity is the norm. In your view, how would that change things?

4. Have you ever done exactly what Yeshua is suggesting? What was the result?

EXERCISES AND MEDITATIONS

1. Think about this exercise carefully. You may want to do it anonymously or you may want to interact directly with another individual who will know what you have done. Plan on giving away (or lending someone) money that they need but don't have. Be generous, but not overwhelming. Make what you give away count for something. If you give it to a stranger, you will probably never know how the money was used. If you give it to someone in need whom you know, you may track the results in some way perhaps. Notice what affect this sort of exchange has on you, the giver, and what affect it has on the receiver of the gift. If you are able, track the results over a longer period of time. Make notes to yourself that you might want to share with others who are perhaps experimenting with you in the same exercise.
2. As westerners we accept a certain worldview about the use of money and finance. Typically in the West we are capitalists and no longer communists or communitarians. We rarely examine our worldview. We simply accept it because everyone else around us does the same. You might want to go online and do some exploration about money and its use on the Internet. For example, you might want to look at the various practices of gift-giving in the indigenous Northwest tribal cultures. Also look at definitions of capitalism, and at "venture capitalism" versus "vulture capitalism," consumerism, production and labor, and corporations. There are many places to look to explore our financial structures.
3. What is your financial or fiscal policy? How should wealth be gained, used, and distributed? You might use these questions as meditations, and as you do, look closely at the teachings of Yeshua, especially in his "Sermon on the Mount."

Matthew 5-7

READINGS FOR INSIGHT

I

Kabir

I don't think there is such a thing
as an intelligent mega-rich person.
For who with a fine mind can look
out upon this world and hoard
what can nourish
a thousand
souls.

II

Pema Chodron
Comfortable with Uncertainty
127

When you open the door and invite all sentient beings in as your guests—and you also open the windows and the walls even start falling down—you find yourself in the universe with no protection at all. Now you're in for it. If you think that just by doing that you are going to feel good about yourself and you are going to be thanked right and left—no, that won't happen. Rather than to expect thanks, it would be helpful just to expect the unexpected; then you might be curious and inquisitive about what comes in the door. We can begin to open our hearts to others when we have no hope of getting anything back. We just do it for its own sake.

III

Lao Tsu
Tao Te Ching
77

The Tao of heaven is like the bending of a bow.
The high is lowered, and the low is raised.
If the string is too long, it is shortened;
If there is not enough, it is made longer.

The Tao of heaven is to take from those who have too much
and give to those who do not have enough.
Man's way is different.
He takes from those who do not have enough to give to those
who already have too much.

What man has more than enough and gives it to the world?
Only the man of Tao.
Therefore the sage works without recognition.
He achieves what has to be done without dwelling on it.
He does not try to show his knowledge.

IV

Pirke Avot
Ethics of the Sages
95

People fall into four types:
Those who say, "What is mine is mine, and what's yours is yours;" this is the average, though some say this is the type predominant in Sodom.
Those who say, "What's mine is yours, and what's yours is mine as well;" this the fool.
Those who say, "What's mine is yours, and what's yours is yours;" this is the saint.
Those who say, "What is mine is mine, and what's yours is mine;" this is the wicked.

LOGION 96

Sapiential Themes

- *Quality, not quantity, is the primary measure in sapiential tradition.*
- *There is an unseen, active agency at work in the universe and in the world of human affairs. Its purpose is to create a form of bread that will feed the world.*
- *The feminine form is used as an expressive image of Sophia at work in her "world-kitchen."*
- *The ideal form of active agency is to work unseen and undercover, silently but powerfully, in the world.*

Yeshua says,

The Father's realm
can be compared to a woman
who takes a tiny bit of yeast,
folds it into dough
and makes great loaves
out of it.
Whoever has ears for this, listen!

Parallel Texts

Matthew 13:35
Luke 13:20-21
John 6:27-39
I Corinthians 5:6
Galatians 5:9

Links

The previous saying about the proper use of money has, perhaps, prompted a series of illustrative logia. It may not seem like much to loan without interest or press for no repayment, but in the end the effects upon the world and the individual may be huge. We cannot judge. A tiny amount of largesse can go a very long way. The Kingdom of Heaven takes whatever is given, however small, and multiplies it.

FOCAL POINT

To illustrate the profound effects that generosity and self giving have upon the world, three primary parables are used in sequence. This first parable illustrates the powerful, hidden effects of the selfless distribution of what little one individual may have. Like a bread maker who works to create an artisan loaf, the active ingredient (the active agency) is hidden away and out-of-sight in the mass of dough, unseen and perhaps even unknown. Nevertheless it acts as an agent of change and expansion in the whole. Something small can have powerful, lasting and even exponential effects.

Notes

The translation using the words "folds it into" is implied in the text where there is a blank spot (called a ***lacuna****). It is commensurate with parallel canonical passages and makes entire sense of the passage. This and the next several logia make use of comparative analogies for understanding the nature and processes of the Kingdom of Heaven (the Father's Realm).*

COMMENTARY

Ideas of what constitutes scarcity and abundance may not be related to empirical data but more to ideology and a certain level of consciousness which sees and defines things in a unique way according to particular point of view.

Our understanding of the divine Realm (the Kingdom of God) and how it works, and the kind of energies and agencies it uses in this world is powerfully illustrated by this saying. In a world where the notion of scarcity and insufficiency predominates, it is difficult to imagine that the Father's Realm (the Realm of the Heaven) can have any effects upon the "real world" of human need and poverty. In a place where we experience remarkable lack, where we guard ourselves against the shortages endemic to the world's system of things, Yeshua's words stand out either fundamentally flawed, untrue, or as some kind of private fantasy of his own. How could abundance be the truth in a world of obvious scarcity?

The image Yeshua uses to reinforce his seeing is one of a woman (a traditional bread maker), providing the daily bread for her family. She has the basic ingredients—perhaps enough for one day or even just one meal from which she will make loaves of bread. The recipe is ancient: take a fistful of flour, add a pinch of yeast, a little salt and enough water, and then let the active agency of the yeast do its work. If you didn't know better you might call it "magic"—but from such a small amount of flour and a tiny bit of yeast, something new and fulsome emerges—something that can feed her family. This is the image Yeshua uses.

The divine Reality is exactly like this. There is a "small, secret ingredient" (an active agency) in the mix. It is folded into the dough of human history and begins to expand inwardly to create a product that is entirely nourishing. We might imagine this secret agent to be the divine energy (or Life), which remains largely unseen and unknown to the untrained eye. Like yeast which is the "hidden secret" of bread makers and is essential for all good bread making, divine agency is hidden from view but effective and necessary. From what seems like so little (almost nothing), something new rises up and feeds the world. It is "bread from heaven" as it were, or bread that has been made out of the inedible dough of the world, made ready through the fires of baking, which will feed the world. We, perhaps, pay undue attention to the small amount of yeast. We ask, "Is it ever enough?" The bread maker knows that with the right application of yeast something larger and nourishing can be produced.

*Charlene Spretnak is an insightful modern writer and feminist who has worked through the contemporary issues of politics, religion, philosopy and finance in the post-modern world. Her **States of Grace: The Recovery of Meaning in the Postmodern Age** (1993) is an invaluable critical analysis of contemporary issues relating to scarcity and abundance.*

Many sapiential insights emerge from these ordinary images. First, there is a form of life that gives fullness to the world. It may look like nothing and seem inert to us, but in the right environment it suddenly "comes alive" and transforms what is around it into something extraordinary. Second, this tiny, secret ingredient is from another Realm—the Realm of Yeshua's Father or Source. Third, a tiny bit of it goes a long way in this world. We should never discount the amount and mistake quantity for those qualities that are to our eyes and understanding, hidden or unknown. Fourth, the most common and ordinary work characterized by us as being feminine may, in fact, be the key to our future. So-called "women's work" in the Father's Realm is regarded as sacred even though it looks to be of little account. What is seen to be small in human society, in the economy of the Kingdom has great worth as it is distributed to nourish the world. In fact, the work and viewpoint of the feminine may be precisely what is being reintroduced to our world as both sapiential teaching and spiritual energy. Finally, this image is like what happens to the dough of the social order on the historical plane when the attributes and actions of generosity from the previous logion are applied. Something marvelous grows and is created.

QUESTIONS FOR REFLECTION

1. Fundamentally, do you see the world in terms of scarcity or abundance? How do you know that this is your worldview? What is your evidence or proof?

2. Have you ever made bread? How does yeast work in bread making? What, in your view, would be the symbolic equivalent for "yeast" being put into the "dough" of this world?

3. If, as Yeshua says, there is hidden action or a hidden agency at work in this world, what have you seen or experienced that agrees with him? Is there any counter evidence?

4. If you consider yourself to be aligned to this sacred work, how is your own life's activity like this woman's?

EXERCISES AND MEDITATIONS

1. Just so that you know how bread-making feels and what the process is like, make a yeast bread of some kind and observe the process carefully. How much difference does yeast make? Try leaving it out. What are the results? Feed someone, including yourself, with the results of your labors. Someone fed in this way may taste the results, but does not know the labor involved. What kind of "secret," then, do you possess?
2. If (as is typically seen) the "feminine activity" of bread-making is understood to be central to the life and work of the Kingdom, meditate on the difference between feminine and masculine activity and achievement in the world. Can you make a comparison? Journal and share your insights.
3. Look at the world carefully. Gather evidence for the "yeasting" (fermentation process) in the world. Yeast actually does ferment bread. It changes the very nature of the dough, as it does in grape juice to make wine. This is the common ingredient between these two foods, and the results are quite amazing. Can you find examples of such "divine fermentation processes" going on in this world and especially in your own life? What are they? Make a list. Collect the evidence.
4. Pray this prayer everyday for a week:

O God,
May I be yeast fit for the bread of this world.
May I be a catalyst for growth and change in the lives of those around me.
May I stay hidden and unseen
but powerful and active in this secret, inner endeavor.
AMEN

Two very good books on bread making are: Jeff Hertzberg and Zoë François' ***Artisan Bread in Five Minutes a Day*** *(2007) and Eric Treuille and Ursula Ferrigno's beautifully illustrated* ***Ultimate Bread*** *(2004).*

READINGS FOR INSIGHT

I

We must not, in trying to think about
how we can make a big difference,
ignore the small daily differences
we can make which, over time, add up
to big differences that we often cannot foresee.

Marian Wright Edelman
Timeless Values

II

We can as individuals do so little to help the sad and suffering in the world—the lonely, bereaved, imprisoned, despised, exiled, sick in mind and body, the cold, the hungry.

Yet we can reach out to those within our knowledge, with courtesy and kindness, an unexpected gift, a visit.

Treating them with the respect they deserve.

Honoring their courage.

Listening to their stories.

For every kindness spreads in a shining circle: See how good people everywhere set rings of light moving across the darkness, rings that link and interlock.

Pam Brown
Timeless Values

III

The aspects of things
that are most important for us
are hidden because of their simplicity
and familiarity.

Ludwig Wittgenstein
Wabi Sabi
102

IV

The beginning of the universe
Is the mother of all things.
Knowing the mother, one also knows the sons.
Knowing the sons, yet remaining in touch with the mother
Brings freedom from the fear of death.

Keep your mouth shut,
Guard the senses,
And life is ever full.
Open your mouth,
Always be busy,
And life is beyond hope.

Seeing the small is insight,
Yielding to force is strength.
Using the outer light, return to insight,
And in this way be saved from harm.
This is learning constancy.

Lao Tsu
Tao Te Ching
52

LOGION 97

Sapiential Themes

- *In the midst of the ordinary world. on our way into the divine Reality, things often happen unbeknownst to us that affect eternal outcomes.*
- *Wisdom's work in the ordinary is often unseen.*
- *Emptiness is a condition that is part of the sapiential unfolding of our lives here on the horizontal plane.*
- *The work of the feminine is key in manifesting the Father's realm, but it may be counter intuitive to rational understanding.*

Yeshua says,

The Father's realm
is like a woman carrying
a jar full of meal.
While she is walking on a path
some distance from her home,
the handle of her jug breaks,
and the meal spills out
behind her on the road.
She is unaware of the problem,
for she has noticed nothing.
When she opens the door of her house
and puts the jar down,
suddenly she discovers it empty.

Parallel Texts

Thomas, 3, 28, 41
Matthew 5:3, 13:31-33
Mark 4:26-29
Luke 13:20-21

Links

In contrast to the previous logion, which expressed the possibility of a greater and growing fullness, this logion expresses a kind of poverty or emptiness. These are perhaps complementary opposites and each constitutes an aspect of what the Realm of Heaven is like. Something unique to the Gospel tradition seems to be expressed in this saying which is found nowhere else in the sayings of Yeshua.

FOCAL POINT

In this household a woman is preparing to make bread, but first she must go out into the wider world beyond her home to secure the necessary ingredients. Inadvertently, on the way home, she loses all that she thought she had gained. Upon entering her house she finds her jar to be completely empty—without knowing it, it has spilled out behind her on the road. Paradoxically, could this not be the precise entry-point that she takes into the reality of the Kingdom? What is the truth about the inner condition of humanity? Must we experience emptiness before fullness? Or is this, instead, a state of exactly the opposite from what should be the case for one seeking entrance there?

Notes

The words ***from her home*** *are not found in the original text, but are nonetheless implied by the parable. This is a complete and quintessential parable whose meaning is koan-like which to the rational mind appears to be a true paradox.*

COMMENTARY

Many of the sayings of Yeshua in the Gospel of Thomas are reminiscent of Buddhist koans. In the oriental world of Buddhism, as Samuel Zinner has explained, a koan is "an intentionally perplexing statement or question that is crafted to encourage the reader or listener to ponder paradoxes which may have no logical, rational solution." (Gospel of Thomas, 47).

The image used in this logion is an ordinary scene in the ancient world. Many households lived simply on daily bread baked after a woman had taken wheat to the miller and returned home with the flour to make loaves for the day.

This hermeneutically complex logion is a true new parable unknown in the Gospel tradition. It is in a form that appears to be koan-like for it challenges our thinking about the world and the future unfolding not only in our own personal life, but for the life of humanity as a whole. As in the previous logion, this saying contains the image of a woman providing food for her family. When she arrives home she discovers a mishap—her jar which had been full of meal is broken and empty. That stark image illustrates something about the nature of the Kingdom. If the previous image was about fullness and abundance, this image appears to be about shortage and emptiness. Are these two complementary images? Do they create a true paradox?

Going about her normal day's work to feed and provide for her family, a woman takes grain to a miller some distance from her home and is returning when this problem arises. She has a cracked jar. Unknown to her it breaks, and through no fault of her own perhaps, the meal spills out behind her on the road. She has noticed nothing and everything seems to her to be fine. She only discovers the problem at the end of her journey when she returns home and puts the jar down. Now, suddenly, she knows what has happened. She understands her predicament and her dilemma. The knowledge of emptiness is a true knowing. She is no longer unaware. The Kingdom of Heaven is somehow like this particular life experience. In the end it makes us aware—we wake up to the truth of things as they are.

One can actually interpret this saying, however, from two viewpoints. The first is a negative one. The woman goes through her whole life-experience and discovers that in the end there has been nothing to it, she is poverty stricken (Logion 3). The second is a positive interpretation—to finally see what is, and to recognize emptiness is, in the end, a breakthrough. This is exactly the state toward which history and the world has been directing her (and by implication, us as well). To know complete emptiness, true poverty, is a gift and, in the Kingdom of Heaven, a true starting point.

Now imagine that the horizontal path that the woman takes through the world ("some distance from home") creates mishaps and she sees indeed that it is all for nothing—she discovers it to be empty. All the activity, then, all the agendas that she had, whether for good or ill, ended up the same way. These presented her with the same outcomes—although during her journey she had noticed nothing (she never discovered that there was a crack in the jar). She lived her life, then, as if everything was normal. But in the end she comes to realize emptiness. For most of us this is the case. Most of us are unaware of this fact—we live in and with an illusion. Life is a form of *Maya* (to use the Sanskrit word for illusion), in which we take something to be real when it is not, and proves to be an illusion or empty.

Could this new realization (this new form of knowing), then, be turned to our advantage? She discovers (as Logion 28 describe it), the complete poverty of her own state at that moment. Might it not be that her knowledge of loss and illusion (or as Yeshua says in Logion 28 and 110) that the human *kosmos* leaves one empty and so one must let it go? This is a great truth. Is this not one of the highest forms of knowledge which prepares us for a new fullness? Emptiness, then, is the condition for the possibility of fullness. This becomes one of the reasons for the historical pilgrimage that she (and we each) must make across the landscape of space and time. We are here to discover what is Real and what is not real. When heretofore, we had noticed nothing, now we can receive the fullness of true knowledge.

QUESTIONS FOR REFLECTION

1. What is your first reaction to this parable? Is it positive or negative? What is Yeshua's intent in telling it?

2. From the standpoint of the Realm of Heaven, is the state of the woman at the end (when she returns home and makes her discovery) a positive or a negative one?

3. Put yourself in the shoes of that woman. What is her inner state? What would you advise her to do?

4. What is the spiritual significance of "emptiness" in the Gospel and later spiritual traditions?

5. Have you ever made a sudden and unexpected discovery like this woman, which perhaps left you stunned and wondering? What was your discovery?

EXERCISES AND MEDITATIONS

1. There are many hermeneutical possibilities to express the meaning of this unique saying. The interpretive doors stand wide open. Since no traditional commentaries are available to us, we get to work with an ancient text as though it is brand new, just as his first students would have heard it the first time. Spend some time in quiet meditating on this saying in the form of a Lectio Divina (sacred reading, prayer and meditation). As you reflect and meditate on it, make a list of the possible interpretations and meanings that can be used to understand what it is seeking to teach us. Try to find as many possibilities as you can. Do not limit them. Brainstorm. What do you discover? Is there a "right" and a "wrong" interpretation, or are we left with a fortuitous ambiguity of meanings which might fit in one circumstance and not another? How could this be?
2. It would be helpful to put this logion into some diagrammatic or artistic form. You might draw a map of the woman's journey, or do a collage of her experience. You could also make a simple line drawing to illustrate it. You could also create a cartoon series out of the parable with "bubble quotations." Any of these would be helpful in entering into this ancient story and seeking to understand its wisdom teaching.
3. You will have noticed no doubt that the subject of "emptiness" is used in opposite ways in the early tradition of Yeshua. Emptiness can mean bereft and lacking, or it can mean cleansed and open. Think about each of these meanings as a spiritual state. In Logia 3, 28, and 41, Yeshua speaks of the former. In the Sermon on the Mount and here in Logion 54 he speaks of "poverty" (spiritually as well as financially).

This approach may run counter to the way we typically interpret sacred texts (trying to find the "one right interpretation)." Jewish tradition in the Talmud uses the exact opposite approach—trying to find as many meanings and interpretations as possible.

READINGS FOR INSIGHT

I

Y. Nomura
Desert Wisdom
62

When Abba Macarius was in Egypt, he found a man with a mule stealing his belongings. Then, as though he were a stranger, he helped the robber to load the animal, and peacefully sent him off saying: "We have brought nothing into the world, and we cannot take anything with us. The Lord has given, and as He has wished, so it has happened. Blessed be the Lord in all things."

II

Dard

Misery and joy have the same shape in this world.
You may call the rose an open heart or a broken heart.

III

Maria Jaoudi
Christian Mysticism East and West
11

In Mahayana Buddhism, *sunyata,* or emptiness, creates wisdom. Without the experience of emptiness we hook into the projections of our mind's ego patterns, and we cannot even come near to the enlightened state. Emptiness, expressed often in Chinese and Japanese art as the empty circle, is the pathway to wisdom. Yet it is not the final stage; returning to the world to embody the Bodhisattva's vow: "However innumerable sentient beings are, I vow: to save them all."

IV

Jalaluddin Rumi

Love's drum has no question and no answer.
The mystery is its emptiness.
Lovers obey no rules.
Love is not a matter of existence,
but rather of absence.

V

Lao Tsu
Tao Te Ching
16

Empty yourself of everything.
Let the mind become still.
Ten thousand things rise and fall
while the Self watches their return.
They grow and flourish and then return to the Source.
Returning to the Source is stillness.
This means returning to what is.
Returning to what is means going back to the ordinary.
Understanding the ordinary: Enlightenment.
Not understanding the ordinary: Blindness creates evil.
Understanding the ordinary: Mind opens.
Mind opening leads to compassion, compassion to nobility.
Nobility to heavenliness, Heavenliness to Tao.
Though the body dies, the Tao will never pass away, there is no danger.

VI

Henry Bayman
The Black Pearl
115

The "emptiness of the phenomenal world
is not the same as the "emptiness" intended for the noumenal world.

LOGION 98

Sapiential Themes

- *Does wisdom include holy war? This logion may speak to the issues involved in spiritual warfare.*
- *Inner strength and not outer force is at the heart of any action that is ultimately effective.*
- *Inner praxis is also at the heart of any outer action.*

Yeshua says,

The Father's realm
is like a man wanting
to kill someone powerful.
So he draws a sword
in his own house
and puts it through the wall
to test whether or not
his hand is actually strong enough.
Then he goes out and slays the giant.

Parallel Texts

Exodus 14:14, 15:3
Deuteronomy 20:2-4
Isaiah 1:19-200
Jeremiah 25:9
Ezekiel 5:17, 6:3
Luke 6:39, 14:39
Matthew 5:29
Ephesians 6:10-20

Links

This is the third logion in a series that describes what the Father's Realm (the Kingdom of Heaven) is actually like (or how it functions and how we function within it). Again, the emphasis is the inner condition and not the external circumstances that matter. Yeshua is teaching on the inner dimensions and not the external forms, and those dimensions exist inside an individual.

FOCAL POINT

Images of the "holy warrior" in a battle against forces greater and more powerful are scattered across the sacred traditions of the world. Perhaps it is because of the rise of civilizations based upon war and conquest (what some have called "Kurgan culture") that these images have been endemic to sacred traditions everywhere and in particular to the Abrahamic faiths. One needs only to be reminded that "holy war" is enjoined in ancient Hebrew Scripture, as it is in the sixth chapter of the letter to the Ephesians in Christian texts. It is certainly understood today to be a part of Muslim culture where the ***muhajadin*** (holy warriors) play an important role in both inner struggle and outer Muslim conquest. This ideal appears also to be at the heart of this logion.

Notes

The word "giant" in this dynamic translation is perhaps metaphorically correct, but it refers to a powerful person, or a person in power who must be vanquished. The term "strong enough" translates "inwardly strong" in the original Coptic text.

COMMENTARY

We do not know who this individual is. He remains anonymous and we do not know what his motivations are. Is he an assassin, in the military, a criminal, or someone who, in a state of rage, is bent on murder? We don't have a clear answer, and it might make a difference as to how we read the text and understand its significance if we did. However, who he is is not the question, but whether he is capable of accomplishing what he has set out to do.

In her history-making book ***Chalice and the Blade****, Riane Eisler suggests that the earliest matriarchal culture of human society was replaced and supplanted by a warrior culture about 7,000 BCE, which she called "Kurgan." Warrior-dominated civilization has been the norm to this day and is reflected in the worlds' sacred traditions.*

Yeshua's words suggest that the key to using force of any kind is inner preparation, which is absolutely necessary if one is going to engage in combat, spiritual or otherwise. The picture is of an individual who has a powerful opponent—an enemy who must be resisted, if not conquered. We could imagine all sorts of scenarios. Perhaps in his day, Yeshua is referring to enemy forces (the Romans) occupying Palestinian lands. Battle and resistance were much on the minds of the Jewish people of his day. However, there are key elements in this text that suggest that the enemy is not outward, but, more importantly, inward. The words "strong enough" express an important original phrase "inwardly strong." While being ambiguous in English perhaps, this phrase seems best rendered with the wording used in the dynamic translation that indicates the amount of power necessary to accomplish the task. However, at the same time, it must be kept in mind that the whole context suggests that the concern is about the degree of inner strength the individual has and the hand must possess this "inner strength." The one who desires to do external work (to have an effect upon the external world), must first stay enclosed on the inside of his own dwelling where the work of inner practice is necessary before it is even possible to confront an external power. But perhaps the enemy (as other sayings in the Gospel of Thomas have suggested) refers to those within one's own household. All these are suggestive of different hermeneutical possibilities.

As we have seen, the previous two logia centered upon a woman at work who is predominant in each. Suppose, then, that this logion with a male at its center may also be a subtle critique about the masculine propensity for violence and domination. By acknowledging this tendency, this saying is also critiquing it. Yeshua reminds the man who is inclined to go out and do battle with an enemy that there is a more fundamental inner work (an inner practice) that is required. The inclination is to think that because we have an opponent, and because we have some degree of strength, we must go immediately and engage in combat. But is that so? Is that the priority? Wisdom has other priorities, but they must start where society is, realizing that one cannot remove the domination-factor in male dominant society immediately. To begin, wisdom must first turn the individual inward.

It may be that there is a slow evolution of the social order away from aggression and war toward more non-violent options.

If we take the position that force is inevitable, and that resistance must be expressed externally, then whatever expression it takes (before dealing with evil in an external way), there must first be the establishment of an inner strength and stability. This principle is also followed in the Letter to the Ephesians, where the "holy warrior" is enjoined not to fight, but to stand and pray against threats from outside. This attitude is clearly reflected in the non-violent teachings of Yeshua found elsewhere in the canonical Gospels, the most remembered being his statement in the face of violent opposition to "turn the other cheek." It is a hard lesson, one not easily practiced. However, there are possibilities of compliance using his wisdom at each point on the spectrum of human response.

Ephesians 6:10-20

Matthew 5:29
Luke 6: 39

QUESTIONS FOR REFLECTION

1. What is your response to this saying? How does it strike you or make you feel?

2. Have you ever had an opponent that you felt must be confronted? What has been your motivation for confrontation?

3. What does inner strength versus outer strength mean? How would you define them? Give an example of someone who has inner strength.

4. How does inner strength work? How do you develop it? What are its practices?

5. Are there any "warrior traditions" that mix the development of both inner and outer strength? How do they do that?

To answer this question in full one might explore the oriental martial arts as an example

EXERCISES AND MEDITATIONS

1. We live in a society where the propensity for violence and war-making is immense. We cannot even imagine a world without war because it is so much a part of human culture. Is it possible to live without war and domination by violence? Can we make such a culture change simply by pointing out the obvious or by protest? What will work to make peace? In a time of meditation and reflection contemplate this problem. Allow yourself to be drawn toward answers and possibilities that may not be immediately obvious. Journal your findings.
2. Mahatma Gandhi began the movement of peaceful non-violent resistance. Explore and research the history and definition of this movement on the Internet. Is there anything you can apply from this concerning your own circumstances? Explore how "non-violent" you are. (Note that non-violence is an inner attitude). Find out what this means.
3. The practice of developing inner strength must come through the experience of real living in the world. We are constantly confronted by resistance and have our own experience of "enemies" (those who wish to do us harm). Developing inner strength by letting these things have an effect upon us without attempting to make them go away so that we do not have to deal with them is a part of deep inner practice. By dealing with them (non-violently) we develop inner strength. Look at your life. Explore the challenges and conflicts that may confront you. Ask yourself, "How could I develop inner strength by accepting certain things and not forcing them away?" Would this necessarily change the external outcome? And if it didn't would it make a difference? Share your experiences and learning with a trusted friend or others who are working on this material with you.

The Letter of James in the Christian Scriptures explores the root causes of war and violence in human society. (James 4:1-3)

*Pema Chödrön's various works deal insightfully with many of these issues. You might wish to consult **Comfortable with Uncertainty** (2003) and **The Places That Scare You** (2005).*

READINGS FOR INSIGHT

I

Pema Chödrön
Comfortable With Uncertainty
145

We train when we're caught off guard
and when our life is up in the air.

II

Kabir Helminski
Living Presence
59

If the essential Self, the soul, is engaged, it has the powers of Being, Doing, Living, Knowing, Speaking, Hearing, and Loving. From essential attributes like these proceed all the qualities that we need to live an abundant life. Within this nondimensional point of the essential Self (nondimensional because it has has its existence in the realm of true Being, which appears to us as nonexistence) is the treasure of all qualities. We may receive what we need to be of service from this treasury through a process of conscious or unconscious activation, but it is our right as human beings to receive consciously. The human being is a channel for the creative power of the universe. Through the use of will—conscious choice—we can activate the qualities and powers of the essential Self.

III

Jalaluddin Rumi
Mathnawi
I, 2195-98

Help me with this ego of mine
that is seeking help from You;
I seek justice from no one
but this justice-seeking self.
I shall not get justice from anyone
except Him who is nearer to me than myself;
for this I-ness comes moment by moment from Him.

IV

Lao Tsu
Tao Te Ching
68, 30

A good soldier is not violent.
A good fighter is not angry.
A good winner is not vengeful.
A good employer is humble.
This is known as the Virtue of not striving.
This is known as the ability to deal with people.
This since ancient times has been known
as the ultimate unity with heaven.

Whenever you advise a ruler in the way of Tao,
Counsel him not to use force to conquer the universe.
For this would only cause resistance.
Thorn bushes spring up wherever the army has passed.
Lean years follow in the wake of a great war.
Just do what needs to be done.
Never take advantage of power.

LOGION 99

Sapiential Themes

- *In the world of wisdom new alliances and networks are formed beyond one's immediate family and kin.*
- *The priority in the sapiential tradition is to know and do the desires of Heaven—the realm transcendent to space and time.*
- *One's own desires are guided by a greater and higher authority than one's individual self.*

His students said to him,

"Your brothers and
your mother are standing
just outside the door."

"My true mother and brothers
are those present right here
who fulfill my Father's desires.
It is they who will get into
my Father's realm," he replied.

Parallel Texts

Matthew 12:46-50
Mark 3:20-22, 31-35
Luke 8:19-21

FOCAL POINT

Links

To be ready for the larger, harder work—perhaps even that of conquest and battle as depicted in the last logion, one must be present—inside the door and ready to do the Father's desires. It might seem that "killing the giant" (or the strongman) would be the will of the Father, but is it? How does one know? Yeshua offers a way into the Father's realm so one can come to know Heaven's desires.

According to various Gospel texts, Yeshua's blood relatives remained nearby throughout his short ministry—watching carefully, perhaps, but it appears they were not in his inner circle, at least not at the beginning. This, of course, can be disputed. Some believe that some of his brothers were students from the beginning. It seems that James (Jacob or Ya'akov) joined the gathering of students toward the end of Yeshua's ministry or very soon after the events that ended his life. This saying suggests that Yeshua had a marginal (and perhaps troubling) relationship with his family and kin. Others were closer to his work and teaching and had kinship with him in a special way—from the position of being "on the inside" of things.

Notes

The word "desire" used here is the same as in the previous logion where the man has the desire to use his sword against a powerful enemy. The significant contrast between the outside and the inside is emphasized in the construction of this Logion.

COMMENTARY

The question is sometimes asked, who is my true family? Who are my real kith and kin? We teach family loyalty to children at a very early age, and then subsequent to that they learn higher allegiance to tribe and nation. But blood relatives, however, stand at the heart of any lists of loyalty for most us. Typically we will stay devoted to family members no matter the circumstances—remembering the old adage "blood is thicker than water."

*In **Jonathan Livingston Seagull**, Richard Bach made the interesting observation that, "The bond that links your true family is not one of blood, but of respect and joy in each other's life. Rarely do members of one family grow up under the same roof."*

Are there circumstances, however, when our blood relatives are no longer as close to us as they once were? Sometimes throughout life experience we find other beings with whom we become closer and more intimate than with our natural family. In the spiritual realm, our blood relatives may stand only at the margins of our commitments, whereas we bond with spiritual kin in an even deeper way. One's closest kin, then, are no longer blood relatives, but come to be those who have gathered with us on the "inside of things"—who are present to us and with us in an interior way. They are true companions, fellow-travelers, "spiritual relatives" helping us fulfill our inner commitments and desires in a way that blood relatives are able to do. It is this kind of spiritual friendship or relatedness that enables us to gain entry into an intimacy unknown in normal social exchanges. This perspective illustrates relationships of relative nearness and distance in an entirely new and different dimension.

We might explore whether or not in the "Communion of Saints" unseen relationships are being formed in us as we live day to day in normal human society. These may be with beings and entities which are deceased or from other dimensions in the hierarchy of being.

The images and teaching of this logion are interesting. For whatever reason, Yeshua's mother and brothers wait for him just outside the door. Either they have not been invited in or they are expressing their own reluctance to join the inner circle (or perhaps to intrude). Before responding to the statement of facts, Yeshua makes an observation about "true relatives" (or spiritual kinship). His observation is that those who stay present in the here and now, and seek to do what the Father desires are counted as his intimates. Yeshua uses this teaching to express the nature of entrance into (and real proximity to) the Father's realm.

It is this "being present to..." and readiness to act on the longings and desires of heaven itself that allows one to know spiritual intimacy and be included in the inner circle of heaven with Yeshua's Father. We each perhaps have experienced what it means to be included in or excluded from some inner circle. Often it is because we have not been chosen in some special way or seen as worthy or acceptable for whatever reason. Perhaps at some point in our lives we have experienced active rejection. In this saying, however, this choice is not made by someone else, it is made by oneself.

The conditions for the possibility of personal relationship to heaven are entirely in one's own hands. We can either make the choice for inclusion in the Realm of Heaven by the way we remain present in the here and now to its inner dimensions and to the desires of ***Abba***, or we can set ourselves on the outside of things. One is either intimate with and in deep relationship with the Father (knowing intimately His desires), or one is not. The Father does not choose this. We choose to come close and be present and then act on the Father's desires. By that choice we experience inclusion or exclusion. It is an interesting way of looking at things. It puts personal responsibility at the heart of the matter.

QUESTIONS FOR REFLECTION

1. Have you ever been on the "outside" of something waiting to come in, or perhaps reluctant to make your entrance? Have you ever been on the inside of something, knowing you were no longer an outsider? Contrast these two states and the feelings attached to each of them.

2. In this world, what keeps a person on the outside? What makes a person an insider?

3. In your view what is the difference between a blood relative and a "true" mother/father or brother/sister in the spiritual world? How would you describe the difference?

4. What does it take to get into the Father's Realm? What are the desires that Yeshua is talking about?

EXERCISES AND MEDITATIONS

In a period of reflection consider the prophetic passage in Micah 6:8 about what God desires. How does this help you to understand what Yeshua is referring to in this logion?

1. Being in a family (and in relationship with others) is an essential part of being human. We cannot live without these social relationships, which are vital to our well-being as well as our spiritual and mental health. How would you describe your relationships to your birth family? Are you on the inside of that family or are you on the outside? Are there other "families of relationships" to which you belong? How are they important to you? Do they trump blood-kin in any way? Reflect on these questions and journal about the "larger spiritual family" to which you belong and toward which you have responsibilities.
2. You might go through the Gospel of Thomas with this question: What does this text tell me about the desires of God and the "will of heaven?" The question is, once we know these desires, are we fulfilling them in practice in daily life? Use this understanding as an exercise for self-reflection and for a re-examination of your life of practice. Keep track of your findings, and share what you are learning with spiritual friends (your relations).
3. How do you imagine your relationships beyond earth and temporal experience as you know it? Are you conscious of these in any way? You might imagine that "heaven" is paying attention to you (to each of us) in its own particular way. In your life-experience, do you have any evidence of this fact?
4. Imagine that you live in two dimensions at once—the outside and the inside. They are very different. One part of your life is very aware of inner Presence, and another part seems distant (or at the margins of that). Notice this dichotomy. How have you experienced this in daily life? How difficult (or easy) is it to attend to each?

Ponder this quote from one of the Jewish sages about human will and divine desire: "Align your will with God's will, and God's will becomes your will. Surrender your will to God's will, and God will surrender others' will to your will." What is your sense of how will or volition in independent beings works? Does this statement help clarify Yeshua's saying?

READINGS FOR INSIGHT

I

Anthony de Mello, S.J.
One Minute Nonsense
9

The father of one of the disciples stormed into the lecture hall where the Master was holding forth. Ignoring everyone present he yelled at his daughter, "You have abandoned a university career to sit at the feet of this fool! What has he taught you?"

She stood up, calmly drew her father outside, and said, "Being with him has taught me what no university ever could—not to fear you and not to be embarrassed by your disgraceful behavior."

II

Valintine Tomberg
Meditations on the Tarot
56

Thus miracles require *two* united wills! They are not manifestations of an all-powerful will *ordaining*, but are due to a new power which is *born* whenever there is unity between divine will and human will. Peter was therefore certainly there for something at the healing of Aeneas at Lydda. The divine will needed his will in order to give birth to the power which raised the paralyzed Aeneas from his bed. ... the work of Redemption being that of love, requires the perfect union in love of *two wills*, distinct and free-divine will and human will.

III

Sarah Rossiter
from "Parabola,"
Summer 2012, 102

As I slept
You entered me, as if I were a desert tent.
And you, a thief who crept by night across dark dunes
To slip inside as I lay empty, pitched on sand.
But when I woke, I found you, here,
Close as my breath, no,
Breath itself, and I, a tent
Lit from within.

IV

Kabir Helmenski
Living Presence
108

Our work is to awaken and realize a spiritual will and presence, a Being that is not coerced by like and dislike, the demands of the personality. ... Our essential will and presence stands outside of time and space, relatively free and pure. This presence is more ourselves than the impulses with which we might identify. Some people may argue that to go with every impulse is natural and spontaneous; on the contrary, this response represents the depths of conditioning and mechanicality. It is not free will, but slavery. Freedom lies in the altogether different direction of conscious will that frees us from separation and opens us to unity.

V

Sana'i

Although we're near, you'd never know it.
Thinking of yourself, our distance only grows greater.
Do you want to reach me?
Then lose yourself.
Walking love's path,
you're either "you," or "me."

LOGION 100

Sapiential Themes

- *Wisdom understands the relative autonomy of various realms and adjusts itself to them.*
- *In traditional understanding the realm of Caesar is that of politics and taxation. The Realm of God is, however, quite different and it is easy to project the human world on the Divine and then turn the Divine Realm into another political system, which it is not.*
- *Yeshua's ownership appears to be distinct from the other two.*

They showed him a gold coin and said,

"Caesar's agents
demand tribute
from us."

He said to them,
"Then give to Caesar
What is Caesar's.
Give to God
what is God's.
And give me
that which is mine."

Parallel Texts

Matthew 22:15-22
Mark 12:13-17
Luke 20:22-26

Links

There are authorities and loyalties to family, friends, society, government and God. The question is, of course, how does one act given these divided loyalties and their demands? It is a difficult question and requires that one exercise discernment in all things.

FOCAL POINT

The world of politics (and political affairs) is a domain with its own rules, laws, and orders. Divine Reality is another realm that transcends this world and possesses other, higher guiding and guarding principles in the hierarchy of being. Between them stands the Wisdom Master who mediates, perhaps, between these two realms. In seeking his wisdom there is a price to be paid. The question is, what is that price and how shall it be paid?

Notes

The word tribute or tax is used here with the implication that something belongs to or is owned by one realm or another.

COMMENTARY

Logion 101 appears to be a test of Yeshua's allegiances—a question about his politics and his loyalties. Is he a trustworthy citizen of the Roman Empire or a subversive? Is he a true son of Israel or a traitor? Where do his loyalties lie? What are his politics in this volatile and difficult region of first-century Palestine? Perhaps this is a trick question. Perhaps the strategy is to entrap him in some statement that will put him at odds with the authorities. How one answers a question like this is a difficult matter demanding keen insight. It is also a matter of practice. If, as he has taught, the Realm of the Kingdom supercedes all other loyalties, then what responsibility does one have to this world's authorities? Since the occupation of their homelands, this had been a troubling question for all Jewish citizens.

Yeshua's answer is astute, but it is not simple. It is nuanced. Yeshua acknowledges authority in multiple realms. In each domain there is a distinct and perhaps unique role for authority. There is, of course, the domain of real-world politics—the realm of Caesar and the Roman Empire. Humans must pay attention to that world and credit it with whatever it is due. There is also the Divine Realm, that which belongs to God, and in that realm a higher authority must be acknowledged and given its due. Finally (and here we have a new phrase added to the Gospel tradition unknown in the canonical texts), Yeshua asks that they give him whatever it is that belongs to him.

In none of these cases, however, does Yeshua say precisely what it is that **must** be given or precisely what the recognition of authority means. The onus is still on the individual under authority to discern and pay tribute however he or she understands it. Tribute certainly in the realm of Caesar is a tax, but is what the Divine wants the same thing, a tax? The tribute that belongs to God is certainly different from what belongs to Caesar. Do we know what that is? Again, what must be given to Yeshua may be altogether distinct from these two. One must make a judgment as to what is precisely required without comment from Yeshua as to the details. Perhaps, in the end, that tribute is altogether personal between student and Master. Each individual develops a unique relationship different from anyone else.

In the Sufi tradition of Ibn al-'Arabi there is a similar theme that each individual is uniquely related to the divine in a way that is shared by no one else but that person. It is often referred to as ***kenotheism**..*

Human beings clearly live in multiple domains. The demands of each domain are perhaps rigorous, but do they overlap, and more importantly, do they contradict? Again, it is unlikely that any definitive answer can be given except through lived experience at any particular location in space or time. But in any case, we are here to serve—to give, and our service and self-giving must be done by understanding the requirements in each domain. We are not here to withdraw, or hold back. Yeshua lives as a testament to such self-giving—even in the realm of Caesar, where he literally gives his own life away. Discernment is the key to an understanding of servanthood and lordship. What is needed is to stay in balance as part of a necessary relationship to all things.

It is interesting that a Shamanic figure in traditional culture is understood to be someone who "walks between the worlds."

Does Yeshua come to mediate between these realms? Perhaps so, for he stands offering himself in service to all—the realm of heaven and the realm of earth (including the political fortunes he must suffer). Therefore, to give Yeshua what belongs to him, one must become a servant. The path of true wisdom is to follow his path of service by understanding these facts and their underlying principles, and then undertaking to walk by his example of discernment.

QUESTIONS FOR REFLECTION

1. What is a tax and what is it used for? Is it a legitimate tribute?

2. When have you experienced divided loyalties between, for example, work and home? What has been the result?

3. If you were going to make a list of items important to you that belonged in each of these categories: Caesar, God, Yeshua, what belongs to Caesar? What belongs to God? What does Yeshua want?

4. There are two paradoxes to consider: First, if, in the end, everything belongs to God, then how can it be that Yeshua designates categories other than God in his teaching? Second, it appears that Yeshua's wisdom is both free and costly. How would you explain this paradox?

5. If Yeshua were to ask you to give what belongs to him, what would you have to give?

EXERCISES AND MEDITATIONS

1. Currently we live in the realm of Caesar, that is, in the world of temporal affairs including culture and society, finance and politics. All of these are regulated by the interactions (and viewpoints) of human beings as they organize themselves politically in space and time. These affairs (including our own lives and agendas on this planet) take up almost all the time that we have just to live and manage our lives. So what is left? Is there any real space for God (for the divine Reality and its Realm)? Where does Yeshua and his wisdom fit into all of this? These are the questions raised by this logion. Sometimes they are difficult to answer in the abstract, but our real relationships to these things can be known in practice. With these questions in mind, graph a pie chart of the time and energy absorbed by each for you. Observe yourself (your own life) from as objective a point of view as is possible. What do you find? Ask yourself this: What is the price of (or "tax" on) wisdom? What does it cost to buy Yeshua's single pearl in Logion 76?
2. An economy is a network of exchanges between citizens and society in a social and political realm, which helps to maintain a flow of goods and services meant for the well-being of the whole order. An economy, however, is usually based on the agendas of those who maintain the system, and at least in a capitalist economy, giving attention to the bottom-line profits and primarily benefiting those who have invested in it. If the divine economy is not based on merit or privileges earned, but on generosity and unearned favor, then what are the networks of exchange in such an unusual system? See if you can understand what the rules are by which that form of economy might operate, especially since you are asked to participate in exchanges of grace.

Multi-national corporations that often appear to be above the law of any nation state may play the role of "Caesar" in our day.

READINGS FOR INSIGHT

I

Tao endures without a name.
Though simple and slight, no one under heaven can master it.
If kings and lords could possess it,
All beings would become their guests.
Heaven and earth together would drip sweet dew
equally on all people without regulation
and all things would take their course.
Once the whole is divided, the parts need names.
There are enough names already. One must know when to stop.
Knowing when to stop averts trouble.
Tao's presence in the world is like a river flowing home to the sea.

Lao Tsu
Tao Te Ching
32

II

There were no clocks in the monastery. When a businessman complained about the lack of punctuality, the Master said, "Ours is a cosmic punctuality, not a business punctuality.

This made no sense to the businessman, so he added, "Everything depends on your point of view. From the viewpoint of the forest, what is the loss of a leaf? From the viewpoint of the Cosmos, what is the loss of your business schedule?"

Anthony de Mello
One Minute Nonsense
117

III

The sage used to say, "Everything is on loan, and a net envelops all the living. The shop is open; the Merchant extends credit. The ledger is open; the hand writes. Whoever wishes to borrow, come and borrow. The collectors make their rounds constantly, day-by-day, collecting payment whether you know it or not. They do not act capriciously. Their judgments are just, and everything is in service to the final banquet."

Rabbi Rami Shapiro
The Ethics of the Sages
53

IV

Reason said,
"We live in a world of six directions—and that's it!"
But Love replied,
"There is a field beyond all that
and I have traveled its path many times.
Reason saw a marketplace and set up shop,
but love trades in another currency altogether—
a consciousness that flows through the arteries of the universe.

—adapted from
Jalaluddin Rumi

V

The real wealth of a nation does not come from mineral resources, but from what lies in the minds and hearts of its people. ...This love-force can be harnessed if we listen to our hearts and minds, and follow its laws of life that lead to a joyous existence.

John M. Templeton
Worldwide Laws of Life
270

LOGION 101

Sapiential Themes

- *Wisdom teaching on one's true origin and source is a continuous theme in this text and other sapiential literature.*
- *Sacred teachings expand the scope of human existence to include a beginning in paradise prior to physical birth.*
- *By contrast, love and its opposite are in view and applied to horizontal relationships. Such opposites seem counterintuitive to us, but may point to a higher loyalty that is not horizontal but vertical.*

Yeshua says,

Whoever does not reject
father and mother
in the way I do
cannot be my student.
Whoever does not welcome
father and mother as I do
cannot be my disciple,
for my mother brought me forth,
but Truth gave me life.

Parallel Texts

Thomas 55, 105
Matthew 10:34-39, 16:24-28
Mark 8:34-9:1
Luke 9:23-27, 14:25-33

Links

The question of ownership and what (or who) belongs to what realm is re-examined here in more detail and perhaps in a more personal way. One's true family of origin is understood to be beyond the scope of the normal relationships that we are used to on earth. One's own birth family is set in a context relative to a higher order. Expressed in a stark way, this saying begins to assert the power of the vertical axis, which is the realm of God as opposed to the horizontal domain and its ordinary human relationships.

FOCAL POINT

The price of wisdom may in the end be separation from one's family—one's nearest kin. On this strange path yearning and desire takes us toward a Realm beyond the norm. The price we pay may look like cold rejection, but there is also another form of receptivity to relationships transcendent to the normal social contracts which open us to a relationship with father and mother at the level of Truth. Physical existence and social conditioning are only one level in which acceptance and rejection may be displayed. The hermeneutics of this passage demand more than acceptance or rejection in normal human exchanges. Openness to Truth at another level is almost totally misunderstood but critical to any one on a wisdom path. Both levels involve issues of our "family of origin," how one understands that, and what one comes to love innately.

Notes

Perhaps due to the passage of time, this text is incomplete. It is impossible to say definitively what its original construction was. There are, therefore, multiple opportunities for interpretation. Hate and love are contrasted here, but their meanings are indeterminate. There are several lacuna in the text (spaces with words missing) which are often filled out by translators in various ways. This translation has kept closer to the text with the words missing.

COMMENTARY

This is a complex and paradoxical Logion. In addition it is hermeneutically demanding in almost every way (theological, sociological and sapiential). There is in it, however, a clear image of what birth in the realm of the Father's Kingdom must mean, and how one can understand that parentage from a wisdom point of view. It appears that there are two streams of life (two axes of existence), one horizontal and one vertical. Parentage along the horizontal axis is a human affair. One must step back, however, from the demands of that axis in favor of another—the vertical—in order to progress on a wisdom path.

The word "reject" (replacing the common translation of "hate") means to refuse to follow the demands and dictates of the social order, specifically the demands of mere human parentage. This, of course, flies in the face of the fifth commandment: *Honor your father and mother, that your days may be long upon the earth which the Lord your God is giving you (Exodus 20:1-17).* But a wisdom path may make a higher demand. This may, in fact be, one of the requirements that Yeshua asks his students to give him as expressed in the previous logion.

One could make a good case that this logion was autobiographical because it expressed Yeshua's own struggle to come to terms with the social and family demands of his day and balance them with the higher authority he was beginning to know and experience. If the story of his early visitation with the elders in the Temple in Jerusalem is accurate, then Yeshua heard that voice and expressed it early on in his spiritual and social formation.

Is this logion autobiographical? Perhaps Yeshua had to move against the social and familial constraints in his own day, and reject the demand to remain at home as the primary bread-winner (if indeed Joseph was dead by that time). Perhaps Yeshua had to listen to a higher authority—the demands of Truth from its original Source (and Mother). Perhaps Yeshua had to be "birthed from Above" as he explains later to a religious leader of his day, Nicodemus. Perhaps Yeshua had to listen to the inner voice which spoke to him with authority above all other demands, even that of the divine Commandment itself. These are interpretive possibilities.

Regardless of how one comes to understand the context, Yeshua acknowledges two birthings and two sources of parentage as well as a hierarchy in the order of Truth. To welcome one stream and resist another is to act in response to higher Truth. To realize that you were brought forth into space-time by an earthly mother, but given birth into a greater Truth and a higher form of life by another mother, is a deep understanding. Although the second word for "mother" is missing in the text it is implied.

What is essential and startling perhaps to the ears of western Christians is that Yeshua acknowledges a Presence who is both feminine in form and in essence the Truth. He has learned truth from this celestial and feminine archetype which has been present to him. In Jewish tradition she was identified as ***Shekhinah*** *(and also Sophia or* ***Hochmah***)*— God's glory and beauty. It is this "Mother" who has taught Yeshua and birthed him into Truth.*

There are, then, two life-forms: a human life-form we all share biologically, and a divine life-form that is indeed ***theomorphic*** in nature. It is our destiny and birth-right to share in this second form spiritually. Both are necessary, but one acknowledges a higher authority than the other. Spirituality trumps biology—or it must when we begin to acknowledge an inner reality. On a wisdom path we begin to hear and acknowledged an inner voice from a source different than the social, human, and biological orders.

The higher Life that Yeshua knew he willingly shared with us. The birth that he had undergone into that Life was an initiation that he catalyzed in the lives of his students. To discover that Source of Life was to know one's true divine parentage. From it an individual could come to understand the nature of the True Self. In the end, one must establish oneness with that Reality. This was at the center of his teaching, at least as it was understood in the tradition of Thomas.

QUESTIONS FOR REFLECTION

1. This saying obviously presents challenges to the long Hebrew tradition of teaching centered on the Ten Commandments which instructs us to "honor our father and mother." Is Yeshua violating this commandment?

2. Do you have a love/hate relationship with your parents in any way? What would make you want to "hate" (or reject) them?

3. How beholden should we be to our natural parents? What is our duty to our parents and where are those limits?

4. Could you ever say that "Truth has brought you forth" or that She is your "mother?" What would that mean, if you did?

EXERCISES AND MEDITATIONS

1. Human relationships are complex affairs. Families are complicated networks of relationship in which we feel either loved or rejected, free or enmeshed. Nothing is ever easy about these relationships whose roots go back generations, and in our own experience exist before we are ever cognizant of them or their many meanings. Think about your family of origin. How has it shaped you to be who you are today? What are positive aspects in that shaping? What do you see as either negative or as being a liability to you now?
2. Imagine another birth process than the natural one which began our life here on earth. Imagine that earth itself is somehow a kind of womb out of which we are being (or will be born) into another realm, realizing a parentage far larger than what we are used to. We tend to think of this world as the whole reality, but when we do we are limiting our vision—limiting the possibilities that we were designed to realize. Examine the poems on the next page in light of another possible future or destiny. What do they tell you about love and rejection? If we are each being birthed into a higher realm, and Truth herself is our true Mother (one possible interpretation of this saying), then how aware are you of this process? Do you notice that you are growing (or being birthed) into truth in new ways? What have you noticed about this? In your experience, what sort of "truth" is this? Is it dogmatic, rational, emotional and mental?
3. In a period of meditation, reflect on the two poems from the "Readings for Insight" and how they answer some of the questions and issues that have been raised by this logion. Journal your insights and if possible share those in a group setting.

Another possible approach for understanding the limitations and consequences of human parentage is to study family-systems patterning in modern psycho-social analysis.

READINGS FOR INSIGHT

I

You have heard it said, "You must hate, and leave, your father and your mother."
Your Mother and your Father are your attachments to beliefs and blood-ties, to your prejudices and to your physical desires and comforting habits.
Don't listen to them! They seem to protect you and provide for you, but, in truth, they imprison you.
They are your worst enemies.
They make you afraid of living in spaciousness.
Know that your body nurtures the spirit and helps it to grow, but then it gives it wrong advice.
Eventually, in peaceful years, the body becomes a vest of chain mail—too hot in summer and too cold in winter.
In another way your physical desires are like an unpredictable associate, whom you must be patient with. That companion becomes helpful when patience expands your capacity to love and feel peace.
Friendship and loyalty have patience as the strength of their connections, but feeling lonely and ignoble indicates that you have not developed patient trust.
Be with those who mix with God just as honey blends with milk and say, "Anything that comes and goes, or rises and sets, is not what I love."
Live in the One who does not rise or set, else you'll be like a caravan-fire left to flare itself out alone alongside the road.

—adapted from Jalaluddin Rumi

II

Little by little, wean yourself.
This is the gist of what I have to say.
From an embryo, whose nourishment comes in the blood,
move to an infant drinking milk,
to a child on solid food,
to a searcher after wisdom,
to a hunter of even more invisible game.

Think how it is to have a conversation with an embryo.
You might say, "The world outside is vast and intricate,
there are wheat fields and mountain passes
and orchards in bloom.
At night there are millions of stars, and there is daytime and sunlight,
the beauty of friends dancing at a wedding.

You ask the embryo why he or she stays cooped up
in the dark with their eyes closed.
Just listen to the answer:
There is no "other world,"
Are you crazy?
I know what I've experienced.
You must be hallucinating.

—adapted from Jalaluddin Rumi

LOGION 102

Sapiential Themes

- *Parable and metaphor play a prophetic role in wisdom tradition.*
- *Traditional wisdom is able to critique conventional religion from a viewpoint beyond the conventions.*
- *Animals of all sorts play mythic roles in wisdom fables and parables.*
- *Cursing and blessing are at opposite ends on a continuum of human experience.*

Yeshua says,

Cursed are your
religious leaders
for they are like dogs
sleeping in the feed bin.
They do not eat
nor do they allow
the cattle to eat.

Parallel Texts

Thomas 39
Matthew 23:13
Luke 11:52

Links

There are certain kinds of relationships (and demands made in those relationships), that must be rejected as unacceptable in the world of contemplative wisdom. Here is one such relationship which falls in the realm of religion itself which is supposedly the "heartland of truth"—the place where truth is born, nourished and passed on to feed future generations. Yeshua sees that rather than being a source, conventional religion actually blocks the nourishing process.

FOCAL POINT

At the heart of Yeshua's critique of the religious establishment of his day are those leaders who prevent ordinary people from entering in and taking proper nourishment. He likens them to dogs, which are deemed unclean by Jewish law. These paragons of religious power are in fact acting in an unclean way at those very places of spiritual enrichment where people come to be fed and nourished. According to Yeshua's way of seeing, conventional religion is, in that circumstance, dangerous and far removed from its sustaining role. This provides a prophetic warning to people in his own time and can be applied just as easily to our own world as well.

Notes

This Logion contains what is apparently a Greek proverb from ancient times concerning "a dog in a manger." The word "manger" is translated here as feed-bin or feeding trough. The word "allow" is missing but implied in the original text.

COMMENTARY

This aphorism may be one of the most damning critiques of conventional religion in recorded history—short, pithy, and to the point. When power and religion combine, it is often a toxic mix. In this case Yeshua sees, in his own world, that when religious leaders have a vested interest in maintaining control, inclusion in the rights and privileges of religion is typically reserved only for those close to the center of power. Everyone else is kept at a distance. But the most damning condemnation of all concerns the actual spiritual state of the religious leaders themselves—they are acting in a state of sleep. They are not awake to spiritual reality and so they are bringing harm to the very ones they are meant to guide. They are unclean dogs who are either ignorant or, perhaps, maliciously asleep.

Negative (or destructive) hierarchies have given a bad name to most religious institutions. There are, however, positive (and constructive) hierarchies that are necessary for all living systems in the human body and deep ecologies within the natural systems of the world. Such hierarchies may be necessary if religion as a social institution is to be of value to seekers.

Exclusion is a tactic typically used in exoteric religion where tight control is maintained at the center as the status quo. Everyone else is kept at bay in the margins. The "uninitiated" are not allowed to receive the privileges that those in power receive. A theological basis is often used as a rationale for this stratification—those who are excluded from the center are said to be unworthy or unacceptable. There are, however, gradations or levels of acceptability—those closer in and most acceptable and those further out and least desirable.

Yeshua is appalled by this. He knows differently. His understanding of divine Reality sees a clear path to God especially for the marginalized and social outcasts. From the divine perspective they are near the center, and the privileged who are actually the alienated and estranged ones, are at the margins. The image he uses is very much a part of rural life in first-century Palestine where stock were kept. Could it be that he had seen (and experienced) this very scene—dogs in the feed-bin who kept the cattle at bay?

In Jewish tradition, dogs are, of course, unclean and so to use that analogy for the leaders of conventional religion in his day is a serious affront. Certainly the word would get out that this was his attitude, and no doubt it added to the resentment that clearly built around Yeshua—an itinerant and unschooled teacher of wisdom unrecognized and unsanctioned by the religious establishment.

So what are we to make of authority in religious convention? Yeshua has given Caesar his due in a previous saying. Instead of cursing Rome, he turns his ire on established religion. Perhaps it is because religious (or sacred) tradition should know better. It should be the most sensitive to the needs of human beings, especially those who feel most estranged from God. You might expect exclusionary treatment from power-politics, but to have religion play such a role when the needs of humanity are so severe is a travesty. Yeshua will have none of it. He expresses the demands of the Kingdom of heaven as he knows it, as well as the insights of wisdom about a tradition that is asleep to its responsibilities and to the needs of those it is meant to serve.

What, then, is to be done? Yeshua does not answer the question in this saying, but in his own reactions to the world around him it is clear that he is constantly making a way for those in need to come close. He is giving them access in every way he can. The next Logion, however, may hold the key to how an individual may respond to exclusionary forces. It may provide the necessary steps for the removal of all obstacles for any human being longing for access to the divine Reality.

QUESTIONS FOR REFLECTION

1. How would you express the meaning of the vivid metaphor of "dogs in the manager" in modern English? Why do you think he is using such a vivid image? What would be the purpose?

2. How do you get a dog removed from a place that is manger-like?

3. Reflecting on Yeshua's use of this metaphor, can you identify any agents in our world foreign to the manager that may be keeping people at bay and away from what they need most in religion?

4. What, in your view, are those agents and how should we address this issue today?

EXERCISES AND MEDITATIONS

1. "Dogs in the manger" is a metaphor. It need not be applied simply to religion, as Yeshua does in this saying, but to any situation where something sits right in the middle of what we most need and we cannot get to it. Imagine, then, your personal situation either past or present—has there ever been, or is there now a "dog in your manger"? It is an important question when it comes to spiritual growth. What is your "manger"?
2. Take some time and illustrate this Logion. It may help to draw a picture or make a diagram of this metaphor in order to more fully understand it. In your diagram or illustration put what you feel is at stake for you, and also what is behind the use of this metaphor by Yeshua that makes it such a vivid description of affairs in the conventional religious world of Yeshua's day.
3. Imagine that the word "cursed" (or "Woe to...") is an exact opposite of the word "blessed." A blessing and a curse stand at opposite extremes. What then would be the blessing that would picture what Yeshua may have in mind? How would it be to work with that image (or that idea) in one's own life or in the spiritual and religious worlds and have it be a blessing?
4. You might want to interview or talk to other people that you know and respect about their experience of this kind of challenge in contemporary religion. Religion clearly plays an important role for individuals in society. How might we begin to respond to this same kind of situation in our day? How do we assist people who cannot approach religion any longer but need its nutritional value?

READINGS FOR INSIGHT

I

In my travels, I came upon a village that had a new temple built over a big well, but no one could draw water from it without paying a price. I asked about this, and this story was told: *One hundred years ago, there was a group of boys that would go to the well to swim, that is, all but one would dive from the top, for one was crippled and could only watch. With all his heart he would wish he was like his friends, that his one arm and leg had not been limp since he was born. One day when it was especially hot, and he was watching his friends swimming and laughing at the bottom of the well, they all turned to him and stared in awe as if seeing something miraculous. The crippled boy turned around and Krishna was standing there smiling wonderfully and said, "It sure is hot today, climb on my back—we will dive in." And they did. Krishna never came up from the bottom of the well, it is said, and when the child who had been on the back of Krishna came up, he was no longer crippled and remained healed the rest of his life.*

The fame of the well spread and many legends and rumors naturally evolved and began to circulate. But the water remained free, and hundreds would travel to drink it and camp there at night and tell the different stories they had heard; the point being, they would be thinking of the Lord and participating in the stories, in a way that helped them most.

A scholar, a lawyer, and a priest arrived one day and all pissed in the water, so to speak. What the priest and scholar wanted people to believe got printed in books, which they also sold along with the water, and of course the lawyer made their insanity legal.

Mirabai
Love Poems from God
264-265

II

Dov Ber was an uncommonly religious man. When people came into his presence, they trembled. He was a Talmudic scholar of repute, inflexible and uncompromising in his doctrine. And he never laughed. He believed firmly in self-inflicted pain and was known to fast for days on end. Dov Ber's austerities finally got the better of him. He fell seriously ill and there was nothing the doctors could do to cure him. As a final resort, someone made a suggestion: "Why not seek the help of the Baal Shem Tov?"

Dov Ber agreed, even though at first he resisted the idea because he strongly disapproved of Baal Shem whom he considered to be something of a heretic. Also, while Dov Ber believed that life was only made meaningful by suffering and tribulation, Baal Shem sought to alleviate pain and openly preached that it was the spirit of rejoicing that gave meaning to life.

It was past midnight when Baal Shem answered the summons and drove up dressed in a coat of wool and a cap of the finest fur. He walked into the sick man's room and handed him the Book of Splendor, which Dov Ber opened and began to read aloud.

He had hardly read a minute when, so the story goes, Baal Shem interrupted him. "Something is missing," he said.

"And what is that?" the sick man asked.

"Soul," said the Baal Shem Tov.

Anthony de Mello
Taking Flight
57-58

III

What good is it if the scholar pores over words and points of this and that but his chest is not soaked dark with love? What good is it if the ascetic clothes himself in saffron robes but is colorless within? What good is it if you scrub your ethical behavior till it shines, but there is no music inside?

Kabir

LOGION 103

Sapiential Themes

- *The theme of blessedness includes an awareness that understands the present moment as well as its connection to one's origins.*
- *Personal sovereignty is intimately related to the divine Sovereignty as it was made manifest and available to humankind from the beginning.*
- *The human **kosmos** has the capacity to steal spiritually from human beings. One must prepare by reaching beyond the human **kosmos**.*

Yeshua says,

Blessed are those who are aware
of the approach of thieves,
who know when and where they will
enter even before they appear,
for then they can arise and prepare
by gathering their sovereignty
about them,
binding to themselves
that which was there from the beginning.

Parallel Texts

Thomas 21
Matthew 24:37-44
Luke 12:39-40
I Thessalonians 5:2
II Peter 3:10
Revelations 3:3, 16:15

Links

*An obvious link between this saying and the previous logion has to do with two states—dogs who are asleep, and someone awake to the present danger. These two elements have been contrasted again and again throughout the Gospel of Thomas, but here an awake being is taking into consideration all that must be done to prepare him or herself for challenges in the environment of the human **kosmos.***

FOCAL POINT

In contrast to the earlier Logion 21, which contains many of the same elements as this saying, Logion 103 begins as a ***Makarios***—the extension of divine blessing, the suggestion of a blessed state of being in which the hearer might find him or herself. Previously Yeshua has warned his students about this possibility of thievery, but now, it seems, this state of blessedness may have been achieved. There is a new depth in the practice of awareness that makes it possible for someone to live awake and aware, as opposed to religious leaders who are said to be asleep as in the previous Logion.

Notes

*There is ambiguity in the text concerning either the time or the place (or both) in which the thieves appear. The word **sovereignty** is used in this text to translate the word **kingdom** in the original. To bind to one's loins is an ancient semiticism which is perhaps equivalent to "rolling up your sleeves" and being prepared for what is to come.*

COMMENTARY

There is agreement on the dangerous nature of earth experience and that it involves suffering, both in the early writings of Ya'akov (James) and in Buddhism as well.

A contemporary example of such an awareness is beautifully expressed in the text by Pema Chödron, ***The Places That Scare You*** *(Shambhala, 2002).*

Dangers and challenges are part of the temporal order. We are surrounded by elements that would do us harm. Those who are awake and aware and truly conscious of the dangers around them, however, can respond, reaching out for help to a power greater than themselves. Only the power of a sovereignty and strength greater than oneself can avail. So to what power does one go? Yeshua says that the ability to deal with the thieving nature of the ***kosmos*** comes from our original inheritance and not from political authority or religious tradition. Our true inheritance, existent from the beginning, is able to withstand the corrosive powers that oppress this world.

Perhaps such external enemies as the power of Roman domination, or the corrosive influence the elitism or exclusivism of the of religious establishment would prove to be an immediate threat to the spiritual well being of the individual in this case. However, it is more likely that the enemy is within, rather than without—that this individual's own inner resistance might prove, in the end, to be overpowering. In either case, these powers act as thieves, stealing spiritual treasure and strength from humankind. They take advantage because the average person remains unaware and is not awake to the threat. The condition of sleep and the power of wakefulness are contrasted here in a powerful way, illustrating what is at stake for human beings in the historical conditions of the world.

The students of Yeshua are being asked to awaken to another reality, and in that awakening to become aware of the true conditions of the external ***kosmos*** as well as to their own inner world. In that state they are to gather to themselves extraordinary power—a sovereignty which is their true heritage from their beginnings prior to their emergence in time. This is a continuous theme in the Gospel of Thomas. Throughout the text Yeshua insists that we can come to know our pre-eternal state—to know what was ours from our origins. It is critical, because it puts one's smaller earthly story into the larger history of one's entire eternal existence. There is immense power in knowing this pre-eternal state—for it is the source of who we are, the source of our eventual sovereignty and the cause of our ability to exercise mastery over the world of impermanence.

If we only know ourselves within the framework of space and time, then we have no superior or transcendent knowledge to draw upon. To see that we are not limited by time and space, but have resources (from our beginnings) beyond them, is to draw upon a larger wisdom, a greater intelligence that belongs to us and to which we belong. This binding (or perhaps, yoke) is a bond that links us to our higher Source, and gives us sovereignty (the capacity to reign over our own affairs and not simply be its victim). It also bestows blessedness, the state of rest where we are not subject to the emotional toll that the world can and often does take. These are, of course, ideal states, but in truth they define the soul's essence, with which when asleep we lose touch. But they also define the states of those who choose now to live in the Realm of the Kingdom (as opposed to some future moment). The ability to exist in the reality of the Kingdom now is the definition of a "saint," but more importantly for Yeshua, it defines a true citizen of the Father's Realm. These states are keys to the Kingdom and to our experience of it in the present age and in the present moment. Understanding this, we have come full circle in Yeshua's explanation of the six states of wisdom which were outlined at the beginning of the Gospel in Logion 2—searching, finding, being troubled, emerging into wonder and awe, reigning in sovereignty, and finding ultimate rest.

QUESTIONS FOR REFLECTION

1. It is common in this world to talk about friends and enemies. We want to be clear who are our allies and who are our opponents. We want to win against our enemies and prevail with our friends. So who or what would you put in those two categories?

2. What kind of thieves or thievery is Yeshua describing here? When have you detected that someone or something has stolen spiritual power away from you? Are these the thieves Yeshua is talking about?

3. There are important verbs used in this text that describe how one stands against such theft. What are they?

4. What would you imagine that being from your beginning or Source is strong enough to prevail against your current enemies or detractors?

EXERCISES AND MEDITATIONS

1. You may or may not have noticed, but this saying suggests an ability to know beforehand both the time and the place of a future event related to one's own life. This is called "pre-cognition" about the future, having to do with a possible future harm or threat. Yeshua suggests here that such knowledge is possible, and we may have never considered it. What is your experience of a pre-cognitive event in your life? Have you ever had something like this happen to you? What spiritual state does this suggest? How might one learn to exercise it? What might be the practice involved? Answers to these questions requires meditation and perhaps discussion with others about this ability and issue.
2. It is hard to imagine perhaps that spiritual thievery exists, but power and sovereignty can be stolen away from us so that we lose the ability to function effectively and forcefully in the world. The question is, of course, who are these thieves, and if they are not all external, then what form might parts of ourselves take to steal from our own wealth? Identifying such thieves and their tactics is part of the discerning process which appears to be implied by this logion.
3. Sovereignty in Logion 103 refers to "kingdom"—the whole Realm of God, and what in one's self is derived from that Realm. The implication is that each individual possesses powers (or links to power) in that Realm, and one can bring that into the present moment. The idea that there are ancient powers and also bindings from the beginning of our existence is part of the mystical theology of this text. In a time of reflection, meditate on that possibility and ask "the Powers that Be" to disclose what these links may be for you. Journal your findings.

Meditate on the following from the ***Tao Te Ching*** *68:*

A good soldier is not violent.
A good fighter is not angry.
A good winner is not vengeful.
A good employer is humble.
This is known as the virtue of not striving.
This is known as the ability to deal with people.
This since ancient times has been known as the ultimate unity with heaven.

How does this passage relate to Yeshua's saying?

READINGS FOR INSIGHT

I

Anthony de Mello
One Minute Wisdom
82

The Master's expansive mood emboldened his disciples to say,
"Tell us what you got from Enlightenment. Did you become divine?"
"No."
"Did you become a saint?"
"No"
"Then what did you become?"
"Awake."

II

Najm ad-Din Daya Razi
Loves Alchemy
159

Before diffusing the light
of the Pleiades
Before stretching the zodiac's band
across the heavens...
From before the beginning of time...
like a flame from a candle,
your love has bound itself to us
with a thousand chains.

III

The Gospel of Philip
Analogue Four
The Luminous Gospels
84

The Anointed One has come! And in coming some he ransoms, others he releases and restores, and there are those whom he rescues. He ransomed strangers and made them his own. Those who came to him, he restored. All this he gave as a self-offering out of his own love and desire. Not only did he willingly give himself at his appearing, from the very beginning of the ***kosmos*** it was his longing to do so. And so now in this way he comes to receive back what he has always loved—releasing all who were held captive by thieves of the soul, redeeming everything in the ***kosmos***, both good and evil.

IV

Thomas Crombie

No man is free who is not
master of his soul and controller of his spirit.

V

Dave E. Smalley

The survival of the fittest is the ageless law of nature, but the fittest are rarely the strong. The fittest are those endowed with the qualifications for adaptation, the ability to accept the inevitable and conform to the unavoidable, to harmonize with existing or changing conditions.

VI

Aristotle

Excellence is an art won by training and habituation. We do not act rightly because we have virtue or excellence, but we rather have those because we have acted rightly. We are what we repeatedly do. Excellence, then is not an act, but a habit.

LOGION 104

They said to Yeshua,

"Come, then,
let us fast
and pray."

He said to them,
"Have I sinned?
Have I been overcome?
No, only when the bridegroom
leaves the bridal chamber,
will it be time to fast and pray."

FOCAL POINT

As is often the case, Yeshua is challenged here by the conventional norms of his day. He is asked to conform to ritual practice. Fasting and prayer are staples in the religious piety of first century Judaism. Does anything supersede it? The insistence that these are the practices that can help those who are most in need of salvation and healing is countered by a claim to an altogether different inner state. That inner reality is described as the state of the "Bridal Chamber"—a way of being in union with and in relationship to divine Reality in an entirely singular manner. Inner intimacy, and not external conformity, is the condition for the possibility of salvation and healing.

Sapiential Themes

- *The mystery and experience of the Bridal Chamber trumps all other forms of praxis in early Christianity.*
- *Fasting and prayer are secondary practices prior to or following the Bridal Chamber experience.*
- *Yeshua's inner life is expressed intimately by this phraseology, which has its source in the Song of Songs of the ancient Hebrew people.*

Links

In the previous logion, the encounter is with thieves who are entering the domicile of the seeker. Perhaps, logically, it must be assumed that such a possibility is the result of some fault of the householder, but here Yeshua suggests something else entirely. Inner experience can be disturbed by outside forces, but for one who knows the Bridal Chamber experience, the inner experience is kept sacrosanct. The experience on the inside is quite different from what his students might have conventionally expected.

Parallel Texts

Song of Songs
Thomas 6, 14, 27
Matthew 9:14-17
Mark 2:18-22
Luke 5:33-39
Gospel of Philip 40-42

Notes

In his response to his students, Yeshua answers the possibility that was represented in the previous saying, of being over-run (or overcome) by approaching thieves. He assures them he has not, but if at any time he should leave the Bridal Chamber, then it would be fitting to fast and pray. There is clear interaction between sayings here which suggest that Yeshua is working from some inner imaginal space that wisdom knows.

COMMENTARY

Fasting and prayer were standard practices in the spiritual lives of the followers of Yeshua in first-century Judaism. They were considered basic, and had a venerable legacy in the common customs of Yeshua's day. Pious Jews were expected to fast and pray, and it is clear that these were practiced by Yeshua himself as is evident in the accounts concerning his temptation in the Judean desert. Fasting and prayer were known as bulwarks against evil. They were used to strengthen the human spirit against the attacks by evil forces. There was no better way to ward off Satanic power (or at least this was the common wisdom of Jewish spirituality). So when Yeshua is asked to engage in these practices during his years of ministry (perhaps as a direct result of his teaching about spiritual thievery), his answer is interesting.

He does not automatically agree to their request. First, he asks them a question about his own state of being. He wants to know if they think he has sinned or has been overcome by evil in some way. Perhaps they do not answer, and so he answers for them with a "No." This may be both a negation of the notion that he is living in a state of sin, or even perhaps the repudiation of a theology based upon sin and redemption as we know it today.

Regardless, he refuses their request to perform practices that they think are necessary. Perhaps they have responded in this way as the answer for their need for protection from the thief in the last logion. Or, in some way, they sense this is required for their well-being in the present moment. In whatever context we might situate this request, Yeshua goes beyond the normal bounds of conventional practice and points to an inner state describing an intimacy that he knows and is somehow experiencing.

The image he uses is one of a bridegroom in a bridal chamber—the residential inner sanctum for love-making for a bride and groom who are able to consummate their union in a sexual way. In that inner chamber fasting and prayer are not central—they have no practical effect—only the intimate knowledge of one another in nuptial relationship is required. This is one of the most vivid and perhaps the strangest of all images describing spiritual marriage—the possibility of intimate relationship between the human and the divine. The term "Bridal Chamber" is the unique way that Yeshua has of talking about this metaphor. To enter the Bridal Chamber is to have intimate "intercourse" with the Divine in a way that is similar to sexual embrace between human beings on earth. Can this be right? Is it correct or even possible to speak of such an intimacy between human beings and the "person or being" of the Divine?

The vivid and startling use of this sexual and poetic image already has a venerable history in the sacred writings of the Hebrew peoples. It is picked up by Yeshua as central to his own experience, and later it will be carried forward in all three of the Ahrahamic faiths as an image for the deepest knowledge that humans can have of the divine Reality.

If and when the time comes that this inner state of union must be left behind—then, it will be time for both prayer and fasting. Until then, the experience of the Bridal Chamber trumps everything else. Yeshua is asserting here that there is a marriage that takes place between the human and the Divine in the inner chambers of the soul. It occurs at the level of the heart which symbolically has been called the "Bridal Chamber." This is the apex (or climax) of contact between the human and the divine, and from that contact an intimacy of union is reached. There is nothing greater than this image to point the way to the deepest immanence that can be known in this world and perhaps beyond it.

QUESTIONS FOR REFLECTION

1. What is your experience with prayer and fasting combined? How have you practiced it? What did you find? How focused do you think spiritual practice today should be on fasting and prayer?

2. There is perhaps no more striking image of intimacy between human beings and the divine Reality than the picture of sexual union in the Bridal Chamber. What is your response to such vivid imagery?

3. Do you have any personal experience of such a mystical state?

4. There appear to be two sets of spiritual values expressed in this saying—religious piety and mystical ecstasy. Do you agree, or would you describe it in some other way?

EXERCISES AND MEDITATIONS

1. Yeshua highlights intimacy with God in his teachings in so many ways. First, he uses the signature phrase "my Father" to describe God as ***Abba***, a beloved parent. Then he clearly speaks of loving God on an intimate level as a form of self-knowing that indicates friendship and even companionship. Finally, he uses the bridal imagery of sexual union as the highest aspect of intimacy. How comfortable are you with the three levels of this intimate imagery and with using any of these terms to describe your own experience with God? How has your own experience grown and expanded to include any (if not all) of this imagery? How would deeper intimacy with God become possible for you? What would it take to reach the highest level of intimacy? What would it mean practically?

How hard is it for you to imagine the Bridal Chamber as the "honeymoon suite" (which is what it clearly refers to in modern parlance)?

2. Spiritual marriage (***hiergamos***) is the term that has been traditionally used in mystical literature to describe intercourse between the human and divine at its deepest and most intimate level. In the wisdom literature of the Hebrew people, the **Song of Songs** was seen as the ancient source of this spiritual understanding and has been used as a foundational document describing the metaphorical "love-play" in this relationship. You might want to read this ancient text from the Hebrew Scriptures with Logion 104 in your mind. Journal your impressions and findings.
3. What would compel someone to leave a Bridal Chamber? Yeshua describes a legitimate use of fasting and prayer when the level of intimacy is broken or is not as high or intense as what occurs in the bridal chamber. Can you distinguish between these two states in your own experience? How would you describe this to someone else?

READINGS FOR INSIGHT

I

The Gospel of Philip
Analogue 50
The Luminous Gospels
100-101

At the river Jordan, Yeshua revealed the great fullness that is the Kingdom of the heavens, which existed before all things. There he was begotten as the son. There he was anointed. There he was restored to fullness of being. And from there he began the great Restoration.

So let us speak then of this great mystery in this way: The Father of All came down and united with "the virgin," and on that day made light shine forth from the fire—revealing to us the power of the Bridal Chamber. Because of this, also on that day Yeshua came into fullness of being, coming forth from the Bridal Chamber as a bridegroom with his bride. It was also in this way that the balance of All was established in Yeshua's heart so that by means of this each of his students might have access to enter into his Rest.

II

Jalaluddin Rumi

The connection to the Friend is secret and fragile.
The image of that friendship is in how you love in the outer world.
It is also in the grace and delicacy,
and the subtle talking together in full prostration outside of time.
When you are there, in that inner chamber,
remember the fierce courtesy of the One you are with.

III

Anthony de Mello
One Minute Wisdom
93

The Master would insist that the final barrier to our attaining God was the word and concept of "God." This so infuriated the local priest that he came in a huff to argue the matter out with the Master.

"But surely the word 'God' can lead us to God?" said the priest.

"It can," said the Master calmly.

"How can something help and be a barrier?"

Said the Master, "The donkey that brings you to the door is not the means by which you enter the house."

IV

Kabir

When the day came—
The Day I had lived and died for—
The Day that is not on any calendar—
Clouds heavy with love showered me with wild abundance.
Inside me, my soul was drenched.
Around me, even the desert grew green.

V

Thomas Traherne
Teachings of the Christian Mystics
135

Your enjoyment of the world is never right, till every morning you awake in Heaven; see yourself in your Father's Palace; and look upon the skies, the earth, and all, as if you were among the Angels. The bride of a monarch, in her husband's chamber, hath no such causes of delight as you.

LOGION 105

Yeshua says,

The one who knows
his true father and mother
will be called
the son of a whore.

Sapiential Themes

- *Origination, a crucial teaching in the wisdom tradition, has to do with genesis and parentage.*
- *The origins of humanity are elsewhere. They are not earthly.*
- *The divine masculine and the divine feminine are at the heart of Yeshua's origins—as they are for each created being.*
- *Society has other standards concerning parentage. Visionary seeing perceives the transcendent sources of human origination..*

Parallel Texts

Thomas 61, 101
John 8:39-47

FOCAL POINT

It appears certain that Yeshua is speaking in this Logion about himself. He says that he knows the stories about who his parents are. He also knows something greater, his true origins. He is aware of the ultimate masculine and feminine source of his being. In the social circles of his day, however, he is called a bastard, or "the son of a whore." This was undoubtedly the taunt leveled at him throughout his entire life. At an early age, he no doubt experienced the blunt force and hurt of this phrase as a form of deep personal pain. This was perhaps the motivation that sent him beyond his own family-of-origin to seek the ground of his being. It is perhaps this which drove him into the Presence of an ***Abba*** that knew him deeply and intimately and with whom he shared deep and intimate friendship.

Links

The issue of sin has been raised in the last Logion. Is Yeshua living in sin? Does it require that he fast and pray? Perhaps from a social point of view in the Jewish world of the first-century Yeshua is "unclean," contaminated by an illegitimate birth, and his "sin" is the result of his birth circumstances. Yeshua rejects both premises. He knows his true parentage. His origins are not earthly, and he has learned that, perhaps, in the Bridal Chamber.

Notes

The use of the definite article for "the" father and "the" mother seems to point to a specific that is beyond "his" particular, natural parents. The term "son of a whore" could have easily been translated as "bastard" which is the slur that was used against Yeshua into his adulthood.

COMMENTARY

This logion may provide us with another of several autobiographical glimpses we have into the personal experience of Yeshua. It is clear from this and other canonical passages that Yeshua's parentage was in question throughout his life. He had certainly heard the expression "bastard" (son of a whore) hurled at him more than once. It may have been a life-long epithet that he was never able to escape, so it shaped his perceptions and left its mark upon his life and teachings. It may have also driven him beyond being simply a victim of social convention to become aware of and sensitive to the pain and suffering of others in a very deep way. Whether or not this epithet wounded him, it is clear that he paid close attention to those living at society's margins in his day. Beyond that, he seemed far more aware than most human beings are of his own his true and divine Source at the center of his being.

This has been cited by Marvin Meyer

There is, of course, a long tradition based upon a quotation found in Origen's **Against Celsus** (1.28;32), which says that Jesus was the "illegitimate" child of Mary. This story circulated throughout the first and second centuries, but was also juxtaposed by the story of his virgin birth. Origen records that Mary 'bore a child from a certain soldier named Panthera.' It is known from a gravestone that a Sidonian archer named Tiberius Julius Abdes Pantera was in fact stationed in Palestine around the time of the birth of Yeshua. Whether or not this particular set of circumstances is historical, it is clear there were serious questions surrounding his birth, and those questions perhaps became the motivation for the young man, Yeshua, to question his earthly as well as eternal origins.

If there was any doubt about his historical parentage, there was no doubt about the deep conviction he had received concerning his own true Origins. He was inexorably drawn beyond cultural conventions and social gossip to understand his and all of humankind's transcendent Source. If people called into question the identity of his mother and father on earth, his own eternal origins were understood and in that understanding he was secure.

In his social world to be born "out of wedlock," was a disgrace, never to be overcome, and not easily managed as a social stigma. Yeshua had, then, to deal with this issue as a constant reminder that for all intents and purposes he himself remained on the fringes of acceptable society. Perhaps that is why he identified so closely with those who for this and other reasons were marginalized in his day. Perhaps this experience is the primal cause of his compassion for those suffering and in need. This may have been at the root of his pursuits of deep compassionate wisdom.

Yes he might be called "the son of a whore," but that expression meant nothing in comparison to knowing his relationship to his true mother and his real father—his Ultimate Origination. For him, the pre-temporal cause of his being was not in doubt, and neither is it for any human being. However, the certainty of our historical parentage may keep us from seeking beyond the literal circumstances of our birth-parents to find and identify with this ultimate Source. Never to question who our earthly parents are may leave the deeper question of who we really are and where we come from unanswered for a life-time. Spiritual meaning and social history are layered in this text. The true cause and circumstance of human origination is central to its teaching. In the rush of our normal day-to-day activities and in the press of our daily needs, we are typically unaware and out of touch with our own true genesis. To live in that ignorance is to be asleep, and to fail our full potential, missing the mark.

QUESTIONS FOR REFLECTION

1. Have you ever been called a name that demeaned you? Describe your experience of this.

2. Have you ever known someone who, for whatever reason, was considered to be an "illegitimate child," born without the benefit of parents with socially accepted marital status? What was it like for them? How do you imagine that experience? What kind of mark would it leave on a person?

One is reminded of the story of ***The Scarlet Letter*** *by Nathaniel Hawthorne.*

3. How close do you feel to your birth-parents? Does the fact that you are said to have originated outside of space and time fundamentally change the way you see them or live in this world?

4. Explain the "motherhood of God" as a concept or as a metaphor. How is God a mother as well as a father?

EXERCISES AND MEDITATIONS

1. We often contemplate the unfolding of our lives into the future. We might even try to imagine our own death and what experiences we will have beyond it. Seldom do we try to imagine what or who we were before we came into physical being. Typically we imagine that we were nothing at all, and came into existence at our birth on earth. The Gospel of Thomas does not hold that view. It imagines that we had a mother and a father prior to our earthly parents. Yeshua was forced perhaps by the circumstances of his life to contemplate his pre-existence before coming into time and to connect with those origins. In a period of meditation push back beyond your own conception and birth on earth to your prior existence. Imagine that you were brought into being in a realm that transcends earth. Imagine that you were sent here from there. Do you have any sense of this, any feelings or intuitions about that possibility ? Do you feel that you may have been on the earth before this in another incarnation? Thomas does not specifically teach the doctrine of reincarnation, but it does express prior existence to your lifetime on earth.
2. Being in a place of intimidation is not easy for any of us. There are various spiritual traditions where followers of the spiritual path deliberately put themselves in this place as a form of deep personal practice. In Russia the "clowns of God" were such a tradition. In Islam the practices of the ***Malamati*** (those who incur blame) were another. In each case individuals endured public humiliation as a test of their own maturity and freedom from an egoic state. We might not wish to practice this as a norm, but we experience it nonetheless throughout our life-time. Notice when this happens to you. What is your reaction? What is your response? Could you "take it" and learn from it?

READINGS FOR INSIGHT

I

Pain is the wind his flags unfurl in,
The desert that the stallions cross and re-cross without check or end,
He is my anguish, and I am his.

Jalaluddin Rumi

II

A bumptious man dismissed a wandering sage by shouting at him, "Be off, nobody knows you here."

"But I know myself," said the sage. "How sad it would be if the reverse were true."

A traditional Sufi saying

III

When a deep injury is done to us,
we never recover until we forgive.

Alan Paton

IV

Define and narrow me down, you starve yourself of yourself.
Nail me into a box of cold words and that box becomes your coffin.
I do not know who I am
I am in astounding, lucid confusion.
I am not a Christian, a Jew or a Zoroastrian.
I am not even a Muslim.
I do not belong to the land or to any known or unknown sea.
Nature cannot own or claim me, nor can heaven, nor India, China, or Bulgaria.
My birthplace is placelessness.
My sign is to have and give no sign.
You say you see my mouth, my ears, eyes, or nose—but they are not mine.
I am the life of Life.
I am that cat, this stone, no one at all.
I have thrown duality away like an old dishrag.
I see and know all times and world as one, one, always one.
So what do I have to do to get you to admit who is speaking?
Admit it and change everything.
This is your own true voice echoing off the walls of God.

Jalaluddin Rumi

V

Last night a friend asked me, "Where is your homeland?"
I said nothing, for what could I say?
My homeland is not Egypt or Syria or Iraq.
My homeland's a place that has never had a name.

Jalaluddin Rumi

VI

Fear fades when facts are faced.

Frank Tyger

LOGION 106

Sapiential Themes

- *Transformation as a result of the practice of unification and integration is at the heart of this Gospel and early Christian wisdom tradition.*
- *This saying may be the quintessential teaching of the Gospel of Thomas—its core statement of purpose.*
- *This logion adds further dimensions to the content of the canonical texts that may have been missed by the other writers.*
- *Nonduality (or Oneness) is central to the vision of Yeshua and at the heart of every mystical tradition.*

Yeshua says,

When you are able
to transform
two into one,
then you too will become
"Son of Humanity,"
and it will be possible
for you to say to a mountain,
"Move," and it will move.

Parallel Texts

Thomas 22, 23, 48, 49, 75
Matthew 17:19-20, 21:18-22
Mark 11:20-25
Luke 17:5-6
I Corinthians 13:2

FOCAL POINT

Links

The kind of knowing that is aware of its origins and source in the way suggested by the previous saying is a prerequisite for the breakthrough in practice and awareness that this logion expresses. Knowing the true Mother and Father who are the Source then leads to the awareness and power of a child of Humanity

At the heart of Yeshua's message is a vision of nonduality—unity and oneness at the core of the universe. This is not simply an idea, it is also a way of being that involves change and transformation at one's center. Far from being just a doctrine, it is a practice that leads to an unfragmented and united Self that is the true nature of the "Son of Humanity." This phrase carries important information about our religious and spiritual heritage. Our origins lie in the "original Adam" (***Adam Kadmon***) who is understood to be the collectivity of the divine-humanity (the "complete being" of humankind that contains every member in the whole and filled with the divine Presence). This entity exists prior to and outside of historical reality. Knowing one's connection to that Being has effects that can move "mountains."

Notes

The term "Son of Humanity" is literally in Coptic "the sons of the Man," indicating, of course, children and not just male sons—though the male designation has weight in the traditional world of the Middle East.

COMMENTARY

We are at a key moment in the Gospel of Thomas. Everything, it seems, has been leading to this logion—preparing for and moving toward those elements that are essential to it. The theme of oneness (and twoness) has been used repeatedly throughout the Gospel text. It is a theme that connects many threads weaving them together into a single tapestry. The primary vision of Yeshua, at least as understood by Thomas, is a unitary vision, where oneness with the whole of reality, and the Source of Ultimate Reality, is seen as the goal on the journey he is taking. This united whole is Yeshua's understanding of the Kingdom—the word "kingdom" defines it as a sovereignty through which this higher authority reigns.

Non-duality is at the core of all metaphysical seeing and teaching. It has various names throughout the sacred traditions. Typically the term "oneness" (as opposed to twoness or duality) is used as a concrete expression of this central idea within the Semitic traditions. Philosophically and metaphysically it appears to be the same.

Oneness is not simply a concept, it is also an operation—a form of transformation. One knows this unity not just conceptually but through the praxis of actually achieving it, by taking separate elements that constitute the realm of twoness and transforming them so that they become a single whole. It is the ability to perform this act—to act in this way (to turn what is two into one) that is the sign of the presence of that Being called the "Son of Humanity." This is the manifestation of a form that has perhaps heretofore been hidden, but is now revealed. The revelation of the complete form of the ***son of the Anthropos*** (as the phrase can also be translated) is something that awaits this act. This ability is what the "child of the Anthropos" is actually able to do. It is the sign of the power and Presence of that entity. The revelation of that Being has been awaiting this activity, which is also its revelation.

This form of humanity is, of course, very mysterious to us. We are not sure, perhaps, what to look for. Based upon Yeshua's own use of the title "Son of Man (Humanity)," one way to understand him is that this Entity makes itself known through him. In the tradition of Yeshua we witness both its manifestation and the activity of transforming two into one. We have seen the signs of it accomplished in just such transformations—taking what is separated in its dualistic forms, and turning them into the manifestations of oneness. Yeshua's powers to heal, to perform acts that we call miraculous are, in fact, ways of understanding unitive transformation as a reconciling and healing force expressed through him in the world through that Higher Power.

Metaphysically, non-dual oneness and the existence of the great Anthropos belong together. As Ken Wilber expresses it, "... (the) observing Self eventually discloses its own source, which is Spirit itself, Emptiness itself. And that is why the mystics maintain that this observing Self is a ray of the Sun that is the radiant Abyss and ultimate Ground upon which the entire manifest Kosmos depends. Your very Self intersects the Self of the Cosmos at large—a supreme identity that outshines the entire manifest world, a supreme identity that undoes the knot of the separate self and buries it in splendor. "
***A Brief History of Everything**, 199*

Sickness, for example, is a sign of loss and fragmentation from wholeness. Yeshua heals by restoring wholeness and unity of being. He heals people into wholeness (or oneness) of being. That is the primary sign of his ministry. But the question is, is he the **only** manifestation of such a possibility, unique and unrepeatable in his capabilities? Some would, of course, say "yes." But he says "no," for he insists that those who follow his path shall do greater things than this—working in the same way.

So it is possible to imagine that the "Children of the ***Anthropos***" are, in the end, a collective of beings united to each other as a single whole and greater than the sum of their individual parts. In truth, the meaning of the term points to a form of humankind that transcends the individual as we know it to be individuated into separate and independent units (a single person), and refers to the collective body of humanity which both predates and proceeds from human existence in space-time. The ***Athropos*** (this collective Body) is, in fact, a celestial being with characteristic features that are almost beyond imagining. Yeshua is claiming to be a "child" of that body, and when called upon, able to "move mountains" if need be.

QUESTIONS FOR REFLECTION

1. Logion 106 is premised upon the capacity to transform two into one—to make duality into a unity. It is a form of practice that is to be done on the personal level. Have you ever been able to unite something that was divided, or create a unity where there was division and duality? Describe that.

2. If "Son of Humanity" (Son of Man) is literally a "Child of the *Anthropos*," how does the creative act you have described above manifested such a transformation (to change one form into another)?

3. What "mountain" may have moved for you? Have you ever made this command? How and when has that happened?

4. Do you have any evidence that you have participated as "a Child of the *Anthropos* in this larger body of humanity?

EXERCISES AND MEDITATIONS

1. Another way of translating this same saying would be: *Whenever you are able to make one from two, then you too will become a son or daughter of the Completed Human, and it will then be possible for you to say to a mountain "Move!" and it will obey you.* Does this translation change anything for you? Does it expand its meaning in some way? This a very dynamic saying inviting you to participate in its action. You are not left out. You are to become a member of this larger body by knowing and practicing the art of oneness. It is critical that the practice of this saying not remain conceptual (only inside your head), but also to become a part of the way you live. What is the secret for such a practice? What have you learned so far? Meditate on this, and journal your responses.
2. Are you currently experiencing an aspect of fragmentation in yourself or in your relationships? How might this saying apply to that situation? Imagine the possibilities for creating oneness.
3. We often imagine that this saying only applies to the human world, but suppose it extends out to include the divisions we experience with all of nature. In your experience where might this apply in the non-human world? Where could you bring this creative act of oneness to bear in the natural order?
4. Transformation is a "change of form" (or being). We see such changes in caterpillars and in pollywogs. Can you image ontological changes in the human world of such magnitude? Have you ever experienced such a change in yourself—in your way of being? It is helpful to clarify what you mean by transformation with examples when you explain this experience to someone else.

READINGS FOR INSIGHT

I

Abba Bessarion, at the point of death, said,
"The monk ought to be as the Cherubim and the Seraphim: all eye."

Only the individual can enjoy "Union with God," a term for the transcendence of all personal identity in favor of the Supreme Identity, which is what Abba Bessarion's "all eye" refers to and what non-dual consciousness means. The goal, if you will, of the evolution of consciousness is found in the realization that there is only One Self expressed in, and manifested through many selves and all of creation. In one of the many paradoxes of mystical reality, this One Self doesn't absorb the individual into an amorphous glob of something or other. Rather, it is the source, substance, and expression of individual identity, meaning, and purpose. Or, to put it another way, the One Self has two faces: human and divine.

Gregory Mayers
Listen to the Desert
88, 100

II

Whoever has the outer law without the inner reality
has abandoned the True Way.
Whoever has the inner reality without the outer law
is nothing but a heretic.
Unite the two, and you will be realized.

A traditional Sufi saying

III

The Perfect Man
is one who, in all perfection,
acts like a slave despite his Lordship.
Then, when he has come to the end of his journey,
Reality places on his head the Crown of Ruler.
He finds eternal life after dying to himself
and begins a fresh path from his End to his Origin.
Clothing himself in the Law like an exterior cloak,
he makes of the Mystic Way his inmost being.
Know that the Truth is the degree of his nature
—he comprehends at once belief and unbelief.
He is adorned with all dazzling virtues,
and praise for his consciousness,
his devotion, his holy calm.
All things are in him, but he is far from everything,
sheltered under the dais of the veils of Mystery.

Mahmud Shabistari

IV

To a disciple who was forever complaining about others the Master said, "If it is peace you want, seek to change yourself, not other people. It is easier to protect your feet with slippers than to carpet the whole of the earth."

Anthony de Mellow
One Minute Wisdom
38

LOGION 107

Sapiential Themes

- *The shepherding image used to describe divine action in the human world is an ancient metaphor from the pastoral people of the Semitic culture.*
- *In this teaching of Yeshua, the ultimate reconciliation of all things is in view. Accordingly, nothing will be lost. Every last being shall be found, which is paralleled in the Bodhisattva tradition of Buddhism.*

Yeshua says,

The divine Realm
can be compared
to a shepherd
who had one hundred sheep.
One of the finest went astray,
so he left the ninety-nine
and went out searching
for it until he found it.
Troubled he said,
"I longed for you more than
the ninety-nine."

Parallel Texts

Psalm 23, 80
Isaiah 40:11
Jeremiah 31:10
Ezekiel 34
Matthew 18:12-14
Luke 15:3-7
John 10:1-16

FOCAL POINT

The parable of the lost sheep is well known in the Gospel tradition. It is a guiding image stemming from the ancient metaphors found in early Hebrew tradition, primarily in the Psalms. God (and the divine realm itself) acts as a guiding force shepherding humanity toward its goal of finding its way back to the homeland, "dwelling in the house of the Lord forever." In the context of the previous Logion concerning the Son of Humanity, we have in this saying an image of what guidance from the person (or being) of the Shepherd is to be. It concerns not just the whole, but each separate part. All the parts or members of that community are to be present. Nothing is lost, nothing is wasted.

Links

Even before you are able to make two into one, or before you have fully become a child of the Human One, even when astray, the Shepherd is there seeking you. This is the divine longing and it precedes everything else. In the end it ***is*** *the way that two are brought together into one. The conjunction of the divine-humanity demonstrates it and in Yeshua works toward it as a goal.*

Notes

The word ***finest*** *may also be translated as "largest." The term* ***found it*** *translates the familiar "seized upon it" that is used throughout the text.* ***Longed for*** *can also be translated as "love" or "desire." The term* ***troubled*** *involves the idea of suffering.*

COMMENTARY

The Hebrew Scriptures have made us familiar with shepherding metaphors. This image is, of course, carried into the Gospel Tradition as well. It seems clear from the previous saying that in order to bring about the transformation of the human race into a unified whole, we need a Shepherd to guide it across the difficult desert landscape of this world. According to this saying, no one, not even the lost, is left out of this process. No one is missing from the whole. The true Shepherd cares for each and all down to the last, single missing sheep in a declaration of both hope, longing and intimacy. But is humanity truly lost?

The subject of "lost humanity" has occupied a central place in Abrahamic thought. Humankind appears to be lost and wandering across a bleak landscape—a desert landscape in fact. The finding (or saving) of the last sheep is a common theme, and the subject of the salvation of the soul becomes the doctrinal formula to express this. The question is, of course, what does lostness mean? Are the sheep "lost in sin," or are they lost in darkness and ignorance? Does finding them mean saving their souls from perdition and hell, or does it mean finding and awakening them in order to bring them back into the light? The answer, of course, all depends upon the theological lens through which one reads this text.

It is noteworthy that in this Logion there are a number of new elements found which are not in the canonical Gospels. The first is that this saying is an illustration of the divine Realm itself (the Kingdom of Heaven). It is in the divine Realm that the flock exists and which is actively pursuing any lost member of that flock. In the canonical Gospels this is also attributed to the will of Yeshua's Father. Second, the description of the lost sheep is of interest. That sheep is called "one of the finest" (or literally, one of the largest). Could it be that this is an apt description of the nature of those sheep who are lost in time, wandering without knowledge of their true homeland? There is something superlative about them. Because they have undertaken the journey through "the valley of the shadow of death," as it were, they are the great ones. Those who agreed to come here from the celestial lands of Paradise, get lost here, and they do indeed need to be sought out and guided by the Shepherd of Humanity.

This logion postulates a deep compassion and kindness expressed by the divine. Albert Schweitzer wrote of this divine quality:

Kindness works simply and perseveringly; it produces no strained relations which prejudice its working; strained relations which already exist, it relaxes. Mistrust and misunderstanding it puts to flight, and it strengthens itself by calling forth answering kindness. Hence it is the furthest-reaching and the most effective of all forces.

*– from **Reverence for Life**, 1969.*

Logion 107 also declares that the Shepherd is troubled, or has gone to a lot of trouble, and expresses the inner motivation which may not have been known before. There was a deep longing for the lost sheep by the Shepherd, more than for the ones who are already safe and sound. Could it be that the value of the lost one is more than the ones who were safe and never in need of the Shepherd's guidance? Could the experience of the lost sheep be of greater value than one who was never lost in the first place? Though this is not said directly, it is implied as a possible interpretation.

Perhaps beyond any of these considerations is the clear indication of a deep intimacy expressed in conversation with the lost sheep that has been found. The Divine not only has a deep longing for the one that is lost, but this longing is conveyed to and felt by the one found. In the modern world we might not consider the relationship between Shepherd and sheep to be one of intimacy, but in the world of pastoral care, there is something akin to it. Humanity is being shepherded with great kindness, great longing, and great care. More than anonymous protection, the Shepherd has a direct relationship with that one sheep—and perhaps in the end we are all that single lost soul.

QUESTIONS FOR REFLECTION

1. Have you ever felt lost, alone, and wandering—having gone astray? What was that experience like for you?

2. Have you also felt that in this seemingly cold and impersonal universe that, in fact, you have been guided by a Presence that is personal to you? What is your experience of this?

3. If you have been tasked with guiding and guarding another human being who becomes lost (or who goes astray), what has been your inner response? Is it anything like the expression in this logion?

4. What has been your sense of something or someone who was lost and is suddenly found, and therefore safe from harm? Do you "long for" that individual more than the rest? Why?

St. Teresa of Avila saw that each follower of the Master is, in fact, another "Christ," perhaps even another Shepherd:

Christ has no body now on earth but yours, no hands but yours, no feet but yours, Yours are the eyes through which to look out Christ's compassion to the world; Yours are the feet with which he is to go about doing good; Yours are the hands with which he is to bless men now.

EXERCISES AND MEDITATIONS

1. In an exercise of meditation and reflection use the translation of Psalm 23 found in the Readings for Insight on the next page as a response to the shepherd's statement in this Logion to form the basis for a new dialogue between you and the Shepherd of Humanity. Imagine that you have indeed been guided throughout your life, as the Psalm says. Now the question is what do you want to say to the Shepherd about the nature of your life? How does the Shepherd respond to you? It might be easy to see this as pure speculation or imagination, but actually the play of the heart and mind in dialogue is something that we are always doing within ourselves. We are always "in conversation" and the question is, do we have an interlocutor? If we do, then tentatively, at least, a real conversation can begin.
2. It is difficult for us to imagine, perhaps, that in interior dialogue a level of trust and unconditional love must first be established between oneself and an Other who cares unconditionally. Often, in our social environment, there are no relationships without "strings attached," and certainly God is perceived in this way as well. So to establish a different relationship is often not easy, and the way toward that kind of trust may be through another human being who acts selflessly to seek us out. The world is full of people lost in the jumble of society—individuals who fall through the cracks. Is it possible to "find" someone like that and become the "known face of the unknown Shepherd" who works through you? See if that is possible.
3. Rewrite Psalm 23 as a personal prayer that reflects your current circumstances.

READINGS FOR INSIGHT

I

1. O God, you are my shepherd,
   nothing needful shall I lack or want.
2. For in the meadows where you make me lie to rest,
   or on the paths you lead beside still waters,
3. My soul revives, refreshed again,
   to follow further the pathways of your Name.
4. Even though the way that I must take leads through the deepest shadows,
   I shall not fear the lurking evil there, nor death.
   Your presence is my rod and staff,
   my comfort and my guide.
5. And in those places where my foes rise up to trouble me
   you spread a table and make a feast;
   Anoint my head,
   and fill my cup to overflowing.
6. So now I know, O Lord, that all my life-long through
   your goodness and mercy flows and follows after me,
   And at the last when journey's done
   your dwelling place shall be my home forever.

Psalm 23
Ancient Songs Sung Anew

II

He desired me so I came close.
No one can come near God unless He has prepared a bed for you.
A thousand souls hear His call every second,
but most every one then looks into their life's mirror and says,
"I am not worthy to leave this sadness."
When I first heard His courting song,
I too looked at all I had done in my life and said,
"How can I gaze into His omnipresent eyes?"
I spoke those words with all my heart,
but then He sang again, a song even sweeter,
and when I tried to shame myself once more from His presence
God showed me His compassion and spoke a divine truth,
"I made you, dear, and all I make is perfect.
Please come close, for I desire you."

Attributed to St. Teresa of Avila by Daniel Ladinsky
Love Poems From God
274

III

The lute began...
My heart snapped its chains.
Something sang from the strings—"Wounded crazy one...come!"
Come, come, whoever you are—wandered, worshiper, lover of leaving—
What does it matter?
Ours is not a caravan of despair.
Come, even if you have broken your vows a hundred times—
Come, come again, come.

Jalaluddin Rumi

LOGION 108

Sapiential Themes

- *Wisdom is imaged as a flowing stream issuing from the mouth of the Master of Wisdom.*
- *The seeker of wisdom is invited into a form of intimacy that deeply ingests what is coming from the Master's mouth.*
- *Intimacy involves mutual exchange between teacher and student leading to reciprocal transformation.*
- *Heretofore this concept of mutual metamorphosis may have been unknown in the stream of wisdom tradition.*
- *In the divine economy nothing is ultimately lost or hidden.*

Yeshua says,

Whoever drinks
what flows from my mouth
will come to be as I am
and I will also come
to be as they are,
so that what is hidden
can become manifest.

Parallel Texts

Psalm 23,
Proverbs 2:2, 6
13:20, 17:24, 18:4
John 4:7-15, 7:37-39
Revelation 22:17

Links

The image of the Shepherd who is troubled until the lost sheep is found, and then confides his own deep longing to the one who is found, raises the sheep into a relationship of reciprocal participation with the Shepherd. In this logion the separation between the species disappears. That gap is bridged as the one "drinks" from the other's mouth and the two come to be defined by and united with the other.

FOCAL POINT

This saying puts the issue of oneness and the Shepherd's search for humanity into an entirely new light. It expresses, perhaps, the longing of the Shepherd in the previous saying, which has been for a new kind of oneness between shepherd and sheep all along. To understand what is being said here, first, we must know what it is that comes from the Master's mouth, Is it not wisdom itself that flows like a spring of water, which is available to anyone who will drink? That which the Shepherd longs to impart and which is the condition for the possibility of oneness is, in fact, the guidance of wisdom from the one who is seeking (and finding) humankind.

Notes

The translation "what flows from my mouth" is literally "out of my mouth." The strong implication is that the drinking in (or deep listening), reciprocal transformation, and revelation of the hidden are all linked together into a seamless whole.

COMMENTARY

Some great mystery of human and divine interaction and participation is deeply expressed in this saying. It is also clear that an unexpected form of intimacy is metaphorically presented here that is both vivid and strange to our ears. Perhaps the image is more easily understood if we recognize that the seeker is drinking from the "waters of wisdom" flowing from the mouth of the Master which, in the end, creates a form of reciprocal transformation in those who are thirsty. Each in some mysterious way is transforming into the other, or, alternatively, each is changing the form of the other substantially in the mirror of mutual reflection and resemblance.

If one carefully examines the image from the previous logion along with an exploration of Psalm Twenty-three, it is evident that the sheep who first appears in that Psalm is no longer a sheep by the end of it—it too has been transformed into something akin to, if not, the same as the Shepherd. Sheep and Shepherd have changed and are transformed and the result is a feast at a table in the house of the Lord. This is, of course, not something that sheep do—feast at a table or live in a house. The Psalm suggests a transformative process—sheep are transformed into beings of another kind who can sit to eat with the Shepherd. Could it be that sheep are themselves being turned into Shepherds?

The sheep come to be what the Shepherd is when they begin to receive what flows from the Shepherd's mouth. They are transformed into the essential nature of the Shepherd himself, and the Shepherd comes to be one with a new kind of "flock" in which there is a new form of unity. This is clearly an unexpected image of metamorphic change. The potential, however, has been there all along. It may have been hidden, but now what was *in potentia* is being made manifest, and the catalyst for the change is Wisdom herself—that which flows from the Master's mouth. Wisdom is transformative—able to make what were two, dissimilar entities a single and united whole.

This unique understanding concerning reciprocal transformation, while perhaps familiar to us today, may have appeared in the Abrahamic traditions first in the teaching of Yeshua (and in particular) in Thomas. There is, however, a closely related thought in the Hindu teaching of the Taittiriya Upanishad:

O Joy!
I am the food of life, and I am the one who eats the food.
I am the eater and the eaten, the two in ONE.
I am the first-born from the world of truth, born before all gods, born in the eye of eternity.
The one who gives me birth, draws me back, I am the food which eats the eater, I am the burning of the Sun!
Whoever knows this, knows the Truth.

See also Logion 5

To say that there is a hidden nature within humankind and that there are potentials within which are unknown to us in our present state of awareness, is to begin to understand the primary force of wisdom teaching concerning the liberation of human consciousness from the prison of limitation which keeps it bound or hidden. We are what we perceive, and if we cannot perceive anything beyond the veil of illusion (constituted by the limits of this world), then we remain imprisoned within those veils. But there are hidden dimensions within—a secret nature which can be known, or better, released—but only by the wisdom which flows from the Master's mouth. Once we receive that wisdom, then we are liberated into a form of being embodied by the Master who has surpassed those limitations, who has realized this potential and is, therefore, acting from those hidden dimensions, and who longs now to draw us forward into the same manifestation.

This transformative possibility has been there for humankind all along—but it has taken the journey into time (becoming "lost in time" and then being found by the Shepherd), to bring the nearness of being held next to the wisdom flowing from the Master's mouth. It is in this nearness that we can deeply listen and be changed. In the end, it is this Wisdom which has catalyzed the potential for transformation in us. The final phrase also appears earlier in the text alongside the assertion concerning resurrection. What is hidden and brought into manifestation is being raised both from death and from sleep into a new form of life and wakefulness.

QUESTIONS FOR REFLECTION

1. When have you drunk deeply from a source of wisdom that was wider and more alive than you had experienced before?

2. What was the effect of such an experience on you?

3. How can two individuals be changed in this way? Do you have any personal examples or experiences of the mutual exchange of wisdom?

4. Do you feel that you have a potential that is hidden perhaps even to yourself?

5. What would it take for what is hidden to be revealed to or in you?

EXERCISES AND MEDITATIONS

Truly, I tell you this, unless a kernel of wheat falls into the ground and "dies" it remains alone, but if it dies it will, in the end, bring forth abundant fruit.
John 12:24

1. Consider your own deep nature. Are you what you imagine yourself to be, or are you a seed of potential that has yet to be revealed? This latter idea is clearly indicated in all of the wisdom teachings of Yeshua. In meditation take the Scripture quote from the sidebar and reflect on its implications. After a period of reflective silence, allow yourself to inwardly enter this teaching. In a journal, write out your insights and understanding of your growth potential.
2. If you were to think of your own life journey as a repository of wisdom, what wisdom do you have to give away to others from your lived experience? Is there something that comes from your mouth (or your life), that is vital even to the wisdom Master—some secret you have learned that perhaps no one else knows? Reflect on these questions. Allow yourself time to evaluate and understand what you might have gained that seems ordinary to you, but might, in fact be unique. What wisdom do you know or that you have (and could express) that is truly your own, hammered out on the anvil of your own life?
3. Who is this "Master" that needs our reciprocal life? We immediately imagine the words "my mouth" to mean the mouth of Yeshua (and certainly this is a reasonable interpretation), there may be other interpretive possibilities as well. For example, another possible understanding is that we are hearing the words of the "higher Self" who is constantly speaking to us intimately (however we understand this higher Self to be). Could it also be that the Master of Wisdom (Yeshua) and your higher Self are, in fact, intimately related already—which is why you are drawn to his teachings? Have you ever heard wisdom being spoken from your higher Self?

READINGS FOR INSIGHT

I

Proverbs 18:4, 13:20

Words of true wisdom are as refreshing as a bubbling brook.
Whoever walks with the wise will become wise.

II

Jalaluddin Rumi
"Like This"
Translated by
Coleman Barks

There is some kiss we want with our whole lives,
the touch of Spirit on the body.
Seawater begs the pearl to break its shell.
And the lily, how passionately it needs some wild Darling!
At night, I open the window and ask the moon to come
and press its face against mine.
Breathe into me, I say.
Then, close the language-door and open the love-window.
The moon won't use the door, only the window.

III

Maria Jaoudi
Christian Mysticism East and West
42

The deeper one's awareness goes, and just as important, the more consistent such an awareness is in one's thoughts and actions, the more one is enabled to connect with the Spirit present in all of life. If one does connect with the Spirit, one is aided by what the world mythologist Joseph Campbell called "the helping hands of the universe."

IV

Jalaluddin Rumi

Love comes sailing through and I scream.
Love sits beside me like a private supply of itself.
Love puts away the instruments,
and takes off the silk robes.
Our nakedness together changes me completely.

V

Jalaluddin Rumi

If you could get rid of yourself just once,
The secret of secrets would open to you.
The Face of the Unknown,
Hidden beyond the universe would appear
On the mirror of your perceptions.

VI

Anthony de Mello
One Minute Nonsense
177

"How joyful the Master seems," a visitor remarked.

Said a disciple, "One always treads with a joyful step when one has dropped the burden called the ego."

LOGION 109

Sapiential Themes

- *Wisdom is considered both a treasure and the treasure house—a storeroom from which all values and virtues come.*
- *In the field of life, what is our own? Do we ever own anything? Perhaps in ignorance we assume ownership.*
- *Ignorance is highlighted in traditional wisdom. Understanding it and discovering how we are involved in ignorance is crucial to wisdom teaching.*

Yeshua says,

The divine Realm
is like a man who owned a field
with treasure hidden away in it.
Unaware of it he died,
leaving it to his son,
who also knew nothing about it.
After taking possession of the land
the son practically gave it away for nothing.
But the one who bought it began plowing
and discovered the treasure,
and immediately started lending
money at interest
to whomever he pleased.

Parallel Texts

Thomas 76, 92
Matthew 13:44
Luke 16:1-8

Links

What was hidden in the previous logion becomes manifest in this saying. The link to this image is that in that field, an unknown treasure suddenly is revealed by the one who plows in the field—who works the field. In both cases there is appropriate action—drinking and plowing. Could it be that these are related actions? In this particular saying knowledge of the treasure is preceded by a deep forgetfulness.

FOCAL POINT

Treasure in the field is a well known image used by Yeshua. Though a similar parable also appears in the canonical Gospels, in this saying there is additional information about the ancestry of the previous owners who never sought for or found the treasure. Apparently they were absent landlords or had other interests that made them careless or unaware. So, though they owned the field, they did not take possession of the treasure. The final owner, however, who worked the field himself, discovered the treasure which he immediately put to good use. This parable may also illustrate the issues of manifestation and revelation mentioned in the previous saying. The last farmer was wise, the others were not, and the outcomes were entirely different.

Notes

The Coptic text says that the son who inherited the land literally "gave it away." The purchaser, however, began working the field, plowing it, and "seized upon" the treasure—(an active act) and, in addition to plowing the field, he began using the money to lend (the original says) "to those he loves."

COMMENTARY

This is another of Yeshua's parables of the Kingdom (the divine Realm), which asserts the presence of a hidden treasure in the very field worked by humankind—a field which is said to belong to a human being. What is particularly true about this treasure, however, is that for generations owners were unaware of it, and so the treasure passed through time without having any effect. It was there all the time, but it was as though it did not exist. Being unaware (or ignorant) of the treasure renders it useless—and so it lies hidden and unused.

To later generations, even the field itself appears to be of little value, and so they sell off their inheritance for practically nothing to someone who perhaps has less than they do, but who is able to plow the field and eventually find the treasure. It is then that things change. The power of the treasure suddenly comes to life. It is put to good use. The farmer becomes an entrepreneur and a financier who is able to use that money to a greater benefit.

So what is this treasure that lies in the field of human potential but hidden away, of which we are unaware? If the previous saying about the manifestation of what has been hidden in humankind is the prelude to this disclosure, then certainly the case can be made that the hidden potential is to become what the Master is—a form of divine manifestation from the *Anthropos*. This is certainly a possibility, though other interpretations, however, are also possible.

The Hymn of the Pearl is an ancient text associated with Oriental Christianity found in the ***Acts of Thomas*** *and is said to have been spoken as a vision on the night before St. Thomas was martyred in India.*

For example, in the canonical Gospels the "talents" about which Yeshua speaks come from a source higher than the servants who receive them, and some are buried in the field. Elsewhere Yeshua speaks about putting treasure away in the heavens. There is also an early image about treasure coming from another source—the **Hymn of the Pearl**—in which it is said that an adventurer from the lands of the Orient travels to Egypt carrying provisions and treasures that have been given him in the East. Interpreted as a metaphor for our journey out of Paradise into time (the lands of the Occident), we carry with us "buried treasure" which we promptly forget about, and therefore cannot use, though it exists and is always potentially available.

We believe we "own" life, and we work it to our benefit sometimes in ignorance and sometimes is awareness. This saying is about the play of both and the result. We are asked both to work the field and distribute what we discover (at interest).

Could it be then that every human being unconsciously carries within wealth and riches from a realm transcendent to space and time? This treasure **is** meant to be found and used, but only by one who has "plowed the field," worked it until it becomes known, and is, therefore, consciously available. When it does become known, it becomes a form of wealth that can be lent out or borrowed by others. It can be used for a greater good. This is, perhaps, an image that suggests that what we possess from our own ancient sources can be of immense benefit to others—though, for them, it is only "borrowed" until they can find their own.

At the heart of this saying, then, is a clarity about two kinds of human beings—those who are aware, and those who are unaware of the treasure within (in the field). The person who becomes aware does so by actively working in the field, seeking to make it productive, and in due course he or she becomes aware (discovers the treasure) and puts that largess to use. This is the task of those close to the wisdom of Yeshua who are active in the field of wisdom.

QUESTIONS FOR REFLECTION

1. What do you make of Yeshua's parable? Do you feel that you understand it?

2. How would you apply this parable to your own circumstances?

3. Which of the three "owners" are you? Is there any treasure you have failed to find in past fields?

4. How are you treating the "field" you are presently living in? How are you making use of it?

5. The parable says that when the new owner discovered the buried treasure he immediately began lending out money. Is that a good thing to do, especially in light of the logion where Yeshua instructs his students to lend money without asking for it back?

EXERCISES AND MEDITATIONS

1. Imagine that your life is not just a history, but a field where life goes on through all the normal human activities. On this field we work and play and live out our existence. Hidden there, Yeshua says is buried treasure waiting for discovery. Have you ever made unexpected discoveries, uncovering items and elements that were in place before arrived? Imagine, then, that the Divine Reality has buried treasure in you. Do you have any idea what that is? Have you found it and used it? It is difficult, certainly, to talk about something you have never discovered—an unknown. But if someone said, "I have seen it with my own eyes, out in that field somewhere is a vast treasure," you might have incentive to go looking for it. How might you do that? Meditate on this conundrum.
2. It may be easier, perhaps, to see the "buried treasure" in someone else's field—to see what they cannot see. Have you ever had that experience? Have you ever helped someone to discover their undiscovered treasure, or their undiscovered potential? How have you done that? Is it an easy thing, or is it difficult? Describe your experience.
3. Pay attention to the human beings around you. Imagine that they are carrying buried treasure put there by the Divine hand. It may be that such treasure lies in the heart of every creature—animals, plants, birds, insects, human beings—and we have simply not noticed it (or thought about it in this in this way). We observe outer activity, but the secret inner life and divine quality is buried deeper still. Look for it. See if you can detect it.

READINGS FOR INSIGHT

I

James Freeman Clark

The only real satisfaction there is, is to be growing up inwardly all the time, becoming more just, true, generous, simple, manly, womanly, kind, active. And this we can all do, by doing each day the day's work as well as we can.

II

Meryl Streep

Integrate what you believe into every single area of your life. Take your heart to work and ask the most and best of everybody else. Don't let your special character and values, the secret that you know and no one else does, the truth—don't let that get swallowed up by the great chewing complacency.

III

Pablo Casals

Each person has inside a basic decency and goodness. If he listens to it and acts on it, he is giving a great deal of what it is the world needs most. It is not complicated but it takes courage. It takes courage for a person to listen to his own goodness and act on it.

IV

Lucie Dupin

Guard within yourself
that treasure, kindness.
Know how to give
without hesitation,
how to lose
without regret,
how to acquire
without meanness.

V

The Prophet Muhammad

A person's true wealth
is the good he or she does in the world.

VI

Jalaluddin Rumi

A friend of Joseph's came to visit him after returning from a long journey. "What have you brought me?" Joseph asked.

"What could I bring you," his friend replied, "that you don't already have? "But," he added, "because you are so beautiful, and nothing exists in all the worlds more beautiful than you, I have brought you a mirror, so you can know the joy at every moment of seeing your own face."

Is there anything that God does not have already that you could give? Is there anything that God could need that you could possibly provide? All you are here for, and the entire meaning of the Path of Love, is to bring before God a heart bright as a mirror, so God can contemplate the divine face within it.

LOGION 110

Sapiential Themes

- *Searching and finding is a primary key for this text—but the content of wisdom depends on what you search for.*
- *This saying is counter-intuitive to the common notion of what is important in this world.*
- *Riches are the highest priority for most individuals. They are at the top of the list of human wants and desires. Yeshua challenges this notion with a radical call for the renunciation of the normal agenda.*
- *Release, surrender, letting go, and detachment are all part of the strategy for transcendent growth into another domain.*
- *The practice of detachment is at the heart of all finding.*

Yeshua says,

Whoever finds
the cosmos
and becomes rich
must ultimately let the cosmos go.

Parallel Texts

Thomas 27, 56, 80, 81, 111
James 1:9-12, 2:5-8, 5:1-6

Links

Finding treasure hidden in a field in the last logion may represent a spiritual process, but that saying may also lend itself to the notion that material gain is of highest value. Yeshua corrects that impression in this saying, and sustains the understanding that there is something vital beyond the human order. Release is the only means for finding it. Letting go represents a different kind of "finding."

FOCAL POINT

The question of true wealth (and and its opposite, poverty), and the quest to find true treasure has been a theme in many of the logia of Thomas. Human beings are concerned about wealth—how to secure it, how to maintain it, and how to keep it from diminishing while they live. It is a primary occupation of the human mind, and a central concern of the social and political world of any age. We spend much of our time on the earth securing wealth. Yeshua sees something entirely different. From a wisdom perspective the letting go of wealth is far more important than its material acquisition and is key to an understanding of the spiritual evolution of the soul.

Notes

This saying is stated as an imperative—one ***must*** *let the human order and the riches it brings go, in order to find a higher state—the Realm of Heaven of which Yeshua continually speaks. There is no other option. This is a wisdom imperative.*

COMMENTARY

The subject of the "***kosmos***" (the human social and cultural conventions that make up the fabric of the civilizations which lie at the heart of human history distinguished from the cosmos of the universe), has appeared in this Gospel a number of times. Finding treasure in the last logion and finding the "cosmos" in this one seems to be juxtaposed. For most individuals, finding riches in the human order (the ***kosmos*** as it is expressed in Greek and Coptic) is the definitive task—it is the supreme purpose of life for most folk. This aim of all our endeavors here on earth (the proverbial "bottom line"), is sabotaged by wisdom itself.

The focus of conscious attention in this world is always targeted toward the goal of succeeding in the *kosmos*—that is, in the human realm. Nothing expresses this objective, perhaps, better than the steady stream of propaganda coming from the commercial centers of the world; the philosophy of commercialism that demands we keep our focus on buying and selling and making more profit in order to steadily increase the bottom line—reminding us of our "true purpose" to promote commercial and monetary growth.

To say that human consciousness is swallowed up by the "beast of commercialism" is not an understatement. We need to be constantly reminded of that, and Yeshua's concise insight gives expression to what lies at the heart of the ***kosmos*** and why it is so critical to understand its inadequacy as the foundation and basic meaning of our lives. Impermanence is built into the nature of our world, and so to construct one's life and base one's true wealth on these shifting sands means that ultimately everything we have worked for will come to nothing. It will all be lost.

*What Yeshua knew (and what all great spiritual teachers have known and declared to be true throughout the generations) was that both the **kosmos** and its riches are temporary and transient elements along the horizontal axis—they are passing through time into oblivion.*

So in light of this, the principle of wisdom is: even in the amassing of riches, which for some will inevitably happen, a higher practice must be in play—it is the practice of letting go. Detachment or non-attachment to the world's wealth in whatever form we may receive it is essential if we are to transcend its hold on our attention. To live with one's consciousness focused only along the horizontal axis of awareness is to become trapped, never allowing consciousness to grow vertically.

As physical creatures we do indeed live on the horizontal axis, and to a great degree we must partake of its many endeavors—being educated, raising families, making a living, being creative and contributing to the common good. We are here in space-time principally for these forms of participation. They are necessary for our becoming, but what spiritual evolution demands is not only participation, but also the higher practice of learning to let go. But letting go of what? Many traditions speak powerfully of letting go of the results of our actions and our typical focus on their results. It is good to act (and to have acted in time), but it is necessary not to hold on to the product or results of those actions as though they were somehow "ours," because, in the end, they will disappear. So learning to act and let go of the results is a art of learning that we practice while living in space and time.

This is clearly the stance that Yeshua took in his own day . He acted decisively and for the common good, but he was also radically able to let go of the results and surrender himself to something higher along the vertical axis—to the Divine Will.

QUESTIONS FOR REFLECTION

1. Have you ever felt yourself to be "swallowed up" by the "beast" of the human order? What is your experience of that?

2. How do you feel about being rich while passing through earth-experience? Is there anything wrong with riches?

3. In your experience have you ever let go of riches? Have you ever been really poor?

4. What is the effect of involuntary poverty? What effect might voluntary poverty have upon an individual?

EXERCISES AND MEDITATIONS

1. We feel like we belong here. When we were younger, perhaps, we felt as if we were permanent features of the world around us—that we are going to be here forever, when in theory perhaps we knew we were not. This is often our experience as we move through the world. We spend a good deal of time in life (at the beginning at least), getting to know and mastering the world around us. We need to have some degree of control over our experience and circumstances, otherwise we feel as if we are mere puppets or victims. However, the time comes when either voluntarily or involuntarily we must let it all go. Reflect on your own experience of this cycle of human experience—the finding and the letting go. Neither are terrible, and both are positive, but the latter may be far more difficult than the former. Meditate on why this is so, and remember that the wisdom tradition offers both counsel and assurance on letting go. How would you summarize this wisdom teaching?
2. In one of his quatrains, Jalaluddin Rumi asks this question and makes a powerful sapiential assertion. In quiet reflection meditate on the meaning (and wisdom) of this poem. Journal your feelings and understanding as you do:

How long will we fill our pockets like children
with dirt and stones?
Let the world go.
Holding it we never know ourselves.
We're never airborne.

READINGS FOR INSIGHT

I

How could the soul not take flight when from the glorious presence a soft call flows sweet as honey... comes right up to her and whispers,
"Rise up now, and come away."
How could a fish not jump immediately from dry land into water when the sound of waves from that ocean springs to its ear?
How could a hawk not fly away, forgetful of the hunt to the wrist of the king as soon as it hears the drum—the king's baton beating again and again—drumming out the signal of return?
How could the mystic not start to dance, turning on him or herself, like an atom in the Sun of Eternity, so as to leap free of this dying world?
Fly away, fly away bird to your native land.
You have leapt free from the cage.
Leave behind these stagnant and marshy waters.
Hurry, hurry, hurry, O bird, to the source of your life.
Your wings are flung back into the winds of God.

Jalaluddin Rumi

II

Our great and glorious masterpiece
is to live appropriately.
All other things, to rule, to lay up treasure, to build,
are at most but little appendices and props.

Michel de Montaigne

III

In the beginning the process of detachment seems cold. When a person sits in meditation or prays by resting in the Spirit she empties herself of everything. How lonely that sounds. But being alone is not necessarily lonely. To detach from your preoccupations is to have faith in the life process and to know that you are a part of it. Through detachment you do not forsake people and your environment. Detachment is a means of connecting with them at a deeper level. For it is not people or things that distract you, but your desires. It is from these desires that you must learn to detach.

Brother Tolbert McCarroll
Notes from the Song of Life
55

IV

Die of surrender, you will live forever.
Be put to death through surrender—death will no longer exist for you.
You will have already died.

A Traditional Persian Saying

V

On this Pathway
The seeker's wealth is poverty.

Yunus Emre

LOGION 111

Sapiential Themes

- *The awareness of the illusory nature of temporal reality is at the heart of many wisdom traditions—what we call "real" quickly passes away.*
- *Central to Jewish mystical practice is to build one's life upon the living principles of the Torah which spring from the Source of all life.*
- *Discovery of the Self—the true nature of one's Ultimate Reality—is at the heart of all wisdom searching.*
- *The above three principles are combined in this saying.*

Yeshua says,

Heaven and earth
will completely disappear
in your presence,
and the one who lives by means
of the Living One
will not see death, because,
as Yeshua says,
"The cosmos is not worthy of the one
who discovers the Self."

Parallel Texts

Thomas 1
Psalm 102:25-27
Isaiah 34:4
Matthew 5:18, 24:34-35
Mark 13:30-31
Luke 21:32-33
Hebrews 1:10-12
Rev. 6:12-14

Links

Letting the ***kosmos*** *go is the theme of the last saying. In this logion we are led to understand that purpose—in order to discover Ultimate Reality. Why one lets go and what one finds in its stead is the theme of these three logia, which contain a concentrated vision of our ultimate state of being and knowing.*

FOCAL POINT

This is a strangely powerful logion combining two (or perhaps three) of Yeshua's sayings in one. The first saying in this logion speaks of the disappearance of heaven and earth in the environment of the divine Presence. The second speaks of a form of spiritual praxis dependent upon that Presence, and the latter reveals why that newly emerging form of life will never know the taste of death. In the third, the ultimate human experience is said to be knowledge of the true Self. When the true Self and the immediate self of our being meet, there is indeed a new form of life.

Notes

This saying is structurally interesting since it appears that Yeshua quotes himself. Disappear is literally "roll up," and presence has the additional word "outer." The emphasis on the discovery of the Self is strengthened by the literal: "the one who seizes upon himself." This is a discovery seized and the ***kosmos*** *is not ready or prepared for the one who makes this discovery.*

COMMENTARY

In the face of Eternity and standing before the divine Presence that dwells everywhere, earth (and perhaps even heaven itself) is only an impermanent manifestation. Everything exists in and is dependent upon the light of that Reality. It is possible, in practice, to live by means of the Living One. It is that Source, that Immortality—the same Immortality which the Presence is—which can overcome all impermanence. Knowing this is a true discovery not easily made. This discovery is not simply an awareness of the immortality of the eternal Presence itself, but of the fundamental awareness that one's own true nature has been eternally held in that eternal Reality from its beginning.

Another interpretive trajectory for this saying is that heaven and earth as distinct and different forms in the way we currently know them will be "rolled up" into one—forming one Ultimate Reality inside the consciousness (or presence) of the knower. They will not longer be separate, but one, and thus Unity will be achieved.

The issue of impermanence was raised by the previous Logion. Now the question is, what perishes and what remains? Is there anything permanent at all or is everything perishing? In the universe of existence, forms are constantly appearing and disappearing. We witness impermanence everywhere—the passing away of temporary forms all around us, even forms that remain for thousands or even millions of years pass out of existence. The heavens and the earth will indeed pass away as impermanent forms. We are told by contemporary astrophysics that the sun, the stars, the galaxies, even the whole universe will move from its present form into what (from our vantage point at least), appears to be non-existence. In time it will cease to be as we know it.

The way in which Yeshua expresses all of this is vital and interesting. He agrees that the heavens and the earth are temporal. He says they will completely disappear. They are passing phenomena, but strangely, there is a witness to their passage which he describes as "your presence." That Presence apparently does not disappear—it remains to watch the passing away. So who is this "witness to impermanence?" Yeshua calls it "Presence," which as we have seen elsewhere, is the way that Thomas often talks about consciousness itself. To be present is to be conscious, and Yeshua seems to be saying here that "you" (his students) will be present (or conscious) to witness these events when they occur. Forms will vanish, but your consciousness (or presence) will remain to witness their disappearance.

Only Presence which possesses deathless consciousness is permanent, all else is passing. The only deathless consciousness is that which issues from the (eternally) Living One, who is also willing to share that life-form and its deathless awareness with everything else.

The question is, of course, does this include everyone—will everyone witness these events—or is this just a select few? Is there some particular form of conscious presence that can be a witness in contrast to a form of consciousness that cannot? The answer appears to be given in the next phrases of the Logion in which Yeshua says this is the form of consciousness (or presence) that lives or is dependent upon the Living One. That presence will not see death because it is connected to its Origin and Source. It is this deathless state of consciousness which allows someone to witness the passing away (or death) of all other forms. A case could then be made that consciousness itself is not a form as such, but the witness of all forms.

Clarity about who just such a person might be is described in the final phrase of the saying, which takes us back into the temporal cosmos and that Entity which stands out from or transcends it—the true Self. The cosmos has its own worth as a temporal phenomenon, but the cosmic-dweller who comes to know or discovers what and who that Self actually is (that it transcends the cosmos), by that very discovery surpasses the cosmos itself.

QUESTIONS FOR REFLECTION

1. How does the impermanence of things affect you? Do you try to keep the things you love fixed and permanent in your life? What happens when things disappear from the fixed form that you have tried to protect?

2. How does your own consciousness seem to you? Is it more fixed or immutable than the things around it? For example, are you aware of the continuity of your own consciousness from childhood until now? Is it the same "you?"

3. What, in your view, would define a real awareness of the true Self? What would make it a false awareness? Does this question make sense to you?

4. Do you feel that you have discovered your Self (or a truer Self beyond what you consider yourself currently to be)?

EXERCISES AND MEDITATIONS

1. If you examine this Logion as a collection of three separate sayings, each one related to and building upon the others, then this wisdom triad helps the listener understand the purpose of life lived in space and time. In a period of personal reflection explore this triad, seeking to understand its complexities. How would you summarize its teaching as a form of insight into the deep wisdom of Yeshua?
2. This logion shares certain viewpoints that are common to Buddhism and Hinduism. Impermanence, for example, is a Buddhist teaching which says that permanence is an illusion we try to keep alive for ourselves. Hinduism speaks of the ultimate form of Selfhood as Atman—a form of consciousness that transcends the state of individual consciousness and includes the conscious Soul of all humanity as a whole. Examine the three sayings in Logion 111 in light of these two teachings, especially the middle passage that speaks of a life-practice dependent upon the Living One—a strong component of the practices of Judaism. Ask yourself, what am I trying to keep permanent, and where are my own illusions?
3. For you to practice what it means "to live by means of the Living One" involves a sense of awareness, wakefulness and openness to transcendent Reality. There are examples in the canonical Gospels that Yeshua himself lived in just this way. See what you can find by reading the Gospel of John. But more importantly, there is your own life, and the question about how to practice this as lived experience. Does this create a sense of dependency, or is this something else entirely? Discuss this important question with colleagues and spiritual friends.

You might want to explore these topics in the traditions of Buddhism and Hinduism as part of a search you make on the Internet. These spiritual approaches toward reality are counter to normal western thinking and require that we explore their significance and their underlying structure of thought from an eastern point of view.

READINGS FOR INSIGHT

I

Bruno Barnhart
Second Simplicity
24

The ultimate reality that is known in contemplative experience and in unitive wisdom has been called simply the *center*. It is the metaphysical center of all reality and also the center of the human person. Corresponding to the presence of this reality at the center of the human person is a unitive Self: *atman*, true self, Christ-self. This is the human person fully participating in the unitive divine Source; it is, therefore, being-in-communication, the person as essentially relational. This unitive reality, as the center of the person, is also the ground of human consciousness. Human consciousness and all of its operations are grounded in a unitive participation in the absolute divine Reality.

II

Yunus Emre

Oh Friend,
when I began to love You,
my intellect went and left me.
I gazed at the rivers, I dove into the seas.
But a spark of Love's fire can make the seas boil.
I fell in, caught fire, and burned.
There is an "I" in me, deeper than me,
whose eyes look at me from inside of me.

III

Bede Griffiths
Return to the Center
16

The whole question is, what is the true Self? What is the true centre of man's being? Is it the ego, making itself independent, seeking to be master of the world, or is there an "I" beyond this, a deeper Centre of personal being, which is grounded in the Truth, which is one with the universal Self, the Law of the universe? This is the great discovery of Indian thought, the discovery of the Self, the Atman, the Ground of Universal Being. It is not reached by thought; on the contrary, it is only reached by transcending thought.

IV

Yoka Daishi

Our Natures,
perfect and pervading, circulate in all natures.
One Reality,
all comprehensive, contains within itself all realities.
The one moon is reflected wherever there is a sheet of water.
And all the moons in all the waters are embraced within the one moon;
The embodied Truth of all the Buddhas enters into my own being,
And my own being is found in union with theirs.

V

Sayfaddin Bakharzi

When the morning of friendship with God begins to dawn, the soul grows distant from the landscape of this world, and you reach a place inside yourself in which each breath of the soul, without any hindrance from your external eyes can catch a glimpse of the face of the Friend.

LOGION 112

Sapiential Themes

- *In Middle Eastern thought, flesh is a technical term having to do with the body-mind connection and its interdependency without input from spirit.*
- *In this saying Yeshua diagnoses suffering as a form of codependency or imbalance between soul and body without the input of Spirit.*
- *Buddhism shared a very similar point of view concerning the nature and purpose of suffering and its causes.*

Yeshua says,

Wretched is the flesh
that is dependent
upon the soul,
and the soul that is
dependent on the flesh.

Parallel Texts

Thomas 29, 87
Mark 10:8
John 3:6
Romans 6:19, 7:14, 8:1-12
I Corinthians 3:1-4

Links

The previous logion expressed a vision about the nature of the true Self. In this saying its counterpoint—the narrow or limited self without any cosmic or universal context is the subject—the egoic self isolated from its original vision or ground of being in the higher Self. Confined to a narrow sense of oneself, without the benefit of true Self-knowledge, one is trapped and lost and wretched—unable to find one's way.

FOCAL POINT

This saying suggests that the relationship between soul and body is both intimate and difficult. Since the flesh is fleeting and its desires are temporary, the soul's dependence upon it creates tension and pain. This is true of any soul that grounds its security or satisfaction on the temporal demands of the flesh. The term flesh being used here is similar to the way it is used in the Epistles of the Apostle Paul. For Paul, the corporeal nature of the human body is not the focus, but the enmeshed relationship between body and soul that creates something he calls "flesh." It is the co-dependency between body and soul in the temporal realm which ultimately makes us miserable.

Notes

The terms flesh and soul are Greek terms used extensively in the early Christian Scriptures. They have broad linguistic and cultural meanings in the Greek-Roman world and equivalents in the Semitic (Hebrew and Aramaic) world with various semantic overlaps.

COMMENTARY

Logion 112 expresses an alternative consciousness different or even opposite from the one that lives by means of the Living One and who discovers the true Self. In terms of the realities that we typically understand, this saying describes a normal state of affairs and a form of consciousness which most human beings here in this world appear to possess—a kind of spiritual codependency—soul-dependence upon flesh, and fleshy dependence upon the soul.

The term ***sarkikos****, which is often translated in English as "carnal," has very much to do with the concept of an internal construction within a human being that ties together both the soul and the body into a psycho-somatic unit that is often expressive of narrow, egoic limits. See the Pauline expression in I Corinthians 3:1-4.*

Like fish who swim in the vast waters of the ocean and yet who, perhaps, cannot conceive of water, human consciousness in its current state cannot conceive of its utter dependency upon these two entities—soul and flesh. This blindness, according to sapiential teaching, constitutes a form of enslavement from which it is not easy to escape. One side of the dependency is the flesh (meaning the body-mind duality of corporeal existence). The other is the self-reflective soul that is aware of that duality but incapable of transcending it. It is clear from our own lived experience that each of these are complexities in themselves, not easily described.

The autonomic nervous system (often called involuntary nervous system) is the electrical system which functions largely below the level of conscious control. It maintains heart rate, digestion, respiratory rate, salivation, perspiration, breathing and swallowing, etc.

The term flesh, as it is used here and in other ancient spiritual texts, does not necessarily mean only the intricacies of the physical body and its myriad functions. It includes the larger relationship of dependence that the body has on the mind and that the mind exercises over the body through the autonomic consciousness that maintains it. This is a complex relationship, one that is intricately interdependent without which we could not physically survive at all. The soul, however, lives beyond the autonomic and the unconscious. It is that entity of personhood that we think of as our "self" existing somewhat independently from the body-mind continuum. The soul, in fact, can reflect on (or think about) the body-mind and can observe itself as distinct from the body, possessing its own forms of functioning and awareness.

If the mind-body and the self (or soul) that is aware of itself as a unit of consciousness within the body is the complete description of a human being, then as Yeshua says, we live in a state of wretchedness. We can, however, awaken to remember that there is a higher state which he describes as "blessedness" (***makarios***).

As Yeshua understands, it is this the terrible limitation (this dependency between soul and flesh) which defines human misery, because in the end these exist as a desolation devoid of spirit or the Higher Self. Without this higher or spiritual Self the soul is wearisome even to itself. Human beings often do not know that their state is one of desolation because they have never experienced the alternative. We may not know blessedness because we have only known the condition of wretchedness and it feels normal to us. It is not the soul's fault, and Yeshua does not seem to be judging humankind. He is simply making an observation of penetrating insight into the nature of the human condition—one that has also been made by other seers and teachers in the East and in the West, ancient and modern.

For example, the Buddha taught that human beings experience suffering precisely because they depend upon the impermanence of both flesh and soul for security which they feel to be permanent. Not to recognize their impermanent nature is to be in the grip of a form of suffering that is not easily relieved, at least until what is permanent and eternal is touched, tasted, and known as the true ground of the Self.

QUESTIONS FOR REFLECTION

1. When in your life have you felt most miserable? What has been the cause of such misery? Did it have anything to do with the insights you find in this saying?

2. Have you ever felt trapped in your own body-mind continuum, unable to escape it in favor of a higher vision or perspective? Why has that form of transcendence been so hard to reach?

3. Do you understand the nuanced meaning of this ancient use of the word "flesh" (the body-mind connection that often traps us and does not allow us to rise to the level of spirit)? How have you experienced this? Is there a relationship between them that is healthy and balanced?

4. If this state is in contrast to the knowledge of the Higher Self expressed in the previous Logion, contrast your experience of each.

EXERCISES AND MEDITATIONS

1. People often live in almost unimaginable states of misery. Sometimes this kind of suffering is imposed by the physical and temporal circumstances which have been created and imposed upon them. Grinding poverty in many places on the earth is just such a state. But even in a land of abundance, where people have access to wealth (or at least the possibility of attaining physical wealth and comfort), individuals can live in a mental state of poverty and wretchedness. What is even worse is the inability to recognize this impoverishment. For example, individuals can live in unrelenting depression, or addiction, or in constant worry and fear. If, as Yeshua suggests, these inner states exist because individual are not able to gain a higher perspective (the viewpoint taken by the higher Self), then these seem quite normal somehow, though they are painful nevertheless. Over a period of a week observe your moods and feeling of well-being and misery or pain. Is there a pattern? How are these triggered? How do they come and how do they go?
2. Self-observation of the relationship between one's own mind and the body is very important if one is not to become a victim of personal patterns of obsession and compulsion. For example, the mind can become obsessed with an idea and drive the body until it fulfills its desires. Or the body can becomes such an object of self-focus (either due to illness, hardships, pain, or even normal need) that the mind is never free to pursue any other thought than the body's need. Again, watch your patterns of behavior to know how these work within the particular and unique structures of your own experience.

You might also want to consider this question: How does an experience of spirit help a human being transcend misery?

READINGS FOR INSIGHT

I

He who has conquered himself by the Self,
he is a friend of himself;
but he whose self is unconquered,
his self acts as his own enemy like an external foe.

Bhagavat Gita

II

The most painful troubles are not outside events but inside gnawings. First, there is wanting to fill up to the brim. Then comes the hunger to have your feelings stroked and to get so lost in your passions that everyone becomes an object. Only one thing will matter, will this person help or hinder your being stroked? Then there is the desire to hold on to whatever you think you have. Next is the belief that it is easier to control situations, people, and even the future than it is to develop trust in yourself and in the life force. Then, there is the temptation to wallow in sadness for not getting things your own way. Then comes the wish to improve your distress by finding an object upon whom you can angrily dump your inner tensions and vital force. Following close behind is the lazy longing to be free of the present moment and to drift aimlessly. Then, there is the opportunity to conceal yourself behind a mask and to strive to look good in the eyes of the universe. Finally, there are moments when it would feel good to deceive yourself into believing in the mask. If you do this, then you will begin to protect your specialness with walls of arrogance, and your separation from life will be complete.

Brother Tolbert McCarroll
Notes from the Song of Life
69-70

III

Sufferings are wings for the bird of the soul;
A bird without wings cannot take flight.
So weep and groan and lament, my friend,
so you can free yourself from this prison
and fly to that placeless place where you will be
free forever in the boundless sky of God.

Sultan Valad
Perfume of the Desert
115

IV

The pain that wins me Enlightenment is of brief term; it is like the pain of cutting out a buried arrow to heal its wound. All physicians restore health by painful courses; then to undo much suffering let us bear a little. But even this fitting course the Great Physician has not enjoined upon us: he heals those who are grievously sick by the most tender treatment.

Shantideva

V

Let your soul be the target of Love's arrow
flying from the bow of the Beloved One's hand.
Let it pass through your soul. Don't bother to shield yourself from Love's weapon.
Its pathway between the two worlds is hidden even from itself,
but its wound is known by a broken-openness.

'Attar

LOGION 113

His students asked him,

On what day
will the kingdom
arrive?

"Its coming cannot be perceived
from the outside," he said.
"You cannot say,
'Look, its over there,' or
'No, here it is.'
The Father's Realm
is spreading out
across the face of the earth,
and humanity is not able
to perceive it."

Sapiential Themes

- *The wisdom tradition contrasts outer perception with inner awareness.*
- *Normative preoccupation with the future is contrasted with immediate awareness in the present moment.*
- *The realities of the Kingdom of Heaven interpenetrate material, spatial, and temporal realities but remain undetected by sensory awareness.*
- *The material world and human history are sites for the manifestation of realities of the Kingdom of Heaven.*

Parallel Texts

Thomas 3, 46, 51
Matthew 24:23-28
Mark 13:21-23
Luke 17: 20-25

FOCAL POINT

To the very end of this Gospel the students of Yeshua are concerned about the physical manifestation of Kingdom. This has to do, no doubt, with theological questions that naturally arose in their time. In light of the instabilities that their world (and Jewish society) were experiencing, Yeshua's students were interested in knowing when the Messiah would return and the Kingdom of Israel be reestablished. Yeshua's answer suggests that they have mistaken physical reality for spiritual reality. The spiritual reality of the Divine Realm is everywhere, yet few (or none) have the ability to see it. It is a serious form of blindness, not easy to overcome.

Links

Perhaps the state of wretchedness which is typical of the human condition prompts the question about a future in which the realities of the Kingdom of Heaven will supplant the current conditions under which humanity lives. Critical to the change in the future would be the arrival of that Kingdom. Yeshua says, however, that it is already present. It is not a future event, but a current happening, though it remains out-of-sight for those unable to perceive beyond the senses.

Notes

A particular kind of perception or seeing is at the core of this wisdom teaching. The ability to perceive the earth in one way or another, and not merely see the human kosmos is critical. The literal term is "earth" which means, perhaps, that both the natural world and the human world are included in this perception. This teaching is understood to be a form of sapiential dialogue not unlike Socrates and the Platonic dialogues where wisdom teaching and learning are expressed through a question and answer format.

COMMENTARY

As an example of what it is like to be oriented simply to the categories of space and time—focused only on physical and temporal events and our usual concerns about "the future," Logion 113 provides us with this vignette. It is a brief exchange comparing the students' perspective with the wisdom way of viewing these same concerns.

His students are anxious about an outer, temporal event—the arrival of the Kingdom that Yeshua had already spoken about. They want to pinpoint the date and perhaps even the place. Perhaps they want him to prophecy about the future and the day the appearance of the Divine Realm can be expected. As is typical of human concerns, we are worried about temporal events in the outer world. Typical of Yeshua, however, is his ability to refocus their question towards an alternative that highlights the perspective of wisdom. The reality of the Kingdom is primarily interior. The establishment of the Kingdom will certainly have external ramifications, but its ultimate reality and core is internal rather than external. In fact, the reality of the Kingdom permeates everything. It is "spread out across the face of the earth," its presence is everywhere, and yet from an external point of view, it is nowhere and undetected by the naked eye and not evident on the surface of things.

"God is a circle whose center is everywhere and circumference is nowhere."
—Blaise Pascal

We want a reality that we can touch, taste, see, hear or smell—that we can point to—either here or there. For us, seeing is believing. If reality does not occupy a fixed point in space and time, then where is it? Can it be real? Can it be true? Is there any reality there at all if it is not empirically verifiable? From Yeshua's perspective, the Father's Realm is not locatable in that way. It is not limited to one geographical location—to a "place" in either space or time. The coordinates of the Divine Realm do not use locations in earth-realms as their primary means of orientation. Yeshua says that Reality is in fact spreading out across the earth.

There is a definition of eschatology—the final unfolding of the universe—which understands that the End and destiny of history is not some event in the far future, but a present reality unfolding in the moment of the Eternal Now. It is an eschatological expression that is "realized" now. The End has come into the middle of time. Something of this way of seeing seems to be imbedded in the teachings of Yeshua and is very prevalent in the text of the Gospel of Thomas.

So where does the Kingdom exist? How does one "find" it? What are its coordinates? Yeshua says that even though it is "everywhere," in truth it is also no-place, except perhaps that it is carried as the interior center of everything. It has inner dimensions or inner coordinates assigned to no fixed place. You cannot point in some direction to find it, except perhaps inwardly, toward the center of the heart. Even then, to locate it there as a fixed dimension is to miss it entirely, for as Yeshua says elsewhere, "it is inside and all around us."

Yeshua has been making the same point from the beginning of this Gospel, and yet his teaching keeps being blocked and misunderstood by this mental perspective. Nothing apparently has changed. His understanding of things keeps being challenged with incredulity. His students want physical evidence—and what he gives them cannot come in this way. They want material and temporal assurances. Yeshua will provide neither, and yet what he does want to give them is closer and more intimate than anything they can materially ask for. He wants not only to change their point of view, he wants to change their very ability to perceive it—their mode of perception. As this and the final logion indicates, for many of his students it has not yet happened. Yet, the change is happening everywhere. The Kingdom is already appearing and spreading out across the earth in the hearts of those who have opened to it. That is a reality which Yeshua now knows and can perceive, perhaps ever so slightly, in his followers.

QUESTIONS FOR REFLECTION

1. Have you ever been able to perceive things that someone else simply cannot see or understand? This is often the case when we are with children who have not yet seen things in the way that adults see them. (The reverse, of course, can also be true).

2. Give an example of spiritual insight and perception that you have had which has been impossible for someone else to know.

3. How important is it to you that your faith or spiritual perceptions be logically or empirically proven? Do you need rational or empirical proof for your faith to make sense?

4. In our day do you think the spiritual reality of the Kingdom of Heaven is increasing or contracting? Is there more evidence of that reality or less of it?

EXERCISES AND MEDITATIONS

1. Yeshua is clearly suggesting that there is another way to view what is going in the world around us. Naturally one would not think that the Kingdom was arriving in his Palestinian world while the Romans were an occupying force and making life very difficult for the Jewish nation. Yeshua sees something far different. He perceives a reality behind the world of appearances. What would it take to perceive in this way? What is the organ of cognition that Yeshua is using? In a period of reflection and meditation, ponder these questions. What answers arrive when you do?
2. In the "Readings for Insight" section there are two very provocative poems that come to us from the Sufi tradition and the heart of Jalaluddin Rumi. These seem to be the forms of seeing that Yeshua is talking about. How do you respond to these poems? How do they fit with Yeshua's own vision of reality? Are they articulating the same thing? Read each poem every day for a week. Allow their meanings and images to have a place inside of you. What do you learn from this exercise? Does it change your perception in any way? How?
3. Consider this passage from the **Tao Te Ching**:

The One who seeks his treasure in the outer world
is cut off from his own roots.
Without roots, he becomes restless.
Being restless, his mind is weak
And with a mind such as this he loses all command below Heaven.

Tao Te Ching
26
Translated by
Jonathan Star

READINGS FOR INSIGHT

I

There was a long drought. Crops dried up. The vineyard leaves turned black. People were gasping and dying like fish thrown up on shore and left there. But one man was always smiling and laughing. A group came and asked him,

"Have you no compassion for this suffering?"

He answered, "To your eyes this is a drought. To me, it is a form of "God's joy." Everywhere in this desert I see green corn growing waist high, a sea-wilderness of young ears greener than onions. I reach out to touch them. How could I not? You and your friends are like the Pharaoh drowning in the Red Sea of your own body's blood. Become friends with Moses, and see this other river-water."

When you think your father or mother is guilty of some injustice,
their faces look cruel. To his brothers, Joseph seemed dangerous.
When you make peace with your father or mother,
they look peaceful and friendly.
The whole world is a container for the forms of this truth.

When someone does not feel grateful, the forms appear to be as they feel. They mirror that anger, that greed, or that fear. So make peace with the universe. Take joy in it. It will turn to gold. Resurrection will be now. Every moment is a new beauty. And there is never any boredom! Instead, an abundant, pouring noise of many springs will come to your ears. The tree limbs will move like people dancing, who suddenly know what the mystical life really is. The leaves snap their fingers like they're hearing music. They are. Right now you see a sliver of light, as from a mirror, shining out from under a felt covering. Think how it will be when the whole thing is open to the air and the sunlight!

There are some mysteries that I cannot tell you just yet.
There's so much doubt everywhere, so many opinions that say,
"What you announce may be true in the future, but not now."
But this form of universal truth that I see says,
This is not a prediction. This is here, in this instant, like cash in the hand!

Jalaluddin Rumi

II

You have gone now to the unseen World.
You broke free of the cage and flew away.
You heard the beat of the drum that calls you home.
You left this plane of humiliation,
this disorienting desert where we often get wrong directions.
You have entered the secret inner garden,
that chamber inside the soul,
and there you have become a strange autumn rose
before the withering winter wind.
The rain is soaking in everywhere from cloud to ground,
that flowing inner silence.
And there you have taken your sweet sleep,
your rest inside the Friend.

Jalaluddin Rumi

LOGION 114

Simon Peter said to them all,

Mary should leave us,
for women are not
worthy of this life."

Yeshua said,
"Then, I myself will lead her,
making her male
if she must become
worthy like you males!
I will transform her
into a living spirit
because any woman changed in this way
will enter the divine Realm."

This is the Good News
according to Thomas.

Sapiential Themes

- *The progression of wisdom points beyond ordinary cultural norms to new horizons and new standards.*
- *Cultural conditioning must be transcended before there is the possibility of true spiritual freedom and equality.*
- *A deeper spiritual teaching and understanding about the nature of the bride and the bridegroom may stand in back of this saying.*
- *Yeshua's actions are aimed at spiritual transformation—turning ordinary human beings into living spirits.*

Parallel Texts

Thomas 22
John 4:27, 12:32
Romans 6:2
I Corinthians 6:17
Galatians 3:28-29
Gospel of Mary Magdalene Dialogue 4

FOCAL POINT

One cannot say for certain how or why this final Logion made its way into the text of the Gospel of Thomas. Some scholars say that it was added later by a community in dispute about the role of women in the nascent church. Others see it as a final (and some say fitting) portrayal of the kind of consciousness that continued to challenge the wisdom teaching of Yeshua—the inevitable resistance that wisdom creates in individuals of a certain consciousness as it moves into common culture. However, in the end, the goal of wisdom is to change consciousness, to add spirit to the human equation, and propel society and humanity forward to a new living point of transcendence and freedom.

Links

The realities of the Kingdom spreading out upon the earth include changing the limited perceptions of someone so important and entrenched as Peter to include women as equal partners and participants. This change is perhaps part of the sea-change that Yeshua is talking about. The very resistance that Peter exhibits is what prevents and inhibits the kind of perception that Yeshua is seeking to achieve across the earth.

Notes

While some believe this Logion is a later addition to the collection of sayings, by reading it ironically and hearing the potential sarcasm in his voice, one might catch something of Yeshua's ultimate intent—to shame Peter into a new way of seeing. Yeshua obviously believes that women ***are*** *worthy despite what Simon Peter believes or says. This text chooses that possibility in the translation.*

COMMENTARY

Confronted with wisdom's radical trajectory, human beings build up an opposition to sapiential teaching, barricading themselves against its demands for self-transcendence. Wisdom will inevitably burst the boundaries of our egoic limitations, but this will be a painful breakthrough. We do not give up (or into) a new reality easily or without a fight. These considerations may be at the heart of this final saying which seems so anticlimactic to much of the wisdom insights expressed so powerfully in the Gospel of Thomas.

It is clear that as Christianity evolved from the teachings of Yeshua, it deviated substantially from his insights, and reestablished another patriarchy based upon church teaching and dogma that substantially saw women as Peter saw them, inferior to men. This is a rejection of Yeshua's wisdom.

In some ways Yeshua's students were in constant conflict with his teaching. Whether it was because of the limitations in their personal level of consciousness, or because of the cultural constraints that were pervasive in that culture, Yeshua's teaching appeared to be antithetical to the conventional perspectives of his students and their culture. When he was gone from the scene opposition and antagonism would surely grow—history, of course, has proven this to be the case. Nothing perhaps signified the power of cultural norms more than the attitudes his students and their culture held about women. Simon Peter, in particular, seems very agitated by Yeshua's tolerance and encouragement of the presence of women, especially in the inner circle. He was most troubled about the presence of Mary Magdalene. From his perspective Yeshua's embrace of women, especially Mary Magdalene, was out of kilter and misguided and had to be fixed.

Feminist theology, which has come to the forefront in our day, begins in women's experience and rejects the patriarchal point of view—the structure of society in which men rule women. The Bible is seen to be a patriarchal text which is in need of critique, and as a consequence whole new and alternative viewpoints emerge which bring balance and correction to a skewed system of life in culture and society. The divine is seen as neither male or female in form, and the language of patriarchy is also corrected to reflect neutrality and balance. Feminist theology is seen to be the reemergence of the voice of Sophia which liberates half of humanity from bondage. Sallie McFague, Elisabeth Schüssler Fiorenza, and Rosemary Radford Ruether are among the important names of contemporary women theologians who champion this point of view.

To put it bluntly, in Simon Peter's view women were inferior and not worthy of the life of the Kingdom that Yeshua is talking about. Yeshua disagrees. One could make the case that there is a heavy use of sarcasm in this saying. Yeshua is saying, "Well then, Peter, if she must become worthy like you males, then I will make her male, if that is what you want."

What is clear from this exchange is that Yeshua is willing to lead Mary Magdalene into the very life of the Kingdom that Peter thinks he has already attained. Peter shows, however, by his very attitude, that he has not attained it. What Yeshua intends to do is to change her not into a male, per se, but a "living spirit." Is it maleness that gives one the privilege of entry into the Kingdom, or is it spirit? Peter seems to think it is maleness. Yeshua disagrees. But if, from Peter's perspective, it is maleness that is required, then Yeshua is even willing to change her gender. So what would Peter say to that proposition? Does he want her to become male?

Perhaps that is what Peter "wants?" He never says one way or the other. It could be that Yeshua's assertion and willingness to even go that far stops Peter in his tracks. Maybe its the tone of voice that Yeshua uses—a retort dripping with sarcasm. We will never know, but it is clear that this saying shows the extent to which Yeshua is willing to go to make the Kingdom available to women and transcend Peter's cultural limitations and consciousness.

In the end, this is truly "Good News," as the last lines of this Gospel attest. It is news that Thomas records and witnesses which brings life and healing to the world. Thomas sees what others, perhaps, did not see. He heard and recorded hard sayings, enigmatic Logia that were difficult for the students of Yeshua to hear and process—the wisdom way of knowing and being that constituted Yeshua's pathway. It is the Good News of Wisdom's voice which eventually becomes the stream of wisdom Christianity.

QUESTIONS FOR REFLECTION

1. What is your personal sense or understanding of this Logion? Does it offend you or give you hope? What do you personally think Yeshua is doing here?

2. What is Peter's mindset or consciousness? What would cause him to respond to Mary Magdalene in this way?

3. If you were in Peter's presence and able to respond to him, what would you say in response?

4. What is this Logion telling us about the relationship between the masculine and the feminine principles inside each of us?

EXERCISES AND MEDITATIONS

1. If one were to see that part of the wisdom tradition's objective is to introduce humanity to divine Sophia, and that in conventional religious terms, this is somehow anathema, because the physical form of a woman is seen to be a challenge to spiritual life (especially for a male)—then Yeshua's challenge for Peter is to begin to integrate the divine Feminine into his life and consciousness. The trajectory of revelation and love is to include and not exclude the feminine, and to balance the feminine with the masculine. In the future, this is where Yeshua's Good News is headed. This is the path of wisdom for future humanity. In a contemplative state, ponder the various streams of teaching that might unfold in the future from the teachings found in the Gospel of Thomas. Can you see other unfoldings possible? Journal your seeing.
2. If truthfulness (seeing the unfolding of truth) is a requirement for any future wisdom work, then attend to the instruction of this quote:

   Truthfulness belongs to insight and not to morality, the need and effort to be truthful: it is a matter of art and imagination. A man can be truthful only to the extent of his sensitiveness and concentration, his generosity and capacity for risk—his intelligence; and they must increase with the effort at truthfulness. A stupid or lazy man cannot be truthful, his stupidity is a denser obstacle than fear or malice. Here and always, stupidity, meanness, lack of imagination is the root crime, the only natural evil.

   Read and meditate on this passage as instruction for any future work in your own sapiential learning. Journal your conclusions. Rewrite this paragraph changing the masculine gender to include all human beings.

Lewis Thompson ***Fathomless Heart: The Spiritual and Philosophical Reflections of an English Poet-Sage****. Berkeley, California: North Atlantic Books, 70-71*

READINGS FOR INSIGHT

I

Sophia moves more easily than motion itself;
By reason of her purity she permeates all things.
She is like a fine mist rising from the power of God,
  the divine radiance streaming from the glory of the Almighty.
Nothing can stain her immaculate purity.
She is the shimmering glow of everlasting Light,
  the flawless mirror of God's power on earth,
  the supreme image of all good things.
Though one, She becomes everything;
  from within Herself, by Her own power,
  She makes all things new.

The Wisdom of Solomon 7:22-30

II

The moment that sweet Sophia—Holy Wisdom—caught my eye
  She washed away my thoughts and has become my heart's companion.
So now I am her slave—my heart and my soul belong to her.
  and they struggle daily to be with her.
Wherever I look it is Her that I see
  in Winter and Spring, in Summer and Fall she surrounds me.
All wisdom comes from knowing her
  and that wisdom means knowing myself.
If we are not learning this lesson,
  we have not been listening to her voice.
And without her voice what is the purpose of religion and piety
  and of reading all the holy books?
It is true, I am no Elijah or Elisha,
  and sometimes I've made a mess of things;
And yet, like Elijah, however little I eat or drink,
  still I am well fed.
The whole universe has her love, her affection inside it.
  And without this deep, deep love, faith hardens into stone.
Since the fire of her love touches everything and everyone,
  it touches me, it touches you and ripens us into our perfection.
With her love, her affection, we are welcomed
  into the single heart of divine love, and the perfect body of humanity.

Inspired by Yunus Emre

III

Those who gain wisdom from truth are liberated beings and a liberated being is one who does not habitually transgress—transgressors being slaves of their own offenses. Truth is our Mother and knowledge of her comes through joining with her. Those to whom Truth is given no longer offend, so the world calls them "free!" They cease their transgressions because they have gained wisdom from truth, which raises the level of their hearts, and having transcended their state in the world, they are free indeed. Love, however, is what uplifts and frees them, and yet in their freedom, knowledge of truth also makes them slaves of love on behalf of those who are not yet ready to live in the freedom of truth. Still it is this knowledge which prepares them so that they too may become free beings.

Gospel of Philip Analogue Sixty-One

Bibliography

A Monk of the West. **Christianity and the Doctrine of Non-Dualism**. (Trs. Alvin Moore, Jr., Marie M. Hansen). Hillsdale, NY: Sophia Perennis, 2004.

Alfeyev, Hilarion. **The Spiritual World of Issac the Syrian**. Kalamazoo, Michigan: Cistercian Publications, 2000.

Aslan, Reza. **Zealot: The Life and Times of Jesus of Nazareth**. NY: Random House, 2013.

Barker, Margaret. **Enoch the Lost Prophet**. London: SPCK, 1988.

Barker, Margaret. **Temple Mysticism**. London: SPCK, 2011.

Barker, Margaret. **Temple Theology: An Introduction**. London: SPCK, 2004.

Barnhart, Bruno. **The Good Wine: Reading John from the Center**. NY: Paulist Press, 1993.

Bauman, Lynn C. **The Hermeneutics of Mystical Discourse**. Arlington, TX: (PhD. dissertation for the University of Texas at Arlington), 1990.

Bauman, Lynn C. and Ward J. Bauman and Cynthia Bourgeault. **The Luminous Gospels: Thomas, Mary Magdalene, and Philip**. Telephone, Texas: Praxis Publishing, 2008.

Bauman, Lynn C. **The Gospel of Thomas: Wisdom of the Twin**. Ashland, Oregon: White Cloud Press, 2002.

Baumer, Christoph. **The Church of the East: An Illustrated History of Assyrian Christianity**. London-NY: I.B. Tauris, 2008.

Besserman, Perle. **Kabbalah and Jewish Mysticism**. Boston and London: Shambhala, 1977.

Bourgeault, Cynthia. **The Wisdom Jesus: Transforming Heart and Mind—A New Perspective on Christ and His Message**. NY: Shambhala, 2008.

Boyarin, Daniel. **The Jewish Gospels: The Story of the Jewish Christ**. NY: New Press, 2013.

Bruteau, Beatrice. **What We Can Learn From the East**. NY: Crossroad Publishing Co., 1995.

Bütz, Jeffrey J. **The Brother of Jesus and the Lost Teachings of Christianity**. Rochester, Vermont: Inner Traditions, 2005.

Bütz, Jeffrey J. **The Secret Legacy of Jesus: The Judaic Teachings that Passed from James the Just to the Founding Fathers**. Rochester, Vermont: Inner Traditions, 2010.

Cameron, Ron. **The Other Gospels: Non-Canonical Gospel Texts.** Philadelphia: The Westminster Press, 1982.

Cheetham, Tom. **After Prophecy: Imagination, Incarnation, and the Unity of the Prophetic Tradition**. New Orleans: Spring Journal, 200y

Cheetham, Tom. **All the World an Icon: Henry Corbin and the Angelic Function of Beings**. Berkeley CA: North Atlantic Books, 2012.

Cheetham, Tom. **Green Man, Earth Angel: The Prophetic Tradition and the Battle for the Soul of the World**. Albany: SUNY Press, 2005.

Cheethm, Tom. **World Turned Inside Out: Henry Corbin and Islamic Mysticism**. New Orleans: Spring Journal, 2003.

Chilton, Bruce and Jacob Neusner, eds., **The Brother of Jesus: James the Just and His Mission**. Louisville, Kentucky: Westminster John Knox Press, 2001.

Chilton, Bruce. **Rabbi Jesus: An Intimate Biography**. NY: Doubleday, 2000.

Chittick, William C. **Imaginal Worlds: Ibn al-'Arabi and the Problem of Religious Diversity**. Albany, NY: SUNY Press, 1994.

Clement, Olivier. **The Roots of Christian Mysticism**. Hyde Park, N.Y.: New City, 1993.

Colless, Brian E. (Translator) **The Wisdom of the Pearlers: An Anthology of Syriac Christian Mysticism**. Kalamazoo, Michigan: Cistercian Publications, 2008.

Corbin, Henry. "Divine Epiphany and Spiritual Birth in Ismailian Gnosis," in **Man and Transformation**. Papers from the Eranos Yearbooks. Bollingen Series XXX, vol. 5. NY: Pantheon Boosk, 1964, 69-160.

Corbin, Henry. **Spiritual Body and Celestial Earth: From Mazdean Iran to Shi'ite Iran** London: I.B. Tauris & Co., 1976.

Corbin, Henry. **The Man of Light in Iranian Sufism.** Boulder & London: Shambhala, 1978.
Crossan, John Dominic. **The Dark Interval**: Towards a Theology of Story. Allen, Texas: Argus Communications, 1975.
Dalrhymple, William. **From the Holy Mountain: A Journey Among the Christians of the Middle East**. NY: Henry Holt and Company, 1997.
Danielou, Jean. **The Theology of Jewish Christianity**. Chicago: Henry Regnery Company, 1964.
Davidson, John. **The Gospel of Jesus: In Search of His Original Teaching**. Rockport, MA: Element, 1995.
Davies, Stevan L. **The Gospel of Thomas and Christian Wisdom.** NY: Seabury, 1983.
Davies, Stevan L. ***The Homepage of the Gospel of Thomas*** **(http://home.epix.net/~miser17/Thomas).**
DeConick, April D. ed., **Paradise Now: Essays on Early Jewish and Christian Mysticism**. Atlanta: Society of Biblical Literature, 2006.
DeConick, April D. **Seek to See Him: Ascent and Vision Mysticism in the Gospel of Thomas**. Leiden: E. J. Brill, 1996.
DeConick, April D. **The Original Gospel of Thomas. With a Commentary and New English Translation of the Complete Gospel**. London/NY: T&T Clark, 2007.
DeConick, April D. **Voices of the Mystics: Early Christian Discourse in the Gospels of John and Thomas and Other Ancient Christian Literature**. NY: T&T Clark International, 2004.
Detweiler, Robert. "What Is a Sacred Text?" **Semeia 31**. Decature, GA: Scholars Press, 1985.
Dionysius The Areopagite. **The Divine Names, and The Mystical Theology**. (Trs. John D. Jones). Milwaukee, Wisconsin: Marquette University Press, 1980.
Elior, Rachel. (trs. David Louvish). **The Three Temples: On the Energence of Jewish Mysticism**. Oxford and Portland, Oregon: The Littman Library of Jewish Civilization. 2004.
Ernst, Carl W. (Translator) **Ruzbihan Baqli, The Unveiling of Secrets: Diary of a Sufi Master**. Chapel Hill, NC: Parvardigar Press, 1977.
Fideler, David. **Jesus Christ Sun of God: Ancient Cosmology and Early Christian Symbolism**. Wheaton, Ill.: Quest Books, 1993.
Fideler, David. **Jesus Christ Sun of God: Ancient Cosmology and Early Christian Symbolism**. Wheaton, Ill.: Quest Books, 1993.
Flusser, David. **Judaism and the Origins of Christianity**. Jerusalem: Magness Press, 1988.
Fujita, Neil S. **A Crack in the Jar: What Ancient Jewish Documents Tell Us About the New Testament**. NY: Paulist Press, 1986.
Fujita, Neil S. **A Crack in the Jar: What Ancient Jewish Documents Tell Us About the New Testament**. NY: Paulist Press, 1986.
Grant, Robert, M. with David Noel Freedman. **The Secret Sayings of Jesus: According to the Gospel of Thomas**. NY: Collins, 1960.
Green, Arthur. **Seek My Face, Speak My Name**. Woodstock, VT: Jewish Lights Press, 2003.
Griffiths, Bede. **Return to the Center**. Springfield, Ill.: Templegate Publishers, 1976.
Griffiths, Bede. **The Marriage of East and West**. Springfield, Ill.: Templegate Publishers, 1982.
Grondin, Michael. **Interlinear Coptic/English Thomas Translation** (www.geocities.com/Athens/9058).
Huxley, Aldous. **The Perennial Philosophy**. N.Y.: Harper and Row, 1944.
Idel. Moshe. **Kabbalah: New Perspectives**. New Haven and London: Yale University Press, 1988.
Izutsu, Toshihiko. **Creation and The Timeless Order of Things: Essays in Islamic Mystical Philosophy**. Ashland, Oregon: White Clous Press, 1994.
Jenkins, Philip. **The Lost History of Christianity: The Thousand-Year Gold Age of the Church in the Middle East, Africa, and Asia—and How It Died**. NY: Harper, 2008.
Jeremias, Joachim. (trs. S. H. Hooke). **The Parables of Jesus**. NY: Charles Scribner's Sons, 1955.
Kadowaki, J.K. **Zen and the Bible: A Priest's Experience**. London: Routledge and Kegan Paul, 1980.
Keenan, John P. **The Wisdom of James: Parallels with Mahayana Buddhism**. NY/Mahwah, NJ: The Newman Press, 2005.
Keizer, Lewis. **The Kabbalistic Words of Jesus in the Gospel of Thomas: Recovering the Inner-Circle Teachings of Yeshua**. Kindle Edition, Amazon Digital Services, Inc.: 2009.

Khalidi, Tarif. **The Muslim Jesus: Sayings and Stories in Islamic Literature**. Cambridge, Massachusetts and London: Harvard University Press, 2001.
King, Karen. **The Gospel of Mary Magdala: Jesus and the First Woman Apostle**. Salem Oregon: Poleridge Press, 2003.
Kingsley, Peter. **In the Dark Places of Wisdom**. Inverness, CA: The Golden Sufi Center, 1999.
Leloup, Jean-Yves. **The Gospel of Mary Magdalene**. Rochester, Vermont: Inner Traditions, 2002.
Leloup, Jean-Yves. **The Gospel of Thomas: The Gnostic Wisdom of Jesus**. Rochester, Vermont: Inner Traditions, 2005.
Leloup, Jean-Yves. **The Sacred Embrace of Jesus and Mary: The Sexual Mystery at the Heart of the Christian Tradition**. Rochester, Vermont: Inner Traditions, 2006.
Louth, Andrew. **Discerning the Mystery: An Essay on the Nature of Theology**. Oxford: Clarendon Press, 1983.
Louth, Andrew. **The Origins of the Christian Mystical Tradition: From Plato to Denys**. Oxford: Clarendon Press, 1981.
Meyer, Marvin. "Be Passersby: **Gospel of Thomas** 12, Jesus Traditions, and Islamic Literature," in J. Ma. Asgeirsson, A DeConick and R. Uro (eds)_, **Thomasine Traditions in Antiguity: The Social and Cultural World of the Gospel of Thomas**. Nag Hammadi and Manichean Studies 59, Leiden: E. J. Brill, 2006, 256-271.
Meyer, Marvin. **Secret Gospels: Essays on Thomas and the Secret Gospel of Mark**. NY: T&T Clark International, 2003.
Meyer, Marvin. **The Gospel of Thomas: The Hidden Sayings of Jesus**. NY: HarperSanFrancisco, 1992.
Meyer, Marvin. **The Nag Hammadi Scriptures.** The International Edition. NY: HarperOne, 2007.
Murphy, Frederick J. **The Religious World of Jesus: An Introduction to the Second Temple Palestinian Judaism**. Nashville: Abingdon Press, 1991.
Murphy, Frederick J. **The Religious World of Jesus: An Introduction to the Second Temple Palestinian Judaism**. Nashville: Abingdon Press, 1991.
Nasr, Seyyed Hossein and Oliver Leaman. **History of Islamic Philosophy**. Routledge History of World Philosophy vol. 1., London and NY: Routledge, 1996.
Nasr, Seyyed Hossein. **Knowledge and the Sacred: The Gifford Lectures**, 1981. NY: Crossroads, 1981.
Nasr, Seyyed Hossein. **The Garden of Truth: The Vision and Promise of Sufism, Islam's Mystical Tradition**. NY: HarperOne, 2007.
Needleman, Jacob. **The Heart of Philosophy**. N.Y.: Alfred A. Knoff, 1982.
Needleman, Jacob. **What is God?** Tarcher, 2009.
Nicoll, Maurice. **Living Time: and the Integration of Life**. Boulder: Shambhala Press, 1957.
Pagels, Elaine. **Beyond Belief: The Secret Gospel of Thomas**. NY: Random House, 2003.
Palmer, Martin. **The Jesus Sutras: Rediscovering the Lost Scrolls of Taoist Christianity**. NY: Ballantine Wellspring, 2001.
Patterson, Stephen J. **The Gospel of Thomas and Jesus**. Sonoma, CA: Polebridge Press, 1993.
Patterson, Stephen J., James M. Robinson, and Hans-Gebhard Bethage. **The Fifth Gospel: The Gospel of Thomas Comes of Age**. Harrisburg, PA: Trinity Press International, 1998.
Ricoeur, Paul. **Essays on Biblical Interpretation**. Philadelphia: Fortress Press, 1980.
Ricoeur, Paul. **Interpretation Theory**: Discourse and the Surplus of Meaning. Fort Worth, Texas: The Texas Christian University Press, 1976.
Riegert, Ray and Thomas Moore. **The Lost Sutras of Jesus: Unlocking the Ancient Wisdom of the Xian Monks**. Berkeley, California: Seastone, 2003.
Robinson, James M., and Marvin W. Meyer (Editors). **The Nag Hammadi Library in English**. NY: Harper and Row, 1988.
Ross, Hugh McGregor. **Thirsty Essays on the Gospel of Thomas**. Longmean, Dorset: Element Books, 1990.
Sanders, James A. **From Sacred Story to Sacred Text**: Canon as Paradigm. Philadelphia: Fortress Press, 1987.
Sanders, James A. **Torah and Canon**. Philadelphia: Fortress Press, 1972.

Scholem, Gershom. **Kabbalah**. NY: Meridian, 1974.
Schuon, Frithjof. **From the Divine to the Human**. Bloomington, Ind.: World Wisdom Books 1981.
Schuon, Frithjof. **Esoterism As Principle And As Way**. (Trs. William Stoddart). Bedfont, Middlesex: Perennial Books LTD., 1981.
Schuon, Frithjof. **Survey of Metaphysics and Esoterism**. Bloomington, Ind.: World Wisdom Books, 1986.
Schuon, Frithjof. **The Transcendent Unity of Religions**. N.Y.: Harper and Row, 1975.
Sells, Michael A. **Mystical Languages of Unsaying**. Chicago and London: The University of Chicago Press, 1994.
Shah-Kazemi, Reza. **Paths to Transcendence According to Shankara, Ibn Arabi, and Meister Eckhart**. Bloomington, Indiana: World Wisdom, 2006
Shah-Kazemi, Reza. **The Other in the Light of the One: The Universality of the Quran and Interfaith Dialogue**. Cambridge, England: The Islamic Text Society, 2006.
Shayegan, Daryush. *Introduction to* **The Green Sea of Heaven: Fifty Ghazals from the Diwan of Hafiz** (by Elizabeth T. Gray). Ashland, Oregon: White Cloud Press, 1995.
Sheppard, Gerad T. **Wisdom as a Hermeneutical Construct**. N.Y.: Walter De Gruyter, 1980.
Sherrard, Philip. **Christianity: Lineaments of a Sacred Tradition**. Brookline, MA: Holy Cross Orthodox Press, 1998.
Sherrard, Philip. **Human Image, World Image: The Death and Resurrection of Sacred Cosmology**. Ipswich, U.K.: Golgonooza Press, 1992.
Sherrard, Philip. **The Eclipse of Man and Nature: An Enquiry into the Origins and Consquences of Modern Science**. West Stockbridge, MA: Lindisfarne Press, 1987.
Steinsaltz, Adin. **The Thirteen Petalled Rose: A Discourse on the Essence of Jewish Existence and Belief**. N.Y.: Harper-Collins Publ. 1980.
Tabor, James D. **The Jesus Dynasty: the Hidden History of Jesus, His Royal Family and the Birth of Christianity**. NY: Simon and Schuster, 2006
Tabor, James D. **The Jesus Dynasty: the Hidden History of Jesus, His Royal Family and the Birth of Christianity**. NY: Simon and Schuster, 2006
Thunberg, Lars. **Microcosm and Mediator: The Theological Anthropology of Maximus the Confessor**. Ejnar Munksgaard Copenhagen: C.W. K. Gleerup Lund, 1965.
Thunberg, Lars. **Microcosm and Mediator: The Theological Anthropology of Maximus the Confessor**. Ejnar Munksgaard Copenhagen: C.W. K. Gleerup Lund, 1965.*
Valantasis, Richard. **The Gospel of Thomas**. London and New York: Routledge, 1997.
Vermes, Geza. **The Authentic Gospel of Jesus**. London: Penguin, 2003.
Von Rad, Gerhard. **Wisdom in Israel**. Nashville: Abingdon Press, 1972.
Warnke, Georgia. **Gadamer: Hermeneutics, Tradition and Reason**. Stanford: Stanford University Press, 1987.
Watts, Alan. **Behold The Spirit: A Study in the Necessity of Mystical Religion**. N.Y.: Random House, 1971.
Watts, Alan. **The Supreme Identity: An Essay on Oriental Metaphysic and the Christian Religion**. N.Y.: Random House, 1972.
White, L. Michael. **From Jesus to Christianity**. NY: HarperSanFrancisco, 2004.
Wilber, Ken. **A Sociable God**. Boulder: Shambhala Press, 1984.
Wilber, Ken. **Eye to Eye: The Quest for the New Paradigm**. Garden City, N.Y.: Doubleday, 1983.
Wilson, Barrie. **How Jesus Became Christian**. NY: St. Martin's Griffin, 2008.
Zibawi, Mahmoud. **Eastern Christian Worlds**. Collegeville, Minnesota: The Liturgical Press, 1995.
Zinner, Samuel. **Christianity and Islam: Essays on Ontology and Archetype**. London: Matheson Trust, 2010.
Zinner, Samuel. **The Abrahamic Archetype: Essays on the Transcendent and Formal Relationships between Judaism, Christianity and Islam**. Cambridge, England: Archetype, 2011.
Zinner, Samuel. **The Gospel of Thomas: In the Light of Early Jewish, Christian and Islamic Esoteric Trajectories**. London: Matheson Trust, 2011.

Author Index

Subject Index